Pacific Passage

Pacific Passage

The Study of American–East Asian
Relations on the Eve of the
Twenty-First Century

edited, and with an introduction by
Warren I. Cohen

COLUMBIA UNIVERSITY PRESS

NEW YORK

COLUMBIA UNIVERSITY PRESS
NEW YORK   CHICHESTER, WEST SUSSEX

Copyright © 1996 Columbia University Press

Library of Congress Cataloging-in-Publication Data

Pacific passage: East Asian relations on the eve of the twenty-first century /
Warren I. Cohen, editor
    p.   cm.
Includes bibliographical references and index.
ISBN   0-231-10406-5 (cloth: alk.   paper).—ISBN   0-231-10407-3
(pbk.: alk. paper)
    1.   East Asia—Relations—United States.   2.   United States—Relations—
East Asia.   I.   Cohen, Warren I.
DS518.8.P336   1996   95-44851
327.7305—dc20   CIP

∞

Casebound editions of Columbia University Press books are Smyth-sewn
and printed on permanent and durable acid-free paper.
Printed in the United States of America
c 10 9 8 7 6 5 4 3 2 1
p 10 9 8 7 6 5 4 3 2 1

Dorothy Borg (1902–1993)

In Memoriam

Contents

Acknowledgments

The conference from which this volume derives was held in April 1994 at the Woodrow Wilson International Center for Scholars, Smithsonian Institution, Washington, D.C. It was funded jointly by the Henry Luce Foundation and the Wilson Center. We are especially grateful to Mary Brown Bullock, Director of Asia Programs at the Wilson Center, and her staff, Jennifer Deming and Li Zhao, for their support—intellectual, financial, and logistical.

Other than those whose work appears in the book, the following scholars and journalists participated in the conference: H.W. Brands (Texas A & M), Mary Brown Bullock (Wilson Center), Chang Su-ya (Academia Sinica), Paul A. Cohen (Wellesley College), Roger Dingman (U. of Southern California), John W. Dower (MIT), Miles Fletcher (U. of North Carolina), Rosemary Foot (Oxford), John L. Gaddis (Ohio University), John W. Garver (Georgia Tech), Waldo Heinrichs (San Diego State University), George Herring (U. of Kentucky), Gary Hess (Bowling Green State University), Jun Iio (Saitama University), Richard H. Immerman (Temple University), Akira Iriye (Harvard), Stanley Karnow (Potomac, Maryland), Burton I. Kaufman (Virginia Tech),

Melvyn Leffler (University of Virginia), Jim Mann (*Los Angeles Times*), Takashi Mikuriya (Tokyo Metropolitan University), Kazuto Oshio (Japan Women's University), Vladimir Popov (George Washington University), Qing Simei (University of Chicago), Michael Schaller (University of Arizona), Michael Sheng (Southwest Missouri State University), Robert Sutter (Congressional Research Service), Kathryn Weathersby (Florida State University), Ka-Che Yip (University of Maryland, Baltimore County) Zhai Qiang (Auburn University at Montgomery), Zhang Shuguang (University of Maryland, College Park)

Contributors

Tadashi Aruga is professor of law at Hitotsubashi University, Tokyo, Japan. He is Japan's leading student of American diplomatic history and has written countless articles on the subject, in English as well as Japanese.

Michael Barnhart, professor of history at SUNY, Stony Brook, serves as editor of the *Journal of American-East Asian Relations*. He is also the author of *Japan Prepares for Total War: The Search for Economic Security, 1919–1941*.

Gordon Chang teaches about Asian Americans at Stanford University. His *Friends and Enemies: The United States, China, and the Soviet Union, 1948–1972* won the Bernath Prize of the Society for Historians of America's Foreign Relations (SHAFR). He has also written several articles on Chinese-American relations, one of which won the Pelzer Prize of the Organization of American Historians (OAH).

Chen Jian is associate professor of history at Southern Illinois University. Among his publications is the recently published *China's Road to the Korean War: The Making of the Sino-American Confrontation, 1948–1950.*

Bruce Cumings, professor of international relations at Northwestern University, is widely ackowledged as the outstanding student of Korean-American relations in the United States. He is best known for his massive two volume *The Origins of the Korean War.*

Marc Gallicchio is associate professor of history at Villanova University. Especially interested in the role of the American military, he is the author of *The Cold War Begins in Asia: American East Asian Policy and the Fall of the Japanese Empire* and several articles on American-East Asian relations, one of which won the Bernath Prize of the Society for Historians of American Foreign Relations.

Charles W. Hayford has taught at Harvard, Oberlin, the Chinese University of Hong Kong, Northwestern University, and the University of Illinois at Chicago. He has written *To the People: James Yen and Village China.*

William Kirby, professor of history at Harvard and chair of the China Council there has written extensively on China's foreign relations during the Republican era. His best known book is *Germany and Republican China.*

Ernest R. May is Charles Warren Professor of History at Harvard, sometime dean of Harvard College and director of the Charles Warren Center. America's most distinguished diplomatic historian, he has devoted much of his time in recent years to teaching policy makers how to understand and use the lessons of the past.

Glenn Anthony May, professor of history at the University of Oregon, is among the leading students of Philippine-American relations, one of the few able to use sources in the Philippines. Among his many publications is a volume he edited, *A Past Recovered: Essays in Philippine History and Historiography.*

Robert J. McMahon is professor of history at the University of Florida. His most recent book was *The Cold War on the Periphery: The United States, India, and Pakistan.* He has also published a collection of essays and documents entitled *Major Problems in the History of the Vietnam War.*

Constantine V. Pleshakov is a section chief at the Institute of U.S. and Canadian Studies, Russian Academy of Social Sciences. At the Advanced Institute, Princeton University, he completed a history of the Cold War from the Russian perspective, written with Vladislav Zubok. In his spare time he writes novels.

Eileen P. Scully is an assistant professor of history at Princeton University. Her doctoral dissertation at Georgetown University was entitled "Crime and Punishment: The U.S. District Court for China, 1906–43."

Nancy Bernkopf Tucker, professor of history and member of the faculty of the School of Foreign Service, Georgetown University, served on the China Desk of the Department of State and in the U.S. Embassy, Beijing, while a Council on Foreign Relations fellow. Her most recent book is *Taiwan, Hong Kong and the United States, 1945–1992: Uncertain Friendships*. She also edited, with Warren I. Cohen, a collection of essays entitled *Lyndon Johnson Confronts the World*.

Introduction

WARREN I. COHEN

This volume is the product of a conference convened at the Woodrow Wilson International Center for Scholars in April 1994. The conference and the book were designed to analyze the accomplishments of the decade or so since the publication of *New Frontiers in American-East Asian Relations* (1983) and to provide a research agenda for the remainder of this century and the beginning of the next. Our efforts were made possible by a grant from The Henry Luce Foundation and matching support from the Wilson Center. The conference was organized by the Committee on American-East Asian Relations, which is chaired by Akira Iriye, funded by the Luce Foundation, and housed at the University of Maryland, Baltimore County. The participants included approximately 50 scholars from China, Japan, Russia, the United Kingdom, and the United States. Offered here are the papers as revised after the conference. Two additional papers were commissioned subsequently to fill in gaps manifested at the conference.

The book, like the conference itself, is dedicated to the memory of Dorothy Borg, whose death in 1993, ended her long reign as doyenne of historians of

American-East Asian relations. *New Frontiers* was the only kind of *festschrift* she would accept. This volume is the only suitable memorial. Many of us worked closely with her over the last 30 years and many of the younger scholars who did not were beneficiaries of the opportunities she created.

In *New Frontiers* we were excited by the opportunity to introduce scholarship from the People's Republic of China and I expressed hope that Chinese archival materials would become more accessible and that the Chinese side would become less opaque. That hope has been realized. The first paper, by CHEN Jian, is in many ways the most exciting. He indicates the extraordinary leap forward in Chinese scholarship as evidenced by his own work and that of scores of other mainland scholars, writing in Chinese, whose work he introduces. Post-1949 Chinese archives are not open, but many valuable collections of documents have been released, many memoirs have appeared, and many Chinese diplomatists have been interviewed by Chinese and foreign scholars. Much of what we have learned appears in Chen's essay; more is apparent in Nancy Bernkopf Tucker's on Chinese-American relations since 1945.

ARUGA Tadashi presents an exhausting survey of the rich literature in Japanese. The range of issues is remarkable. The improvement in the quality of Japanese writing on American-East Asian relations has been extraordinary since Aruga and I began collaborating in 1969. In the early 1970s we had surrendered the idea of a volume of translated Japanese essays because we were unable to find a sufficient number with which to impress American scholars. Scores of superb works have appeared since and Aruga introduces them all.

Beyond anything any of us anticipated in 1982, Soviet documents are also being released—arguably on a more systematic basis than the Chinese. Russian historiography, however, lags far beyond the Chinese. Constantine Pleshakov indicates some of what is currently available in Russian, but also the multitude of problems confronted by scholars in the former Soviet Union. Politics still drives the research agenda and it will probably be another decade before we see Russian work comparable in quality to that being produced by Chinese historians.

It became clear at the conference that it was time to include the story of Asian Americans in the international history of American-East Asian relations and Gordon Chang volunteered to write the needed essay. Chang offers a wonderfully conceived piece in which he first reviews the work of diplomatic historians, noting the disappearance of immigration issues and the role of Asian Americans in the work of many of us writing in the Cold War era. He then surveys the rich new field of Asian American studies and places it in the context of Asian-American relations.

Eileen Scully volunteered after the conference to write an article on 18th and 19th century Chinese-American relations. Hers is an elegantly written argument for incorporating social science methodology, especially as used by social historians, in the writing of the history of international relations. In addition to surveying the relatively thin literature on the years before the twentieth century, she offers a blueprint for new approaches.

Charles Hayford follows Scully's advice while focusing on Chinese-American cultural relations from 1900 to 1945. His conception of an American Raj in China is fascinating and provocative. Like Scully, he examines literature too often ignored by diplomatic historians and provides insights they should find valuable. In a complementary essay, William Kirby forces us to see Chinese-American relations in the larger context of China's relations with the world. Suddenly the United States seems to shrink in importance, a perspective new to those who have worked primarily with a bilateral paradigm. In addition he offers us a valuable guide to materials that may be found in Chinese archives.

Reviewing scholarship on American relations with Japan and Korea in these same years, Michael A. Barnhart starts in 1945 and looks backward. His unique perspective serves to underscore the fact that far fewer American than Japanese scholars are working in this period. Nonetheless, interest in issues relating to the origins and conclusion of the "Pacific War" persist.

For the years since 1945 there is a vast literature on both Chinese-American and Japanese-American relations. Nancy Bernkopf Tucker discusses the "continuing controversies" in writings on Chinese-American relations despite—or because of—the enormous amounts of documentation that have become available since the *New Frontiers* volume. The Chinese materials to which Chen Jian refers have been used very differently by American scholars and by Chinese emigre scholars freed from the restraints of the Beijing regime. And, for four or five years before the Tiananmen disaster of 1989, Chinese officials had been speaking with considerable candor to Chinese and Western scholars, providing additional insights into Chinese behavior in the 1940s and 1950s. Tucker details striking advances that have been made in the study of the Eisenhower and Johnson years—much of it her own—and notes the considerable amount of work on the 1970s and 1980s that has already proved possible. As she reports, the Kennedy Library continues to pose problems for researchers.

Marc Gallicchio's essay on Japanese-American relations since 1945 moves beyond the *New Frontiers'* focus on the occupation to discuss the abundant literature on the peace and security treaties and the wide range of work on the economic issues that followed. Nonetheless, issues related to the occupation continue to draw attention and Gallicchio outlines the various arguments with remarkable precision. Here, too, the work of emigre scholars has contributed to more profound understanding of the relationship.

Virtually untouched in the *New Frontiers* volume were American relations with the Philippines and with Vietnam. On this occasion Glenn Anthony May offers an impressive summary and analysis of Filipino as well as American scholarship on Philippine-American relations from beginning to end. He notes how little use American scholars have made of either Filipino scholarship or archival materials and evinces little patience with the large body of ethnocentric literature produced in the United States.

Robert J. McMahon reviews the extraordinarily rich literature on American relations with Vietnam. He notes that unlike other topics considered at the conference, work on Vietnam focuses on an event rather than a relationship. Little is written that does not eventually confront the questions of why the United States became involved in the war and why it failed to achieve its objectives. With characteristic judiciousness he explicates the "liberal realist," "radical revisionist," and "conservative revisionist" positions. In addition, he notes the evident lack of information and analysis of the Vietnamese side of the confrontation and the need to answer questions pertaining to the relationship between the needs of state and those of society in the United States.

Bruce Cumings took time off from his efforts to prevent war between the United States and North Korea to review the literature that has appeared since his pioneering essay on the historiography of Korean-American relations in *New Frontiers*. He was not pleased with what he found. It is clear that the language barrier continues to hamper work by western scholars and too little work by Korean scholars is accessible. We hope that Korean scholars will be able to join us for our next survey of the field.

No conference at the Wilson Center is ever complete without one policy-relevant session to meet the needs of the Washington foreign policy elite. Ernest R. May agreed to speak on the subject of "American-East Asian Relations in the Twenty-first Century." He graciously allowed us to include that address in this volume.

As has been evident for the last quarter of a century, the field of American-East Asian relations has been in the forefront of the historical profession. Scholars working in this area have been quick to use American archival materials as soon as they leave the hands of reluctant declassifiers. When available, they have used British, Chinese, Filipino, Japanese, Korean, and Russian documents. They have begun to collect Vietnamese documents. They are open to suggestions of new approaches and include some who have adopted the most arcane methods of social historians, cultural historians, and art historians—and even of political scientists and sociologists. Some have used world systems theory and others experiment with the methods of Michael Foucault and Edward Said. No one scholar can do it all, although a handful like Bruce Cumings, Michael Hunt, Akira Iriye, and William Kirby come close. Most, however, have benefitted from the efforts of other adventurous colleagues. From time to time some among us will play Cassandra and bemoan our lack of progress, our inability to do all and know all. Certainly Dorothy Borg, had she lived, would have tolerated no complacency. The holes in our knowledge revealed in the following essays would have prompted her to demand a half dozen or more conferences to fill these and find others. We honor her memory by rejecting complacency and continuing the search for young scholars to bring into the field and new methods to expand it.

Warren I. Cohen
July 1995

Pacific Passage

Part One

Chapter One

Sino-American Relations Studies in China

CHEN JIAN

The 1980s and early 1990s witnessed in China rapid development in the study of Sino-American relations. The first major indication of such development came in November 1985, when more than seventy scholars from all over China gathered at Fudan University in Shanghai to hold the "First National Conference on Sino-American Relations," presenting nearly thirty papers covering a variety of topics.[1] Three years later, at the "Second National Conference on Sino-American Relations," held at Nanjing University in July 1988, more than forty papers were presented.[2] In the meantime, two book series on Sino-American relations, with Professor Ding Mingnan and Professor Wang Xi, respectively, as the chief-editors, were inaugurated in the mid-1980s, and within their framework, more than twenty monographs and translations have since been published.[3] Meanwhile, between the early 1980s and early 1990s, several hundred articles about American-East Asian relations were published in Chinese journals.[4]

Along with these achievements are the establishment and rapid development of new research institutions. According to the statistics offered by Li

Shenzhi, former vice president of the Chinese Academy of Social Sciences and president of the Chinese Association for American Studies, as of 1990 more than seventy American studies institutions, research departments, and research groups had been established at China's universities, colleges, and provincial and municipal academies of social sciences, many of which put the study of Sino-American relations at the top of their agenda. On the basis of this institutional growth, in 1989, a nationwide organization, the Chinese Association for American Studies, was established to coordinate scholarly activities in the field. In March 1994, initiated by a group of Sino-American relations scholars in Beijing, the "Society for Scholars of Sino-U.S. Relations" was established. The society's first activity was to convene a national symposium on Sino-American Relations, March 27–29, 1994, aimed at "reviewing the results of the study of the history as well as the current situation of Sino-U.S. relations in the past decade."[5] It is no exaggeration to claim that the study of Sino-American relations in China has been flourishing since the early 1980s.

The direct driving force underlying this scholarly development, in retrospect, was a politically oriented one, related to the flowering of the "opening and reform" era in China in the early 1980s, which has stimulated Chinese scholars' increasing willingness to "re-understand America while at the same time re-understanding China." In Li Shenzhi's words, "The United States is one of the most important countries in today's world; its strength in science and technology, as well as its economic and military power, has been the number one in the world for over half a century; and it has played so important a role (be it good or bad) in international politics that no other country could ignore it. When we Chinese have opened our door to the outside world, it is natural that how to understand America is to us an urgent task."[6]

Indeed, almost all Chinese students of Sino-American relations emphasize that the necessity of promoting study in this field lies in the importance of the field itself. With the end of the Cold War era, such issues as the disputes over human rights, the controversies resulting from trade relations, and different approaches toward the arms control and proliferation problem, all of which had long been overshadowed by other more prominent issues under Cold War circumstances, emerged to hinder a smooth development of Sino-American relations in the post Cold War era. From a Chinese perspective, how to understand the dynamics of U.S. foreign policy in general and U.S. China policy in particular becomes an issue of immediate importance.

While these politically oriented utilitarian considerations have created conditions for a quantitative growth of the field, they have brought about at the same time a research environment that is not necessarily favorable to the field's qualitative improvement—political "correctness" may well overwhelm scholarly virtue to become the standard of criticism and judgment. There-fore, these concerns, if not properly handled, could bias scholars' way of thinking, thus serving as a new source of misunderstandings and mispercep-tions.

As a matter of fact, even during the age of "reform and opening to the out-side world," the inner world of most Chinese scholars is still influenced (if not dominated) by their previous training and experience. For example, the dog-matic Marxist methodology of class analysis, which had been the prevailing theoretical guideline for all historical studies in China during the Mao era, may continue to demonstrate its influence on scholars' efforts to form per-spectives. This "inner restriction," combined with the above-mentioned "out-side restrictions," will leave its indelible stamp on the field's development.

Consequently, if we review China's Sino-American relations studies in the past decade, it is not difficult to find that while a substantial number of new publications have accumulated, few of them can be regarded as innovative or path-breaking. While it is true that Chinese scholars have tried very hard to design new research topics, dig into new source materials, and develop new questions and answers, the restrictions existing both in scholars' own minds and in the research environment made it difficult for fresh and critical schol-arly perspectives to emerge. In this sense, Sino-American relations study in China still faces the task of defining and refining the field's mission and scope. In this essay, I will describe recent Chinese scholarship on Sino-American relations by dividing it into nine different periods, introducing new points of views, new interpretations, and new sources, while at the same time noting the remaining problems and suggesting possible strategies for future improvement.

The Early Relationship: Before 1844

Chinese scholars have seldom treated Sino-American relations before 1844, the year when the Treaty of Wangxia was signed, as a central part of their study. However, in order to trace the origins of the contacts between China and America and, for scholars of modern Chinese history, to explore how China's closed pre-modern society had been opened by foreign influences and power, this period cannot be ignored. Since the early 1980s, a few monographs and articles have been published on this topic, focusing on Sino-American trade relations and the early activities of American missionaries in China.[7]

One of the basic features of early Sino-American trade relations is that while American merchants came to do business in China, the reverse was not true. The questions Chinese scholars try to examine are: Why did American merchants come to China? How should one define the "nature" of their activities in China?[8] How did these activities influence the development and changes of Chinese society?

In answering the first question, Wang Xi and Tsou Mingteh, and Qiao Mingshun argue that the driving force of American merchants coming to China could be found in North America's special conditions in the late eighteenth and early nineteenth centuries. After the War of Independence, while such European powers as Britain and France had placed tighter restrictions on trade with North America, the early development of American capitalism required raw materials, markets, and new capital. Under these circumstances, the Americans saw new significance in trade relations with China, and the United States government encouraged and supported merchants to do business in East Asia.[9] As a result, after the *Empress of China*'s successful voyage to China in 1784, Sino-American trade relations developed.[10] In analyzing the "nature" of American merchants' activities in China, Qiao Mingshun and several other scholars argue that as a large portion of the profit from the China trade was later used as industrial investment back home, "America's trade relationship with China played an important role in primitive capital accumulation in the development of American capitalism." It is thus of a capitalist nature.[11]

In terms of the impact of Sino-American trade relations upon the development of Chinese society, most Chinese scholars believe that it was insignificant. They argue that Chinese society in the late eighteenth and early nineteenth centuries was still a closed one based on a self-sufficient economy (which had been further enhanced by the Manchu dynasty's efforts to shut foreign influence out of China). As early American exports to China were mainly luxuries, they touched only a very small portion of China's upper classes. Later, when the American merchants joined the British in transporting and selling opium to China, they began to have some influence upon China's social life, especially in some southern provinces. But overall, the structure of China's traditional society was barely challenged.[12]

During this period, American missionaries to China faced a difficult situation created by the Manchu dynasty's policy of forbidding any missionary activities on its territory. Several Chinese scholars point out that American missionaries' activities in China had to stay underground, often combined with the activities of English missionaries. Their influence upon Chinese society, if any, was therefore very limited. They had thus developed an extreme hostility toward not only the laws forbidding missionary activities but also toward the entire Chinese legal system. Consequently, their criticism of the "cruelty" and "inhumanity" of the Manchu dynasty's legal system turned out to be one of the most important initial forces driving foreign powers to impose extraterritoriality on China.[13]

What should be noted here is that most Chinese students involved in the study of Sino-American relations during this period are "scholars of American history." The focus of their study is the analysis of the logic and development of America's political, economic, and cultural policies toward China. The sources they have used in most cases are secondary works by Western scholars. Some of their studies have indeed touched upon the influence of American merchants' and missionaries' activities in China on the internal development of Chinese society, but this has never become these scholars' main concern. Their work covers a period earlier ignored by Chinese scholars. Their perspectives, though, are hardly fresh.

From the "Treaty of Wangxia" to the "Open Door": The Late Nineteenth Century

In the second half of the nineteenth century, Sino-American relations developed in a context in which the structures of both Chinese society and Chinese foreign relations were experiencing dramatic and profound transformations. The background of Chinese scholars involved in the study of Sino-American relations during this period has changed accordingly: "scholars of American history" have now been joined by "scholars of modern Chinese history."

The two groups of scholars ask different research questions, use different sources, and have different scholarly concerns. For scholars of American history, what is important is how to understand the logic and dynamics underlying the development of U.S. "strategies of aggression" against China in the context of changing American-East Asian relations in the late nineteenth century. Their studies therefore focus on such topics as the signing of the Wangxia Treaty and the emergence of the treaty system, Americans' changing attitude toward Chinese immigrants and the making of the Chinese Exclusion Act of 1882, the introduction of the "Open Door" policy, the American involvement in the suppression of the Boxer Uprising, and Washington's role in the signing of the Boxer Protocol. In other words, American policy is the main subject.

In contrast, modern Chinese historians try to treat the exchanges between China and the United States as an integral part of understanding China's crisis in the late nineteenth century, and their main concern is how to comprehend the scope and depth of the crises facing China's state and society in the broad context of the shock waves produced by the encounters between Chinese and Western cultures. Therefore, their studies focus more on such topics as why Chinese students went to study in the United States and how they influenced Chinese modernization after their return home; the emergence and development of American business enterprises in China and their impact on China's economy and society; American missionaries' activities in China under the treaty system; and the influence of the newspapers published and schools run by Americans in China on China's course of modernization. Generally speaking, the first group of scholars base their studies on openly published American documents and secondary Western sources, while the sources used by the second group usually include Chinese archives and other documents, contemporaries' diaries, correspondence and memoirs, and other books and newspapers published at that time. This pattern of different research emphases and use of sources can also be found in the two groups of historians' studies covering other periods.

In the 1980s, most Chinese scholars, as had their predecessors in the past three decades, continued to view U.S. policy toward China in the late nineteenth century as economic and political aggression conducted under the protection of the unequal treaty system, serving the interests of rising American capitalism and imperialism. In their studies about the signing of the Treaty of Wangxia and the making of the unequal treaty system, Qiao Mingshun and other scholars argue that like the other Western powers, Americans aimed to bring China into the international system controlled by the Western powers through political, economic and, if necessary, military means. The making of the treaty system made China a semi-colony of all Western powers, including the United States, thus setting up a pattern of unequal exchanges between China and America.[14]

It is within this framework of interpretation that most Chinese scholars have viewed Chinese laborers going to North America in the late nineteenth century as victims of the unequal relations between China and the United States. Zhu Jieqin, while arguing that Chinese laborers had played an important role in the exploration and development of the American West, points out that the anti-Chinese tendency that had gradually developed in America in the late nineteenth century (which reached a peak in 1882 with the passage of the Chinese Exclusion Act) epitomized China's increasingly inferior position in the eyes of the Americans.[15] Wu Mengxue further linked this issue to the development of America's extraterritoriality in China, stressing that the American request for privileges and rights in China "expanded from protecting American defendants to supporting American plaintiffs, from challenging Chinese jurisdiction over American residents in China to preventing the Chinese government's protection of Chinese residents in the United States, and from trampling upon Chinese sovereignty . . . to interfering with China's internal affairs."[16]

This criticism of the "U.S. imperialist policy" continues to dominate Chinese studies of the "Open Door" policy introduced at the turn of century. Since the early 1950s, Chinese scholars had consistently regarded the "Open Door" policy as a specifically designed imperialist policy serving Washington's attempt to "penetrate the Chinese market and interfere with China's internal affairs." In the early 1980s, Xiang Liling, Wang Xi, and Luo Rongqu provided a revisionist perspective. They pointed out that among all imperialist powers, the United States was the only one that had not demanded any territory from China, and that the introduction of the "Open Door" policy had contributed to the protection of China's territorial integrity and administrative sovereignty. However, these arguments were angrily criticized by Ding Mingnan and others as an "attempt to drag the studies in the field backward."[17] Since then Ding Mingnan has published several articles to argue that the "Open Door" policy was a logical outgrowth of America's aggressive policy toward China starting with the signing of the Treaty of Wangxia, and that this policy was designed to allow American imperialist interests to further penetrate the Chinese market when America was then economically strong but politically and militarily relatively weak.[18]

If the fate of the Chinese nation is the main concern underlying the first group of historians' studies, the perceived impact on China's course of modernization dominated the second group of historians' thinking. Against this background, how Chinese students went to the United States and what role they had played after returning home become important. Most Chinese scholars have related their research on this issue to the rise and decline of the "Self-Strengthening" movement. They usually do not treat the activities of the students going to the United States as part of Sino-American relations; rather, they prefer to link their experiences with those of Chinese students going to Europe and Japan.[19] They highly praise the role played by these students after they had returned home, arguing that these students (such as Rong Hong [Yung Wing]) brought to China new ways of thinking in dealing with China's ever-deteriorating national crisis. However, they also point out that the reform efforts made by the returning students had always been hindered by political and social forces which did not want to see progressive changes in China, thus making the personal experience of most of the returning students a profound tragedy. They had neither the strength to transform China nor the influence to change the unequal relationships between China and the United States and the other Western powers. From a long-range perspective, though, the failed efforts of the returning students did leave behind them valuable lessons useful for future reformers.[20]

American business enterprises in China have been another focus of modern Chinese historians' attention. The infrastructure of the Sino-American economic relationship began to change after the signing of the Treaty of Wangxia: in addition to bilateral trade relations, increasing numbers of American businessmen came to invest and open new business enterprises in China. All of this, while an important aspect of Sino-American relations in the late nineteenth century, became also an integral part of the profound economic and social changes China was undergoing. In two articles on the development of Shanghai's steamboat industry in the 1860s and 1870s, Yu Xingmin and Chen Jian investigate the role played by American steamboat merchants. After the opening of the Shanghai port, the steamboat industry possessed increasing importance and began to attract foreign capital, especially from Britain and the United States. Although the British merchants were more powerful in terms of their financial strength, the Americans proved more able to handle the existing Chinese network of business, as well as in utilizing traditional Chinese channels of trade and transportation.

The American steamboat merchants thus gained an upper hand in their competition with the British merchants. The American penetration of Shanghai's steamboat industry, in turn, had virtually transformed the precapitalist nature of Shanghai's water transportation business, thus contributing to the emergence of a new mode of production, a capitalist mode of production, in the Shanghai area. This also explains in a sense why one finds in Shanghai and other ports along the Yangzi River stronger local support for the "Self Strengthening Movement" than in many other places in China.[21]

American missionary activities in China and the resulting cultural exchanges between China and America also caught modern Chinese historians' attention. Before the early 1980s, Chinese scholars always treated this issue as a case of U.S. imperialist cultural aggression against China. Since then, many scholars, especially those of the younger generation, have begun to view this issue from the perspective of how it influenced China's course of modernization.[22] While continuing to point out that missionaries' activities had been protected by extraterritoriality and the treaty system, and that the pressures from missionaries had been a constant source for extending extraterritoriality, these scholars emphasize the other side of American missionaries' China experience: the cultural confrontations caused by the Western invasion of China meant also the introduction to China of new information and ideas. The missionaries' activities had actually opened a window through which the Chinese could access the outside world. They had thus contributed to the growth of elements of modernity in Chinese society.[23] This contribution, among other things, was demonstrated in American missionaries' sponsorship in establishing new schools and publishing newspapers and books.

In examining the role played by missionary schools, Luo Rongqu and Liang Biying believe that while there is no doubt that the American missionaries took education as a tool for religious conversion, missionary schools nevertheless represented a fatal blow to China's thousand-year old education system and produced large numbers of new talents who would play important roles in promoting China's course of modernization.[24] Chen Jiang, in his study about Young John Allen (Lin Lezhi) and *Chinese Globe Magazine*, argues that American missionary newspapers in China introduced Western technology and ideas to the Chinese readership; and that Lin's efforts to pursue compromises between Christianity and Confucianism further created a practical way for Western ideology to enter Chinese society. Missionary newspapers thus became a forum for cultural exchanges between Chinese and Westerners.[25] Wang Weijian and Liang Biying use the same perspective to evaluate American missionaries' involvement in book translation and publication, emphasizing that it contributed significantly to changing Chinese scholars' closed cognitive structure that had long been dominated by the tradition of institutionalized Confucianism.[26]

It is apparent that underlying Chinese scholars' standards of criticism are deep concerns for China's national independence and course of modernization. When they criticize American policy, it is in most cases because they see in this "imperialist" policy the harm done to China's sovereignty and integrity (and, interestingly, those scholars who attach positive meanings to the "Open Door" policy argue that this policy had been favorable to maintaining China's administrative sovereignty and territorial integrity). And when they praise such American activities as investment in business and involvement in Chinese education, they believe them to be useful for promoting China's modernization.

In Face of the Chinese Revolution: The Early 20th Century

The failure of the 1898 reform symbolized in China the end of the "age of reforms." Afterward, "continuous revolutions" would dominate China's twentieth-century history. While how to face the rising revolutionary tide in China presented serious challenges to the Americans, how to evaluate

America's existence and influence in China became an important issue that Chinese revolutionaries could not afford to ignore. The relationship between the rising Chinese revolution in the early twentieth century and America's policy toward China thus caught the attention of many Chinese scholars (in this case, mostly, modern Chinese historians).

The best study about Chinese-American relations on the eve of and during the 1911 Revolution remains Qing Simei's 1981 award-winning article, "A Study of U.S. Policy toward China on the Eve of the 1911 Revolution," which was based on extensive use of American diplomatic documents and Chinese archives.[27] On the eve of the 1911 Revolution, according to Qing Simei, the Manchu dynasty struggled to cope with the daily deteriorating internal and external situation, and badly needed a stable international environment. To achieve such an environment, the Manchu government repeatedly pursued support from the United States, hoping that the American backing would enhance the international resources available to the Manchu's struggle for survival while at the same time checking Japan's and Russia's attempt to divide up China's Northeast. However, the Theodore Roosevelt and Taft administrations, restricted by America's limited military power and political influence in East Asia, failed to offer the Manchu government the backing it needed. Consequently, although the Americans had no sympathy for the Chinese revolutionaries led by Sun Yat-sen, U.S. policy toward China did not facilitate constitutional reform, thus playing a role in the Manchu dynasty's final downfall.

If the United States showed no sympathy with, let alone support for, the 1911 Revolution, the keynote of American policy toward the "Great Revolution" of the 1920s under the banner of the CCP-GMD (Guomindang or the Nationalist Party) "united front" was open hostility. In "A Study of the Imperialists' Relationship with the Shanghai Coup of 1927," Shen Yu drew a picture of how Washington coordinated with London to use every means available to check China's revolution. During the initial stage of the "Great Revolution," according to Shen Yu, the Americans were not quite certain about the distinctions between the CCP and Jiang Jieshi's GMD, and Washington thus refused to recognize the revolutionary government in Guangzhou (Canton). When the Northern Expedition had reached the middle and lower reaches of the Yangzi River, the Americans even tried to use gunboats to stop the spread of revolution. But when the Northern Expedition Army occupied Shanghai in spring 1927, the Americans, for the purpose of maintaining their own commercial interests there, began to adopt a cautious attitude. After Jiang Jieshi's anti-Communist coup in April 1927, the Americans quickly realized that Jiang was a counter-revolutionary, and provided him with their support.[28] Niu Dayong, while sharing Shen's view in criticizing the reactionary nature of American policy toward China during this period, argues that in dealing with the "Great Revolution," Washington had more common interests with Tokyo than with London. He stresses that the very purpose of Washington's policy was "how to soften and split the Chinese revolution and revolutionaries, how to induce the Chinese bourgeoisie to lead the revolution to a path of evolution, and how to contain the spreading influence of communism." Niu believes that American policy was an important element in the making of the counter-revolutionary tide emerging in China with Jiang's reactionary coup of 1927.[29]

It is noteworthy that these Chinese scholars' interpretations of U.S. China policy during the 1920s differ dramatically from the views held by such American scholars as Dorothy Borg, Warren I. Cohen, and Akira Iriye.[30] American scholars point out that important changes in American policy toward China occurred during the 1920s, under the Coolidge administration, emphasizing that as a response to the rising tide of Chinese nationalism after the May Fourth Movement, policymakers in Washington were more willing than other Western leaders to understand revolutionary nationalism and make concessions to it, and that while American businessmen did demonstrate hostility toward China's national revolution, American missionaries and journalists in China were sympathetic to the revolution. However, Chinese scholars disagree with these views, stressing that America's China policy had continuously demonstrated its counter-revolutionary nature.

It is here we can find that, in addition to national fate and the course of modernization, there exists a third criteria of judgment in Chinese historians' evaluation of American policy toward China: America's understanding of and attitude toward the Chinese revolution, especially the Chinese Communist revolution. In the article "America and China's Three Revolutions," Tao Wenzhao, a historian of modern Chinese history and of American diplomacy,[31] offers a comprehensive description of these criteria. First of all, he points out that as a historical phenomenon, the Chinese revolution developed out of the fundamental problems facing China's state and society, representing an inevitable response to China's national crisis and need for modernization. Therefore, in a historical perspective, the revolution has been both just and legitimate. He then argues that the Americans, as the result of their historical tradition, cultural values, and considerations of practical interests, were not in a position to understand the historical necessity of the Chinese revolution, and that the U.S. government consistently took a hostile attitude toward the Chinese revolution at different stages of its development. Consequently, according to Tao Wenzhao, a stage had been set for the total confrontation between China and the United States that would emerge in the late 1940s and early 1950s.[32] As I shall discuss in several later sections of this essay, Chinese scholars will take the American attitude toward the Chinese revolution as a crucial criterion in their study of a series of other questions, especially of the ones concerning the relationship between the Chinese Communist Party (after 1949, the People's Republic) and the United States.

From the Manchurian Incident to Hiroshima: The War Years

The Manchurian Incident of September 18, 1931 symbolized the beginning of the breakdown of the Washington Conference system,[33] and would lead East Asia and the whole world to a global catastrophe. In terms of its impact on the development of Sino-American relations, from this point on China and the United States would gradually become allies during the Second World War. Until the early 1980s, Chinese scholars had usually emphasized that America's pre-war policy in East Asia had been one designed for making a "Far Eastern Munich." In the past decade, many Chinese scholars (especially modern Chinese historians) have tried to put more emphasis in their studies of America's China policy before Pearl Harbor on analyzing America's changing domestic situation and global strategy.

What were U.S. East Asian strategy and China policy during the Manchurian Incident? How should they be evaluated? Different views exist among Chinese scholars. Hu Dekun, Liu Tianchun, and Wang Mingzhong argue that restricted by the Great Depression and influenced by the deep-rooted anti-Sovietism, the Hoover administration carried out a policy of appeasement toward Japan's attempt to invade China's Northeast. In an overall sense, even with the introduction of the Stimson Doctrine, the United States had actually given tacit consent to the changed status quo caused by Japan's aggression against China. On a global scale, such a policy had created an age that was characterized by the Western democracies' appeasement of aggressors, which would reach its peak at Munich in the late 1930s.[34]

Yi Xianshi and Gao Erying have offered an alternative interpretation. They argue that considering that the management of the Great Depression was Washington's top priority and that none of the Western democracies had prepared for an international crisis like the one that erupted in September 1931 in Manchuria, Stimson's "nonrecognition" doctrine was the only policy option available to Washington during the Manchurian crisis. This policy, in its essence, was a reflection of the confrontation between America's "Open Door" principle and Japan's desire to establish its hegemony in China and

East Asia. The practical effect of this policy, these scholars point out, is the role it played in containing, rather than appeasing, Japan's aggression against China. From a long-range perspective, it is through the logic of this policy that one finds the first hint that China and the United States would become allies during the Second World War.[35]

These divergences among Chinese scholars have been further demonstrated in their interpretations of America's East Asian strategy and China policy during the four years between the Lugou (Marco Polo) Bridge Incident in July 1937 and Pearl Harbor in December 1941. Until the early 1980s most studies argue that such strategy and policy were in their essence a "Far Eastern Munich," designed to pursue compromises with Japan. These studies criticize the Americans as selfish and short-sighted, causing them to continue to sell strategically important materials to Japan (such as oil), and to fail to boycott Japan's aggression even morally.[36] These studies, however, are seldom supported by firsthand Chinese or American sources, and are usually highly speculative.

New interpretations putting emphasis on the confrontation between the United States and Japan began to emerge in the mid-1980s. Wang Side and Li Julian point out in an influential article, "The Changing U.S. Far Eastern Strategies Prior to the Pacific War," that only by linking America's East Asian strategy and China policy to Washington's anti-fascist "Europe first, Asia second" global strategy will one be able to understand them properly. They argue that as the United States, especially after France's downfall in summer 1940, had to use its main resources to deal with Nazi Germany's challenges in the West, President Roosevelt had no other choice but to seek temporary compromises with Japan. However, because of the anti-fascist nature of America's global strategy, the confrontation between the United States and Japan turned out to be inevitable.[37] Now, this line of interpretation has gradually become the main stream among Chinese scholars.

For Chinese-American relations from 1941 to 1945, most Chinese scholars focus their attention on CCP-U.S. relations, which I will discuss in the next section. In a few studies about GMD-American relations, Chinese scholars follow a pattern: they usually praise the U.S. support to China's War of Resistance against Japan, while at the same time criticizing Washington's failure to check Jiang's anti-Communist activities. Under the influence of this pattern, understandably, the Jiang-Stilwell controversy received attention. While General Stilwell has been widely praised for his "far-sighted vision" in dealing with Jiang and his corrupt regime, top policymakers in Washington have been criticized for their failure to back the general, and, again, this failure is usually attributed to the "imperialist nature" of U.S. strategy in East Asia, as well as to the Americans' lack of understanding of China's real situation.[38]

The Making of a Total Confrontation:
The Late 1940s and Early 1950s

China and the United States walked out of the Second World War in 1945 as allies; only five years later, however, the two had turned into adversaries on the Korean battlefield. The confrontation would not end for another twenty years, until President Richard Nixon's visit to China in 1972. Why did the confrontation develop? Was there any chance that the Sino-American confrontation might have been prevented? These questions have concerned both Chinese and American historians for a long time.

For Chinese scholars, these questions had been politically sensitive.[39] Until the mid-1980s, their answers had been predictable: they always argued that U.S. imperialist hostility toward the Chinese revolution had led to the Sino-American confrontation. As such hostility reflected the imperialist nature of U.S. China policy, it was impossible for the U.S. government to pursue an accommodation with the Chinese Communist regime. Chinese scholars welcomed the "lost chance" thesis introduced by many American scholars in the 1970s, largely because they found it to be compatible with their interpretations of the origins of the Sino-American confrontation.

Since the mid-1980s, the situation has undergone some subtle change. While the generalization that Washington's pro-Jiang and anti-communist reactionary policy had set a stage for Sino-American confrontation has continued to be the dominant thesis in Chinese scholarship, many scholars, especially those of the younger generation, have tried to use new sources and new case studies to give more nuance to this generalization. Their studies, though, in most cases focus on criticizing U.S. policy toward China and the perceptions underlying it.

The 1944–1946 period has attracted many Chinese scholars' attention in the past decade. Most believe that U.S. Ambassador Patrick Hurley's mediation of the CCP-GMD controversy served America's strategic goals in East Asia: on the one hand, Washington did want to see the CCP forces play a role in fighting against the Japanese in the last stage of the Pacific War; on the other hand, however, it was Washington's established goal to let Jiang Jieshi control China and, therefore, CCP forces should be put under Jiang's leadership. It was this pro-Jiang policy-line, in retrospect, that would eventually lead to the conflict between the CCP and the United States.[40]

In the discussions of General George C. Marshall's mediation in China, most scholars argue that Washington carried out a policy of supporting Jiang while at the same time trying to avoid a large-scale civil war in China that might have involved the United States. Therefore, Marshall's strategy was designed to force the GMD government to make some concessions of secondary importance to the CCP so that the party would be incorporated into a GMD-dominated regime. These scholars thus argue that Marshall's mediation was no more than a continuation of Hurley's anti-Communist policy.[41]

These arguments about the origins of the Sino-American confrontation are developed further when the 1949–1950 period becomes the focus of discussion. Most Chinese scholars believe that Washington's hostility toward the new China precluded the possibility of a Chinese-American accommodation. Zi Zhongyun, Tao Wenzhao, and Wang Jisi are typical in this regard. Using documentary sources they collected in the United States, they emphasize that there existed profound conflict between Washington's desire to establish America's hegemony in East Asia and the CCP's determination to pursue China's national liberation. Although policymakers in Washington had hoped to encourage a split between Beijing and Moscow, their approach toward China was by nature anti-Communist and counterrevolutionary, and they would never tolerate China's emergence as a revolutionary power in the East.[42] Tao Wenzhao concludes in a recent article that American hostility to the Chinese revolution was so deep that there existed little chance in 1949–1950 for a Sino-American accommodation to be achieved.[43]

It is within this context that Zi Zhongyun and several other scholars sharply criticize U.S. policy toward Taiwan. Zi Zhongyun points out that during 1949–1950 U.S. policy toward Taiwan wavered between choices from direct military intervention to supporting a regime established by a non-Communist third party; it is also true that President Truman and Secretary of State Dean Acheson had excluded Taiwan from America's Western Pacific defensive perimeter. But Washington had never given up the idea of using America's political influence (if possible) or military power (if necessary) to prevent Taiwan from falling into the hands of the Chinese Communists. Truman's decision to send the Seventh Fleet into the Taiwan Straits after the outbreak of the Korean War was a natural outgrowth of Washington's previous policy toward Taiwan.[44]

While trying to dig deeper into the factors underlying such mistaken U.S. policies toward China, in contrast to scholarship of earlier periods which put emphasis on political and ideological motives, the Chinese scholarship of the past decade pays more attention to historical-cultural elements, which were related but not identical to ideology. Zi Zhongyun, Tao Wenzhao, and Yuan Ming, for example, argue that it was the deep-rooted American misperception of the CCP and China that led to confrontation. The United States, as a rising world power in the twentieth century (after the end of the Second World War, the leading world power), had a profound sense of superiority in face of a backward China, which prevented the Americans from putting themselves into the shoes of the Chinese when necessary. The American understanding of the CCP was even less adequate. The profound influence of America's anti-revolutionary tradition combined with the emerging Cold War mentality to place policymakers in Washington in a position where they were unable to understand the nature and promising prospect of the Chinese Communist revolution. Therefore, Washington's suspicion of and hostility toward the CCP was by no means accidental.[45]

Related to Chinese scholars' sharp criticism of American policy toward China is their strong desire to determine which side should take the main responsibility for the Sino-American confrontation. Almost every Chinese scholar makes it clear, in one way or another, that the main responsibility to avoid confrontation lay with the American side. Li Shenzhi uses explicit language to summarize Chinese scholars' position on this issue: "The United States should take the main responsibility for the making of the Sino-American confrontation, while the China [the CCP] side bore little duty, or, more accurately speaking, no duty at all [to prevent it]."[46] While such a strong sense of maintaining political "correctness" in one's study will probably strengthen the researcher's argument, it will inevitably serve as a source of bias and misunderstanding.

In a scholarly environment like this, Chinese scholars demonstrate an interesting approach toward the "lost chance" thesis introduced by American scholars. Some are willing to embrace this thesis, as it has placed the responsibility for the making of the confrontation squarely on Washington; others argue that Washington's hostility toward the Chinese revolution had been so profound that there was never any chance that the confrontation could have been averted.[47]

Methodologically speaking, however, this approach has brought about a real paradox: by making the Americans fully responsible for the coming of the Sino-American confrontation, these scholars have actually treated the CCP's foreign policy simply as a passive reaction to the policy of the United States, and they have thus implied that American policy is the source of all virtues as well as evils in the world. If something went wrong somewhere, it must have been the result of a mistake committed by the United States.

It is obvious that the CCP's policy toward the United States is an integral part in the study of the making of the Sino-American confrontation. However, scholarly efforts in this regard have long been hindered, among other things, by the lack of access to primary Chinese sources. Only in recent years has there been any release of documents, and then only on a highly selective basis.[48] In the meantime, Niu Jun, He Di, Zhang Baijia and, especially, Yang

Kuisong, have published studies about the CCP's policy toward the United States, all of which have benefited from new Chinese sources.[49] In general, however, the CCP's policy toward the United States remains a weak aspect in Chinese studies of the making of Sino-American confrontation.

The Confrontation in Korea, 1950–1953

In late October 1950, Mao Zedong and the Beijing leadership decided to send Chinese troops to Korea to fight against the American-headed UN forces marching rapidly toward the Chinese-Korean border. This direct Chinese-American confrontation would last until July 1953, when an armistice agreement was finally reached at Panmunjom, leaving Korea's political map virtually unchanged from prewar lines. In the past decade, a variety of new Chinese sources have become available to scholars, making new studies (but not necessarily the emergence of new perspectives) in the field possible.[50]

Why did China enter the Korean War, and what were Beijing's war aims? Almost all Chinese scholars argue that the Beijing leadership did not welcome the Korean War because China faced difficult tasks of economic reconstruction and political consolidation at home and wished to give priority to liberating the Nationalist-controlled Taiwan. They stress that the Chinese decision to enter the Korean War was simply a reaction to the threats to China's security interests created by the UN forces' march toward the Yalu. While most scholars believe that the American decision to cross the 38th parallel triggered China's intervention, some scholars even assume that if the UN forces had stopped at the parallel, China's intervention could have been averted. Accordingly, they argue that China's aims in participating in the Korean War were no more than the defense of the safety of the Chinese-Korean border.[51]

New Chinese sources, however, challenge many aspects of these interpretations. For example, Beijing's active preparations for entering the war started as early as mid-July, 1950, almost two months before General MacArthur's Inchon landing.[52] In defining Beijing's war aims while making the decision to send troops to Korea in early October 1950, Mao Zedong made it clear that he aimed to drive the American forces out of the Korean peninsula so that not only China's security interests but also the interests of the "Eastern revolution" would be best served.[53] He would not give up the goal of pursuing a total victory in Korea until mid-1951, when the Chinese troops in Korea had suffered a major setback in their fifth offensive campaign.[54] The considerations underlying the Beijing leadership's decision to enter the war were obviously much more complicated and ambitious than the simple defense of the Chinese-Korean border.

How, then, did the Korean War end? Chinese scholars argue almost unanimously that it was because of China's initiative that the Korean War finally was concluded. New Chinese sources indicate that when the negotiations for an armistice started in July 1951, Chinese leaders and negotiators anticipated that the war would soon end.[55] Xu Yan, Qi Dexue, Meng Zhaohui, all leading scholars of Korean War history, argue that it was because the Americans were unwilling to walk out of the war without claiming a victory that the conflict continued for another two years. Xu Yan and Qi Dexue particularly point out that in November 1951, Mao Zedong and Zhou Enlai believed that an armistice in Korea could be reached by the end of the year, and they failed to anticipate that the POW issue would become the single remaining obstacle to hinder the reaching of an armistice agreement. When the POW issue did emerge, the Beijing leadership understood that this was "a serious political struggle" they could ill afford to lose. Both Xu Yan and Qi Dexue point out that the military conflict of the last 18 months in Korea, in Beijing's perspective, was of a clear political nature.[56]

Particularly of note is that in this context the Beijing leadership dramatically escalated the propaganda campaign to condemn Washington's "dirty biological war" in North Korea and in China's Northeast. According to new Chinese sources, in early 1952 both Chinese People's Volunteers' commanders in Korea and top Chinese leaders in Beijing truly believed that the Americans had used biological weapons against the Chinese and North Koreans. On February 18, 1952, for example, Nie Rongzhen sent to Mao and Zhou a report pointing out that there existed clear evidence that the Americans had been engaged in biological warfare in Korea.[57] The next day, Mao read the report and instructed Zhou Enlai to "pay attention to this matter and take due measures to deal with it."[58] As no evidence has ever been produced on the American side to confirm the Chinese version of the story, what really happened in Korea in the winter of 1951–1952 must be regarded as one of the most mysterious aspects of the Korean War. In any case, though, there is no doubt that the Beijing leadership did find in this matter an effective weapon with which to confront Washington's use of the POW issue to gain a politically superior position.

Did American nuclear power play a role in forcing the Beijing leadership to accept an armistice? There is no evidence in new Chinese sources to show that the Beijing leadership, while formulating the strategies to end the war, paid any special attention to whether the Americans would use nuclear weapons in Korea, although Beijing's military planners might have considered this possibility. The Beijing leadership's basic conviction was that the Korean conflict would be determined by ground operations, not by the use of the atomic bomb.[59] From a historical perspective, the direct military conflict in Korea crystallized the confrontation between China and the United States.

The Confrontation Continues: The 1950s and 1960s

Throughout the 1950s and 1960s, the conflict between China and the United States continued to develop. In 1954–1955 and 1958, the two countries were involved in crises over the Taiwan Straits. The Chinese-American ambassadorial talks, starting in 1955, did create a channel of communication between Beijing and Washington, but failed to bring the two sides any closer together. In the mid-1960s, with the gradual escalation of the Vietnam War, China and the United States were again brought to the brink of a direct confrontation.

Xu Yan stresses in his study that Mao's central concern was how to prevent the Taiwan issue from becoming a "forgotten issue." After the end of the Korean War and the First Indochina War, Mao realized that there existed also the danger that the status quo in the Taiwan straits might be finalized, and he therefore ordered the shelling of the GMD-controlled offshore islands in order to bring the Taiwan question to the attention of the international community. Mao, however, had no intention of involving China in another direct confrontation with the United States. When the crisis situation escalated in the Taiwan Straits area, Mao ordered the PLA forces to try their best to avoid engaging in conflict with the Americans. Xu Yan argues that as the first Taiwan crisis had resulted in widespread international concern over the Taiwan question, Mao's and the Beijing leadership's management of the crisis should be regarded as a success.[60]

This study, together with the information offered by other new Chinese sources, such as the memoirs by the persons concerned, have drawn for the first time a fresh (though still far from complete) picture about how the Beijing leadership perceived and managed the first Taiwan crisis and Sino-American relations in the mid 1950s. However, the interpretations of the Beijing leadership's motivations seem to have major omissions. No one, for example, has linked China's domestic situation during this period with the Beijing leadership's management of the Taiwan question. In actuality, in 1954 and 1955, Mao and the Beijing leadership were preparing for a "total socialist transformation" of China's state and society, and they sought the means to mobilize both the Party and the Chinese masses to participate in this new stage of China's continuous revolution. Did Mao see in the tensions created by the Taiwan Straits crisis a source of strong justification of his new revolutionary designs at home?

An unexpected result of the first Taiwan Straits crisis was the Chinese-American ambassadorial talks, first conducted in Geneva and then in Warsaw. Ambassador Wang Bingnan's memoir is the single most important Chinese source covering this important event. Wang recalls in the memoir how and why he was selected as the Chinese representative. He also reveals how Zhou Enlai dictated the strategies to him on how to handle the talks. In a few places he even touches upon interesting details.[61] In an overall sense, though, the information offered by Wang, as that offered by other similar memoirs published in China in the past decade, is highly selective. When scholars want to cite it, they should therefore carefully double check it.

Xu Yan and He Di offer the best study about the second Taiwan Straits crisis. He Di emphasizes that Taiwan's status was the central element in Mao's consideration of how to manage the crisis. [62] While sharing much of He Di's interpretation, Xu Yan attaches more importance to Mao's domestic considerations in explaining his management of the crisis. In summer 1958, at several Party conferences, the CCP leadership made the decision on nationwide communization and radically increasing China's production and capital accumulation targets. It is within this context that Mao ordered large-scale shelling of the Nationalist positions on Jinmen and other offshore islands. Accompanying the shelling, an anti-Jiang and anti-U.S. campaign emerged, making "we must liberate Taiwan" its central slogan. Mao obviously believed that the shelling would be helpful in gaining the popular support for his radical strategies of transforming China's politics, economy, and society in a short period.[63] Xu Yan's interpretation is supported by Mao's recently released manuscripts. For example, Mao stressed in early September 1958 that "despite its disadvantageous side, a tense [international] situation could mobilize the population, could particularly mobilize the backward people, could mobilize the people in the middle, and could therefore promote the great leap forward in economic construction."[64]

In the late 1950s and early 1960s, when Sino-American relations remained hostile, the split between Beijing and Moscow surfaced. In several new Chinese sources, it is reported that during Nikita Khrushchev's visit to Beijing in October 1959, he had emotional debates with Mao and other CCP leaders on, among other things, the assessment of the international situation in general and the "American threat" in particular: while Khrushchev put emphasis on the possibility of a peaceful coexistence with Western countries, Mao and the other Chinese leaders stressed the need of using revolutionary means to struggle against the "U.S. imperialists and their lackeys." This difference of opinion between Chinese and Soviet leaders would continue to exist and further develop in the early 1960s, widening the gap between Beijing and Moscow.[65] Although new Chinese sources have not yet offered a basis for comprehensive studies about the relationship between Beijing's confrontations with Washington and its split with Moscow, it is at least safe to say that how to assess "the nature of the U.S. imperialism" and the "American threat" was a key element in the emergence of the Sino-Soviet controversy.

The escalation of the Vietnam War in the mid-1960s again brought China and the United States to the verge of a direct military confrontation. While no Chinese study has offered a comprehensive review of the Beijing leadership's strategies to handle the deteriorating situation in Vietnam caused by increasing American military involvement there, several new Chinese sources make it possible to piece together a picture about how Beijing leaders perceived the "American threat" and, accordingly, how they defined the goals and means while committing China to "assist Vietnam and resist America."[66] I argue that by combining China's domestic needs and international commitments, while at the same time drawing lessons from China's intervention in Korea, the Beijing leadership adopted a three-point strategy in early 1965 in coping with the escalating crisis in Vietnam: First, China would offer any support that was requested by Hanoi, including dispatching military forces to defend North Vietnam. Second, China would give clear warnings to the Americans, so that the United States would not feel free to expand its ground operations into the North. Third, the emphasis of Chinese strategy would be put on avoiding direct military confrontation with the United States if possible; but if the Americans brought the war too close to China's borders, China would not shrink from a confrontation. This strategy did contribute to avoiding another direct Chinese-American military confrontation, but it also sowed the seeds for the future split between Beijing and Hanoi.[67]

The Road to Rapprochement:
The Late 1960s to Early 1970s

In the late 1960s, Sino-American relations seemed to have reached a low ebb with the development of the Cultural Revolution in China, as well as the escalation of America's military involvement in Vietnam. Indeed, the relations between the two sides seemed to be so tense that even the decade-long Sino-American ambassadorial talks in Warsaw were discontinued in 1968. However, starting in early 1969, the earliest clues for a Sino-American rapprochement began to emerge.[68] When President Nixon expressed his intention not to exclude Beijing from the international community, Mao sent out his message about his willingness to deal with top American leaders by entertaining the American journalist Edgar Snow at the Gate of Heavenly Peace.[69] Starting with "ping pong diplomacy" in spring 1971, a series of exchanges occurred between Beijing and Washington, finally leading to Nixon's visit to China in spring 1972, which signaled the end of the confrontation between China and the United States that had lasted for more than twenty years.

Why did policymakers in Washington adopt a policy of rapprochement with Beijing after more than two decades of confrontation? Chinese scholars generally attribute the causes to two key factors. First, within the context of the global confrontation between the United States and the Soviet Union, especially facing the cruel reality that the Soviet nuclear power had placed overwhelming pressure on America's global strategic status, both Nixon and Kissinger believed that a rapprochement with Beijing would help Washington to improve dramatically America's strategic status in a confrontation with the Soviet Union. Second, Nixon's intention of pulling American forces out of Vietnam represented another important motivation for Washington to approach Beijing. Policymakers in Washington hoped that a new relationship with Beijing would help strengthen American's bargaining power with the Vietnamese Communists.[70]

Why and how, then, did Mao and the Beijing leadership find rapprochement with the United States desirable while the Cultural Revolution was continuing in China? One answer could be found, several Chinese authors argue, in the escalation of the confrontation between China and the Soviet Union and, therefore, Beijing's need to strengthen its position in facing the Soviet threat, now perceived by Mao and many other leaders in Beijing as China's most dangerous enemy.[71]

This interpretation has been supported by the memoirs of Xiong Xianghui, Zhou Enlai's long-time associate in the ministry of foreign affairs, who offers a detailed first-hand account about how the ideas of pursuing rapprochement with the United States first came into being.[72] According to him, in April 1969, "following Chairman Mao's ideas," Zhou Enlai instructed Marshals Chen Yi, Nie Rongzhen, Xu Xiangqian, and several other veteran CCP leaders and PLA commanders to form a "study group" to "have a comprehensive review" of the international situation, and Xiong was assigned by Zhou to coordinate the group's activities. In the summer and fall of 1969, this group met seven times to discuss the international situation and China's strategy to deal with it. Finally, the group suggested that in order to counterbalance "the threat from the Soviet Union," China needed to "improve its relations with the United States." As suggested by several other Chinese sources, he attributed the reasons why Mao became willing to pursue a new relationship with the United States in early 1969 to the deterioration of the Sino-Soviet relationship at that time.[73]

However, Xiong's recollections, while providing valuable information, at the same time raise a series of new questions. For example, why did Mao assign the task of reviewing China's foreign policy in general and its policy toward the United States in particular to a group of veteran revolutionaries, all of whom had been the target of criticism during the Cultural Revolution? Nowhere in Xiong's memoirs or in other new Chinese studies can one find a persuasive answer to this question. Equally questionable was Lin Biao's position toward Sino-American rapprochement as claimed by Xiong and some other Chinese scholars: he, according to them, opposed contacts with the United States. But, was Lin Biao truly an opponent of rapprochement with the United States? If so, how can one interpret the fact that the "571 Program," allegedly the "reactionary coup plan" formulated by Lin Liguo, Lin Biao's son, favored the softening of Mao's radical domestic and international policies? These questions are still awaiting answers.

"Ping pong diplomacy" in spring 1971 turned out to be a key step toward the Sino-American rapprochement. New Chinese sources made it very clear that Mao and Zhou favored Chinese ping pong players' contacts with the American players and, then, with Mao's approval, the American ping pong delegation was invited to visit China. Mao intended to use this move to send a signal to Washington, which policymakers in Washington recognized.[74]

On Richard Nixon's visit to China, Chen Dunde offers a comprehensive, yet not always reliable, account.[75] The studies by Gong Li and Wei Shiyan, in comparison, are based on both interviews and documentary sources and thus more reliable.[76] Particularly noteworthy is Gong Li's citation of the CCP Politburo's circular justifying the party's decision to invite Nixon to visit China, as well as the party's strategies to handle the visit.[77] Also useful are the recollections of Zhang Yufong, Mao's "daily-life secretary" in the 1970s, which record how Mao suddenly decided to meet Nixon only hours after his arrival in Beijing.[78] In an overall sense, it should be pointed out, these sources are more descriptive than interpretive.

From Normalization to the Post-Cold War Era: The Late 1970s to the Early 1990s

The study of this period of Chinese-American relations in China, understandably, has been focused on political relations, and the year 1989 constitutes a clear dividing line.While the pre-1989 scholarship focused mainly on how to explain and justify the smooth development of Sino-American relations since 1972 (although analysis of problems and conflict, especially of those related to the Taiwan question, did exist), since then the literature has become much more critical of American policy toward China, and its focus turns toward a critical review of the political, historical, and "cultural" exploration of the apparent and potential problems existing between China and the United States.

The pre-1989 scholarship is best summarized in a collection of articles, *Zhongmei guanxi shinian* (A Decade of Sino-American Relations), published in 1989.[79] All contributors to the volume were leading scholars in different fields of China's American studies, and articles selected to be published in the volume covered almost every aspect of Chinese-American relations: political, economic, strategic, diplomatic, military, and cultural. In analyzing the diplomatic and strategic relations between China and the United States, several scholars argue that common concerns of maintaining a strategic stability in the Asian-Pacific area had served as a crucial element in determining the smooth development of the relations between Beijing and Washington. Top leaders in both countries, regardless of their partisan backgrounds or domestic priorities, had always maintained the consensus that a friendly Sino-American relationship was the cornerstone for stability not only in the Asian-Pacific region but throughout the world. Some scholars further made it clear that so long as the Soviet Union remained a threat or potential threat to the security interests of both China and the United States, any problem that was to emerge in Sino-American relations would be overshadowed.[80]

Contributors to this volume also believed that the prospect for improving Sino-American relations had been further guaranteed by the expanding economic relations between the two countries. They stressed that while the Americans had never been willing to give up the dream of the "China market," China's economic reforms and opening to the outside world have created for the first time in history a reality that might match this American dream. These scholars saw the development of Sino-American economic relations in the late 1970s and 1980s as merely a modest beginning of a historical process that would reach its maturity only in the last decade of the twentieth century and, possibly, not until after the turn of the century. Their prediction of the future development of Sino-American relations was therefore very optimistic.[81]

In the fields of political contacts and cultural exchanges, contributors to this volume sensed the possibility of potential conflict between China and the United States. These scholars all realized that differences in political interests, ideologies, and cultural values had distanced the two countries in the past, and would continue to bring about problems in their relations in the future. However, while some of these scholars argued that the common interests in strategic concerns and economic exchanges between the two countries made these differences only of secondary importance, others argued that further contacts between the Chinese and the Americans would help bridge these gaps between the two peoples.

It is on the Taiwan issue that the contributors to this volume expressed the greatest concern about the future development of Chinese-American relations. Several scholars argued that if the Americans continued to fail to understand that the Taiwan issue was by its essence related not only to China's national interests but also to the Chinese people's conviction of China being a unified nation, and that the Taiwan issue was part of China's internal affairs, the prospect of a closer Sino-American cooperation would be jeopardized.[82]

The Tiananmen tragedy in 1989, together with the collapse of the Soviet Union and the end of the Cold War, changed dramatically the environment of Sino-American relations and created a series of new problems for Beijing and Washington. When Sino-American relations entered a period of difficulties, the tone of Chinese scholarship changed accordingly. While most Chinese scholars continue to argue, usually in rather abstract terms, the importance of a smooth development of Sino-American relations for China's course of modernization, as well as for the maintenance of stability in the Asian-Pacific region, some extreme points of view have penetrated the field. Excluding the official-sponsored propaganda that can hardly be defined as "scholarship" according to any standard, two new themes should be mentioned here. First, the Americans do not have a proper understanding of the "characteristics" of China's tradition and culture, which, together with profound American-ethnocentrism and superpower mentality, has caused America to try to impose its values and codes of behavior on the Chinese.[83] Second, the Americans do not want to see the emergence of a unified and powerful China, and it is America's long-range, strategic goal to keep China economically backward, politically divided, and militarily weak, so that America would be able to maintain its dominant position in the international economic and political system.[84] In general, the post-1989 scholarship is much less optimistic about the future of Chinese-American relations.

Toward Establishing New Scholarly Perspectives

The development of Sino-American relations studies in the past decade in China is striking. With the establishment of new institutions and new access

to useful sources, Chinese scholars, especially scholars of the younger generation, have made major efforts to widen the scope of the field while at the
same time developing new theses in their studies. However, these developments are more quantitative than qualitative in nature. Three main problems
have lingered in the field, which are hindering further improvement of Chinese scholarship on Sino-American relations.

First, although many Chinese scholars have stressed the need to widen
researchers' vision by making such important aspects as the cultural and
social developments part of the mainstream of Sino-American relations studies, the reality is that the Chinese scholarship emerging in the past decade
remains focused on political relations. Not only have politics and political
economy remained the focus of most scholars' studies, but also, and worse,
predetermined political judgements have restricted (if not dominated) scholarly vision.

Second, when Chinese scholars criticize the American ethnocentrism
demonstrated both in American policy toward China and American scholars' studies of Sino-American relations, they need to notice that ethnocentrism exists in the Chinese conceptual world as well, making bias, misperceptions, and misinterpretations possible. This danger is further deepened
by the fact that most Chinese scholars, restricted by China's political settings
and confined by their own highly politically oriented training, have been
accustomed to focus their criticism on American policies toward China, and
they have seldom criticized the PRC's policy toward the United States. Unless
this danger is fully appreciated, the prospect for the field's further progress
could be dim.

Finally, the further development of Chinese studies on Sino-American
relations, especially those related to the post-1949 period, depends on the
opening of Chinese archival sources, so that all scholars, both Chinese and
foreign, will have equal and free access to the documentary data that will serve
as the basis of authentic scholarship. As long as the current situation of documents being released only on a selective basis (and, sometimes, released for
purposes other than making the truth known) continues, there is always the
possibility that a study might be misled by its incomplete data bases. As a
result, the field as a whole will continue to suffer.

NOTES

1. For a survey of the conference, see Wang Lizhong, "A Scholarly Conference on Sino-American Relations Convened in Shanghai," *Shijieshi yanjiu dongtai* (Trends in World History Studies), no. 5 (1986); for the conference proceedings, see the Editorial Committee of

the Series on Sino-American Relations and the History Department of Fudan University eds., *Zhongmei guanxi lunwenji* (A Collection of Research Papers on Sino-American Relations, hereafter cited as Lunwenji), vol. 2 (Chongqing: Chongqing Press, 1988).

2. For a survey of the conference, see Tao Wenzhao, "A Report on the Conference on Sino-American Relations," *Jingdaishi yanjiu* (Studies on Modern Chinese History), no. 6 (1988); for the conference proceedings, see the Editorial Committee of the Series on Sino-American Relations and the Johns Hopkins-Nanjing University Center for Chinese-American Studies eds., *Zhongmei guanxi lunwenji* (A Collection of Research Papers on Sino-American Relations), vol. 3 (Nanjing: Nanjing University Press, 1992).

3. Wang Xi, chief ed., "Zhongmei guanxi yanjiu congshu" (The Series on the Study of Sino-American Relations, Shanghai: Fudan University Press); and Ding Mingnan, chief ed., "Zhongmei guanxishi yanjiu congshu" (The Series on the Study of the History of Sino-American Relations, by various presses). The first series covers both historical and current topics, and the second series is historically oriented.

4. For a bibliography, see Yang Yusheng and Hu Yukun comp., *Zhongguo meiguoxue lunwen zhongmu* (A Guide to Essays on American Studies in China, Shenyang: Liaoning University Press, 1991), Part Seven; see also Tao Wenzhao, "Sino-American Relations Studies: The Past Decade in Retrospect," *Lunwenji*, 3: 282–307.

5. The letter by Zi Zhongyun (President of the Society for Scholars of Sino-U.S. Relations) to announce the society's establishment, July 1993.

6. Li Shenzhi, preface to Yang Yusheng and Hu Yukun comp., *Zhongguo meiguoxue lunwen zhongmu*, 1–2.

7. The most detailed study on Chinese-American trade is Wang Xi and Tsou Mingteh, "Sino-American Trade before the Opium War," *Fudan xuebao* (The Journal of Fudan University), nos. 4–5 (1982); a revised version of this article is published in Wang Xi ed., *Zhongmei guanxishi luncong* (The History of Sino-American Relations: Selected Essays, Shanghai: Fudan University Press, 1985), 93–146. Other main publications covering this topic include Qiao Mingshun, *Zhongmei guanxi diyiye* (The First Page of Sino-American Relations, Beijing: Press of Social Science Documents, 1991); Qiao Mingshun, "A Brief Discussion of Sino-American Relations before 1840," *Lunwenji*, 2: 1–18; Qi Wenying, "On the *Empress of China*'s Successful Voyage to China," *Lunwenji*, 2: 19–32; and Luo Zhitian, "Early Contacts between China and the United States, 1784–1839," *Meiguo yanjiu congkai* (Series on American Studies), no. 2 (1986).

8. Many Chinese scholars, as a result of their training, have been accustomed to applying a Marxist methodology of class analysis to their study of history, focusing on defining the "nature" of human activities. In the study of Sino-American relations, this phenomenon also widely exists.

9. Wang and Tsou , "Sino-American Trade before the Opium War," 93–94; Qiao Mingshun, *Zhongmei guanxi diyiye*, chs. 1–2; and Jiang Xiangze and Wu Jipeng et al., *Jianmin zhongmei guanxi shi* (A Brief History of Sino-American Relations, Xian: Shaanxi People's Press, 1989), chapter 1.

10. See, for example, Wang and Tsou, "Sino-American Trade before the Opium War," 94–96; Qi Wenying, "On the *Empress of China*'s Successful Voyage to China," *Lunwenji*, 2: 19–32; and Tao Wenzhao, *Zhongmei guanxi shi* (A History of Sino-American Relations, 1911–1950, Chongqing: Chongqing Press. 1993), 2–4.

11. Wang and Tsou, "Sino-American Trade before the Opium War," 127–130; Qiao Mingshun, *Zhongmei guanxi diyiye*, p. 3.

12. Qiao Mingshun, *Zhongmei guanxi diyiye*, p. 153; Luo Rongqu, "The Introduction of New American and Western Bourgeoisie Culture into China," *Lunwenji*, 1: 36–37.

13. Wu Mengxue, *Meiguo zaihua lingshi caipanquan bainianshi* (A Century's History of U.S. Extraterritoriality in China, Beijing: The Press of Social Science Documents, 1992), ch. 1.

14. Qiao Mingshun, *Zhongmei guanxi diyiye*, ch. 7; Wu Mengxue, *Meiguo zaihua lingshi caipanquan bainianshi*, part II; Xiong Zhiyong, "Sino-American Diplomacy and the Signing of the Wangxia Treaty," *Jingdaishi yanjiu*, no. 2 (1989).

15. Zhu Jieqin, "The Role Played by Chinese Immigrants in America's Development in the Late 19th Century," *Lunwenji*, 1: 159–160; Hao Guiyuan, "The Qing Government's Dealings with the United States on the 'Chinese Exclusion Act' Issue," *Meiguoshi lunwenji* (Essays on American History, Beijing: People's Press, 1983); Cao Qian, "America's 'Chinese Exclusion' Policy and the Qing Government's Attitude," *Huaqiao lishi* (History of Overseas Chinese), no. 4 (1986).

16. Wu Mengxue, *Meiguo zaihua lingshi caipanquan bainianshi*, 69.

17. For a discussion, see Luo Rongqu and Jiang Xiangze's review essays in *New Frontiers in American-East Asian Relations*, edited by Warren I. Cohen (Columbia University Press, 1983); see also Tao Wenzhao, "Sino-American Relations Studies: The Past Decade in Retrospect," 286–287.

18. See, for example, Ding Mingnan, "A Historical Examination of America's Open Door Policy toward China," *Lunwenji*, 2: 115–134; see also Qiao Mingshun, "American Monopoly Capitalists and the Making of the Open Door Policy," *Hebei daxue xuebao* (Hebei University Journal), no. 3 (1986). For a different argument, see Yan Siguang, "Discussions of America's Open Door Policy," *Meiguo yanjiu* (Journal of American Studies), no. 3 (1987).

19. See, for example, Li Xishuo, *Jingdai zhongguo de liuxuesheng* (Overseas Chinese Students in Modern China, Beijing: People's Press, 1987); and Huang Jizhong and Yu Xingmin, "The Dispatch of Chinese Students to Study Abroad during the Period of the Self-Strengthening Movement," *Huadong shida xuebao* (The Journal of East China Normal University), no. 3 (1981).

20. Li Xishuo, "Chinese Students Going to America in Late Qing and Early Republican Period," *Shixue yuecan* (History Studies Monthly), no. 4 (1982); Hu Fuxing, "The First Dispatch of Chinese Students to Study Abroad and its Significance," *Jiangxi shida xuebao* (Journal of Jiangxi Normal University), no. 4 (1985); Huang Zhizheng, "The Contribution of Chinese Students Returning from the United States to the Spreading of Scientific Knowledge During the May Fourth Period," *Jingdaishi yanjiu*, no. 2 (1989); Yuan Honglin, "On Rong Hong [Yung Wing]," *Lunwenji*, 1: 239–271; and Xu Luhang, "The Influence of Boxer Indemnity Students on China's Development," *Lunwenji*, 3: 21–32.

21. Yu Xingmin and Chen Jian, "Steamboat Industry and Steamboat Merchants in Shanghai in the 1860s," *Zhongguo shehui jingjishi yanjiu* (Chinese Social and Economic History Studies), no. 3 (1983); and "American Steamboat Merchants in Shanghai in the 1860s and 1870s," ibid., no. 3 (1985).

22. An interesting example in this regard is Gu Changsheng's revision of the title of his study on missionary activities in China. In the 1970s, this study started under the title "A History of How Imperialists Used Religion to Invade China." When this study was finally completed and published in the early 1980s, its title became *Chuanjiaoshi yu jindai zhongguo*"(Missionaries and Modern China, Shanghai: Shanghai People's Press, 1981).

23. See, for example, Luo Rongqu, "The Introduction of New American and Western Bourgeoisie Culture into China," *Lunwenji*, 1: 33–60; Guo Changsheng, *Chuanjiaoshi yu jingdai zhongguo*.

24. Luo Rongqu, "The Introduction of New American and Western Bourgeoisie Culture into China"; Liang Biying, "American Missionaries and Modern China's Cultural Contacts with the West," *Lunwenji*, 3: 1–8.

25. Chen Jiang, "Young John Allen and *Chinese Globe Magazine*," *Lunwenji*, 2: 61–84.

26. Wang Weijian, "W.A.P. Martin and the Tong Wen Guan in Beijing," in Wang Xi ed., *Zhongmei guanxi luncong*, 194–229; Wang Weijian, "W.A.P. Martin in 1900," *Lunwenji*, 2: 85–114; Liang Biying, "American Missionaries and Modern China's Contacts with the West," *Lunwenji*, 3: 1–20; and Chen Jiang, "Young John Allen and *Chinese Globe Magazine*."

27. Qing Simei, "A Study on U.S. Policy toward China on the Eve of the 1911 Revolution," *Lunwenji*, 1: 186–225. For a recent study of Chinese-American relations during the 1911 Revolution, see Tao Wenzhao, *Zhongmei guanxi shi*, ch. 1, part 1.

28. Shen Yu, "A Study on the Imperialists' Relationship with the Shanghai Coup of 1927," *Lishi yanjiu* (History Studies), no. 4 (1984); "U.S. Policy toward China during the Period of the the Northern Expedition," *Lunwenji*, 2: 204–230.

29. Niu Dayong, "The Connections Between U.S. China Policy and the April 12, 1927 Coup," *Lishi yanjiu*, no. 4 (1985); "U.S. Policy Toward China and the Failure of the Great Revolution," *Lunwenji*, 2: 231–256; and "U.S. Policy Toward the Northern Expedition and the Establishment of the U.S.-Jiang Relations," *Jingdaishi yanjiu*, no. 6 (1985). For a discussion about the establishment of the relations between Jiang's Nanjing government and the United States, see Guo Xixiao, "The Nanjing Incident and Sino-American Diplomacy," *Lishi yanjiu*, no. 5 (1992).

30. Dorothy Borg, *American Policy and the Chinese Revolution*, 1925–1928 (New York: Octagon Press, 1968); Warren I. Cohen, *America's Response to China* (New York: Columbia University Press, 3rd ed., 1990), ch. 4; Akira Iriye, *After Imperialism: The Search for a New Order in the Far East, 1921–1931* (Cambridge: Harvard University Press, 1965).

31. After being a researcher at CASS's Institute of Modern History for over a decade, Tao Wenzhao became deputy director of CASS's Institute of American Studies in early 1994.

32. Tao Wenzhao, "America and China's Three Revolutions," *Zhonggong dangshi yanjiu* (CCP History Study), no. 2 (1990).

33. For two recent studies on the making of the Washington conference system and its connections with the development of Sino-American relations, see Xiang Liling, *Zhongmei guanxi shang de yici quzhe: cong bali hehui dao huashengdun huiyi* (A Tortuous Experience in the Development of Sino-American Relations: From Paris Conference to Washington Conference, Shanghai: Fudan University Press, 1993), and Tao Wenzhao, *Zhongmei guanxishi*, ch. 2.

34. Hu Dekun, "The Manchurian Incident and the Policy of Appeasement," *Wuhan daxue xuebao* (The Journal of Wuhan University), no. 3 (1979); Liu Tianchun, "The Plot of Far East Munich and China's War of Resistance against Japan," *Zhongguo shekeyuan yanjiushengyuan xuebao* (The Journal of the Graduate School of CASS), no. 4, (1985); and Wang Mingzhong, "The Manchurian Incident and the Stimson Doctrine," *Meiguoshi lunwenji, 1981–1983* (A Collection of Essays on American History, 1981–1983, Beijing: Sanlian Press, 1983).

35. Yi Xianshi, "On America's Response to the September 18th Incident," *Zhongmei guanxishi luncong*, 315–327; Gao Eryin, "Open-doorism versus the Continental Strategy: American-Japanese Diplomacy around the September 18th Incident," *Lunwenji*, 2: 257–279.

36. See, for example, Liu Tianchun, "The Plot of Far Eastern Munich and China's War of Resistance against Japan"; Feng Chunming, "American Policy toward China during the War of Resistance against Japan), *Mingguo dangan* (Republican Archives), no. 3 (1986).

37. Wang Side and Li Julian, "The Changing U.S. Far Eastern Strategies Prior to the Pacific War," *Lunwenji*, 1: 289–310; see also Wang Side and Chen Jian, "China's War of Resistance against Japan and the Changing Strategies of the Major Powers," *Shehui kexue zhanx-*

ian (Social Science Front), no. 3 (1985); Ren Donglai, "The Road to a Sino-American Anti-Japanese Alliance," *Nanjing daxue xuebao* (The Journal of Nanjing University), no. 1 (1992).

38. According to incomplete statistics, more than forty articles have been published on General Stilwell and the Jiang-Stilwell controversy. The most notable ones include Wei Chuxiong, "The Stilwell Affair and Its Causes," *Jindaishi yanjiu*, no. 1 (1985); He Di et al., "The Evolution of U.S. China Policy during the Last Stage of the War of Resistance against Japan," *Zhongmei guanxi luncong*, 311–335.

39. The background differences between historians of modern China and historians of American diplomacy, as noted in earlier sections of this paper, no longer make any significant sense in explaining the different views held by scholars in their studies on PRC-U.S. relations. One explanation is that the political sensitivity of the questions under discussion has overwhelming influence upon the research environment, as well as on scholars' conceptual realm, making scholars' background differences insignificant.

40. The best study on this topic is Niu Jun, *Cong heerli dao maxieer* (From Hurley to Marshall, Fuzhou: Fujian People's Press, 1988). See also Xiang Liling, "Hurley and Roosevelt's Policy toward China," *Meiguoshi lunwenji,1982–1983*; Xiang Liling, *Zhuanzhe de yinian: Heerli shihua ye meiguo duihua zhengce* (A Year of Transition: The Hurley Mission and U.S. Policy toward China, Chongqing: Chongqing Press, 1988); Yang Lixian," Hurley's Mediation and the Turning Point of Wartime Sino-American Relations," *Beijing shida xuebao* (Journal of Beijing Normal University), no. 1 (1987); Tao Wenzhao, "Hurley's Mission to China and the Making of America's Supporting Jiang and Opposing Communist Policy," *Jingdaishi yanjiu*, no. 2 (1987); and Tao Wenzhao, *Zhongmei guanxishi*, ch. 7.

41. Niu Jun, *Cong heerli dao maxieer*; Niu Jun, "Marshall's Mission in China and the Civil War in the Northeast," *Lunwenji*, 3: 166–190; Tu Chuande, "U.S. China Policy during the Postwar Period and the Marshall Mission to China," *Lunwenji*, 1: 336–349; Tao Wenzhao, "Marshall's Mission to China and the Truman Administration's China Policy," *Lunwenji*, 2: 412–429; Wang Guanhua, "American Policy toward China after the End of World War II and Marshall's Mission to China," *Nanjing daxue xuebao* (The Journal of Nanjing University), a special issue on modern and contemporary international relations, 1987; for a discussion focusing on the CCP's management of the Marshall mission, see Yang Kuisong, "The GMD-CCP Negotiations and the Marshall Mission to China," *Lishi yanjiu*, no. 5 (1990).

42. The most important study on the topic is Zi Zhongyun, *Meiguo duihua zhengce de yuanqi he fazhan, 1945–1950* (The Origins and Development of American Policy toward China, Chongqing: Chongqing Press, 1987); see also Shi Yinhong, "The Truman Administration's Policy toward the New China: From Hostility to War," Ph.D. dissertation, Nanjing University, 1988; Wang Jianwei, "American Policy toward China on the Eve and after the New China's Founding," *Lunwenji*, 2: 449–470; and Tao Wenzhao, *Zhongmei guanxishi*, ch. 8.

43. Tao Wenzhao, "The Recognition Issue and U.S. Policy toward China, 1949–1950," *Lishi yanjiu*, no. 4 (1993).

44. Zi Zhongyun, "Test of History: U.S. Policy toward Taiwan around the New China's Founding," *Lunwenji*, 1: 350–367; Shi Yinhong, "The Truman Administration's Policy toward China and the Taiwan Issue," *Lunwenji*, 2: 471–493.

45. Zi Zhongyun, *Meiguo duihua zhengce de yuanqi he fazhan, 1945–1950*; Yuan Ming, "America's Conception of China Policy around the New China's Founding," *Lishi yanjiu*, no. 3 (1987); Wang Jisi, "U.S. Policy toward China and Its Consequences, 1945–1955," *Meiguo yanjiu*, no. 1 (1987).

46. Cited from Zhang Baijia, "A Review of the Seminar on the History of Sino-American Relations, 1945–1955," *Lishi yanjiu*, no. 3 (1987), 40.

47. See, for example, Tao Wenzhao, "The Recognition Issue and U.S. Policy toward China, 1949–1950."

48. For example, *Zhonggong zhongyang wenjian xuanji* (Selected Documents of the CCP Central Committee, 18 vols., Beijing: CCP Central Academy Press, 1989–1993).

49. Niu Jun, *Cong Yan'an zouxiang shijie: zhongguo gongchandang duiwai guanxi de qiyuan* (From Yan'an Marching toward the World: The Origins of the CCP's External Relations, Fuzhou: The Fujian People's Press, 1992); He Di, "The CCP's Changing Policy toward the United States, 1945–1949," *Lishi yanjiu*, no. 3 (1987); Zhang Baijia, "New China's Foreign Policy," *Guoshi yanjiu cankao ziliao* (Reference Materials of PRC History Studies), no. 2 (1993); Yang Kuisong, "The Soviet Factor and the CCP's Policy toward the United States in the 1940s," *Chinese Historians*, vol. 5, no. 1 (Spring 1992); and Yang Kuisong, "The Ward Case and the Finalization of the CCP's Policy toward the U.S.," *Lishi yanjiu*, forthcoming. Among these scholars, Yang Kuisong has made the most extensive use of previously unavailable Chinese archival sources.

50. These new sources include personal memoirs by those who were involved in Beijing's intervention in Korea, official academic publications using classified documents, openly or internally published collections of CCP Central Committee's and regional bureaus' documents, and the internally published collections of Mao Zedong's papers. While it is apparent that these sources have created new opportunities for fresh studies, it is also clear that they were released on a selective basis and, sometimes, for purposes other than a desire to have the truth known. For a more detailed discussion of these new sources, see Chen Jian, *China's Road to the Korean War: the Making of Sino-American Confrontation, 1948–1950* (New York: Columbia University Press, 1994), 5–6.

51. See, for example, Qi Dexue, "A Survey of the CPV's Strategic Goals in the War to Resist America and Assist Korea," *Zhonggong dangshi yanjiu*, no. 6 (1989); Yao Xu, *Cong yalujiang dao banmendian* (From the Yalu River to Panmunjom, Beijing: People's Press, 1985).

52. See Mao Zedong's remarks, July 7, 1950, *Jianguo yilai Mao Zedong wengao* (Mao Zedong's Manuscripts since the Founding of the People's Republic, Beijing: The Central Press of Historical Documents, 1987) 1: 428; Mao Zedong to Gao Gang, August 5 and 18, ibid., 1: 454, 469.

53. See, for example, Mao Zedong to Stalin, October 2, 1950, *Mao wengao*, 1: 539–541.

54. For a more detailed discussion, see Chen Jian, "China's Changing Aims during the Korean War, 1950–1951," *The Journal of American-East Asian Relations*, 1, no. 1 (Spring 1992): 8–41.

55. Mao Zedong to Peng Dehuai, Gao Gang, and convey to Kim Il-sung, July 2, 1951, *Mao wengao*, 2: 381; Chai Chengwen and Zhao Yongtian, *Banmendian tanpan* (Panmunjom Negotiations, Beijing: People's Liberation Army Press, 1992), 150–151, 169–170.

56. Xu Yan, *Diyici jiaoliang* (The First Test of Strength, Beijing: Chinese Television and Broadcasting Press, 1990), ch. 7; Qi Dexue, *Chaoxian zhanzheng juece neimu* (Inside Story of the Decisionmaking During the Korean War, Shenyang: Liaoning University Press, 1992), chs. 5–6.

57. Nie Rongzhen's report to Zhou Enlai and Mao Zedong, February 18, 1952, *Nie Rongzhen junshi wenxuan* (Selected Military Papers of Nie Rongzhen, Beijing: People's Liberation Army Press, 1992), 365–366. The editor of this volume put the date of this report as February 28. However, according to other sources, the date should be February 18.

58. Mao Zedong's remarks on Nie Rongzhen's report, February 19, 1952, *Jianguo yilai Mao Zedong wengao*, 3: 239.

59. See, for example, Qi Dexue, *Chaoxian zhanzheng neimu*, p. 314.

60. Xu Yan, *Jinmen zhizhan* (The Battle of Jinmen, Beijing: Chinese Television and Broadcasting Press, 1992), ch. 4; and "The CCP Central Committee's Strategies in Handling the Struggles in the Southeastern Coastal Areas in the 1950s," *Zhonggong dangshi yanjiu*, no. 2 (1992), 54–57.

61. Wang Bingnan, *Zhongmei huitan jiunian huigu* (Nine Years of Sino-American Ambassadorial Talks, Beijing: The Press of World Affairs, 1985).

62. He Di, "The Evolution of the People's Republic of China's Policy toward the Offshore Islands," in Warren I. Cohen and Akira Iriye eds, *The Great Powers in East Asia, 1953–1960* (New York: Columbia University Press, 1990), 222–245.

63. Xu Yan, *Jinmen zhizhan*, ch. 5.

64. Mao Zedong's Speech to the Supreme State Council, September 5, 1958, *Jianguo yilai Mao wengao*, 7: 389–390.

65. See, for example, Quan Yanshi, *Mao Zedong he Heluxiaofu* (Mao Zedong and Khrushchev, Beijing, 1992).

66. Useful studies include Shi Yingfu, *Mimi chubing yare conglin: yuanyue kangmei jishi* (Sending Troops Secretly to the Sub-tropical Jungles: A Factual Account of Assisting Vietnam and Resisting America) (Beijing: People's Liberation Army Literature Press, 1990), Wang Xiangen, *Kangmei yuanyue shilu* (A Factual Account of Resisting America and Assisting Vietnam, Beijing: International Cultural Development Press, 1990), and Li Ke and Hao Shengzhang, *Wenhua dageming zhong de renmin jiefangjun* (The People's Liberation Army During the Cultural Revolution) (Beijing: CCP Historical Materials Press, 1989), 408–409. The second volume offers one of the best accounts of China's military development from the mid-1960s to the mid-1970s. As the authors were alleged to have released confidential information without proper authorization, the book was withdrawn from circulation shortly after its publication.

67. See Chen Jian, "China's Involvement with the Vietnam War, 1964–1969," *The China Quarterly*, forthcoming.

68. Interestingly, one of the first signs of Beijing's new attitude toward Washington was that in January 1969 *Hongqi* and *Renmin ribao*, the official journal and newspaper of the Chinese Communist Party, published Richard Nixon's inauguration speech, in which the U.S. president mentioned that the United States would not encourage the exclusion of any country (including China) from the world community. In 1969, with Mao's approval and under Zhou's direct supervision, Beijing started to reassess its relations with the United States. New Chinese sources prove that Mao personally approved the publication of Nixon's speech. See Gong Li, *Kuayue honggou: The Evolution of Sino-American Relations, 1969–1979* (Zhengzhou: Henan People's Press, 1992), p. 40.

69. Mao Zedong, *Mao Zedong zhuxi yu sinuo de tanhua* (Chairman Mao Zedong's Talks with Edgar Snow, Beijing: People's Press, 1971).

70. Gong Li, *Kuayue honggou*, ch. 2. This book is one of the best comprehensive studies done by Chinese scholars on this issue.

71. See, for example, Gong Li, *Kuayue honggou*, 20–34; Xie Yixian et al., *Zhongguo waijiao shi, 1949–1979* (A History of Chinese Diplomacy, 1949–1979, Zhengzhou: Henan People's Press, 1988), 377–378.

72. Xiong Xianghui, "The Prelude to the Opening of Sino-American Relations," *Zhonggong dangshi ziliao* (CCP History Materials), no. 42 (June 1992), 56–96.

73. Ibid.; Gong Li, *Kuayue honggou*, 23–25.

74. See, for example, Qian Jiang, *Ping pong waijiao shimo* (The Complete Story of the Ping Pong Diplomacy, Beijing, 1987).

75. Chen Dunde, *Mao Zedong, Nikesong zai 1972* (Mao Zedong and Nixon in 1972, Beijing: Kunlun Press, 1988). Chen is a movie director.

76. Gong Li, *Kuayue honggou*, chs. 4 and 5; Wei Shiyan, "The Inside Story of Kissinger's Secret Visit to China," in *Xinzhongguo waijiao fengyun*, 2: 33–45.

77. Gong Li, *Kuayue honggou*, 102–108.

78. Zhang Yufong, "Random Recollections on Chairman Mao's Last Years," in *Mao zhuxi yishi* (Chairman Mao's Stories, Changsha: Hunan Literature Press, 1989), 9–11.

79. The Institute of American Studies, CASS, and Chinese Association for American Studies, eds., *Zhongmei guanxi shinian* (A Decade of Sino-American Relations, Beijing: Shangwu Press, 1989).

80. Zhang Jingyi, "The Security Factor in Sino-American Relations: Retrospect and Prospect"; Li Pei, "The Security Relations between China and the United States since the Establishment of Diplomatic Relations"; Zhuang Qubing, "The Soviet Factor in U.S. Policy Toward China" ibid., 38–52, 53–64, 66–81.

81. Zi Zhongyun, "The Basis for Sino-American Relations," ibid., 17–37.

82. He Di, "American-Taiwan Relations in the 1980s," ibid., 82–109; see also Zi Zhongyun and He Di eds. *Meitai guanxi sishinian* (Forty Years of American-Taiwan Relations, Beijing: People's Press, 1991).

83. See, for example, Hua Qingzhao, "The Prospect of American Culture Influence in Asia," Meiguoshi yanjiuhui tongbao (Chinese Association of American Studies Newsletter), no. 51 (June 1992); Ji Hongsheng ed., *Zhongmei guanxi wushinian* (Sino-American Relations in the Past Fifty Years, Shanghai: Baijia Press, 1993), 205–208;

84. The extreme expression of this view can be found in He Xin's discussion about the post Cold War international situation and American foreign policy, collected in his *Shiji zhijiao de zhongguo yu shijie* (China and the World at the Turn of the Century, Chengdu: Sichuan People's Press, 1991) (He Xin is a researcher affiliated with CASS. In 1991 he became a member of China's National People's Consultative Conference). However, many other Chinese scholars share in different degrees a view like this. For example, in two review essays on Edward Said's recent book, *Culture and Imperialism* (New York: Knopf, 1993), the authors argue that such concepts as "hegemony" and "imperialism" are far from out of date. Rather, according to them, the imperialist "mentality' and "spirit" has found new expressions in the post-Cold War era. See Zhang Kuan's and Qiao Jun's review essay in *Dushu* (Books Reading), no. 9 (1993) (*Dushu* has been a widely recognized intellectual forum in China since the early 1980s).

Chapter Two

Japanese Scholarship in the History of U.S.–East Asian Relations

ARUGA TADASHI

This overview of recent Japanese scholarship in the history of U.S.-East Asian relations aims to introduce major monographic works and research trends during the last fifteen years. As historical scholarship reflects and helps shape the current intellectual climate and public mood, this essay will also pay attention to the intellectual environment in which Japanese historians have been working. There are some problems in defining "Japanese scholarship." For example, Akira Iriye's writings, both English and Japanese, are influential in the Japanese academic community. Since he has his academic base in America, and since his scholarship is well known internationally, this essay will not usually discuss his work. There are a number of doctoral dissertations submitted by Japanese students to American universities. They may be part of American scholarship as well as Japanese scholarship. This essay will usually mention these dissertations but mainly introduce their authors' Japanese publications. This essay refers only occasionally to Japanese contributions to academic journals and books published in English in the United States. There are a number of Chinese and Korean scholars who studied at Japanese universities and have been active in the Japanese academic community. Their relevant works published in Japan will be mentioned in this paper as part of scholarship in Japan.

Unless it is necessary for an explanation of the historiographical background, this overview will not discuss works published before 1980. Any reader interested in Japanese works in diplomatic history published before 1980 should consult the two reference books edited by Sadao Asada (his name will usually be referred to as Asada Sadao in this paper), *Japan and the World, 1853-1952: A Bibliographic Guide to Japanese Scholarship in Foreign Relations*,[1] which contains historiographical essays as well as bibliographies regarding Japanese foreign relations from the opening of Japan to the San Francisco peace settlement, and its sister volume, *International Studies in Japan: A Bibliographic Guide*,[2] which serves as a guide to Japanese works on major aspects of Japanese foreign relations after the San Francisco peace settlement and on international history and area studies not directly related to Japanese foreign relations.

Shigaku zasshi, a monthly journal of historical studies in Japan, features in each May issue review essays on Japanese scholarship published in the various fields of history during the previous year. Particularly useful for the purpose of this overview are review essays on Japanese scholarship in modern Japanese history. But there is also some relevant information in essays on Japanese scholarship in North American history and modern East Asian history.

With some exceptions, this essay romanizes Japanese personal names in the family name—given name order.[3] This may cause some confusion, since most Japanese reverse this order when they romanize their names and because many internationally active Japanese are known by names in the Westernized name order. To avoid confusion, the family name of a Japanese author will be printed in capital and small capitals when his/her full name appears in bibliographical citations in endnotes.

1. Japan and the United States: The First Encounter

The U.S.-Japanese relationship was asymmetrical at the beginning. The arrival of the *Kurofune* (black ships), the American squadron commanded by Commodore Matthew Perry in 1853, not only led to the opening of Japan to foreign intercourse but also triggered a profound political and social upheaval that culminated in the demise of the Shogunate regime and the creation of the more progressive Meiji regime. For the United States, on the other hand, the dispatch of Perry's fleet to Japan was a minor political event in an era of growing sectional tensions, even if it was no minor adventure for its navy.

Because of the importance of external impact in the 1850s and 1860s, many Japanese scholars have studied the initial phase of Japan's external relations.[4] Katō Yūzō's *Kurofune zengo no sekai* and *Kurofune ihen*[5] offer a broad and perceptive discussion of the first U.S.-Japanese encounter. Katō relates the dispatch of Perry's fleet to Japan to the traditional role of the U. S. navy to provide Americans abroad with diplomatic protection. Instead of subscribing to economic interpretions of the dispatch of Perry's mission, Katō emphasizes the navy's bureaucratic interest in carrying out this mission. Confronted with the reduction of naval expenditure after the Mexican War, the navy wanted to maintain its level of strength by emphasizing the need to protect the safety of American vessels and seamen in Asia and by appealing to the nationalistic urge to precede Britain in diplomatic contact with Japan.

Yamaguchi Muneyuki's *Perii raikō zengo*[6] points out that Japanese officials, forewarned of Perry's arrival by the Dutch, remained relatively cool during his presence in Edo Bay. The author also notes that the local people were not overly alarmed. The only times the Japanese were much agitated were when Perry led a part or the whole of his squadron deep into the bay to put pressures on the Shogunate.

As Katō points out, it was very important for U.S.-Japanese relations for the two nations to avoid war at their first encounter, and indeed they succeeded in opening intercourse peacefully. It is Katō's view that both sides wanted to avoid armed conflict. Although Perry used forceful diplomacy backed by his "black ships," he had no intention of violating the government's instruction to use force only in self-defense. The Shogunate's prime minister, Abe Masahiro, and his colleagues wanted to avoid war to maintain Japan's national dignity by accepting Perry's minimum demands. Katō's two books, although both are small and overlapping in contents, are seminal in suggesting problematiques for the first U.S.-Japanese encounter: What were their mutual perceptions, their views of the world situation, and their diplomatic strategies and negotiation tactics? And how did mutual communication develop and how was agreement reached? More substantial work should be done along these lines.

Mitani Hiroshi's articles provide a detailed analysis of the foreign/defense policy of the Shogunate government during the 1850s.[7] Before Perry's arrival, Abe Masahiro had tried to revive the Shogunate decree ordering all *daimyō* (feudal lords) to repulse foreign vessels by force, but had refrained from doing so when he found his defense advisers and many daimyo opposed. Mitani argues that Abe changed his mind because he had wanted to restore the decree to reaffirm the legitimacy of the policy of national seclusion, but was inclined to respond flexibly when foreign warships actually appeared.

It would be no problem if foreign warships, like those commanded by Commodore Biddle in 1846, were willing to return without persisting in demanding national intercourse. When a foreign squadron persisted in its demand and appeared too formidable to fight, Japan should avoid fighting and accept the minimum demands of the visitor as a means of gaining time to increase her military strength to reestablish the policy of national seclusion. For Abe, the treaty of amity of 1854 was a partial temporary modification of the traditional policy. Mitani regards Abe's successor Hotta Masayoshi as a leader who genuinely believed that Japan would not be strong and wealthy without foreign trade. Hotta committed himself to the policy of opening the nation gradually to foreign commerce by concluding commercial treaties first with the Netherlands and Russia. He wanted to conclude a similar treaty with the United States, but Townsend Harris skillfully persuaded him to accept a more radical treaty of commerce. Because of its severe nature, this treaty incited an opposition movement that would shake the authority of the Shogunate regime.

Because the U.S.-Japanese relationship had begun without war, and because of British and French activities in China, many Japanese began to feel that the United States was more benign than other western powers. Accepting the American version of American history, they regarded the American War for Independence as a heroic war against a cruel enemy and admired the Americans for their victory in the war and for their speedy development into a powerful nation.

Nevertheless, it is unfortunate that U.S.-Japanese relationship began with America's forceful diplomacy backed by naval power. When Japanese later looked back upon the episode of the first encounter, many of them felt that it was a humiliating experience: Japan was compelled to accept U.S. demands under the threat of force. This feeling still persists among the Japanese. Thus Kishida Shū, a psychoanalyst, argues[8] that Japan was "raped" by the United States at the beginning of their relationship. According to Miwa Kimitada, Admiral Yamamoto Isoroku, the commander of the combined Japanese naval fleets during World War II, allegedly said he had entered the navy to obtain revenge for Commodore Perry's intrusion.[9]

Because of its impact, Perry's fleet became in Japanese eyes the symbol of the Western military power that threatened Japan and East Asia in the middle of the nineteenth century. Ueyama Shumpei, a Kyoto intellectual, argued in the 1960s that the shock of the *Kurofune* experience led the Japanese to an obsessional pursuit of power which culminated in the "Greater East Asian

War."[10] More recently, Inose Naoki, a writer and critic, writes that because of the *Kurofune* shock the Japanese have always felt and still feel that "there is somewhere beyond the sea horizon a mythical zone from which a unsettling mist of *gaiatsu* [external pressure] is emanating."[11]

Although the United States lost political interest in Japan during the Civil War and Reconstruction eras, many Americans, along with Europeans, came to Japan to help modernize the country. Many of them were *yatoi*, that is, people employed by the Japanese national government, local authorities or private companies. Many others were Christian missionaries. Because diplomatic relations between Japan and the United States became less important during this era, the contributions of individual Americans to Japanese modernization and their personal experiences in Japan became a more significant aspect in broadly defined U.S.-Japanese relations during the last several decades of the nineteenth century. Mori Arinori, the first Japanese minister in Washington,[12] worked hard to invite American experts to Japan.

A number of Japanese scholars have taken interest in the study of *yatoi*, and joint Japanese-American research conferences were held twice: first at Rutgers University in 1975 and second in Toyama in 1986. The proceedings of the Rutgers conference were published both in English and Japanese; the proceedings of the Toyama conference were published in Japanese.[13]

American *yatoi* played a major role in developing Hokkaido, the northern island of Japan, since the governor of Kaitakushi (Hokkaido Development Agency) employed mostly Americans because of their experience in developing the American West. Fujita Fumiko discusses leading Americans employed by Kaitakushi: their contributions to the development of the island, their personal relationships with the Japanese, and their views of Japanese culture. Fujita recognizes three types of Americans: those who believed in the universal application of the American way, those who wanted the Japanese to retain their traditional culture, and those who recognized both peculiar and universal qualities in Japanese culture. She contends that the third type of Americans struck the most responsive chord in Japan. She also compares the development of Hokkaido with the American West and points out the absence of a robust frontier spirit in the Japanese case as the most significant difference. It was an enterprise guided and promoted from above by the Meiji government.[14]

Kohiyama Rui studied American women who worked in Japan as missionaries during the 1870s and 1880s.[15] Her book offers an example of women's studies in Japan. She explains that the efforts of American missionary women were successful in developing education for Japanese women in those decades because the Japanese government busied itself in establishing the educational system for men and left the field of women's education to private initiatives. It was not until the mid-1890s that the Japanese government started the policy of developing secondary education for women. Thereafter the role of American missionary women in Japanese education declined. The author suggests, however, that the ideal of middle-class American womanhood influenced the official motto for female public education, to bring up good wives and wise mothers.

As Kohiyama points out, however, the Japanese concept of family was different from that of the Americans. Several Japanese women educated by American teachers became socially active, but all had difficulty in Japanese society because of their faith and their liberal way of life. Women's studies will illuminate certain less studied aspects of U.S.-Japanese transnational relations, such as: the attitudes of the various Japanese women's associations to issues of U.S.-Japanese relations, the transnational relations between American and Japanese women's associations, and the roles of American-educated women in prewar and postwar Japan. An interesting book relating to the last topic is Kuno Akiko's biography of Ōyama (Yamakawa) Sutematsu, the Vassar College-educated wife of Ōyama Iwao, a prominant army general of Meiji Japan.[16] Sutematsu's letters written to her best American friend supplied Kuno with invaluable sources for this biography.

2. Japanese in America

The study of the experience of Japanese immigrants and their descendants in the United States was not a thriving branch of American studies in Japan until around 1980; the study of Japanese emigration was a minor field in modern Japanese history.[17] During the last fifteen years, however, research on Japanese emigration and ethnic Japanese abroad has burgeoned. The recent growth of Japanese literature dealing with Japanese emigration and ethnic Japanese in America, like the development of the study of Americans in Meiji Japan, is a manifestation of increasing Japanese awareness of the importance of intercultural relations. "Internationalization" was a fashionable catchword of the 1980s in Japan. As Togami Muneyoshi observed in 1985, international themes, such as Japanese experiences overseas, became in vogue in the Japanese media.[18]

Several general histories of Japanese immigrants in Hawaii and the mainland have been translated from English, while Japanese authors have also written on this topic during these years. Among more specific studies, particularly interesting is Notoji Masako's study of the *issei* (first-generation) Japanese who settled as farmers in the Yakima Valley in Washington.[19] Notoji traces their community's quest for ethnic identity during the four prewar decades. They tried to soften anti-Japanese sentiment among white Americans by eagerly adopting the American way of life. They wanted to be decent members of American society and their children to become good citizens of the United States. At the same time, Issei Japanese tried to maintain their morale by bolstering their racial pride and implanting it in the minds of their American-born children. Americanization, argues Notoji, did not weaken Japanese-consciousness, but instead strengthened it.

Japanese immigrants were not only farmers and laborers. As Tachikawa Kenji pointed out, there was an American fever among Japanese youth at the beginning of the twentieth century.[20] Many believed that the United States was a paradise for poor students where they could earn enough to support themselves while studying in school. One of the writers who spread such an image of America was Katayama Sen, a radical who later became an activist for international communism. After a sojourn of more than ten years in the United States, he returned to Japan to publish a magazine that propagated simultaneously both the idea of America as a paradise for the ambitious poor and the gospel of socialism. He was a socialist, but he loved America's open society in which he believed everyone could gain a fair reward for hard work.

Among those who went to the United States to receive higher education around the turn of the century were Asakawa Kanichi (Kanichi Asakawa) and Kiyoshi Kawakami (K. K. Kawakami), both of whom chose to remain in America and were married to American women: Asakawa became a highly respected medievalist at Yale, and Kawakami became a journalist specializing in East Asian international affairs. Abe Yoshio's biography of Asakawa includes chapters on Asakawa's opposition to the course of Japanese imperialism after the end of Russo-Japanese War and his appeal to President Roosevelt to send a personal telegram to Tenno Hirohito to avoid a Japanese-American war in 1941.[21] In addition, there is an article by Ohata Tokushiro, a diplomatic historian, that discusses Asakawa's criticism of Japanese foreign policy.[22] K. K. Kawakami's name may be familiar to students of U.S.-East Asian relations from the 1910s through the 1930s because his signed articles appeared very often in American news magazines. The former socialist lost his political faith and always defended Japanese foreign policy and military actions in Asia. His biography by Komori Yoshihisa describes with some sympathy the difficult position of a Japanese journalist living in the United States and writing both for the American and Japanese media in an age of turbulent international affairs.[23]

Another young man who went to the United States to study was Kiyosawa Kiyoshi, who soon began to work as a reporter for Japanese community newspapers in Seattle and San Francisco. Kiyosawa later returned to Japan and was active in Japanese journalism during the interwar period. He is remembered as a diplomatic critic who emphasized the importance of friendly relations with the United States against the trend of the 1930s. Kitaoka Shinichi wrote a good biography of Kiyosawa and discussed in a separate article his activities as a reporter/writer for Japanese-language community papers.[24] Kitaoka maintains that the basic views Kiyosawa espoused as a diplomatic critic were shaped during his years in Seattle and San Francisco. His article also touches on the mentality of Japanese immigrant communities through Kiyosawa's critical eye.

Japanese language newspapers published in Japanese immigrant communities are invaluable sources for the study of Japanese immigration. They shed much light on the life of Japanese immigrants: problems they faced, ethnic identity they developed, their responses to anti-Japanese movements, their contacts with Japanese consulates, as well as their attitudes toward Japanese foreign policy. Tamura Norio, Shiramizu Shigehiko and their associates made a very informative survey of early Japanese-language newspapers in the United States in 1986.[25] Tamura also published a history of Japanese-language newspapers in the United States.[26] These publications will stimulate studies based on those newspapers as source materials.

As Japanese-language newspapers were very important for the life of immigrant communities, so were religious teachers. Inoue Nobutaka divides Japanese religions active in the United States into three groups.[27] The first-wave group is the Honganji faction, the dominant Buddhist sect in Western Japan, which followed closely the flow of Japanese immigrants around the turn of the century. The second-wave group, such religions of relatively new origin as Tenrikyō and Konkōkyō, began its activities in the United States in the 1920s when Japanese communities achieved a degree of maturity. The third-wave group consists of new religions, such as Sekai kyuseikyō and Sōkagakkai, which began their activities in the 1950s. Sōkagakkai, known as Nichiren Shoshu America (NSA) in the United States, has made the most vigorous efforts to spread its faith outside the Japanese community and has achieved some success.

Nakamaki Hirochika discusses not only religions of Japanese origin but also ethnic Japanese Protestant churches in California.[28] Although his focus is on the present-day state of traditionally ethnic Japanese Protestant churches, Nakamaki also discusses the origins of these churches. Some Japanese immigrants became Christians because they met pastors who treated them kindly; others were converted because they thought that conversion would help them gain acceptance in American society. But Japanese-speaking pastors were necessary to spread Protestantism among Japanese immigrants. A number of Japanese graduates from theological institutes in Japan and America were engaged in missionary work among the Japanese immigrants in Hawaii and the mainland from the 1890s. Thus Protestant religion transplanted to Japan by American missionaries was retransplanted in Japanese immigrant communities in Hawaii and North America by Japanese missionaries. Their activities are described in detail in *Hokubei Nihonjin kirisutokyō undō-shi*,[29] the report of a joint research project organized by Doshisha University's Institute for the Study of Humanities.

3. Conflict and Cooperation in Asia and the Pacific

Japan and the United States both joined in imperialist power politics in the 1890s. They soon became competitors in China, although both tried to control their conflict. Japan's difficulty in adjusting its interest with America's lay in the fact that the United States, unlike other imperialist powers, did not claim any sphere of influence in China and was unwilling to recognize Japan's sphere openly. All the U.S.-Japanese agreements on China, from the Root-Takahira Agreement to the Nine Power Treaty, were ambiguous compromises between Japanese special interest and American principles of the open door.[30] The United States practiced territorial imperialism and the policy of maintaining an exclusive sphere of influence in the strategically important Caribbean region and obviously considered the Eastern Pacific above the equator its own sphere. Japan did not challenge U.S. annexation of Hawaii or the Philippines, and the United States was willing to recognize Japan's supremacy in Korea. Before Japan's acquisition of her sphere in South Manchuria, Japan and the United States tolerated each other's imperialism. The Taft-Katsura agreement demonstrates the point.

Nagata Akifumi has written a book on U.S. policy toward Korea, or U.S.-Japanese-Korean relations, during the administration of Theodore Roosevelt.[31] An outgrowth of his M.A. thesis based on Korean, as well as Japanese and American primary sources, the book depicts vividly the pathetic and vain endeavor the Korean royal court made to obtain U.S. diplomatic intervention against Japanese encroachment on Korean independence, relying on the American promise of good offices in case of Korean troubles with a third party in the U.S.-Korean Treaty of 1882. He also examines the available sources concerning Taft's visit to Japan and concludes that there was, in spite of Raymond Esthus's view to the contrary, an informal Japanese-American understanding, approved by President Roosevelt, that assured Prime Minister Katsura Taro of American support for the Anglo-Japanese alliance and for Japan's claim to supremacy in Korea. Nagata's doctoral dissertation illuminates the impact of Wilson's advocacy of national self-determination upon the Korean nationalist movement at home and abroad and describes in detail American and Japanese responses to the March 1st movement in Korea.[32] Although American official response was mild, the aroused interest of Congress and the American media in the Korean situation was one important factor that influenced Japanese post-March 1st policy toward Korea.

As Nagata mentions in his book, Katsura wanted the United States to act as an informal partner in the Anglo-Japanese alliance and Taft agreed with him. Once Japan acquired a foothold in Manchuria, however, conflict began to develop between the two countries. American business interests in South Manchuria began to complain that the Japanese were trying to monopolize commercial opportunities in the region. One American diplomat who felt betrayed by Japan was Huntington Wilson who was then in the U.S. legation in Tokyo. He returned to Washington as the third assistant secretary in 1906, but he was not consulted when the Root-Takahira agreement was signed. It was after Taft had become President that Wilson, now the assistant secretary under Secretary Knox, succeeded in establishing regional divisons permanently in the reform of the State Department in 1909. He designed toward China a dollar diplomacy which had anti-Japanese connotations. In an article written in 1989, Kitaoka Shinichi discusses the Taft administration's China policy focusing on the role of Huntington Wilson and the East Asian specialists in the Far Eastern Division.[33] He argues that the East Asian specialists, with Wilson's support, shaped Taft's China policy and their policy failed because they held a China-centered view and did not take the general context of international politics into account. Kitaoka notes, however, that Wilson's view of American East Asian policy changed in 1911 since he had learned to view American interest in China in the context of overall American foreign policy. It is Kitaoka's view that there was a drawback in the creation of regional divisions in the State Department, for it resulted in American foreign policy often being shaped by the narrow views of regional specialists.

In this connection, Mitani Taichirō's observation may be mentioned here.[34] In his contribution to a forthcoming survey history of U.S.-Japanese relations, Mitani observes that since its founding the Far Eastern Division was staffed mostly by China specialists. Before the Pacific War, Mitani says, the State Department had only two Japan specialists, Joseph Ballantine and Eugene Dooman. Thus he implies that Japan tended to be slighted in policymaking within the Division.

Kimura Masato discusses the exchange of visits between the business communities in the Pacific coast of the United States, Japan, and China during the years between 1905 and 1911.[35] It is Kimura's view that the Japanese business community thought of its relations with the American counterpart in the context of Japan-American-Chinese relations. He focuses on the Pacific coast business communities because they were particularly interested in East Asian trade and made efforts to strengthen their trade relations with Japan and China. Their influence upon Washington was limited, but their activities had considerable influence in Japan and China. Also interesting is Kimura's biography of Shibusawa Eiichi, a very influential leader of the Japanese business community who acted as a kind of unofficial diplomat to preserve friendly relations between Japan and the United States in the early twentieth century.[36] There have been some, but not many, studies of technological transfer from the United States to Japan in the early twentieth century. As for the introduction of American technology into Japanese electrical industry, Hayashi Yoshikatsu has published articles based on his doctoral dissertation.[37]

Influenced by William Appleman Williams, several Japanese historians adopted the thesis of open-door imperialism to explain the American expansionist strategy for the twentieth century. But the open-door thesis has been replaced recently by world-system theory among those historians. Matsuda Takeshi discussed Woodrow Wilson's policy toward the China consortiums first in the framework of open-door imperialism but later from a viewpoint of the world system theory. In several articles as well as his doctoral dissertation on Wilson's policy toward the new four-power China consortium,[38] Matsuda makes clear that policy makers in the Wilson administration worked for the creation of a new consortium to prevent unilateral Japanese financial assistance to the Chinese government, which they feared might result in Japanese political and economic hegemony in China. It was a policy of coopting Japan into an international regime to restrain her unilateral action.

As for the Japanese 'Twenty-One Demands,' Hosoya Chihiro's pioneering analysis of American response to the demands[39] has been supplemented by Kitaoka. Kitaoka regards Kato Takaaki, the architect of the Twenty-One Demands, as a practitioner of old diplomacy who did not understand the coming of the new era.[40] Kato was familiar, he argues, with the British style of diplomacy and calculated the British response. But Kato, unfamiliar with Wilsonian diplomacy, failed to anticipate the American response. Because not much has been published recently on U.S.-Japanese or U.S.-East Asian relations of the World War I years, the publication of Hosoya Chihiro's earlier essays in book form, including two essays on wartime U.S.-Japanese diplomatic relations, is particularly welcome.[41]

In a newly written introductory chapter, the author, the dean of Japanese diplomatic historians, succinctly summarizes Japanese foreign policy during the interwar years. A large segment of the Japanese elite, particularly in the military, entertained an ambivalent attitude toward Pax Anglo-Americana, combining realistic acceptance of the new realities with submerged resentment against the "have nations." Only a part of the Japanese elite positively defined Japan's role as a responsible partner in maintaining the new international order. The shallow commitment of the Japanese elite to the post-World War international order, together with the rise of Chinese nationalism that seemed to threaten Japanese vested interests in China, drove Japan toward military expansionism in the 1930s. In another chapter, Hosoya observes that by 1928 the United States and Britain began to think of coopting China as a partner in the Washington system, but Japan could not go along because of her obsession with special interests in Manchuria. After the failure of Tanaka diplomacy, which tried to forge a common stand with Britain to protect their interests in China, the army began to think of a military action as the only means to achieve Japan's objectives.

As for the Washington Conference of 1921–22 and the international system that emerged from it, Asada Sadao's collection of his monographic essays[42] is the most important contribution since the publication of *Washinton taisei to Nichi-Bei kankei* [43] in 1978. Asada's book is particularly strong regarding the politics and diplomacy of naval limitation. Most of the chapters in this book were published elsewhere, some in English, during the past twenty years, but the author rewrote them for this book, incorporating substantial revisions based on new research. The first chapter of his book discusses the influence of Alfred T. Mahan upon U.S.-Japanese relations. The author contends that Admiral Mahan, serving as a propagandist for naval expansion, had to stress the possibility of a war with Japan in the future. He suggests Mahan's argument was exploited by the Japanese navy as well as the American navy to defend their respective bureaucratic interests after World War I and thus eventually led to the Pacific War, fulfilling his prophecy of a Japanese-American war.[44]

In a chapter of considerable length Asada compares the Japanese and American decisionmaking processes at the Washington Conference. Two effective leaders, Katō Tomosaburō, minister of the navy, and Charles Evans Hughes, triumphed over the restraint of bureaucratic politics on both sides, and succeeded in reaching a rare durable naval limitation agreement. Asada points out that under the peculiar Japanese system only an a senior naval statesman like Katō was able to exercise "civilian control" by proxy over the military. In another chapter Asada discusses U.S.-Japanese detente at the Washington Conference as the result of the converging process of the foreign policy views of Tokyo and Washington. While Tokyo departed from the old diplomacy to accept the new diplomacy of peaceful international cooperation, Washington moved back a little from Wilsonian new diplomacy toward Rooseveltian old diplomacy.

As Asada observes, statesmanlike leadership in the Japanese navy declined after the Washington Conference. At Geneva and London, it was more difficult to control the militants in the navy.[45] His book contains a detailed analysis of infighting within the navy as well as army-navy conflicts in the 1930s. He was very critical of the weak navy leadership that took an indecisive attitude during the crisis leading to the Japanese-American war.

Asada's book also devotes one chapter to the issue of Japanese immigration and discusses it in the broad racial and cultural, as well as diplomatic, context of U.S.-Japanese relations. As he points out, no substantial interest was involved in this issue. Japan did not want to send emigrants to the United States and was willing to restrict emigration, and the inflow of a few hundred Japanese immigrants per year would not really affect American life, even in California. But this became a very important issue for Japan because the Japanese, just freed by unequal treaties, were sensitive to an unequal treatment of their nationals by Western countries and regarded it as a matter of national dignity. The total exclusion of Japanese immigration was very important as a political symbol for West Coast politicians. This chapter contains a most thorough discussion of the immigration issue and includes several interesting observations. For example, Asada states that Japanese liberals of the day, Taisho liberals, felt betrayed by Americans in 1924 because they had had a blind spot in their understanding of the United States, that is, their rationalist underestimation of the strength of American racism. He argues that the Japanese diplomatic elite also did not take American racism toward Japanese seriously, considering it a transient phenomemon.

There are several works focused on specific topics relating to the immigration issue. Kagawa Mari published a series of articles on the controversy over San Francisco's attempt to segregate Japanese students in public school.[46] An article by this writer examined the enactment of the anti-Japanese clause in the immigration act of 1924.[47] He emphasizes the political weakness of the Coolidge administration as the major direct cause that brought forth the anti-Japanese legislation in 1924, and regards Ambassador Hanihara's ill-fated letter as Hughes's desperate attempt to reinforce the weak position of the administration with external pressure.

Matsumura Masayoshi studied the failure of Japanese public diplomacy to counter anti-Japanese immigration movements.[48] It was a mere waste of money because propaganda activities through news agencies founded by a covert fund of the Japanese government incurred the resentment of the American public. A student of public diplomacy, Matsumura published a book which described in detail the success of Kaneko Kentaro's public diplomacy in the United States during the Russo-Japanese War.[49]

As Hasegawa Yūichi points out, the enactment of the Japanese (Asian) exclusion clause in 1924 stimulated the rise of Asianism in Japan.[50] But this Asianism was an expression of Japanese nationalism rather than Asian internationalism, and as Hasegawa observes, it turned into Japanese hegemonism and unilateral expansionism in Asia. In this connection, a thoughtful article by Ōnuma Yasuaki on the Japanese proposal to include the principle of racial equality in the League of Nations Covenant should be mentioned. He calls the principle "an ideal far away," not only because there was no possibility of its adoption at Paris but also because the Japanese themselves discriminated against other Asians.[51]

Although the enactment of the Japanese exclusion clause deeply wounded Japanese, it did not immediately destroy friendly relations between the two governments. Mitani Taichirō writes that, in spite of the impact of the anti-Japanese immigration legislation, U.S.-Japanese relations were not destroyed "because there were common political and economic interests between the two countries and because there were strong will and power to maintain common interests on both sides."[52] Iino Masako and Bamba Nobuya observe that there was some prospect that the anti-Japanese immigration clause might have been repealed in the 1930s if Japan had not invaded Manchuria and if depression had not hit the United States.[53] Takahashi Katsuhiro describes Japanese diplomatic attempts to get the anti-Japanese immigration clause repealed.[54]

4. The 1930s and the Pacific War

The Manchurian Incident that took place in 1931 was a major turning point in U.S.-Japanese relations. Once Japan had forcibly detached Manchuria from China, it was no longer possible to reach an agreement with the United States regarding China policy. It was a great blow to the framework of the Washington treaties. A number of Japanese historians, particularly those on the left, adopted the concept of the "Fifteen Years War," emphasizing that Japan continued to pursue an aggressive policy even during the apparent interlude between the Manchurian Incident and the Sino-Japanese War of 1937. Eguchi Keiichi is the most articulate proponent of the concept of the "Fifteen Years War."[55] Since Japan did not become totalitarian immediately or did not move directly from the Manchurian Incident to the Sino-Japanese War, however, several recent works by Japanese scholars of a younger generation are explicitly critical of or implicitly opposed to the concept of the "Fifteen Years War." Sakai Tetsuya contends that much of the Taisho Democracy system and of the Washington system survived the Manchurian Incident and argues for the necessity of studying Japanese politics from 1931 to 1937 as the process that led to the eventual collapse of these systems.[56] Inoue Toshikazu points out that Japan sought for a while an international reconciliation on the basis of fait accompli in Manchuria: a detente with China and improved relations with the United States and Britain.[57] Katō Yōko regards the 1930s as a period in search of itself, a period of uncertainty.[58]

While Sakai's book does not touch on U.S.-Japanese relations, Inoue and Katō discuss Japanese policy and attitudes toward the United States more extensively. Inoue argues that Japan's withdrawal from the League of Nations should be understood in terms of Japanese pursuit of international cooperation instead of her quest for unilateral action, because it was international cooperationists in the ministry of foreign affairs, not unilateralists, who decided to withdraw to save the face of Britain and small nations in the League without being sanctioned and to reconstruct friendly relations with them outside the League. Japan wanted to improve her relations with the United States by cooperating in matters of foreign economic policy immediately after the inauguration of President Franklin Roosevelt. Japan also succeeded partially in reestablishing normal relations with China. Hirota Koki was eager to improve Japanese relations with Britain and the United States while seeking their recognition of Japanese political interests in China. His proposal of an Anglo-Japanese nonaggression pact, according to the author, was really a part of his scheme of a new Anglo-American-Japanese entente. Thus an attempt to pursue Japan's China policy within an international framework survived until it became untenable in 1936 because of political activities of the army in Northern China and the hardening of Chinese attitudes toward Japan.

Katō's discussion seems quite original. She points out American foreign policy of the 1930s had two salient principles: reciprocal trade and neutrality. The principle of reciprocity, because of its bilateral approach and its support for liberal international trade, appeared to be congenial to the Japanese, who preferred bilateralism to multilateralism and were afraid of losing foreign markets in the era of the British imperial preference. She also notes that the Japanese foreign ministry seriously considered a reciprocal trade agreement with the United States before the outbreak of the Sino-Japanese War.

According to Katō, the neutrality laws of the United States defined the character of the Sino-Japanese War as an undeclared war. China did not declare war because she did not want those laws applied to the conflict. Neither did Japan, since she felt that an undeclared war would be less offensive to the Americans than a declared one. Under an undeclared war, Japan could not officially establish a military government in the occupied areas; she set up puppet regimes there and tried to rule the areas indirectly despite the complaints of theater commanders. Katō also discusses Hiranuma Kiichiro's approach to the United States in 1939, which intended to find a way out of the war in China in diplomatic cooperation with the United States. Mitani Taichirō's comments on Hiranuma are very incisive.[59] Mitani calls it a dual diplomacy of trying to improve Tokyo's relations with Washington while strengthening its ties with the Berlin-Rome axis. He says Hitler and Stalin as well as Hiranuma played the game of dual diplomacy, and Hiranuma turned out to be the loser.

Among Japanese works dealing with American economic foreign relations with East Asia in the 1930s, there are several articles relating to the silver policy of the United States, some of which are included in *Chūgoku no heisei kaikaku to kokusai kankei*[60] But the most significant contribution in this field is Mitani's article on the demise of the four-power consortium.[61] He traces financial diplomacy among China, the United States, Britain, and Japan over China loan issues from 1933 to 1937. It is his view that while no country acted to honor the spirit of the four-power consortium in the 1930s, the facade of the consortium was maintained because the State Department did not want to alienate Japan completely. There was ambivalence, he observes, in the official American attitude toward Japan during those years.

As Japan's undeclared war against China continued, Japan had to take into account the possibility of Anglo-American economic sanctions. Watanabe Akio studied an interagency committee set up to discuss how to cope effectively with such sanctions.[62] The committee could find none because Japan's dependence upon imports from America for strategic materials was so great. This dependence was vividly described by an article by Suzuki Akira.[63] If so, why was Japan's policy not restrained by the fear of economic sanctions in the early phase of the Sino-Japanese War? Because, says Watanabe, Japanese policymakers did not feel for long that the threat of economic sanctions was immediate and concrete. The threat, he implies, was not made early and concretely enough to be effective.

Studies in Japanese foreign relations leading to the Pacific War were very much stimulated by two binational conferences. One was a conference of Japanese and American scholars held at Lake Kawaguchi in 1969, which produced *Pearl Harbor as History* in 1973.[64] The other was a conference of Japanese and British scholars which met in London in 1979, which resulted in the publication of *Anglo-Japanese Alienation* in 1982.[65] During the London Conference and after, Hosoya Chihiro stated the thesis that the Pacific War was really an Anglo-Japanese war rather than an American-Japanese war.[66] His point is well taken in the sense that Japanese military action in China threatened British interests most seriously and that Japanese military expansionists, who wanted to sweep away British influences in China, later began to covet the resources of British-dominated Southeast Asia. The military's increasing interest in Southeast Asia, stimulated by German military success in Western Europe, is described well in Hatano Sumio's political and military history of Japan from 1931 through 1945.[67] As this book and Nomura Minoru's book on the Japanese military indicated, military expansionists in the Japanese army were far less hostile toward the United States than toward Britain, and hoped for a while that the United States would not align with Britain if Japan collided with the latter in Southeast Asia.[68] The navy argued that an Anglo-Japanese war would inevitably involve the United States. This argument was seemingly realistic, but it was actually motivated, as Asada's book mentioned above and other Japanese studies have made clear, by a bureaucratic desire to obtain more budget and resource allocation for the navy.[69]

Since Britain could not hope to restrain Japan, she tried to strengthen her ties with the United States and induce the latter to take a common stand against Japan. Articles by Ikeda Kiyoshi[70] trace British policy toward Japan from 1937 to 1941, and relate it to her attempts to get cooperation from the United States. As Germany was Britain's primary enemy, however, her policy toward Japan was of course formulated in the broad context of her global policy. Confronted with Japan's militancy in 1941, Churchill desired U.S. military intervention against Japan, expecting that it would also lead to its full participation in the war in Europe. But it was reasonable, too, for Britain to seek to gain time in the Pacific while fighting a deadly war against Germany. Shiozaki Hiroaki contends that there was in the second half of 1940 and the first half of 1941 a covert British attempt to appease Japan with the intention of concentrating both American and British power against Germany.[71] He identifies William Wiseman as the central figure of this scheme and argues that Wiseman was close to J. M. Drought and alleges he was behind the effort of the so-called "John Doe Associates" for a U.S.-Japanese detente.

Mitani Taichirō mentions that in addition to Ikawa Tadao and Iwakuro Hideo who worked with the John Doe Associates, there was also an attempt by Hashimoto Tetsuma, a former right-winger who apparently had the support of former premier Hiranuma and some army officers, to improve U.S.-Japanese relations in 1941.[72] Noting the existence of conservative pro-Americans as well as liberal pro-Americans, Mitani suggests that recurrent covert attempts to improve Japanese relations with the United States in the era of overt partnership with the axis powers reflected some uneasiness among the Japanese conservatives in aligning Japan fully with the upstart fascist states which they could not embrace wholeheartedly.

Sudō Shinji studied the whole process of U.S.-Japanese negotiations in 1941.[73] In this first Japanese work to fully utilize the Hornbeck papers, Sudō focuses on perception gaps between Tokyo and Washington. He points out that while the Tripartite Pact was important for Americans as an ideological symbol, Japanese leaders did not understand the American reaction, regarding the pact as a means of power politics. Nor, he maintains, were Japanese leaders aware of Washington's accumulated distrust of Tokyo, since they did not consider Japan's war in China particularly immoral. Sudō analyzes the U.S.-Japanese negotiations of 1941 in detail, and explains that Hull gave up the idea of proposing a modus vivendi at the end of the final negotiations because he believed intelligence reports of a large Japanese convoy heading southward. As for Japanese Proposal B, which Sudō does not discuss much, Kamiyama Akiyoshi's research note sheds light on the question of when the Japanese ambassadors were instructed to include in the Proposal B the promise of the withdrawal of the Japanese forces from southern Indochina.[74]

Soon after the outbreak of the Pacific War, Japanese and Japanese Americans were removed by a presidential order from their residence in the West Coast to the relocation camps. This episode has been studied in Japan as part of the history of ethnic Japanese in the United States. The most significant among such studies is a book-length research paper by Murakawa Yoko and Kumei Teruko.[75] It is a study of *ki-Bei Nisei* (second-generation ethnic Japanese who had spent part of their life in Japan before the war) who chose to return to Japan during the war. On the basis of extensive interviews, the authors conclude that those Nisei expatriated themselves, not because of their sentimental attachment to Japan, but because of their resentment against the United States which had removed them to relocation camps.

Although the Pacific War inflamed racist feelings, the United States had to deny racism against the Asians to secure their support in its war against Japan. Therefore, the United States eliminated discrimination against the Chinese in the naturalization and immigration laws of 1943. In a study that compares the movement for Japanese relocation in 1941–42 with the movement for the repeal of discrimination against the Chinese in 1942–43, Yui Daizaburo concludes that pro-Chinese groups were able to win public support because they emphasized the importance of the Chinese people as allies, not the principle of racial equality or that of fair treatment of all Asians.[76]

Once discrimination against the Chinese had been removed, however, it was difficult not to do the same for other friendly Asians. Thus, discrimination against the Filipinos and the Asian Indians were eliminated from the law of the land in 1946. The repeal of discrimination against all Asians including the Japanese in the U.S. naturalization law, however, had to await the development of the Cold War in Asia.

The most significant recent publication on the Pacific War in Japan is *Taiheiyō sensō*,[77] the product of a four-day international conference held at Lake Yamanaka in November 1991. In a sense, the conference was a new version of the Lake Kawaguchi Conference, which produced *Pearl Harbor as History*. Unlike the previous conference, which was binational, however, this was truly an international conference. Comparing it with the previous conference, Ernest May summarizes its characteristics in his concluding remarks as follows.[78] First, while papers of the 1969 conference were influenced by the "bureaucratic politics" approach, papers of the 1991 conference recognized that Japan and the United States were in some respects unitary actors. Second, papers of 1991 paid far more attention to the regional and world environments in which the Japanese-American conflict erupted. Third, discussion in the 1991 conference revealed real narrowness for other choices at each of the four turning points in the collision course leading to Pearl Harbor. Fourth, discussion in the 1991 conference made clear that the Pacific War was a living event not only in the minds of scholars but also in the minds of the citizens and public officials in the Pacific countries. As subjects left for further research, May listed several topics, such as the influence of broad economic trends on political events, the role of racism in the war, and public moods and their influence on high politics.

May also raised the question of how the advice of experts in a specific nation might have changed policy decisions. Taking note of the appearance of a book about a future Japanese-American war, he expressed his hope that scholars would be able to lessen risks of future collisions among the Pacific powers. In a brief written statement submitted to that conference, this writer stated that even now Japanese and Americans held different views on the Pacific War, and feared that this difference might become a source of U.S.-Japanese psychological frictions in the future.[79] American scholars would not debate whether they should give some other name to the Pacific War. But the problem of naming has been seriously discussed by Japanese historians.[80] To be sure, very few knowledgeable Japanese scholars claim that the Pacific War was a righteous war for the liberation of Asia. But there are still some non-specialist writers who maintain that Japan fought to give Asian peoples an opportunity to liberate themselves from Western imperialism, agreeing with

Hayashi Fusao who argued in the 1960s that the war was the culmination of Japan's hundred years war against Western imperialism.[81]

More Japanese are less self-righteous but like to think that there was something in the Japanese cause that might at least partially redeem Japan from her aggression. Miwa Kimitada's study of the intellectual history of the Pacific War reflects this strand of national sentiment.[82] There were similarities, as Akira Iriye pointed out, between the principles declared in the Atlantic Charter and those of the Declaration for Greater East Asia of 1943, which was a Japanese attempt to formulate the war purposes comparable to the former.[83] Miwa contends the Declaration for Greater East Asia was more advanced than the Atlantic Charter in enunciating some principles, such as independence for Asian nations and opposition to racial discrimination. He is inclined to think there were two meanings in Japan's war, liberation as well as aggression. As Yasuda Toshie's study indicates, Foreign Minister Shigemitsu Mamoru was very serious about the declaration and hoped it might serve as a basis for negotiating an honorable termination of the war in the future.[84] But her study also makes it clear that other Japanese leaders took the declaration only as a piece of wartime propaganda. Whatever merit could be found in the principles enunciated by Japanese officials and ideologues, it should pale in the face of actual Japanese behavior in Asia.

Besides, any idea of an international order cannot be separated from the nature of the domestic regime that propagated it. There was nothing internationally appealing in the authoritarian, militaristic regime of wartime Japan or the totalitarian regime of her axis partners. The axis victory would have been a fatal setback to the cause of liberal democracy in the world. Many Japanese, however, overlook this aspect of the war. Since Japan has committed herself to liberal democracy, Japanese should emphasize a liberal democratic perspective when they look back to the Pacific War.

In the short paper mentioned above, this writer referred to the Pearl Harbor attack[85] and the atomic air raid against Hiroshima and Nagasaki as the most symbolic events that highlight perception gaps between the two nations about the Pacific War. Asada's recent article discusses the perception gap regarding the atomic air raids.[86] While a majority of Americans consider the use of the atomic bombs against Japan justifiable as a war measure in the context of the Pacific War, most Japanese feel that if they should apologize for Pearl Harbor, Americans should do the same about Hiroshima and Nagasaki. Asada is sympathetic with this Japanese sentiment, but points out that his examination of high-school history textbooks in the two countries indicates that teaching about Hiroshima and Nagasaki is more substantial and meaningful in the United States than in Japan.

5. The Occupation and the Peace Settlement

By the 1970s Japanese scholars could look back at the occupation period with a degree of objectivity, U.S. archival sources were opened to scholarly research and well-documented studies of the occupation and the peace settlement became possible. Carol Gluck has written that most of the younger Japanese scholars who had begun to study the occupation in the 1970s had "preferred to seek the concrete, the empirical," and "to make clear the substance of occupation policy from the viewpoint of the mechanism of policymaking and the special characteristics of the policy context."[87] This trend in Japanese scholarship continued during the 1980s, when two younger scholars, Iokibe Makoto[88] and Igarashi Takeshi[89], mentioned by Gluck, published books based on their 1970s research.

Iokibe's book is a detailed two-volume study of wartime planning for postwar American policy. The basic frame of reference of his study is the principles of the Atlantic Charter vs. the victors' peace to be imposed upon the vanquished. Examining the records relating to the Cairo and Teheran conferences, he points out that the opinion of East Asian specialists in the State Department had no influence upon American policy in those conferences. FDR was concerned primarily, he contends, with securing a system of long-term cooperation with the major allies, without much attention to the principles of the charter. He was willing to offer Chiang the Ryukyus and Stalin the Kuriles if they desired them. One of the important questions he takes up is the meaning of the policy of demanding unconditional surrender. He traces how the policy evolved from its inception toward the Potsdam Declaration. In the sense that Japan accepted the conditions set forth in the declaration, her surrender was not unconditional. There is also a book-length study by Morita Hideyuki, which focuses on wartime planning of the occupation policy in the State Department.[90] He is also interested in the wartime views of American intellectuals who seemed to be influenced by the radical analysis of Japanese society by Japanese leftists who stayed in Yan'an[91]

Yui Daizaburō contributes a more extended study of American intellectuals' wartime planning for postwar policy toward Japan, emphasizing wartime discussion among the members of the American Institute of Pacific Relations.[92] Yui is sympathetic with those who stood for a complete democratization of Japan and stressed the importance for the occupation authorities to encourage and support people's movements for drastic change. He regrets their idea of postwar reform in Japan was not carried out. Although Washington's initial directives directed MacArthur to encourage democratic movements from below, the general ignored this aspect of the directives and increasingly depended on the cooperation of the Japanese bureaucracy and conservative elements for governing Japan. Democratization during the occupation was thus incomplete, and the authoritarian conformist mentality of the Japanese survived.[93]

Nakamura Masanori is another historian interested in the wartime planning of postwar policy toward Japan. His particular interest is in the origins of the idea of retaining the emperor (*tennō*) as the symbol of reformed Japan. He studied the role of Joseph Grew as well as the development of the idea.[94] Although Grew entertained the idea of remaking the emperor as the symbol for the reborn nation, Nakamura does not find his direct influence in the process in which the term *shocho* (symbol) was incorporated into the draft Japanese constitution. He suspects that the American lawyers who drafted the document were inspired by the British Charter of Westminster. He also points out that the deleted article of the Potsdam Declaration, which suggested a possiblity of constitutional monarchy for postwar Japan, was written by Stimson, not by Grew. Yamagiwa Akira also supports this point.[95]

As for Stimson's relations with Japan, Iokibe published a powerful essay focusing on his personality and statesmanship with a historian's perceptive eye.[96] Stimson, who played important, but unpopular, roles in crucial occasions in U.S.-Japanese relations during the Showa era, yielded much to Japan in the London Naval Conference because of his trust in Wakatsuki's statesmanship. He became the foremost hardliner against Japan, when she embarked upon the road to military expansionism; in 1945, when Japan was on the verge of defeat, he returned to an understanding attitude toward Japan, particularly on the issue of the emperor's status. He also saved Kyoto from nuclear bombing by persuading the military to avoid Japan's cultural capital. Iokibe admires Stimson for his statesmanship which not only aimed to pursue national interest in the best sense of the term but also remembered a statesman's responsibility to humanity. There are more discussions of the origins of the postwar symbolic emperor by Toyoshita Narahiko, Matsuo Takayoshi, and several others.[97] While most of these scholars emphasize the collaboration between MacArthur and the emperor, Takahashi Hikohiro points out its indigenous social democratic origins.[98] Toyoshita and Matsuo both regard the famous Hirohito-MacArthur meeting of September 1945 as the historic occasion in the process of its creation. The latest study on Emperor Hirohito by Yoshida Yutaka[99] describes joint efforts by Hirohito himself, his close advisers, and GHQ officials to protect him from war criminal indictment. The forging of this collaboration had an immense importance for postwar Japan. It guaranteed a smooth enforcement of drastic reform measures and greatly contributed to the stability of the postwar Japanese regime. Thus, in this writer's view, the collaboration had positive historical effects in Japan. But there was also a drawback to it. As Yoshida stresses, this collaboration tended to obscure the problem of Japanese responsibility for the war, and Japan still has much to do in dispelling the distrust of Asian neighbors.[100]

Interesting in this connection is Kōsaka Masataka's observation that Hirohito played a very important role from the end of the war to the San Francisco Peace, when he ceased to be a sovereign ruler.[101] Noting that Hirohito met MacArthur eleven times, Kōsaka implies that their meetings were important communication channels between the two nations. Hirohito also sent his confidant to the general to convey his message discreetly. In September 1947, he conveyed to William Sebalt, MacArthur's political adviser, through Terasaki Hidenari his desire that the United States be willing to retain its control over Okinawa in a bilateral agreement. This episode is suggestive of his political ideas. According to Miyamoto Seigen who studied the making of America's Okinawa policy, however, the emperor's message had no significant influence upon Washington's policy.[102] As Ota Masahide maintains, it was Washington's established policy to detach Okinawa from Japan on a long term basis.[103] George F. Kennan favored the emperor's proposal for a while. After his talks with General MacArthur, Miyasato points out, he changed his mind and became an advocate for permanent American control of the islands on the basis of the Potsdam Declaration.

Igarashi's book cited above deals with the occupation and the planning for peace with Japan in the Cold War setting. His book adopts the dual concept of "international cold war" and "internal cold war" as the basic framework to connect the two levels of political dynamics. There was, as he notes, a gap in 1947 between the Cold War reorientation of global American policy and the draft peace treaty, which retained the wartime aims of keeping postwar Japan weak. He analyzes the political process through which America's Japan policy was redirected to conform to the global Cold War policy. He emphasizes the role of Kennan's policy planning staff, the architects of the Cold War policy, in taking the initiative in reorienting America's Japan policy. According to the author, however, GHQ's labor policy, which curtailed the government workers' rights in 1948, was GHQ's local response to the internal Cold War situation in Japan and accepted hesitatingly by Washington, as Labour governments in Britain and the Pacific commonwealth nations were very critical of the policy.

He also discusses how Yoshida Shigeru developed the postwar Japanese foreign policy posture, the combination of a clear political commitment to the American side and a passive stance in military cooperation, which conformed to the dual political conditions of the international Cold War and the internal one, the peculiarity of the latter being the strength of the forces supporting Article 9 of the peace Constitution. This policy posture was inevitably accompanied, he points out, by an air of secret diplomacy in U.S.-Japanese security problems.

The lack of candor in Japanese politics of rearmament is also stressed by Ōtake Hideo.[104] Although Yoshida took a passive attitude toward the rearmament issue, he considered that an independent nation should have armed forces. Ōtake contends that Yoshida wanted to take time to enlighten the Japanese public to the necessity of a constitutional revision which would allow Japan to possess forces for national defense. But he had to follow the tactics of deception adopted by GHQ which hurried the Japanese to organize the so-called police reserve at the outbreak of the Korean War. Then, Ōtake argues, Yoshida had to repeat the same tactics when he created the self-defense forces in 1954, thus perpetuating the lack of candor in Japanese politics over security issues.[105]

The dual concepts of the international and internal cold wars employed by Igarashi were originally proposed by Sakamoto Yoshikazu as a frame of political analysis.[106] However, although useful, the concepts are confusing because of the ambiguity of the concept of internal cold war. Sakamoto himself, aware of the need to emphasize the liberalism of the opposition, does not use the term domestic cold war in his more recent article. Instead, he simply points out that the Japanese bipolar political alignment was quite different from the international cold war bipolarity, because it was primarily conflict between "the anti-communist reactionaries" and "the liberal democrats who regarded co-existence with the Left as an acid test for Japanese liberal democracy."

Sakamoto takes the view that when GHQ became allied to anti-communist reactionaries, it was those progressive liberals who contributed to "naturalizing" postwar reforms through their opposition to GHQ's "reverse course" policy. This article, the lead article in *Nihon senryō no kenkyū*,[107] edited by Sakamoto himself and Robert E. Ward, the result of a Japanese-American joint project also published in English, succinctly expresses the views and sentiment of many Japanese intellectuals who were young liberals in the 1950s. Because of his keen awareness of the strength of reactionary forces in postwar Japan, Sakamoto wonders how it was possible for the planners of the occupation to think that drastic reforms introduced during a short period of the occupation could survive after its end. Thus he argues that they had no plan for post-occupation, or post-reform, Japan and suggests that this lack of post-reform plan, as well as the Cold War, gave an opportunity for Japanese reactionaries to attempt revising or reversing postwar reforms.

In the preface to this book, Sakamoto writes that there was a slight difference of interest between the Japanese and American participants in the joint project. Whereas the Japanese participants who had experienced the occupation in their youth had the viewpoints of the occupied, some of the Americans had really taken part in the occupation and therefore had viewpoints of the occupiers. The Japanese considered the occupation and postwar reforms as a process of self-transformation; the Americans tended to look at them as a kind of grand experiment in political engineering from outside. Such difference, however, is not pronounced in the final product.

The product of another joint Japanese-American project, *Nichi-Bei no Shōwa*[108] reviews the Showa era as a whole. It is this writer's impression that while several Japanese contributors to this book tend to emphasize the drastic nature of postwar reform, some American contributors, notably Chalmers Johnson and John Dower, emphasize continuity from prewar Japan to postwar Japan. The degree of continuity/discontinuity can be evaluated differently, depending on which aspect of the Japanese life is considered. Iokibe Makoto classifies the various aspects of the postwar reform into three categories: Japan-initiated (e.g. labor union law reform), Japan-initiated but GHQ-enhanced (e.g. agricultural land reform), and GHQ-imposed (e.g. constitutional reform), and contends that such classification will be useful in measuring continuity/discontinuity between prewar Japan and postwar Japan.[109]

The most notable among recent works on the Japanese occupation seems to be Toyoshita's.[110] His book discusses the establishment of the unique occupation regime in Japan, America's virtual one-power control, in a comparative perspective. The author of a detailed study of the occupation of Italy and an advocate of comparative studies, Toyoshita includes discussion of the Allied occupation regimes in Germany, Italy, and three East European countries. Toyoshita's comparative studies focus on interactions between the occupier and political forces in the occupied country and the process of forging the occupation regime through collaboration between the occupier and some of these forces. He is critical of the double standards in American policy, which excluded the Soviet Union from the Italian occupation and monopolized power for itself in Japan, while strongly protesting the Soviet attempt to exclude the United States and Britain from East European countries.

Yui, Nakamura, and Toyoshita cooperated to organize a study group for comparative occupation studies some years ago, and part of the result of their research was published in *Rekishigaku kenkyū* in 1988, and the final product was published in book form.[111] This project includes a study of the Philippines liberated from the Japanese rule and a study of U.S. and Soviet occupation policies toward Korea.[112] An earlier book in comparative occupation studies, edited by Sodei Rinjirō,[113] the author of a well known Japanese book on MacArthur, discusses the wartime Japanese occupation in Southeast Asia in comparison with the American occupation in the Asia-Pacific region: Japan, Okinawa, Korea, and Micronesia. It also includes lively discussion on the two key figures in the occupation of Japan, MacArthur and Yoshida.

Such a focus upon Yoshida as the key person in the shaping of postwar Japan is controverted by Shindō Eiichi.[114] He regards Ashida Hitoshi as a liberal who wanted to rebuild Japan on a new liberal constitution and compares him favorably with Yoshida, who was in his view an anti-communist conservative. Thus he emphasizes the contribution made by the coalition of Ashida liberals and Katayama socialists to postwar economic liberalism and social democratization. Kitaoka would not argue with Shindō about Yoshida's conservatism or anti-communism, but his interest is in the world view of Yoshida the diplomatist.[115] He considers Yoshida's world basically shaped in the heyday of the Anglo-Japanese alliance. Thus he stood for cooperation with Britain before the war, alliance with America after the war.

Besides comparative studies of the occupation, there have been a number of studies on specific aspects of reform under the occupation regime, such as educational reform and religious freedom. There are two monographic studies, one by Suzuki Eiichi and the other by Kubo Yoshizo,[116] on educational reform leading to the Fundamental Education Act. Both emphsize the leadership of GHQ in reform; Kubo mentions that GHQ entertained for a short while the idea of letting the emperor write a new educational rescript to facilitate reform. A book edited by Ikado Fujio[117] is a good collaborative study in MacArthur's policy on Japanese religions and the conditions of Japanese religions during the occupation. All these books remind the readers how much the Japanese owe the liberal democratic features of Japan today to the basic framework laid by reform during the occupation. Although Japanese scholars still use the term "reverse course," they recognize that it did not go far and generally kept the basic framework of postwar reform intact.

As for the San Francisco Peace Settlement, Hosoya Chihiro's *Sanfuran-shisuko kōwa eno michi*[118] will remain long as the standard work in Japan. His book is centered on the description and analysis of the development of American peace policy, but it also gives a detailed analysis of Japanese and British policies and describes with skill interactions among American, British, and Japanese policies. He emphasizes the American inability in 1949 to take the diplomatic initiative in the Japanese peace issue because of the negative attitude of the military, and stresses the importance of Dulles's role in solving this impasse. He recognizes that a series of meetings held during his visit to Tokyo in June 1950 was crucial in the process of consensus building within the U.S. government. His book ends with a chapter on the "Yoshida letter" of January 1952. Yoshida spoke in the Diet of the possibility of opening some kind of relationship with the People's Republic, and appeared to tilt toward the British policy toward China. Dulles, becoming very uneasy, decided to put Yoshida on a leash by forcing the reluctant leader to send him a letter dictated by himself. The book also examines whether Yoshida really made any commitment regarding rearmament in his January 1951 meeting with Dulles, and concludes that he conveyed explicitly, contrary to his claim, his intention to take an initial step toward rearmament after the peace treaty became effective. Yuan Ke-Qin takes a different view regarding the Yoshida letter.[119] In the letter, he maintains, Yoshida simply repeated what he had promised Washington and went further than Dulles's draft in criticizing the People's Republic.

Another volume on the San Francisco Peace is a collection of articles edited by Watanabe Akio and Miyasato Seigen.[120] This volume attempts to put the peace settlement in an international context, studying the policies of various countries toward peace with Japan. As for the U.S-Japanese Security Treaty of 1951, there are several articles supplementing Hosoya's book. Very revealing is Igarashi Takeshi's article,[121] which examines the attitudes of major policymakers in Washington, particularly in the Joint Chiefs of Staff. It illuminates how their perceptions of the Far Eastern crisis influenced the shaping of the security treaty. It clarifies, for example, the background of the "Far East" clause inserted into the treaty. A part of Kan Hideki's book discusses Washington's idea of a Pacific security treaty and relates it to the making of the U.S.-Japanese Security Treaty.[122] As for the administrative agreement which accompanied the security treaty, Miyasato Seigen's article is very informative.[123]

6. The Cold War and U.S.-East Asian Relations

The increasing opening of post-World War II American sources to scholarly research stimulated Japanese studies not only in the occupation of Japan and the peace settlement but also for U.S.-East Asian relations in general. Anticipating the rapid archival opening of wartime and postwar American documents and other primary sources, Nagai Yōnosuke, a leading Japanese scholar of international politics, took the initiative in the 1970s in planning a research project to study the international environment of postwar Japan. As a part of the research project, an international symposium was held in Kyoto in 1975, and the papers contributed to the symposium were published in English in 1977.[124] A dozen scholars who participated in the project began to publish their works in the *Kokusai kankyō* series. Nagai himself wrote *Reisen no kigen*[125] for the series in 1978. Nagai discussed the origins of the Cold War in Europe and its impact on international relations in East Asia. He noted that the "line of containment" in Asia differed from the "line of demarcation" at the 38th parallel in Korea and the 17th in Indochina. The "line of containment" was the "defensive perimeter" calculated from a strategic cost-benefit analysis. It was a realistic policy, but Truman discarded this policy of limited containment at the outbreak of the Korean War. The question is why did he do so?

Nagai argues that there had been mounting dissatisfaction in the public mood, rising impatience with the gap between the two lines, which was rooted in American experience and tradition. Thus Truman responded instinctively to the outbreak of the Korean War and decided to intervene. It is Nagai's view that the North Koreans began the war because they were optimistic about their military strength in the existing balance of power, but pessimistic about future power relations in the peninsula. The Soviet Union was willing to let them invade the South as it seemed to involve little risk of a third world war. But Nagai says the invasion served as the catalyst for the globalization of American Cold War policy.

Okonogi Masao's *Chōsen sensō*,[126] another book in the series, is a more detailed examination of U.S. policy toward Korea before and during the Korean War. He recognizes ambivalence in U.S. policy toward the Republic of Korea before the war, but does not consider, as Nagai did, that Korea was outside the line of containment. Since the United States had helped create the South Korean regime, it had an important political stake in the security of South Korea.[127]

Okonogi did not discuss policies of Moscow, Pyongyang, and Beijing toward the Korean War much because of the very limited availability of sources. Relying on some revealing sources on the communist side, however, two books focused on Beijing's role in the Korean War appeared more recently. Hiramatsu Shigeo's *Chūgoku to Chōsen sensō*,[128] a collection of articles on the military role of the People's Republic, maintains that Beijing was more positively involved in the outbreak of the war than Allen Whiting thought, since the ethnic Korean troops, which Beijing transferred from the People's Liberation Army to the North Korean Army, played an important role in the North Korean offensive against South Korea. More interesting is Zhu Jianrong's *Mō Takutō no Chōsen sensō*,[129] a monograph on Beijing's Korean War policy focused upon the question why Beijing decided to enter it. Based on sources accessible and personal interviews, this book offers a very detailed analysis of Mao Zedong's thinking and decisions, and Beijing's negotiations with Moscow. Zhu considers that Mao decided to intervene primarily because he wanted to defeat Washington's aggressive intent against China by stopping the U.S. forces in Korea. Mao deeply feared, says Zhu, that the American conquest of North Korea would stimulate her counterrevolutionary offensive against his regime and encourage anticommunist elements in mainland China. In a review essay, Wada Haruki argues that the Chinese Communists entered the Korean War as a continuation of their own revolution.[130] As for the Soviet attitude toward the war, Oh Choong Keun argues that the Kremlin chose to be absent from the Security Council to avoid clarifying its own position on the North Korean invasion, because it did not expect the U.S. would be ready to send forces to Korea.[131] Nakatsuji Keiji illuminates another aspect of the Korean War, Syngman Rhee's resistance against the U.S. armistice policy, which reflected the South Korean leader's frustration with the loss of American support for national unification and his fear that the American commitment to South Korea's security might not be strong enough.[132]

Yano Tōru has studied the Cold War in Southeast Asia.[133] Yano emphasizes cultural varieties within the region, indigenous factors in national and regional politics, and the complicated nature of regional international relations in the early Cold War years. The very idea of Southeast Asia as a region, he suggests, was for the first time defined and popularized by the United States during the Cold War era. He regards the United States as the country which, traditionally uninterested in and unfamiliar with this region except the Philippines, tended to approach it with a universalist image of the Cold War.

There are studies of narrower scope with a focus on U.S. policy toward Indochina. Miyasato Seigen studied America's Indochina policy, mostly during the Truman administration, within a framework of bureaucratic decisionmaking analysis.[134] Matsuoka Hiroshi emphasizes Dulles's dilemma in Indochina, that is, his inability to win over both European colonialist powers as partners and Asian nationalists as friends to the American side.[135] Matsuoka contends that Dulles, disappointed by Britain and France in 1954, began to look to Japan as a potential partner in the U.S.-led Pacific order.

The newest book on American policy toward the Indochina crisis of the 1950s is Akagi Kanji's *Vetonamu sensō no kigen*[136], a study based on extensive research in U.S. archival sources. While Miyasato's study in decisionmaking focuses on officials of secondary rank, Akagi's and Matsuoka's books focus on top leaders. This difference may reflect the fact that Indochina had not been a critical issue during the Truman era. As for the key reason why the Eisenhower administration did not intervene in the Indochina War, Akagi contends that it was the infirm French commitment to continuing the war with ground forces. In a brief overview of Eisenhower's post-armistice policy in Vietnam, he states that Eisenhower and Dulles seem to have been overly optimistic about stabilizing the Ngo Dinh Diem regime and opened the way toward the Vietnam War. This phase of Eisenhower's policy in Vietnam deserves a full-length study. Interestingly, Akagi does not discuss at all the diplomacy of the Geneva conference of 1954 which produced the Indochina armistice. This oversight may be deliberate, reflecting the fact that Washington did not have any serious interest in it. However, this conference, the first of big-power multilateral diplomacy during the Cold War era in which the People's Republic participated, reflected the complicated nature of Southeast Asian international relations of the mid-1950s. It may take some time before the history of the first Indochina crisis can be written with a truly multilateral approach based on multiarchival research. As Yano points out, the Soviet Union had only peripheral interest in Southeast Asia, and the shadow of the People's Republic loomed larger over the region. Shutō Motoko describes how the United States and the People's Republic struggled for influence over Indonesia in the first half of the 1960s in her book on Indonesian nationalism.[137]

Neither Matsuoka's book nor Akagi's directly deals with the Vietnam War. Compared with the vast amount of scholarly American literature on the Vietnam War, Japanese scholarly literature has been strikingly meager. This may reflect the fact that Japan was not directly involved in the war, whereas for Americans it was an American war and a traumatic national experience. Besides, Japanese scholars tend to see it in an international context or in the context of Vietnamese history. This makes it more difficult for them to write scholarly books not only in terms of sources but also in terms of historical perspectives. Reflecting on changes in the post-Vietnam world, Japanese intellectuals cannot hold on to the naive glorification of national liberation they used to express. The best Japanese overview of the war now available, *Rekishi to shiteno Betonamu sensō*, written by Furuta Motoo, a specialist in Vietnamese history, reveals the historical perspective of the new age.[138] Although he considers that justice was on the side of revolutionary Vietnamese, he thinks it natural for many people today to ask whether national independence might have been achieved without so much sacrifice. Recognizing an ironic turn of world history after the war, Furuta considers that the end of the war marked the end of an age. When the cause of nationalism triumphed over imperialism, the age in which the idea of the nation-state had shone came to an end. When a war for national liberation achieved a great victory, it began to lose its charm in the world. When a socialism of poverty and equality won the war, such a socialism began to lose the support of the people. The Vietnam War itself, he argues, contributed much to this ironic turn of history.

As Watanabe Akio points out, Japanese economic planners had been thinking that Japan should reenter the Southeast Asian market to achieve her economic recovery since the occupation period.[139] Eisenhower seemed to take a similar view when he said in 1954 that the fall of dominos in Southeast Asia would affect Japan. The Eisenhower administration favored an increase of Japanese trade with the region and helped Japan improve her relations with Southeast Asian countries. As Yoshikawa Yōko's study shows, for instance, the U.S. government also helped Japan negotiate a reparation agreement with the Philippines.[140] Because of the lack of Japanese funds for investment in Southeast Asia, the Japanese government repeatedly proposed to Washington a joint economic development of Southeast Asia during the 1950s. Everytime Washington gave the cold shoulder to the Japanese approach. This aspect of U.S.-Japanese diplomacy in the 1950s is told by Shimizu Sayuri's article and also by Hiwatari (Hayashi) Yumi's.[141]

One of the major diplomatic issues between Japan and the United States, which also involved American policy toward China, was the problem of control of trade with the communist countries. Katō (Yasuhara) Yoko provides the first book-length study of COCOM and CHINCOM based on extensive research.[142] Her book is a detailed history of trade control in the Truman era. She pays particular attention to the process of Japan being integrated into these systems and their impact upon Japan's trade policy. Her book is much less detailed in the discussion of trade control in the Eisenhower era. This part of the story, the problem of relaxing the "China Differential" in 1955–57, is given more detailed analysis in Takamatsu Motoyuki's recent article.[143] Takamatsu also has published substantial studies of U.S. human rights diplomacy toward Asian countries.[144]

There are a number of articles, but few book-length studies on U.S.-Chinese relations.[145] For that matter, no book-length study has been published with regard to post-Korean War U.S. policy toward Korea. There is no monographic study, for example, of the role of the United States in normalizing the relationship between Japan and the Republic of Korea.[146] The most significant Japanese book-length study of U.S.-Chinese relations belongs to the field of comparative diplomatic studies and was first published in English. This is *Normalization with China* by Ogata Sadako, a scholar-diplomat who now serves as UN High Commissioner for Refugees.[147] From interviews with many Americans and Japanese who took part in the normalization processes, Ogata reconstructs U.S. and Japanese processes and compares them. Since her book was published in the United States, it is assumed that the book is known widely to specialists in East Asian affairs.[148]

Also of interest is Ijiri Hidenori's critical survey of the intellectual history of modern China studies in the United States since the beginning of the 1970s.[149] Ijiri traces fluctuations in American intellectuals' images of contemporary China, relating them to changes in China as well as those in American domestic trends and U.S. external relations. He emphasizes that their understanding of China has been affected by their sentiment toward China. Are these fluctuations particularly conspicuous among American intellectuals compared with Europeans and Japanese, or with regard to China compared with Japan? His answers are affirmative since he considers China to have been historically a special country to Americans. American intellectuals' image of Japan has also changed toward the end of the 1980s. According to Mizobe Hideaki, however, Japan as well as China have been special countries for Americans, as they needed either China or Japan to satisfy their national sense of civilizing mission and maintain a national identity different from Europeans.[150] Thus their favor shifted from one country to the other several times.

Homma Nagayo critically reviews revisionist interpretations of Japan and stresses the danger in the new American dichotomy of regarding Japan as "not like us," as an alien among the advanced nations.[151] Homma calls upon the Westerners to recognize that the Christian civilization, despite its past glory, can no longer dictate the standard of human values and must cooperate with the other peoples to develop new ways and manners for global coexistence. The problem is whether Japan, confronted with American universalism, will be able to present the world with something that is different but still has a universal meaning. Noting that modern Japan has often been confronted with the challenge of American universalism, Nakanishi Hiroshi examines Konoe Fumimaro's famous 1918 essay, in which he expressed his opposition to the Anglo-American idea of a pacifist international order that seemed to favor the "have" nations, as an attempt to meet the challenge of Anglo-American universalism by universalizing several principles suitable to Japan.[152] Nakanishi regards Konoe's as an understandable but unsuccessful attempt, but fears that Japanese today are no better than Konoe in this regard. "What can Japan speak about her own national experience?" asks Sakamoto Takao, addressing the same question.[153]

7. Japan and the United States after the San Francisco Peace Settlement

The development of U.S.-Japanese relations from the beginning of the Cold War to the middle of the 1950s is given a well balanced treatment by Ishii

Osamu[154] Due attention is given to economic issues in U.S.-Japanese bilateral relations. Kamiya Fuji provides another survey history of U.S.-Japanese relations, and with a longer time span.[155] As Ishii points out, the United States in the first half of the 1950s felt uncertain of its future direction. Washington was not satisfied with Tokyo's efforts in rearmament, but more concerned with uncertain Japanese political direction and with unimpressive Japanese economic performance which would increase political uncertainty. Washington watched Japanese negotiations with the Soviet Union with an uneasy eye as peace with the Soviet Union might confuse Japan's political orientation further. Tanaka Takahiko, in a recently published study on the restoration of Soviet-Japanese diplomatic relations, suspects that the United States did not want a Soviet-Japanese peace settlement because of the fear that it might stimulate Japanese interest in opening diplomatic relations with the People's Republic.[156]

A binational issue on which Tokyo took the diplomatic initiative was the revision of the security treaty. A magnum opus on this issue is Hara Yoshihisa's *Sengo Nihon to kokusai seiji.*[157] From numerous interviews with Kishi Nobusuke, Fujiyama Aiichiro, Togo Fumihiko, and many others including those who were on the side of the opposition movement, Hara reconstructs the political process which led to the ratification of the new security treaty and the resignation of the Kishi cabinet. His framework is the political dynamics of postwar Japan which tied domestic politics closely with what he called the U.S.-Japanese security system. Since it was the aim of the United States to retain this system, that is, a Japan closely tied to the U.S. political and security interest, the United States was willing to respond to a Japanese request to revise the security arrangement, if it would help strengthen the political and military relations of the two nations. In 1955, Dulles flatly rejected Foreign Minister Shigemitsu's proposal to revise the "one-sidedness" of the security treaty. As Hara's book reveals, Shigemitsu made the proposal in a very abrupt manner. Apparently he did not consult the Cabinet about it, and his two colleagues in the mission, Kono Ichiro and Kishi Nobusuke, did not know it until he raised the issue in a conversation with Dulles. Sakamoto Kazuya's recent article gives more information about Shigemitsu's proposal which included the gradual withdrawal of U.S. forces from Japan.[158]

In 1958, Dulles was willing to respond positively to the request of Kishi, who he expected would be a powerful and reliable leader. Kishi wanted to revise the security treaty primarily because of political, not military, reasons. In 1958, however, the Foreign Ministry officials were thinking that only a modest revision through an exchange of official letters would be possible. Kishi wanted to conclude a new security treaty, which was supported by

Ambassador Douglas MacArthur III, the promoter of treaty revision on the U.S. side. Because the Foreign Ministry had not yet prepared a new treaty draft, it was agreed that the American side would propose one as a basis for negotiations. It is clear therefore that the American ambassador had anticipated Kishi's preference and had been prepared for the negotiations. This much was known about the beginning of the negotiations since the publication of Togo's *Nichi-Bei gaikō 30-nen*[159] in 1982, a brief, but very informative memoir by a former diplomat. But Hara's book puts muscles and skin to the skeleton provided by Togo's memoirs.

Hara describes in detail the complicated game of LDP (Conservatives) intraparty maneuvering between Kishi and faction chieftains. But his analytical description of the opposition movement is very revealing, too. He points out that the JSP (Socialists) wanted to develop ties with Beijing, because the LDP had Washington behind it, and the Communists had Moscow. When Asanuma Inejiro visited China in March 1959, he was therefore persuaded by his left-wing advisers to insert in his statement that famous phrase "American imperialism is the common enemy of the Japanese and Chinese peoples." Because of his ambition for the JSP chairmanship, Asanuma, an affable rightwing socialist, was captured by the JSP left-wingers. Hara observes that the established groups in the opposition movement, such as the JSP leaders and the Sohyo labor leaders, did not expect that they could prevent the treaty ratification. They were pessimistic because their ability to mobilize the masses was limited. When the government passed the new treaty through the lower house by a dubious procedure, the opposition was given a sacred cause for its movement, the defense of parliamentary democracy. Angry mass movements flared up. The sudden flareup of a mass protest movement finally forced the Kishi Cabinet to resign. With its resignation, the mass movement lost the target for anger and rapidly subsided, and the new treaty was in effect. Hara explains the rapid rise and fall of mass protests this way. Basically agreeing with Hara, Kamiya mentions a psychological factor: Japanese nationalism might have needed one emotional eruption of this kind against the United States. This writer shares the same speculation. Another factor was a widespread public distrust of Kishi, who had been a minister in the Tojo Cabinet.[160]

Kishi was the last prime minister in postwar Japan who had been prominent in goverment or politics in the prewar and war years. The end of the Kishi Cabinet was the end of an era. Since that time, Japanese politics has been in the hand of the politicians who emerged in politics, bureaucracy, or business in postwar Japan, and who therefore were more accustomed to postwar democracy and the 1947 constitution. Because of the turmoil in Tokyo in June 1960, Eisenhower was not able to make the first presidential visit to

Japan. Hara's book traces communications regarding his visit between the Japanese government, the U.S. embassy in Tokyo, and the State Department. Recently Hara has published a handy book[161] which deals with the same subject, but with emphasis on U.S.-Japanese relations. It is written for nonprofessional readers, but he uses newly released U.S. documents which he did not use in his previous work.

Overlapping partly with Hara's books is Hiwatari Yumi's study, which focuses on Ikeda Hayato, who succeeded Kishi as the prime minister.[162] Her major interest is the Ikeda Cabinet, but she traces Ikeda's political career in the context of postwar Japanese politics and U.S.-Japanese relations. She discusses politics and diplomacy during the Kishi era and Ikeda's position on political and diplomatic issues. Hiwatari suggests that although Dulles valued Kishi's political stance, he had some fear of Kishi's Asianist orientation. Dulles responded negatively to Kishi's proposal for joint aid to Southeast Asia, Hiwatari contends in this book and also in her article,[163] partly because he feared that once Kishi had succeeded in capturing the Southeast Asian market with American aid, Kishi might turn out to be an Asianist rather than an advocate of a long-term close relationship with the West.

According to Hiwatari, Ikeda, an economic growth-first conservative, did not feel the necessity of close security ties with the United States. He supported the security treaty revision only because he believed that Japan needed American friendship to promote her economic development and prosperity, and expected that the economic clause in the new treaty would be helpful. It may be said that Ikeda did not view the world in terms of the Cold War but of a Pax Americana, and it was his aim to pursue Japanese economic development, depending upon the Pax Americana. Hiwatari is critical of Ikeda's diplomacy, which lacked any idea of Japan contributing to the world by sharing the burden of international public responsiblity with other nations. Fortunately for him, the United States, still confident of its own power, was tolerant of a self-centered Japanese policy, considering Japan harmless because of its dependence upon the United States.

The latest significant scholarly book on postwar U.S.-Japanese relations is Kōno Yasuko's *Okinawa henkan o meguru seiji to gaiko*,[164] a well researched work in the politics and diplomacy of the Okinawa problem. There have been a number of scholarly works relating to Okinawa in U.S.-Japanese relations. American policy toward Okinawa in the early postwar years was studied by Miyasato Seigen in the 1960s and 1970s, and more recently by Ota Masahiro.[165] There is also Matsuda Yoshitaka's substantial study of the socioeconomic aspect of postwar Okinawa under the U.S. administration.[166]

Kono's book covers the early history of the Okinawa problem in the first several chapters. She traces the combined political processes of diplomatic negotiations between the United States and its allies and between the United States and Japan, and of bureaucratic politics within the U.S. government, which finally produced the Okinawa clause (Article 3) of the San Francisco peace treaty as a compromise and left the future status of Okinawa to be decided in the development of post-peace U.S.-Japanese relations. Therefore, according to the author, the Okinawa problem during the early post-peace years was defined by the character of Japanese foreign policy. Because of the lack of Japanese consensus on security issues and the passive rearmament policy of the Yoshida government, the State Department, which was willing to support the early reversion of Okinawa under certain conditions, agreed with the military in the policy of long-term control of the islands. Thus, the initiative in opposition to the status quo in Okinawa was taken by the Okinawan people themselves, and the rise of the opposition movement in Okinawa increasingly influenced the Japanese political process and forced the Tokyo government to take up the Okinawa problem in diplomacy and domestic politics, while Washington gradually began to recognize the importance of the problem. The analysis of this process occupies the central, and the most interesting, part in Kono's book. She has only one long chapter to analyze the Okinawa reversion issue during the Sato Eisaku administration because available sources are limited. Interesting for the study of the diplomacy of the Okinawa reversion is Wakaizumi Kei's very revealing memoir of the scholar who served as Sato's secret liaison with Kissinger on the Okinawa issue from 1967 through 1969.[167]

U.S.-Japanese economic frictions started with the textile wrangle in 1970 and recurred one after another until they became very serious by the beginning of the 1990s. On the issue of economic frictions, much has been written in Japan. This paper will not discuss them since most of them are not historical studies. Besides, the best studies on earlier cases, collaborative works by Sato Hideo, I. M. Destler and others, were published both in English and Japanese.[168] Katō Yoko's book cited before contains a chapter on the Toshiba affair of 1987–88, a unique case which combined an economic friction with the Cold War issue.[169] She points to a wide perception gap between Japanese and Americans. Since there had been no strong military fear of the Soviet Union in Japan, Japanese were not sensitive to the issue of restricting exports to the Soviet Union and therefore perceived the Toshiba clause in the newly revised U.S trade act as a form of Japan bashing.

The end of the Cold War has reminded us that the "Cold War" was the most appropriate term for Atlantic-European international relations. It began in Europe and ended there. It was fought in Europe. Hot wars took place in East Asia. No bipolar alignment existed in Pacific-East Asian region. The Soviet Union did not dominate the communist countries there. A Cold War even developed between the Soviet Union and the People's Republic. Thus the great change in the Soviet Union had a limited impact upon most of these countries, and the one-party rule by the Communists has been able to survive in them. Nor was there any unity or homogeneity among the American allies in East Asia and the Pacific. 1972, the year of Sino-American rapprochement and the normalization of Sino-Japanese relations, was a great watershed, probably greater than 1989 or 1991, in Pacific-East Asian international relations.[170] The Cold War era may be called the "long peace" in the sense that there was no third world war. But Ishii Osamu argues that the Cold War achieved a degree of stability and globalism which might be called an international system only in the middle of the 1950s as the result of the East-West division of security spheres in Europe, the possession of thermonuclear weapons by both superpowers, the return of East-West diplomacy, and the diffusion of the Cold War into the periphery.[171] It may be said that the struggles for filling the power vacuum left by the vanquished German and Japanese empires were over by 1955, and a new phase of the Cold War started in that year.

One limited impact of the end of the Cold War upon Pacific-East Asian international relations is the increasing politicization of U.S.-Japanese trade frictions. In 1990, Shimokobe Atsushi, then president of the National Institute for Research Advancement (NIRA), concerned with the future of U.S.-Japanese relations, thought of sponsoring research projects on the history of U.S.-Japanese relations, since he feared that Japanese had begun to forget the past. He entrusted Hosoya Chihiro with the task of organizing several research projects.[172] The products of these research projects are expected to be published soon. It is hoped that their publication will have some constructive impact on the Japanese understanding of U.S.-Japanese relations.

Japanese scholarship in the history of U.S.-East Asian relations has produced a number of substantial works in the past fifteen years. Most, regrettably, are not internationally well known because Japanese scholars, of course, publish their works largely in Japanese. Japanese scholars doing research in Japanese foreign relations since the 1950s are also handicapped by the slow opening of Japanese diplomatic archives.[173] While documents made available to the scholarly community are very useful, the actual opening of the Foreign Ministry documents is far behind the 30 year rule proclaimed in 1965 and their release has been done very conservatively. The Japanese government should learn that a reasonable openness of the public records to the scholarly community will bring a long-term benefit to Japanese public policy. Japanese scholars have an obligation to persuade the Japanese government in this respect.

Acknowledgment

This writer would like to thank Professors ASADA Sadao and IGARASHI Takeshi, who kindly read this manuscript and gave him valuable comments.

NOTES

1. ASADA Sadao, ed., *Japan and the World, 1853–1952: A Bibliographic Guide to Japanese Scholarship in Foreign Relations* (New York: Columbia University Press, 1989).

2. Asada Sadao, ed., *International Studies in Japan: A Bibliographic Guide* (Tokyo: Japan Association of International Relations, 1988). Since most of the Japanese publishers are located in Tokyo, the place of publication will hereafter be shown only when the particular book was published somewhere else.

3. Since it is the Japanese custom to put the family name first and the given name second, Western Japanologists usually romanize Japanese personal names in that order. This paper adopts their practice with some exceptions. When English works by Japanese authors are cited in the following endnotes, their names appear as they do in their particular books, articles, and dissertations. Another exception is the name of Japanese authors whose permanent professional base is outside Japan and who write in English extensively.

4. HAYASHI Yoshikatsu, "Nihon ni okeru Nichi-Bei kankeishi kenyū no jōkyō" [The State of Japanese Scholarship in the History of Japanese-American Relations from 1853 to 1941], *Amerika kenkyū shiryō sentā nenpō*, no. 9 (1986): 44–75, is a useful historiographical essay combined with a bibliographical guide. This annual publication of the University of Tokyo's Center for American Studies usually features review essays and bibliographical guides on aspects of American studies in Japan.

5. KATŌ Yūzō, *Kurofune zengo no sekai* [The World at the Time of Kurofune's Arrival] (Iwanami Shoten, 1885; Chikuma Shobo, Bunko, 1994), Kurofune ihen, *Perii no chōsen* [The Kurofune Affair] (Iwanami Shoten, Sinsho, 1988). *Perii wa naze Nihon ni kitaka* [Why Did Perry Come to Japan?] (Shinchōha, 1987) by Somura Yasunobu, a naval geopolitics specialist, is informative but not inspiring. There is no solid Japanese work on the American side of this first encounter.

6. YAMAGUCHI Muneyuki, *Perii raikō zengo: Bakumatsu kaikokushi* [The Age of Kurofune Arrival] (Perikansha, 1988).

7. MITANI Hiroshi, "Kōka-Kaei nenkan no taigai seisaku" [Foreign Policy of the Koka and Kaei Years] *Nenpō kindai Nihon kenkyū*, no. 7 (1985, pub. by Yamakawa Shuppansha): 1–39; "Kaikoku katei no saikento" [A Reconsideration of the Process of Opening the Nation] *Nenpō kindai Nihon kenkyū*, no. 10 (1988): 1–20.

8. KISHIDA Shū with D. K. Butler, *Kurofune gensō: Seishin bunsekigaku kara mita Nichi-Bei kankei* [Black Ship Trauma: U.S.-Japanese Relations Seen from Psychoanalysis] (Toreviru, 1986).

9. MIWA Kimitada, "Yamamoto Isoroku wa Perii ni fukushū shita" [Isoroku Yamamoto Revenged Himself on Perry] in Amerika to Nihon, ed. Jochi Daigaku (Sophia Univer-

sity) *Amerika-Canada Kenkyujo* (Sairyūsha, 1993), 15–50; "Perii 'daiyon no shokan'," [Perry's 'Fourth' Letter Handed to the Bakufu Officials in July 1853], *Kokusai seiji* [International Relations], V102 (Feb. 1993): 1–21. Miwa contends that Perry indeed insulted the Japanese by offering them white flags to use when they wanted to surrender in case of war. He suspects that because of its insulting nature Perry kept silent about the episode in his report and that Japanese Americanists, too, ignored it for the sake of U.S.-Japanese friendship. This episode does not seem to this writer to be more insulting than his tactics of forceful diplomacy, since if Perry offered white flags, he simply wanted to keep a means of communication by telling the Japanese beforehand how to signal for a cease-fire in case of war.

10. UEYAMA Shumpei, *Daitōa sensō no imi* [The Meaning of the Great East Asian War] (Chūō Kōronsha, 1964).

11. INOSE Naoki, *Kurofune no seiki* [The Black Ship Century] (Shōgakukan, 1993). The quotation is from p. 512.

12. MOTOHASHI Tadashi, *Nichi-Bei kankeishi* [A History of Japanese-American Relations] (Gakushuin Daigaku, 1986) contains an interesting chapter on Mori Arinori's American studies during his tenure in Washington.

13. The collection of the papers written for the Rutgers Conference was translated and published in Japanese as Ardath W. Burkes, ed. *Kindaika no suishinshatachi: Ryōgakusei, oyatoi gaikokujin to Meiji* [The Modernizers: Oveerseas Students, Foreign Employees, and Meiji Japan] (Kyoto: Shibunkaku Shuppan, 1990). As its subtitle indicates, this volume pays considerable attention to Japanese overseas students during the late Edo and early Meiji years. Its original English edition was published by Westview Press in 1985. The papers submitted to the Toyama Conference were published as SHIMADA Tadashi, et al., eds., Za yatoi [The Yatoi] (Shibunkaku Shuppan, 1987).

14. FUJITA Fumiko, *Hodaido o kaitaku shita Amerikajin* [The Americans Who Developed Hokkaido] (Shinchōsha, 1993), is based on her dissertation, "'Boys be Ambitious!'—Americans Who Worked in the Japanese Frontier, 1871–1882," City University of New York, 1988. Its revised version will be published by Greenwood Press.

15. KOHIYAMA Rui, *Amerikajin fujin senkyoshi: Rainichi no haikei to sono eikyo* [The 19th-Century American Women's Foreign Mission Enterprise and Its Encounter with Meiji Japan] (Tokyo Daigaku Shuppankai, 1992)

16. KUNO Akiko, *Rokumeikan no kifujin Ōyama Sutematsu: Nihon hatsu no ryūgakusei* [Lady Sutematsu, Rokumeikan Socialite: The First Japanese Woman Student in America] (Chūō Kōronsha, 1988). An English edition of this book was published by Kodansha International, Tokyo, in 1993.

17. This section, "Japanese in America," is adapted from this writer's review essay, "Editor's Introduction," for the *Japanese Journal of American Studies*, No. 3 (1989), (hereafter JJAS) which featured "Japanese Immigrants and Japanese Americans," but incorporates new materials. This volume of JJAS publishes several articles relating to the featured topics. For more detailed historiographical essays with bibliographical guides on Japanese emigration to Hawaii and the continental United States, Japanese immigrants, and Japanese Americans in Hawaii and the mainland, see KUMEI Teruko and IINO Masako," Nihon ni okeru Nihonjin Imin Nikkei Amerikajin Kenkyū" [Japanese Studies on Japanese Immigrants and Japanese Americans] *Amerika Kenkyū Shiryō Sentā Nenpō* 3 (1990): 18–42.

18. TOGAMI Muneyoshi, ed., *Japaniizu-Amerikan: Ijū kara jiritsu eno ayumi* [Japanese Americans: From Emigration to Settlement] (Kyoto: Mineruva Shobō, 1985). This book is the result of a joint research project including American as well as Japanese scholars.

19. Masako NOTOJI, "From Graveyard to Baseball: The Quest for Ethnic Identity in the Prewar Japanese Immigrant Community in the Yakima Valley," JJAS, no. 3 (1989): 29–63.

20. TACHIKAWA Kenji, "Meiji kohanki no tobei netsu" [An American Fever in the Second Half of the Meiji Period], Shirin, 69, no. 3 (1986): 71–105; "Jidai o fukinuketa tobeiron: Katayama Sen no katsudō o megutte" [Going to America as a Social Phenomenon of the Age: On Sen Katayama's Activities], Pan, no. 4 (Spring 1987): 96–123.

21. ABE Yoshio, 'Saigo no Nipponjin': Asakawa Kanichi no shōgai [The 'Last Japanese': The Life of Asakawa Kanichi] (Iwanami Shoten, 1983).

22. ŌHATA Tokushirō, "Asakawa Kanichi no Nihon gaikō hihan" [Asakawa Kanichi's Criticism of Japanese Foreign Policy], Kokusai seiji, vol. 102 (Feb. 1993); Asakawa Kanichi kenkyūkai, ed., Asakawa Kanichi no sekai [The World of Asakawa Kanichi] (Waseda Daigaku Shuppanbu, 1993).

23. KOMORI Yoshihisa, Arashi ni kaku [He Wrote in a Storm] (Mainichi Shinbunsha, 1987).

24. KITAOKA Shinichi, Kiyosawa Kiyoshi: Nichi-Bei kankei eno dōsatsu [Kiyosawa Kiyoshi: Insights into U.S.-Japanese Relations] (Chūō Kōronsha, Sinsho, 1986); "Kiyoshi Kiyosawa in the United States: His Writings for the San Francisco Shinsekai," JJAS, no. 3 (1989): 65–87.

25. TAMURA Norio and SHIRAMIZU Shigehiko, eds., Beikoku shoki no Nihongo shinbun [Early Japanese-language Newspapers in the United States] (Keisō Shobō, 1986).

26. Tamura, Amerika no Nihon-go shinbun [Japanese-language Newspapers in America] (Shinchōsha, 1991).

27. INOUE Nobutaka, Umi o watatta Nihon shūkyō [Japanese Religions Abroad] (Kōbundo, 1985).

28. NAKAMAKI Hirochika, Nihon shūkyō to Nikkei shūkyō no kenkyū: Nihon, Amerika, Burajiru [Studies in Japanese Religions at Home and Abroad: Japan, America and Brazil] (Tōsui Shobō, 1989).

29. Doshisha Daigaku Jinbun Kagaku Kenkyūjo [The Humanities Institute, Doshisha University], ed., Hokubei Nihonjin kirisutokyō undō-shi [A History of the Japanese Christian Movement in North America] (PMC Shuppan, 1992).

30. This ambiguity in Japanese-American agreements on China and their precarious nature were stressed by Sadao ASADA "Japan's 'Special Interests' and the Washington Conference, 1921–1922," American Historical Review, 67, no.1 (October 1962): 62–70.

31. NAGATA Akifumi, Seodoa Rūzuveruto to Kankoku [Theodore Roosevelt and Korea] (Miraisha, 1992);

32. Nagata, "Chōsen dokuritsu undō to kokusai kankei" [The Korean Independence Movement of 1919 and International Relations], Doctoral dissertation, Hitotsubashi University, 1994.

33. KITAOKA Shinichi, "Kokumushō Kyokutō-bu no seiritu: Doru gaikō no haikei," [The Creation of the Far Eastern Division in the State Department: A Background of Dollar Diplomacy] in Nenpō kindai Nihon kenkyū, 11 (1989): 1–38.

34. MITANI Taichirō, "Taishō demokurasii to Washinton taisei" [Taisho Democracy and the Washington System] in Nichi-Bei kankei tsushi, ed. Hosoya Chihiro on behalf of the National Institute for Research Advancement [NIRA] (to be published by Tokyo Daigaku Shuppankai in 1995)

35. KIMURA Masato, Nichi-Bei minkan keizai gaiko, 1905–1911 [Japanese-American Transnational Economic Diplomacy] (Keio Tsushin, 1989).

36. Kimura, Shibusawa Eiichi (Chūō Kōronsha, Shinsho, 1991).

37. HAYASHI Yoshikatsu's article which appeared in Sundai Shigaku, no. 61 (1984–85):

31–73, was part of his dissertation, "The Introduction of American Techonology into the Japanese Electrical Industry: Another Aspect of Japanese-American Relations at the Turn of the Century," University of California, Santa Barbara, 1986.

38. MATSUDA Takeshi's articles that appeared in *Seiyō shigaku*, no. 112 (1978): 1–17, and no. 113 (1979): 33–43, and *Shirin*, vol. 65, no. 3 (1982): 1–30, are based on his dissertation, "Woodrow Wilson's Dollar Diplomacy in the Far East," University of Wisconsin, 1977.

39. HOSOYA Chihiro's article, " '*Nijūichi kajō yōkyū' to Amerika no taiō*" [The Twenty-One Demands and American Response], originally published in *Hitotsubashi Ronsō*, vol. 43, no. 1 (1959), is reprinted in his book cited in note 41.

40. KITAOKA Shinichi, "Nijūikkajō saikō: Nichi-Bei gaikō no sōgo sayō" [A Reconsideration of the Twenty-One Demands: Interaction of Japanese and American Foreign Policies], *Nenpō Kindai Nihon Kenkyū*, no. 7 (1985): 119–50.

41. HOSOYA Chihiro, *Ryōtaisenkan no Nihon gaikō* [Japanese Diplomacy: From World War I to World War Two] (Iwanami Shoten, 1988).

42. ASADA Sadao, *Ryōtaisenkan no Nichi-Bei kankei: Kaigun to seisaku kettei katei* [U.S.-Japanese Relations during the Interwar Period: The Navies and Policy Making Processes] (Tokyo Daigaku Shuppankai, 1993).

43. HOSOYA Chihiro and SAITŌ Makoto, eds., *Washinton taisei to Nichi-Bei kankei* [U.S.-Japanese Relations Under the Washington System] (Tokyo: Daigaku Shuppankai, 1978). This is a very useful collection of papers presented to the conference of Japanese and American scholars on Asian-Pacific international relations during the 1920s, which was held in Kauai, Hawaii, in 1976. This conference gave due attention to economic and cultural aspects of Japanese-American relations of the 1920s. It is regrettable that an English edition of these papers was not published.

44. Much of the contents of of this book is available in English. In addition to his contribution to *Pearl Harbor as History*, see particularly: "Japanese Admirals and the Politics of Naval Limitation: Katō Tomosaburō vs. Katō Kanji," in *Naval Warfare in the Twentieth Century*, ed. Gerald Jordan (London: Croom Helm, 1977), 141–66; "The Revolt Against the Washington Treaty: The Imperial Japanese Navy and Naval Limitation, 1921–1927," *Naval War College Review*, 46, no. 3 (Summer 1993): 82–97; "From Washington to London: The Imperial Japanese Navy and the Politics of Naval Limitation, 1921–1930," 82–97; (with Sumio HATANO) "The Japanese Decision to Move South (1931–1941), in *Paths to War: New Essays on the Origins of the Second World War*, eds. Robert Boyce and Esmond E. Robertson, (London: Macmillan, 1989), 383–407.

45. KOIKE Seiichi emphasizes that the building program of auxiliary warships restrained internal conflict within the navy. Koike, "Washinton kaigun gunshuku kaigi zengo no kaigun bunai jōkyō" [Internal Politics in the Navy before and after the Washington Naval Limitation Conference], *Nihon Rekishi*, no. 480 (May 1988): 68–84.

46. KAGAWA Mari, "Sanfuranshisuko ni okeru Nihonjin gakudo kakuri mondai" [The Segregation of Japanese Pupils in San Francisco Public School System], *Hōgaku seijigaku ronshū*, no. 5 (Summer 1990): 171–207; ibid., no.7 (Dec. 1990), 285–324; ibid., no.9 (Summer 1991): 227–266; ibid., no.10 (Sept. 1991), 113–144.

47. ARUGA Tadashi, "Hai-Nichi mondai to Nichi-Bei kankei" [The Japanese Exclusion Question and U.S.-Japanese Relations] in *Senkanki no Nihon gaikō* [Japanese Diplomacy during the Interwar Period], eds. Akira IRIYE and ARUGA Tadashi (Tokyo Daigaku Shuppankai, 1984): 65–96.

48. MATSUMURA Masayoshi, "Shippai no kōhō gaikō: Taishō-ki Nihon no imin haiseki o meguru tai-Bei 'keihatsu undō' " (A Failure in Publicity Diplomacy: the Japanese Attempt

to 'Enlighten the American Public' to Prevent the Enactment of Anti-Japanese Immigration Laws), *Teikyō Daigaku Kokusaibunka Gakka Kiyō*, 3 (March 1991): 15–59.

49. Matsumura, *Nichi Ro Sensō to Kaneko Kentarō: Kōhōgaikō no kenkyū* [Kaneko Kentaro and the Russo-Japanese War: A Study in Public Diplomacy] (Rev. ed., Shinyūdo, 1987).

50. HASEGAWA Yūichi, "1924 nen ni okeru datuō nyūa ron no fujō" [The Rise of Japanese Asianism in 1924], Kokusai seiji, vol. 102 (Feb. 1993): 99–113.

51. ŌNUMA Yasuaki, "Harukanaru jinshubyōdō no risō" [Racial Equality: An Ideal Far Away—the Japanese Proposal to Include a Racial Equality Clause in the League Covenant and the Japanese Views of International Law], in *Kokusaiō, Kokusairengō, to Nihon*, ed. by Ōnuma (Kōbundō, 1987), 427–80.

52. See Mitani's chapter in Nichi-Bei kankei tsūshi cited in note 32.

53. IINO Masako and BAMBA Nobuya, "Imin mondai o meguru Nichi-Bei-Ka kankei" [The Immigration Question and Japanese-American and Japanese-Canadian Relations] in *Taiheiyō Ajia ken no kokusaikeizai funsō-shi*, ed. HOSOYA Chihiro (Tokyo Daigaku Shuppankai, 1983), 85–112.

54. TAKAHASHI Katsuhiro, "Beikoku hai-Nichi iminhō shūsei mondai to Chū-Bei taishi Debuchi Katsuji" [Ambassador Debuchi Katsuji's Efforts for the Repeal of the Japanese Exclusion Clause], *Nihon Rekishi*, no. 523 (Dec. 1991), 59–75.

55. EGUCHI Keiichi, *Jūgo-nen sensō shōshi* [A Short History of the Fifteen Years War] (New edition, Aoki Shoten, 1991). See this new edition for his defense of the "Fifteen years War" thesis.

56. SAKAI Tetsuya, *Taishō demokurashii taisei no hōkai* [The Collapse of the Taisho Democracy System] (Tokyo Daigaku Shuppankai, 1992).

57. INOUE Toshikazu, *Kiki no naka no kyōcho gaikō* [Cooperative Diplomacy in Crisis] (Yamakawa Shuppansha, 1994)

58. [NOJIMA] KATŌ Yōko, *Mosaku suru 1930 nendai: Nichi-Bei kankei to rikugun chūkensō* [1930 in Search of Itself: U.S.-Japanese Relations and the Army Officers of the Middle Ranks] (Yamakawa Shuppansha, 1994).

59. MITANI Taichirō, "Senzen senchūki Nichi-Bei kankei ni okeru shin-Nichiha gaikōkan no yakuwari: J. Balantain to E. Douman ni tsuite" [The Role of Pro-Japanese American Diplomats in U.S.-Japanese Relations before and during the Pacific War: Joseph Ballantine and Eugene Dooman], *Gaikō fōrumu*, nos. 36–39 (Sept.–Dec. 1991). See particularly no. 37 (Oct. 1991): 82–90, for this problem.

60. NOZAWA Yutaka, ed., *Chūgoku no heisei kaikaku to kokusai kankei* [Currency Reform and International Relations] (Tokyo Daigaku Shuppankai, 1981).

61. MITANI Taichirō, "Kokusai kinyū shihon to Ajia no sensō" [International Financial Capital and Wars in Asia], in *Nenpō kindai Nihon kenkyū*, no. 2 (1980): 114–58.

62. WATANABE Akio, "Ei-Bei ni yoru keizai seisai no kiki to Nihon no taiō" [The Danger of American and British Economic Sanctions and the Japanese Response, 1937–39], Nenpō kindai Nihon kenkyū, no. 7 (1985), 221–24.

63. SUZUKI Akira, "Nihon senji keizai to Amerika" [The Japanese War Economy and the United States], *Kokusai seiji*, 97 (May 1991): 103–18.

64. Its Japanese edition is HOSOYA Chihiro, et al., *Nichi-Bei kankeishi: Kaisen ni itaru 10 nen, 1931–1941* (4 vols., Tokyo Daigaku Shuppankai, 1971–72). These conferences were possible because since the 1950s Japanese scholars had developed studies in political and diplomatic history leading to the Pacific War. Their most significant product was the eight-volume *Taiheiyō sensō e no michi* (Asahi Shinbunsha, 1962–63). Many monographic essays in this series remain valuable. They have been selectively translated into English and pub-

lished in five volumes by Columbia University Press under the editorship of James W. Morley between 1976 and 1994.

65. Its Japanese edition is *Hosoya, Nichi-Ei kankeishi, 1917–1949* (Tokyo Daigaku Shuppankai, 1982).

66. Hosoya, "Taiheiyō sensō towa Nichi-Ei sensō dewa nakatta ka" [Was not the Pacific War really an Anglo-Japanese war?], *Gaiko shiryōkan shiryō*, no. 10 (Oct. 1979). Hosoya's articles relating to Japanese diplomacy during the Interwar Period are collected in his book cited in note 41. The essay cited above is not printed in this book.

67. Hatano Sumio, 'Daitōa sensō' no jidai [The Era of the 'Great East Asian' War] (Asahi Shinbunsha, 1988). Thoroughly familiar with the sources of the Japanese military, Hatano is one of the most productive and reliable scholars in Japanese foreign and military policy from the Manchurian Incident through the Pacific War. Hatano explains important Japanese foreign policy decisions and statements as products of domestic politics brought forth without serious consideration of their international implications. His articles contributed to journals and collaborative books are too numerous to cite here. His other book relating to Japan's road to the Pacific War is *Bakuryō tachi no Shinjuwan* [Army Staff Officers' Pearl Harbor] (Asahi Shinbunsha, 1991). Hatano also cooperated with Kurihara Ken in editing the documents relating to Japanese attempts to end the Pacific War, *Shūsen kōsaku no kiroku* [The Record of Maneuvers to Terminate the War] (2 vols., Kōdansha, 1986).

68. Nomura Minoru, *Taiheiyō sensō to Nihon gunbu* [The Pacific War and the Japanese Military] (Yamakawa Shuppansha, 1983).

69. In addition to Asada's book cited in note 42, see Moriyama Masaru, "Kaigun chūkensō to Nichi-Bei kōshō" [The Navy Officers of the Middle Ranks and U.S.-Japanese Negotiations], *Kyūshū shigaku*, no. 99 (1991); "Kokusaku sakutei no seiji katei" [Political Process of National Policy Making], ibid., no. 102 (1991)

70. Ikeda Kiyoshi, "Nichi-Ei kankei to Taiheiyō sensō, 1937–1941" [Anglo-Japanese Relations and the Pacific War, 1937–1941], Hogaku, vol. 46 (1983): 619–58; vol. 51 (1988): 859–900.

71. Shiozaki Hiroaki, *Nichi-Ei-Bei sensō no kiro: Taiheiyō no yūwa o meguru seisenryaku* [Crossroads of the Anglo-American-Japanese War: Political and Military Strategies of Appeasement in the Pacific] (Tokyo, Yamakawa Shuppansha, 1984).

72. The source is cited in note 59.

73. *Nichi-Bei kaisen gaikō no kenkyū: Nichi-Bei kōshō no hottan kara Haru nōto made* [A Study of U.S.-Japanese Diplomacy Leading to the Outbreak of the War: From the Beginning of U.S.-Japanese Negotiations to the Hull Note] (Keiō Tsūshin, 1986).

74. Kamiyama Akiyoshi, "1941 nen Nichi-Bei kōshō ni kansuru Gaikō shiryōkan bunsho" (Documents of the Diplomatic Record Office Relating to the Japan-U.S. Talks in 1941), *Gaikōshiryōkanpō*, no. 4 (March 1991): 44–58.

75. Murakawa Yōko and Kumei Teruko, *Nichi-Bei senji kōkansen, sengo sōkansen 'kikoku'sha ni kansuru kisoteki kenkyū* [A Study of the 'Japanese' Repatriates and Expatriates from the United States during and after World War II], (Toyota Zaidan Josei Kenkyū Hōkokusho 025, Toyota Zaidan, 1992).

76. Yui Daizaburō's paper contributed to the NIRA project report on "Ethnic Factors in the History of U.S.-Japanese Relations" (to be published in 1994). Part of his paper was published in English as "From Exclusion to Integration: Asian Americans' Experiences in World War II," *Hitotsubashi Journal of Social Studies*, vol. 24, no. 2 (Dec. 1992): 55–67.

77. Hosoya Chihiro, et al., eds., *Taiheiyō sensō* [The Pacific War] (Tokyo: Daigaku Shuppankai, 1993).

78. Ernest R. May, "Sokatsu" [Overview], ibid., 655–69.

79. Its English version, "Reflections on the Impact of the Pacific War on Japanese-American Relations," *Japan Forum*, vol. 4, no. 1 (April 1992): 69–72.

80. During the Pacific War, the Japan government officially called it *Daitōa sensō* [Greater East Asian War]. After the war, MacArthur renamed it as *Taiheiyō sensō* [Pacific War]. Most Japanese and the media commonly use the name Pacific War. So do officially approved history textbooks. But the problem of naming has been much discussed among the Japanese historians and intellectuals. Intellectuals on the right usually refer to the war as the Greater East Asian War. Some people not on the right, however, do not like to use the name Pacific War, because they think the name connotes an American perception or interpretation and/or because they feel that the name slights the importance of Asia in the war. Ueyama Shumpei used the wartime name for the war in his book (cited in note 10) published in 1964. But he was not a rightist nor had he any intention of glorifying Japan's war. A historian on the left, the late Shinobu Seizaburō, once wrote that the name Greater East Asian War was better than the Pacific War because the former gave due importance to Asia. Japan fought the United States in the Pacific, but its real aim was to drive out Britain from East Asia and dominate the region. He said to use the name was one thing and to justify the war was quite another. Other leftists and liberals feel it is repugnant to use the wartime name. Ienaga Saburō says, for example, he likes to call the war the "Fifteen Years War" combining it with Japanese aggressions in China in 1931 and after 1937. For practical reasons, however, he settles with the internationally accepted name Pacific War. Some other scholars, like Kisaka Junichirō, dissatisfied with the name Pacific War, but disliking the War for Greater East Asia, advocate calling the war the Asian-Pacific War. Others do not consider this name inclusive enough and argue for calling the war "the Asian-Pacific Theatre of the Second World War," indicating its connection with the war in Europe.

81. HAYASHI Fusao wrote two volumes entitled *Daitōa sensō kōtei ron* [The Greater East Asian War Justified] (Banchō Shobō, 1963, 1964). Among recent publications, *Haisha no sengo* [Postwar for the Vanquished: Napoleon, Hitler and Shōwa tennō] (Chūō Kōronsha, 1989) by IRIE Takanori, a professor of comparative literature and culture, is sympathetic to Hayashi's hundred years war thesis. Although he does not claim justice for Japan's war, stating that there is no just war, Irie strongly defends modern Japan's foreign policy and her decision for war in 1941.

82. MIWA Kimitada, *Nihon: 1945 nen no shiten* [Japan: A Viewpoint of 1945] (Tokyo Daigaku Shuppankai, 1986). Also see "Nichi-Bei Higashi Ajia-kan no sōkoku" [Conflict between Japanese and American views of East Asia] in *Shōwashi no gunbu to seiji*, ed. MIYAKE Masaki (5 vols., Daiichi Hoki, 1983), 3: 195–232, and his own articles in the two books he edited: *Nihon no 1930 nendai* [The 1930s for Japan] (Saikōsha, 1980) and *Saikō Taiheiyō sensō zengo* [The Era of the Pacific War: Reconsidered] (Sōseiki, 1981).

83. Akira Iriye, *Power and Culture: The Japanese-American War* (Cambridge: Harvard University Press, 1981).

84. YASUDA Toshie "Daitōa kaigi to Daitōa sengen o megutte" [On the Conference of Greater East Asian Nations and the Joint Declaration], *Hōgaku kenkyū*, 63, no. 2 (1990): 369–422. SHINOBU Seizaburo, *Taiheiyō sensō to "mou hitotsu no Taiheiyō sensō"* [The Pacific War and "another Pacific War"] (Keisō Shobō, 1988) also discusses critically this conference and the declaration in the context of the wartime resistance of Asian peoples against Japan.

85. Although many Japanese do not feel Japan was particularly guilty of aggression against the United States because Japan was a weaker power and roundly defeated, and because they believe the United States, too, was an imperialist power, they nevertheless have

a psychological reason, as they know Japan made the surprise strike against Hawaii, to believe that Japan was forced to fight or maneuvered to attack Pearl Harbor. Any American author who implicates President Roosevelt in a conspiracy theory always finds a responsive audience in Japan. KONNO Tsutomu, a TV documentary director, wrote *Sinjuwan kishū: Rūzuberuto wa shitte itaka* [The Surprise Attack at Pearl Harbor: Did Roosevelt know it?] (Yomiuri Shinbunsha, 1991), the best Japanese book on this subject. He concludes that FDR and several advisers had vague information about the presence of a Japanese fleet in the Pacific that might be aiming at Hawaii, but did not take it seriously, assuming that Japan would make major strikes against Southeast Asia.

86. ASADA Sadao, "Kinokogumo to kokumin shinri—Genbaku tōka o meguru Nichi-Bei gyappu, 1945–1992" [The Mushroom Cloud and National Psyches: Japanese and American Perceptions of the A-Bomb Decision, 1945–1992], in *Amerika to Nihon*, ed. Jochi Daigaku Amerika-Kanada Kenkyujo (Sairyusha, 1993), 81–107. Its English version will be published in the *Journal of American-East Asian Relations*.

87. Carol Gluck, "Entangling Illusions—Japanese and American Views of the Occupation," in *New Frontiers in American-East Asian Relations*, ed. by Warren I. Cohen (New York: Columbia University Press, 1983), 169–236. The quotation is from p. 176. For a historiographical discussion of postwar U.S.-Japanese relations with a bibliographical guide to Japanese literature on the subject, see *Amerika kenkyū shiryō sentā nenpō*, no. 11 (1988): 39–70. For a review essay on major Japanese studies on the occupation, see Sadao ASADA "Recent Works in the American Occupation: The State of the Art," in JJAS, no. 1 (1981): 175–91.

88. IOKIBE Makoto, *Beikoku no Nihon senryō seisaku: Sengo Nihon no sekkeizu* [U.S. Occupation Policy toward Japan: Designs for Postwar Japan] (2 vols., Chūō Kōronsha, 1985). Part of this work was published in English: "American Policy towards Japan's 'Unconditional Surrender.'" JJAS, no. 1 (1981): 19–54. Iokibe edited two sets of a microfiche edition of U.S. documents relating to occupation policy. The first series is *The Occupation of Japan: U.S. Planning Documents, 1942–1945* (Maruzen and CIS, 1987). The second series compiles documents from 1945 and after. His *Nichi-Bei sensō to sengo Nihon* [The Japanese-American War and Postwar Japan] (Osaka: Osaka Shoseki, 1989) is written for a general audience.

89. IGARASHI Takeshi, *Tai-Nichi kōwa to reisen: Sengo Nichi-Bei kankei no keisei* [The Peace with Japan and the Cold War: The Formation of Postwar Japanese-American Relations] (Tokyo Daigaku Shuppankai, 1986). He has published several articles relating to the occupation and the peace settlement, which were not printed in this book. Part of his work on the occupation was published in English: "Peace-Making and Party Politics: The Formation of the Domestic Foreign-Policy System in Postwar Japan," *Journal of Japanese Studies*, 11, no. 2 (Summer 1985): 323–56; "MacArthur's Proposal for an Early Peace with Japan and the Redirection of Occupation Policy toward Japan," JJAS, no. 1 (1981): 55–86; "The American and Japanese Constitutions," in *The U.S. Constitution and the Constitutions of Asia*, ed. Kenneth W. Thompson (Lantham, MD: University Press of America, 1988), 37–52.

90. MORITA Hideyuki, *Tai-Nichi senryō seisaku no keisei: Amerika kokumushō, 1940–1944* [The Formulation of American Occupation Policy towards Japan: U.S. Department of State, 1940–1944] (Fukuoka: Ashi Shobō, 1982).

91. Morita, "Amerika keizai kyūshinha chishikijin no sengo tai-Nichi kōsō" [The Ideas of American Economic Radical Intellectuals on Postwar Japan], *Kagoshima Daigaku Jinbungakka ronshū*, no. 29 (1989): 35–56; no. 31 (1990).

92. YUI Daizaburō, *Mikan no senryō kaikaku: Amerika chishikijin to suterareta Nihon*

minshuka kōsō [Incomplete Reform During the Occupation: American Intellectuals and an Abandoned Plan for Democratic Japan] (Tokyo Daigaku Shuppankai, 1989).

93. Similarly interested in the fate of liberal American intellectuals involved in East Asian affairs is NAGAO Ryūichi, *Amerika chisikijin to Kyokutō: Ratimoa to sono jidai* [American Intellectuals and the Far East: Lattimore and His Time] (Tokyo Daigaku Shuppankai, 1985).

94. NAKAMURA Masanori, *Shōchō tennōsei eno michi: Beikoku taishi Gurū to sono shūhen* [The Road to the Symbolic Tennō Institution: Ambassador Grew and his Circle] (Iwanami Shoten, 1989).

95. YAMAGIWA Akira, "Potsudamu sengen no sōan ni tuite" [On the Original Draft of the Potsdam Declaration], *Yokohama Shiritsu Daigaku ronshū, Jinbun*, 37, nos. 2–3 (1986).

96. Iokibe, "Sutimuson: Nichi-Bei Kankei no Shōwa o kimeta otoko" [Stimson: The Man Who Shaped U.S.-Japanese Relations of the Shōwa Era], *Asteion*, no. 11 (Winter 1989): 22–52.

97. TOYOSHITA Narahiko, "Tennō wa nani o katatta ka: Tennō-Makkāsā kaiken no rekisiteki ichi" [What Did Tennō Tell MacArthur? The Historical Meaning of the Tennō-MacArthur Meeeting], *Sekai*, no. 537 (1990), 232–51; no. 538 (1990), 105–17; MATSUO Takayoshi, "Kōsho Shōwa tennō-MacArthur gensui dai-ikkai kaiken," [The First Tennō-MacArthur Meeting: An Examination of Documents] *Kyoto Daigaku Bungakubu Kenkyū Kiyō*, no. 29 (1990); MIWA Takashi, "GHQ minsei kyoku no shōchō tennōseido sekkei no ichi haikei" [A Background for the Designing of the Symbolic Tennō Institution by GHQ's Civil Government Section], *Saitama Daigaku Kiyō*, vol. 39, no. 1 (1990).

98. TAKAHASHI Hikohiro, "Shōchō tennō-sei no keisei yōin" [The Symbolic Tennō Institution and the Reasons for Its Emergence], *Rekishigaku kenkyū*, no. 605, 1–13. See also Nakamura's *Sengoshi to shōchō tennō* [Tennō as Symbol in Postwar Japanese History] (Iwanami: Shoten, 1992) for the acceptance of tennō as symbol by a large majority of the Japanese people during the occupation period.

99. YOSHIDA Yutaka, *Shōwa tennō no Shūsen-shi* [Shōwa Tennō and the End of the War] (Iwanami Shoten, Shinsho, 1992).

100. Relating to this war responsibility issue, Nakamura regrets that Hirohito's desire to retire was thwarted first by MacArthur and then by Yoshida Shigeru. See his book cited in note 94.

101. KŌSAKA Masataka, "Purologu: 1926–1945" [Prologue to An Era] in Nichi-Bei no Shōwa [Shōwa—Japan and America], edited by KŌSAKA Masataka and YAMAZAKI Masakazu (TBS Buritanika, 1990), 24.

102. MIYASATO Seigen, *Amerika no taigai seisaku kettei katei* [Foreign Policy Making in the United States] (San-ichi Shobō, 1981). See pages 217–228.

103. OTA Masahide, "Amerika no sengo Okinawa seisaku" [U.S. Policy Toward Postwar Okinawa], in *Nihon senryō no kenkyū*, ed. Robert E. Ward and SAKAMOTO Yoshikazu [Studies in the Occupation of Japan] (Tokyo Daigaku Shuppankai, 1987).

104. ŌTAKE Hideo, *Saigunbi to Nashonarizumu* [Rearmament and Nationalism], (Chūō Kōronsha, Shinsho, 1988)

105. The lack of candor also characterized Japanese negotiations for the Mutual Security Aid Act of 1954 with the United States. The Japanese government spoke of the MSA aid as economic aid, but it was clearly military aid, as Yasuhara Yōko's article indicates. Yasuhara, "Keizai enjo o meguru MSA kōshō" [U.S.-Japanese Negotiations for an Economic Aid under the MSA Program], *Amerika kenkyū*, no. 22 (1988).

106. See his article in *Kōza Gendai: Reisen* [Series on Contemporary Era: the Cold War] (Iwanami Shoten, 1963), 331–70.

107. The book is cited in note 103 above. The English version of this book is *Democratizing Japan: The Allied Occupation*, eds. Ward and Sakamoto (Honolulu: University of Hawaii Press, 1987).

108. This book is cited in note 96 above. It was edited by the editors of *Asteion* and *Daedalus* with the support of the Suntory Foundation.

109. Iokibe, "Senryō kaikaku no san ruikei" [Three Types of Reform Introduced during the Occupation], *Leviathan*, 6 (1990): 97–120.

110. TOYOSHITA Narahiko, *Nihon senryō kanri taisei no seiritsu* [The Emergence of the Control System for Occupied Japan] (Iwanami Shoten, 1992). His study of the occupation of Italy, *Itaria senryō-shi josetsu: Sengo gaikō no kiten* [A Study of the History of the Occupation of Italy: The Starting Point for Postwar Diplomacy] (Yūhikaku, 1984).

111. See *Rekishigaku kenkyū*, no. 600 (1989): 1–77; Yui, Nakamura, and Toyoshita, eds., *Senryō kaikaku no kokusai hikaku* [Comparative Studies on Reforms in Occupied Areas: Japan, Asia and Europe] (Sanseidō, 1994).

112. NAKANO Satoshi, "Beikoku no Firipin saisenryo" [The American Reoccupation of of the Philippines], ibid., 27–55, and his article in *Rekishigaku kenkyū*, no. 600: 57–67, are attempts to answer why democracy failed to develop in the postwar Philippines. LEE Ke-tae, "Bei-So no Chōsen senryō to Nanboku bundan" [The Occupation of Korea by USA and USSR and the Korean Partition], in *Senryō kaikaku no kokusai hikaku*, 56–84, and his article in *Rekishigaku kenkyū*, 68–77, critically discuss U.S. and Soviet policy toward Korea. As for American policy toward postwar Korea, there is a study which discusses it in the context of the American strategy of integrating the Pacific region: LEE Jong-Won, "Sengo Beikoku no Kyokutō seisaku to Kankoku no datsu-shokuminchika" [Postwar U.S. Policy towards the Far East and Decolonization in Korea], in *Iwanami kōza: Kindai Nihon to shokuminchi* (8 vols., Iwanami Shoten, 1993), vol. 8.

113. SODEI Rinjirō, *Sekaishi no naka no Nihon senryō* [The Occupation of Japan in World History] (Nihon Hyōronsha, 1985). Sodei's biographical study of MacArthur was published by Chūō Kōronsha in 1974.

114. Shindō, "Ashida Hitoshi to sengo kaikaku," [Ashida Hitoshi and postwar reform], *Kokusai seiji*, vol. 85 (May 1987): 55–72. This volume features "the Occupation of Japan: Studies from Various Viewpoints." Another article worth noting in this volume is MASUDA Hiroshi's which illuminates the making of the purge directives, "Kōshoku tsuihō rei o meguru Beikoku no seisaku" [The Formulation of Purge Directives, SCAPIN-550 and 548], 73–96.

115. Kitaoka, "Yoshida Shigeru no gaikō: Senzen to sengo" [Yoshida Shigeru's Foreign Policy: Prewar and Postwar], *Gaikōshiryōkanpō*, no. 7 (March 1994): 1–23.

116. SUZUKI Eiichi, *Nihon senryō to kyōiku kaikaku* [The Occupation and Educational Reform in Japan] (Keisō Shobō, 1983); KUBO Yoshizo, *Tai-Nichi senryō seisaku to sengo kyōiku kaikaku* (Sanseido, 1984).

117. IKADO Fujio, *Senryō to Nihon shūkyō* [The Occupation and Religions in Japan] (Miraisha, 1993). Part I of this book includes Igarashi Takeshi's essay on the beginning of the postwar cultural exchange program between the United States and Japan, an aspect of postwar U.S.-Japanese relations not much studied. It may be mentioned here that HOSOYA Masahiro has published several articles based on his dissertation, "Selected Aspects of the Zaibatsu Dissolution in Occupied Japan, 1945–1952," Yale University, 1982.

118. HOSOYA Chihiro, *Sanfuranshisuko kōwa eno michi* [The Road to the San Francisco Peace] (Chūō Kōronsha, 1984).

119. YUAN Ke-Qin, "Gaiatsu riyō gaikō toshiteno Yoshida shokan" [The Yoshida Letter as Diplomacy Utilizing External Pressure] *Hitotsubashi ronsō*, 107, no. 1 (1992): 91–118.

120. WATANABE Akio and MIYASATO Seigen, eds., *Sanfuranshisuko kōwa* [the San Francisco Peace] (Tokyo Daigaku Shuppankai, 1986).

121. Igarashi, "Nichi-Bei Anzen hoshō jōyaku no teiketsu to Chōsen sensō no kage" [The Conclusion of the U.S.-Japanese Security Treaty of 1951 and the Shadow of the Korean War], in *Kokka to shimin*, ed. Kokka Gakkai (Yūhikaku, 1987), 195–231.

122. KAN Hideki, *Bei-So reisen to Amerika no Ajia seisaku* [The American-Soviet Cold War and America's Asian Policy] (Kyoto: Mineruva Shobō, 1992), ch. 4.

123. Miyasato, "Gyōsei kyōtei no sakusei katei" [Making of the Administrative Agreement between the United States and Japan], *Kokusai seiji*, vol. 85 (May 1987): 133–50.

124. The English publication is *The Origins of the Cold War in Asia*, ed. by Yonosuke NAGAI and Akiria IRIYE (Tokyo Daigaku Shuppankai and Columbia University Press, 1977).

125. NAGAI Yōnosuke, *Reisen no kigen: Sengo Ajia no kokusai kankyō* [Origins of the Cold War: The International Environment of Postwar Asia] (Chūō Kōronsha, 1976). The volumes in the *Kokusai kankyō* series were published by Chūō Kōronsha from 1978 to 1985. The books by Iokibe, Okonogi, and Yano cited in notes 88, 126, and 133 were among them. Akira Iriye's *Power and Culture: The Japanese-American War* was first published in Japanese in this series.

126. OKONOGI Masao, *Chōsen sensō* [The Korean War] (Chūō Kōronsha, 1985).

127. At one time the Korean War was an ideologically controversial subject in Japan. When Shinobu Seizaburō, a historian on the left, wrote in 1965 that North Korea had started the war as a war of national liberation, his thesis was favorably noted by the more conservative Kamiya Fuji, but bitterly criticized by his ideological colleagues who believed that it had been a war of aggression started by the American imperialists. The Japanese left gradually accepted Shinobu's thesis. By the middle of the 1970s, the origins of the Korean War became far less controversial among Japanese intellectuals. Shinobu, *Chōsen sensō no boppatsu* [The Outbreak of the Korean War] (Fukumura Shuppansha, 1969). His thesis was first published in *Sekai*, no. 237 (Aug. 1965): 18–32. His interpretation that the initiative to start a full scale war in the peninsula was on the Northern side was supported by FUJI Kamiya, *Chōsen sensō* [The Korean War] (Chūō Kōronsha, Shinsho, 1966).

128. HIRAMATSU Shigeo, *Chūgoku to Chōsen sensō* [China and the Korean War] (Keisō Shobō, 1988).

129. ZHU Jianrong, *Mōtakutō no Chōsen sensō* [Mao Zedong's Korean War] (Iwanami Shoten, 1991).

130. WADA Haruki, "Chōsen sensō ni tuite kangaeru" [Reflections on the Korean War], *Shisō*, no. 795 (Sept. 1990): 6–29.

131. OH Choong Keun, "Chōsen sensō to Soren—Kokuren Anpo rijikai kesseki o chushin ni" [The Korean War and the Soviet Union: The Soviet's Absence at the UN Security Council], *Hōgaku kenkyū*, vol. 65, no. 2 (1992): 131–53.

132. NAKATSUJI Keiji, "Chōsen teisen to Bei-Kan kankei—reisen ni kakureta betsunaru sensō" [The Korean Armistice and U.S.-ROK Relations: A Struggle beneath the Cold War], *Shisō*, no. 791 (May 1990): 42–71.

133. YANO Tōru, *Reisen to Tōnan Ajia* [the Cold War and Southeast Asia] (Chūō Kōronsha, 1986).

134. MIYASATO Seigen, *Amerika no taigaiseisaku kettei katei* [Foreign Policy Decision Making Process in the United States] (Sanichi Shobō, 1982)

135. MATSUOKA Hiroshi, *Daresu gaikō to Indoshina* [Dulles Diplomacy and Indochina] (Dobunkan, 1988).

136. AKAGI Kanji, *Vetonamu sensō no kigen: Aizenhawā seiken to daiichiji Indoshina sensō*

[Origins of the Vietnam War: The Eisenhower Administration and the First Indochina War] (Keio Tsushin, 1991).

137. SHUTŌ Motoko, *Indonesia: Nashonarizumu henyō no seiji katei* [Indonesia: Political processes of Transforming Indonesian Nationalism] (Keisō Shobō, 1993).

138. FURUTA Motoo, *Rekishi to shiteno Betonamu sensō* [The Vietnam War as History] (Ōtsuki Shoten, Shinsho, 1991).

139. Akio WATANABE "Southeast Asia in U.S.-Japanese Relations," in Akira Iriye and Warren I. Cohen, eds., *The United States and Japan in the Postwar World* (Lexington: University of Kentucky Press, 1989), 80–95.

140. YOSHIKAWA Yōko, *Nip-Pi baishō kōshō no kenkyū* [A Study of Japanese-Philippine Reparation Negotiations] (Keisō Shobō, 1990).

141. SHIMIZU Sayuri, "Posuto-kōwa ka no Nichi-Bei kankei: Tonan ajia keizai kaihatsu kōsō o chūsin ni" [Post-Peace U.S.-Japanese Relations in the 1950s: On Plans for Economic Development in Southeast Asia], in *Amerika to Nihon*, 177–201. See also her PhD dissertation, "Creating People of Plenty: The United States and Japan's Economic Alternatives," 1952–1958 (Cornell, 1991). For Hiwatari's works see the next section and notes 162 and 163.

142. KATŌ (Yasuhara) Yōko, *Amerika no sekai senryaku to COCOM* [America's Global Strategy and COCOM] (Tokyo: Yūshindō, 1992). The main part of her book is based on her dissertation: Yoko YASUHARA "Myth of Free Trade: COCOM and CHINCOM," (University of Wisconsin, 1984).

143. TAKAMATSU Motoyuki, "Chaina difarensharu kanwa mondai o megotte no Aizenhawā seiken no taiō" [The Eisenhower Administration's Response to the China Differential, 1955–1957], *Kokusai seiji*, vol. 105 (Jan. 1994): 60–79.

144. Takamatsu, "Kankoku ni taisuru jinken gaikō no tenkai" [U.S. Human Rights Diplomacy towards Korea] in Amerika gaikō to jinken, ed. ARUGA Tadashi (Nihon Kokusalmondai Kenkyujō, 1992), 207–64; "Kātā-Rēgan Ryōseiken ni yoru Tai-Phiripin jinken gaikō no tenkai," [U.S. Human Rights Diplomacy Toward the Philippines During the Carter and Reagan Administrations] *Tezukayama Daigaku Kyōyō Gakubu Kiyō*, no. 31 (1992): 367–92.

145. Takamatsu, "A Comparative Analysis of the Eisenhower Administration's Responses to Two Taiwan Straits Crises in 1954–55 and 1958," *Amerika kenkyū*, no. 21 (1987), 129–46 is a study based on archival research. See also his "Daiichiji Taiwan kaikyō kiki to Aizenhawā-Daresu no tairitsu" [Eisenhower, Dulles, and the First Taiwan Straits Crisis], *Ajia kuōtari*, vol. 10, no. 2 (Spring 1978): 1–32. See also Usami Shigeru's work cited in note 148.

146. Lee Jong-Won has completed a manuscript which relates an analysis of Japan-Republic of Korea relations to America's East Asia policy in the 1950s.

147. Sadako OGATA, *Normalization with China: A Comparative Study of U.S. and Japanese Processes* (Berkeley: University of California Press, 1988). A Japanese edition was published in 1992.

148. The Carter administration's policy on the formal recognition of the People's Republic was also studied by USAMI Shigeru in several articles, among them: "Bei-Chū kokkō juritsu to Bei-Ka jōyaku no shori" [The Establishment of Formal Relationship with the People's Republic and the Problems relating to the Termination of the Treaty with the Republic of China], *Ajia kuōtari* (Oct. 1985): 14–36; and "Bei-Chu kokko juritsu to Chaina robii no teiko" [Resistance of the "China Lobby" to Establishing a Formal Relationship with the People's Republic], *Kokusai mondai*, no. 330 (Sept. 1987): 56–71. He plans to publish a book-length study.

149. IJIRI Hidenori, *Gendai Amerika chishikijin to Chūgoku* [Responses of Contemporary American Intellectuals to China] (Kyoto: Mineruva Shobō, 1992).

150. MIZOBE Hideaki, "Nichi-Bei tairitsu no seiji shisōshiteki kōsatsu" [On the Psychohistorical "Truth" of Japanese-American Rivalry], *Nonpō kindai Nihon kenkyū*, vol. 11 (1989): 243–66.

151. HOMMA Nagayo, "Nihon 'Tasha ron' no kiken" [Danger in the Thesis that Japan Is 'Not Like Us'], *Gaikō fōrumu*, no. 13 (Oct. 1989): 12–21.

152. NAKANISHI Hiroshi, "Konoe Fumimaro 'Ei-Bei hon'i no heiwashugi o haisu' ronbun no haikei: Fuhenshugi eno taiō" [The Intellectual Background of Konoe's Essay, "Opposed to the kind of Pacifism favorable to Britain and America": A Response to Universalism], *Hōgaku ronsō*, vol. 132, Nos. 4–6 (1993): 235–56.

153. SAKAMOTO Takao, *Nihon wa mizukara no raireki o katariuruka* [What Can Japan Speak about Its Own National Experience?] (Chikuma Shobō, 1994).

154. ISHII Osamu, *Reisen to Nichi-Bei kankei* [The Cold War and U.S.-Japanese Relations] (Japan Times Press, 1989).

155. KAMIYA Fuji, *Sengoshi no naka no Nichi-Bei kankei* [U.S.-Japanese Relations in the Postwar History] (Shinchōsha, 1989).

156. TANAKA Takahiko, *Nis-So kokkō kaifuku no kenkyū* [A Study of the Reestablishment of Soviet-Japanese Relations] (Yūhikaku, 1993).

157. HARA Yoshihisa, *Sengo Nihon to kokusai seiji: Anpo kaitei no seiji rikigaku* [Postwar Japan and International Politics: The Political Dynamics of the Security Treaty Revision] (Chūō Kōronsha, 1988).

158. SAKAMOTO Kazuya, "Shigemitsu hō-Bei to Anpo kaitei kōsō no zasetsu" [Shigemitsu's Visit to the United States and the Failure of His Plan to Revise the Security Treaty], *Mie Daigaku Hōkei ronsō*, 10, no. 2 (1992): 23–58. Shigemitsu's proposal conveyed to Washington through the American ambassador before his visit included the eventual withdrawal of all U.S. forces from Japan in accordance with the progress of Japanese rearmament, although his proposal in Washington was more cautious.

159. TOGO Fumihiko, *Nichi-Bei gaikō 30-nen* [The Thirty Years of U.S.-Japanese Diplomacy] (Sekai no Ugokisha, 1982).

160. For Kamiya's view, see his book cited in note 155. For this writer's view, see Tadashi ARUGA, "The Security Treaty Revision of 1960," in Iriye and Cohen, eds., *The United States and Japan*, 61–79. Since many Japanese opposed to the new security treaty in 1960 did not expect or hope that this kind of self-assertion would result in the deterioration of Japanese-American relations, it may be said that their behavior revealed a mentality of dependence. For the concept of "mentality of dependence," see Takeo DOI THE ANATOMY OF DEPENDENCE (Kōdansha International, 1973).

161. Hara, *Nichi-Bei kankei no kōzu* [The Design of U.S.-Japanese Relations] (Nihon Hoso Shuppan Kyokai, 1991).

162. HIWATARI (Hayashi) Yumi, *Sengo seiji to Nichi-Bei kankei* [Postwar Japanese Politics and U.S.-Japanese Relations] (Tokyo Daigaku Shuppankai, 1990).

163. Hiwatari, "Kishi gaikō ni okeru Tōnan Ajia to Amerika" [Southeast Asia and the United States in Kishi's Foreign Policy], *Nenpō kindai Nihon kenkyū*, vol. 11 (1989): 211–242.

164. KŌNO Yasuko, *Okinawa henkan o meguru seiji to gaikō* [Politics and Diplomacy of the Okinawa Reversion] (Tokyo Daigaku Shuppankai, 1994).

165. For Misayato's work, in addition to the book cited in note 5, see *Amerika no Okinawa tōchi* [The American Rule in Okinawa] (Iwanami Shoten, 1966). For Ota's works, see note 101.

166. MATSUDA Yoshitaka, *Sengo Okinawa shakai keizai-shi kenkyū* [A Study of the Social and Economic History of Postwar Okinawa] (Tokyo Daigaku Shuppankai, 1981).

167. WAKAIZUMI Kei, *Tasaku nakarishi o shinzemto hossu* [I would like to believe there was no other policy choice] (Bungei Shunjusha, 1994).

168. Hideo SATO I.M. Destler, Priscilla Clapp, and Haruhiko Fukui, *Managing an Alliance: The Politics of U.S.-Japanese Relations* (New York: Brookings, 1976); and Destler, Fukui, and Sato, *The Textile Wrangle: Conflict in Japanese-American Relations, 1969–1971* (Ithaca, NY: Cornell University Press, 1979); Destler and Sato, eds, *Coping with U.S.-Japanese Economic Conflicts* (New York: Lexington Books, 1982).

169. Her book is cited in note 142. See Chapter 9, 241–270.

170. This writer discussed major characteristics of Asian international politics during the Cold War era in his paper for the Seminar on Okinawa Reversion: Its Long-Term Significance in U.S.-Japanese Relations, May 13–14, 1992, Tokyo.

171. ISHII Osamu, "Reisen no '55 nen taisei'"[The "System of 1955" in Cold War History], *Kokusai seiji*, vol. 100 (Aug. 1992): 35–53.

172. Hosoya invited four scholars, Igarashi Takeshi, Akira Iriye, Miyasato Seigen, and this writer, to cooperate with him in organizing five research groups. A group directly supervised by Hosoya himself was engaged in writing a history of Japanese-American relations. Part of this group drafted a detailed cholonology of Japanese-American relations and collected documents to edit a documentary history of Japanese-American relations. The Igarashi group was engaged in research in the influence of American political thought upon modern Japan; the Miyasato group was engaged in comparative studies in Japanese and American diplomatic styles; the Iriye group, composed of American scholars, conducted research on relations between social change and foreign affairs in the two nations; and the Aruga group, a binational group, conducted research on ethnic factors in the history of Japanese-American relations. A survey history and a documentary history of Japanese-American relations will be published by Tokyo Daigaku Shuppankai. The other research papers will be published by NIRA itself.

173. In December 1975, the Ministry of Foreign Affairs declared that the Ministry would make public its diplomatic records following a lapse of thirty years in response to a growing demand from the academic world. The first release of postwar Japanese diplomatic records was made in May 1976; and the eleventh release, the last to the date, was made in October 1991. Documents of more than 400,000 pages have been transferred to the Diplomatic Record Office to make them available to the public. Some documents of 1960, such as those relating to the cancellation of President Eisenhower's visit, are open to the public, but records relating to negotiations for the security treaty of 1960 are still withheld. While records relating to Japanese application for a UN membership are said to be very valuable, documents relating to the Northern Islands issue and the Soviet-Japanese negotiations in 1955–56 have been kept from the public. Even when a group of documents relating to a particular subject was released, many scholars complain some important documents appeared to have been withheld. As diplomatic issues become quite varied, important diplomatic documents will be increasingly in the hands of agencies other than Foreign Ministry, such as the Ministry of Finance or the Ministry of International Trade and Industry. The Ministry of Finance has the office of financial history and publishes its official history, the multivolume postwar *Shōwa zaiseishi* [A History of Governmental Finance]. The 20-volume financial history of the occupation period is now complete, while six of the twenty volumes for the period from 1952 through 1973 have been published. A limited number of documents used for writing a particular series of the Ministry's official history are to be opened to general researchers at the office when the publication of the series is

completed. MITI has also been publishing its official history, the 17-volume *Tsūshō sangyōshi* [A History of Japanese Policy in International Trade and Industry] which covers from 1945 through 1979. Regretably, MITI and other agencies seem to have far less interest than the Foreign Ministry in preserving and releasing their documents for the use of the scholarly public.

Chapter Three

East Asian Conundrum: Geopolitics and Ideology in the Mirror of Russian Historiography

CONSTANTINE V. PLESHAKOV

.

1.

The development of East Asian studies in Russia has followed the general pattern of social science progress in this part of the world. Since the crisis of Soviet society was accelerated by *perestroika* in the mid-80's, Russian historiography[1] in general, be it the history of science or political theory, has experienced three distinct stages.

The first stage could be called the stage of *realpolitik*. In 1985–87 the Soviet Union acknowledged that it was facing an all-embracing crisis from notoriously inadequate agricultural production to a stagnant and counterproductive foreign policy. Lip service was paid to modernization in the framework of the "socialist choice." This modernization implied reconciliation with the outside world, and the creation of a favorable environment for modernization efforts. The Soviet leadership, under the pressure of Mikhail S. Gorbachev and his ambitious, though not overly sophisticated team, had agreed to the universalization of the worldview, forsaking Soviet particularism. The notions of "new political thinking," "common humanitarian values" and "interdependent world" were introduced into Soviet foreign policy and, correspondingly, to academic discussions. This universalization of mentality implied a definite retreat from ideology and the ascendance of *realpolitik* as the general approach to international affairs. *Realpolitik* seemed good enough to pull the USSR out of the swamp of crisis and self-inflicted isolation. From then on this principle (though the term was rarely used) came to be regarded as a pivot for foreign policy thinking. Ideology was desacralized, and pragmatism (combining geopolitics and economic needs) became the mainstream.

History and political science were there to support the new doctrine with their inadequate, but volatile forces. Having been nursed at least for two decades by the intellectuals, pragmatism was now introduced as state practice. The intellectual logic of the doctrine was based, first of all, upon the concept of equal responsibility of East and West for the Cold War. The first wave of revisionism flooded the Soviet publications. However, unlike diehard anti-Communists, the cautious and evasive majority of historians started examining Soviet policy from the balance-of-power angle.

For East Asian studies it meant total reappraisal of relations with all nations of the Far East. The academic community had acknowledged the existence of the northern territories problem in Soviet-Japanese relations. The argument, however, ran along *realpolitik* lines. The USSR, the historians argued, was right to keep the disputed territories for two reasons. First, their transfer to the USSR in 1945 had been the result of the concert of great powers' interaction in 1945, and Stalin was blamed for not having sealed the deal at the San Francisco 1951 conference. Second, the necessity to keep the islands now was described in terms of their strategic importance for the Soviet Navy (especially nuclear submarines) which otherwise, the experts argued, would be locked in the Sea of Japan with Vladivostok of no use as a naval base.

Relations between Moscow and Beijing were another East Asian affair of paramount importance. However, the leadership of the Soviet Union, feeling very vulnerable, divided on the issue and, not willing to give the Chinese any idea of what was going on in the milieux of Soviet China experts, had simply introduced a moratorium on any publications on modern China. The continuing undercurrent of dispute had been influenced by a paradigm of geopolitics and ideology. The conservatives (both in leadership and in academia) were arguing consistently that China was an ideological enemy, undermining the socialist world by its corrupted bourgeois reform and also harming the national interests of the Soviet Union in geopolitical terms by what they called an alliance of China with the United States. The reformers were insisting that China was an *ally* in ideology, for both countries faced the problem of modernization, of reforming socialism, and that the USSR could not afford to have a hostile China in geopolitical terms. However, in the ideology-geopolitics paradigm, ideology was the side which suffered, for in 1985–88 it was politically incorrect to stress the significance of ideological affinity or contradictions.

The third issue was that of the two Koreas. The dispute again was never made public. The conservatives would follow more or less the same argument they used with China. North Korea, they pointed out, was an ally both in ideological and in geopolitical terms. In ideological terms the Soviet Union, having a divided nation in its own military bloc—Germany—and facing a delicate problem of a divided China, could not afford to endorse capitalist choice vs. socialist one. In geopolitical terms, they contended, it would be absurd to weaken the military cooperation with the North with the American army present in South Korea in the vicinity of Soviet borders. They also indicated that alienation of Moscow from Pyongyang would mean playing into Chinese hands, pushing Kim Il Sung away from a fragile equilibrium between the PRC and the USSR. The reformers suggested that an alliance with one of the most notorious totalitarian regimes in the world did not help to apply humanistic makeup to the Soviet face. They also insisted that reconciliation with Seoul offered Moscow a unique geopolitical leverage on the Korean peninsula, making the USSR the only nation having normal relations both with the North and with the South.

The *realpolitik* period had opened the way to pluralism at least in the narrow layer of elites, and now it was no longer a heresy to disagree with the previous policy or with the views of the majority, as long as one cared about the national interests of the country." However, this period did not find a full reflection in the publications of the time (because of censorship) and did not produce any considerable scholarly effort (for the same reason).

The second stage of Soviet social science development during *perestroika* could be called a stage of emotional revisionism. It lasted approximately three years (1989–1991) and again never brought important scholarly results or political gains. The flood of anti-Communism and anti-Sovietism, dammed up by the state apparatus for so many years, was finally let loose. The euphoria of sudden freedom of speech was so breathtaking that it overwhelmed serious research. Even the elites of the society first had to get accustomed to the feeling of speaking up. The most evident facts, known to the West for decades and only whispered and hinted at in Moscow parlors before, now had to be established in the society and in its allegedly enlightened academia. The epicenter of the historical debate was far away from East Asia; it was concentrating upon the Molotov-Ribbentrop pact and the consequences of the partition of Eastern Europe with Nazi Germany.

At the same time the East Asian experts, too, had started admitting the facts, denied for decades. The number one question was a pathetic debate over "Who started the Korean War?" To admit in public that it had been the North was already a political and emotional breakthrough. But issues of historical interest—such as the role of Stalin and Mao in unleashing the war, and the real scale of the Soviet involvement in it—were not discussed: first, the archives were still closed and, second, the childish but understandable excitement at the opportunity to call black black was there.

But simultaneously the political scientists had started an overt campaign for establishing diplomatic relations with Seoul. A consensus was soon reached that it was necessary to build a diplomatic corridor for an important economic and geopolitical partner, and the only thing which was under dispute was how to do that—i. e., how to keep from alienating North Korea totally , to avoid pushing it into Beijing's embrace—and what to demand from Seoul in exchange for recognition. In 1990 diplomatic relations were established; the political scientists had fulfilled their role, but the historians had not entered the scene yet.

As far as Japan was concerned, attempts were made to suggest that the notorious northern territories remained in the domain of ideological myths and not in the realm of geopolitics. Expectations were running high: Japan was supposed to pay a handsome ransom for the disputed islands. However, here ideological myths (of the territorial integrity of the USSR, which was soon to perish *in toto*, and of the sacred nature of territorial gains paid for by millions of dead during World War II) prevailed, and Gorbachev's leadership never approached a resolution of the issue.

The political scientists, however, had reached a breakthrough regarding China. By late 1988 a consensus was formed that it was better to have China geopolitically neutral (the fears of American strategic involvement in the area had diminished significantly by that time). Ideological considerations were more complicated. Gorbachev's visit to China to normalize relations between the USSR and the PRC came in May 1989, on the eve of the Tiananmen massacre, when the center of Beijing was already occupied by the protesters. In this context Gorbachevians regarded China as an ideological ally, i. e. a socialist country, venturing major reform and struggling for stability against the irresponsible mob of liberals. The liberals were expressing their solidarity with the Chinese protesters persecuted on Tiananmen, regarding them as allies in the struggle against communist totalitarianism. Very little historical research on modern China was nevertheless performed: the archives did not participate in the freedom of speech movement.

The third stage in social science arrived with the collapse of the USSR in late 1991 and continues today. It could be defined as the period of primary processing of information. Both political scientists and historians had to digest the tide of the new. First, the new ideological and geopolitical situation of Russia had to be considered and put into some methodological perspective. Second, the contradictory process of opening of the archives started. Third, interaction with the world academic community has become limited only by financial considerations; that permitted Russian scholars to integrate into world academia with its resources of both questions and answers. Fourth, a search for a new historical methodology started. So far the results have been few. However, this period promises to create a basis for a social science *Resorgiamento* in Russia and should be described in length.

2.

The range of sources used by contemporary Russian historians is very uneven. Some sources, known to the West for many years, are entering the ivory towers of Russia historians only now. Others, found in Russia itself, are new to the world academic community. The documents used are very uneven in quality, and the rumors about the avalanche of new and sensational sources in Russia are slightly exaggerated.

The sources already used by Western historians are still of some considerable value for their Russian colleagues, for they can put them into a purely Russian perspective and suggest the interpretation of the insiders. The best example of such sources is Nikita S. Khrushchev's memoirs.[2]

Simultaneously the publication of other memoirs has started. They vary from highly revealing (though not so much so on East Asia) transcripts of talks with Vyacheslav M. Molotov presented by Felix Chuev[3] to marginal memoirs of people involved in East Asian affairs in the 1940s and 1950s.[4] However, the memoirs published were heavily influenced by commercialism and certain publications should be treated with extreme caution.

The son of Laventy P. Beria, the head of Stalin's secret police, has published memoirs *My father—Lavrenty Beria*.[5] This book bears a clear imprint of "family revisionism." Beria is portrayed as the wisest Soviet leader of Stalin's era, the chief pragmatist of the Soviet Union. There is some rationale in interpreting Beria's personality in terms of pragmatism, but the sensational flavor of the publication demands caution. There is some discussion of East

Asia in the book, which must be doublechecked: Sergo Beria describes the
situation, for instance, when Stalin was prepared to order a preemptive strike
against American vessels in 1950, having been warned by intelligence sources
that the U.S. was going to land forces in Korea. Beria allegedly made Stalin
change his mind, emphasizing the plausibility of nuclear retaliation by the
Americans.[6]

The American audience was shocked by Soviet spymaster Pavel Sudoplatov's book, *The Special Tasks*, mainly because it accused the American scientific community of collaborating with Soviet intelligence. The offending part
of the book differs greatly from others both in its style and in its very laconic
description of the operation (the absence of details, for instance, is very sus-
picious). There is every reason to believe that this portion of the book is
mainly the product of American coauthors' entrepreneurial skills. The only
reference to East Asia also looks strange: Sudoplatov argues that Stalin had
unleashed the Berlin crisis of 1948 to divert the attention of the West away
from the Communist offensive in China.[7] This idea looks extremely questionable, given tension in the relations between Mao and Stalin in 1948. In
any case, this book in general should not be discarded, for it is persuasive in
describing the inner life of the Soviet secret police and intelligence.

The memoirs published by the veterans of the Soviet offensive in the Orient who are still active in politics can not be regarded as reliable, especially the
books about the Afghan war. The former head of KGB intelligence, Leonid
Shebarshin, has published his memoirs, mostly consisting of Kipling-like
descriptions of the exotic Orientals.[8] The memoir of a hawkish general, Boris
Gromov,[9] is the most advanced military version of what happened in
Afghanistan. The major value of the book is the top secret documents from
the archives, including the minutes of the Soviet leadership's discussion of the
situation in Afghanistan prior to intervention.

Finally, some archival materials were released after 1991. However, the
expectations of full access to the Cold War materials (at least as far as the for-
ties and fifties were concerned) proved to be unrealistic. The most important
archives—the Presidential (also known as Kremlin), containing all Politburo
documents plus Stalin's papers, are still protected for reasons not altogether
clear. It is highly improbable that the documents of the Stalin era could be a
source of a potential political or personal trouble for people in power. All
major decisions of the hermit of the Kremlin are well known, and historians
are interested primarily in motivations and the decisionmaking process. Old-
timers who could have vested interests in not releasing those documents by
now have completely lost any influence in Moscow. Neocommunist opposition was not regarded as a significant political factor before the parliamentary

elections of December 1993 and, therefore, did not influence the decision to keep the Kremlin archives closed. Few exceptions are made, but none of the historians who have entered the archives through the back door (Dmitri Volkogonov, the author of Stalin's biography and very important personally in handling the Russian archives, was one of them) returned with anything revealing.

The KGB opens its archives only when this secret order, not touched in its core by transformations, is willing to release a particular document or file, sometimes pursuing the familiar goal: disinformation. One of the loudest cases was Volkogonov's "investigation" in the KGB archives on Alger Hiss, after which he came out with a definitive statement of Hiss's innocence, which was immediately shaken by findings in the Hungarian archives. So much for the KGB archives' openness.

All other major archives—two sharing the funds of the Communist Party Central Committee (correspondingly before and after 1952), that of the Foreign Ministry and of the Ministry of Defense, are totally unpredictable. Personal deals with the archivists, joint projects giving archives face or money, blind chance, chaos compete with political considerations, traditional secretiveness, and arbitrariness of the staff characterize their operations. This results in some interesting findings, scandals (as in "the Morris case" when for reasons unknown the American researcher was granted access to a document which *should* have remained classified because of its ticklish nature, the context of Russo-American relations, and the modern reading of the Vietnam issue in general) and unexpected crackdowns compromising proclaimed openness.[10]

One should not forget that 1991–1993 looked much more hopeful for the archives' openness than the years to come. In 1991–1993 the liberals in Moscow came the closest to being in charge and they wanted to establish the image of Russia as an open society. Today, with the nationalistic opposition driving Yeltsin to be more Catholic than the Pope, the archives are likely to be even more reluctant about sharing the secrets of a great power—especially East Asian materials. Yeltsin's leadership has found itself confronted by political problems in the Far East which surpass its ability to cope with the challenge. The uncertainty of the partnership with the U.S. is backed by hostility toward Japan and utter bewilderment at the developments in China and on the Korean peninsula

This does not mean that the Russian archives will return to sullen silence, but researchers should be prepared for unexpected setbacks. However, the progress of independent thinking in Russia (which, naturally, introduces more opportunities to all camps, liberals being only one faction of them)

promises the emergence of new Russian historiography even in the absence of key documents and evidence.

3.

The most intriguing and acute struggle of ideas occurs these days in Russian political science. History, having told Russian society what the Western community knew long ago, is somehow on the margins of social science. There are good reasons for that: Russian society, in a desperate search for a post-Soviet identity, for a definite set of priorities in foreign policy, for a stable place in the shaking and generally hostile world, is more interested in prognosis than in the autopsy of the past. However, one can still distinguish between different trends of thinking in historical studies and statements.

The neocommunist camp is maintaining old Soviet phobias supported by new evidence. A participant in the Soviet Air Force combat missions in Korea says that the goal of the Soviet intervention was "to shield the sky of North Korea from the flights of American aircraft and thus protect the borders of the Soviet Union from afar."[11] The diabolic image of the United States, unacceptable even during the last years of the USSR's existence, is reintroduced. The same witness testifies that the American army was living by the "laws of a wolf' pack" and even claims that American pilots, parachuting during combat, were shot by other Americans.[12] The Soviet hostility toward ungrateful Chinese has not been forgotten. The readers are told a James Bond story of Chinese treacherousness: when Soviet YaK-17 aircraft were stationed in China, the Chinese would put two sleeping pills (the amount is known precisely) in the cabin which would evaporate during the flight, the pilot to become intoxicated and crash.[13]

The *Realpolitik* school is playing cautiously with revisionism, tending to judge Soviet policy according to the effect it had on the great power status of the country. A retired Soviet diplomat, also involved in scholarly research, admits that Moscow was playing the Xinjiang and Manchuria card in the 1940s, that Stalin was overrating the role of the American troops in China in 1945, and that Stalin was unwilling to cooperate with the Guomindang after the war with Japan was over. At the same time we will find the familiar Soviet stereotype of a good Roosevelt in the triangle "USSR-USA-China."[14] The *Realpolitik* school in general would emphasize geopolitics and indicate that ideological considerations were often an obstacle to rational behavior.

The Revisionist school is reappraising Soviet history in general, sometimes coming out with very serious works[15], based upon new archival research. It is the most promising trend, the development of which is made difficult by unpredictable access to the Russian archives. However, scholars, when faced by the closed doors of the depositories, address themselves to the witnesses of the Soviet foreign policy. Probably, the most sensational finding was made by Sergei N. Goncharov, who has pulled out of obscurity one Ivan V. Kovalev, Stalin's personal representative to China in the late 1940s, who preserves not only memories of those fateful years, but also documents from his personal archives. In his talks with Goncharov, the former proconsul described Stalin's dealings with Mao Zedong and other Chinese leaders, giving important evidence on Stalin's motivations and the process of finding a new *modus vivendi* in East Asia.[16] The book published by Sergei Goncharov, John W. Lewis, and Xue Litai[17] is the first joint attempt to address the issue of Soviet decisionmaking in 1950. However, notwithstanding that the Kovalev papers are a breakthrough, the book lacks other revealing Soviet evidence concerning Stalin's China and Korea policy. This is by no means the fault of the authors, but this is the reason not to call this book a definitive one on the Soviet role in the Korean War.

There were some other interesting findings, i. e. the memoirs of a Soviet diplomat, A. I. Elizavetin, about the Alexey N. Kosygin–Zhou Enlai talks in the Beijing airport on September 11, 1969, plus the publication of the minutes of these talks.[18] A survivor of several Soviet leaders, Nikolai T. Fedorenko has published his account of talks between Stalin and Mao in 1949–1950 (in a sense, counterbalancing the memoirs of the Chinese interpreter Shi Zhe, published in China). Miscellaneous reminiscences on Sino-Soviet comraderie have appeared, reporting, for example, how Academician (and later Ambassador to China) P. F. Yudin was editing Mao's works, combing them for non-Marxist statements.[19] Mao in general ignites a lot of interest among the historians.

Summing up, one has to conclude that the major interest of the Russian historians is located in Stalin's policy toward Europe; scholarship on East Asia in still lagging behind.

4.

Political science is booming in modern Russia. Its impact upon decisionmaking is dubious, but it is a fact that the political scientists create an environment in which Russian leaders of different political orientations grow or, for that matter, fade away. In political science (plus writings close to this genre, but polluted by the venom of ideological vengeance and rivalry) one can find several distinct camps: neocommunists, conservatives, extreme nationalists, moralists, and liberal nationalists.

Neocommunists are indisputably in the margins of all social processes; their fixation upon the restoration of the Soviet Union is unlikely to attract the support of the masses. Their success in the December 1993 parliamentary elections is explained merely by the existence of a large age cohort that will soon fade away.

Conservatives are not to be lumped with extreme nationalists; their prophet is Alexander Solzhenitsyn who preaches the return to Holy Russia, probably uniting Ukraine and Belarus, but not pursuing broad expansion. The conservatives would favor the idea that Russian civilization is close to Asian, in opposition to the corrupted West, the source of spiritual pollution and political provocations. Sergei Kara-Murza would insist that the eurocentrism of Russian politics, initiated by Gorbachev and developed by Yeltsin's leadership, is bankrupt. In all directions Russia faces the American threat.[20] A well-known orientalist, Gennady Chufrin, firmly states that Russia does not need Western democracy, but it desperately needs the "authoritarian-pluralistic model," developed by the ASEAN countries.[21]

Extreme nationalists are aggressive, they favor the idea of Russian Reconquista, and the Devil incarnate for them is the United States, against which they are even willing to cooperate with Islamic fundamentalism, a stronghold of morality in the world of dissolved spirituality. Major-General Viktor Filatov, fired from his position even by the Russian military, advocates cooperation with Iraq, giving various arguments in favor of this alliance. He insists that Iraq has been helping Moscow to escape the COCOM limitations for years: Iraq was buying weapons from Moscow, sold oil to countries "like" Japan and then informed its customers: "You, Japan, will keep a certain sum of money, the Soviet Union will give you the list of items it needs and you will deliver these items without delay."[22] Yeltsin's foreign policy is described by them as absolutely pro-American.[23] America is a "crazy country; a depositary for social waste from all over the world; a parasite-country with ersatz-products, ersatz-culture, ersatz-morality."[24]

Moralists have been representing the views of the Russian leadership in 1991–1993. Their credo was immediate integration into the Western community, agreeing to all concessions the West demanded. Nodar Simoniya, arguing that Russia should face the Asia-Pacific region, insisted that Russia should break with "pseudopatriotism" and normalize relations with Japan,[25] i.e., to solve the northern territories problem without delay and without exploiting the issue of the hurt national feelings of Russians.[26]

Liberal nationalists would argue that some sort of nationalism is vital to modern Russia, that this nationalism should be combined with liberal principles in politics. They perceive Russia as a cornerstone of stability in the Eurasian heartland and would insist that the West acknowledge that this is Russia's function. At the same time they would introduce a Monroe doctrine of sorts, indicating that the territory of the former USSR is the sphere of exclusively Russian interests and should be perceived as such by the rest of the world.

Alexei Bogaturov insists that the world in general is going through a crisis as a manageable system. Revising postwar history, he argues that in Yalta and Potsdam "a conspiracy of the mighty" and not confrontation occurred and that only later the principles of joint management of the world by the great powers were forsaken. He introduces a new (for Russia) reading of the Sino-Soviet crisis of 1969 (unable to find any solid evidence, he just attracts the attention of the researchers to the problem of whether the Kremlin seriously considered bombing Chinese nuclear facilities after the border clashes). He describes the U.S. role in the Far East at that time in positive terms, stating that the escalation of the crisis had been prevented not only by the USSR, but also by the U.S., which had firmly declared the escalation of Sino-Soviet conflict to be unacceptable.[27] This historical allusion is not incidental, for liberal nationalists would place their hopes upon cooperation with the United States in introducing the new world order, whatever that might mean.[28] However, some of them are skeptical about the prospects of partnership with the U.S. in the Far East, seeing too many contradictions between the two countries in an area (that does not lead to an anti-American conclusion, but rather simply withholds East Asia from the sphere of possible cooperation).[29]

. . .

5.

This brief review of the current Russian studies on East Asian affairs demonstrates both the variety of views and the vital significance of the area for Russia. In the domain of history, where a researcher can work without haste and the pressure of political needs, the research agenda is broad and intriguing.

Sino-Soviet relations are of a major interest here. The interrelations among Moscow, the Chinese Communists, and the Guomindang at the last stage of civil war in China were followed by the duel of Stalin and Mao. Contradictory reports and evidence on the Stalin-Mao relationship (with contradictions existing not only between Chinese and Russian historiography, but also inside Russian academia) make it urgent to reassess such a major event as Mao's visit to the USSR in 1949–1950. Relations with China under Khrushchev to a great extent remain a blank spot: that includes different issues, from Soviet participation in the Chinese nuclear program, to Moscow's reaction to the Quemoy and Matsu crisis of 1958, and finally to the reasons for the final split.[30] A special study should be made of the attempts to mend the relationship after Khrushchev's downfall. The Sino-Soviet border conflicts of 1969 and corresponding military buildup should be a top research priority too, for they could clarify both the Soviet and the Chinese view of geopolitics in the modern world.

The Korean War is not satisfactorily depicted from the Soviet angle yet, though, probably, only materials from the Presidential archives could clarify the Soviet position in 1950–1953. It would be intriguing to probe the issue to see how Pyongyang has been balancing between Moscow and Beijing since the early 1950s. It would be challenging also to do research on the Soviet attitude toward Taiwan during the Sino-Soviet confrontation and to see whether Moscow has always adhered to the principle of a single China and to what extent it was tempted to back Taibei vs. Beijing. Russo-Japanese relations, unfortunately, will not be a promising field of research until the northern territories issue is settled and archival research ceases to be impeded.

NOTES

1. The bulk of East Asian studies has been concentrated in Moscow even under the Soviet regime, so in a way in this field historiography was always Russian. Three other major centers of East Asian research—St. Petersburg, Khabarovsk, and Vladivostok—are situated on the territory of the Russian Federation too. Some research on East Asia has been done in Tashkent (Uzbekistan) and Kiev (Ukraine) as well.

2. Their publication has started in "Voprosy istorii," 1990, no. 2 and will last for an indefinite period of time.

3. Chuev has published only a portion of the transcripts and, probably, the full text of them could be of more interest to an Asia expert.

4. B. S. Abakumov, "Sovietskiye letchiki v nebe Korei," in *Voprosy istorii*, no. 1 (1993); A. M. Ledovsky, "Na diplomaticheskoy rabote v Kitaie v 1942–1952 gg," in *Novaya i noveishaya istoriya*, no. 6 (1993).

5. Sergo Beria, *Moi otets—Lavrenty Beria* (Moscow: Sovremennik, 1994).

6. Ibid., 402–405

7. Pavel Sudoplatov and Anatoli Sudoplatov, *Special Tasks: The Memoirs of an Unwanted Witness* (Boston: Little, Brown, 1994), 210.

8. L. V. Shebarshin, *Ruka Moskvy* (Moscow: Tsentr-100, 1992), 182–184.

9. B. V. Gromov, *Ogranichenny kontingent* (Moscow: Progress. 1994).

10. See *New York Times*, April 12, 13, 1993, for "Morris" story.

11. Abakumov, "Sovietskiye letchiki v nebe Korei," 129.

12. Ibid., 133.

13. Ibid., 130.

14. Ledovsky, "Na diplomaticheskoy rabote," 109–130.

15. L. Ya. Gibianski, "Kak voznik Kominform. Po novym arkhivnym materialam," in *Novaya i noveyshaya istoriya*, no. 4 (1993): 131–152.

16. *Dialog Stalina s Mao Zedunom*, in *Problemy Dalnego Vostoka*, no 6 (1991); nos. 1–3 (1992).

17. Sergei N. Goncharov, John W. Lewis, and Xue Litai *Uncertain Partners: Stalin, Mao and the Korean War* (Stanford: Stanford University Press, 1993).

18. A. I. Elizavetin, "Peregovory A. N. Kosygina i Zhou Enlaia v pekinskom aeroportu," in *Problemy Dalnego Vostoka*, no. 5 (1992), no. 1 (1993).

19. N. T. Fedorenko, "Kak akademik P. F. Yudin redaktiroval Mao Zeduna," In: *Problemy Dalnego Vostoka*, no. 6 (1992).

20. Sergey Kara-Murza, "Tainiya ideologiya perestroiki," in *Nash sovremennik*, no. 2 (1992): 110.

21. Gennady Chufrin, "V kakom politicheskom opyte nuzhdaetsya Rossiya," in *Nash sovremennik*, no. 9 (1993): 148.

22. Viktor Filatov, "Pochemu i ch'i tanki rasstrelyali Verkhovny Sovet Rossii," in *Molodaya gvardiya*, no. 1 (1994): 28.

23. Alexander Krotov, "Russkaya smuta," in *Molodaya gvardiya*, no. 1, (1994): 13.

24. Nikoay Kotenko, "Cherny oktiabr," in *Molodaya gvardiya*, no. 1, (1994): 21.

25. N. Simoniya, "Razmyshleniya o vneshney politike Rossii," in *Problemy Dalnego Vostoka*, no. 2 (1993): 11.

26. In contrast to that, pro-communist sympathizers would stress the "responsibility" of the Japanese side for "artificially" preventing the progress in Russo-Japanese relations. (M. L. Titarenko and B. T. Kulik, "Vneshnyaya politika Rossii: dalnevostochny vektor," in *Problems of the Far East*, no. 1 (1993): 23.

27. A. Bogaturov, "Krizis mirosistemnogo regulirovaniya," in *Mezhdunarodnaya zhizn*, no. 7 (1993): 31–33.

28. See also A. D. Bogaturov, et al., "Vashington i postosevtskiye gosudarstva," in *SShA: ekonomika, politika, ideologiya*, no. 12 (1993); no. 1 (1994).

29. I. Kobrinskaya, "Vneshnyaya i vnutrennyaya politika Rossii," in *Mezhdunarodnaya zhizn*, no. 9 (1993): 68.

30. In the fall of 1995, Harvard University Press will publish a book coauthored by Vladislav Zubok and myself, in which we use some revealing documents from the Communist Party Central Committee archives, though this is just the beginning of the archival study of the Sino-Soviet conundrum.

Part Two

Chapter Four

Asian Immigrants and American Foreign Relations

GORDON H. CHANG

Seventy years ago, Eliot G. Mears, the director of the first scholarly study of attitudes toward Asian immigrants in this country, emphasized the importance of domestic sentiment for American relations with Asia. He observed: "In the field of Oriental-American relations, the significance of California is out of all proportion to its area and population. The attitude of California and Californians has largely determined American foreign policy toward the Oriental."[1]

Mears wrote from California, the center of hostility toward Asians in the United States, at the historical culmination of decades of virulent anti-Asian immigrant sentiment. Just the year before, Congress had passed what became known as the 1924 Immigration Act that, along with the 1882 Chinese Exclusion Act and other federal legislation, virtually ended all legal immigration from China, Japan, Korea, India, and Southeast Asia. A decade later, the United States restricted the entry of Filipinos into the country. Washington slowly began to dismantle these discriminatory policies in the midst of World War II, starting with the acts directed against the Chinese—the anti-Chinese laws

were an embarrassment at that historical moment when China was the puta-
tive heroic ally of America. Mears may have overstated his case in claiming the
importance of California in influencing Washington's policy toward Asia, but
he did not exaggerate in drawing attention to the prominence of the immigration question (for want of a better phrase) in American relations with Asia
at the time that he wrote.

In the same vein, George F. Kennan, in his classic work *American Diplomacy, 1900–1950*, observed that the "long and unhappy story" of United
States-Japan relations in this century was constantly troubled by the fact that
the United States "would repeatedly irritate and offend the sensitive Japanese by our immigration policies and the treatment of people of Japanese lineage . . . in this country.[2] Mears, a sociologist, and Kennan, a diplomatic historian, writing for different purposes but arriving at similar conclusions,
both emphasized the relevance, even centrality, of the "immigration question" to diplomacy in pre-war American-East Asian relations.

While the immigration issue occupied the attention of specialists and the
general public alike for decades in the first part of this century, American
diplomatic historians have devoted considerably less attention to the subject
since World War II. In recent years, diplomatic historians, in fact, have often
found the immigration question to be of relatively small importance to their
work; for example, papers delivered at the 1994 Wilson Center conference
that produced this volume, with only one exception, cited few works that
explored the immigration issue or even suggested the possibility of future
work in this area. What is remarkable is that many contemporary diplomatic
historians have virtually no familiarity with this issue even though it had been
a lively question for two earlier generations of their predecessors. Now with
Asians becoming the fastest growing minority in the United States and Asian
immigration again becoming a controversial public issue, it is appropriate to
review the historiography of the attention given to Asian immigration in
American diplomatic history literature and to the ways historians have
thought about Asian immigrants and foreign relations and diplomacy.

Unlike other essays in this present volume that focus on research conducted principally in the 1980s and early 1990s, this effort will review the
place American diplomatic historians have given (or not given) to Asian
immigrants over the decades in their work, the treatment of this question
since 1980 in scholarly literature, especially in the field of Asian American
studies, and the position this question may occupy in future research into
American-East Asia relations. This essay makes no claim to be comprehensive and cite every work that speaks to Asian immigration and United States
foreign policy, but will instead examine general trends and representative

works. The essay is also weighted toward work on American relations with China or Japan.[3]

My hope is that this review will be of use principally to historians of American-East Asian relations who may find the second half of this essay more useful than the first; but I also hope that Asian Americanists, many of whom are unfamiliar with political and diplomatic history, will find these thoughts of interest, especially those in the first half.

Before World War II

Remarkable in surveying the early, classic work on American relations with Asia is the prominence given to the immigration question and the influence of American domestic prejudice toward Asians on the making of United States policy. For example, one of the first and most important works on American-East Asia relations, Tyler Dennett's *Americans in Eastern Asia* (1922), devotes a full chapter to "Asiatic Immigration and American Foreign Policy." Attempting to correct mistaken notions, Dennett wrote that, "Asiatic immigration in the United States viewed historically is much more than a domestic question; it has exercised a marked influence on foreign policy." In his work, he examined Chinese, Korean, and Japanese immigration to the United States and their policy implications.[4] Another classic work in the field, A. Whitney Griswold's *The Far Eastern Policy of the United States* (1938), made the same point and bluntly raised the issue of race: anti-Asian immigration legislation, he wrote, and "the germs of race prejudice had polluted American relations with both China and Japan, and had profoundly influenced the development of the Far Eastern policy of the United States." In his view, restricting Asian immigration to the United States had been as important an objective to Washington as had been a secure Far East to resist European designs and commercial advantages.[5] Two other pioneering specialists in the field of American relations with Asia, Payson Treat and Yamato Ichihashi, also devoted considerable attention to Japanese immigrants and their treatment in the United States in their studies,[6] and a third historian, one of the enduring figures in diplomatic history who also taught at Stanford, Thomas A. Bailey, published his first book with a title that again emphasizes the point made above, *Theodore Roosevelt and the Japanese-American Crises: An Account of the International Consequences Arising from the Race Problem on the Pacific Coast* (1934).[7]

Common to the work of these early diplomatic historians, foreshadowing the work of Kennan and others who believed that popular sentiment in

America often complicated, if not damaged, the development of a consistent and genuinely self-interested foreign policy, is the view that passions at home adversely affected American relations abroad with China and in particular Japan. Anti-Asian immigration legislation, political demagogy, and widespread mistreatment of Asian immigrants created unnecessary frictions, in their views. The authors, who were all critical to varying degrees of the United States and American popular attitudes, believed that the prejudices had far-reaching implications. As Bailey wrote, United States-Japan relations experienced a half-dozen crises from 1905 to 1909 as a result of American mistreatment of Japanese in this country. These crises, in Bailey's view, severely "taxed the conciliatory powers of the two governments" and "on several occasions came uncomfortably near to precipitating war." The Japanese attitude, on the other hand, had been characterized, "by a high degree of patience, forbearance, and courtesy," according to Bailey. The unhappy result was the ending of an supposed "golden age" of United States-Japan relations.[8]

Of principal interest to these early American historians was the extent and the ways in which the immigration question affected policy and diplomatic relations generally. They were usually less interested in the felt or lived experiences of the immigrants themselves, or were interested in them only in so far as these experiences were necessary to understand the seriousness of the conflicts, the reactions of Japanese and Chinese officials, and the attitudes of white American citizens.

After World War II

The Second World War appears to be a turning point in the study of American-East Asia relations. The classic studies of the war in the Pacific, its causes, and its aftermath that were completed in the immediate postwar period gave relatively little attention to the immigration question or even to its legacy in American-East Asian relations. Herbert Feis virtually ignores the dimension of immigration in his *The Road to Pearl Harbor* (1950) and *The China Tangle: The American Effort in China from Pearl Harbor to the Marshall Mission* (1953), as does Tang Tsou in *America's Failure in China, 1941–1950* (1963). The Cold War's concern with high-level policymaking or perhaps the disappearance of immigration as a source of conflict in postwar American-East Asian relations (or in American domestic life generally, for that matter) for several decades accounted for the retreat. Whatever the reason, one could read a number of very important books on American-East Asian relations written in the 1950s and 1960s without learning that immigration conflicts and immigrant experiences had been a critical part of the history. John K. Fairbank devotes no attention to the immigration question in the first edition of his durable *The United States and China*.[9] The same is the case with two other important books, Marilyn Young's *The Rhetoric of Empire: American China Policy, 1895–1901* (1968), Thomas McCormick's *China Market: America's Quest for Informal Empire, 1893–1901* (1967), both of which examine the period when the immigration question was prominent in United States-China relations. (Of note is that it seems that immigration did not interest a number of what have been called revisionist diplomatic historians, such as Gabriel Kolko, as in his critique of progressivism, *The Triumph of Conservatism* (1963), and William A. Williams in his *Tragedy of American Diplomacy* (1959). The essays evaluating the development and current state of scholarship in American-East Asian relations in *American-East Asian Relations: A Survey* edited by Ernest May and James Thomson, Jr. and Roger Daniels's essay, "American Historians and East Asian Immigrants,"[10] confirm that diplomatic historians devoted relatively little attention to the problem of Asian immigration in the two decades following World War II. Even as late as 1983, an acclaimed study of Theodore Roosevelt and Woodrow Wilson, who both had much to do with immigration and race, found it possible to discuss the presidents and virtually ignore the exclusion from and mistreatment of Asian immigrants in the United States.[11]

To be sure, some diplomatic historians in the postwar period continued to examine the interrelationship of immigration and diplomacy, and the history of Asian immigrants themselves, as a way of understanding the dynamics of American-East Asian relations. Hilary Conroy especially comes to mind with his *The Japanese Frontier in Hawaii, 1868–1898* (1953) and his later co-edited work with T. Scott Miyakawa, *East Across the Pacific: Historical and Sociological Studies of Japanese Immigration and Assimilation* (1972). It may also have been forgotten in light of his later extensive work in other areas, but Robert Divine's first book, *American Immigration Policy, 1924–1952* (1957) focused on immigration as well. Divine studied the making of American immigration policy and identified four principal elements in policy formation: the economic welfare of the nation, the rise of social and racial issues, the influence of nationalism and lastly foreign policy itself. He emphasized, echoing Tyler Dennett some twenty-five years earlier, that while the popular perception in America had been that immigration was a purely domestic matter, "more perceptive individuals realized that immigration was an international process which transcended national boundaries" and which could have broad international implications. Divine studied, in particular, immigration laws as they related to Chinese, Japanese, Filipinos and Koreans. Many of Divine's observations speak directly to us today, when the country has renewed anxieties about immigration policy.[12]

One contemporary diplomatic historian who has devoted consistent attention to the immigration question has been Akira Iriye, who, as part of his ongoing exploration of the cultural dimension of American-Japan relations, has been sensitive to the possibilities of having the Japanese immigrant experience help illuminate the study of diplomacy. He has examined the history of Japanese immigration as a way of grappling with the sometimes elusive question of "culture," and by so doing has gone beyond attention to immigration as an influence on formal policy or to popular American attitudes about immigrants and race. As Iriye once provocatively advanced, the question in the early twentieth century was not only whether Japanese and Americans could coexist "as two separate nations across the Pacific but also living together in the United States."[13] By posing the question in this way, Iriye opened the investigation of the Japanese immigrant as a way of investigating what he believed was the very core of the troubled relationship between Japan and the United States. The Japanese immigrant therefore was elevated from being treated in historical literature as a passive "object" of social forces to an active historical "subject" whose words and actions speak to our interests about the past.[14]

Iriye developed his ideas in several of his works, most notably in *Pacific Estrangement: Japanese and American Expansion, 1897–1911* (1972), which explores at some length the experience of Japanese in America and the American exclusionist movement as an important dimension in the relationship. As Iriye found, because "the self-image of Japanese in America was almost identical with that in the homeland,"[15] Japanese immigrant writings were especially useful in developing insight into the cultural conflicts that plagued American-Japan relations in the early twentieth century. Iriye found that the conflict over immigration policy, which deeply embittered the Japanese, had international consequences long after exclusion ceased to be a major political issue for Americans. Iriye's work (along with Delber L. McKee's book on America's early-twentieth century China policy which contains interesting material on Chinese Americans)[16] suggests that the historical material generated by the immigrant experiences of other groups could be employed in similarly imaginative ways. Michael Hunt made an explicit call for such work in the 1981 conference evaluating the state of scholarship in American-East Asian relations. "The subject of Chinese immigration to the United States," Hunt noted, "stands out as a promising area of research. . . . It is an excellent example of what is to be gained by shifting the primary focus of inquiry away from official relations. In this case, not immigration policy but the immigrants themselves—their origins and experiences, their allies and antagonists within the United States—belong at the center of inquiry."[17]

By the mid-1980s, perhaps because of the growth of popular and scholarly interest in the place of race and ethnicity in American life, a steady stream of work that spoke to the immigration question began to appear in diplomatic history literature. Historians had produced studies of attitudes toward Asians in America over the years,[18] but now diplomatic historians began to elevate race, ethnicity, and racial prejudice to a position of central importance in American foreign relations. These works include Michael Hunt, *Ideology and U.S. Foreign Policy* (1987), Paul Gordon Lauren, *Power and Prejudice: The Politics and Diplomacy of Racial Discrimination* (1988), and Alexander DeConde, *Ethnicity, Race, and American Foreign Policy* (1992). All three books devote attention to the examination of American-East Asian relations and Asian immigrants in America. With regard to race as a factor in foreign relations, the viewpoints in these books extend from the cautious DeConde, who still finds that race has been and "remains a prominent ingredient in [America's] relations with a large part of the world," to Lauren who comes close to agreeing with W. E. B. DuBois's bold declaration that race was "the problem of the twentieth century."[19]

Before moving to literature generated out of research into Asian American history, two further examples of recent work, both by Asianists, should be mentioned here to illustrate the creative possibilities in exploring what loosely may be called the immigrant experience. John Dower's *War Without Mercy: Race and Power in the Pacific War* (1986) investigates how race was involved in various dimensions, from high politics to popular culture to mass attitudes, on both the American and Japanese sides in the Pacific War. Dower uses the incarceration of Japanese Americans into American concentration camps during the war to help understand the entire racial character of the war. A book of a very different nature is *Land Without Ghosts: Chinese Impressions of America from the Mid-Nineteenth Century to the Present*, translated and edited by R. David Arkush and Leo O. Lee. Most of the selections in this work are excerpts from the written observations of short-term visitors to America from China, mainly diplomats and intellectuals, but included are voices of individuals who were very much a part of the Chinese American community for months or even years during their stays in the United States. Arkush and Lee note the relevance of their book for several different purposes, among these being the study of United States-China relations.[20]

Asian American Literature

Since the early 1970s, a new genre of historical literature relevant to, although not usually explicitly directed toward, understanding American relations with Asia has developed out of the field of Asian American studies. While the study of Asians in America was certainly not new—serious sociological and historical work appeared as Asians arrived in numbers in the mid-nineteenth century—extensive and intensive study developed as a result of the growth of "ethnic studies." The field has rapidly developed in sophistication and in the numbers of practitioners—attendance at the annual meeting of the Association for Asian American Studies, the professional association for the field, averages around five hundred persons.

The following is an overview of the work in the field as it relates to understanding American-East Asian relations. (In recent years there has been a heightened awareness of the linkages between Asian Americans and Asia in many different fields, including literature and cinema. In 1994, the Asia Society of New York held an unprecedented exhibition of contemporary Asian American artists. According to a description on the catalog's jacket, exhibited works speak to several diverse themes: "traversing cultures, situation, speaking to and of Asia, and addressing East/West interaction.")[21] An indication of this awareness in academic work is the expansion of the book review sections of both *Amerasia Journal*[22] and the *Journal of American-East Asian Relations* to include books generated from the other field. The following will be limited to work that speaks to traditional historiographic concerns.

I identify five general scholarly approaches that have been used to understand the social and historical experience of Asians in American and the significance of that experience. These approaches appeared in rough chronological order, but are still adopted today. A particular work may not fall neatly into one category and may employ several approaches—the categories, admittedly, are broadly descriptive and simply for discussion purposes.[23]

The first is diplomatic history, which was discussed above, and there are some diplomatic historians who are continuing to write about Asian Americans. Recent and representative examples of this include the work by Wayne Patterson on Koreans in America, especially his book, *The Korean Frontier in America: Immigration to Hawaii, 1896–1910* (1988), Sandra Taylor's biography of Sidney L. Gulick, an American missionary and campaigner for friendlier United States-Japan relations in the early twentieth century and *Jewel of the Desert: Japanese American Internment at Topaz* (1993), and several essays by other authors that have recently appeared in the *Journal of American-East Asian Relations*.[24]

The second approach might be characterized simply as "immigrant experience" history. Produced by social scientists as well as historians of the recent past, this history focused on the migration, transition, and experiences of recent Asian immigrants to America. Examples of early work that addressed foreign relations concerns are, Mary Coolidge, *Chinese Immigration* (1909) and Bruno Lasker, *Filipino Immigration to Continental United States and to Hawaii* (1931). Principal attention was given to the difficulty of transition from the homeland to a new life in America, to the efforts to assimilate and contribute to America, to the triumph over adversity, and, in some instances, to policy implications. A current version of this approach is *East to America: A History of the Japanese in the United States* (1980) by Asianist Robert A. Wilson and Bill Hosokawa which is an overview of Japanese Americans.

At present, the literature on Southeast Asian refugees and immigrants is especially noteworthy and growing rapidly. As the titles of the following recent works show, they are often as much about life in Asia as they are about the experience in America: James M. Freeman, *Hearts of Sorrow: Vietnamese-American Lives* (1989); Usha Welaratna, *Beyond the Killing Fields: Voices of Nine Cambodian Survivors in America* (1993), John Tenhula, *Voices from Southeast Asia: The Refugee Experience in the United States* (1991), and Sucheng Chan, *Hmong Means Free: Life in Laos and America* (1994). Most of this work relies heavily on oral interviews. This literature can be helpful in understanding the recent American military involvement in Southeast Asia, the personal experiences of those who were deeply affected by the contact, the attitudes toward various local political forces, and the refugee issue which has now become widely controversial in the country.

The third approach is the diaspora. Area specialists interested in Asian Americans often favored this perspective, which means examining the experience of Asians in America principally through the lens of the national, cultural, or social experience of their respective homelands. Often, the experience of Asians in America was compared with the history of transplanted Asians in other countries. Prominent examples of this approach are S. W. Kung, *Chinese in American Life: Some Aspects of Their History, Status, Problems, and Contributions* (1962); Kazuo Ito, *Issei: A History of Japanese Immigrants in North America*, trans. Shinichiro Nakamura and Jean S. Gerard (1973); Stanford M. Lyman, *The Asian in North America* (1970); and Hyung-chan Kim, ed., *The Korean Diaspora: Historical and Sociological Studies of Korean Immigration and Assimilation in North America* (1977). Recent expressions of this type of work are two books by Henry Shih-shan Tsai, *China and the Overseas Chinese in the United States, 1868–1911* (1983) and his text *The Chinese Experience in America* (1986), and Alan Takeo Moriyama, *Imingaisha: Japanese Emigration Companies and Hawaii, 1894–1908* (1985).

Many of the articles in *Chinese America: History and Perspectives*, the journal published by the Chinese Historical Society of America, also take this approach. The work of Him Mark Lai, a principal editor of the journal, is particularly distinguished in this area. See for example his "Kuomintang in Chinese American Communities before World War II," in Sucheng Chan, ed., *Entry Denied: Exclusion and the Chinese Community in America, 1882–1943* (1991).[25] Other works which examine the relationship of Chinese Americans to Chinese politics are L. Eve Armentrout Ma, *Revolutionaries, Monarchists and Chinatowns: Chinese Politics in the Americas and the 1911 Revolution* (1990) and Ren-qiu Yu, *To Save China, To Save Ourselves: The Chinese Hand Laundry Alliance of New York* (1992). These works explore the complex interrelationship of identity and local and international politics, and show that social history can help illuminate international history and vice versa.

Because of the attention to cultural identity and immigrant social and political ties with their lands of ancestry, diaspora literature may be of particular usefulness to diplomatic historians interested in the place of ethnicity in international relations. In addition, many of these works use Asian language sources which may otherwise be inaccessible to some historians.

The fourth approach is a part of the new social history, which has flourished over the last couple of decades and seeks to understand the history of everyday men and women in America, including racial minorities, and their efforts to forge meaningful, self-defined lives. Asian Americanists, responding to longstanding American prejudices that accepted Asians in America as only foreigners or as perpetual aliens, have produced a body of literature that has emphasized the *Americanness* of the experience here. (Work that studies mass anti-Asian reactions and racial ideology might also be listed in this category.) One of the early examples of this literature in Asian American studies was by Victor and Brett deBary Nee, who are Asianists ironically. Their book, *Longtime Californ': A Documentary Study of an American Chinatown* explicitly broke with a traditional inclination to see the Chinese in America as simply as extensions of China.[26] They wrote to help reclaim a portion of the American experience for Chinese Americans. Their book, they wrote, "is about a community and a people whose roots extend deep into the American past. Most Americans know of San Francisco's Chinatown, yet few can claim an understanding of this community, the role which its people played in the making of the American West, and the rich tradition and culture which it spawned in its one hundred and twenty year history."[27] Yuji Ichioka, a leading historian of Japanese Americans, described his book on the Issei, the first generation of Japanese in America, as being a history "of a racial minority struggling to survive in a hostile land." It was also "labor history," as he put it. Despite these self-descriptions, Ichioka's book is also adept at placing the story in the context of the American-Japanese political interaction.[28]

Most of the work of leading Asian American historians falls into this category of new social history. Without going into extended descriptions of their work and in danger of committing the unforgivable sin of omission, the following are some of the more important recent book-length works on Asian Americans that may be of particular interest to diplomatic historians: Roger Daniels, the leading specialist on the forced relocation of Japanese Americans during World War II, continues to produce extensive work on this subject, including the reissuing and updating of his comparative work, *Concentration Camps: North America, Japanese in the United States and Canada During World War II* (revised edition 1989) and his text *Asian America: Chinese and Japanese in the United States since 1850* (1988); Sucheng Chan, *This Bittersweet Soil: The Chinese in California Agriculture, 1860–1910* (1986) contains a fine assessment of nineteenth-century Chinese emigration and her text, *Asian Americans: An Interpretive History* (1991) capably utilizes the existing literature in the field. The volume she edited, *Entry Denied*, cited above, also contains excellent essays on policy and the consequences of exclusion for Chinese in America. *Strangers From A Different Shore: A History of Asian Americans* (1989) by Ronald Takaki is another fine text. His *Iron Cages: Race and Culture in 19th-Century America* (1979) has sections that explore the international dimension of American racial ideology and Asians.[29]

Two other recent books specifically explore the relationships of social history and policy, immigration and local law, and politics. These are Bill Ong Hing, *Making and Remaking Asian America Through Immigration Policy, 1850–1990* (1993) and Charles J. McClain, *In Search of Equality: The Chinese Struggle Against Discrimination in Nineteenth-Century America* (1994).

The fifth and last category is one that has gradually taken shape over the last decade. I call it "transnational," which may sound a bit fuzzy, but I use it to describe a literature that seeks to break from the imposed definitions of a nationally based historicism, which is what tends to characterize the diaspora or American social history approaches. This category includes work that is comparative or "world systems," or strives to understand Asians in America as part of a growing number of "internationalized" people in the Pacific Rim whose lives do not fall neatly into a specific national pattern. These perspectives are nicely discussed in a single volume that includes essays by Evelyn Hu-Dehart, a Latin Americanist who is comparing the experiences of Chinese in North and South America, Gary Y. Okihiro, an Africanist who has also become a specialist in Asian American history, and Sucheta Mazumdar, an Asianist, who explores the relationship of Asian American studies and Asian studies. *Asian Americans: Comparative and Global Perspectives* is edited by Shirley Hune, Hyung-chan Kim, Stephen S. Fugita, and Amy Ling (1991).[30]

A collection of historical and sociological essays that is guided by a world systems approach is Lucie Cheng and Edna Bonacich, eds., *Labor Immigration Under Capitalism: Asian Workers in the United States Before World War II* (1984). A recent volume reflects the growing interest in the concept of a Pacific Rim and the place of Asian migration and Asian Americans in that emerging system. That volume's editor, Arif Dirlik, contends in his own essay that the "problems of Asian-American history are also problems in the history of an Asia-Pacific regional formation.[31] One of the more provocative articulations of this perspective is contained in a series of wide-ranging essays by Gary Okihiro, who in his words seeks to call "into question the exceptionalist streak of Asian American studies by positing a global dimension to Asian American history from the Orientalism of the ancient Greeks to European imperialism and the world-system, from America to Asia, from the Pacific to the Indian and Atlantic oceans, from California to the Caribbean and American South. The Asian American immigrant, like his sojourner stereotype, should be relegated to the dustbin of Eurocentrisms."[32]

What may be the future of the study of Asian immigrants and diplomatic history, of the relationship between Asian American studies and work on American-East Asian relations?

It seems clear that interaction between the two will steadily develop for several reasons. For one, the growing integration of the Pacific Rim as a region is encouraging the development of new ways of thinking and new paradigms regarding social interaction and history. For both Asian Americanists and diplomatic historians, this development will encourage each to learn methodologies, literatures, and historical questions from the other.

The Pacific Rim is currently witnessing a drama of extraordinary economic transformation and development as well as human migration. A useful reference in this regard is James T. Fawcett and Benjamin V. Carino, eds., *Pacific Bridges: The New Immigration from Asia and the Pacific Islands* (1987), which contains essays covering social, demographic, economic, and political aspects of the new immigration. Asian migration to the United States is rapidly increasing the Asian American population and changing American society and culture—in 1970 Asians were a mere 0.7% of the U.S. population but by 1990 they increased to almost 3%, or six and one half million persons. By 2020, the Asian American population is expected to rise to 20 million nationally and as has been seen in the past, this population will continue to have many links to their lands of ancestry.[33] All this will certainly result in heightened interest in the Asian American population and their past and present place in the foreign relations of the United States with Asia.

Secondly, scholarly interest in race, ethnicity, and culture in international affairs has risen significantly with the end of the Cold War. Replacing the preoccupation with high policy and leadership decisionmaking, is attention to the broader social dynamics of foreign relations. Whatever one thinks of Samuel Huntington's suggestion that foreign relations in the post-Cold War era may best be understood as a "clash of civilizations," his view is indicative of the expanded interest of social scientists in studying the ethnic and cultural dimensions of foreign relations. Since historians always examine the past with interests and concerns generated by our current preoccupations, we should expect a growing convergence, though not merging, of interests of Asian Americanists and American-East Asian specialists as the Pacific Rim grows closer as a region in political, economic, and human terms.[34]

Notes

1. Eliot G. Mears, "California's Attitude Towards the Oriental, reprinted from *The Far East*, 122, *The Annals of the American Academy of Political and Social Science* (November 1925): 1–15. Mears directed the Survey of Race Relations centered at Stanford University.

2. George F. Kennan, *American Diplomacy* (Chicago: University of Chicago Press, 1984 expanded edition), p. 49.

3. Overviews of earlier work completed in China and Japan on the history of emigrants from those countries to the United States can be found in the essays by Kwang-ching Liu, Robert S. Schwantes, and Akira Iriye in Ernest R. May and James C. Thomson Jr., eds., *American-East Asian Relations: A Survey* (Cambridge: Harvard University Press, 1972; and in the essays by Michael Hunt and Akira Iriye in Warren I. Cohen, ed., *New Frontiers in American-East Asian Relations: Essays Presented to Dorothy Borg* (New York: Columbia University Press, 1983). Also, see the essay by Tadashi Aruga in this volume for recent Japanese scholarship. I do not examine literature about the Asian subcontinent or its emigrants in this essay.

4. Tyler Dennett, *Americans in Eastern Asia: A Critical Study of United States' Policy in the Far East in the Nineteenth Century*, (New York: MacMillan, 1922), Chapter 28 and p. 535.

5. A. Whitney Griswold, *The Far Eastern Policy of the United States*, (New York: Harcourt, 1938), p. 8. Chapter 9 in its entirety is devoted to the immigration question.

6. Payson Treat, *Japan and the United States, 1853–1921*, (Stanford: Stanford University Press, 1928). Treat was one of the first Asianists in academia in the United States. Yamato Ichihashi, *Japanese in the United States: A Critical Study of the Problems of the Japanese Immigrants and Their Children* (Stanford: Stanford University Press, 1932). In 1928, Ichihashi had published *The Washington Conference and After: A Historical Study*. Ichihashi had attended the 1922 Conference as a member of the Japanese delegation.

7. Also see, Rodman Paul, *The Abrogation of the Gentlemen's Agreement* (Cambridge: Harvard University Press, 1936).

8. Bailey, *Theodore Roosevelt*, pp. 1–3, 331.

9. His fourth edition published in 1980 devotes a few sentences to nineteenth-century American reactions to Chinese immigrants in the United States, p. 319. In contrast, two other surveys, Warren I. Cohen, *America's Response to China: An Interpretive History of Sino-American Relations* (New York: Wiley, 1971) and Michael Schaller, *The United States and China in the Twentieth Century* (New York: Oxford University Press, 1979) both give greater attention to the immigration question.

10. May and Thomson, eds. *American-East Asian Relations*; Roger Daniels, "American Historians and East Asian Immigrants," *Pacific Historical Review* 43 (1974): 448–72.

11. John Milton Cooper, Jr. *The Warrior and the Priest: Woodrow Wilson and Theodore Roosevelt* (Cambridge: Belknap Press of Harvard University, 1983). Compare Cooper's treatment with other studies of Roosevelt, such as Howard K. Beale, *Theodore Roosevelt and the Rise of America to World Power* (Baltimore: Johns Hopkins University Press, 1956); Raymond A. Esthus, *Theodore Roosevelt and Japan* (Seattle: University of Washington Press, 1966); Charles E. Neu *An Uncertain Friendship: Theodore Roosevelt and Japan, 1906–1909* (Cambridge: Harvard University Press, 1967). These all study the immigration question during the Roosevelt administration in depth.

12. Robert A. Divine, *American Immigration Policy, 1924–1952* (New Haven: Yale University Press, 1957).

13. Akira Iriye, "From the Washington Treaties to Pearl Harbor: 1922–1931," in May and Thomson, eds., *American-East Asian Relations*, pp. 221–242.

14. Regarding objects and subjects of history, see Daniels, "American Historians and East Asian Immigrants."

15. Iriye, *Pacific Estrangement: Japanese and American Expansion, 1897–1911* (Cambridge: Harvard University Press, 1972), p. 138. Iriye again drew attention to the importance of studying immigrant material in his essay, "Americanization of East Asia: Writings on Cultural Affairs Since 1900," in Warren I. Cohen, ed., *New Frontiers*, pp. 45–75. Also see the volume he edited, *Mutual Images: Essays in American-Japanese Relations* (1975) which contains an essay by Don Toshiaki Nakanishi on Japanese-American views of Japan. Nakanishi later became the director of the Asian American Studies Center at the University of California, Los Angeles.

16. Delber L. McKee, *Chinese Exclusion versus the Open Door Policy, 1900–1906: Clashes over China Policy* (Detroit: Wayne State University Press, 1977).

17. Michael H. Hunt, "New Insights But No New Vistas: Recent Work on Nineteenth-Century American-East Asian Relations," in Cohen, ed., *New Frontiers*, pp. 17–43.

18. Some of the most important of this work on images includes, Harold I. Isaacs, *Scratches on our Minds: American Images of China and India* (New York: John Day, 1958); Stuart Creighton Miller, *The Unwelcome Immigrant: The American Image of the Chinese, 1785–1882* (Berkeley: University of California Press, 1969); and Robert F. McClelland, Jr., *The Heathen Chinee: A Study of American Attitudes toward China, 1890–1905* (Columbus: Ohio State University Press, 1970). Among the more recent literature are studies of African-American views of Asians in America. See, for example, the several essays by David Hellwig, "Afro-American Reactions to the Japanese and Anti-Japanese Movement, 1906–1924," *Phylon* 38 (1977): 93–104; "Black Leaders and United States Immigration Policy, 1917–1929," *Journal of Negro History* 66 (1981): 110–27; and "Black Reactions to Chinese Immigration and the Anti-Chinese Movement, 1850–1910," *Amerasia*, 6 (1979): 25–44. And see, Arnold Shankman, *Ambivalent Friends: Afro-Americans View the Immigrant*, (Westport CT: Greenwod, 1982).

19. An early work, often overlooked, is Rubin Francis Weston, *Racism in U.S. Imperial-*

ism: The Influence of Racial Assumptions on American Foreign Policy, 1893–1946 (Columbia: University of South Carolina Press, 1972). Race is a sub-theme in my own work, *Friends and Enemies: The United States, China, and the Soviet Union, 1948–1972* (Stanford: Stanford University Press, 1990).

20. The authors make an explicit effort to link their study to the understanding of United States-China relations by extensively quoting Warren Cohen on the importance of understanding national images in their Afterword. Arkush and Lee, *Land Without Ghosts: Chinese Impressions of America from the Mid-Nineteenth Century to the Present* (Berkeley: University of California Press, 1989), pp. 299–303.

21. The Asia Society Galleries, *Asia/America: Identities in Contemporary Asian American Art* (New York: Asia Society Galleries, Abbeville Press, 1994). See in particular, the essay by historian John Kuo Wei Tchen, "Believing is Seeing: Transforming Orientalism and the Occidental Gaze," which reflects upon a hundred years of development of Asian and American identities.

22. The Asian American Studies Center at the University of California, Los Angeles publishes *Amerasia Journal*, which is the most important periodical on Asian American studies. It is multidisciplinary in its contents.

23. I do not include local, family, and popular history in this discussion. Much of it is excellent, but is extensive and beyond the immediate purposes of this review essay.

24. See, for example, Yelong Han, "An Untold Story: American Policy toward Chinese Students in the United States, 1949–1955," (Spring 1993), 2:1, 77–99; Izumi Hirobe, "American Attitudes toward the Japanese Immigration Question, 1924–1931," (Fall 1993), 2:3, 275–301; and Qingjia Edward Wang, "Guests from the Open Door: The Reception of Chinese Students into the United States, 1900s-1920s," (Spring 1994), 3:1, 55–75. My own work in Asian American history may fall into this category as well. See " 'Superman is about to visit the relocation centers' and the Limits of Wartime Liberalism," *Amerasia Journal* (Spring, 1993); and my forthcoming book on Yamato Ichihashi.

25. Lai regularly publishes in *Chinese America* and recently published in Chinese a major history of the Chinese in America, *Cong Huaqiao Dao Huaren—Ershiji Meiguohuaren Shehui* (Hong Kong: San lien shu tien, yu hsien kung ssu, 1992). He is translating it for an English language edition. He is also the author of *A History Reclaimed: An Annotated Bibliography of Chinese Language Materials on the Chinese of America* (Los Angeles: Resource Development and Publications, Asian American Studies Center, UCLA, 1986) and co-author with Genny Lim and Judy Yung of *Island: Poetry and History of Chinese Immigrants on Angel Island, 1910–1940* (San Francisco: Hoc Doi, San Francisco Study Center, 1980).

26. See Gunther Barth, *Bitter Strength: A History of the Chinese in the United States, 1850–1870* (Cambridge: Harvard University Press, 1964).

27. Nee and Nee, *Longtime Californ'* (Stanford: Stanford University Press, 1986 reissued edition), p. xi.

28. Yuji Ichioka, *The Issei: The World of the First Generation Japanese Immigrants, 1885–1924* (New York: Free Press 1988).

29. The texts by Chan and Daniels have useful bibliographic sections. Other recent historical work by Asian Americanists that may interest diplomatic historians include Evelyn Nakano Glenn, *Issei, Nisei, War Bride: Three Generations of Japanese American Women in Domestic Service,* (Philadelphia: Temple University Press, 1986), Valerie Matsumoto, *Farming the Home Place: A Japanese American Community in California, 1919–1982* (Ithaca: Cornell University Press, 1993), Gary Okihiro, *Cane Fires: The Anti-Japanese Movement in*

Hawaii, 1865–1945 (Philadelphia: Temple University Press, 1993), and Judy Yung's forthcoming book on Chinese American women. One might place the extensive literature on the internment of Japanese Americans in this category as well.

30. Also see *Amerasia Journal* 15, no 2. (1989), which is devoted to "Asians in the Americas."

31. Arif Dirlik, *What Is In A Rim? Critical Perspectives on the Pacific Region Idea*, (Boulder, CO: Westview Press, 1993). Dirlik's essay is entitled, "The Asia-Pacific in Asian-American Perspective," pp. 305–329.

32. Gary Y. Okihiro, *Margins and Mainstreams: Asians in American History and Culture* (Seattle: University of Washington Press, 1994).

33. See, Leadership Education For Asian Pacifics, Inc., *The State of Asian Pacific America: A Public Policy Report, Policy Issues to the Year 2020* (Los Angeles, 1994).

34. Samuel P. Huntington, "The Clash of Civilizations?" and "Response: If Not Civilizations, What?" in *Foreign Affairs* 72, no. 3 (Summer 1993): 22–49 and 72, no 5 (Nov./Dec. 1993) :186–194.

Chapter Five

Still Strangers at the Gate: Recent Scholarship on Pre-1900 Sino-American Relations

EILEEN P. SCULLY

In his 1983 review of the literature on nineteenth-century American-East Asian relations, Michael H. Hunt concluded that the previous decade's contributions had provided some useful insights but "no striking new vistas, leaving the basic contours of the field unchanged."[1] In Hunt's estimation, the tenacious grip of modernization theory, and near uniform adherence to a statist conception of the international order, had led to the neglect of realms below and beyond the state-to-state level, such as informal contacts, material culture, and popular perceptions. Similarly, chronic "ethnocentrism and a narrow preoccupation with diplomacy," had obscured the extent to which the 'special relationship' was historically a multi-faceted, "dynamic process of interaction in which Chinese attitudes, initiatives, and responses play[ed] a crucial part."[2]

By way of correctives, Hunt recommended that scholars seek a more cosmopolitan vantage point on events; exercise greater precision in the use of organizing concepts, such as "imperialism"; show greater interest in cultural and economic interactions; construct comparisons across regional special-

ties; give more attention to the identity and activity of indigenous collaborators; focus on the generation and impact of cross-cultural images; and look
more closely into the lives and legacies of "mercenaries, political advisors, and
cross-cultural adventurers and intermediaries" in U.S.-China relations.[3]

A review of the literature since 1983 indicates broad agreement upon, and
clear progress toward, these research objectives, particularly in the areas of
missionary studies, commercial relations, and cross-cultural perceptions.
New questions, broader conceptual frameworks, and diminished ethnocentrism have made the landscape of pre-1900 Sino-American relations more
variegated, more populated, more nuanced, and more vibrant. This willingness to broaden the scope of diplomatic history, and openness to interdisci-
plinary approaches, is what puts the field of U.S.-East Asian relations more
generally on the "cutting edge of the historical profession," according to Warren I. Cohen, whose own 1992 *East Asian Art and American Culture* attests to
this vitality.[4]

Yet, a look at the scholarship also indicates that in many respects historians of pre-1900 Sino-American relations are still 'strangers at the gate,' laboring energetically—though ultimately in vain—to penetrate the inner layers of
Chinese society through barriers of language, culture, knowledge, privilege,
and historical experience. A persistent reluctance to abandon American
exclusivity for a comparative, internationalist approach; a resistance against
engaging the most recent literature in Chinese social history; and a general
skepticism about the revolution in the social sciences, together seem to
imprison scholars in the same small, anomalous enclaves that once circum-
scribed the universe of the transplanted missionaries, diplomats and businessmen whom they now study.

Michael Hunt's 1983 *The Making of a Special Relationship: The United States
and China to 1914* is by now the starting point for the study of U.S.-China
relations prior to the First World War. The work has been justifiably praised
for its multiarchival, multidisciplinary approach, its attention to the Chinese
side of things, and its expansive sense of what constitutes diplomatic history.
A synthesis of the existing literature, fortified by the author's own work in
Western- and Chinese-language primary sources, and supplemented by bibliographic essays for each chapter, *The Making of a Special Relationship* offers
a baseline against which all subsequent work for the pre-1900 period may be
assessed, in terms of both methodological scope and interpretative value.

Arrell M. Gibson's *Yankees in Paradise: The Pacific Basin Frontier* (1993)
significantly broadens the geographic and demographic context for early
Sino-American contacts beyond the mercantile, East-coast "open door con-

stituency" identified by Hunt and others.[5] The author, who died before completing this book, depicts these early contacts as a continuation of American westward expansion, and he argues that the Pacific Basin was carved out by overlapping waves of pioneers, including maritime fur traders, cattlemen, mining and agrarian interests, missionaries, soldiers, and literary figures. Though his treatment of U.S.-China relations is derivative, based largely on Warren I. Cohen's well-known *America's Response to China*, Gibson's unique contribution is this sweeping, imaginative Pacific Basin frontier as a basic framework for understanding the movement of American goods, culture, and sojourners toward China's ports early in the nineteenth century.[6]

The commercial component of this broader movement is now more thoroughly understood, thanks to the publication since 1983 of numerous monographs and articles on early U.S.-China trade. Prepared for the 1984 bicentennial anniversary of the first commercial voyage between the U.S. and China, Philip C. F. Smith's *The Empress of China* draws from a wealth of previously untapped primary sources, and appears to be the definitive work on the subject.[7] Two other recent works explore the role of New York and Philadelphia in the China trade.[8] James R. Gibson's 1992 thoroughly documented, and broadly conceived *Otter Skins, Boston Ships and China Goods: The Maritime Fur Trade of the Northwest Coast, 1785–1841* illuminates a vital area of early U.S.-China commerce.[9] Gibson highlights Anglo-American rivalry, vividly describes the Canton market, traces trade patterns over time, and concludes that ultimately the exchange was unequal as Americans gained capital essential for development, but Northwest Indians, Hawaiians and Chinese suffered only disease, disorder, and decline.

Gibson addresses what continue to be the paramount questions in the study of U.S.-China trade prior to 1900, that is, the relative importance of this trade to both partners over time, and the extent to which this trade—conducted under the auspices of unequal treaties—was exploitative and imperialist. The most comprehensive treatment of these issues in the last decade is *America's China Trade in Historical Perspective: The Chinese and American Performance* (1986), which grew out of a 1976 conference at Mt. Kisco sponsored by the national Committee on American East Asian Relations. Co-edited by Ernest May and the late John K. Fairbank, the book seeks to "separate myth from fact" on these questions through an empirical examination of China's exports to the United States (tea and silk), American exports to China (cotton textiles, cigarettes, petroleum), and the historical [un]importance of each partner in the overall trade and investment portfolio of the other.[10]

Succinctly stated, the overriding thesis of *America's China Trade in Historical Perspective* is that the case study of U.S.-China trade simply does not fit the paradigm of exploitative Western imperialism in the third world that is the mainstay of dependency theory. This argument comes in response not only to the critique of American diplomacy issued during the Vietnam era by "New Left" historians, but also to the continuing debate in Chinese history as to whether indigenous economic development was stimulated or retarded by the Western presence. The book provides the most recent, and most persuasive iteration to date, of what is generally called the "Harvard school" of thought on these questions. Briefly stated, this view—which has long dominated the study of early Sino-foreign relations—sees the Western enterprise in China as painful, but ultimately beneficial for that country's long-term "modernization," inasmuch as cultural, intellectual, and socioeconomic characteristics inherent in that society limited its developmental potential.[11] Essays straddling the nineteenth and twentieth centuries by Hao Yen-p'ing, Robert Gardella, and Lillian Li bring into the literature of Sino-American relations some of the most recent Chinese and Western scholarship on the question of whether China's "opening" to the West weakened or sustained indigenous "sprouts of capitalism," a theme taken up in greater detail in Hao Yen-p'ing's 1986 *The Commercial Revolution in Nineteenth-Century China: The Rise of Sino-Western Mercantile Capitalism*, and William T. Rowe's two-volume study of Hankow.[12]

Li, Hao and Gardella collectively conclude that: a) The tea and silk trades were mutually profitable, but never vital to either partner; b) This trade worked within the structures of the Chinese economy, and did not skew it into dependency, as was the case in plantation-style colonialism in India or Latin America; c) There was some hardship on the Chinese side when land and labor were given over to cash crops, and unfavorable rates of exchange deflated indigenous currency; d) However, commercial profits played a crucial role in "self-strengthening" projects (railroads, communications, steamships and military defense) in each country; e) Chinese enthusiastically responded to opportunities opened by foreign trade; f) but, ultimately, competition from Japan and India, together with what are described as China's inherent precapitalist deficiencies, mired that country in relative backwardness.

Li's sanguine assessment of the Western impact on China's silk trade, drawn from her 1981 monograph on the subject, is challenged in Robert Y. Eng's 1986 *Economic Imperialism in China: Silk Production and Exports, 1861–1932*. Taking a middle road between the "Harvard school" modernization approach and the critique of Western imperialism found in publications such as the *Bulletin of Concerned Asian Scholars*, Eng argues that the technical stagnation of the industry owed to the inextricable combination of imperialism's pernicious effects and China's own internal problems [13] A more thorough indictment of Western capitalism as the source of China's modern woes can be found in Alvin Y. So's 1986 study of the South China silk district, which examines the subject from the world systems perspectives developed by Immanuel Wallerstein and Ferdinand Braudel. As in earlier efforts by other scholars to apply a world systems framework to East Asia, theory and doctrine overwhelm data with provocative, but ultimately unconvincing, results.[14]

U.S.-China textile trade has been thoroughly investigated by Kang Chao and Bruce Reynolds, whose essays in *America's China Trade* very usefully put this subject in a global context. Both authors generally ascribe the vicissitudes of that exchange to comparative advantage and "accidental factors," rather than to the sort of political-military coercion or corporate-government collusion the authors see on the part of Great Britain and Japan in their dealings with China. Consistent with the conclusions of the book as a whole, Cheng Chu-yuan's profile of the very substantial U.S. petroleum trade with China from 1876 to 1949 argues that, notwithstanding some negative impacts on indigenous development, in the final balance the result for China was positive. "The influx of gasoline and liquid fuel facilitated the mechanization of handicrafts," and "[t]he substitution of kerosene for vegetable oil as a household illuminant released millions of tons of vegetable oils for exports."[15]

Sherman Cochran's far-reaching essay on the British American Tobacco Company (BAT), the subject of his 1980 published dissertation, *Big Business in China: Sino-Foreign Rivalry in the Cigarette Industry, 1890–1930*, asserts that BAT's enormous success and deep penetration into the Chinese economy down to the village level owed largely to its reliance on cheap, skilled indigenous labor, and entrepreneurial Chinese intermediaries operating with a high degree of autonomy. Although the company's ruthless campaign against its indigenous competitors in China qualifies as economic imperialism—a censure directed at little else in *America's China Trade*—BAT's other activities were less so, inasmuch as they did not drain wealth from that country, BAT-associated laborers were no worse off than others around them, and the company worked with, rather than against, indigenous structures and market forces.

Concluding essays by Peter Schran and Mira Wilkins emphasize the relative insignificance of U.S.-China trade, and foreign trade more generally, in the history of each of the two partners, whether in terms of gross national product or strategically vital goods. Wilkins, in particular, asserts in her discussion of American-headquartered multinationals that although these enterprises made China more important to the U.S. political system than might otherwise have been the case, the impact of corporate interests on

China policy was diffuse, inconsistent, and always modified by other contending forces within American domestic politics.

The strength of *America's China Trade* is the emphasis on empirical data, the effort to ground analysis in Chinese-language sources and Chinese social history, and the use of a broad historical and international context. However, few authors in the work deal directly with the unequal treaty structure of domination beyond noting its existence, or using its incremental additions as chronological landmarks. Further, the issue of American involvement in, and benefit from, the trade in opium and in Chinese "coolie" labor is finessed rather than confronted directly. This is particularly egregious when one considers the observation by a historian of American business in China, Jacques M. Downs, that "by the late 1830s, opium was the basis of East-West commerce. It balanced the payments and was the economic foundation of the Canton foreign community." According to Downs, in the Sino-foreign nexus, "everyone needed" opium to one degree or another.[16]

Finally, although acknowledging the widespread criticism in recent years of the modernization model, these historians continue to rely on an implied Western model of development, one that implicates China's own inherent characteristics as the basic source of its modern fate, an interpretation they shore up through comparisons to Japan. The fact that Japan was able to throw off the unequal treaties and tariff restrictions by the turn of the century, while China could not until 1943—and then only because of the Allies' wartime needs—is taken as just one more bit of support for the central tenet of the Harvard school's argument, i.e. that China's own internal deficiencies, rather than Western imperialism, are to blame for the turn of events into revolution and civil war.

There seems to be general agreement in the field, though, with John Fairbank's assessment that "the American approach to China was a phenomenon of the mind and spirit more than of the pocketbook," as "bouts of American enthusiasm for trade and investment in China originated" less from historical realities or concerted pressure from entrenched economic interests than from "a mind-set that believed in economic expansion."[17] Similarly, the drift away from narrowly construed diplomatic histories of U.S.-China relations prior to the issuance of the Open Door notes at the turn of the century suggests broad acquiescence as well to Fairbank's persuasive argument that it is a "misconception" to speak of an "America China policy" prior to 1898, inasmuch as the U.S. functioned wholly within a framework defined, refined and upheld by the force of British global predominance.[18]

Consensus on these issues has increased attention to the generation, nature and impact of Sino-American mutual images and to the activities and identities of cross-cultural intermediaries, both areas of great promise.[19] Research on these topics has been facilitated by the publication of two enormously useful reference works: *Christianity in China: A Scholars' Guide to Resources in the Libraries and Archives of the United States*; and Kathleen Lodwick's index to the *Chinese Recorder*.[20]

A. Owen Aldridge's 1993 *The Dragon and the Eagle: The Presence of China in the American Enlightenment* fills in an important gap in the literature on mutual images by demonstrating that in the 120 years between the birth of Benjamin Franklin in 1706 and the death of Thomas Jefferson in 1826 "information about the history and culture of" China was "widespread and readily available."[21] In this early period, the author argues, there was a mixture of praise and contempt, but little hint of the racism that infused later images.

Aldridge successfully disproves the contention in earlier works that Enlightenment-era Americans knew little about China, and he modifies the argument made by Harold Isaacs, Tyler Dennett, and others, that positive, idealized images of China prevailed almost exclusively in this period.[22] In addition, the work appears to confirm one of the main tenets of Stuart C. Miller's 1969 *The Unwelcome Immigrant: The American Image of the Chinese*, i.e. that the benign images of these years were overtaken by the contemptuous and disparaging images generated by businessmen and missionaries frustrated in their efforts to "open" China to Western influence.[23] According to Aldridge, "the China trade, by bringing the United States into direct contact with Chinese people and products," led to "a drastic change in attitude toward the Middle Kingdom in all sectors of American society," as China "had become a nation to be exploited rather than" admired.[24]

Colin Mackerras's *Western Images of China* draws heavily from the ideas of Michel Foucault and Edward Said to posit a direct correlation between negative images of China and Western imperialist goals. The assertions Mackerras makes about the relation of power and knowledge in Western perceptions of China are important and will no doubt stimulate further research on the subject. However, the author's implied definition of "images" is unhelpfully vague, his use of Foucault and Said is mechanical, and he fails to show persuasively why and how some images prevailed over others at a given moment.[25]

America Views China: American Images of China Then and Now (1991), its editors note, is about straightforward "innocent [and] ... honest" images, in the sense that the contributors are "not into" the "science of imagery" as debated by various historians, including Akira Iriye.[26] Among essays covering the pre-1900 period, of interest are those by Jacques Downs and Raymond F. Wylie, examining the commercial and missionary sources of enduring American attitudes toward China, as well as brief pieces by Raymond G. O'Connor and Jonathan Goldstein exploring the impact of imported Asian objects d'art, chinoiserie and the advent of photography on Western perceptions and attitudes.[27] The latter are best read in conjunction with the first part of Warren I. Cohen's *East Asian Art and American Culture* (1992), which puts the subject in the context of the unequal relationship between the two societies.[28]

United States Attitudes and Policies toward China. The Impact of American Missionaries, also a foray into the study of image making and transmission, tries, for the most part unsatisfactorily, to find a middle ground between New Left condemnations of American "cultural imperialism," and the self-serving justifications of nineteenth- and early twentieth-century missionaries themselves.[29] Written originally for a 1987 conference at the University of San Diego sponsored by the Asia Pacific Rim Institute, these essays examine the forces at work in the production of images about China by missionaries in the field, and in their transmission by local American mission boards to home audiences to solicit moral and financial support.

Of particular note are Jessie G. Lutz's profile of Karl Gützlaff, a Prussian missionary who wrote widely for American audiences in the 1830s; Lawrence D. Kessler's study of the complex relationship between what men in the field reported and what their sponsors chose to emphasize; and, Kathleen L. Lodwick's examination of the images of China put out by missionary and secular presses at Hainan station. In essays published in *United States Attitudes and Policies toward China*, *America Views China*, and elsewhere, Murray A. Rubinstein makes important contributions to the thesis laid out earlier by Stuart C. Miller and others that missionary groups frustrated by Ch'ing restrictions generated derogatory images of Chinese justifying the use of force and heightened Western aggression.[30]

The most thorough and historically grounded treatment of the subject of mutual images and cross-cultural brokers is *Christianity in China: Early Protestant Missionary Writings* (1985), a volume originating from a 1978 conference centered around the Harvard-Yenching Library's substantial missionary archives. Co-edited by Suzanne W. Barnett and John Fairbank, this work explores Sino-foreign interaction "on the operating level where Christianity met its Chinese public."

Christianity in China can be seen as a philosophical companion piece to *America's China Trade*, discussed earlier.[31] As Fairbank's introduction to the former intimates, the analogy driving the analysis here is the profile of the British American Tobacco Company compiled by Sherman Cochran, who (as noted above) emphasized the substantial and decisive role of indigenous brokers in that company's successful penetration to the village level. Each of the nine essays contributes to the overall thesis of the book that, although drawing some of its persuasiveness from the force of Western arms, "Christianity in China from the first was a Sino-foreign enterprise," and acquired its historical momentum in that setting over the course of the nineteenth century above all from indigenous sources.[32]

Selections by Daniel H. Bays, Jane Kate Leonard, Jessie G. Lutz, Fred W. Drake, and Evelyn S. Rawski look at the adaptation of the Christian message to the China context. Very much like the advertising managers of the British American Tobacco Company described by Cochran, it would appear that Protestant missionaries learned what sold the product and what did not in the China market. Accenting congruities rather than conflicts and contradictions, and speaking from within Chinese cultural norms, worked best, as Bays shows in his discussion of the most enduring and widely read Christian tract in China.

Adaptation in turn changed missionaries' sense of themselves and their purpose. Jane Leonard argues in her essay that secularization and simplification led to a pragmatic focus on education, "creat[ing] a class of missionary-scholars . . . who ultimately played a vital role as cultural mediators in the treaty ports after the Opium War."[33] This same process is discussed in Adrian Bennett's study of the early China career of Young J. Allen, and an interesting variation on the theme is presented in Charles W. Weber's detailed study of Baptist educational work in this same period, both published under separate cover.[34] In a large sense, though, adaptation to the China setting meant letting indigenous brokers and converts set the agenda, according to Evelyn Rawski, who finds that "in the short run, Chinese perspectives and values shaped the form and content of the mission primary-school curriculum."[35] So too, the pragmatism of missionary entrepreneurs fatally compromised the Christian enterprise in the eyes of Chinese and of home sponsors, a point well made in Jessie Lutz's contribution to this volume.

The essay by Fred Drake presents missionaries in what has come to be the Harvard school's characteristic view on the subject, i.e. that these cultural frontier folk served as inadvertent subversives, firing "intellectual artillery" at the Confucian fortress, spreading chaos and dissension in the ranks of Ch'ing society, all with the best of intentions. The practical bent of missionaries, and their own sense of the inextricability of Christianity, Western civilization, and Western power, provided interested Chinese with a particularly pragmatic blend of knowledge, and led them to question the very core of their own society. Whereas integrating China into their world view challenged Westerners, Drake argues, Chinese efforts to come to terms with the West unleashed a process so profound and tumultuous as to undo the traditional order.

Barnett and Charles W. Hayford take up the genesis, content, and impact of the mutual images transmitted by missionary entrepreneurs, such as Walter Medhurst and Arthur Smith, both to Chinese and to their home audience. Both underscore the tendency among Americans to see their values and experience as universally valid. Hayford subjects Smith's classic *Chinese Characteristics* to the critical analysis favored by literary deconstructionists, concluding that Smith was unable to transcend his own middle-class experience as a reference point on China. This in turn led Smith—and generations of his readers—to the insoluble paradox that the primary obstacle in China to Christianity and all that it historically brought (prosperity, industry, equality, stability, etc.) was Chinese society's "Chineseness," i.e. its fatal lack of middle-class Christian values, such as punctuality, precision, public mindedness, perseverance, and patience.

Beyond the subject of images, two selections in *Christianity in China* provide exceptionally rich underlying conceptualizations and provocative conclusions, each with important implications for the study of pre-1900 Sino-American relations. In his "Christianity and Chinese Sects: Religious Tracts in the Late Nineteenth Century," Daniel Bays explores the interaction and over-. lap of sinicized Christianity and Chinese sectarian heterodoxy, a theme he raised in a 1982 *Ch'ing-shih wen-t'i* article.[36] Drawing on contemporary tract literature, and Chinese-language published archives on missionary cases, Bays demonstrates that a convergence of cosmological themes, normative values and membership appeal made indigenous sectarianism Christianity's major "point of access" into nineteenth-century Chinese society.

Complementing this discussion is P. Richard Bohr's in-depth look at one of the earliest Chinese converts to Christianity, Liang Fa, known to historians most for his authorship of the tract that introduced Christianity to the anti-Ch'ing Taiping rebels. Bohr portrays Liang Fa's "moral quest" as the story of "how a Chinese convert found in Protestantism what he had been seeking in China" and Confucianism, i.e. filial piety and moral sincerity, the promise of individual salvation and social transformation, and a vantage point on his own society other than that offered by the historic "center of the world" self-image. This portrait resonates with studies of other Chinese drawn to Western ideas and mores, such as Paul A. Cohen's examination of Chinese "Christian" reformers.[37]

These essays by Bays and Bohr merit close study. Bays, in particular, manages a feat seemingly beyond the reach of most American forays into missionary studies in putting the archival efforts and conceptual innovations of Western Chinese social historians—such as Elizabeth Perry, Susan Naquin, Frederic Wakeman, and G. William Skinner—in the service of U.S. diplomatic history. Naquin and Perry, for example, have explored the social, familial, and geographical dynamics of sectarianism. Bay's portrayal of Chinese Christianity as part of the heterodox tradition, together with Bohr's sophisticated profile of a man he characterizes as the embodiment of the Christian convert, provide a bridge to Perry's and Naquin's work that makes it possible to talk about at least one aspect of the "American impact" on China in analytically sophisticated, socially complex, and historically precise terms.

Still, construing nineteenth-century Sino-foreign relations as "the meeting of cultures" and depicting Western missionary activity in late Ch'ing China in terms of the "Sinification of Christianity," strikes many in the field as ignoring the unequal structure within which Sino-foreign relations unfolded. Indeed, the proof adduced in *Christianity in China* and *America's China Trade* to demonstrate the virtual absence of Western imperialism is taken by others as evidence of "informal imperialism," i.e. the unequal relationship between two or more countries, involving the indirect rule through indigenous collaborators, on the basis of a treaty structure which allows outside veto power over essential political, economic, foreign policy, and military decisions. True, China was not divided up in the manner of colonial Africa, or transformed into a plantation-based economy in the Caribbean or Latin American mode. Yet, as Jürgen Osterhammel argues in his 1986 essay, "Semi-Colonialism and Informal Empire in Twentieth-Century China: Towards a Framework of Analysis," beginning in the mid-nineteenth century Sino-foreign relations bore many of the earmarks of imperialism: legally autonomous foreign enclaves; extraterritoriality; racial discrimination; a foreign military presence; repeated interventions in domestic politics; foreign tariff, revenue collection and customs controls; large-scale loans, foreign investments and indemnities; and collaborative indigenous elites.[38]

The utility of the concept of informal imperialism has been expanded in recent years by the work of the late Ronald Robinson, who construed the process as a series of interconnecting linkages between: a) metropolitan states and their own domestic constituencies; b) metropolitan states and indigenous collaborators; and, c) indigenous collaborative elites and their own domestic constituencies. This model highlights the importance of resistance in the target society, and the concessions metropolitan states have to make to their collaborators in order to continue pursuing "imperialism on the cheap."[39] This approach begins with imperialism as a premise, much like dependency theory, but its complexity and its emphasis on indigenous forces, enables scholars to move beyond history as victimization.

A 1991 *Pacific Historical Review* article by Paul Harris represents the most far-reaching attempt in the last decade to reconceptualize American activities in late Ch'ing China using this framework of informal imperialism as a premise.[40] Borrowing from Johan Galtung's 1971 seminal essay on a "structural theory of imperialism," Harris argues that the relationship of nineteenth-century American Protestant missions to their target Chinese audience reproduced and depended upon the same inequalities of power and dominance present in other facets of Sino-foreign relations, whether economic, diplomatic, or military.

Though missionaries tried in many cases to maintain functional autonomy from their merchant and military counterparts, they shared an "imperial culture" which linked all of these groups to the larger Western penetration process. What joined China-based missionaries to this process was less "conscious intentions and formal policies," than it was "the deeper, cultural forces that shaped missionary behavior." For Harris, then, the central question is not whether missionaries "served as advance agents, subversives, propagandists, salespeople, or in any other particular way of use to other imperialists," but rather whether they "shared the beliefs, values, and attitudes of imperialists" and, second, whether they in fact acted like imperialists in the ways they went about securing their position and accumulating converts.[41]

American Protestant missionary strategies of conversion varied, notes Harris, but all ultimately depended upon unequal treaties enforced through military, political, and economic pressure on the Ch'ing. Similarly, over time these strategies tended to gravitate around the goal of producing dependent, collaboration-minded, indigenous converts. So too, although many missions did not perform the essential functions leading scholars now ascribe to cultural imperialism—such as propagating capitalist consumption values and mores—these same individuals "continued to send out unintentional messages associating Christianity with material comfort and affluence" simply by insisting upon reproducing American home-life abroad.[42]

A similar, but more historically grounded, approach to these same issues is found in Jane Hunter's 1984 *The Gospel of Gentility: American Women Missionaries in turn-of-the-Century China*.[43] Using archives from the American Board of Commissioners for Foreign Missions, Yale Divinity School, the Claremont Oral History Project, and the Woman's Foreign Missionary Society, Hunter argues persuasively that partaking in the spoils of the unequal treaty system eventually overrode the self-deprecating, subordinating "habits of femininity" American missionary women brought with them to China, as "colonial status" and "imperial gratifications" gradually imbued them with "colonial temperaments."[44]

Hunter's study is pioneering in its examination of the interaction of gender, class, national affiliation, and race in the crucible of semi-colonialism.

She presents in rich detail and refreshingly undogmatic terms how the experience of managing a household in the imperial setting, i.e. on the foundation of cheap indigenous labor, elitist paternalism, and caucasian racial pretensions, in turn shaped the mistress-servant paradigm through which female missionaries eventually mediated overall relations with their intended Chinese audience.[45]

Though Hunter's work is more informed by social history perspectives than are the selections in *Christianity in China*, it falls short, as Hunter herself acknowledges, on the twofold question of indigenous participation in missionary activities, and the American missionary impact on China or on particular Chinese. Explicitly stating the limited nature of her source base on this subject, Hunter observes in her discussion on "Chinese Women and Christian Identity," that female missionaries drew female converts from lower classes with combinations of religious offerings and social and economic assistance, a view which resonates with earlier published and unpublished work by Daniel Bays and others on the appeal of Christianity in China to indigenous women. High-class patronage from the Chinese treaty port elite was also a factor in the equation, underscoring the general point that "both Chinese and American women discovered that the margins of others' societies could encourage collective pride, national consciousness, and female autonomy discouraged at the center of their own."[46]

Missionary studies could benefit greatly by crossing the lines of regional specialties into comparative history. A 1987 special issue of *American Ethnologist*, for example, takes up the "Frontiers of Christian Evangelism" in various parts of the third world, in search of commonalities and contrasts. An essay by the late Morton Fried in that issue offers a good overview of the history of foreign missionaries in China, but leaves ample room for more focused investigations of issues of gender and cultural imperialism.[47] Similarly, the work of Jean and John Comaroff on Christianity and colonialism in South Africa investigates "the generic nature of mission agency in the colonial process," and makes a useful distinction between missionary influence in formal political settings versus their impact on informal, everyday activities.[48] Interestingly, ethnologists' oral interviews offer valuable insights to historians on, for example, the ambivalence of foreign religious groups toward the development of an indigenous church, or the dissonance would-be converts experience between the simplicity missionaries preach, on the one hand, and the high standard of living these same foreigners struggle to maintain when in the field, on the other.[49]

The suggestion that participation in the unequal treaty system meant complicity in Western imperialism, whether by definition (Harris) or by experience (Hunter), has far-reaching implications for the study of Sino-American relations. It challenges one of the central organizing principles of most works on U.S. diplomacy and Americans in China, i.e. the oscillation of American policy between the polarities of idealism and realism, or what Hugh Deane calls in his 1990 work "good deeds and gunboats."

Typical of the genre, Deane's *Good Deeds and Gunboats: Two Centuries of American-Chinese Encounters* condemns U.S. policy in general, but hails the prescience and tenacity of a few "true [American] friends of China. [50] Deane, an American journalist in China during the 1930s and 1940s, and co-founder of the United States-China Peoples Friendship Association, recounts the lives and times of an historic pantheon of particular Americans—for example, Amasa Delano, Mark Twain, Edgar Snow, and Joseph Stilwell—who "were not seduced by the pleasures and prejudices of treaty port life and who were drawn to the cause of a likable people struggling against national humiliation and the cruelties of a society in which a few oppressed and fleeced the many."[51] For Deane, these "friends of China," including nineteenth- and twentieth-century botanists, journalists, intellectuals, and officials, symbolize, "the better side of America—populist and reformist impulses, concern for social justice abroad as well as at home, [and a] generous readiness to help those in trouble. . . ."

Though written from a distinctly different point of view, and in a more scholarly tone, David L. Anderson's very useful and informative 1985 biographical history, *Imperialism and Idealism: American Diplomats in China, 1861–1898*, is organized around these same essential dichotomies.[52] Not unlike Tyler Dennett and Whitney Griswold before him, Anderson portrays U.S. China policy as being historically torn between "American ideals and self-interests." Each of the nine U.S. ministers in Peking he examines are shown to embody various of the "fundamental and paradoxical elements in America's historical and cultural identity that in turn shaped the dualities in American China policy."[53] As suggested by the title of Anderson's Epilogue, "The Dilemma Becomes the Policy in John Hay's Open Door Notes," the author views "Hay's initiatives" as "blend[ing] masterfully the ideals and self-interests of the United States," finally bringing to a close the constant oscillation between imperialism and idealism that characterized the period 1861 to 1898.[54]

Those who write from the perspective of the informal imperialism model see in all of this a fundamental confusion between "idealism" and what might be called "imperial angst." It is true that from time to time Americans experienced pangs of conscience and acute anxiety over the inconsistencies between their country's revolutionary, anti-colonial heritage and its counter-revolutionary, expansionist foreign policy. The tension between these contrary pulls mediated America's rise to global hegemony, dictating compromises along the way, but did not change the essential nature of the imperial process itself. In other words, American gunboats and good deeds—its self-interests and ideals—are best viewed as two ways of going about the same thing, each with its own assets and liabilities. This is the argument made in Philip Darby's 1987 study of British and American approaches to Asia and Africa from 1870 to 1970. Darby sees expressions of moral responsibility—certainly a mainstay of U.S. China policy—as one of the "three faces of imperialism."[55]

Stepping back from the literature of the past decade, it would seem, then, that scholars best able to travel into the hinterlands of Chinese society do so with a narrow set of questions, while those with broader and more complicated questions seldom venture beyond the margins, for one reason or another. An enormously promising research vein could be tapped by, somehow, bringing together the social history concerns evident in *The Gospel of Gentility* and the close-in, multiarchival, multilingual approach featured in the explorations by Daniel Bays and Richard Bohr of Chinese Christian converts, noted above. This research strategy would enable students of Sino-American relations to take advantage of the conceptually sophisticated, richly detailed local histories and "from the bottom up" social analyses being produced by Western China historians, such as Frederic Wakeman, Joseph Esherick, Mary Rankin, Gail Hershatter, Elizabeth Perry, and Susan Naquin.

For example, private Sino-American disputes in China—involving land, fraud, contracts, debts, and violence—could be examined as an arena of interaction. As Britten Dean pointed out in 1981, the Tsungli Yamen Archive at the Academia Sinica's Institute of Modern History in Taiwan has documentation for Sino-American contact at the local level, sources which give hints as to the "operation of local bureaucracies, . . . local power structure[s], and working relations with and attitudes toward foreigners."[56] This local perspective offers an exciting reconceptualization of the history of the State Department in China, for example, as suggested by the almost parenthetical observation by Marilyn Blatt Young in her *The Rhetoric of Empire* that the U.S. Consul in Amoy functioned in the style of a Confucian district magistrate—diverting (illegally obtained) immigration fees to the upkeep of a local militia.[57]

Second, together with archival material from U.S. and Chinese sources, both published and unpublished, these items provide the details necessary to locate particular Sino-American conflicts within the local and social history case studies reconstructed by Western Chinese social historians, not only in time and place, but also in terms of class, gender and clan.[58] Hypotheses drawn at this point in the research process could then be tested against, for instance, a recent volume edited by Joseph Esherick and Mary Rankin on patterns of elite dominance in late imperial and Republican-era China which identifies the sources of gentry power as land, irrigation control, local relief efforts and civil activity, and suggests that local elites showed great adeptness in utilizing the foreign presence to shore up their position.[59]

More generally, one of Chinese social history's themes that is particularly promising for specialists in early Sino-American relations is that of brokerage as an enduring and central phenomenon in modern China. According to Esherick and Rankin, freelance brokerage often offered ostensibly powerless individuals or groups "an empowering role," because "in areas where elite brokers were weak or unwilling to serve, nonelite individuals could rise to perform brokerage roles and thereby gain power over local arenas."[60] Concomitantly, those outside of elite-mass client-patron relations, such as sectarian bands, the roving poor, transient workers, disbanded soldiers, and criminals threatened elite hegemony. Sino-American relations specialists might make a contribution to this work by investigating to what extent Americans and U.S. policy reinforced or challenged existing vertical patron-client ties.

Studies that explore the membership appeal of Christian missions for disaffected, alienated, impoverished, or oppressed Chinese individuals are just the beginning of such an effort. In my own study of American extraterritoriality and consular corruption in China, I have found that the privileges available to all U.S. nationals in China made every American there a potential broker—whether prostitute, vagabond, transient worker, disbanded soldier, confidence man, or saloon keeper—because there was a tremendous market in commodified foreign privileges, whether for the buying and selling of land, establishment of business, contracting of debts, escape from legal jurisdictions, gunrunning, or opium dealing.[61]

Why, we might then ask, is the subject of Sino-American cross-cultural brokerage being conceptualized such that "rice Christians" and "beachcombing adventurers" are invariably consigned to the footnotes? If the last decade saw progress in overcoming what Michael Hunt described as ethnocentricism and statism, the agenda for the future might fruitfully call for a struggle against the tendency to assume that only articulate, purposeful, generally "respectable" people can make real international history.

NOTES

1. Michael H. Hunt, "New Insights But No New Vistas: Recent Work on Nineteenth-Century American-East Asian Relations," in Warren I. Cohen, ed., *New Frontiers in Ameri-*

can-East Asian Relations. Essays Presented to Dorothy Borg (New York: Columbia University Press, 1983), 17.

2. Ibid., 17, 24.

3. Ibid., 17, 18, 19, 22, 26–28, 32, 33.

4. Warren I. Cohen, "The History of American-East Asian Relations: Cutting Edge of the Historical Profession," *Diplomatic History* 9, no.2 (Spring 1985): 101–112.

5. Arrell M. Gibson (with the assistance of John S. Whitehead), *Yankees in Paradise, The Pacific Basin Frontier* (Albuquerque: University of New Mexico Press, 1993).

6. Warren I. Cohen, *America's Response to China: A History of Sino-American Relations* (NY: Columbia University Press, 1990, 3d edition).

7. Philip C. F. Smith, *The Empress of China* (Philadelphia: Philadelphia Maritime Museum, 1984).

8. David S. Howard, *New York and the China Trade* (New York: Columbia Publishing Company, 1984); Jean G. Lee, *Philadelphians and the China Trade, 1784–1844* (Philadelphia: Philadelphia Museum of Art, 1984) supplements but does not displace Jonathan Goldstein's *Philadelphia and the China Trade, 1682–1846: Commercial, Cultural, and Attitudinal Effects* (University Park, PA: Pennsylvania State University Press, 1978).

9. James R. Gibson, *Otter Skins, Boston Ships and China Goods: The Maritime Fur Trade of the Northwest Coast, 1785–1841* (Seattle: University of Washington, 1992).

10. Ernest R. May and John K. Fairbank, eds., *America's China Trade in Historical Perspective: The Chinese and American Performance* (Cambridge: Harvard Studies in American-East Asian Relations [11], 1986).

11. For a thorough discussion of the historiography, see: Paul A. Cohen, *Discovering History in China: American Historical Writing on the Recent Chinese Past* (New York: Columbia University Press, 1984), esp. 1–148; Robert Marks, "The State of the China Field, or, the China Field and the State," *Modern China* 11, no.4 (October 1985); Edward Said, *Orientalism* (New York: Vintage Books, 1979); Joseph Esherick, "Harvard on China: the Apologetics of Imperialism," *Bulletin of Concerned Asian Scholars* 4 (December 1972): 9–16; Andrew J. Nathan, "Imperialism's effects on China, Ibid., 3–8; Victor D. Lippit, "The Development of Underdevelopment in China," *Modern China* 4 (1978): 251–328; Tim Wright, "Imperialism and the Chinese Economy: A Methodological Critique of the Debate," *Bulletin of Concerned Asian Scholars* 18 (January–March 1986): 36–45.

12. Hao Yen-p'ing, *The Commercial Revolution in Nineteenth-Century China: The Rise of Sino-Western Mercantile Capitalism* (Berkeley and Los Angeles: University of California, 1986); William T. Rowe, *Hankow: Commerce and Society in a Chinese City, 1796–1889* (Stanford, CA: Stanford University Press, 1984), and *Hankow: Conflict and Community in a Chinese City, 1796–1895* (Stanford, CA: Stanford University Press, 1989).

13. Lillian M. Li, *China's Silk Trade: Traditional Industry in the Modern World, 1842–1937* (Cambridge: Council on East Asian Studies, Harvard University, 1981); Robert Y. Eng, *Economic Imperialism in China: Silk Production and Exports, 1861–1932* (Berkeley, CA: Institute of East Asian Studies, University of California, 1986). Of limited use is the overview of the subject in David G. Brown, *Partnership with China: Sino-Foreign Joint Ventures in Historical Perspective* (Boulder, CO: Westview Press, 1986).

14. Alvin Y. So, *The South China Silk District: Local Historical Transformation and World-Systems Theory* (Albany, NY: State University of New York Press, 1986). For a more succinct statement of the thesis, see Alvin Y. So, "The Process of Incorporation into the Capitalist World-System: The Case of China in the Nineteenth Century," *Review* (Journal of the Braudel Center), 8, no.1 (Summer 1984): 91–116. The best-known earlier application of world systems theory is Frances Moulder, *Japan, China and the Modern World Econ-*

omy (Cambridge: Cambridge University Press, 1977). On the world systems theory, see: Terence Hopkins and Immanuel Wallerstein, eds., *World-Systems Analysis* (Beverly Hills, CA: Sage Publications, 1982); Angus McDonald, "Wallerstein's World Economy: How Seriously Should We Take It? (Review Article)," *Journal of Asian Studies* 38 (May 1979): 535–40.

15. Cheng Chu-yuan, "The United States Petroleum Trade with China, 1876–1949," *America's China Trade*, 206.

16. Jacques M. Downs, "The Commercial Origins of American Attitudes toward China, 1784–1844," in Jonathan Goldstein, Jerry Israel, and Hilary Conroy, eds., *America Views China: American Images of China Then and Now* (Bethlehem: Lehigh University Press, 1991), 60–61.

17. Fairbank, "Introduction," *America's China Trade*, 7.

18. John K. Fairbank, " 'American China Policy' to 1898: A Misconception," *Pacific Historical Review* 39 (November 1970): 409–420.

19. These explorations of American images of China are balanced by two works focusing on Chinese perceptions of America: *Land Without Ghosts. Chinese Impressions of America from the Mid-Nineteenth Century to the Present*, R. David Arkush and Leo E. Lee, trans. and eds., (Berkeley: University of California, 1989), translated excerpts drawn from the travel notes of nineteenth- and twentieth-century Chinese traveling in the United States; and Charles A. Desnoyers' 1991 *Pacific Historical Review* article, "Self-Strengthening in the New World: A Chinese Envoy's Travels in America," based upon the journal of Ch'en Lan-pin, the first Chinese Minister to the United States. Much awaited as well is the publication of Chang-fang Chen's dissertation, "Barbarian Paradise: Chinese Views of the United States, 1784–1911" (Indiana University 1985).

20. Archie R. Crouch, et al., eds. *Christianity in China: A Scholars' Guide to Resources in the Libraries and Archives of the United States* (Armonk, NY: M. E. Sharpe, 1989); Kathleen Lodwick, *The Chinese Recorder Index: A Guide to Christian Missions in Asia, 1867–1941* (Delaware: Scholarly Resources, Inc., 1986).

21. A. Owen Aldridge, *The Dragon and the Eagle. The Presence of China in the American Enlightenment* (Detroit: Wayne State University, 1993), 210.

22. See Hunt's discussion of this debate over early images in *The Making of a Special Relationship*, page 320, bibliographic essay.

23. Stuart C. Miller, *The Unwelcome Immigrant: The American Image of the Chinese, 1785–1882* (Berkeley, CA: University of California Press, 1969).

24. Aldridge, *Dragon and Eagle*, 119.

25. Colin Mackerras, *Western Images of China* (Oxford and Ontario: Oxford University Press, 1991).

26. Jonathan Goldstein, Jerry Israel, and Hilary Conroy, eds. *America Views China: American Images of China Then and Now*, (Bethlehem: Lehigh University Press, 1991)

27. See also Downs' "Fair Game: Exploitive Role-Myths and the American Opium Trade," *Pacific Historical Review* 16, no. 2 (May 1972): 133–49; and his "American Merchants and the China Opium Trade, 1800–1840," *Business History Review* 42 (Winter 1968).

28. Warren I. Cohen, *East Asian Art and American Culture. A Study in International Relations* (New York: Columbia University Press, 1992); see also Irene E. Cortinovis, "China at the St. Louis World's Fair," *Missouri Historical Review* 72, no. 1 (1977): 59–66. Insights on the current debates in this field of research may be found in "The World on Exhibition," a special section in the *Comparative Study of Society and History* 31, no. 2 (April 1989): 193–236.

29. Patricia Neils, ed. *United States Attitudes and Policies Toward China. The Impact of American Missionaries* (Armonk, NY: M. E. Sharpe, 1990).

30. See also, Rubinstein's "The Wars They Wanted: American Missionaries' Use of *The Chinese Repository* Before the Opium War," *American Neptune* 48 (1988): 271–282; Stuart Creighton Miller, "Ends and Means: Missionary Justification of Force in Nineteenth Century China," in John K. Fairbank, ed., *The Missionary Enterprise in China and America* (Cambridge: Harvard University Press, 1974), 249–282.

31. Suzanne W. Barnett and John K. Fairbank, eds., *Christianity in China: Early Protestant Missionary Writings* (Cambridge: Harvard Studies in American-East Asian Relations [9], 1985).

32. Ibid., 2, 8.

33. Ibid., 59

34. Adrian A. Bennett, *Missionary Journalist in China: Young J. Allen and His Magazines, 1860–1883* (Athens: University of Georgia Press, 1983); Charles W. Weber, "Conflicting Cultural Traditions in China: Baptist Educational Work in the Nineteenth Century," in Neils, ed., *United States Attitudes and Policies Toward China.*

35. Rawski, in Barnett and Fairbanks, *Christianity in China,* 151.

36. Daniel H. Bays, "Christianity and the Chinese Sectarian Tradition," *Ch'ing-shih wen-t'i* [since renamed *Late Imperial China*] 4, no. 7 (June 1982): 33–55.

37. Paul A. Cohen, "Littoral and Hinterland in Nineteenth Century China: The 'Christian' Reformers," in John K. Fairbank, ed., *The Missionary Enterprise in China and America* (Cambridge: Harvard University Press, 1974), 197–225. In particular, see Cohen's assessment that for the Chinese individuals he examines: "Christianity . . . was an important dimension of the overall experience of acculturation. It helped them to wrench free from the old culture and was instrumental in enabling them to pioneer a reformist approach. When it came to specific reform ideas, however, the Christian contribution proved negligible. Indeed, it would be fair to say that intellectually the 'Christian' reformers were scarcely Christian at all." (Ibid., 200).

38. Jürgen Osterhammel, "Semi-Colonialism and Informal Empire in Twentieth-Century China: Towards a Framework of Analysis," in Wolfgang Mommsen and Jürgen Osterhammel, eds., *Imperialism and After: Continuities and Discontinuities* (London: Allen & Unwin, 1986), 290–314.

39. Ronald Robinson, "The Excentric Idea of Imperialism, with or without Empire," in *Imperialism and After,* 267–289; Ronald Robinson, "Non-European Foundations of European Imperialism: Sketch or a Theory of Collaboration," in Roger Owen and Bob Sutcliffe, eds., *Studies in the Theory of Imperialism* (London: Longman 1977 [1972]), 117–40

40. Paul W. Harris, "Cultural Imperialism and American Protestant Missionaries: Collaboration and Dependency in Mid-Nineteenth-Century China," *Pacific Historical Review* 60 (August 1991): 309–38.

41. Ibid., 311–12.

42. Ibid., 333–34.

43. Jane Hunter, *The Gospel of Gentility: American Women Missionaries in Turn-of-the-Century China* (New Haven, CT: Yale University Press, 1984).

44. Ibid., xvi-vii, 265.

45. Ibid., 165.

46. Ibid., 255.

47. Morton Fried, "Reflections on Christianity in China," *American Ethnologist* 14, no. 1 (Feb. 1987): 94–106.

48. Jean Comaroff and John Comaroff, "Christianity and Colonialism in South Africa," *American Ethnologist* 13, no. 1 (Feb 1986): 1–22.

49. See, for example: Jack E. Nelson, *Christian Missionizing and Social Transformation:*

A History of Conflict and Change in Eastern Zaire (New York: Praeger, 1992), 3–4, 6, 7, 73–76, 137, 167–79.

50. Hugh Deane, *Good Deeds and Gunboats: Two Centuries of American-Chinese Encounters* (San Francisco, China Books; Beijing; New World Press, 1990).

51. Ibid., 196.

52. David L. Anderson, *Imperialism and Idealism: American Diplomats in China, 1861–1898* (Bloomington, Indiana: Indiana University Press, 1985).

53. Ibid., viii.

54. Ibid., 171.

55. Philip Darby, *Three Faces of Imperialism: British and American Approaches to Asia and Africa, 1870–1970* (New Haven, CT: Yale University Press, 1987).

56. Britten Dean, "Sino-American Relations in the late 19th Century: The View from the Tsungli Yamen Archive," *Ch'ing-shih wen-t'i* 4, no. 5 (June 1981): 77–107.

57. Marilyn Blatt Young, *The Rhetoric of Empire: American China Policy, 1895–1901* (Cambridge: Harvard University Press, 1968), 100.

58. On the American side, State Department consular records for this period are available on microfilm. On the Chinese side, there is, for example: Chang Kuei-yung, ed., *Chiao-wu chiao-an tang* [Archives on Mission Affairs and Mission Incidents] (Taipei: *Chung-yang yen-chiu yuan, chin-tai shih yen-chiu so*, 1974–81), 7 volumes in 21 parts.

59. "Introduction," Joseph W. Esherick and Mary Backus Rankin, eds., *Chinese Local Elites and Patterns of Dominance* (Berkeley, CA: University of California Press, 1990), 6.

60. Ibid., 323.

61. Eileen P. Scully, "Crime, Punishment and Empire: The U.S. District Court for China, 1906–43" (Ph.D. Dissertation, Georgetown University, 1993); Scully, "Taking the Low Road to Sino-American Relations," *Journal of American History* (1995) and Scully, "On Distinguishing Dirt from Policy: American Consular Corruption in Late Ch'ing China," an article in progress.

Chapter Six

The Open Door Raj: Chinese-American Cultural Relations 1900–1945

CHARLES W. HAYFORD

Like the British in India, Americans in China formed a Raj. They developed an informal set of loosely related institutions, not organized by the American government, financed either by private enterprises or voluntary contributions. These institutions included denominational missions, schools and hospitals, business enterprises, newspapers, travel agencies, all of which enrolled many Chinese; their constituency was trans-Pacific, with contributors, clients, audiences, and victims in both countries. By the 1920s some families and organizations stretched back a generation or two—"old China hands," as newcomers came to call anyone who had come to China on an earlier boat than themselves. This Open Door Raj provided historical meaning, role, and vocabulary in which members worked, whether they resented, resisted, exploited, or boosted it. Neither completely independent nor completely dependent on stateside support, it was not exactly "Chinese" and not exactly "not Chinese"—it was a Chinese-American hybrid.[1]

Much of its regal attitude was lifted from the British, as reflected in its vocabulary: "coolie," "mandarin," "schroff," "paddy," "chit," "cot," "bungalow," "loot," "typhoon"; these and many more came from Hindi, Malay, Persian, or Arabic through the British Raj, promoting the flavor of a unique and exotic Orient somewhere East of Aden.[2] The Yankee Raj also inherited a long-standing argument which used culture to justify imperialism. Thomas Babington Macaulay famously argued in the 1840s that the British must educate "interpreters," a "class of persons, Indian in blood, and color, but English in taste, in opinions, in morals, and in intellect," who would present the native masses with modern culture.

At the same time, much American exceptionalism came from seeing the British as what America was exceptional *from*. China was never a formal colony; Sun Yat-sen called it a "hypo-colony," and Mao said it was a "semi-colony." Americans in China convinced themselves that they represented an *idea*, not cannonballs; like McKinley, they wanted to "uplift, Christianize, and civilize." Some British in India, like Rudyard Kipling, wanted an independent Anglo-Indian Raj and developed an "illusion of permanence." Americans in China thought they would love China and leave it—an illusion of *impermanence*.[3] This self-concept of representing civilization, of godfathering a new nation, was the cultural stance of United States-China relations.

Historians of China and American-East Asian relations have explored this web of culture, politics, and psychology,[4] perhaps to a fault.[5] Under the rubric of "Americanization," Akira Iriye's 1981 field review remarked on an "outpouring" of works that "go beyond conventional diplomatic history to deal with economic, intellectual, and other aspects" in the broad category of "cultural affairs."[6]

Michael H. Hunt's *The Making of A Special Relationship: The United States and China to 1914* is the charter work in combining diplomatic history with cultural analysis.[7] Hunt shows how businessmen, missionaries, and diplomats formed a three-legged constituency. They germinated an "Open Door ideology" that defined China in terms of two struggles: the first, a Chinese domestic struggle between progressive reform and feudal inertia; the second, a struggle that pitted the selfish imperialism of Britain, Russia, and Japan against the benevolent policies of the United States.

The two struggles were fused by a "paternalistic vision" of "defending and reforming China" (p. ix)—only Yankee reform could stave off imperialism. This "special relationship" (Hunt uses the term ironically) was built on expansionism, paternalism, and racism. Sentimentality did not prevent the State Department from demanding equal concessions from China; missionaries, businessmen, and travelers did not hesitate to use extraterritorial privileges. The final cornerstone of recent studies of culture and diplomacy is Akira Iriye's oeuvre, especially *Power and Culture*. Iriye defines Wilsonianism as both a cultural stance and a political strategy consisting of "gradualist reforms, global interdependence, international cooperation, and coupling of material well-being with political maturity."[8]

Separate from this appreciation of culture in diplomacy, the decade of the 1980s also saw a surge of cultural studies: "critical," "post-modern" and "post-colonial"—or, in the case of China, perhaps we could say "post-semi-colonial" or "post-hypo-colonial"—studies, to which academic prospectors have come with gold-rush fervor.[9] These studies are cynical about the "Enlightenment project" and see the civilizing mission as a mask for conquest. For instance, the subaltern group in South Asian studies and theorists of colonial Africa show how the concepts "nation," "race," "gender," and "class" were invented in the imperialist context; they formed a cultural thought system, or "discourse," which bounded, formed, and shaped belief, thought, and action. After formal liberation from European political control, a "derivative discourse" still energized the oppression of the formerly colonized peoples by indigenous leaders.[10]

Edward W. Said established the term "Orientalism" to excoriate Western political institutions and scholarship which culturally constructed an "Other" in order to subdue it by violence, treating Asia as an exotic unchanging essence. Said's 1993 *Culture and Imperialism*, however, is wary of treating the West and Western scholarship as itself an unchanging and unambiguous essence; the discussion of literary texts and political stances—or, literary stances and political texts?—more ambivalently explores an "imperial attitude" which includes both "redemptive force" as well as the "waste and the horror of Europe's mission in the dark world."[11]

Said richly explores this tugging duality between enlightenment sweetness-and-light and lustful, dark, imperialism—the same consideration which runs through Chinese and American discourses, and which recent scholarship explores. Paul Cohen shows that the question of the Boxers raised "what has very possibly been the central issue of cultural identity in the last century or so of Chinese history: the ambivalence with respect to the West." In times when they were in an anti-imperialist mode, Chinese historians and novelists presented Boxers as heroes; at other times, when equally patriotic Chinese (sometimes even the same ones) looked to the West for tools with which to build their nation, the Boxers were presented as superstitious, anti-modern, and xenophobic peasants, whose "feudal" culture held China back.[12]

Our review of the field begins in 1900 on a note of change, ambiguity, and clashing histories. The nativism shared by Boxers, gentry-literati, and officials was matched by the American Board of Commissioners for Foreign Missions

(ABCFM) support for American Marines burning and looting Chinese villages in a sort of "heart of darkness" scenario. This clash dissolved in the years after 1900 with a speed and thoroughness matched only by the reconciliation between the United States and imperial Japan in the 1940s. As Iriye's *Power and Culture* suggests, such diplomatic reconciliation was authorized by underlying agreement on values such as the power of enlightenment to validate an elite. The Empress Dowager posed for photographs with the diplomats' wives at tea; government officials and the Manchu court looked to Japan as a model for a modern polity and society; literati put their sons into new schools and their money into railroad stocks; villagers were taxed to pay the indemnities and policed into place.[13]

In these few years, Hunt's three constituencies each turned a corner: the missionaries found a Young China for their new Social Gospel of science and education; business developed from coastal peddling to manufacture and inland selling; diplomats saw themselves as working out America's Rise to World Power. Scholarly studies of these constituencies in the Open Door Raj look at several general questions: 1) Possible influence on American foreign policy. 2) Participation in Chinese thought, society, or policy—how Americans worked (in Jonathan Spence's now obligatory phrase) "to change China." 3) The light that Chinese-American relations shed on the general nature of cultural imperialism, the colonial (or semi-colonial) moment. In particular, there is a thread of concern with the problem, much theorized in the cultural studies literature, of how to define what is authentically Chinese.[14]

1. Protestant Mission—From Christ to Culture:

William R. Hutchison's *Errand to the World: American Protestant Thought and Foreign Missions* is a model cultural and intellectual history that shows missionaries to have been as much motivated by theology as Marxists were by ideology. Mission administrators of the ABCFM had learned the religious cost of successful social involvement in Hawaii. In that island paradise royal reformers had drawn missionaries away from spiritual concerns and made them worldly administrators of churches and government. A similar lesson emerged from mission experience with American Indians. The ABCFM sent mechanics and farmers to educate the wandering tribes into the American Way of Life and settle them as farmers; but acceptance of Jesus was made impossible by government racism and white land grabbing. The standard-issue mission argument then became a precocious cultural relativism:

"Native" civilizations were perfectly capable of absorbing Christianity without Americanizing their politics or culture. The job of the missionary was evangelization not social reform, presenting only "Jesus and him crucified."[15]

By around 1900, mainstream Protestants and their middle class supporters subverted this position; they came to feel that the Gospel could not take root in an unreconstructed society. Arthur Smith's *Chinese Characteristics* (1894) teetered on the brink of this change. Smith had come to China 1872 and worked for a trans- (or non-) national Christianity: "Christ was an Asiatic," he pointed out. Yet, on the other hand, only Christianity, Smith argues in 1894, can make China modern, and Christianity was embodied in what we would call American Middle Class Way of Life. The characteristics Smith notes by "absence" or "indifference" form a virtual checklist of the concepts in which the new middle class defined themselves (time, politeness, cleanliness, nerves, truthfulness).[16]

Henry Luce and other newly arrived young college graduates wanted to bring modern education to the urban middle class, to build a new Chinese nation in which Christianity could then take its proud paternal place. Irwin Hyatt called this new strategy "bourgeois elitism." The Social Gospel of John R. Mott's Student Volunteer Movement caught the imagination of idealistic, world minded young Americans. YMCA physical education, health work, and science campaigns involved young Chinese, especially since the Y was the first mission organization to turn control over to a Chinese, David Z. T. Yui, Harvard '10. Mott's 1913 evangelical tour of China played to packed houses, and Yuan Shikai told Mott that friends of the Y were saying "Confucius would have been a 'Y' man."[17]

The influence of missionaries on policy is frequently debated. Patricia Neils's useful overview concedes that it is "impossible to measure scientifically the impact of American missionaries on U.S. attitudes and policies toward China." James Reid's *The Missionary Mind and American East Asia Policy 1911–1915* opens with the observation that "considered historically, American East Asian policy may be distinguished by its lack of clear-sightedness." While he presents much useful material on the structure of China mission support networks in the U.S. and the ideas that traveled through them, Reid does not show that actual government policy was changed in response to missionary pressure, nor what a "clear-sighted" U.S. policy might have accomplished if missions had not existed. Rather, what emerges is that makers had to explain their policies to a public which took Christian ambitions far more seriously than did the policymakers themselves.[18]

The History of Christianity in China Project, sponsored by the Henry Luce Foundation and directed from 1985–1992 by Daniel Bays, does not start from the "missionary enterprise," an extension of Western history, but focuses on Christianity as a part of Chinese history. This again raises the question of how to draw the line between "Chinese" and "not Chinese." The work of the project covers both international cultural relations and domestic Chinese developments. Sometimes, as in the case of the "Little Flock" and "True Light" movements, independent Christian *churches* repudiated both Chinese government and mission contacts. In other cases, as in Emily Honig's studies of Cora Deng (Deng Yuzhi), a Christianity learned under YWCA auspices led to a lifelong religious orientation to social activism and support of the 1949 Revolution.[19] An imbalance toward Protestants has begun to be redressed with studies of Catholic missions.[20] Jane Hunter's sophisticated study explores the White *woman's* burden, the intertwined but differing Chinese and American feminisms in the spread of the "gospel of gentility."[21]

2. The Diplomacy of Uplift

Diplomacy, from the Macartney Mission of 1793 to the Marshall Mission of 1946, presented itself in terms of power and realism, but, as Andrew Nathan observes, foreign relations must include cultural and economic interactions, since "military and diplomatic responses were shaped by internal cultural and economic concerns."[22] Washington and missionaries talked uplift; Qing diplomats feared American gunboats, indemnities, and extraterritoriality.

Eileen P. Scully is producing a lively debunking of American pretensions, and deftly wielding the tools of gendered analysis. She mines the records of the United States District Court in Shanghai for a "bottom up" view of the whores, gamblers, sharks, and beachcombers who peddled their extraterritorial privileges to Chinese clients who used treaty law to enforce private debt collection. They created a market for "technologies of power" (a phrase drawn from Michel Foucault), the use of which enabled Chinese purchasers to move differently—usually more profitably and exploitatively—within their own society. Chinese collaborators and compradors altered "the balance of power in Confucianism's pivotal relationships" and freed themselves from the "reciprocity clauses of Confucian-based social arrangements." (This seems to idealize Chinese culture as harmonious and whole.) Respectable imperialists attacked these "wayward treaty port Americans" for giving America a bad name, embarrassing America's clients among the Chinese elite, and making it harder to bring China into a profitable market relationship. The lowlife brigade struck back by using Congressional consular reforms to remove judges or diplomats who crossed them.[23]

3. The Business of Uplift

Traders, entrepreneurs, investors, and salesmen also saw themselves in cultural terms. One advertising executive explained that during the Great War he had learned the necessity of "selling" America to the world, showing the nations that we were "warring against war; that we sought no aggrandizement of territory; that what we desired was the destruction of arbitrary power and the reign of law based on the consent of the governed—that and nothing more."[24]

Sherman Cochran, *Big Business in China: Sino-foreign Rivalry in the Cigarette Industry, 1890–1930* [25] is an exemplary study of the rivalry between the British-American Tobacco Company (BAT), an early multinational conglomerate, and the Chinese-owned Nanyang Brothers Tobacco Company. Under the American tycoon James Duke, BAT showed that the China market was not always a myth; the company fabricated a multicultural network of compradors, agents, shopkeepers, and peasants, all but the last of whom prospered. Polemics pit "imperialism" against "economic nationalism," but Cochran tests these generalizations category by category, finding a complex picture of foreign and Chinese interaction rather than one-sided exploitation. Commercial rivalry built a market for nicotine addiction which surpassed the market for Christianity.

There is still room for studies of individuals, enterprises, and new professions which spread the American Dream while making a fortune. An ambiguous spirit haunts Alice Tisdale Hobart's *Oil For the Lamps of China*; the frustration of the hero, based on Hobart's own husband, a sales executive for Standard Oil, reflects her serious attempt to deal with China's messy and menacing revolutionary nationalism. Less reflective was the advertising pioneer Carl Crow, best remembered for his *400 Million Customers* but also the author of many books which presented China to Americans. Jerry Israel's insightful essay notes that "Crow's China had no misery, wretchedness, poverty or . . . revolution." Crow thought of himself as a "friendly democratic American, not as a privileged, threatening white." He looked for 'Four Hundred Million Customers,' but perhaps found 'Four Hundred Million Number One Boys.'" Israel claims Crow "created many household images Americans held about the Chinese," but again we see no proof or examples.[26]

Nationalism and the Sinification of Progress

The American Raj was marked by the self-conscious, often self-deluding attempt to indigenize, to educate Chinese "interpreters." In 1912 the young

John Leighton Stuart attended the new Provisional National Assembly in Nanking and reported that 90 percent of the assemblymen were Western educated and 25 percent were professing Christians. Having heard such accounts, the President of the Remington Typewriter Company wrote the State Department to ask "now that China has become a Christian country, how soon will it be before English becomes the national language?"[27]

But in the 1920s the Raj was redefined by Chinese revolutionary nationalism, British withdrawal, Japanese expansionism, and competition from the Bolsheviks. The thoughtful began to doubt that a modern China could look just like Kansas City after all. Sun Yat-sen complained that the United States had abandoned progressive China: "America was the inspiration and example when we started the revolution to abolish autocracy and corruption in high places," but when he came back to power again in Canton, fifteen American gunboats parked off the Shameen to enforce payment of customs as indemnities. "In the twelfth year of our struggle toward liberty, there comes not a Lafayette but an American Admiral."[28]

Much recent scholarship has dealt with this rethinking of politics, culture, and history. Nicholas R. Clifford asks: was Shanghai an "imperialist parasite" or "China's future"? Clifford exposes Shanghailanders by showing them in action, or rather obstructive nonaction, opposing not only emerging Chinese nationalism but also the realistic British Foreign Office policy of accommodation with the new Nanking Government. He paints the Shanghai Mind as a "particularly unpleasant and inefficient combination of bigotry and narrowness of vision."[29] James Huskey describes the common class interests between middle-class Chinese and foreign "cosmopolitan" businessmen in Shanghai which unified them against the "parochials" on either side. He concludes that the new configuration was a "fundamental transformation from the old culture of colonialism to the beginning of an equalitarian relationship between Chinese and foreign businessmen."[30]

Unlike Shanghailanders described by Clifford, liberal missionaries tended to support Chinese nationalism, which they saw in the sense of patriotic unity, not as radical nationalism in the sense of anti-foreignism. On the Chinese side, Jessie Gregory Lutz shows significant differences between the two anti-Christian movements that followed May Fourth. The 1920–1922 Anti-Christian Movement derided religion in general; Christianity and Buddhism were equally superstitious. The Movement to Restore Educational Rights of 1924–1928, however, was used by both the Nationalists and the Communists during the May 30th Movement and Northern Expedition to recruit for their organizations and express hard-shell anti-imperialism.[31]

In March 1927, Northern Expedition soldiers looted Nanking University and shot its Vice President when he refused to give up his gold watch. Lutz sees this "Incident" as another dramatic turning point for foreigners. It was not exactly the Chinese equivalent of the Sepoy Mutiny of 1857—actual casualties were not high, only six foreigners, compared to dozens of demonstrating Chinese killed in the Shanghai May 30, 1925 Incident and incidents at Shakee and Wanhsien—but a "shadow of the Boxer Rebellion influenced the perceptions of many." Gunboats under consular orders quickly drained the Yangtze Valley of missionaries.

The reaction at home was strong: contributions to missions had already been falling, and recruitment slackened off, with 1926 numbers only half of 1920. By July, only 500 of 8,000 Protestant missionaries remained at their posts and never recovered their original number. Negative stereotypes of the missionary among Americans came to the fore at this point. Lutz confirms Dorothy Borg's judgment that Shanghailanders' calls for big stick diplomacy only influenced Washington *against* intervention.[32]

Political nationalism now defined and policed boundaries of cultural Chineseness; for Christians, this politicization created and enforced a choice between religion and nation. Dealing with Chinese nationalism in the jaws of Japanese militarism was a major concern. Frank Rawlinson became a key mediator in Protestant mission thought as he built the Shanghai *Chinese Recorder* into the main forum for debate on how to grapple with Chinese nationalism. A "topical biography" by his son, John Lang Rawlinson, does not make broad theoretical claims but gives a rich day-by-day account of a central life and writings. Rawlinson saw no problem in supporting Chinese national unity, especially against Japanese imperialism. Tragically, but aptly symbolic, Rawlinson was killed on a Shanghai street in 1937 by a Japanese bomb.[33]

Curiously, the only other full-dress scholarly biography of a twentieth-century American missionary is of John Leighton Stuart, discussed below. We do have John Hersey's well-researched *The Call*, a novel cast in the form of journal and biography, with footnotes. The hero, David Treadup—an apt name—is based on six actual missionaries who ran the Social Gospel *cursus honoris*, including Roscoe Hersey (the author's father), Fletcher S. Brockman, Lewis Gilbert, and Hugh W. Hubbard. John Fairbank called the book an "epitaph for 120 years of Protestant missions in China. . . . the great American experience of semicolonialism," which was a "fine thing if you can get it, as we could, without a sense of guilt for having set it up." Treadup's crisis of faith at the end of the novel and the eve of the 1949 revolution does face up to the guilt. Like so many others in the Raj, he found that he was too "Chinese" to fit back into America but not Chinese enough for the Revolution.[34]

John S. Service renders another filial boon in editing his mother's charming, shrewd memoirs of family life and Y activity in Chengtu. The epigraph quotes Sherwood Eddy, another of John Mott's recruits: "in our missionary purpose there was never any thought of a harsh dogmatism, of forcing our religion down the throats of an unwilling people," and there were "no ideas of a narrow orthodoxy of 'perishing millions' who were eternally lost." Service himself recalls that when he visited Yen'an, the Communist leader Chen Yi greeted him enthusiastically as the son of his old Y English teacher! The implicit argument is that the Student Volunteer Movement and the YMCA fit into China's long revolution.[35]

A rosier nostalgia is conjured up by John Espey's memoir of Shanghai mission life. On a visit to the U.S., his sister plaintively asked their mother when they were going "home"—to China. The tales are exotic, droll, sometimes instructive of the implicit racism of the situation: Young Master Espey and his sister taught a table boy raw from the village to speak English and to embody what they saw as the "true nature" of China—looking authentically inscrutable and moving about in "the Oriental glide for which Chinese servants have ever more been justly world-famous." He defects to a richer family, explaining: "But my two dear friends, surely you know that an English-speaking table boy is paid at least three times as much as a Chinese-speaking one?" These musings do not bite into the colonial situation as does J. G. Ballard's autobiographical *Empire of the Sun*[36] but perhaps I underestimate Espey's ironic Presbyterian guile: "The more I think of it," he remarks, "the more I realize how essentially responsible my sister and I were for making Oozong conscious of the habits of his own race, for making him, indeed, really Chinese. Without us, he would probably never have known the true qualities of his own nationality."[37]

The neglect of Pearl S. Buck is strange but being redressed (a major biography is forthcoming). Cardinal in the phenomenon of "the United States and China," Buck is not discussed in any of the four editions of John Fairbank's book by that name; *The Good Earth*, the American Raj's answer to Kipling's *Kim*, appears only in the bibliography of its 1948 edition. Buck's life and work were the subject of a 1992 symposium on the centennial of her birth at her alma mater, Randolph-Macon Women's College. In the conference keynote address, James C. Thomson, Jr., recalled the Nanking University enclave of his youth and the place of "Aunt Pearl" in it. He remarks that she "remains the most influential Westerner to write about China since thirteenth century Marco Polo"—without, again, being able to specify what that influence was. *The Good Earth* was written while Buck lived only a few hundred miles from Mao's Autumn Harvest Uprisings and was married to the world's leading agronomist of China. In my contribution to the symposium, I argued that the book rejects both progressive reform and class revolution in favor of an Orientalist view of the Chinese farmer (not "peasant") as autonomous and eternal.[38]

The influence of *The Good Earth* is related to the influence of travel writing; like "natives" pictured in the *National Geographic*, Wang Lung and O-lan became "comfortable strangers."[39] There is a dauntingly technical but valuable literature of critical studies approaches to travel and travel writing. Especially suggestive is Peter Bishop, *The Myth of Shangri-la: Tibet, Travel Writing and the Western Creation of Sacred Landscape*. Starting from the proposition that in "one sense, landscape does not exist," and that we "inescapably shape the world, even if only with our minds and not our hands," Bishop traces the transformation of Tibet in Western writings from a "geographically grounded sacred place to a placeless utopia."[40] Arthur Waldron's *The Great Wall* includes a look at tourists who fell for the whopper that The Wall was the only human structure visible from space but still wanted to see it close up.[41]

Much remains to be written on the American military; its interactions with Chinese counterparts, impact on Chinese and American public perceptions, and shaping of later doctrine could well be explored. Dennis L. Noble, *The Eagle and the Dragon: The United States Military in China, 1901–1937* is a useful starting point, based on English language secondary works and archives, with extensive bibliographical notes.[42]

The Open Door Raj, based on cultural ideals, was proud of the thirteen Protestant and three Catholic universities and the many thousands of primary and secondary schools. But Marianne Bastid, in a recent study of foreign educational practices and systems in China, echoes the ever present ambivalence: was Chinese adoption of Western education and professional training "servitude or liberation?"[43] Yenching University and Peking Union Medical College were developed in the 1910s as capstone institutions for mission networks begun fifty years earlier; the move from the village to the capital was a change both in geographical location and social strategy.

Yenching was transformed under John Leighton Stuart, the mission counterpart of BAT's James Duke. Shaw Yu-ming's biographical critique portrays Stuart as the doyen of the Raj: "the most genuine and rock-solid representative of Christian, Western, and American civilizations." Born in Hangchow in 1876 to missionary parents, Stuart noted later that it would be "difficult to exaggerate the aversion" he felt to the evangelistic work he had seen his father perform ("haranguing crowds of idle, curious people in street chapels or temple fairs, selling tracts for almost nothing. . . .") or burying himself in a Chinese village. Shaw explores Stuart's affinity with Woodrow Wilson, who heard Stuart preach in Washington during World War I; the President reported he was moved by "the most amazing and inspiring vision" of a "great sleeping nation suddenly cried awake by the voice of Christ." Stuart collaborated with Wu Lei-ch'uan and Chao Tzu-chen in developing a liberal, post-mission Christology with Chinese characteristics. This accommodation got him into hot water stateside, but his Sino-American network, which raised money both in China and North America, developed a university acceptable for China's new professionals and patriotic middle class.[44]

William Hung, a self-styled "latter day Confucian" and a Christian, joined Stuart as Dean at Yenching to pursue what Philip West called a "cosmopolitan ideal." He appropriated Western scholarly techniques for the Harvard-Yenching Sinological Index Series (his native Fukienese "*yin-dek*" (Mandarin *yinde*) became the Chinese term for "index"). Others were less fortunate in cultural cross-breeding; returned students and Western-trained faculty were called intellectual compradors with a reputation for social snobbery and dead intellectual aping of their foreign masters. The daughter of one Yenching sociologist recalls the museum-like re-creation of American middle-class life in their faculty house, complete with violin lessons and doilies on the dining room table.[45]

The educator, poet, and politico Tao Xingzhi, seen as a disciple of John Dewey, is a key example of an American returned student who stopped wearing a Western suit and tie in favor of Chinese clothes. Hubert O. Brown's firm and imaginative study finds that Tao actually took no courses at Columbia from Dewey, and that there is "nowhere in Tao's vast bibliography any sort of systematic discussion of Dewey's educational thought," of which Tao sometimes showed a "profound misunderstanding." Tao fought "two dead educations," one traditional Chinese, the other the uncreative importation of American models. Tao did identify with American Progressivism, and he championed a wide range of teaching reforms, such as kindergartens, creative dramatics, and "little teachers." But his most important achievement was the "associative living" school in a village outside Nanking, which drew on Dewey, but more on Wang Yangming and James Yen.[46]

Many studies deal with developing professions and the production of knowledge which would be both modern and authentically Chinese.[47] Mary Brown Bullock's *An American Transplant: the Rockefeller Foundation and The Peking Union Medical College* examines the attempt to provide a "Johns Hopkins for China." The Rockefeller Foundation aimed to replace both outmoded missionary medicine (which one adviser accused of serving only the "coolie constituency") and traditional Chinese practice. The metaphor in Bullock's title suggests incompatibility between two cultural organisms, but her complex story is the eventual, almost inadvertent contribution of elitist, professionalized, medicine to the Chinese Revolution: the "actual issues are not impact but *adaptation*, not response but *assimilation*" (xix). Bullock indeed lays out the populist and nationalist charges: the untoward side effects of professionalization even in America, where it reduced the number of women and black doctors; the false hybrid "Chinesey" architecture of the PUMC building; the elitist curriculum, taught in English (the library's first purchase was 50,000 German language monographs); the charge that the foundation was a tool of the exploitative "Oil King"; the 1926–1949 total of only 324 graduates for a country of hundreds of millions. But a "clear pattern of sinification" shows that PUMC graduates turned quickly to Chinese problems. The "medical Bolshevik" John Grant championed state medicine; his students C. C. Chen and Marion Yang both raised professional standards and spread their work to the villages. As J. D. Rockefeller, Jr. asked after the Communist takeover of PUMC, "who are we to say that this may not be the Lord's way of achieving the intent of the founders?"[48]

By the 1930s, although most college and universities in China did not offer PhD study, and had to rely on foreign doctoral programs (an enduring feature of Chinese higher education), most academic disciplines developed the national societies, journals, undergraduate programs, and the turf wars and personal feuds that define professional maturity; they were also attacked as foreign and elitist.

American money and Chinese autonomy pushed and pulled in the development of an "Anglo-American oriented social science establishment." Chiang Yung-chen's "Social Engineering and the Social Sciences in China, 1898–1949" (PhD thesis, Harvard University, 1986) is a case study of the "production of knowledge, academic entrepreneurship, and philanthropy" in a cross-cultural setting. The study argues that the "modern notion of social engineering" is a "reincarnation of traditional Confucian elitism." Chiang makes shrewd use of the Rockefeller and other archives to catch the personalities, bureaucratic rivalries, and research strategies in Fei's Xiaotong's Sociology Department at Yenching, Franklin Ho's Institute of Economics at Nankai, and Chen Hanseng's "radical Marxist" agrarian research enterprise at the Academia Sinica and the Institute of Pacific Relations.[49] Randall Stross skeptically dissects American and American-trained Chinese professional agriculturalists, most notably John Loessing Buck and Shen Tsung-han, who only gradually and fitfully progressed towards a farm science suited to China.[50]

Two 1990 monographs deal with those dilemmas that inhabit the Sino-American frontier of culture and diplomacy—urban elitism vs. village populism, professional values vs. indigenous tradition—choices the cultural politics of nationalism cast as imperialism vs. patriotism, American vs. Chinese.

My own *To the People: James Yen and Village China* analyzes Yen as a "trans-Pacific liberal." Yeh Wen-hsin's *The Alienated Academy: Culture and Politics in Republican China, 1919–1937* examines the educational cultures of government and private (mainly Christian) colleges, dealing primarily with domestic events, not foreign relations. Yet even Yeh notes that many of her own governing assumptions were dictated by the "powerful insights" of Joseph R. Levenson on Westernization and consequent "deracination" of new intellectuals, professionals, financiers, industrialists, engineers, and other members of the new intellectual elite. But her fascinating case-by-case examination of the various academic cultures portrays a more complex picture, with neither a single set of urban institutions in higher education nor an "unequivocal process toward Westernization."[51]

James Yen (Yan Yangchu) was not formed by the May Fourth attack on culture; Chinese culture *was* what Chinese *did*. Like Mao Zedong (his almost exact contemporary) Yen started with a foreign doctrine that had to be taken away from urban intellectuals to produce practical village results. C. C. Ch'en's village health work used graduates from Yen's People's Schools to invent a system of "de-professionalized" health care; Qu Junong theorized a People's Education; Xiong Fuxi created an influential People's Theater; Franklin C. H. Lee (Li Jinghan) led an innovative rural survey, which also recorded *yang ko*; government, private banks, and village leaders built economic cooperatives. Taken as a whole, this was one possible "sinification of liberalism."

Warren I. Cohen, *East Asian Art and American Culture* is an imaginative, suggestive examination of how study of Asian art took professional form in the twentieth century and affected how Americans saw Asia. Cohen draws productive parallels with the making of foreign policy; money, personality, and contingency count as much as abstract "culture." Some scholars and dealers were bandits, looting Chinese art for profit; others were genuine and creative in developing cultural relations based on intellectual equality and mutual benefit. However, unlike the situations in medicine or sociology, foreign trained Chinese PhD's did not establish professional art history in China before the war.[52]

The "Revolution Paradigm" and Losing China

By the 1930s, Chinese government nationalism pre-empted the Raj in China; Japan's "Asia for the Asiatics" campaign spelled the end of white man's empire; and, most important, Mao's China loomed. The professional foreign correspondent and area specialist were getting set to oust the missionary, traveler, and treaty port resident as China definers and culture mediators; the new professionals forged new keywords, ideas, and historical narratives to re-represent revolutionary China (some of the disregard for Pearl Buck as an amateur and a woman springs from this adversarial relation with new professionals). Pearl Buck, Carl Crow, Ida Pruitt, and Walter Judd, each continued to speak for China through the 1940s; they were important, in ways we still have not worked out, in defining a picture of poor little China and big bad Japan.[53] But it was Pearl Harbor and not Pearl Buck that drew the U.S. into the Pacific War.

The problems of defining China culturally and dealing with it politically were intertwined—the politics of representation and the representation of politics. Mutual perceptions or "images" are a starting point. A recent survey of Western images of China defined an "image" as "a view or perception" which holds "sufficient priority with the viewer to impinge upon the consciousness." John Fairbank objected that "images" thus include "practically everything written, said, or visually represented about China"; "what we call fact and what we call opinion are inextricably mixed together" in "the "ultimate television mentality."[54] Moreover, "image" too easily implies that there is a rock-like "reality" against which the image is to be tested, or that the shortcomings of any image can be corrected by adding more facts.

The Institute of Pacific Relations (IPR) provides a key view of the drive to professionalize—regularize, justify, and theorize—the production of knowledge about Asia by getting it into the hands of experts armed with social "science" tools. Founded at a Honolulu conference in 1925, the IPR was also an example of YMCA devolution from the ministerial to the professional. Edward Carter, for instance, had been recruited from Harvard by John R. Mott, worked for the Y in India and World War I France, and then joined The Inquiry, a Y front group working on American racial and labor problems. We have some scholarly studies of (and shelves of writings by) Owen Lattimore, Karl Wittfogel, Chen Hansheng, Fred Field, E. H. Norman, T. A. Bisson, but not a full-dress life and hard times of the organization.[55] John K. Fairbank, a minor actor in the early years of the IPR, became central in professionalizing both journalistic and academic China knowledge; he has received due attention, not least from himself. Paul Evans's biographical study concludes that Fairbank's historical vision was of a "titanic clash of civilizations, each with its own traditions, aims, and means" which could only be mitigated when the two sides developed historical perspective.[56]

In the 1920s and 1930s China journalists had likewise begun to professionalize. The younger generation implicitly pushed aside the spokespeople of the Raj by being more professional, offering a China based on regularized theory. Thomas Millard, founder of the *China Weekly Review*, had been an "adventurer, a romantic, a muckracker, and a progressive," in the words of Mordechai Rozanski. But J. B. Powell, Millard's successor, is described by his son Bill as both a ringleader of the "Missouri mafia" and a concerned professional who raised the standards of Shanghai journalism. Of the fifty Missouri School of Journalism graduates who visited China, Powell enticed thirty to stay on. The *Weekly Review* became a politically involved but not partisan outlet, with eventually more than half of its readers being Chinese.[57] Edgar Snow, Agnes Smedley, and Anna Louise Strong are honored in Beijing with a "Three S Society" and in North America by respectful biographies.[58]

They are also charged with foisting a "revolution paradigm" on Americans or providing "validation" of Mao from the outside.[59] Early in the 1980s, Stephen MacKinnon organized a conference *cum* reunion for some forty surviving wartime China correspondents and diplomats to assess their experience and achievements. John Fairbank challenged the self-congratulatory mood: "from the point of view of history, this reunion should be a wake. The American experience in China [during the 1940s] was a first-class disaster for the American people . . . . It's perfectly plain that we all tried, but we failed . . . . We could not educate or illuminate or inform the American people or the American leadership in such a way that we could modify the outcome . . . ." Correspondents disagreed; as one said, "we did a pretty goddamn good job."

The biggest obstacle, they contended, was not their own ignorance, linguistically impaired reliance on interpreters, detachment from peasant China, Nationalist censorship, or gatekeeping editors at home, but the parochiality of a Great American Public more concerned with the mishaps of any hometown boy than the fate of any Chinese city. The story that got the most play at home during the war concerned the clever Chinese in Chungking who could make eggs stand on their small ends during the Lunar New Year![60]

My attempt to join the linguistic *turnverein*, "The Storm Over the Peasant: Orientalism, Rhetoric, and Representation in Modern China," tries to explain the process in which Orientalist China of the Raj is replaced by progressive, revolutionary China. It uses keyword, metaphor, and story as more specific and manageable than "image." The keyword "peasant" is hard to find in American writing about China before the 1920s; the man with the hoe was a "farmer," as in F. H. King's 1911 *Farmers of Forty Centuries* ("peasant" doesn't appear in *The Good Earth*). "Peasant" drives out "farmer" by the mid-thirties. This change was, I argued, part of a re-construing of the "Orientalist" story of

China—unique, exotic, and autonomous country populated by farmers, fights progress—into the liberal progressive story—feudal land of peasants looks forward to 1789. Theodore White opens Chapter One of *Thunder Out of China* (1946) with "the Chinese peasant was born in the middle ages to die in the twentieth century."[61]

Snow, Belden, and White did not invent the revolution paradigm, in which traditional China suddenly became retrospectively feudal, but they were taken up into it in the same way as were many Chinese. How this reconstruing process affected American public perceptions and policy formation is yet to be explored; but surely, as remarked by John Fairbank in the quote above, the inability of journalists and diplomats to communicate to the stateside audience has to do with the incompatible paradigms they used.

The 1940s was what Akira Iriye called a decade of "de-Americanization." By 1945, China and the United States were "on the brink of disaster" marked by an "abysmal lack of reciprocity and mutual respect."[62] In India, for better or for worse, the British Raj would leave the framework of a modern nation. In China, the American Raj left little, except perhaps the cultural opening for a brief Soviet Raj. As late as 1949, the American Secretary of State, Dean Acheson, wrote that American efforts to save China from violent and destructive revolution were in vain because World War II had "destroyed the emerging middle class which historically has been the backbone and heart of liberalism and democracy." When Ambassador John Leighton Stuart, now labeled a "cultural imperialist," left China, Mao Zedong wrote the epitaph:

> Leighton Stuart is a symbol of the complete defeat of U. S. policy of aggression. Leighton Stuart is an American born in China; he has fairly wide social connections and spent many years running missionary schools in China; he once sat in a Japanese gaol during the War of Resistance; he used to pretend to love both the United States and China and was able to deceive quite a number of Chinese.

Stuart was rightly called the "forgotten Ambassador," whose political influence in Washington was about the same as in China—none.[63]

The real lost chance or lost China (if not the lost horizon) was a Shangri-la middle-class liberal kingdom, the China in American minds.

NOTES

1. In addition to Hunt, Making of a Special Relationship (below): Albert Feuerwerker, "The Foreign Presence in China," *Cambridge History of China* (Cambridge University Press 1983) Volume 12, Part I, 128–207. For comparative thoughts, see Michael Adas, *Machines*

as the Measure of Men: Science, Technology, and Ideologies of Western Dominance (Ithaca: Cornell University Press, 1989); Patricia Nelson Limerick, *The Legacy of Conquest: The Unbroken Past of the American West* (New York: Norton, 1987).

2. Cf. Ivor Lewis, *Sahibs, Nabobs, and Box Wallahs: A Dictionary of the Words of Anglo-India* (New Delhi: Oxford University Press, 1993).

3. Macaulay, "Minute on Education (1835)," reprinted in *Sources of Indian Tradition* (New York: Columbia University Press 1958), quote at p. 45 and p. 49; Francis Hutchins, *The Illusion of Permanence: British Imperialism in India* (Princeton: Princeton University Press, 1967). Other cultural studies include: Lewis Wurgraft, *The Imperial Imagination: Magic and Myth in Kipling's India* (Middletown, Connecticut: Wesleyan University Press, 1983); Gauri Viswanathan, *Masks of Conquest: Literary Study and British Rule in India* (New York: Columbia University Press, 1989).

4. See "Essay on the Historical Literature," in Michael H. Hunt, *Ideology and U. S. Policy* (New Haven: Yale University Press, 1987); Michael H. Hunt, "Ideology," (pp. 193–201), and Akira Iriye, "Culture and International History," (pp. 214–225), in Michael J. Hogan and Thomas G. Paterson, eds., *Explaining the History of American Foreign Relations* (Cambridge: Cambridge University Press, 1991). For a psychological-anthropological concept of culture, see Michael Harris Bond, editor, *The Psychology of the Chinese People* (Hong Kong: Oxford University Press 1986), with an extensive bibliography of works in English and Chinese, 296–351; *Beyond the Chinese Face: Insights from Psychology* (Hong Kong: Oxford University Press, 1991); Zhongdang Pan, Steven H. Chaffee, Godwin C. Chu, and Yanan Ju, *To See Ourselves: Comparing Traditional Chinese and American Cultural Values* (Boulder: Westview Press, 1994).

5. Judith B. Farquhar and James L. Hevia, in "Culture and Postwar American Historiography of China," *positions* 1, no. 2 (Fall 1993): 486–525, criticize as "essentialist" the use of "culture" to explain Chinese characteristics as uniform and predictable which are actually political and contingent.

6. Akira Iriye, "Americanization of East Asia: Writings on Cultural Affairs Since 1900," in Warren I. Cohen, ed. *New Frontiers in American-East Asian Relations* (New York: Columbia University Press, 1983), 45—75, quote on p. 45, quoting from his "The 1920s," in Ernest May and James C. Thomson. Jr., *American-East Asian Relations: A Survey* (Harvard University Press, 1972), 242.

7. Michael H. Hunt, *The Making of A Special Relationship: The United States and China to 1914* (New York: Columbia University Press, 1983).

8. Akira Iriye, *Power and Culture: The Japanese American War, 1941–1945* (Cambridge: Harvard University Press, 1981), 132. I have sketched my view of this "Transpacific Liberalism" in *To The People: James Yen and Village China* (New York: Columbia University Press, 1990), xi-xii.

9. See, for instance, Gyan Prakash, "Writing Post-Orientalist Third World Histories of the Third World: Perspectives from Indian Historiography," *Comparative Studies in Society and History* 32, no. 2 (April 1990): 382–408; Patrick Williams and Laura Christman, eds., *Colonial Discourse and Post-Colonial Theory* (New York: Columbia University Press, 1994).

10. Partha Chatterji, Nationalist Thought in the Postcolonial World: A Derivative Discourse (Delhi: Oxford University Press, 1986), and *The Nation and Its Fragments: Colonial and Postcolonial Histories* (Princeton: Princeton University Press, 1993; 282 pp.). Kwame Anthony Appiah, *In My Father's House: Africa in the Philosophy of Culture* (Oxford: Oxford University Press, 1992); Henry Louis Gates, Jr., editor, *"Race," Writing, and Difference* (Chicago: University of Chicago Press, 1986); Dominick LaCapra, editor, *The Bounds of Race: Perspectives on Hegemony and Resistance* (Ithaca: Cornell University Press, 1991).

11. Edward Said, *Culture and Imperialism* (New York: Knopf, 1993); Zhang Longxi's "The Myth of the Other: China in the Eyes of the West," *Critical Inquiry* 15 (Autumn 1988): 108–131 fears that Foucault & Co. will treat all Western writing as essentially the same.

12. "The Contested Past: The Boxers as History and Myth," *Journal of Asian Studies* 51, no. 1 (1992): 82–113, quotes at p. 107.

13. Douglas R. Reynolds, *China, 1898–1912: The Xinzheng Revolution and Japan* (Cambridge: Council on East Asian Studies, Harvard University, distributed by Harvard University Press, 1993).

14. Cf the list of scholarly concerns in Jia Qingguo, "Between Sentiment and Reason: The Study of Sino-American Relations in China," in Priscilla Roberts, ed., *Sino-American Relations Since 1900* (Hong Kong: Centre of Asian Studies, Hong Kong University, 1991), 17–37.

15. William R. Hutchison, *Errand to the World: American Protestant Thought and Foreign Missions* (Chicago: University of Chicago Press, 1987). Bob [sic] Whyte, *Unfinished Encounter: China and Christianity* (London: Harper-Collins, 1988) is a thoughtful Marxist survey, including ample references.

16. Charles W. Hayford, "Chinese and American Characteristics: Arthur H. Smith and the Respectable Middle Class View of China," in Suzanne Barnett and J. K. Fairbank, eds., *Christianity in China: Early Missionary Writings* (Cambridge: Harvard University, Committee on East Asian Studies 1985).

17. Hayford, *To The People*, 66, 19, 41–42. The Y campaigns are dramatized in John Hersey's *The Call* (New York: Knopf, 1985).

18. Introduction, Neils, ed., *United States Attitudes and Policies Toward China: The Impact of American Missionaries* (Armonk, New York: M. E. Sharpe, 1990), 19. Neils also provides a useful bibliographical essay. James Reid, *The Missionary Mind and American East Asia Policy 1911–1915* (Cambridge: Council on East Asian Studies, Harvard University, distributed by Harvard University Press, 1983), quote at p. 1. Also, Robert Crunden, *Ministers of Reform: The Progressives' Achievement in American Civilization, 1889–1920* (New York: Basic Books, 1982), Ch. 8, "A Presbyterian Foreign Policy."

19. Daniel H. Bays, ed., *Christianity and China, The Eighteenth Century to the Present: Essays in Religious and Social Change* (Stanford: Stanford University Press, forthcoming).

20. Thomas Breslin, *China, American Catholicism, and the Missionary* (University Park: Penn State University Press, 1980); Jean Paul Wiest, *Maryknoll in China: A History, 1918–1955* (Armonk, New York: M. E. Sharpe, 1988). Jonathan Spence, *The Memory Palace of Matteo Ricci* (New York: Knopf, 1984) views Christianity as new but not culturally incompatible with Chinese values, while Jacques Gernet, *China and the Christian Impact* (Cambridge: Cambridge University Press, 1985) sees innate and fundamental incompatibilities. Erik Zrcher, in *Bouddhisme, Christianisme, et societe chinoise* (Paris: 1990), emphasizes politics, particularly the insistence on papal jurisdiction, over culture.

21. Jane Hunter, *The Gospel of Gentility: American Women Missionaries in Turn-of-the-Century China* (New Haven: Yale University Press 1984); Marjorie King, "Exporting Femininity Not Feminism: Nineteenth Century American Women Missionary Women's Efforts to Emancipate Chinese Women," in Leslie Flemming, ed., *Women's Work for Women* (Boulder: Westview Press, 1989).

22. "Implications for Foreign Relations of Some Recent Trends in the Western Historiography of Republican China," (AAS Convention, Boston, April, 1987; revised version of paper prepared for Second International Conference on Sinology, December 1986, Academia Sinica, Taiwan), 2.

23. Eileen P. Scully, "Taking the Low Road to Sino-American Relations," *Journal of American History* (forthcoming) drawing on her "Crime, Punishment, and Empire: The

United States District Court for China, 1906–1943" (PhD Dissertation, History Department, Georgetown University, 1993).

24. Charles W. Hart, *Foreign Advertising Methods* (New York: De Bower, 1928), xii. The book, dedicated to Herbert Hoover, includes chapters on "Advertising in the Orient" and "Movies and Missionaries" as good ways of moving the goods.

25. Sherman Cochran, *Big Business in China: Sino-foreign Rivalry in the Cigarette Industry, 1890–1930* (Cambridge: Harvard University Press, 1980).

26. Jerry Israel, "Carl Crow, Edgar Snow, and Shifting American Journalistic Perceptions of China," in Jonathan Goldstein, Jerry Israel, and Hilary Conroy, eds., *America Views China: American Images of China Then and Now* (Bethlehem: Lehigh University Press; London and Toronto: Associated University Presses, 1991), with an Introduction by Hilary Conroy and Suggested Readings by Jonathan Goldstein, 148–168, quote at p. 153. In the same volume, also Sandra Hawley, "The Importance of Being Charlie Chan," is sensible and informative on a touchy subject.

27. Yu-ming Shaw, *An American Missionary in China: John Leighton Stuart and Chinese-American Relations* (Cambridge: Harvard University Press, 1992), 30; Hayford, *To the People*, xi, 58, 19.

28. To Fletcher Brockman of the YMCA, *New York Times* (July 22, 1923), quoted in Hayford, *To the People*, 61.

29. *Spoilt Children of Empire: Westerners in Shanghai and the Chinese Revolution of the 1920s* (Hanover and London: Middlebury College Press, 1991), 240, and "A Revolution is Not a Tea Party: The Shanghai Mind(s) Reconsidered," *Pacific Historical Review* 59 (November 1990): 501–526.

30. "The Cosmopolitan Connection: Americans and Chinese in Shanghai During the Interwar Years," *Diplomatic History* 11 (Summer 1987): 227–242. There is an important commentary, "On Social History, the State, and Foreign Relations," by Michael Hunt and Charles R. Lilley, 243–250.

31. Lutz, *Chinese Politics and Christian Missions: The Anti-Christian Movements of 1920–28* (Notre Dame, Indiana: Cross Cultural Publications, 1988). Also, Yip Ka-che, *Religion, Nationalism, and Chinese Students. The Anti-Christian Movement of 1922–1927* (Bellingham, WA: 1980); Liao Kuang-sheng, *Antiforeignism and Modernization in China, 1860–1980: Linkage Between Domestic Politics and Foreign Policy* (Hong Kong: rev. ed., The Chinese University Press, 1984).

32. Lutz, 232–245. Buck is quoted on the Incident at p. 235. Hersey, *The Call*, graphically portrays the Incident, while Richard McKenna, who served on a Yangtze gunboat a few years later, re-creates the incident in *Sandpebbles* (New York: Harper, 1954).

33. Rawlinson, *The Recorder, and China's Revolution: A Topical Biography of Frank Joseph Rawlinson, 1871–1937* (Notre Dame, Indiana: Cross Cultural Publications, Book One, Book Two, 1990). Also Rawlinson: "Frank Rawlinson, China Missionary, 1902–1937: Veteran Deputationist," in Neils, ed., *United States Policies and Attitudes Toward China*, 111–132; The Recorder is now carefully indexed: Kathleen Lodwick, *The Chinese Recorder Index: A Guide to Christian Missions in Asia, 1867–1941* (Wilmington, Delaware: Scholarly Resources, Inc., 1986).

34. Hershey, *The Call*; reviews by John Fairbank, "Mission Impossible," *New York Review* (May 30, 1985): 17–18 and Jonathan Spence, "Emissary in the East," *New Republic* (May 13, 1985): 28–30 (quote on p. 17).

35. Grace [Boggs] Service, *Golden Inches: The China Memoir of Grace Service* (Berkeley: University of California Press, 1989), quote at n. 9.

36. J. G. Ballard, *Empire of the Sun* (New York: Simon and Schuster, 1984).

37. John Espey, *Minor Heresies, Major Departures: A China Mission Boyhood* (Berkeley, Los Angeles, Oxford: University of California Press, 1994), consisting of "all the chapters I wish to preserve from *Minor Heresies, Tales Out of School* and *The Other City*." Quotes from pp. 92–94.

38. James C. Thomson, Jr., "Pearl S. Buck and the American Quest for China," and Hayford, "The Good Earth, Revolution, and the American Raj in China," in Elizabeth J. Lipscomb, Frances E. Webb, and Peter Conn, eds., *The Several Worlds of Pearl S. Buck: Essays Presented at a Centennial Symposium, Randolph-Macon Woman's College, March 26–28, 1992* (Greenwood Press, 1994). There are also serious but partial studies: Paul A. Doyle, *Pearl S. Buck* (New York: Twayne, revised edition, 1980) reports the writings; Nora Stirling, *Pearl Buck: A Woman in Conflict* (Piscatawney, New York: New Century, 1983), is shrewd about the person but uninformed about both China and the American context; Michael Hunt, "Pearl Buck—Popular Expert on China, 1931–1949," *Modern China* 3, no. 1 (January 1977): 33–64; Stross, *The Stubborn Earth* has an illuminating chapter on J. L. (Mr. Pearl) Buck; Hutchison, *Errand to the World* treats her role in "re-thinking missions"; John Dower, *War Without Mercy: Race and Power in the Pacific War* (New York: Pantheon, 1986) describes her activities with Eleanor Roosevelt to fight racism during World War II. Prof. Peter Conn of the University of Pennsylvania has finished *The Woman Who Invented China: A Cultural Biography of Pearl S. Buck*.

39. The phrase is from Catherine Lutz and Jane L. Collins, *Reading National Geographic* (Chicago and London: University of Chicago Press, 1993).

40. Peter Bishop, *The Myth of Shangri-la: Tibet, Travel Writing and the Western Creation of Sacred Landscape* (Berkeley: University of California Press, 1989), 1, ix; Mary B. Campbell, *The Witness and the Other World: Exotic European Travel Writing, 400–1600* (Ithaca: Cornell University Press, 1988); Mary Louise Pratt, *Imperial Eyes: Travel Writing and Transculturation* (London and New York: Routledge, 1992); David Spurr, *The Rhetoric of Empire: Colonial Discourse in Journalism, Travel Writing, and Imperial Administration* (Durham: Duke University Press, 1993).

41. Arthur Waldron, *The Great Wall* (Cambridge University Press, 1989).

42. Dennis L. Noble, *The Eagle and the Dragon: The United States Military in China, 1901–1937* (Westport, Conn.: Greenwood Press, 1990). Also: Frederick Wakeman, "American Police Advisers and the Nationalist Chinese Secret Service, 1930–1937," *Modern China* 18, no. 2 (April 1992); Gu Xuejia, "PRC Historiography on Chennault and the Flying Tigers During the Anti-Japanese War," in Roberts, ed., *Sino-American Relations Since 1900*, 284–295; Michael Schaller, *Douglas MacArthur: The Far Eastern General* (Oxford: Oxford University Press, 1989); Bernard D. Cole, *Gunboats and Marines: The United States Navy in China, 1925–1928* (London: Association of University Presses, 1983); John N. Hart, *The Making of an Army "Old China Hand": A Memoir of Colonel David B. Barrett* (Berkeley: Institute of East Asian Studies, 1985); Robert W. Barnett, *Wandering Knights: China Legacies, Lived and Recalled* (Armonk, New York: M. E. Sharpe, 1990).

43. In Ruth Hayhoe and Marianne Bastid, eds., *China's Education and the Industrialized World: Studies in Cultural Transfer* (Armonk, New York: M. E. Sharpe, 1987), which also includes: Delia Davin, "Imperialism and Diffusion of Liberal Thought: British Influence on Chinese Education"; Ruth Hayhoe, "Past and Present in China's Educational Relations with the Industrialized World"; and a "Select Bibliography of Chinese Education and its International Relations." Ruth Hayhoe "A Chinese Puzzle," *Comparative Education Review* 33, no. 2 (May 1989): 155–175, relates cultural theory to comparative education.

44. Shaw, *An American Missionary in China: John Leighton Stuart and Chinese-American Relations*, quotes at pp. 311, 33–37.

45. Susan Chan Egan, *A Latter Day Confucian: Reminiscences of William Hung* (1893–1980) (Cambridge: Council on East Asian Studies, Harvard University, 1987). Philip West, *Yenching University and Sino-Western Relations, 1916–1952* (Cambridge: Harvard University Press, 1976); Catherine [Yang] Wei, *Second Daughter* (Boston: Little, Brown, 1985), describing her father, Cato Young (Yang K'ai-tao); Hayford, *To the People*, 56, 123. Another insightful autobiography is Chih Meng [Meng Zhi], *Chinese-American Understanding: A Sixty-Year Search* (New York: China Institute in America, 1981).

46. "American Progressivism in China: The Case of Tao Xingzhi," in Hayhoe and Bastid, eds., *China's Education and the Industrialized World*, 120–138, quotes at p. 126. Tao is treated extensively in Hayford, *To The People*.

47. For the growth of the professions and professional education, with extensive bibliographical references, see E-tu Zen Sun, "The Growth of the Academic Community 1912–1949" *Cambridge History of China*, Volume 13, *Republican China*, Part 2 (Cambridge: Cambridge University Press, 1986): 361–420.

48. Mary Brown Bullock, *An American Transplant: the Rockefeller Foundation and The Peking Union Medical College* (Berkeley: University of California Press, 1980); quote at p. 209. Also: C. C. Chen [Chen Zhiqian], M. D. , in collaboration with Frederica M. Bunge, *Medicine in Rural China: A Personal Account* (Berkeley: University of California Press, 1989); AnElissa Lucas, *Chinese Medical Modernization: Comparative Policy Continuities, 1930s-1980s* (Praeger, 1982); Dr. G. H. Choa, *"Heal the Sick": The Protestant Medical Missionaries in China* (Shatin, N. T., Hong Kong: The Chinese University Press, 1990); Karen Minden, *Bamboo Stone; The Evolution of a Chinese Medical Elite* (Toronto: University of Toronto Press, 1994); Laurence Schneider, "The Rockefeller Foundation, the China Foundation, and the Development of Modern Science in China," *Social Science and Medicine*," 16 (1982): 1217–1221, and "Using the Rockefeller Archives for Research on Modern Chinese Natural Science," *Chinese Science* 7 (December 1986): 25–31, available from the Archive Center (15 Dayton Avenue, Pocantico Hills, North Tarrytown NY 10591–1598); Frank A. Ninkovich, "The Rockefeller Foundation, China, and Cultural Change," *Journal of American History* 70, no. 4 (March 1984); James Reardon-Anderson, *The Study of Change: Chemistry in China, 1840–1949* (Cambridge: Cambridge University Press, 1991).

49. Also, R. David Arkush, *Fei Xiaotong and Sociology in Revolutionary China* (Cambridge: John K. Fairbank East Research Center, Harvard University Press, 1981); Georges-Marie Schmutz, *La sociologie de la Chine: matriaux pour une histoire, 1748–1989* (Berlin: Peter Lang, 1993); Leo Douw, "Chinese Rural Sociology in the 30s: On the Acculturation of Social Scientists' Political Attitudes," in Kurt Werner Radtke and Tony Saich, eds., *China's Modernisation: Westernization and Acculturation* (Stuttgart: Franz Steiner Verlag, 1993), 83–109; Michael Hsin-huang Hsiao, "From Europe to North America: The Development of Sociology in Twentieth Century China," in David S. Goodman, ed., *China and the West: Ideas and Activists* (Manchester: Manchester University Press, 1990): 130–146.

50. Randall Stross, *The Stubborn Earth: American Agriculturalists on Chinese Soil, 1898–1937* (Berkeley: University of California Press, 1986).

51. Yeh Wen-hsin, *The Alienated Academy: Culture and Politics in Republican China, 1919–1937* (Cambridge: Council on East Asian Studies, Harvard University Press, 1990), quotes at pp. xii-xiii; Hayford, *To the People*. Jonathan Spence reviewed them together in the *New York Review* (August 1991), reprinted in *Chinese Roundabout: Essays in History and Culture* (New York: Norton, 1992), 259–276, which includes "Gamble in China," on Sydney Gamble's career and photographs of 1920s China.

52. Warren I. Cohen, *East Asian Art and American Culture* (New York: Columbia Uni-

versity Press, 1992). For the professionalization of archeology, see Kwang-chih Chang, *The Archeology of Ancient China* (New Haven: Yale University Press, 4th edition, 1986), 4–21.

53. Marjorie King, "Ida Pruitt: Heir and Critic of American Missionary Reforms Efforts in China," pp. 133–148; Tony Ladd, "Mission to Capitol Hill: A Study of the Impact of Missionary Idealism on the Congressional Career of Walter H. Judd," pp. 263–283, both in Neils, *United States Attitudes and Policies*; Lee Edwards, *Missionary for Freedom: The Life and Times of Walter Judd* (New York: Paragon House, 1990).

54. "Review," of Colin Mackerras, Western Images of China (Hong Kong: Oxford University Press, 1989) *China Quarterly* 123 (September 1990): 559–561, quote at p. 561.

55. Hayford, *To the People*, 69–71 & 252 n. 22; Paul Hooper, *Elusive Destiny: The Internationalist Movement in Hawaii* (Honolulu: University of Hawaii Press, 1980) and "The Institute of Pacific Relations and the Origins of Asian and Pacific Studies," *Pacific Affairs* 41 (Spring 1988): 67–92; William Holland, "Source Materials on the Institute of Pacific Relations," *Pacific Affairs* 58, no. 1 (Spring 1985): 91–97; John B. Condliffe, "Reminiscences of the Institute of Pacific Relations," (Institute of Asian Research, University of British Columbia, 1981); Frederick V. Field, *From Right to Left: An Autobiography* (Westport, Conn.: Lawrence Hill, 1983); Fairbank, *China Bound*, esp. 322–324; Chiang Yung-chen, "Social Engineering and the Social Sciences," ch. 4; James Cotton, *Asian Frontier Nationalism: Owen Lattimore and the American Policy Debate* (Manchester: Manchester University Press, 1989); Owen Lattimore, compiled by Fujiko Isono, *China Memoirs: Chiang Kai-shek and the War Against Japan* (Tokyo: University of Tokyo Press, 1991; distributed by Columbia University Press); Robert P. Newman, *Owen Lattimore and the "Loss" of China* (Berkeley: University of California Press, 1992). John Thomas, *Institute of Pacific Relations* (Seattle: University of Washington Press, 1974) is limited to the IPR experience under McCarthyism.

56. Paul Evans, *John Fairbank and the American Understanding of Modern China* (New York and Oxford: Basil Blackwell, 1988), quote at pp. 324–329; John K. Fairbank, *China Bound: A Fifty-year Memoir* (New York: Harper & Row, 1982).

57. See below, MacKinnon and Friesen, 23–26.

58. Tracy B. Strong and Helene Keyssar, Right in Her Soul: The Life of Anna Louise Strong. (Random House 1984); Jan and Steven MacKinnon, *Agnes Smedley: The Life and Times of an American Radical* (University of California 1988); Harold R. Isaacs, *Re-Encounters in China: Notes of a Journey in a Time Capsule* (Armonk, New York: M. E. Sharpe, 1985). A. Tom Grunfeld, as part of his project on the pre-war "Friends of China," edited and annotated Milly Bennett, *On Her Own: Journalistic Adventures from San Francisco to the Chinese Revolution, 1917–1927* (Armonk, New York: M. E. Sharpe, 1993).

59. Ramon H. Myers and Thomas A. Metzger, "Sinological Shadows: The State of Modern Chinese Studies in the United States" *Washington Quarterly* (Spring 1980): 87–114; David Apter and Tony Saich, *Revolutionary Discourse in Mao's Republic* (Cambridge: Harvard University Press, 1994), 90, 354 n. 36; Jonathan Mirsky, "Message from Mao," *New York Review* February 16, 1989, 15–17, review of John Maxwell Hamilton, *Edgar Snow: A Biography* (Bloomington: Indiana University Press, 1988). Also, Jerry Israel, " 'Mao's Mr. America': Edgar Snow's Images of China," *Pacific Historical Review* 47 (February 1978): 107–121, partially incorporated in his article in Goldstein et. al., eds., *America Views China*.

60. Stephen R. MacKinnon and Oris Friesen, *China Reporting: An Oral History of American Journalism in the 1930s and 1940s* (Berkeley: University of California Press, 1987), 184, 4, 123.

61. Hayford, "The Storm Over the Peasant," (forthcoming). The "linguistic turn" is briefly introduced and usefully weighed in JoAnne Brown, *The Definition of Profession: The*

Authority of Metaphor in the History of Intelligence Testing, 1890–1930 (Princeton: Princeton University Press, 1992).

62. Steven I. Levine, "On the Brink of Disaster: China and the United States in 1945," in Harry Harding and Yuan Ming, eds., *Sino-American Relations, 1945–1995—A Joint Reassessment of a Critical Decade* (Wilmington: Scholarly Resources, 1989): 3–13.

63. Dean Acheson, "Letter of Transmittal," *United States Relations with China . . .* (Department of State, Washington D. C. 1949), vi; Mao, "Farewell, Leighton Stuart!" *Selected Works* (Peking: Foreign Languages Press, 1969), 4: 433–440; Lawrence Kessler, "Review," *China Review International* 1, no. 1 (Spring 1994): 243–247; Kenneth W. Rea and John C. Brewer, eds., *The Forgotten Ambassador: The Reports of John Leighton Stuart, 1946–1949* (Boulder: Westview Press, 1981); John C. Brewer and Kenneth W. Rea, "Dr. John Leighton Stuart and U. S. Policy Toward China, 1946–1949," pp. 230–244, and Edmund S. Wehrle, "John Leighton Stuart's Role in the Marshall Negotiations: The Kalgan Crisis," pp. 245–262, both in Neils, ed., *United States Attitudes and Policies.*

Chapter Seven

Chinese-American Relations in Comparative Perspective, 1900–1949

William C. Kirby

The definition and periodization of historical fields are always problematic. "Sino-American relations" may or may not be a distinct subspecies of modern international relations, a bilateral relationship with distinguishing (even "special") features of political, cultural, and economic relations. This has long enough been the subject of popular and academic dispute. What is clear is that the historical study of this relationship has become an important academic concern on both sides of the Pacific: first in the United States and Taiwan, and most recently in the People's Republic. What is not immediately clear, at least to an outsider to the field, is why that should be the case for much of the period under review in this essay. The years from 1900 to 1949 do not constitute a clear-cut "era" of Chinese-American relations. For the large part of this period, Sino-American relations were nowhere near the center of attention of the political leadership of either China or the United States. There were few apparent continuities over these decades, apart from the fact that a few American troops arrived in China at the beginning of this period and many more were leaving at the end of it. But perhaps that is the point: the final years of this period witnessed a state-led revolution of the foreign relations of both China and the United States, the clearest manifestation of which was the Chinese-American alliance from 1942 to 1945. One casualty of this was a historical Chinese-American relationship dominated by spheres of cultural and economic interaction in which governments had played a minor role.

One way to approach the history, historiography, and research agendas of this period of Chinese-American relations is to place them in some comparative perspective. As a historian of modern China, I might contribute best to this discussion in three ways: by offering a narrative overview of what appears to have distinguished the American role in China's foreign relations in these years, compared to that of other nations; to review the general state of the larger field of Chinese foreign relations as well as of Sino-American relations; and to suggest, from the perspective of modern Chinese historical studies, prospects for new research that might contribute to our understanding of Chinese-American relations.

1. Overview of the Period[1]

There are important reasons why the alliance between China and the United States in World War II has dominated scholarship on Sino-American relations. For the United States, entry in the Pacific War began three decades of military and political conflict in East Asia, and embroiled this country in Chinese political struggles in a manner that continues today. All this was (and is) a subject of intense domestic political debate, and there is a strong domestic orientation in the historical concerns of American scholarship on Chinese-American relations of the 1940s. This is one explanation for the near-total reliance by American historians on American source materials to write the history of that alliance.[2]

The centrality of the alliance for China is equally clear. Most important, it permitted the survival of a Chinese nation-state that had only begun to be organized at the beginning of this century. It also brought China into global political systems in an unprecedented manner. For China, which had no experience as an "ally," in the modern military-diplomatic sense of the term, the alliance ushered in twenty years in which it sought security and economic development in close association with what would later be called "superpowers"—first the United States and then the Soviet Union. But in Chinese scholarship as in American scholarship, it is the *internal* political ramifications of Chinese-American relations that have garnered—and continue to attract—the most attention.[3]

Missing in much of the literature is a historical and comparative sense of the distinguishing features of this alliance and above all of the bilateral relationship which it altered fundamentally. The alliance was—it is seldom enough recalled—a shotgun marriage, born of sudden necessity, not the culmination of a long-term relationship. It was a strategic alliance to resist a common enemy, with little basis for cooperation beyond that. Although the strategic objective, Japan's defeat, would be attained, the alliance came to be resented by both sides: by a United States divided at home about its entanglement in Chinese domestic politics; by a Chinese Nationalist regime that grew dependent domestically as well as internationally on its powerful ally; and by the Communist opponents of the Nationalists, who resisted the continuation of American influence in China after the anti-Japanese alliance had served its purpose.

Before the 1940s, despite significant levels of Sino-American contact in the private sphere, there was no infrastructure of cooperation between governments. This had to be erected hastily and in the absence of a treaty of alliance spelling out mutual objectives and responsibilities. Unlike the cases of other significant relationships between China and foreign powers—for example, the cases of Sino-Soviet, Sino-German, and even Sino-Japanese relations[4]— there was very little experience in either mutual cooperation or conflict at the government level.

If there had ever existed a "special relationship" between the Chinese and American peoples, the disinterested observer of the 1920s or 1930s would never have said the same of their governments. Chinese-American political relations were correct and, within limits, friendly. However, the United States was content to follow Great Britain's lead and maintain a united front of the powers in dealing with issues such as treaty revision. Although in 1932 the United States took the lead in articulating the "nonrecognition" of Japanese conquests in Manchuria, for the next six years thereafter U.S. policy was driven by conceptions of limited American interests and power in East Asia and a desire to avoid antagonizing the region's main power, Japan. Particularly during the years 1934–37, the United States took pains to avoid even the appearance of assisting China, responding in a most submissive fashion to Japan's opposition to international cooperation with China.[5]

In this period there were few political or personal links between Washington and Nanjing. It was not America that the new Nationalist government admired or emulated after its formation in 1927. Regarding China's apparent ideological proclivities in the 1930s, it was not with praise that American sources in China discussed the growth of "fascism à la Chine." Nor did the United States follow the example of several European countries by deepening trade and other links through the large number of foreign advisers serving in various official capacities in Chinese governments. On the contrary, the State Department declined to associate the United States with American advisers in China, and rejected Chinese requests for a mission of aviation instructors. One result of this was that the United States, unlike either Germany or the Soviet Union, began the period of its closest partnership with China without experience in managing an official or quasi-official advisory effort in China. The sudden, large-scale U.S. military presence in China had no foundation upon which to build, and began without any real definition of its role.

The Chinese government believed that U.S. public opinion was more sympathetic to China than was the U.S. government. But what did it matter? If Chiang Kai-shek hoped to gain more than sympathy by forcing the fight against Japan in August 1937 to the Shanghai area, within range of American cameras, he was terribly mistaken. U.S. public opinion did not become interventionist, and in any event U.S. policy did not change. A neutralist United States declined invitations to mediate the Sino-Japanese war, pursued a passive diplomacy at the Brussels Conference, and refused to let Japanese brutalities, even the Nanjing Massacre, alter basic policy.

Cultural exchanges between China and the United States certainly far surpassed in scope those between China and any other nation in this period. But they had no obvious effect upon cooperation between governments. The activities of U.S.-funded educational institutions played an important part in the explosive growth of Chinese higher education in this period, while the majority of Chinese who went abroad to study went to the United States. American educational models could be found in a range of private Chinese and Sino-foreign institutions, bringing along with them such innovations as for-profit night schools and extracurricular sports.[6] Unlike the case of the smaller but more focused German cultural effort in China, however, these activities were not directed toward areas of mutual national interest or toward the creation of specific constituencies in government. And when the Chinese government sought external models for the reform of higher education, it was from European, not American models that it drew its inspiration.

American economic interests in China also offered little basis for cooperation between governments. For much of the period under review, the United States stood in second or third position among China's trading partners. But this trade was statistically of marginal importance to both economies.[7] More to the point, for the most part it was—unlike Sino-German or even Sino-Soviet trade, for example—of marginal importance to both governments, seldom involving commodities of strategic significance to either side. From the perspective of the two governments in the mid-1930s, the most important item traded was silver, but high-level disputes, not cooperation, marked Sino-American negotiations on the silver question.[8] In the same period, the U.S. frequently turned down Chinese requests for government-to-government loans. The one exception to the officially negative American rule on credit to China, the Cotton and Wheat Loan of 1933, was defended as a means of exporting otherwise unsalable goods.

U.S. investment in China reached its high point in 1930 and then declined steadily during the period of China's most intensive pursuit of foreign investment. Most such investment took place where Chinese governments least wanted it, under extraterritorial privilege. Very little went for manufacturing enterprises, and few of these took place in sectors given high priority by Chinese economic planners (an exception being the role of American firms in the electrical manufacturing industry).[9] For its part the U.S. government did little to promote Sino-American economic cooperation. Americans seeking to do business in China were granted little of the home-government support, such as investment guarantees, enjoyed by their European competitors.

The best-known Sino-American economic joint venture during this period did not prove to be a model for bilateral cooperation. The China National Aviation Corporation, a joint enterprise between Curtiss Wright Co. (and later Pan American) on the one hand, and the Chinese Ministry of Communications on the other, was founded as a civilian carrier in 1930. Adhering to the letter but ignoring the spirit of the 1929 Chinese joint venture law, C.N.A.C. was managed by the American side as if it were a wholly owned subsidiary. It never served as a vehicle for technology transfer. The status of equipment provided by the U.S. side was a source of constant dispute; and throughout the company's existence there occurred only the most limited training of Chinese pilots, navigators and mechanics. Worse, the Chinese government discovered that its majority ownership of the firm meant little when American pilots, being "neutrals," refused to fly during the early months of the Sino-Japanese war. The perceived failure of this Sino-American approach to joint ventures gave birth to an alternative model: limiting the foreign role to technical assistance in state-owned Chinese enterprises. This became the dominant form of Sino-foreign economic joint ventures under both Nationalist and Communist rule.[10]

China became important to American policymakers *only* when their strategic assessment of Japan's intentions and abilities changed after 1938 and as the East Asian struggle became linked diplomatically with the European theater, which was Washington's central focus of concern. Perhaps if it had been possible to limit cooperation to the main area of common interest—the military struggle against Japan—the wartime Sino-American alliance might have worked to greater mutual satisfaction. But the propaganda and myth-making dictated by the war—some of which came to be believed by policy-makers—obscured the limited degree to which the interests of the United States and China ran parallel.

Franklin Roosevelt's ambitions for a united, liberal China whose foreign policy would be pro-American as a matter of reflex bore no resemblance to any Chinese government. His desire to treat China as a "great power" was one reason why the U.S. relinquished its extraterritorial rights in China in 1943. The policies by which the Chinese government expected to *attain* great power status, however, were often in opposition to American interests. Its postwar plans called for state-led, military-industrial development in an increasingly "socialized" (*shehuihua*) economy, in which foreign and Chinese capital would be channeled to the needs of the state. Paradoxically, it was in support of "private enterprise" in China that the U.S. government finally became interventionist in commercial matters. The difficult negotiations (1943–46) for a commercial accord to succeed the old treaty system revealed the size of the gap between Chinese and American interests. By the end of the Second World War—before the complications of Chinese civil war—it was clear enough that the prospects for postwar Chinese-American cooperation were not good.[11]

To conclude this survey: Sino-American relations for most of the first half of the century were without major bilateral conflicts of the kind found, for example, in Sino-British, Sino-Soviet or (especially) Sino-Japanese ties. Nor had there been an experience of intense cooperation at the official level, as was the case in Sino-German and (in two periods) Sino-Soviet relations. Before the late 1930s the relationship was simply not of central significance to either side. Non-state cooperative activity by Chinese and American individ-uals and institutions certainly stood at a high level. But one lesson of this peri-od is that such non-state intercultural or economic activity does *not* auto-matically strengthen official relations.[12]

By the end of the war, the most dynamic sectors of Chinese-American relations—non-state cultural and economic interaction—had, in any event, become "officialized," and thereby fundamentally transformed. The State Department's new Division of Cultural Relations began operations in China;[13] Chinese students and trainees sent to the U.S. were chosen in the context of the "war production" effort;[14] and economic relations became, for the duration of the war, a matter between governments. After the war, with extraterritoriality gone and the Chinese government in a position to enforce its authority on what one may term the internal frontiers of Chinese foreign relations, Chinese laws began to govern and increasingly restrict the activities of Americans in China. They still do.

2. States of the Field

If the above overview of Chinese-American relations is even remotely accurate, it is no accident that the most influential recent work in the history of Chinese foreign relations does not centrally concern the United States, at least for the period before 1940. Similarly, it is not by chance that much of the best new work in Chinese-American relations has focussed on cultural and economic ties. Although, as we shall see, there has been significant work in diplomatic history, both the larger field of China's foreign relations and the subfield of American-Chinese relations are distinguished by an emphasis on a broadly conceived "international" history.

Modern China's Foreign Relations

Distinctions between the study of the foreign policies of states and the foreign relations between peoples, including their governments (that is, between diplomatic and international history), have long been implicit in studies of modern China. Indeed, it is striking how small has been the influence in China studies of the "realist" school of foreign relations, which treats states as rational actors pursuing permanent interests and emphasizes the *Primat der Außenpolitik* as an organizing principle. The history of the Opium War, for example, has never been written as a contest purely of power politics between the British government and the Qing court; indeed it is incomprehensible without reference to the economic interests of unsavory opium traders and their Chinese networks—the "non-state actors" (to use more recent academic language) who were protagonists in that drama. Similarly, historians have recognized that in the latter part of the nineteenth century, the formal diplomatic agenda between China and foreign powers was determined in good measure by the impact of the unofficial but often problematic foreign relations resulting from the settlement of Europeans in China and Chinese in North America.

The most influential modern historians of China's foreign relations have thus viewed foreign policy as but one aspect of their subject.[15] In the West, they have generally not inclined toward highly theoretical approaches based on international relations theory, in either its Anglo-American or continental manifestations.[16] In China as in the rest of the former Eastern bloc, on the contrary, one theoretical approach has been most influential: the Marxist-Leninist-Stalinist tradition, which integrates the study of social, economic, and military forces by stressing the economic and class dimensions of foreign relations. Thus an "imperialist" West, so defined by the dominance of "state-monopoly capitalism," may confront a "semi-feudal" China, and give rise *inter alia* to a dependent, "compradore" bourgeoisie. In China, the "imperial-ism" model descended from Lenin dominated until recently the debate on all forms of Sino-foreign interaction—wars, trade, and "open doors." Not a few Chinese social scientists still define China's historical *and* contemporary for-eign relations with capitalist countries in terms of conceptions of "imperial-ism."[17] However, the pathbreaking work of Wang Xi, now carried forward by a new generation of Chinese scholars of Sino-American relations and even of CCP history, has introduced a new, archival-based empiricism that has chal-lenged inherited orthodoxies.[18]

In strong contrast to the Marxist tradition is an antimaterialist methodol-ogy, in vogue in the West in the past two decades, that places foreign relations within a broader matrix of international communication, and emphasizes the cultural construction of foreign policy through the study of how nations per-ceive each other. Here the role of "images," "perceptions," "belief systems," and "cognitive maps" is central, and the diplomatic historian becomes cognitive psychologist. As important as the interests and actions of other nation-states is the "set of lenses" through which information about them is viewed.[19] This approach is applied compellingly by Youli Sun in his revisionist account of China's "appeasement" diplomacy during its search for anti-Japanese alliances in the 1930s. Sun emphasizes the cultural construction of Chinese foreign policy. In Sun's study, "imperialism" remains the central conception around which Chinese foreign policy is conceived, but it proves an evolving term with alternative cultural and intellectual definitions.[20]

The importance of a multitextured approach to foreign relations (includ-ing foreign policy) is nowhere more important than in the study of Sino-Japanese relations, at once the most influential and most complicated of China's international relationships. The domestic aspects of China's Japan policy in the 1930s and the evolving role of "public opinion" in policy debate and formulation are at the heart of Parks Coble's finely crafted study.[21] Don-ald Jordan emphasizes how economic disputes, particularly Chinese boycotts, worked (and were manipulated) in a rapidly changing political and emotion-al climate to push China and Japan further toward political and military con-frontation in the early 1930s. If it is now taken for granted that economic sanctions do not work, or work very poorly, as a diplomatic instrument in international relations, this is in no small measure because of the failure of international sanctions to impede Japanese expansion in China in the 1930s. Jordan takes the treatment of sanctions a step further by asking: did Chinese economic sanctions against Japan, in the form of the boycotts of 1931–32, not only fail to deter Japanese aggression but in fact help to bring it about in the first place? Although the boycotts had more psychological than economic impact on Japan, Jordan's suggestion that China was co-responsible for the struggles that took place on its soil in 1931–32 is enough to ensure that this book will be the subject of heated discussion.[22]

A methodologically inclusive approach may be seen in Akira Iriye's masterful volume of essays on Chinese-Japanese relations in the nineteenth and twentieth centuries. Iriye divides the study chronologically and thematically into three periods where relations were defined primarily, he argues, in terms of "power," "culture," and "economics." Readers may be surprised that Iriye finds that "culture" primarily defined this relationship during the Republican era. His point is to demonstrate that the political and military relations that culminated in the slaughter of the eight-year Sino-Japanese war are inexplicable without reference to cultural and intellectual transformations in both China and Japan. Certainly it is only in the context of Iriye's rich, textured narrative, in which Chinese-Japanese relations are part of a global tapestry, that one can begin to think of the invasion of Manchuria and the rape of Nanking as "cultural" phenomena.[23]

All this does not mean there is no room for, or good work done, in the study of China's foreign *political* relations, in which one may note several trends. In the history of power politics, there is now greater respect for the overall performance of Chinese governments in the dangerous international environments of the first half of the twentieth century. The diplomacy of the Nationalist government of the 1930s and 1940s has been the latest to undergo a form of historiographical rehabilitation. It was, after all, the first Chinese government to enter into modern international political alignments of any significance. Its successive alignments or alliances with three of the world's most powerful nations (Germany, the Soviet Union and the United States) in order to protect itself against the fourth (Japan), appear as greater achievements as Chinese and foreign documents on these relationships have become available. Certainly the achievements of the Nationalist regime in international economic policy—ranging from the regaining of tariff autonomy to the end of extraterritoriality to the first Sino-foreign economic joint ventures acceptable to Chinese economic nationalism—have long been underappreciated in Western historiography, though the proceedings of two recent conferences may begin to redress that.[24]

Revisionist themes in diplomatic history of a more traditional sort are evident also in the first major scholarly study of wartime (i.e. 1937–45) Sino-Soviet relations, by John W. Garver. Chiang Kai-shek emerges from Garver's pages as a shrewdly opportunistic negotiator whose diplomatic successes were out of any proportion to his effective military power. His success in obtaining significant Soviet material assistance in 1937–39, in regaining Xinjiang from Soviet influence in 1943, and in using the U.S. to pressure Moscow into countenancing China as a "great power" in the final stages of the war, are all highlighted in this study, which gives Chiang Kai-shek high marks as an international statesman.[25] Garver's findings have in part been contested by Odd Arne Westad, who suggests overriding, anti-communist, domestic priorities in Chiang's negotiations with Moscow, and by Xiaoyuan Liu's nuanced analysis of Chiang's multiple motivations.[26] (How any of these interpretations will stand up once Soviet materials are fully declassified and available remains an open question.) For one part of the story, at least, Garver's account may be augmented by Andrew D. W. Forbes's fascinating account of struggles for local and provincial control in Xinjiang.[27]

It is possible to write a straight diplomatic history of high calibre, as Garver has done for the war period and as He Jun has written for the prewar years,[28] of Nationalist China's relations with the Soviet Union, because the pattern of Sino-Soviet relations has been one of the unremitting primacy of politics. From the founding of the Soviet state, there was no truly "private" dimension to its foreign relations. The historiography of China's other international relationships has the task, by contrast, of addressing the informal as well as the formal, the internal as well as the international, dimensions of Chinese relations with foreigners.

Here the wide ranging and analytically rigorous study by Jürgen Osterhammel, *China und die Weltgesellschaft*, which focuses on the interplay of economic and political relations, has no equal in any language, though alas, for lack of an English translation, too few readers in the U.S. and Britain.[29] Also stimulating in the realm of comparative cultural and intellectual history is Frank Dikötter's analysis of the construction of modern Chinese racial nationalism.[30] In monographic studies of bilateral relationships, the most interesting contributions to China's "international history" have appeared above all in the realm of cultural studies, as practiced for example in Françoise Kreissler's outstanding study of German cultural activity in China; or in the fundamental contributions of Kuo Heng-yü, Mechthild Leutner, Bettina Gransow and others to an integrated study of Sino-German relations from colonial to contemporary times.[31]

Chinese-American Relations

Although several recent studies add considerably to our knowledge of U.S.-China policy at the beginning and end of the Republican era—the work of Nancy Bernkopf Tucker is particularly notable here[32]—the historiography of Sino-American relations, even more than that of Sino-foreign relations, has come to emphasize the primacy of foreign *relations* over foreign *policy*. The large majority of recent works addresses subjects outside the realm of high politics.

The missionary impulse remains a central theme in Chinese-American relations, even as the history of Christianity in China is being rewritten with a more China-centered perspective. It is striking that academic literature on missionaries seldom takes religious beliefs seriously. This is changing as we begin to see Christianity in China not simply in the context of social-work missions and imperialism, but also as an important *Chinese* religious movement. The work of Joseph Esherick on the origins of the Boxer Rebellion shows how important it is to research indigenous religious traditions;[33] the History of Christianity in China Project, headed by Daniel Bays at the University of Kansas, is the first to record how Christianity, too, found a place among "indigenous" Chinese religions.

Missionary work of a more secular sort is documented by recent works—including novels—revolving around the history of the YMCA in China.[34] Technical missionaries, if one may use that term, are the subject of Randall Stross's research on American agriculturalists in China and (in the tradition of works by James C. Thomson and Peter Buck) on the limits of technological advice in the absence of broader social change.[35] Military advisers and mercenaries—can we consider the euphemism 'military missionaries'?—were cultural go-betweens of another kind. In the field of Sino-American relations, attention has focused almost exclusively on the politics of the Stilwell and Wedemeyer missions of the 1940s, usually with a strongly partisan perspective.[36] The institutional and cultural (as opposed to personal and political) history of these missions remains to be written.[37]

Journalists and academics constituted another (sometimes overlapping) set of intercultural interlopers: interpreters of China for American public opinion. Two recent works on American journalists set out alternative approaches to the topic.[38] *China Reporting* is an oral history based on a conference of journalists, diplomats, and scholars, all of whom could claim direct experience or knowledge of the China reporting scene in the 1930s and 1940s. The book offers readers a form of "mass memoir" of China reporters together with judicious commentary on the part of the editors of these journalists who are not a particularly introspective—not to mention self-critical—lot. One journalist who is more read about than read these days was Agnes Smedley, whose complicated life and times have now been rendered by Stephen and Janice MacKinnon. They treat Smedley as a distinctly "American radical," while describing well the European and Asian political arenas in which this dynamic woman made her career. The appearance of the Smedley biography, Robert Newman's biography of Owen Lattimore, Paul Evans's study of John Fairbank, and Fairbank's own study, with Richard Smith and Martha Coolidge, of his mentor H. B. Morse, may suggest a new market for the study of historical China-watchers[39]

The field of Sino-American studies has been active also in reviewing the history of educational relationships. *Educational Exchanges*, edited by Joyce Kallgren and Denis Simon,[40] contains several important studies of U.S.-China cultural relations over time. Mary Bullock's investigation of Chinese who studied in the U.S. before 1949 places more recent events in historical perspective, arguing that patterns of earlier exchanges provided the foundation for the rapid growth of educational cooperation since 1978. The more detailed (and, with around 50 tables, quantified) study of contemporary exchanges published under the auspices of the U.S. Committee on Scholarly Communication with the People's Republic of China[41] offers but a few pages on earlier times, but will be a valuable source for future historians. The relative importance of cultural and (especially) educational exchanges in the history of Sino-American ties is attested to by the new set of essays edited by Priscilla Roberts, in which these themes are given pride of place and space in a large conference volume.[42]

As a result of this interest in cultural exchanges, scholars of American relations with China have been in the vanguard in writing the history of modern Chinese education. They have described vibrant educational interchange and the remarkable growth and innovation of Chinese institutions of higher learning in a period that permitted young Chinese students to be trained *in China* at the highest international standard.[43] The academic results have been measured discipline-by-discipline: we now have monographic studies of the development of sociology, biology, botany, genetics, chemistry, agronomy, geology, medicine, and economics during the Republican period.[44] The dominance of cultural over diplomatic studies certainly has something to do with academic fashion in the United States, which has put diplomatic historians on the defensive. It may also be the result of a perception that the diplomatic story has been "told," and more than once too often. It has indeed been told, but with one-sided reliance on American source materials. Indeed it is striking to recall that the major works that defined the study of Chinese-American relations in China's Republican era until recent years had to be based on little or no Chinese archival evidence. Works that disagreed on the nature of the pre-1949 Communist movement were united in their inability to use the main collections of Party historical materials in the CCP/PRC Central Archives [*Zhongyang dang'anguan*] or Central Military Commission Archives [*Zhongyang junwei dang'anguan*]. In the few cases before the 1980s in which Chinese diplomatic documents were made available to scholars, it was on a highly selective basis and usually to make a point in an international scholarly/political dispute (as in the never-ending Stilwell controversy).[45]

Since the late 1970s, however, the archive gap has been closing. There has been a revolution in the professional organization and public access of Republican-era archival materials on both sides of the Taiwan Strait. The Second Historical Archives in Nanjing and several major provincial and municipal archives in the PRC, as well as the Academia Historica [*Guoshiguan*] and the Institute of Modern History of the Academia Sinica on Taiwan, have now developed state-of-the-art storage facilities, preservation programs, cataloguing systems, and—most important—a new willingness to retrieve documents for scholarly use.[46] At the same time, Beijing's Central Archives have permitted the publication of volumes of documents on the Chinese Communist movement and on the founding years of the PRC.

The impact of this newfound archival openness on historical studies of twentieth-century China has been stunning, as old fields are revisited and new ones initiated. If ten years ago scholars despaired of gaining any substantial access to Republican archives, the danger today may be of a surfeit of materials, even if full, public access to archives, including their catalogues and finding aids, is still by no means the rule. Certainly few serious research proposals in Republican Chinese history can now omit mention of the multiple archival collections in China and Taiwan that might bear on a topic.[47]

Gradually these developments are also opening new frontiers in the historiography of Chinese-American diplomatic relations of the 1940s. It is now possible to add Chinese Nationalist as well as Chinese Communist documentation to the long-open American materials on this period. So far the biggest impact has been in the study of the external activities of the pre-1949 Chinese Communist Party. The publication of documentary materials from the Beijing Central Archives in such journals as *Dangde wenxian* has permitted Michael Hunt to revise considerably our understanding of the evolution of Chinese Communist foreign policy.[48] In the People's Republic, studies of Communist Party history and of Chinese-American relations have come together through the work of Yang Kuisong and others.[49] In the West, several recent works have gone far toward studying postwar China, its Communist revolution, and its Civil War in a wider global setting.

Making careful use of Chinese materials from Taiwan and the PRC as well as American sources, Xiaoyuan Liu describes an important and heretofore neglected topic, Chinese and American wartime planning for postwar East Asia: the sometimes incoherent, always incomplete, and above all inconsistent conceptions of the postwar order in East Asia held by the victorious allies (China, the United States, and the Soviet Union). Offering a nuanced analysis of Chinese and American decisionmaking processes, Liu paints a detailed, unflattering portrait of the political workings of the Sino-American alliance, and adds texture to our understanding of a relationship that has previously been analyzed primarily in Americano-centric terms of military leadership (Stilwell episode) or political mediation (Hurley, Marshall, etc.).[50]

Odd Arne Westad explores the interaction between great power and domestic Chinese politics in the latter half of the 1940s, discussing the origins of the Chinese Civil War in the context of the international forces that partly shaped it and determined its timing.[51] This is a work that shows how the use of newly available materials, in this case from the Chinese and Soviet sides, can offer fresh perspectives on events, processes, and personalities that have been written about many times before. He shows how both Chinese parties had trouble adjusting their strategies to the emergence of the Cold War, and at the same time how great-power perceptions of developments on Chinese territory exacerbated the mutual suspicions of the Soviet and American leadership. He too establishes the nearly universal ineptitude (at best, limited vision and gross miscalculation) that was the mark of leading policymakers in all four corners, that is, in Chungking, Yenan, Moscow, and Washington.

In fleshing out the international dimensions of the civil war, Westad builds upon, but does not supplant, Steven I. Levine's exceptional study of the CCP victory and Nationalist defeat in Manchuria.[52] Although not based on the most recently available archival materials, Levine's unparalleled control of Chinese (Communist *and* Nationalist), Soviet, and American sources sets the struggle in its regional, national and international settings. In raising again, albeit in a scholarly rather than polemical tone, the old "who lost China?" debate, Levine suggests that a more decisive American involvement in the first postwar years might have allowed the Nationalist government to survive in Manchuria, and, by extension, nationwide. For the civil war, he stresses, was decided in Manchuria, and by conventional warfare. The communist revolution there was not a peasant revolution, but an urban-based political movement that mobilized urban and rural social forces to serve military-political ends. It mobilized its resources better and faster than its Nationalist adversaries, and applied them more intelligently to military strategy. This is a complicated story, splendidly narrated. It is also one of the very few works that straddles scholarly divisions in the field, contributing in an important way to the historiography of both Nationalist and Communist China, not to mention to international history (and all this by a political scientist).

3. Opportunities for Future Research

If the best work discussed above—that of Steven Levine, for example—has any lessons for future work, it is to avoid the tyranny of "field" and "period," and to be conversant both with disciplinary developments and with the central intellectual trends of each "national" field that forms part of an "international" topic.[53] To put it more simply: it is difficult to be a historian of Chinese-American relations without being, at least to some degree, a serious historian of both China and the United States and of modern international relations. New research on the 1940s for example, goes increasingly beyond bilateral, Chinese-American relations to incorporate the dynamic relationships of all relevant international actors. It is multidimensional and multi-archival. It is also shaped increasingly by academic agendas in Chinese historical studies. Looking to the future, it may be useful to speculate on how several new trends in the study of modern China may affect research on its foreign relations.

Continuity and Change Across 1949

The first and perhaps most obvious development is that the political "markers" for twentieth-century Chinese history now matter much less than they used to. The year 1949 has long been the central date for twentieth-century China in a manner that was not unlike the use of 1789 as a dividing point in French and European history. On the Chinese mainland, not only was a New China proclaimed; there was also a new term that went beyond the concept of "revolution," with the cyclical implications of that term (both in Chinese and English). This was "liberation." In China, "liberation" became a synonym for "1949." A few naive Western scholars have used it that way. With less drama, a new era was begun on Taiwan by what was left of the Republic of China, which could hardly glorify its tenure on the mainland. Indeed, as that government redefined success in terms of the provincial economy, it reinforced the idea of a "break" of 1949 by cutting Taiwan's communications with the rest of China for nearly forty years and more thoroughly than the Japanese ever had during their half-century rule of the island.

In the United States in particular, the perception of a mid-century "break" was widened by divisions of labor between academic disciplines that study China; 1949 marked the boundary between history and the allegedly "harder" social sciences. Scholars of pre-1949 China were trained by different mentors, in different methodologies, than their counterparts in "contemporary" fields. Those who study Taiwan were often another category altogether. Until recently, historians of Nationalist China and of the pre-1949 Communist movement have proceeded as separate intellectual efforts, each, in different ways, anticipating the great "transition" of 1949. (For organizational as much as intellectual reasons, this trend is less noticeable in European universities, where even political scientists who study China may be housed in institutes of sinology.)

The strong separation between pre- and post-1949 Chinese history is fading. Scholars have come to terms with the historical limitations of Communist rule on the mainland—which in its recent decade of "reform" has harkened back to many pre-1949 patterns—and with the robust success of the reincarnated Nationalist regime on Taiwan. Scholarship on pre-1949 China has increasingly endeavored to "understand the countercurrents which contended in the Republican period and the diverse legacies that they left."[54] Chinese archival materials of the 1940s and (to some small degree) of the early 1950s have become available at a time when it is possible to interview historical actors. This combination allows for a reassessment of the transition from Nationalist to Communist rule on the Chinese mainland and degrees of continuity or change in different sectors of Chinese life.

The nature of the pre-1949 Nationalist regime, for example, is being reassessed to the degree that it (in scholarship at least) bears resemblance less to interwar European corporatist or fascist experiments than to postwar East Asian developmental states, of which it may be seen as a problematic predecessor.[55] Just how problematic remains to be seen. New work by Julia Strauss,[56] with superb case studies of the Salt Gabelle, the Finance Ministry, the Examination Yuan, and the Foreign Ministry, offers a more detailed view than any previous study on the inner workings of Chinese government bodies during the Republican era. Strauss describes a variety of institutional strategies for creating strong, professional government organizations that sought (with various degrees of success) insulation from political (i.e. party) interference. Her work and that of others[57] may provide the basis for serious comparative work on the political systems of the Nationalist and subsequent Communist regimes.

Several studies currently under way seek to address explicitly issues of continuity and change across 1949 for specific social groups and institutions. A 1994 conference at Harvard University brought together scholars who have worked on both sides of the 1949 divide and both sides of the Taiwan straits to explore what changed, for whom, and for how long during the Chinese upheavals in the middle of our century. What difference, for example, did "liberation" from Guomindang to Communist rule make for Shanghai industrial workers? How was their lot different from industrial workers in Taipei? How were organizations and individuals of former governments incorporated (or not) into the new regimes? How did the leading political parties change under circumstances of victory and defeat? And how do we measure constancy or change in national policy? These are among the questions that the resultant conference volume must address.[58]

What are the implications for the study of foreign relations of this trend to ignore the 1949 boundary? There appear to be several. One is to rethink, as Michael Hunt has done, the external relations of the pre-1949 Chinese Communist Party and of the People's Republic of the early 1950s. If Hunt is right to conceive of the emergence of a specifically Chinese *Communist* foreign policy, one may anticipate patterns of continuity between CCP relations with the Comintern before 1943 and PRC relations with the Eastern bloc after 1949. On another front, any attempt to study "Chinese Nationalist" foreign relations must now take the Taiwan period seriously, and as an integral part of twentieth-century Chinese history. Historians never accorded the study of U.S. relations with Taiwan attention commensurate with the importance of the topic and the availability of source materials on it. The American-ROC relationship from 1950 to 1979 was one of unusually successful collaboration—be it in military, political, economic, or cultural affairs—between the same two governments that had been such unhappy allies in World War II. It may well have been the high point of Chinese-American cooperation in this century. Nancy Bernkopf Tucker's new book is the first to treat this relationship seriously as history.[59]

As noted earlier, American scholars have already begun to research continuities in Sino-American intellectual exchange before and after 1949, with focus on institutions. This is undoubtedly a growth area, not just for the study of universities, foundations, and research institutions but also of ministries and quasi-governmental organizations that have been central to Sino-American exchange. Julia Strauss's work, cited above, contains the first detailed study of the Chinese foreign ministry under Nationalist rule—a cosmopolitan and internationally connected organization that did everything *except* make foreign policy. On the American side, a comparative study of the self-

appointed "leadership" groups that seek periodically to define American policy toward China—from the China-America Council of Commerce and
Industry of the 1940s to the various "national committees" of the present—
would make interesting reading.

Internal Frontiers of Chinese Foreign Relations

The increasing rejection of politically defined "fields" and "periods" has led
also to work that ignores the Party-State centered narratives of Nationalist or
Communist historiography. In political history, Roger Jeans and others have
traced the historical lineage of opposition parties, and argued that the two
"ruling parties" have largely obscured the history of organized alternatives to
one-party dictatorship. The opposite of dictatorship was not, it is suggested,
necessarily "chaos."[60]

Periods and movements that were once derided as "chaotic" and "disunit-
ed" in twentieth-century China are also being reassessed, not the least because
unity, too, has been shown to have had enormous costs. Marie-Claire Bergère
calls the period from 1916 to 1927 (once known as the "warlord period") one
of "spontaneous modernization," as contrasted to the failed attempt at mod-
ernization-from-above that had marked late Qing reforms and Yuan Shikai's
brief rule.[61] Spurred both by the competitive opportunities opened by the
First World War and by the collapse of state authority, Chinese capitalism
emerged as an independent economic and social force in China and—we may
add—as a distinctive variant of capitalism internationally.

The dynamics of this period of economic growth, if one adds the findings
of Thomas J. Rawski, have important implications for the study of foreign
economic relations. Disproving earlier theories of the "stagnation" of the Chinese national economy during the Republican era, Rawski traces a pattern of
sustained economic expansion of the national economy during the period
1912–1937 that was "rooted in the expansion of foreign trade."[62] He shows
how demand for agricultural exports stimulated an already commercial agricultural sector and how a host of changes designed to facilitate foreign trade
had a positive impact on the economy as a whole. Although Bergère suggests
the development of an internationally connected Chinese bourgeoisie was
possible *because* political instability impeded the reestablishment of a strong
state, and Rawski implies that impressive growth occurred *despite* "impotent
governments, internal disorder, and external threats,"[63] for both analyses, the
state was at most a marginal contributor to what Bergère calls an "economic
miracle."[64]

Such work has spurred exciting new research on the cities that were the hubs of economic growth and the central meeting places between Chinese, Americans, and other strangers in the first part of the twentieth century China. The so-called "treaty ports" were the most visible products of China's relative weakness in power relations with the West as well as the breeding grounds of new social classes with international connections. The heyday of the treaty ports was, not coincidentally, the period of Chinese capitalism's (first?) "golden age"; of China's first—and last—independent worker's movement; and of intellectual dynamism and academic institution-building by an intelligentsia not tied to the state. It was here, between the fall of the Qing and the rise of the Nationalist state, that we have the best examples of the world of China's "private" foreign relations. Here was permitted as never before or since independent contact with foreigners and foreign institutions. Here, in China's closest equivalent to European city-states, emerged urban civic cultures (if not quite an independent civil society) with an enlarged "public sphere" and with distinctive political and social institutions.[65] Shanghai—at once an international and a Chinese city—has been a natural focus of new work. In the study of that metropolis alone Elizabeth Perry has reopened the field of labor history, which had lain dormant in the West since the work of Jean Chesneaux; Frederic Wakeman has brought to light the dark, underworld struggles of the police and their adversaries; Emily Honig has investigated migrant culture, Jeffrey Wasserstrom student culture, Wen-hsin Yeh banking culture—all assisted by archival sources that were not open to research just a few years ago.[66]

The international social history of these cities remains to be written. The "sojourners" studied by Wakeman, Yeh and others consist of the Chinese bankers, industrialists, workers, students, journalists, gangsters and prostitutes who gradually came to think of themselves as "Shanghai people." It is not the Shanghai of international sojourners—of businessmen, adventurers and refugees from around the globe—which form the topic of Nicholas Clifford's recent work.[67] But surely it is the history of the *interaction* between these worlds that is the missing story of modern Sino-foreign relations. To take an example from the history of Sino-German relations: Jork Artelt's detailed study of German-ruled Qingdao,[68] an essential contribution ten years ago, will now provide the foundation upon which a multinational, multiarchival urban history of that city can be written.

The international business history of modern China also largely remains to be written. This field offers probably the best entrance into the study of Sino-foreign cooperation and competition. The relative paucity of work on Chinese-American business relations seems unfortunate, not only because of the scope of private American business activity in pre-Communist China but also because the economic archives of both public and private companies (including foreign firms) comprise the largest and most accessible bodies of documentation available to scholars: to the sizeable holdings of the Second Historical Archives, Nanjing, and the Institute of Modern History, Taipei, may now be added the Business History Archive of the Shanghai Academy of Social Sciences.[69] The excitement of the field will be evident to any reader of Sherman Cochran's marvelous account of cutthroat competition in the Chinese match industry, comparing how three firms, of different nationalities and business cultures, sought to light up the Shanghai market.[70]

Another new frontier for the study of Chinese-American relations is surely the field of legal history. The proliferation of domestic and international commercial transactions in modern China, aided by the inauguration of a hierarchical system of modern courts, brought with it a significant growth of litigation, which was further facilitated by a growing body of civil law that would finally be promulgated in the Civil Code of 1929. Although the Code owed much to continental models, British and American influence was notable in commercial law. Chinese lawyers began to be trained in law faculties, preeminent among them the (American-styled) Suzhou University Comparative Law School at Shanghai. All this had particularly striking effects in China's commercial and industrial center, Shanghai, where the coexistence of Chinese, foreign, and Sino-foreign courts added a competitive element in encouraging people to sue each other.[71] The legal interactions of Chinese and Americans under and after extraterritoriality constitute an ongoing and important story in Sino-American relations, but they remain largely unexamined.[72]

Archives

This leads to a final comment on sources. Every historical field is periodically made over by access to new archival material, particularly the type of material that governments, businesses, and private individuals intended to keep secret: what Marc Bloch called "the evidence of witnesses in spite of themselves."[73] We have seen how this process has reinvigorated the study of U.S.-Chinese diplomatic relations in the 1940s and promises to benefit new work on the cultural and business interactions that were the heart of Sino-American relations before 1940. Sino-American relations in the first half of the twentieth century can now be studied from both the Chinese and American perspectives. For pre-1949 China, then, the "archive gap" has closed considerably. The question now is: what will be the state of Chinese historical materials of the years after 1949?

Chinese history—diplomatic and otherwise—did not end in 1949, although most Chinese archives consider that year to be the end-point for historical research. But the quality of scholarship on the post-1949 period, as for the period under review in this essay, will depend in good measure on the quality of source materials, which depends in turn on the further opening of archives. This is not a matter of concern just, or even primarily, for Western scholars. For the present, despite a new PRC archive law and several draft laws on Taiwan,[74] the history of the field seems, unfortunately, to be repeating itself: just when the step-by-step opening of Chinese Republican archives brings the hope that the international imbalance of archival materials will be addressed, even greater imbalance has developed for the years after 1949.[75] American diplomatic materials are largely (if imperfectly) opened through 1963. British Foreign Office documents written on (and in) China are declassified through the year 1964. Those of the German Democratic Republic and its party leadership are catalogued and open through the year 1989 (the happy result of a fallen government); those of the pre-1991 Soviet Union are opening more gradually, but opening nonetheless.[76] But although the large majority of extant Chinese archival material deals with the years after 1949,[77] these documents remain sealed, for all practical purposes. To be sure, the recent, partial publications of CCP "party-historical" and PRC foreign policy documents of 1950s and 1960s can be useful to historians, although as source materials they are highly controlled and selective. But while the archives of the imperialists as well as of the socialist brothers now welcome historians, those of post-1949 China remain, so far at least, solely in the hands of its official historiographers.

Notes

1. This section is based on my essay: "China's Search for a Partner: Relations with Germany, the Soviet Union, and the United States, 1928–42," in Harry Harding, ed., *Patterns of Cooperation in Modern China's Foreign Relations* (in preparation).

2. Thus even now there is no account by an American historian that makes a serious effort to employ the range of accessible Chinese documentation, either as published in Taipei or available in the Second Historical Archives in Nanjing. In this the field is behind that, for example, of Chinese-Soviet relations: see John W. Garver, *Chinese-Soviet Relations, 1937–1945: The Diplomacy of Chinese Nationalism* (Oxford: Oxford University Press, 1988).

3. Cf. Xiang Rong, "Lun menhu kaifang zhengce" [On the open door policy], *Shijie Lishi* no. 5 (1980); *Lun dangdai diguozhuyi* [On contemporary imperialism] (Shanghai: Renmin, 1984). On the domestic Chinese uses of such analysis in policy analysis see the excellent analysis by David Shambaugh, *Beautiful Imperialist: China Perceives America, 1972–1990* (Princeton: Princeton University Press, 1991), 53ff.

4. The most helpful overviews of Sino-American relations in this period remain:

Dorothy Borg, *The United States and the Far Eastern Crisis of 1933–1938* (Cambridge: Harvard University Press, 1964); Warren I. Cohen, *America's Response to China* (New York: Columbia University Press, 1990); Ta-jen Liu, *History of Sino-American Relations,1840–1974* (Taibei: China Academy, 1978); Michael Schaller, *The U,S, Crusade in China, 1938–1945* (New York: Columbia University Press, 1979); Zhang Zhongfu, *Sinian laide Meiguo yuandong waijiao* (U.S. Far Eastern policy in the past four years) (Chongqing, 1941); idem., *Meiguo zhanqiande yuandong waijiao* (U.S. Far Eastern policy before the war) (Chongqing, 1944); and Li Changjiu, ed., *Zhong Mei guanxi erbainian* (200 years of Sino-American relations) (Beijing, 1984). The two best sources on Sino-Soviet relations of this period are: He Jun, "Lun 1929–1939 nian de Zhong Su guanxi" (Sino-Soviet relations, 1929–39), dissertation, Nanjing University, 1986; and John W. Garver, *Chinese-Soviet Relations*. Other general sources include: Tian Peng, *Zhong E bangjiao yanjiu* (Research in Sino-Russian relations) (Shanghai, 1937); and *1931–1945 nian de Zhong Su guanxi* (Sino-Soviet relations, 1931–45) (Beijing, 1957), a Chinese translation of a Soviet volume. Secondary literature on Sino-German relations in this period includes: William C. Kirby, *Germany and Republican China* (Stanford: Stanford University Press, 1984); John P. Fox, *Germany and the Far Eastern Crisis* (New York, 1982); *Deguo zhu Hua guwentuan gongzuo jiyao* (Summary of the work of the German military advisory mission in China) (Taibei: Guofangbu shizhengju, 1969); and Zhang Qiyun, ed., *Zhong De wenhua lunji* (Symposium on Sino-German cultural relations) (Taibei: Wenhua daxue, 1966). On Sino-Japanese relations the integrative essays of Akira Iriye, *China and Japan in the Global Setting* (Cambridge: Harvard University Press, 1993), replace everything else.

5. See Borg, *Far Eastern Crisis*, 1–45, 75–76; Bao Huaguo, *Guoji zhengzhi yu Zhong Ri wenti* (International politics and the Sino-Japanese question) (Shanghai, 1934), 226–53, 297ff.

6. Cf. Wen-hsin Yeh, *The Alienated Academy* (Cambridge: Council on East Asian Studies, Harvard University, 1990).

7. Peter Schran, "The Minor Significance of Commercial Relations between the United States and China, 1850–1931," in Ernest R. May and John K. Fairbank, eds., *America's China Trade in Historical Perspective* (Cambridge: Harvard University Press, 1986), 258.

8. Borg, *Far Eastern Crisis*, 121–137.

9. See Schran, "Commercial Relations," 244, and Mira Wilkins, "The Impact of American Multinational Enterprise on American-Chinese Economic Relations," 1786–1949," in May and Fairbank, *America's China Trade*, 286.

10. See William M. Leary, Jr., *The Dragon's Wings* (Athens, Ga.: University of Georgia Press, 1976); Bodo Weithoff, *Luftwerkehr in China* (Wiesbaden: Harrassowitz, 1975); and Jack C. Young, "Joint Venture and Licensing in Civil Aviation: a Sino-American perspective," *Stanford Journal of International Studies* 15 (1979).

11. See William Kirby, "Planning Postwar China: China, the United States and Postwar Economic Strategies," *Proceedings of the Conference on Sun Yat-sen and Modern China* (Taibei, 1986).

12. The history of China's other bilateral relationships in this period also indicate that there are no easy rules to be made about connections between trade and cultural contact, on the one hand, and political/strategic alignment, on the other, though there may have been patterns unique to each relationship. Akira Iriye argues that in the 1920s Sino-Japanese cultural relations deepened despite the deterioration of political relations, with "more Chinese and Japanese civilians [being] in contact with one another than ever before"; Donald Jordan has recently emphasized how during the same period economic disputes (particularly Chinese boycotts) pushed China and Japan further toward political and military

confrontation in the early 1930s. In the case of Sino-German relations in the 1920s and 1930s, which in some ways foreshadowed China's ties with the European Community in the 1980s, cultural and economic ties among elites could grow in part because there was no "power," or strategic element central to the relationship. See Akira Iriye, *China and Japan in the Global Setting*; Donald A. Jordan, *Chinese Boycotts versus Japanese Bombs: The Failure of China's "Revolutionary Diplomacy," 1931–32* (Ann Arbor: The University of Michigan Press, 1991).

13. See Wilma Fairbank, *America's Cultural Experiment in China, 1942–1949* (Washington: U.S. Department of State, Bureau of Educational and Cultural Affairs, 1976).

14. See William Kirby, "Minguo shiqi Zhongwai jingji jishu hezuo: Meiguo zhanshi shengchan guwentuan huan Hua, 1944–1946" [Sino-foreign economic and technical cooperation in Republican China: the U.S. War Production Mission to China, 1944–1946] in Zhang Xianwen et al., eds., *Minguodangan yu minguo shi xueshu taolunhui lunwenji* [Proceedings of the Conference on the Archives and History of Republican China] (Beijing: Dangan chubanshe, 1988).

15. This is a generalization that would hold true, in different ways, for historians as different as Hu Sheng and John K. Fairbank. Within the field of Sino-American relations, the leading example of an inclusive approach to foreign relations is Michael H. Hunt, *The Making of a Special Relationship: The United States and China to 1914* (New York: Columbia University Press, 1983).

16. For a stimulating overview of one part of the literature, in terms of its relationship to theory, see Jürgen Osterhammel, "The Place of the CCP in the Chinese Foreign Relations Past: Sketch of a Preliminary Framework," paper presented to the Conference on the CCP's External Relations, Woodrow Wilson Center, Washington, D.C., July 1992.

17. Cf. Xiang Rong, "Lun menhu kaifang zhengce" [On the open door policy], *Shijie Lishi* no. 5 (1980); *Lun dangdai diguozhuyi* [On contemporary imperialism] (Shanghai: Renmin, 1984).

18. A field arguably begun by Wang Xi, "Luelun Zhong Mei guanxi shi de jige wenti" [Brief discussion of several questions on the history of Sino-American Relations], *Shijie lishi*, no. 3 (1979), is now very large and influential indeed, particularly in the field of Sino-American relations, but also in the study of foreign relations generally and even of CCP party history. Impressive recent examples include the work of He Di, Niu Jun, Zi Zhongyun and Yuan Ming. For an overview see Yuan Ming, "Cross-Century Assignment: Past and Prospects of the Study of the History of Sino-American Relations in China," paper presented to the Conference on the CCP's External Relations, Woodrow Wilson Center, Washington, D.C., July 1992.

19. See Ole Holsti, "The Belief System and National Images," in James N. Rosenau, ed., *International Politics and Foreign Policy* (New York: The Free Press, 1969). More recently see Richard Little, ed., *Belief Systems and International Relations* (Oxford: Oxford University Press, 1990). For an excellent review of the literature see Shambaugh, *Beautiful Imperialist*, 17–20.

20. Youli Sun, *China and the Origins of the Pacific War*, (New York: St. Martin's Press, 1993).

21. Parks M. Coble, *Facing Japan: Chinese Politics and Japanese Imperialism, 1931–1937* (Cambridge, Mass.: Council on East Asian Studies, 1991).

22. Jordan, *Chinese Boycotts Versus Japanese Bombs*.

23. Iriye, *China and Japan in the Global Setting*.

24. See Harding, *Patterns of Cooperation*.

25. Garver, *Chinese-Soviet Relations*.

26. See Odd Arne Westad, *Cold War and Revolution: Soviet-American Rivalry and the Origins of the Chinese Civil War* (New York: Columbia University Press, 1993); Xiaoyuan Liu, "A Partnership for Disorder," manuscript.

27. Andrew D. W. Forbes, *Warlords and Muslims in Chinese Central Asia: A Political History of Republican Sinkiang, 1911–1949* (Cambridge: Cambridge University Press, 1986).

28. He Jun, "Lun 1929–1939 nian de Zhong Su guanxi." (Note 4 above.)

29. Jürgen Osterhammel, *China und die Weltgesellschaft. Vom 18. Jahrhundert bis in unsere Zeit* (Munich: C. H. Beck, 1989). On the Republican era see also his stimulating "Semi-Colonialism and Informal Empire in Twentieth-Century China: Toward a Framework of Analysis," in Wolfgang J. Mommsen and Jürgen Osterhammel, eds., *Imperialism and After: Continuities and Discontinuities* (London: Allen & Unwin, 1986).

30. Frank Dikötter, *The Discourse of Race in Modern China* (Stanford: Stanford University Press, 1992).

31. Françoise Kreissler, *L'Action culturelle allemande en Chine. De la fin du XIXe siècle à la Seconde Guerre mondiale* (Paris: Editions de la Maison des sciences de l'homme, 1989); Kuo Heng-yü, ed., *Von der Kolonialpolitik zur Kooperation. Studien zur Geschichte der deutsch-chinesischen Beziehungen* (Munich: Minerva, 1986).

32. Daniel M. Crane and Thomas A. Breslin, *An Ordinary Relationship: American Opposition to Republican Revolution in China* (Gainesville: University Presses of Florida, 1986); Nancy Bernkopf Tucker, *Patterns in the Dust: Chinese-American Relations and the Recognition Controversy, 1940–1950* (New York: Columbia University Press, 1983. See also Edwin W. Martin, *Divided Counsel: The Anglo-American Response to Communist Victory in China* (Lexington: University Press of Kentucky, 1986).

33. See his *The Origins of the Boxer Uprising* (Berkeley: University of California Press, 1987).

34. See John Espey, *Minor Heresies, Major Departures: A China Mission Boyhood* (Berkeley: University of California Press, 1994); John Hersey, *The Call* (New York: Knopf, 1985). See also the forthcoming study by Kimberly Risedorph.

35. R. E. Stross, *The Stubborn Earth: American Agriculturalists on Chinese Soil, 1898–1937* (Berkeley: University of California Press, 1986). James C. Thomson, *While China Faced West* (Cambridge: Harvard University Press, 1969); Peter Buck, *American Science and Modern China* (Cambridge: Cambridge University Press, 1983).

36. Of which the best example remains Barbara Tuchman, *Stilwell and the American Experience in China* (New York: Macmillan, 1971).

37. Such is not the case, however, with the significant German military mission to the Nationalist government during the period 1928–38, which for the past fifteen years has been the subject of detailed research not only on its leadership but also on its organization, institutional culture, and influence on a range of military, economic, ideological, and political matters. See for example, Bernd Martin, ed., *Die deutsche Beraterschaft in China, 1927–1938* (Düsseldorf: Droste, 1981); Hsi-Huey Liang, *The Sino-German Connection: Alexander von Falkenhausen between China and Germany, 1900–1941* (Assen: Van Gorcum, 1978); and my *Germany and Republican China*.

38. Stephen R. MacKinnon and Oris Friesen. *China Reporting: An Oral History of American Journalism in the 1930s and 1940s* (Berkeley: University of California Press, 1987); and Janice R. MacKinnon and Stephen R. MacKinnon, *Agnes Smedley: The Life and Times of An American Radical* (Berkeley: University of California Press, 1987).

39. Robert P. Newman, *Owen Lattimore and the "Loss" of China* (Berkeley: University of California Press, 1992); Paul M. Evans, *John Fairbank and the American Understanding of Modern China* (New York: Basil Blackwell, 1988); John King Fairbank, Martha Henderson

Coolidge, Richard J. Smith, *H. B. Morse and China: Customs Commissioner and Historian, 1855–1934* (Lexington: University of Kentucky Press, forthcoming).

40. Joyce K. Kallgren and Denis Fred Simon, eds., *Educational Exchanges: Essays on the Sino-American Experience* (Berkeley: Institute of East Asian Studies, 1987).

41. David M. Lampton, et al., *A Relationship Restored: Trends in U.S.-China Educational Exchanges, 1978–1984* (Washington, D.C.: National Academy Press, 1986).

42. Priscilla Roberts, ed., *Sino-American Relations Since 1900* (Hong Kong: University of Hong Kong Centre of Asian Studies, 1991).

43. On the diversity of the higher educational enterprise in China see Wen-hsin Yeh, *The Alienated Academy*.

44. See Bettina Gransow, *Geschichte der chinesischen Soziologie* (Frankfurt: Campus Verlag, 1992); Françoise Kreissler, "Deutsch-Chinesische Kooperation im Hochschulwesen: Das Beispiel der Tongji Universität," in Kuo and Leutner, eds., *Beiträge zu den deutsch-chinesischen Beziehungen* (Munich: Minerva, 1986), 10–32; Mary Bullock, *An American Transplant: The Rockefeller Foundation and Peking Union Medical College* (Berkeley: University of California Press, 1980); Idem., "The Legacy of the Rockefeller Foundation in China," paper presented to the American Historical Association annual meeting, 1990; Peter Buck, *American Science and Modern China, 1876–1936* (Cambridge: Cambridge University Press, 1980); Chiang Yung-chen, "Social Engineering and the Social Sciences in China, 1898–1949," Ph.D. dissertation, Harvard University, 1986; William J. Haas, "Gist Gee: A Life in Science and in China," Ph.D. dissertation, Harvard University, 1990; James Reardon-Anderson, *The Study of Change: Chemistry in China* (New York: Cambridge University Press, 1991); Laurence A. Schneider, "The Rockefeller Foundation, the China Foundation, and the Development of Modern Science in China," *Social Science in Medicine* 16 (1982); Yang Tsui-hua, "Geological Sciences in Republican China, 1912–1937," Ph.D. dissertation, State University of New York at Buffalo, 1985.

45. See for example Ching-chun Liang, *General Stilwell in China, 1942–1944: the Full Story* (New York: St. John's University Press, 1972).

46. See, among other publications: *Dangdai Zhongguo de dang'an shiyeh* (Beijing: Zhongguo shehui kexue chubanshe, 1988); *Zhongguo dang'an fenlei fa* (Beijing: Dang'an chubanshe, 1987); *Zhongguo dang'an nianjian* (Beijing: Dang'an chubanshe, 1992-); Lu Shou-chang, *Xiandai shiyong dang'an guanli xue* (Taibei, 1983); *Guoshiguan gaikuang* (Taibei: Guoshiguan, 1984). Professional and scholarly periodicals reviewing the state of archival work include: *Dang'an gongzuo* (Beijing); *Dang'an yanjiu* (Beijing); *Dang'an qingbao* (Beijing); *Dang'anxue tongxun* (Beijing); *Shanghai dang'an gongzu* (Shanghai) and *Jindai Zhongguo yanjiu tongxun (Taibei)*.

47. See Frederic Wakeman, Jr., "Chinese Archives and American Scholarship on Modern Chinese History," and William Kirby, "Notes on the Opening of Archives and Western Scholarship on Republican China," papers presented to the Conference on Modern Chinese Historical Archives, University of California at Berkeley, August 1994.

48. Michael H. Hunt, "The Genesis of Chinese Communist Foreign Policy: Mao Zedong Takes Command, 1935–1949," Occasional Paper no. 42 of Asia Program of the Woodrow Wilson Center, 1991. The Conference on the CCP's External Relations was convened at the Wilson Center in July, 1992. See his *The Genesis of Chinese Communist Foreign Policy* (New York: Columbia University Press, 1995).

49. See for example Yang Kuisong, "The Soviet Factor and the CCP's Policy toward the United States in the 1940s," in *Chinese Historians* 5, no. 1 (Spring 1992): 17–34.

50. Xiaoyuan Liu, *A Partnership for Disorder: China, the United States, and Their Policies for the Postwar Disposition of the Japanese Empire, 1941–45* (in preparation).

51. Odd Arne Westad, *Cold War and Revolution: Soviet-American Rivalry and the Origins of the Chinese Civil War* (New York: Columbia University Press, 1993).

52. Steven I. Levine, *Anvil of Victory: The Communist Revolution in Manchuria, 1945–48* (New York: Columbia University Press, 1987).

53. This is a less articulate phrasing of Michael Hunt's charge to U.S. diplomatic historians in "Internationalizing U.S. Diplomatic History: A Practical Agenda," *Diplomatic History* 15, no. 1 (1991): 1–11.

54. See Andrew J. Nathan, "Some Trends in the Historiography of Republican China," *Republican China* 17, no. 1 (1991): 119.

55. Quite different examples would be A. J. Gregor, et al., *Ideology and Development: Sun Yat-sen and the Economic History of Taiwan* (Berkeley, 1981), and W. Kirby, "Continuity and Change in Modern China: Chinese Economic Planning on the Mainland and on Taiwan, 1943–1958," *Australian Journal of Chinese Affairs* 24 (July 1990); Laurence Schneider, paper on the history and legacy of the Academia Sinica, presented to the annual meeting of the Association for Asian Studies, March, 1989.

56. Julia Strauss, *Strong Institutions in Weak Polities: Personnel Policies and State Building in China, 1927–1940* (Oxford: Oxford University Press, 1995).

57. Chang Jui-te, *Zhongguo jindai tielu shiye guanlide yanjiu: zhengzhi cengmiande fenxi* [Railroads in modern China: political aspects of railroad administration, 1876–1937] (Taibei: Zhongyang yanjiuyuan jindaishi suo, 1991).

58. Marie-Claire Bergère and William Kirby, eds., *China's Mid-century Transitions: Continuity and Change on the Mainland and Taiwan, 1946–1955* (in preparation).

59. Nancy Bernkopf Tucker, *Taiwan, Hong Kong and the United States, 1945–1992: Uncertain Friendships* (New York: Twayne, 1994).

60. Roger B. Jeans, ed., *Roads Not Taken: the Struggle of Opposition Parties in 20th Century China* (Boulder, Colorado: Westview Press, 1993).

61. Marie-Claire Bergère, "Cycles of Modernization and State-Society Relations in Modern China (1842–1949), in Yu-ming Shaw, ed., *Chinese Modernization* (San Francisco: China Materials Center, 1985), 73. See, above all, her *The Golden Age of the Chinese Bourgeoisie, 1911–1937* (New York: Cambridge University Press, 1989).

62. Thomas J. Rawski, *Economic Growth in Prewar China* (Berkeley: University of California Press, 1989), 344.

63. Ibid., 347.

64. Bergère, *Golden Age*, 63ff.

65. See David Strand, *Rickshaw Beijing: City People and Politics in 1920s China* (Berkeley: University of California Press, 1989); Christian Henriot, *Shanghai, 1927–1937* (Berkeley: University of California Press, 1993); Frederic Wakeman, Jr. and Wen-hsin Yeh, eds., *Shanghai Sojourners* (Berkeley: Institute of East Asian Studies, University of California, 1992); and in a general review of literature, William T. Rowe, "The Public Sphere in Modern China," *Modern China* 16, no 3 (1990): 309–329.

66. Elizabeth J. Perry, *Shanghai on Strike* (Stanford: Stanford University Press, 1993; Jean Chesneaux, *The Chinese Labor Movement, 1919–1927* (Stanford: Stanford University Press, 1968); Frederic Wakeman, Jr., *Shanghai Police* (Berkeley: University of California Press, 1994); Emily Honig, "Migrant Culture in Shanghai: In Search of a Subei Identity"; Jeffrey Wasserstrom, "The Evolution of Shanghai Student Protest Repertoire," both in Frederic Wakeman, Jr., and Wen-hsin Yeh, *Shanghai Sojourners* (Berkeley: Institute of East Asian Studies of the University of California, Berkeley, 1992); Wen-hsin Yeh, "Corporate Space, Communal Time: Everyday Life in Shanghai's Bank of China," paper presented at the Luce

Seminar on Commerce and Culture in Shanghai, 1895–1937, Cornell University, August 1992.

67. *Spoilt Children of Empire* (Hanover, NH: University Press of New England, 1991).

68. *Tsingtau. Deutsche Stadt und Festung, in China,1897–1914* (Düsseldorf: Droste, 1984).

69. One English-language publication from the latter is Zhang Zhongli, et al., *The Swire Group in Old China* (Shanghai: Shanghai People's Publishing House, 1990).

70. Cochran, "Three Roads into Shanghai's Market," in Wakeman and Yeh, *Shanghai Sojourners*, 35–75.

71. Tahirih V. Lee, "Courts and Commercial Dispute Resolution in Early Twentieth Century Shanghai." Paper presented to the Association for Asian Studies, April 1990; Alison Conner, "Legal Education During the Republican Period in China: The Comparative Law School of China." Paper presented to the American Society for Legal History, February 1990.

72. On Sino-American controversies over corporate law see William Kirby, "China, Unincorporated: Company Law and Business Enterprise in Twentieth-Century China," *Journal of Asian Studies*, forthcoming.

73. Marc Bloch, *The Historian's Craft* (New York: Vintage, 1953), 61.

74. For the PRC's Archive Law see: *Zhonghua renmin gongheguo dang'anfa* (Beijing: Dang'an chubanshe, 1988). It promises a thirty-year rule of declassification, to which, however, there are many exceptions (particularly for foreigners). A more welcome sign is the recent decision by the Guomindang Party Historical Commission *(Dangshihui)* in Taiwan to open its archive through to the year 1961.

75. For a reasoned analysis based on quite incompatible source bases see Gordon H. Chang and He Di, "The Absence of War in the U.S.-China Confrontation over Quemoy," *American Historical Review* 98, no. 5 (December 1993): 1500–1524.

76. See Mark Kramer, "Archival Research in Moscow," and Kathryn Weathersby, "New Findings on the Korean War," both in *The Cold War International History Project Bulletin* No. 3 (Fall 1993); Mark Bradley and Robert Brigham, "Vietnamese Archives and Scholarship on the Cold War Period: Two Reports," Working Paper No. 7 of the Cold War International History Project, Woodrow Wilson Center (September 1993); Shuguang Zhang and Jian Chen, *Chinese Communist Foreign Policy and the Cold War in Asia: New Documentary Evidence, 1944–1950* (Chicago: Imprint Publications, 1995).

77. This is true at the local as well as the national level: see *Shanghaishi dang'anguan jianming zhinan* (Beijing: Dang'an chubanshe, 1991).

Chapter Eight

Driven by Domestics:
American Relations with Japan and Korea, 1900–1945

MICHAEL A. BARNHART

A little more than a decade ago, Waldo Heinrichs surveyed "new frontiers" in American-East Asian relations for the first half of this century. He came to two principal conclusions. A. Whitney Griswold's interpretation of a cycle of overcommitment, overextension, and retreat appeared finally overthrown by recent scholarship that emphasized the deliberately limited nature of America's role in East Asia from 1900 to 1941, at least. And this period had not been an arena for breakthrough research, or even copious research, given the rush of scholars old and new to the postwar years.

These two conclusions remain unchallenged in their essence, but they have been amended by scholarship over the past decade in ways that invite further explorations of this field if any investigators can be lured away from the documentary riches of the Cold War.

My examination begins in a period of such riches and proceeds backward chronologically to underline my argument that America's relations with Japan and Korea from 1945 to 1900 were "driven by domestic" forces and nearly always dominated by exceptionally small constituencies within the American and Japanese governments throughout these years.

These two considerations might seem contradictory. An examination of small constituencies should emphasize the elite or at least elitist nature of American or Japanese policymakers and their relative detachment from other concerns. It should stress the "Driven by Domestics" cloistered nature of those policymakers, and their aloofness or even disdain for broader, domestic considerations. By the same token, assertions that the relationship between the American and Japanese governments was driven primarily by domestic concerns within each country, one might think, would lead to a consideration of just how wide those concerns were, from immigration, opium smuggling, and plain old racism to the role of the media, missionaries, and the old-fashioned military, too.

In fact, there is nothing contradictory in this picture. Many constituencies were involved in the framing of relations between Japan and the United States. And all of them were involved, when they were involved, because of their domestic concerns. In fact, it is fair to say that at no point did either government make a serious effort to address the domestic concerns of the other throughout this period. In this sense, it seems accurate to say that there was no real diplomacy of this sort, at least on a consistent basis, throughout these entire forty-five years.[1] Nor were there any private domestic constituencies in any position to consider undertaking such an effort, much less to carry one out.[2] No one should be greatly surprised that these years were characterized by war—once Japan's dominant, domestic concerns pointed in that direction, and once America's room for possible concession was restricted by reminders of the need to couch its foreign policy in terms of Wilsonian principles—preceded by crisis preceded by mistrust. Nor should we be surprised that peace dominated American-Japanese relations after this era: both nations' domestic imperatives (now joined by those of South Korea)[3] pointed in this direction. The thrust of recent scholarship on these American-Japanese relations between 1945 and 1900 focuses upon these domestic imperatives and why they contributed to war and what came before.

Japan was a defeated nation by July 1944, as the fall of the Tojo Cabinet (as much as of Saipan) clearly indicated. Why then the continuation of thirteen months of agony until the conditional surrender of mid-August 1945? Why the employment of two atomic bombs against Japan at that time? These questions continue to generate many studies and just as many controversies. One of the most satisfying of those studies, Leon Sigal's *Fighting to a Finish*, offers persuasive answers to these questions for the United States Government. His analysis also goes far toward suggesting why Japan's authorities acted as they did during that fateful summer.

Sigal offers a stark portrait of two nations willing to wage unrelenting war long after the conflict's outcome was obvious. But that is precisely the point. No one doubted that Japan would be defeated by the summer of 1944. No one knew under what terms that defeat would occur. Sigal makes clear that the Americans understood that the preservation of the institution of the Imperial Throne was central for Japan. Why did Washington refuse to offer such preservation in the summer of 1944 and why did it do so a year later?

The answer is simply that Washington was not of one mind in 1944, and barely so a year later. The United States Army strongly opposed any conditional peace terms to Tokyo. It was on sound ground. The dynamics of the Grand Alliance argued overwhelmingly for no separate peace and no concession whatsoever to any Axis foe.[4] As importantly, the Army's leaders believed that any war ended by air or seapower alone would be disastrous for their institution's survival into the postwar era. Old-line army versus Army Air Forces (AAF) frictions only strengthened this conviction, and made the assembly of any reasonable terms to Japan more complex. The AAF and Navy, as Sigal explains, were content to let bombing and blockade bring Japan to terms not because either understood the nature of Japan's dynamics of surrender, but because both understood that such a victory guaranteed them a place in the postwar American defense establishment.[5]

If the United States Army's institutional instincts made Japan's conditional surrender difficult, the Imperial Japanese Army's desire for survival made it impossible. The Imperial Army understood perfectly well that America's war aims allowed it no life. The critical phrase of the Potsdam Declaration, after all, called explicitly for the unconditional surrender "of all Japanese armed force."[6] It had every reason to devise and maintain a wartime strategy that insisted upon the suicide of the nation, too.[7] This critical issue has been explored by a number of recent works, though still incompletely. One of the most recent is Stephen S. Large's examination of *Emperor Hirohito and Showa Japan*.[8] Despite much greater accessibility to Japanese documents,[9] Large departs in no substantial way from Robert J. C. Butow's conclusions of forty years ago, although the emperor's reluctance to part with the services of Prime Minister Tojo Hideki in the summer of 1944 comes through much more clearly than before.[10] In this most recent account, the emperor remains a deeply troubled figure during the critical month of August 1945, badly shaken by the news of the destructiveness of the Hiroshima bomb, and acutely concerned that even his direct intervention in cabinet decisions might not bring the Imperial Army's assent.[11]

These domestic Japanese factors ought to be weighed within the still lively debate over the wisdom of America's dropping the two atomic bombs, though there is little sign of such weighing.[12] Two essays have forcefully argued that the oft-cited casualty figure of a half million Americans if the bombs had not induced surrender was grossly inflated after VJ-Day.[13] There remains ample room for a bi-archival examination of the interworkings of the surrender process, including why the Americans strongly believed that their losses, and those of the Japanese, nevertheless would be quite high.[14]

Of course, there were estimates of possibly high casualties made by various Japanese in late 1941, while contemplating war against the United States. Here again, it was the Imperial Army that played the central role, in this case in the decision for war. According to one controversial interpretation,[15] its generals were equally concerned with domestic reform and war against the West. Hoping to use war fever to secure the adoption of a set of fundamental economic and political changes within the Empire (a set that would enable them to mobilize that Empire long enough to sustain a stalemate against the Americans), they placed Tojo Hideki in power in October 1941. Tojo might have succeeded, at least in realizing the army's domestic goals, but for the unexpectedly swift setbacks of the late spring of 1942.

There still are no studies of contemporary American perceptions of domestic change within Japan during the Second World War.[16] American wartime propaganda easily equated Tojo with Hitler and Mussolini. Whether experts in the government deduced a growing system of fascist-like controls, and whether they believed that excising the Imperial Army would remove those controls, remains unclear. Yet examinations of American planning for Japan's surrender note that somehow certain Americans understood that there were elements of Japan's leadership that could and would collaborate with the United States once the war was over.[17] These Americans were able to appeal to those elements only sporadically and incompletely. The imperatives of American domestic politics made anything more impossible. But they made the attempt, and historians of this period need to ask why they thought it worthwhile. Many studies of Japanese politics and policy-making have stressed the quite strong degree of consensus among Tokyo elites, civilian and military alike, favoring imperial expansion especially at China's cost and at the expense of friction or worse with the West. They may well be right. But their rightness only redirects attention to Joseph Grew and others who felt sure that there were some Japanese, and important ones, who could be trusted, in Grew's phrase, to bring Japan back within the Anglo-American orbit. Where did Grew's idea come from?

By the same token, it may be too obvious to point out that by 1945 Americans so distrusted the Japanese military that they meant to obliterate it forever. But why? John Dower's powerful account, *War Without Mercy*, accurately details the savagery of the Pacific War.[18] He is doubtless correct to point out that race was the crucial difference in that savagery. Yet he has difficulty explaining the swiftness of the change in American attitudes once the war was over, especially since there was no Nazi Party in Japan to serve as a lightning rod for hatred, racial or otherwise.

The answer may well be within Dower's own evidence. American, and Western, attitudes toward wartime Japan were almost invariably expressed in terms of attitudes toward the Japanese military and its unexpected prowess and, later in the war, fanaticism. The dissolution of that military may well have been the ideal solution for a peaceful occupation. If so, American occupation plans for Japan were considerably more lenient than Morgenthau's for Germany. Ironically, while the Imperial Army sought to meld itself with the state in an age of "total war," Americans thought that it would be a relatively easy matter to separate army from state—forever. It may be that these American assumptions about wartime Japan derive much more from American assumptions about human nature than a dedicated analysis of the political structure of the foe.[19] In any event, these attitudes toward the Imperial Army and Navy seem to have combined with Grew's desire for preservation of the Emperor System to make a postwar accommodation, and alliance, far more likely than it otherwise would have been.[20]

However, it is still not clear when the demonization of the Japanese military took place in American eyes. Nor is there full understanding of the blindness of American wartime strategies to manipulating the Japanese domestic political constellation, given that demonization. There are, though, several new studies of the origins of the Pacific War, such as the trenchant examination of 1941 in Waldo Heinrich's *Threshold of War*.

Heinrichs' account is praiseworthy on a number of scores. It reemphasizes how pitifully small was the amount of military force at the disposal of Franklin Roosevelt throughout 1941, whether for aid, deterrence, or, in the end, use. It lucidly shows the pivotal nature of German-Soviet relations that year, carefully tracing the rise and decline of American confidence in the USSR's ability to survive from June through December. Only through this global perspective does the shift and nuance of American policy toward Japan become clear.[21] And it becomes clear, likewise, that that shift and nuance rarely had anything to do with American readings of the Japanese polity.

Even the rarities are illuminating. American Secretary of State Cordell Hull agreed to use Father James Drought's "Draft Understanding" of April as a basis for opening discussions with Nomura Kichisaburo hoping to "tilt the balance" within Tokyo against Japanese hardliners such as Foreign Minister Matsuoka Yosuke.[22] At that instant, Matsuoka was in Europe attempting to negotiate a grand bloc of Germany, Italy, the Soviet Union, and Japan. When, within a day, word came that Matsuoka had obtained Stalin's consent to a neutrality pact, Hull quickly discarded his strategy of attempting to influence the balance of forces within the Japanese Government, though he did elect to continue the discussions with Nomura.

Roosevelt too was willing to permit the discussions to continue. But because Japan had nothing to fear from the north, and therefore might strike British, French, and Dutch positions to its south, he refused to weaken the Pacific Fleet. Indeed, at that very early point, Roosevelt seems to have decided to employ Hull's talks as a means to play for time in the Pacific (or, as he would say later in the summer, to "baby the Japanese along"). In this respect, the Hull-Nomura meetings must be counted a resounding success. It is not so clear that they were nearly as useful as they might have been. The Americans were aware of Matsuoka's volatility, but dismissed him as a lightweight player for exactly that reason and rejoiced when he was dismissed from office in mid-July.

This interpretation, in retrospect, is curious. That Matsuoka had used the negotiations to stake out a very strong line against the United States (and in favor of Japan scrupulously adhering to its alliance obligations with Germany) was viewed as simply playing politics—and Matsuoka played and lost. That the Imperial Army attached a monitor, in the person of Colonel Iwakura Hideo, to Nomura to ensure that Japan's position on both the Axis and China did not waver was barely noticed in Washington. Only Joseph Grew believed that a new round of talks with Nomura would affect Japanese policy, that is, would alter the domestic balance within Japan. His strongest pitch, an endorsement of a summit meeting between Roosevelt and Prime Minister Konoe Fumimaro, fell on deaf ears.

Other accounts have noted the extreme reluctance of Roosevelt's advisers, such as Stanley Hornbeck,[23] to favor the summit out of doubts that Konoe could assure the Japanese military's concurrence in any agreement. Heinrichs stresses that Roosevelt was lukewarm. A summit was possible or not. Roosevelt appears not even to have considered whether Konoe could make good on any promises made there. The central aim remained to play for time so that the United States could aid its de facto allies in Europe and complete a crash buildup in the Philippines.[24] Such a buildup was all the more useful since it provided a convenient and well-used dumping ground for Douglas MacArthur, keeping him out of American domestic politics and Roosevelt's hair.[25] Once Washington believed that the Soviets would survive 1941 and that the Japanese were not likely to invade Siberia, there was little reason to consider concessions to Japan at Britain's and China's expense. For a Japan that could wait no longer, a Japan on the periphery of American foreign policy concerns in 1941,[26] that meant war.[27]

Throughout 1941 Roosevelt had a consistent view of Japan. It was economically weak and therefore a secondary threat to American security. And it was in the grip of a military establishment bent on territorial expansion to remedy that weakness. It is not clear how much earlier Roosevelt had arrived at such a reading, but it is certain that it made him, and many of his advisers, reluctant to consider any attempts to manipulate internal divisions within Japan to America's advantage. This reluctance may have been a missed opportunity, for this writer's study, *Japan Prepares for Total War*,[28] confirms that there were considerable internal differences, even (or especially) between the Japanese armed services in 1940 and 1941.

Roosevelt was correct to view Japan as economically vulnerable and at least part of its military determined to change that condition. Outlining the struggles of the Imperial Army to set Japan on a path toward self-sufficiency is a primary purpose of *Japan Prepares*. This study also emphasizes that those struggles were essentially over when the Marco Polo Bridge Incident of July 1937 developed into a full scale war with China by that year's end. Japan would become weaker, and more dependent upon America, in each of the next four years, while the "total war" officers would prove unable to build upon the legislative successes of 1938[29] that the war fever would bring them. The Americans missed this entirely. Indeed, quite a few Far Eastern experts believed that the same officers who sponsored the drive to autarky actually favored, and had even planned, the attack on China.[30]

The Japanese were hardly experts themselves in calculating the American factor into their foreign relations of these key years from 1937 to 1945. Ironically, the manner in which the Americans fought Japan ensured that the Imperial Army would remain a powerful force in Japanese politics from Pearl Harbor until the surrender. By 1944, although the navy was ready for peace, by that time it was an enfeebled force that had to be rescued twice by the emperor's intervention: the famous one of August 1945 that led to the end of the war, and Hirohito's opposition to a formal merger of navy with army in April.[31]

The Imperial Army knew little about America. For it, from 1941 on, as for Roosevelt during that year, the German-Soviet situation was the key to Japan's position in a global settlement. Early hopes for a German victory, or a German-Soviet negotiated peace, died late and hard. Even after Germany's defeat, as has been well documented for decades now,[32] the Imperial Army believed that Soviet mediation would retrieve a measure of survival for empire and army. In many respects, the final verdict on the "total war" ideology of 1941–45 must be that it fostered an almost deliberate blindness toward the opponent's domestic requirements with suitably radical implications for ending the war. This was a fatal flaw for Japan (and merely a bad one for the United States).

The fiftieth anniversary of the Pearl Harbor attack endured a renewal of the sharp debate over responsibility for American unpreparedness. The attacks involved, however, were anything but surprise ones. Edwin T. Layton, Admiral Husband E. Kimmel's intelligence officer in Hawaii on the day of infamy, defends Kimmel and himself with a long demonstration of how little information Washington shared with Hawaii. Layton places much of the blame at Admiral Richmond Kelly Turner's doorstep, terming Turner an intelligence amateur and grasping empire-builder. Although much of Layton's account deals with the intelligence-gathering minutiae, he also speculates that Hull's "ultimatum" of November 26, 1941 was President Franklin Roosevelt's doing. Roosevelt's sudden harshness, Layton argues, was due to Winston Churchill's sharing information gathered from British codebreaking operations that demonstrated Japanese bad faith. This conclusion is directly challenged by a British account which maintains that Churchill deliberately withheld information from Roosevelt to ensure American entry into the war.[33] Layton's defense of Kimmel inspired a spirited rebuttal from Henry C. Clausen, an attorney who led the War Department's investigation of the Pearl Harbor debacle. In Clausen's view, Kimmel was both fool and knave, charges equally applicable to Layton, for refusing to share intelligence with the Army before the attack.[34]

In stark contrast to the still-blazing controversy over American blame and responsibility for the Pearl Harbor attack, there appears to be an emerging consensus, at least in Japanese scholarship, concerning the nature of American-Japanese diplomacy in late 1941. That is, consideration of the United States itself played a relatively minor role in much of Japan's overall diplomacy before Pearl Harbor. Japanese scholars have increasingly come to regard the Hull-Nomura negotiations as merely another exercise of Anglo-American appeasement, driven by the same logic that suggested initial accommodation with Hitler before drawing a line. The distinguished scholar Hosoya Chihiro has gone so far as to suggest that in some respects the Pacific War was more a conflict with England than America.[35] Akira Iriye takes an even broader perspective. Asking how the Sino-Japanese struggle of 1931 became an international war of 1941, in which China had many allies and Japan none of value, he examines the breakdown of the "Washington System" in East Asia and the Pacific and its growing links to the German question in Europe.[36]

Just as Japan was rarely a primary consideration of America's foreign relations, America seldom occupied center stage in Tokyo's policy deliberations. This was especially true for the Imperial Army, which regarded the Americans, and their presence in the Philippines, as an unwanted nuisance to the Southward Advance in 1940 and American measures of encouragement of China in 1938 and 1939 as unnecessary steps prolonging Chiang Kai-shek's resistance.[37] The army only accepted the navy's premise of Anglo-American indivisibility and the need to include the United States in warplans by the summer of 1941. Even then, it pressed for a shoestring operation in the south and essentially got one. China and the Soviet Union remained far more important even after Pearl Harbor until the USSR's attack of August 1945 at last compelled the generals to confront the Americans fully.[38] In many respects, the Imperial Army remained driven by its domestic institutional concerns. Since the army dominated Japanese foreign policy making after 1937, it seems fair to agree with the thrust of Hosoya's argument.

It is an argument with another implication: If neither the United States nor Japan held the central position in the other's foreign-policy making, and if the top leadership of both countries turned to each other only rarely and under the most extreme situations, what characterized the day-to-day relationship between these countries? For most of these years, the American-Japanese interface was a quite narrow one, with Lilliputian constituencies. Some of these were, of course, directly concerned with that relationship, such as the State Department's Far Eastern advisers and their Japanese counterparts. More were Americans and, occasionally, Japanese who encountered the other infrequently. When they did, it was nearly always in an atmosphere of hostility, as a number of recent studies make clear.

Americans paid little attention to Japan between 1933 and 1937. But the attitudes of Roosevelt's Secretary of State, Cordell Hull, were remarkably consistent toward Japan. Already by 1933 he was convinced that Japan was a law-breaking nation. The United States had to oppose Tokyo not out of any concrete interests in East Asia, but because aggression was wrong wherever it occurred. Hull understood that a quiet withdrawal from that region was an option, but one he never seriously considered, nor one, in all likelihood, that Roosevelt would have permitted.[39] There was no real "Oriental crossroads of decision" throughout the 1930s or, for that matter throughout the half century under discussion.[40] Even America's Ambassador to Japan, Joseph Grew, did not advocate yielding up American principles and rights, and he was vigilant in protesting infringements upon those rights by Japan.[41]

There were, however, some arguments for a fundamental reassessment of America's Japan policy. Arthur Waldron has rendered a signal service to the field by editing, with extensive introduction and annotation, John V. A. Mac-

Murray's long memorandum of the summer of 1935.[42] Much of the memo traced the breakdown of the Washington treaty system in East Asia, blaming the United States and China for abandoning treaty obligations and forcing Japan to extreme measures in defense of its interests. MacMurray did not well discern the Japanese domestic political situation, either as it affected the Manchurian Incident of 1931 or Tanaka Gi'ichi's rise to the prime minister ship four years earlier. But he was excruciatingly correct when he asserted, "On both sides there is some bitterness of feeling. But we, who live in a large country with natural resources that make us relatively self-sufficient and between oceans that give us ready access to the markets of all the world and at the same time form a barrier against invasion, can scarcely realize how much more the Japanese are concerned about us than we are about them."[43] . . . And how much more China meant to Japan than the United States. MacMurray was ignored.

Instead, Hull's State Department hewed very closely to the line laid down by Henry Stimson during the Far Eastern crisis of 1931–33. The United States would reserve the right to object to Japan's encroachments upon China and American rights and principles there, but it would do nothing to obstruct those encroachments. This is an old story; new scholarship does not fundamentally revise it. Still, it would be useful to know why the old story is true. As Howard Jablon observes, Roosevelt's New Deal was remarkably eclectic, consistently experimental, and deliberately new in its domestic programs.[44] Why did it avoid new thinking for American-Japanese relations?

General studies of the New Deal are of no help on this score. The fiftieth anniversary of Roosevelt's first inauguration sparked publication of a number of collections assessing his programs. Of all these, a single chapter addresses the foreign policy of the New Deal. Arnold A. Offner neatly draws parallels between American appeasement of both Germany and Japan early in the New Deal. He too notes that in large measure Roosevelt followed Hoover's policy toward Tokyo. Offner does tantalize with his observation that Grew was distressed with Japan's "war psychology" in 1934 and that the German victories of 1940 were "strong wine," as if a normal and sober Japan had no differences with the United States.[45] But there is no connection here or elsewhere with the change and newness of much of the New Deal at home compared to its foreign relations' staid conservatism. Historians in other fields venture not even speculation. For example, Michael A. Bernstein's expert analysis of the American economy during the Great Depression stops at the water's edge. Alan Brinkley's essay on "The Idea of the State" raises obvious questions for perceptions of other nations and relations with them, but Brinkley draws back from such a discussion.[46] It is somewhat depressing that no works have built upon, or sought to amend, Lloyd Gardner's *Economic Aspects of New Deal Diplomacy*, now thirty years old.[47]

Studies focussed upon Roosevelt's diplomacy perforce cover his relations with Japan. Yet here too connections between the New Deal at home and American foreign relations are seldom made. Frederick Marks offers a blistering criticism of Roosevelt and his advisers as ambivalent and deceptive.[48] Time and again, Marks argues, Roosevelt held out hopes for an American-Japanese accommodation only to snatch them back whenever the Japanese reached out. In an echo of Griswold's central theme, Marks maintains that Roosevelt refused to coordinate his diplomacy's means to its ends. The United States would not accept détente with Japan, nor would it prepare to accept the consequences of eventual confrontation. Curiously, Marks too declines to link Roosevelt's diplomacy to his domestic concerns. He argues that New Dealers placed their faith in disarmament, personal diplomacy, and public disapprobation on moral grounds to safeguard the peace. If these posturings somehow failed, economic pressure was sure to work. Conveniently, they assumed that Japan, like Germany and Italy, was economically weak and on the brink of collapse.

This is an interesting line of analysis to pursue, but it does require pursuit. It seems remarkable that American diplomats and their superiors would be so supremely confident that time was on their side, and that *Japan* was ready to collapse in the dark days of the mid-1930s.[49] Yet we still do not have a systematic exploration of New Deal diplomats' views of the American system, nor any survey of American perceptions of Japan, and the Japanese economy and economic reforms, during these years. Marks justifies Japanese expansionism as driven in part by population pressures. This canard ought to have been laid to rest some time ago in any historian's analysis, but it would be interesting to determine how seriously Americans took it at the time and used it to justify their confidence that time would work against Japan's program of expansion.

In sum, there still is no satisfactory account explaining why American policy toward Japan failed to shift in the transition from Hoover to Roosevelt. This realization ought to redirect attention to the crises of 1931–32 in Manchuria and Shanghai. Were these defining events in this half-century of American-Japanese relations, or did they merely confirm and solidify existing antagonisms?

Justus D. Doenecke's *When the Wicked Rise* is well placed to answer these questions.[50] His account makes clear that most Americans, even those who regularly considered foreign policy questions, rarely thought about Japan. The Manchurian crisis excited few. Those few viewed Japan far more in terms of ideals and principles than from a reasoned consideration of America's actual interests (as MacMurray had criticized). Both Henry Stimson and Dorothy Detzer, of the Women's International League for Peace and Freedom, believed that Japan's acts endangered the rules of international relations that had been laboriously constructed over the past thirteen years to avoid future wars. Both wanted stronger action than Washington delivered, but President Herbert Hoover was reassured that over time Japan would stumble and weaken, so it was best to note disapproval and do nothing more.[51]

The Japanese attack on Shanghai drew much more attention. More than three thousand Americans lived in the city and 1,300 Marines were stationed there. American labor counseled against any direct action, which would only benefit wealthy corporate interests, not the United States generally. But intellectuals rallied behind the application of economic sanctions after Japan cavalierly bombed nonmilitary targets. Harvard president A. Lawrence Lowell and professor Francis B. Sayre (Woodrow Wilson's son-in-law) supported sanctions against Tokyo. They were joined by Wilson's former Secretary of War, Newton D. Baker, who was sometimes mentioned as presidential timber for the 1932 contest. Columbia University President Nicholas Murray Butler headed a Committee on Economic Sanctions.

For all this intellectual horsepower, there is little evidence that any of these advocates considered the likely effect of sanctions on Japan—meaning on the domestic balance of forces within Japan. Stimson informed Detzer that patience was the best way to encourage Japanese liberalism, strange words from the author of the Borah letter. *The New Republic* editor Bruce Bliven predicted that sanctions would drive Japan to state socialism, autarky, and alliance with Germany and the Soviet Union. Yet Bliven himself already was terming the government of Japan a "military dictatorship."[52]

Recent scholarship has little to say as to whether Americans believed Japan to be such a dictatorship before September of 1931, as little work has been done for the period before that year.[53] There is a tantalizing suggestion along these lines, however, in Edward Miller's *War Plan* ORANGE. Miller traces in great detail the evolution of War Plan ORANGE, the American Navy's operations plans for war against Japan. Miller recounts a history of permutations in Plan ORANGE, led at different periods by "thrusters," "cautionaries" or "defensives." Even so, what is most remarkable about that warplan's history is how very little its assumptions about Japan changed from 1906 to 1941 (and later). Born in the aftermath of the immigration crises and war scares of 1906–7, the plan presumed unlimited economic warfare against a totally mobilized Japan, led by a ruthless military supported by a docile population. An initial Japanese strike would remove the American bases in the western Pacific and allow Japan freedom to expand against China and the resource-rich western colonies to the south. An American counteroffensive, coordinated with a tightening blockade, would force the Imperial Navy into a decisive battle, which it would lose. Thereafter, economic strangulation would doom Japan. No actual invasion would be necessary, even though the Imperial Army would remain intact on the home islands and in China.[54]

It is certainly possible to regard this scenario as uncannily predictive. But it seems more useful to ask how such fundamental notions about Japan could have gone unchallenged through such decades of change. American planning against every other nation changed often, and often substantially, between 1906 and 1941. But ORANGE, when it was altered, came in response to new weapons and capabilities, or to development (or lack thereof) of various Pacific bases, American and Japanese, or the vagaries of the budget (invariably American). The Taisho crisis, the rise and fall of Hara Kei, the Tanaka-Shidehara debates, the Ìsumi purge—none is reflected in ORANGE planning. Nor does ORANGE provide much by way of detail concerning precisely how, or even why, Japan should surrender. The Imperial Army, it was presumed, would simply give up without a fight as if it were in the service of the state, American-style. For a plan that posited a ruthless military and docile population, this premise was the most peculiar of all.

Another virtually unchanged premise of ORANGE revolved around its jump-off point, the "Eastern Pacific Bastion" of Pearl Harbor. The United States Navy never worried about Hawaii's vulnerability after 1914 and the completion of the Panama Canal, although some concern remained about the safety of shore installations in case of a Japanese carrier raid.[55] This attitude would have come as news to the Japanese studied in John Stephan's *Hawaii Under the Rising Sun*.[56] Stephan rightly argues that Yamamoto Isoroku correctly judged Hawaii's importance, making it the target of the Pearl Harbor Attack Plan and the ill-fated Eastern Operation that ended at Midway in 1942. He examines the debates within the Imperial Navy over the viability and desirability of actually invading Hawaii. He notes that 1940 planning papers made Hawaii part of Japan's Greater East Asia Co-Prosperity Sphere and that Hawaii, along with Mindanao, was to be annexed into the Japanese Empire.[57]

This combination should not seem curious. Both areas were heavily settled by Japanese. Indeed, people of Japanese descent made up forty percent of Hawaii's total population, the largest single ethnic group. Many retained close ties to Japan, with some even serving in the emperor's military. The Japanese government took pains to cultivate this connection. Hawaiian donations to the National Defense Fund of Japan were routed to the same prefecture, sometimes the same village, that the contributors (or their ancestors) had come from. In 1940 Japan sponsored a congress of "Overseas Compatriots" at which Matsuoka proclaimed them Japan's "first line of overseas expansion."[58] Nor was this idle talk. Stephan's account makes quite clear that not only Japan but also the Japanese themselves regarded the diaspora as irretrievably Japanese and nothing else. Quite a few in Japan believed that the Americans would not greatly regret the loss of Hawaii, since it was not really American in the first place. In 1945, some Hawaiian Japanese refused to believe that their homeland had surrendered.

Taking account of rumors of War Plan ORANGE and possible Japanese responses to it under the Washington treaties, Hector Bywater wrote his famous *The Great Pacific War* in 1925.[59] That book's reception in American, British, and Japanese naval and even literary circles is traced in an engaging if sometimes necessarily speculative study by William Honan.[60] Honan does not prove that Bywater's novel inspired the actual drafting of Admiral Yamamoto Isoroku's attack plan fifteen years later. But he does provide a detailed analysis of why Bywater, and many others, thought a Pacific war likely, and why many, at least in the 1920s, did not.[61]

Although the United States Navy may not have worried about Japan or the Japanese in Hawaii after 1914, Hawaiian Americans—the planters—had been deeply concerned a decade before. Japanese laborers on their plantations were hardly docile. They engaged in strikes and often left the fields as soon as they could to live and prosper in the towns. In addition, the planters did not want Hawaii to be too Japanese.[62] So they looked elsewhere for workers. Whites were preferable, but experiments with Portuguese went poorly. By late 1903, the planters struck upon the solution: Koreans. Recruited by an American businessman, aided by Washington's Minister to Korea and a band of missionaries there, some seven thousand Koreans entered Hawaii—illegally—until their emigration was halted by 1905 not by American officials but rather Japan's tightening colonial grip over their homeland. It is an amazing story in all its detail.[63]

One such detail was the Gentlemen's Agreement of 1907 ending Japanese[64] emigration to the United States. This was merely one step of many, as Mitziko Sawada's recent study makes clear.[65] The Japanese Government was keenly sensitive to American charges that it was exporting its undesirables. The Meiji oligarchs went to considerable lengths to formalize and control the issuance of passports. In 1900, Tokyo introduced a (temporary) ban on emigration to the United States. Its 1907 initiative simply followed this same line and, a year later, Japan even agreed to establish a system registering Japanese nationals residing in the United States to bar those present on non-migrant (hi-imin) status, such as students, from becoming emigrants.

Of course, immigration was not the only case of "managed trade" between Tokyo and Washington. William Miles Fletcher's *The Japanese Business Community and National Trade Policy, 1920–1941* is primarily a study of growing cooperation between Japanese businessmen, especially from the textile industry, and a growing economic bureaucracy in the government.[66] But it also illuminates several important episodes in American-Japanese relations from the end of the First World War through the Second. One is surprised to find leading business groups referring to the London Economic Conference of 1933 as "a problem of life and death," as they campaigned for stable exchange rates and lower tariffs worldwide.[67] Their commitment to free trade as a matter of principle was not deep. Within a year they had joined with the government to pass and apply the Law to Protect and Regulate Trade designed, as Finance Minister Takahashi Korekiyo put it, to achieve "the modest aim" of avoiding large balance of trade deficits with certain nations.[68] Interestingly, the business community was rarely interested in the United States.[69] American criticisms during the Manchurian crisis sparked business interest in China as a market and source of raw materials (especially cotton).[70] Washington's increasing economic pressures of 1940–41 merely accelerated and deepened a business-government collaboration already well underway, a collaboration that nearly a decade before had worked to force American companies out of Japan.[71]

In many respects, this story is a microcosm of American-Japanese relations throughout these years. When either nation troubled to give the other more than a cursory glance, it was usually within the context of wider problems, usually European for Washington and continental Asian for Tokyo. It can safely be said that at virtually no point did either have a sound understanding of the other's primary concerns in the international arena. And neither much troubled to investigate the other's domestic imperatives, much less attempt to use those to its advantage.

It may be time to examine nonofficial relations more closely, as the immigration and, to an extent, business studies have done. Closer studies of Japanese immigrants on the American mainland, especially the ones who stayed, would be helpful.[72] Intercultural exchanges need attention, too. The Institute for Pacific Relations is one obvious focal point; Japanese students at American universities another. There were tourists from both countries who left records, largely unlooked at.[73] Some traveled over newly established air routes by the end of this period, not counting the still largely untapped source of the experiences of soldiers and sailors, both Japanese and American, who encountered each other and, sometimes, each other's homelands at first-hand.[74] Nor is it always necessary to examine direct, literally interpersonal, contact. Sharon Nolte's study of Japanese liberalism offers ways for students of American-Japanese relations to track the exchange of ideas and influences, which was by no means a one-way street.[75]

At the intergovernmental level, though, Americans and Japanese spoke monologues through these decades. The United States Navy simply assumed that somehow Japan would surrender after ORANGE's economic strangulation was successfully executed. American planters pursued their ways to replace Japanese workers with Korean, oblivious to imperial developments in East Asia. Professional pacifists, well-intentioned academics, and Henry Stimson were appalled by the implications of the Manchurian crisis for their international peace structure, but it might as well have been challenged by Lower Slobbovia[76] as Japan, for all the analysis that attempted to deduce Tokyo's motivations, or a political system that permitted such motivations and their easy translation into policy. The Japanese were no more perceptive. The Imperial Navy, which insisted in 1940 that the United States could not be sheared away from Great Britain, did not arrive at this conclusion from a careful analysis of trends in London and Washington, but rather out of a need to justify itself and its own warplans for any southward advance.[77] The Imperial Army of 1941 barely gave the long-term implications of an attack on the Philippines much thought. The forlorn Japanese in Hawaii, disbelieving America's victory of 1945 even as they looked over a Pearl Harbor bursting with American power, displayed a blindness that typified relations across the Pacific for a half century. This is not to say that the Pacific War was inevitable. It just so happened that both nations' domestic imperatives made such a war quite likely. It was a terrible war, but it did ensure that the story of American-Japanese relations after 1945 would be quite different from the infrequent glances, touches and blows that characterized those before Hiroshima.

Acknowledgment

The author would like to thank Professors Roger Dingman and W. Miles Fletcher III for comments on an earlier version of this work.

NOTES

1. The exceptions—times of real dialogue in the sense of respect for the other government's domestic position—were quite limited. The United States (but not Japan) in the summer of 1945 and Japan (but not the United States) during the various immigration difficulties of the first quarter of the century.

2. There were sporadic efforts of this kind, nearly always undertaken by American members of the clergy. The most famous was the Walsh-Drought initiative of 1941. But missionary sorts also tried to lessen the consequences of American immigration restrictions through much of the period. See, for example, Izumi Hirobe, "American Attitudes Toward the Japanese Immigration Question, 1924–1931," *The Journal of American-East Asian Relations* (Fall 1993) 2: 275–302, and the works by Sandra Taylor, cited below.

3. For some of the early confusions in American-Korean relations, see Hong-Kyu Park, "From Pearl Harbor to Cairo: America's Korean Diplomacy, 1941–1943," *Diplomatic History* 13 (Summer 1989): 343–358.

4. This dynamic affected terms with Germany as well, of course. Churchill's willingness to keep alive consideration of a possible settlement with a non-Nazi German regime was never popular with the Americans, who seemed (and still seem) to equate militarism with military regimes and to have difficulty believing that civilian regimes could be militaristic.

5. The AAF was acutely conscious of the need to plan carefully and well in advance for the postwar demobilization, which had to be well handled to assure it a secure peacetime future. Yet even in early August 1945, its demobilization planners and highest officers—including those privy to the atomic bomb project—did not believe that the war against Japan would soon be over. See Jacob Vander Meulen, "Planning for VJ-Day by the US Army Air Forces and the Atomic Bomb Controversy," *The Journal of Strategic Studies* 16 (June 1993): 227–239.

6. There are at least speculative grounds for concluding that the German Army understood that an army regime in Germany would be welcomed by the West. Italy came to a similar, and correct, conclusion, and Japanese elites closely studied the occupation of Italy for signs that at least an anti-communist regime would be tolerated. However, the Imperial Army had associated itself too closely with radical reform, not conservatism, within Japan, just as the old "Imperial Way faction" had predicted in the early 1930s, and a reform fundamentally antithetical to the sort of global order preferred by the United States, as Cordell Hull had made clear (or thought he had made clear) during his discussions with Admiral Nomura in 1941. By 1944 and 1945 the army had no escape hatches whatsoever and acted accordingly. Its desire for a final Armageddon with America should surprise no one.

7. For that matter, the issue of suicide itself, whether institutional or individual, has not received sustained attention from historians. One preliminary foray can be seen in Louis Allen, "The Campaigns in Asia and the Pacific," *The Journal of Strategic Studies* 13 (March 1990): 162–192. Allen goes so far as to argue that *shinpū* (the employment of suicide attacks, popularly known as *kamikaze*) was Japan's chief contribution to the high strategy of war, as it would have made the Allied invasions of the home islands "unspeakably costly." Watanabe Shoichi explores the cultural background of this phenomenon in *The Peasant Soul of Japan* (New York: Macmillan, 1989). See also Shunsuke Tsurumi, *An Intellectual History of Wartime Japan, 1931–1945* (London: KPI Ltd., 1986), ch. 9. A personal testament to the practice may be found in Ugaki Matome, *Fading Victory* (Pittsburgh: University of Pittsburgh Press, 1991). Admiral Ugaki, Chief of Staff of the Combined Fleet from August 1941 to April 1943, took his own life in a suicide mission on August 15, 1945. His translated diaries make for fascinating reading. For an example of a famous Japanese pilot who refused to complete a suicide mission, see F. G. Notehelfer, "A Matter of Transcendence: War Experiences and the Transformation of Japanese and American Fighter Pilots," in James W. White, Michio Umegaki, and Thomas R. H. Havens, eds., *The Ambivalence of Nationalism: Modern Japan between East and West* (Lanham, Md.: University Press of America, 1990).

8. Stephen S. Large, *Emperor Hirohito and Showa Japan: A Political Biography* (London: Routledge, 1992).

9. Four of these documentary collections are reviewed in Large, "Emperor Hirohito and Early Showa Japan," *Monumenta Nipponica* 46 (Autumn 1991): 349–368. One collection includes the emperor's recollections of key events as recorded in early 1946.

10. Put simply, the emperor believed that only Tojo could keep the Imperial Army under control in the event of Japan's capitulation. He employed the same reasoning to strongly favor Tojo's appointment as Prime Minister in October 1941: here was a leader who could control the army come what may.

11. For dissenting views, which blame the emperor for being informed of Japan's foreign policies throughout the war, and allowing his office to be used by the ultranationalists, see John W. Dower, "Showa as Past, Present, and Future," in his *Japan in War and Peace* (New York: New Press, 1993) and a less scholarly, more vigorous attack in Edward Behr, *Hirohito: Behind the Myth* (London: Hamish Hamilton,1989).

12. Japan is barely mentioned in the skillful historiographic survey, J. Samuel Walker, "The Decision to Use the Bomb," *Diplomatic History* 14 (Winter 1990): 97–114.

13. See Rufus E. Miles, Jr., "Hiroshima: The Strange Myth of Half a Million American Lives Saved," *International Security* 10 (Fall 1985): 121–140 and Barton J. Bernstein, "A Postwar Myth: 500,000 U.S. Lives Saved," *Bulletin of The Atomic Scientists* 41 (June/July 1986): 38–40. These articles show that the half million figure was a postwar concoction. They do not demonstrate that the use of the atomic bombs was unnecessary, either in an abstract sense or in the views of American policymakers at the time. See the Vander Meulen article for evidence of AAF demobilization planning, in addition to three other articles illuminating the extent to which the United States was prepared to go to secure the unconditional surrender of Japan's military: Marc Gallicchio, "After Nagasaki: General Marshall's Plan for Tactical Nuclear Weapons in Japan," *Prologue* 23 (Winter 1991): 396–405; John Ellis van Courtland Moon, "Project SPHINX: The Question of the Use of Gas in the Planned Invasion of Japan," *The Journal of Strategic Studies* 12 (September 1989): 303–323; Barton J. Bernstein, "America's Biological Warfare Program in the Second World War," *The Journal of Strategic Studies* 11 (September 1988): 292–317. Gallicchio explores the willingness of the American military, including George C. Marshall, to consider the use of concentrated atomic bombings as preparation for an American invasion. Van Courtland Moon observes that Marshall was at least willing to discuss the use of gas warfare to take the fight out of Japanese fanatics in the home islands. Bernstein explores plans for the use of defoliants to destroy Japanese crops, possibly to begin in September or October 1945.

14. A good place to begin that examination would be with an analysis of the lessons both sides drew from the bloody fight on Okinawa from March to July 1945. There is little on the Japanese side and, surprisingly, not much more on the American. Miles's article argues that American casualty estimates were based upon extrapolations from the Luzon campaign. A fine starting point for Okinawa is Ian Gow with H. P. Willmott, *Okinawa 1945: Gateway to Japan* (London: Grub Street, 1986).

15. Namely this writer's *Nihon rikugun no shinchitsujokōs ōto kaisen kettei* ["The Imperial Army's New Order and Japan's Decision for War,"] *Taiheiyō sensō [The Pacific War]*, ed. Hosoya Chihiro, Homma Nagayo, Akira Iriye, and Hatano Sumio (University of Tokyo Press, 1993): 33–44.

16. There have been fine studies of the war itself. An outstanding one-volume survey of that war can be found in Ronald Spector, *Eagle Against the Sun: The American War with Japan* (New York: The Free Press, 1985). Among Spector's contributions is a trenchant analysis of the role (American) intelligence played in the war. A narrower study on this

topic alone based on fine research is Edward Drea, *MacArthur's ULTRA: Codebreaking and the War Against Japan* (Lawrence: University Press of Kansas, 1992).

17. Besides Sigal, there is Masanori Nakamura, *The Japanese Monarchy, 1931–1991: Ambassador Grew and the Making of the "Symbol Emperor System"* (Armonk, NY: M. E. Sharpe, 1992).

18. John Dower, *War Without Mercy: Race and Power in the Pacific War* (New York: Pantheon Books, 1986). See also James J. Weingartner, "Trophies of War: U.S. Troops and the Mutilation of Japanese War Dead, 1941–1945," *Pacific Historical Review* (February 1992) 61: 53–68.

19. Some of these assumptions are explored in Michael H. Hunt, *Ideology and U.S. Foreign Policy* (New Haven: Yale University Press, 1987).

20. However, it was an accommodation and alliance that was by no means an unalloyed victory for Japanese conservatives. As to the point, Grew himself favored dramatic change in an occupied Japan. See Steven Schwartzberg, "The 'Soft Peace Boys': Presurrender Planning and Japanese Land Reform," *The Journal of American-East Asian Relations* (Summer 1993) 2: 185–216. Grew's thoughts were shared and articulated by Edwin O. Reischauer, *My Life between Japan and America* (New York: Harper & Row, 1986).

21. For a somewhat different tack, see Frederick W. Marks III, "The Origin of FDR's Promise to Support Britain Militarily in the Far East—A New Look," *Pacific Historical Review* 53 (November 1984): 447–460. Marks argues that Roosevelt extended his guarantee by early October 1940.

22. Waldo Heinrichs, *Threshold of War: Franklin D. Roosevelt and American Entry into World War II* (New York: Oxford University Press, 1988), 51. For the role of China: Warren I. Cohen, *Nichi-Bei kanken ni okeru Chūgoku yōin* ["The Issue of China in Japanese-American Relations"] in Hosoya, et al., *Pacific War* 67–86.

23. There still is no full-length published study of Hornbeck.

24. These two objectives sometimes conflicted. Heinrichs implies that at least part of Stimson's determination to build up American airpower in the Philippines stemmed from his fear that if the planes were not sent there they would be diverted to British or Soviet forces and lost to the Army.

25. Michael Schaller, *MacArthur: The Far Eastern General* (Oxford University Press, 1989), ch. 4.

26. It is significant that Warren F. Kimball's new synthesis of Roosevelt's diplomacy barely mentions Japan. *The Juggler: Franklin Roosevelt as Wartime Statesman* (Princeton: Princeton University Press, 1991).

27. A useful survey of Japanese studies on this period can be found in Matsuda Takeshi, "The Coming of the Pacific War: Japanese Perspectives," *Reviews in American History* (December 1986) 14: 629–652.

28. Michael A. Barnhart, *Japan Prepares for Total War: The Search for Economic Security, 1919–1941* (Ithaca: Cornell University Press, 1987).

29. The best known example would be the National General Mobilization Law of 1938. It was barely noticed in American quarters, save as another example of Japan's slide into militarism.

30. Inflexibility in American policy toward Japan is a central theme in Jonathan Utley, *Going to War with Japan, 1937–1941* (Knoxville: University of Tennessee Press, 1985). Utley's account is the best yet in, among other things, discussing the oil embargo wrangle of the summer of 1941. An interesting side note on the Japanese view of the oil question is Kunio Katakura, "The Yokoyama Mission: Japanese Diplomacy for Oil, 1939," *The International History Review* 8 (May 1986): 263–269. A sampling of the debates over the origins

of the war can be found in Hilary Conroy and Harry Wray, eds., *Pearl Harbor Reexamined* (Honolulu: University of Hawaii Press, 1990).

31. Nomura Minoru, *Taiheiyō sensō to Nihon gunbu* (Yamakawa Shuppansha, 1983). For details on this and many other Japanese works, see the splendid collection by Asada Sadao, *Japan & the World, 1853–1952* (New York: Columbia University Press, 1989).

32. See the reprint of the 1946 original of Japanese Foreign Ministry documents relating to the surrender in Kurihara Ken and Hatano Sumio, eds., *Shūsen kōsaku no kiroku* (Kōdansha, 1986).

33. Edwin T. Layton, *"And I Was There" Pearl Harbor and Midway—Breaking the Secrets* (New York: Morrow, 1985); James Rusbridger and Eric Nave, *Betrayal at Pearl Harbor: How Churchill Lured Roosevelt into World War II* (New York: Summit Books, 1991), 144. Layton performs other analytical acrobatics, including an astounding supposition that the Soviet Union had broken Japanese codes and that a Soviet vessel spotted the Japanese fleet bound for Pearl Harbor and reported it to Stalin. Rusbridger and Nave agree with Layton that Britain was not entirely forthcoming with the Americans, but British records for this area and period remain closed in 1994.

34. Henry C. Clausen with Bruce Lee, *Pearl Harbor: Final Judgement* (New York: Crown, 1992), a hopeful title if ever there was one. Additional Japanese documents concerning the planning and execution of the attack appear in Donald M. Goldstein and Katherine V. Dillon, eds., *The Pearl Harbor Papers: Inside the Japanese Plans* (Washington: Brassey's, 1993).

35. Hosoya Chihiro, "Britain and the United States in Japan's View of the International System, 1937–1941," *Anglo-Japanese Alienation, 1919–1952*, ed. Ian Nish (Cambridge: Cambridge University Press, 1982). Louis Allen's article follows this line, too, suggesting that quite important segments of the "Pacific War" dealt with Asia and represented, for Britain, the last real colonial war it would fight. R. J. C. Butow, "Marching off to War on the Wrong Foot: The Final Note Tokyo Did *Not* Send to Washington," *Pacific Historical Review* 43 (February 1994): 67–79, is an interesting reexamination of the conclusion of the Hull-Nomura negotiations

36. Akira Iriye, *The Origins of the Second World War in Asia and the Pacific* (New York: Longman, 1987). See also his impressive survey, *The Globalizing of America, 1913–1945*, The Cambridge History of American Foreign Relations, vol. 3 (New York: Cambridge University Press, 1993). Further illustration of the international dimension of the East Asian state system can be found in Ian Nish, *Japan's Struggle with Internationalism: Japan, China and the League of Nations, 1931–3* (London: Kegan Paul International, 1993) and, appropriately, a collection of studies honoring Professor Nish's retirement, T. G. Fraser and Peter Lowe, eds., *Conflict and Amity in East Asia* (London: Macmillan, 1992).

37. Just how important any token of American support was to Chiang, and a remarkably broad range of Chinese, is made clear in Youli Sun, *China and the Origins of the Pacific War, 1931–1941* (New York: St. Martin's, 1993), especially ch. 7.

38. There still is no sustained scholarly study in English on the Imperial Army, war planning, and wartime politics.

39. The case for a Roosevelt vigorously interested in containing Japan with British help is built in Richard A. Harrison, "A Neutralization Plan for the Pacific: Roosevelt and Anglo-American Cooperation, 1934–1937," *Pacific Historical Review* 42 (February 1988): 47–72.

40. Cordell Hull, *Memoirs*, 1:290–1, cited in Howard Jablon, *Crossroads of Decision: The State Department and Foreign Policy, 1933–1937* (Lexington: The University Press of Kentucky, 1983), 62.

41. For example, in 1933 Grew objected to proposed Japanese controls over the petroleum industry in Manchuria. Interestingly, he was much more concerned with the issue as

a violation of the "Open Door" than as a sign of the Imperial Army's dedicated drive for self-sufficiency. Jablon *Crossroads of Decision*, 58.

42. Arthur Waldron, ed., *How the Peace Was Lost* (Stanford: Hoover Institute Press, 1992).

43. Ibid., 133.

44. Jablon, *Crossroads of Decision*, 64.

45. Arnold A. Offner, "Appeasement and Aggression: The New Deal and the Origins of the Second World War," *Fifty Years Later: The New Deal Evaluated*, ed. Harvard Sitkoff (New York: Knopf, 1985), 199, 202.

46. Michael A. Bernstein, "Why the Great Depression Was Great: Toward a New Understanding of the Interwar Economic Crisis in the United States," and Alan Brinkley, "The New Deal and the Idea of the State," *The Rise and Fall of the New Deal Order, 1930–1980*, Steve Fraser and Gary Gerstle, eds. (Princeton University Press, 1989). Iriye, in *Globalizing*, discusses the role of Charles Beard and other American critics and thinkers in insisting upon priority for resolution of domestic problems, as well as the virulent xenophobia of Father Coughlin and others. Much work remains in this area.

47. (Madison: University of Wisconsin Press, 1964). A. Romasco's *The Politics of Recovery* dissects the domestic presures on Roosevelt during the London Economic Conference with precision and insight. There is nothing comparable for American-East Asian relations during these years.

48. Frederick Marks, *Wind Over Sand* (Athens: University of Georgia Press, 1988).

49. Many Japanese in these years were certain that liberal capitalism was collapsing. See, for example, this writer's *Japan Prepares*, ch. 3 and William M. Fletcher III, *The Search for a New Order* (Chapel Hill: University of North Carolina Press, 1982).

50. Justus D. Doenecke, *When the Wicked Rise: American Opinion-Makers and the Manchurian Crisis of 1931–1933* (Lewisburg: Bucknell University Press, 1984).

51. Ibid., chapter 1.

52. Ibid., chs. 2–4. Interesting parallels can be found in Sandra C. Taylor, "The Ineffectual Voice: Japan Missionaries and American Foreign Policy, 1870–1941," *Pacific Historical Review* (February 1984) 53:20–38. A group of American missionaries in Japan protested American reinforcements at Shanghai, arguing that this step aided Japanese militarists and made the work of "liberal-minded" Japanese more difficult. Taylor, 30. Taylor's major study, *Advocate of Understanding: Sidney Gulick and the Search for Peace with Japan* (Kent State University Press, 1984) makes clear that there was much suspicion about Japan well before 1931, much of it associated with the immigration issue. Taylor's work makes clear how important the American immigration act of 1924 was in discouraging such advocates on both sides of the Pacific. Her conclusions are reinforced by a number of seminal studies on Japanese thinkers. See Thomas W. Burkman's analysis of Nitobe Inazō in J. Thomas Rimer, ed., *Culture and Identity: Japanese Intellectuals During the Interwar Years* (Princeton: Princeton University Press, 1990), ch. 10. Also, Shin'ichi Kitaoka, "Prophet Without Honor: Kiyosawa Kiyoshi's View of Japanese-American Relations," in White, et al., *The Ambivalence of Nationalism*.

53. One exception is Timothy P. Maga, "Prelude to War? The United States, Japan, and the Yap Crisis, 1918–22," *Diplomatic History* (Summer 1985) 9:215–232. Maga concludes that the crisis was no such prelude, but did indicate the growing frictions and clash of interests between Tokyo and Washington. There is little indication in his study that Americans had clearly distinguished between an aggressive, dangerous Japanese military and "liberal-minded" Japanese during that crisis, however. Maga's is the only article devoted to American-Japanese relations for the 1900–1945 period in the past decade of *Diplomatic History*.

54. Edward S. Miller, *War Plan ORANGE: The U.S. Strategy to Defeat Japan, 1897–1945* (Annapolis: Naval Institute Press, 1991), 4.

55. Naval planners never worried about the safety of the fleet at Pearl Harbor. It was judged quite capable of taking care of itself. Ibid., 48.

56. John J. Stephan, *Hawaii Under the Rising Sun: Japan's Plan for Conquest after Pearl Harbor* (Honolulu: University of Hawaii Press, 1984).

57. Ibid., 79.

58. Ibid., 49.

59. Hector C. Bywater, *The Great Pacific War: A History of the American-Japanese Campaign of 1931–33* (Boston: Houghton Mifflin, 1925).

60. William H. Honan, *Visions of Infamy: The Untold Story of How Journalist Hector C. Bywater Devised the Plans that Led to Pearl Harbor* (New York: St. Martin's, 1991). A broader survey of similar matters was undertaken by Mark R. Peattie, "Forecasting a Pacific War, 1912–1933: The Idea of a Conditional Japanese Victory," in White, et al., *The Ambivalence of Nationalism*. Peattie, too, notes the importance of the 1924 immigration law.

61. For example, Sir Frederic Maurice, a distinguished veteran of the First World War, argued that Japan's poverty of resources would never allow even the illusion of victory. Honan, *Visions of Infamy*, 171.

62. Early studies of Japanese immigration to Hawaii suggest why the planters wanted to avoid additional Japanese. The Meiji regime closely and ably controlled emigration, and erected an overseas apparatus to look after the interests of Japan and Japanese emigrants. Although these protections were more often directed against unscrupulous Japanese, especially one notorious bank, that exploited the emigrants, the specter of the Japanese state's effectiveness affected the planters' desires for more Japanese workers. Alan Takeo Muriyama, *Imingaisha: Japanese Emigration Companies and Hawaii, 1894–1908*. (Honolulu: University of Hawaii Press, 1985).

63. Wayne Patterson, *The Korean Frontier in America: Immigration to Hawaii, 1896–1910* (Honolulu: University of Hawaii Press, 1988). An examination of American acquiescence to Japan's tightening colonial grip is John Edward Wilz, "Did the United States Betray Korea in 1905?" *Pacific Historical Review* (August 1985) 54: 243–270. A useful survey of early American-Korean relations can be found in John Edward Wilz, "Encountering Korea: American Perceptions and Policies to 25 June 1950," *A Revolutionary War: Korea and the Transformation of the Postwar World*, ed. William J. Williams (Chicago: Imprint Publications, 1993): 13–82. A longer examination of the early years is Jongsuk Chay, *Diplomacy of Asymmetry: Korean-American Relations to 1910* (Honolulu: University of Hawaii Press, 1990). A useful collection of research materials appears in Scott S. Burnett, ed., *Korean-American Relations: Documents Pertaining to the Far Eastern Diplomacy of the United States: III: The Period of Diminishing Influence, 1896–1905* (Honolulu: University of Hawaii Press, 1989).

64. And thus Korean emigration as well, since Koreans then traveled under Japanese passports.

65. Mitziko Sawada, "Culprits and Gentlemen: Meiji Japan's Restriction of Emigrants to the United States, 1891–1909," *Pacific Historical Review* (August 1991) 60: 339–360.

66. The wartime culmination of these sorts of trends is summarized in John W. Dower, "The Useful War," in Carol Gluck and Stephen R. Graubard, eds., *Showa: The Japan of Hirohito* (New York: Norton, 1992) and explored further in W. Miles Fletcher III, *Taiheiyō sensō no Nihon keizai e no eikyō* ["The Pacific War's Impact on Japan's Economy"] in Hosoya, et al., 371–392.

67. (The University of North Carolina Press, 1989), 90.

68. Fletcher, *The Search for a New Order*, 102.

69. Reasons for the lack of interest in at least one important sector are given in William D. Wray, *Mitsubishi and the N.Y.K., 1870–1914: Business Strategy in the Japanese Shipping Industry* (Cambridge: Harvard University Press, 1984). Trans-Pacific traffic was small and largely unprofitable before the completion of the Panama Canal, confined as it was to shipments to Seattle or San Francisco, usually from Shanghai in the N.Y.K.'s case, and then overland by rail. Ironically, this kind of sea-land route is enjoying a substantial rebirth in the 1990s. The need for an analysis of Pacific basin economic flows and transactions from 1900 to 1941 is compelling.

70. Ibid., 105.

71. Mark Mason, *American Multinationals and Japan: The Political Economy of Japanese Capital Controls, 1899–1980* (Cambridge: Harvard University Press, 1992). Mason catalogs an impressively comprehensive set of those capital controls during this entire period. Two questions arise. First, how were American companies able to overcome Japanese resistance at all, early in this century. Second, why was the "cooperative diplomacy" of the 1920s not joined by a lowering of such resistance? Mason recounts the astounding statistic that by 1929 American foreign direct investment was greater in China than Japan. A fascinating personal account of Japanese business in the United States appears in Haru Matsukata Reischauer, *Samurai and Silk: A Japanese and American Heritage* (Cambridge: Harvard University Press, 1986). Reischauer's less well known grandfather was Arai Rioichiro, who became the first direct exporter of American cotton to Japan. Arai, whose business led him to live near New York, received much better treatment personally after Japan's victory over Russia in 1905.

72. One model for such studies is Yuji Ichioka, " 'Attorney for the Defense': Yamato Ichihashi and Japanese Immigration," *Pacific Historical Review* 50 (May 1986): 192–225.

73. An example of such a look, from a British perspective, is George Feaver, ed., *The Webbs in Asia: The 1911–12 Travel Diary* (London: Macmillan, 1992).

74. Notehelfer's work marks a good start in this regard for the Pacific war era. Similar work, for a much earlier such exchange, can be briefly found in James R. Rechner, *Teddy Roosevelt's Great White Fleet* (Annapolis: Naval Institute Press, 1988).

75. Sharon H. Nolte, *Liberalism in Modern Japan: Ishibashi Tanzan and His Teachers, 1905–1960* (Berkeley: University of California Press, 1987); K.H. Nute, *Frank Lloyd Wright and Japan: The Role of Japan in the Shaping of Frank Lloyd Wright's Organic Architecture* (New York: Routledge, 1994); Warren I. Cohen, *East Asian Art and American Culture: A Study in International Relations* (New York: Columbia University Press, 1992).

76. With apologies to L'il Abner.

77. The depth of feeling against the United States among many senior officers of the Imperial Navy is expertly developed in Sadao Asada, "From Washington to London: The Imperial Japanese Navy and the Politics of Naval Limitation, 1921–30," *Diplomacy and Statecraft* 4 (November 1993): 147–191. Early Japanese interest in the South Seas appears in Mark R. Peattie, *Nan'yō: The Rise and Fall of the Japanese in Micronesia, 1885–1945* (Honolulu: University of Hawaii Press, 1988), ch. 2.

Chapter Nine

Continuing Controversies in the Literature of U.S.-China Relations Since 1945

NANCY BERNKOPF TUCKER

During the 1980s and early 1990s several exciting developments enlivened scholarship in the area of American-Chinese relations since 1945, among them the declassification of vast collections of evidence regarding the development of policy toward China, the adoption of new perspectives and techniques, and the entry of Chinese scholars into the arena. On the American side the cables, letters, memoranda, and reports released by presidential libraries, the State Department, Defense Department and Central Intelligence Agency have opened new vistas on the troubled interaction between the United States and China in the Cold War years. Whereas in the 1970s historians were limited to modest accumulations of documents for the Truman period, by the end of the decade not only had releases from the Truman archives become a torrent but the Eisenhower Library rapidly caught up and surpassed it in supplying new sources. By the end of the 1980s, archivists at the Lyndon Johnson Library were also making important strides in opening files, leaving the John F. Kennedy Library as the single significant barrier to research in presidential records. As for the National Archives, classification continued to limit State

Department materials to the pre-1958 period and military records to the early 1960s. The result, nevertheless, has been a series of discoveries about the actual policies American officials pursued between 1945 and 1969 in sometimes striking contrast with the earlier assumptions of historians.

Although the struggle to open U.S. documentary records has not been without tumult and challenge during the past decade,[1] more extraordinary has been the advent of access, however limited, to archival holdings in China and the former Soviet Union. Completely unanticipated when scholars met for the *New Frontiers* [2] conference, reforms in China, the end of the Cold War and the collapse of the Soviet empire have not only added crucial events to the history that must be studied but also created an atmosphere more conducive to serious historical inquiry. The resulting flow of documents and memoirs have proven of mixed reliability, as researchers such as He Di and Steven M. Goldstein have cautioned, but have nevertheless broadened horizons considerably.[3] The scholarship utilizing this abundance of information and these new insights has been significant, stimulating, and markedly different from books and articles completed in the 1970s and before.

Fresh approaches in methodological terms have also made this new literature unusually exciting. This is not traditional historical dialogue between foreign ministries. The literature of the 1980s looks at cultural interaction as well as military confrontation. It takes seriously the influence of public opinion, of domestic pressure groups (including ethnic minorities) and the insights provided by psychological analysis. New perspectives have been borrowed from political science as well as from social history. Diplomatic historians have also been using the critical tools provided by the Wisconsin school of William Appleman Williams's followers who emphasize the economic roots of policymaking. This inclusiveness has yielded a literature more sophisticated than that of earlier times, one that interweaves narrative with fresh analytical perceptions, which neither ignores the key role of individuals and contingency nor the significance for policymaking of the dynamics of psychology, economics, or culture.

Finally there is the unprecedented arrival of Chinese scholars on the stage of serious, nonpolemical historical analysis in the years since Deng Xiaoping inaugurated reforms in China at the end of the 1970s. Despite the setback for scholarship in China as a result of the political repression following the 1989 Tiananmen Massacre, several young, well-trained and imaginative historians have continued to revolutionize the way Chinese examine their own history and their relations with the U.S.

In 1988 Robert McMahon asked the question, in an important historiographical article,[4] whether a synthesis had emerged in the literature concerning the Cold War in Asia. He concluded that pursuit of consensus regarding the troubling issues in the field was premature given the many problems still to be explored, the archival materials still untapped, and the vast differences among interpretative approaches still largely unreconciled. Six years later McMahon's critique remains true not only of the larger arena of American-East Asian relations but also of exploration of United States relations with China. Discovery and controversy are the norm rather than any fresh, satisfying, and widely accepted paradigm.

The most basic controversy has been over the nature and roots of American and Chinese policy. Did Washington invariably permit Cold War considerations to dictate decisions regarding China as it allowed the U.S.-Soviet confrontation increasingly to dominate the making of policy toward Europe? Or did officials still engage in bilateral policymaking shaped by more traditional considerations among which was apathy regarding developments in China? Debate regarding the globalization of Washington's postwar vision has gripped the general literature on U.S. foreign relations. The uncertainty about China involves the need to make Chinese history part of world history and the contradictory imperative to recognize those factors that prevent U.S.-China relations from being lost in a monolithic model of communism and an all-encompassing American response to it. Clearly the quickening tide of Cold War confrontation in Europe and the Middle East sensitized U.S. policymakers to potentially threatening Soviet behavior in Asia. But it remains unclear when and whether the Soviet menace became dominant and swept nuanced decisionmaking before it.

On the Chinese side similar issues of ideology and pragmatism have emerged to bedevil interpretive coherence. There is little doubt that the Chinese Communists both by inclination and necessity looked to Moscow for sustenance and guidance. Nevertheless, scholars have found the force of nationalism a jarring counterpoint to alignment and alliance. How the balance was achieved for a leadership immersed in revolution, devoted to sovereignty, and determined to build a strong nation continues to fuel controversy.

Therefore, not only has the question of when the Cold War came to Asia and how quickly it eclipsed other imperatives for decisionmaking remained unresolved, but so too has the related issue of the so-called "lost chance" continued to engage scholars. Harry Harding has suggested that conferees at a pathbreaking conference on Sino-American relations held in Beijing in 1986 believed that in the late 1940s

The Chinese, frustrated by the injustices and inequalities in their society, the slow pace of their country's modernization, and their subordinate position in the international system, were engaged in a massive domestic revolution, the aim of which was to overthrow the existing political and economic order and to replace it with a new set of leaders and institutions. The United States, in contrast, . . . was showing a renewed interest in outward expansion and brought to its relations with Asia a distaste for revolutions in general and for Communist movements in particular. [Thus] the cleavage between the two sides was simply too wide for them to work out . . . [demanding] a degree of maturity, sophistication, and mutual understanding that neither country then possessed in adequate measure.5

In reality scholarly disagreement survives regarding the possibilities for an accommodation of modest parameters which could have facilitated interchanges such as trade even as political and ideological frictions remained.

If some analysts, then, see ideology and experience as precluding alternatives for the governments of the period, others identify greater flexibility. Akira Iriye noted in his controversial essay "Was There a Cold War in Asia?" that "the United States chose not to engage the Soviet Union in a cold war in [China] . . . during these years. *There was a cold war perception but no cold war*."6 Subsequent research demonstrated that Iriye's nuanced approach fit well the realities of what happened, for instance, at Yalta.

Whereas historians have long agreed that during the Yalta conference in February 1945 Roosevelt sought to sustain working relations with Stalin to meet wartime demands and provide for a peaceful future, new studies demonstrate that FDR did not sell China down the river to accomplish these goals. Odd Arne Westad asserts that the agreements signed at Yalta actually followed logically from the events of the preceding months and were not the mistakes of a senile, dying man.7 John W. Garver goes further to assert that although "domestic political considerations required that Chiang [Kai-shek] later plead surprise and outrage at this Soviet-American diktat . . . , Chiang had long sought American mediation and had indicated to Roosevelt general approval of several of the key elements which were embodied in the Yalta agreement." Moreover, according to Garver, "the roots of specific terms of the Yalta agreement traced back to Chiang's 1940 offer of alliance with the Soviet Union."8

Yalta in this rendition loses much of the Cold War edge of earlier analyses as do events in Manchuria when studied by Steven I. Levine. According to Levine, fears of Soviet ambitions in Manchuria led to George Marshall's mediation mission in 1945, but the United States quickly recognized that this was not a Cold War battleground necessitating commitment of lavish resources and concerted resistance. Fortuitously, Moscow, understanding that the U.S. would not intervene to guarantee a Kuomintang victory, chose to circumscribe, although certainly not dispense with, its own assistance to the CCP. The Soviet Union proved critical to CCP success in the end, and Marshall never truly performed as an impartial mediator because of the Soviet factor, but in the short-term Marshall concluded that containment did not need to be applied in Manchuria.[9]

When then did the Cold War arrive in China? To both Garver and Westad the origins of Cold War policies related intimately to domestic Chinese politics. Each makes much of the strategies employed by Chiang Kai-shek to manipulate the great powers. Garver posits an effort simultaneously to involve the United States in Chinese affairs and to assure the Soviet Union that the Kuomintang would remain neutral in Soviet-American confrontations and welcome continuing assistance from Moscow.[10] Westad argues that Chiang's early success in securing support from both Washington and Moscow dissipated during 1946. As relations worsened between the U.S. and USSR globally, Chiang lost the ability to monopolize patronage because each of the powers insisted on exclusivity. In the end, the Chinese civil war "originated with the emergence of the Cold War," insists Westad, even though this seems to underestimate the legacy of earlier struggle and the urgency of contemporary internal disarray.[11]

Chinese scholars have tended to see Mao Zedong's disillusionment with the United States beginning soon after the World War II coalition of powers fractured. Few writing in English still subscribe to an undifferentiated portrait of American policy as invariably supporting repression and reaction.[12] Nevertheless, although they concede that tensions existed also in Sino-Soviet relations given Stalin's continuing determination to protect the cradle of the revolution at all costs, the antagonism felt for the United States was of a different sort, far more profound, according to Yang Kuisong.[13]

Did Chinese Communist disenchantment in the mid-1940s make impossible any subsequent improvement in U.S.-China relations? Steven Goldstein has repeatedly argued the "no chance" thesis, stating forcefully his view that for ideological reasons no accommodation could have occurred between the U.S. and the CCP.[14] Similarly Shaw Yu-ming contends that Mao and Zhou had made clear, even without John Leighton Stuart's aborted trip to Peking, that CCP commitment to the Soviet Union was total.[15] Huang Hua told Warren I. Cohen in a 1986 interview that his discussions with Stuart during 1949 were never expected to produce accommodation but rather were meant to prevent a U.S. invasion of China.[16] And Ho Zhigong reports that Huang told him an additional motive was to undermine resistance to CCP takeover by suggesting a U.S. intention to abandon the Nationalists.[17] He Di, however, argues that awareness of irreconcilable tensions and objectives, in fact, occurred only gradually between 1944 and 1949 and that during those years opportunities for better relations were missed.[18] Moreover, Zhai Qiang rejects an exclusive emphasis on the centrality of ideology, asserting that "although ideology and historical remembrance helped shape the CCP's foreign policy, geopolitical considerations were of paramount importance." Thus "the CCP had not excluded establishing diplomatic and trade relations with Western countries."[19] And Lowell Dittmer, a careful student of Chinese politics, suggests that although Mao professed to be uninterested "the CCP leadership was prepared to offer low-profile diplomatic relations and an opportunity for dialogue" but was "too weak to resist bloc discipline" and "too needy to decline Soviet aid in the context of Western isolation and American blockade."[20]

How early, then, did the United States follow a Cold War path? There were very good reasons for Washington's opposition to civil war in China quite apart from concern about Soviet expansionism. After decades of struggle the country lay prostrate, its people and economy exhausted and the ramifications of continuing political instability, famine, and fighting profound for all of East Asia. Given these conditions, Washington ought entirely to have devoted its energies to bolstering the KMT regime. So much more so had the Cold War been on policymakers' minds. Qing Simei, in a fascinating attempt to apply the sociology of knowledge to international relations, demonstrates that instead the U.S. undermined its ally by imposing the 1947 commercial treaty on an unwilling population. This arrangement, which damaged Kuomintang credibility and violated both Nationalist and Communist visions for the development of the political economy of East Asia, predominantly served American business interests and suggested a disregard for political and strategic priorities.[21]

Nevertheless Marc S. Gallicchio contends that anti-Soviet convictions played the critical role in policy choices for the U.S. as early as 1945. Indeed, Gallicchio's Harry S Truman is far quicker to jump to conclusions about parallels between communist behavior in Asia and Europe than much recent literature has suggested. This Truman, who harks back to an earlier portrait of a quick tempered, unreflective president, reacted profoundly to Soviet involvement in northeast Asia and, as a result of the continuing crises buffeting U.S. leaders during 1945, simply interprets all revolutionary action as Soviet subversion.[22]

By the time Dean Acheson became Secretary of State in January 1949 the collapse of Nationalist fortunes in China could not be arrested. Although this is clear in retrospect, at the time various individuals and groups still hoped to save Chiang Kai-shek from oblivion. Was Acheson one of these people? There seems to be general agreement that Acheson disliked Chiang and shared the spreading assessment of Nationalist rule as corrupt and ineffective. He sent Livingston Merchant to Taiwan early in 1949 to see whether the overthrow of Chiang might bring new and more desirable leaders to the fore. But Merchant concluded that a coup could not be carried out given the generalissimo's iron grip on local politics. The fate of Chiang, the Nationalists and Taiwan seemed inseparable.[23]

From this juncture analyses diverge regarding the importance given to Taiwan and the lengths to which the Truman administration would go to preserve Nationalist rule. Whereas Robert McMahon declared optimistically in his 1988 essay that scholars had reached consensus on the view that "prior to the Korean War, the Truman administration contemplated accommodation with Beijing to a much greater extent than previously recognized" no genuine meeting of the minds appears to have occurred.[24] Those who have examined Acheson's policies most intensively in the European context, such as Melvyn Leffler,[25] portray an undifferentiated Acheson who pursued the Cold War with as much determination in Asia. According to David McLean, who dismisses the importance of bureaucratic, Congressional or public pressures upon leaders at the time, Acheson's ideological commitment to democratic idealism allowed only a momentary dalliance with pragmatic action, and forced a quick abandonment of any effort at accommodation.[26] Robert Blum asserts that the disparity in Washington's response to communism in Europe and Asia followed from limited resources and familiarity with Europe rather than indifference to Asia.[27] In my work, on the other hand, I have demonstrated that Acheson could be a cold warrior in Europe where the stakes were high and follow quite a different path in China where his objectives and the national interests were not significantly engaged, where he and the American people were apathetic and ignorant and where he hoped to promote a breach between Peking and Moscow.[28]

The examination of economic policies along with strategic and political goals reveals Acheson's flexibility. Yoko Yasuhara and I have exploited commercial records to demonstrate the importance of economic imperatives. Confronted by efforts within the administration to place strict controls on commerce with the Communist Chinese, Acheson saw trade as a lure to split the Chinese from Soviet control. He thought about the possibility that Mao might prove to be another Tito and recognized, in any case, that Chinese markets and raw materials were critical to Japanese economic recovery which he considered a high priority.[29]

In the spring of 1950 Acheson held the line against any American effort to rescue the Kuomintang on Taiwan in spite of mounting pressures in the nation and among his own advisers to do something. Although Bruce Cumings and June Grasso have posited conspiracy, having written about plots and plans hatched by those who could not bear to see Taiwan fall, they have not been able to prove that Acheson did more than listen sympathetically, even occasionally with some interest, and then turn them down flat.[30] This was true even as some of his most moderate China experts grew pessimistic about the potential of better relations with the Communist Chinese.[31]

Accordingly, the administration made clear its willingness to accept what intelligence agencies predicted would be an inevitable CCP assault and KMT collapse. It communicated this posture through a State Department circular telegram of December 1949, Harry Truman's January 5, 1950 news conference remarks, and Acheson's infamous January 12, 1950 National Press Club speech placing Taiwan and Korea outside the American defensive perimeter. Although Bruce Cumings insists that it is a misconception that Korea and Taiwan were excluded, he does concede that the concept of such a perimeter was not new with Acheson. At the same time he rejects John Gaddis's argument that Acheson was simply reiterating a military-strategic policy previously adopted by the military, the NSC and the president, and instead sees the January speech as based in political economy.[32]

Ironically recent research in Chinese sources indicates that, contrary to U.S. intelligence estimates, China was not prepared to attack Taiwan that summer. Lacking trained personnel and equipment, Beijing had begun to plan for an invasion in the summer of 1951.[33] Moreover, it appears that the Acheson speech, which Republican opponents of the Truman administration vigorously denounced as an invitation to war on the Korean peninsula, actually did serve as reassurance to China and the Soviet Union that their objectives in East Asia might be met without U.S. interference.[34] On the other hand, according to Sergei N. Goncharov, John W. Lewis and Xue Litai, whose collaboration brought a unique multinational thrust to their analysis, Stalin, throughout this period, remained preoccupied with the necessity of preventing reconciliation between Washington and Beijing. Anything that might facilitate better Sino-American understanding and eliminate points of friction must be sabotaged, including American acquiescence in China's conquest of Taiwan or Beijing's admission to the United Nations. Such developments would be most unwelcome, undermining the PRC's dependence upon the USSR.[35]

Throughout 1949 and early 1950 Communist leaders had debated the likelihood of American military intervention on behalf of the Nationalists. According to Yang Kuisong and Chen Jian, Mao and the CCP concluded in 1949 that the threat of U.S. invasion had receded given its passivity while PLA forces eliminated the last KMT resistance.[36] Zhang Shu Guang, Chen Xiaolu,

Jonathan Pollack, Hao Yufan and Zhai Zhihai, on the other hand, emphasize Mao's sense of encirclement and his conviction that an American assault would come from either Korea, Taiwan or Indochina in the near future. To Pollack, Hao and Zhai Zhihai anxiety about being surrounded was critical to Mao's decision to intervene in Korea since, if war with the U.S. was inevitable, it would better be fought in Korea where the logistics were more favorable to China.[37] Goncharov, Lewis and Xue propose yet another interpretation, claiming that Mao, although worried that Washington would intervene, could not admit this to Moscow given his assurances to Stalin that a Soviet-supported Chinese attack on Taiwan would not trigger an American response.[38]

Rosemary Foot makes clear that throughout the Korean conflict bureaucratic and public pressures in the United States for an attack on China mounted. U.S. officials did contemplate air and naval action against China in the early days of the Korean War. Moreover, "those early discussions of retaliation served to bring the administration dangerously close to expanding the war" on several later occasions including proposals to use atomic warheads to force acceptance of an armistice agreement.[39] Edward Keefer stresses the bankruptcy and desperation of an American policy which contemplated escalation of a localized conflict into a nuclear assault on the PRC simply because Washington could find no other way to secure peace.[40]

American policymakers at the time were quick to assume a Chinese role in the North Korean invasion and recent studies have continued to question the degree of China's foreknowledge and involvement.[41] Nikita Khrushchev insisted in his memoirs that Stalin turned to Mao for advice on whether the Soviet Union should approve Kim Il-sung's war and that Mao urged support.[42] More recent research in newly opened Soviet archives shows that Stalin did, in fact, hesitate in encouraging Kim—he was not pushing to test American resolve[43]—but is less clear regarding Mao's role. Kathryn Weathersby indicates, from her reading of a confidential 1966 Soviet report, that Stalin acted in part out of distrust of Mao and that Kim got Mao's approval for his operation during an April 1950 visit to Beijing.[44] Chinese scholars Hao Yufan and Zhai Zhihai, on the other hand, assert that although Kim informed Mao of his general determination to reunify Korea, he did not tell Mao about his military plans or the date on which he would launch his effort. Furthermore, China's lack of preparedness, they insist, demonstrates that the Chinese did not know. Beijing, absorbed in domestic problems, paid little attention to developments on the peninsula, had only one army in the border area which was engaged in agricultural production, and had launched a general demobilization of the People's Liberation Army, not a buildup for possible war in

Korea. Mao, moreover, understanding in general terms that Kim wished to reunify his country, opposed the idea.[45] On the other hand, Anthony Farrar-Hockley emphasizes redeployment of Chinese forces north in the spring of 1950,[46] and Chen Jian flatly rejects the argument that Mao opposed Kim's militant proposal.[47] William Stueck places his emphasis on the external assistance that the North Koreans received for prosecuting the war a significant proportion of which, even before China's intervention, came from Beijing.[48]

Chinese intervention came as a surprise to the Americans because they ignored Chinese warnings, failed to understand the security threat they were posing to Beijing, and discounted the ability of China to mount a serious war effort. When the moment arrived, the U.S. government once again assumed that Beijing acted at Moscow's behest. Weathersby's research suggests that Stalin did pressure the Chinese Communists to enter the war, a point contested by Zhang Shu Guang whose research relies on Chinese, not Soviet, sources.[49] It is clear that China had good, independent reasons for making its commitment to North Korea among which Hao, Zhai Zhihai, Chen, Pollack, Thomas J. Christensen, and others stress rational security calculations.[50] Mao, in particular, believed that action was necessary and compelled agreement from other leaders to the risky course.[51] Michael Hunt and Zhang depart from this focus on carefully reasoned decisionmaking. Utilizing methodologies borrowed from political psychology, deterrence theory and cultural studies, they emphasize the confusion, cultural misunderstanding, and contingency which proved decisive factors in both Beijing and Washington.[52]

Once in the war Mao looked less at national defense and domestic stability, and, like the American leadership in Washington, inflated his goals which, for Mao, came to include U.S. departure from Taiwan and a Chinese seat in the United Nations.[53] The realities of the struggle, however, quickly disabused him of these ambitions and there are indications that the Chinese sought an earlier settlement to the conflict than Stalin wanted. Burton Kaufman argues that the United States missed an opportunity for a cease-fire and negotiated settlement in 1951.[54] Rosemary Foot explores the difficulties Americans had in accepting the idea of a compromise peace or in responding seriously to Communist Chinese hints that progress could be made on particular issues.[55]

Instead, Washington sought to coerce an end to the war by threatening to use nuclear weapons.[56] But it is not clear whether the Chinese took the possibility of a nuclear attack seriously. Whereas Daniel Calingaert argues that the American tactic was effective, other scholars believe that Beijing did not find U.S. warnings credible, either because they underestimated the potential damage or thought world opinion would restrain Washington.[57] It also remains unclear whether Eisenhower really would have used the bombs or whether his was simply an example of masterful diplomacy, an interpretation scoffed at by Rosemary Foot in her superb review of the literature on the war.[58] In the end, the war raised Chinese international prestige considerably although at a terrible cost in lives and strain on the domestic economy.[59]

Eisenhower administration policy toward China, beyond the problems caused by the Korean War, until recently was thought to embody the firm Cold War stand held by the United States against the expansion of communism in Asia. From the unleashing of Chiang Kai-shek in Ike's first state of the union address to Washington's support for the Nationalists in two dangerous and unnecessary crises over the offshore islands, the personnel, the policies, and the public attitudes of the 1950s assumed that monolithic communism dictated Chinese behavior.[60] The destructive McCarthyite pall cast over U.S.-China relations in the 1950s has received painstaking study in the intellectual biography of the persecution of Owen Lattimore. Paul Evans also uses intellectual history to pursue some of the same issues in the life of John Fairbank.[61] And venturing even further outside the traditional province of diplomatic history, William O. Walker shows how the anticommunism of American officials, particularly Harry J. Anslinger, commissioner of the Federal Bureau of Narcotics, interfered with antiopium campaigns in Asia. Despite Beijing's efforts to eradicate poppy production at home, its denial of drug trafficking and the lack of evidence that it sought to undermine the West through narcotic sales, Anslinger persisted in wild accusations. His continuing "misrepresentation of the PRC's antiopium records," asserts Walker, "contributed to the development of U.S. security policy early in Eisenhower's administration" as it had under Truman.[62]

Eisenhower revisionism, however, has not only altered assessments of the president's leadership style, but also has challenged earlier assumptions about his view of China and his administration's policies toward the Chinese.[63] Similarly, scholars have looked again at John Foster Dulles, a "limited Dulles renaissance" Robert Divine calls it, and have traded the common portrait of a ferocious cold warrior, for a picture of a more reasonable and cautious diplomat.[64]

Fundamental to this reassessment has been a widespread recognition that Eisenhower and Dulles were more flexible regarding China than heretofore assumed. David Allan Mayers, Gordon H. Chang, and I have proven that neither Eisenhower nor Dulles thought communism was monolithic.[65] Eisenhower believed the United States ought to conduct trade with the PRC and that its representatives should sit in the United Nations.[66] Dulles pursued a "two Chinas" policy, accepting the reality of communist control on the mainland and seeking to curb Chiang Kai-shek's fantasies of returning there. Far from being an uncritical exponent of the Nationalist cause, Dulles held serious reservations about Chiang and released him immediately after Eisenhower's provocative and risky State of the Union declaration setting Nationalist forces free.[67] In addition to distancing the U.S. from Chiang, John Lewis Gaddis has argued that Dulles hoped to divide China and the Soviet Union by applying a "wedge strategy" that would force the two together, demonstrate Moscow's inability to meet Chinese needs, and produce sufficient friction to sever the alliance.[68] From Waldo Heinrichs's perspective, however, the indifference to Asia shared by Eisenhower and Dulles, as it had been earlier by Truman and Acheson, "encouraged illusion, and illusions about East Asia generated their own persisting, self-inflicted wounds."[69]

Whatever the underlying attitudes may have been, the central policies and problems of the period revolved around the offshore islands crises of 1954–55 and 1958. Traditional assessments of these events suggested episodes of Chinese expansionism thwarted by U.S. willingness to take China to the brink of war.[70] A far more nuanced story has been pieced together in recent years.

To begin with in neither crisis was Beijing really determined to seize Jinmen and Mazu. In each instance, it sought rather to make a political point to the world community regarding the status of Taiwan as a part of China. According to the work of He Di and Gordon Chang, who emphasize the importance of cultural misperception in the Sino-American relationship, the Chinese never even saw the encounter of 1954–55 as a crisis.[71] In 1954, contend He, Xue, Lewis, Thomas E. Stolper, and I, the Chinese Communists sought to frustrate an American effort to gain adherents to its "two Chinas" policy and particularly to discourage Washington from signing a mutual defense treaty with the Nationalists by demonstrating that the U.S. risked being dragged into dangerous confrontations in Asia. Beijing, however, did not want conflict directly with the U.S. and turned to ambassadorial talks to defuse the crisis.[72]

In contrast to the judiciousness attributed to the Communist Chinese there remains controversy over the performance of Dwight Eisenhower. According to Gordon Chang, the president came close to instigating war. Rejecting the view articulated by Stephen Ambrose and Leonard Gordon that Ike's handling of the crisis was masterful, Chang indicts the president for unnecessary and unwise provocation and confusion. Both by his ambiguity regarding U.S. intentions and through his plan to substitute a naval blockade for garrisoning of the offshore islands Ike irresponsibly risked miscalculation leading to disaster.[73] Marc Gallicchio, on the contrary, praises Eisenhower for restraining the Joint Chiefs of Staff and being "thoroughly frustrated by what he perceived as the Chiefs' inability to understand his policy of reducing tensions in the straits."[74] Even the provision of Sidewinder missiles to Taiwan, says Gallicchio, was meant strictly as a defensive action designed to keep the U.S. out of war.[75]

The British also thought the Americans had acted recklessly, fearing Washington might blunder into war with China over indefensible and unimportant territories because of a mistaken belief that these islands were critical to the psychological welfare of the population on Taiwan and U.S. credibility in Asia.[76] Washington and London had long diverged on China policies from recognition of the PRC to support for Chiang Kai-shek.[77] In 1954 British opposition to U.S. offshore island policy manifested itself in its reluctance to support John Foster Dulles's UN initiative codenamed ORACLE, its reservations regarding the Mutual Defense Treaty, and its horror at the use of nuclear threats. But British criticism moderated significantly between the first and second crises as a result of Whitehall's determination to repair Anglo-American relations seriously strained by the 1956 Suez Crisis.[78]

On the other hand, my own research has made clear that much of the belligerence demonstrated by Eisenhower and Dulles was rhetorical rather than substantive. The administration secretly placed restrictions on how Chiang could use American aid. The mutual defense treaty that Washington signed with Taipei in 1954 was granted reluctantly.[79] Ambassadorial talks continued throughout the Eisenhower years.[80] And although the administration encouraged small-scale raids to discomfort the Communist regime, it never had any intention of authorizing seriously destabilizing operations lest the United States be dragged into a war with China. Threats to use nuclear weapons were made but the will to carry through did not exist. Moreover, even though Dulles did believe economic pressures on Beijing were useful, he agreed to a loosening of trade restrictions at the behest of the British and Japanese.[81] Scholars have also used the offshore islands crises to comment on U.S. government decisionmaking and especially the relationship between the executive branch and Congress. Anna Nelson and John Rourke have looked at Congressional willingness to defer to Eisenhower by giving him the Formosa Resolution that permitted almost any action he wanted to take in the Taiwan Straits.[82] Robert Accinelli, however, emphasizes Ike's "strict congressionalism" alongside Congress's compliance, arguing that the president understood that Congressional support had to be cultivated and that his actions must be constrained to some degree by awareness of what Congress would tolerate.[83]

Unresolved remains the dilemma of what the impact on policy might have been of a president and his secretary of state who actually were relatively reasonable men. Robert Divine concedes, for instance, that "it would

be difficult ever again to present Dulles as the inflexible and dogmatic ideo-
logue he appeared to be to many contemporaries, as a bull who carried
around his own china shop, in Churchill's view." And yet, Divine doubts that
American policies were very much affected since the thrust of developments
was narrowly anti-Communist throughout.[84] This critique, however, ignores
the dangers avoided and discounts the political necessity of a belligerent
public facade.

As new documents have softened the Cold War profile of Eisenhower and
Dulles policy toward China, recent revelations regarding John F. Kennedy
have made clear that he took a far tougher stance toward Beijing than heretofore imagined. The early literature about the young president written by veterans of Camelot suggested that, had he lived, Kennedy would have opened
diplomatic relations with China.[85] The first serious study to contradict that
claim came from Warren I. Cohen in his 1980 biography of Dean Rusk.[86]
Since then other scholars such as Thomas G. Paterson have rejected the heroic narrative of the Kennedy years and focused on a less effective and more
dangerous man.[87] Gordon Chang, in particular, posited a president obsessed.
Kennedy believed the Chinese to be fanatics and feared the atomic bomb that
they were in the process of developing. Chang goes so far as to suggest that
Kennedy was responsible for an approach to the Soviets for a joint strike
against Chinese research facilities, an assertion McGeorge Bundy, based on
his White House access, indirectly refutes.[88] Chang contends U.S. action
served to "transform the [Sino-Soviet] dispute into an irrevocable split" and,
in turn, radicalized Chinese behavior particularly sharpening Beijing's anti-
Americanism.[89]

Others who also are critical of Kennedy have not made quite so bold a case.
Building upon Cohen's revelation that JFK guaranteed Chiang Kai-shek use
of the U.S. Security Council veto to prevent PRC entry into the United Nations
(something Dulles had consistently refused to do), they have shown an
administration largely hostage to the Cold War. Kennedy doubted the legitimacy of the Sino-Soviet split, feared Chinese expansion into southeast Asia,
and explored new initiatives toward China largely, in James Fetzer's words, to
"find alternative measures to contain China."[90] Kennedy's fears of a nuclear
armed China were echoed in a public opinion that, according to Leonard
Kusnitz, saw the Chinese as putting world peace in more serious jeopardy
than the Soviets.[91] War between China and India merely confirmed indict-
ments of China's aggressiveness and undermined the efforts of those like John
Kenneth Galbraith who had favored a more sympathetic U.S. view of China.[92]
Although participants like Dean Rusk continue to retail the unsubstantiated
story that Eisenhower threatened the new president with political mayhem

should he recognize the PRC or allow it to be admitted to the UN, it would seem that Kennedy did not need to be coerced into taking a hostile line.[93]

At the same time there were moments of greater vision. Many members of the administration recognized that China would endure and most preferred pursuing a "two Chinas" policy. They endorsed the idea of shipping food to the Chinese people, given famine conditions in the PRC, and favored exchanging journalists. In 1962 during the third Taiwan Straits crisis, Kennedy reassured Beijing privately and publicly that the United States would not support the Nationalists in attacking the mainland.

It may, in fact, be the case that during both the later Eisenhower and post-Cuban missile crisis Kennedy years the government perceived utility in creating an image of a fearsome, irrational China. Focusing on the importance of public opinion and interest groups in the making of U.S. foreign policy, Leonard Kusnitz and I both note the advantages such perceptions had for explaining efforts to improve relations with the Soviets. "Washington's vigilance on the China front satisfied much of the emotional xenophobia abroad in the land," allowing Washington freedom to seek working relations with a more stable and constructive leadership in Moscow.[94]

Lyndon Johnson's preoccupation with Vietnam dictated his administration's interaction with China and in turn has shaped the literature on Johnson administration policy in Asia. There has been a great outpouring on the war but little on U.S.-China relations. Determined to defeat Hanoi, LBJ had little energy left to devote to relations elsewhere in the area. In fact, my own research indicates that the president allowed his obsession with Vietnam to dictate his policies toward other Asian states, making assistance in the war the key to trade, aid, and support from Washington. LBJ even briefly considered the use of uniformed Nationalist Chinese troops in southeast Asia and, after rejecting that alternative, he did welcome covert participation by Taiwan.[95] The China factor, of course, loomed large in Johnson's analysis of why the Vietnamese continued to fight and, Gordon Chang argues, administration officials saw defeat of the north as a lesson vital to curb radical communism as espoused by Beijing in contrast to Moscow's increasingly rational approach to world affairs.[96]

Nevertheless LBJ understood that the fighting in Vietnam could not be allowed to challenge Chinese security directly, provoking intervention as Washington had in Korea. Thus, to the military establishment's chagrin, the president insisted upon curbing tactics on the battlefront by which the U.S. might have blundered into a wider war.[97]

In contrast to the antagonism felt over the Vietnam issue and Chinese support for national liberation struggles more generally, there were also changes in Washington that served to deescalate tensions. Roger Hilsman's December 1963 speech, which may or may not have been properly cleared by higher authorities, and may or may not have been feasible had Kennedy lived, did suggest greater flexibility in American policy. Indeed, what Hilsman said or how much it reflected actual policy was less important than that the world and the U.S. news media chose to see it as a departure and welcomed the new tone. Progress was, however, not steady with developments such as the explosion of China's atomic bomb, the fall of Khrushchev and the beginning of the Chinese Great Proletarian Cultural Revolution producing an environment hostile to even limited reconciliation. But, as Kusnitz's work shows, Americans slowly began to see that security itself necessitated China's presence in international forums.[98] Senate Foreign Relations Committee hearings in 1966 put China specialists on record as advocating better Sino-American relations and LBJ called for reconciliation in a dramatic July 1966 speech which was followed by relaxation of the U.S. ban on travel and on informal contacts between American and Chinese diplomats. Serious change would, however, await the Nixon administration.

Another facet of Sino-American relations which has sometimes been overlooked has been covert activities. Throughout the period from 1950 to 1972 Washington collaborated with the Nationalists to try to destabilize the Beijing regime.[99] Such operations proceeded under the guiding hand of the armed forces as well as the Central Intelligence Agency and involved small-scale "butcher and bolt" raids, high-technology spy plane missions, leafleting, radio broadcasts, and listening stations.[100] The CIA, as William M. Leary and William Stueck show, even acquired its own airline to carry out intelligence operations[101] and supported an insurgent Nationalist military force in Burma.[102] Although the U.S. proved most energetic during periods of heightened tension, such operations continued even at times when more open policies were being considered among White House and State Department personnel.

For the period of reconciliation, both rapprochement and normalization, the literature has only recently begun to provide serious analysis of the problems encountered by Americans and Chinese seeking to pursue a new order. Most of it, not surprisingly, has been written by journalists and political scientists who are less discomforted by the absence of archival materials than are historians. Much of the rest consists of memoirs by participants in the policy process. Nevertheless, it is further testimony to broad continuing lack of interest in China, that in a review of works on American foreign policy since 1969, wherein Vietnam, Central America, and the Middle East receive serious attention, Robert Schulzinger never discusses China even though many would say Sino-American relations were a foreign policy triumph for Richard Nixon and a signal success for an often beleaguered Jimmy Carter.[103]

By far the best and most comprehensive of the extant works is the thoughtful, perceptive study by Harry Harding significantly entitled *A Fragile Relationship*. Covering the landscape from 1972 to 1992, Harding argues that Chinese-American interaction has been volatile throughout those two decades with recurring crises producing an unpredictable and uneasy association characterized by damaging mood swings and too often on the verge of breaking down entirely. Steven I. Levine has been less struck by fragility than by resilience, contending that U.S.-China relations are in much better condition than could have been anticipated given conflicting national interests and domestic priorities.[104]

Among the reasons that Harding and others have declared relations between Beijing and Washington to have been delicate and uncertain was the genesis of rapprochement in antipathy toward Moscow rather than in compatible world views and shared values. This marriage of convenience seemed a viable defense against Soviet expansionism for China when the worsening split with Moscow led to border clashes in 1969.[105] Beijing feared the Soviets would use their Brezhnev Doctrine to justify a military restoration of socialism in China as they had in Czechoslovakia in 1968.[106] John Garver disputes this emphasis on the military aspects of deterrence, believing that American analysts should focus more on the broader political dynamics motivating Chinese leaders, given that they actually emphasized self-reliance in countering Soviet armed forces. Nonetheless, the political issues he deems central do include the Chinese desire to intensify U.S.-Soviet rivalry as well as to recover Taiwan.[107] On the American side, Banning Garrett and Bonnie Glaser convincingly demonstrate the increasing emphasis placed on military ties with Beijing by Henry Kissinger and James Schlesinger.[108] Sadako Ogata similarly stresses this aspect of U.S.-Chinese relations in her comparative study—a focus which, she demonstrates, was in striking contrast to the motives of the Japanese government in pursuing its own normalization with China.[109]

Both the United States and China also had a range of other motives for pursuing improved relations. Richard Nixon and Henry Kissinger hoped to use Beijing to secure a negotiated peace with Hanoi. They sought to secure Chinese participation in arms control agreements. Scholars have noted China's growing interest in modernization and the concomitant desire to acquire technology along with access to western, especially American, markets. United States attention to the long fabled China market also grew as the domestic economy suffered recession. For both sides, the realignment of military threats under the new circumstances meant significant savings in military expenditures with the added bonus of forcing the Soviet Union to increase its own military budgets to cope with the heightened menace of a coalition on its Asian frontier.[110]

There remains another subsidiary debate in the literature that generates considerable passion: the question of who in the Nixon administration masterminded the China initiative. Henry A. Kissinger and Richard M. Nixon have both laid claim to this distinction.[111] Kissinger biographer Walter Isaacson notes early signs from both men with Nixon proposing better relations with China in his 1967 *Foreign Affairs* article, and Kissinger writing similar verbiage into a speech for Nelson Rockefeller in 1968. My work on U.S. relations with Taiwan demonstrates that already in 1965 Nixon talked of the need to improve relations with the PRC although he knew his remarks would be overheard by Nationalist Chinese intelligence operatives.[112] Robert Schulzinger, another biographer of Kissinger, credits the national security adviser with greater vision, regarding China, than men such as Dean Rusk and greater courage in pursuing a new relationship than Richard Nixon.[113] But Isaacson's Kissinger proved reluctant to act and Nixon had to keep after him to realize the opening.[114] Other participants have been determined to place the process in perspective, believing that Kissinger has, in fact, exaggerated his own importance and maligned the State Department which he excluded from the rapprochement process, scornfully complaining about the lack of initiative and imagination among career diplomats.[115] Indeed, H. R. Haldeman's diaries show Kissinger and Nixon consciously and maliciously excluding Secretary of State William Rogers from crucial meetings and working to prevent State Department officials from getting any credit for the opening to China.[116]

Contention between Nixon and Kissinger and between the White House and State Department over who should be credited with rapprochement has, not surprisingly, ignored the Chinese role. Declassification of Richard Solomon's Rand history of the normalization process, however, provides new insights, demonstrating that Beijing successfully manipulated all the major American players and utilized divisions among them to shape policies more advantageous to the PRC.[117]

Diplomatic relations did not follow until 1978. In the United States China policy fell victim to the Watergate scandal. In China proponents of the opening to the U.S. were unhappy with improvements in Washington's relations with Moscow including SALT I, the Helsinki Accords, technology transfer and grain sales. Then both Mao Zedong and Zhou Enlai died in 1976 and Deng Xiaoping was purged, eliminating the last key advocate of ties with the U.S. Momentum gathered again, however, with the advent of the Carter adminis-

tration, the restoration of Deng and the worsening of relations between Beijing and Hanoi.[118]

Two of the primary players at the end of the 1970s on the United States
side, Secretary of State Cyrus Vance and National Security Adviser Zbigniew
Brzezinski, warred with one another for control of policy and the president.
They adopted antagonistic approaches regarding China and subsequently
recorded these differences in hostile memoirs published in 1983. Brzezinski,
who proved the winner in the power struggle, claims credit for realizing the
breakthrough with Beijing which he urgently pushed to secure strategic leverage over the Soviet Union.[119] To Vance, Brzezinski's aggressive posture unnec-
essarily threatened relations with the Soviet Union, particularly the SALT II
negotiations, and therefore seemed ill-considered. Vance did not oppose bet-
terment of relations with Beijing but advocated a process that would not
endanger his priority regarding detente.[120]

Neither Vance nor Brzezinski spend much time worrying about the
impact of recognition of the PRC upon the Nationalist Chinese in Taiwan. In
fact, the Carter administration, most analysts agree, treated the Taiwan
regime very badly.[121] Chiang Ching-kuo did not receive word of the shift in
relations until a 2 A.M. visit from the American ambassador just hours before
the formal announcement was made. Nevertheless, the Nationalist Chinese
had never been prone to passive acceptance of U.S. decisions and throughout
the period, both before and after normalization, they attempted to shape
American political, military, and economic policies.[122] A coalition of their
supporters and those outraged by the precipitous change of policy, about
which the administration never consulted Congress, collaborated on drafting
of the Taiwan Relations Act which placed the new informal links on a solid
foundation.[123]

Regardless of the official U.S. diplomatic posture toward Taiwan, the 1970s
and 1980s proved to be extraordinary decades for economic and political
developments on the island, facilitated in part by American involvement. The
debate over the degree of U.S. responsibility for the Taiwan economic miracle has engaged historians, economists, and political analysts for many
years.[124] There is also a continuing question of U.S. political and military
obligation to the Nationalists, which has been argued fiercely by Martin L.
Lasater, A. James Gregor, and Robert L. Downen.[125] General agreement does
exist concerning the extraordinary progress made and the challenges for the
United States posed by Taiwan's success whether that be in connection with
trade imbalances, membership in GATT, military sales, or the growing independence movement.[126]

The election of Ronald Reagan, in contrast to the dismal Carter years,

ought to have been an occasion for unadulterated pleasure for the Nationalist Chinese. He had long been a proponent of Free China and during the election campaign pledged to restore formal recognition to Taipei. The realities
proved quite different. When the arduous contest for the president's mind
ended, Washington continued to favor Beijing in its policies although Taiwan
did have a somewhat more secure position than Jimmy Carter had accorded
it. Reagan had in the interim, however, managed not just to disappoint Taipei
but also to anger Beijing. The administration refused to supply Taipei with
advanced jet fighter aircraft, a debate carefully analyzed by A. Doak Barnett.[127] But questions of technology transfer and Taiwan arms sales also produced frictions with Beijing at the same time that a lessening of the Soviet
threat to Chinese security and an economically driven preference for peaceful relations generally, devalued alignment with Washington, leading to a
more independent foreign policy posture.[128] The transition became clear in
the arduous negotiation of the August 17, 1982 communique, described in
detail by Secretary of State Alexander Haig in his memoirs. As a result, Reagan conceded that though arms sales to Taiwan would continue they would
not exceed in quality or quantity sales made since 1979.[129]

After Haig's abrupt resignation, the new secretary, George Shultz, put less
emphasis on the importance of China and the strategic triangle. He reasoned
that exaggerated concern in the U.S. regarding maintenance of the relationship, rather than what such ties would yield, gave the Chinese too much leverage. Instead, he explains in his memoirs that he sought to balance enticements
such as technology transfer with a firm line on Taiwan and other questions
involving America's fundamental values.[130] The emphasis, therefore, shifted
from strategic to economic cooperation and accorded more weight to China's
place in regional affairs than its uncertain global role. According to Garrett
and Glaser, "Washington consented to Beijing's desire to publicly deempha-
size the strategic aspects of the relationship while quietly expanding them." At
the same time, they conclude that Washington fundamentally altered the
existing American approach to Sino-Soviet affairs as "day-to-day calculations
of tactical moves in relations with China were no longer seen as necessary or
efficacious in managing relations with Moscow."[131]

On the Chinese side fewer details have emerged regarding the play of politics and personality in the formulation of foreign policy, whether regarding
China's normalization strategy or other foreign affairs issues. Chinese decisionmaking has not been dissected by any of the participants in the way that
Kissinger or Brzezinski, Haig or Shultz have illuminated (or obfuscated)
American deliberations. Nonetheless, for the 1980s greater access to Chinese
sources has allowed scholars from the United States to analyze developments

with more assurance than heretofore as is evident in A. Doak Barnett's important study on *The Making of Foreign Policy in China*.[132]

This was the period in which both sides believed that contacts had matured and could be maintained on an even, upward track.[133] Economic restructuring in China created new markets and openings for foreign investment. Educational exchange flourished with tens of thousands of Chinese seeking higher education in the United States and hundreds of Americans pursuing research and teaching opportunities in the PRC.[134] As interactions between Americans and Chinese increased, the literature seeking to examine and explain it also became more diverse. Scholars explored nontraditional aspects of international exchange using nontraditional approaches. The collected essays in Joyce Kallgren and Denis Fred Simon's *Educational Exchanges* by American scholars and practitioners long immersed in informal interaction with the Chinese contemplate the importance of cultural, academic, and scientific relations and U.S. philanthropic efforts to promote private cooperation. Their focus on such issues highlight the financial, institutional, and psychological investment by Americans in China and clarify both the euphoria and despair that has at times characterized American views of the Chinese. Similarly David Arkush and Leo Lee deal with the problems generated as Chinese from the PRC traveled to the United States where the startling differences in cultural values and customs created both better understanding and increased misperception that sometimes carried over into the realm of international relations.[135] David Shambaugh demonstrates this taking the analysis of intellectual and cultural disparities into his examination of China's America watchers.[136]

Still, genuine normalization has not yet come to U.S.-China relations. After the brief euphoric period of the mid-1980s, the disaster of the Tiananmen Massacre made clear that fundamental problems in the relationship had never been resolved.[137] Since 1989 the repercussions of Tiananmen coupled with the collapse of the Soviet Union and the end of the Cold War have created an atmosphere in which, given the absence of larger strategic imperatives, frictions over human rights, arms proliferation, and trade deficits could not be ignored or dismissed. Although U.S.-China relations remain important for reasons of trade, arms control, regional security, environment, drug trafficking, and future developments in resource exploitation and immigration,[138] none of these issues has been compelling enough to justify the sort of "creative ambiguity" that Roger Sullivan believes characterized the relationship in the past. Americans, he asserts, must no longer accept "meaningless diplomatic formulations" which disguise basic disagreements and ought to work for the end of communist rule in China.[139]

Steven Levine, lamenting the disillusionment that has divided the China watching community in the U.S. since 1989, categorizes critics as either "denouncers" such as Sullivan or "debunkers" like Bruce Cumings or me.[140] The denouncers "see China as an atavistic anomaly" whereas the debunkers argue that "given a new world order in which threats are not as dire or as neatly defined . . . the United States does not need China as much and will be both less generous and less forgiving."[141] Few China analysts go as far as Sullivan in calling for U.S. policies to hasten the fall of the communist regime, but more hostility has been expressed by China watchers than had been evident in many years, giving greater license to dedicated detractors of the PRC such as Steven Mosher.[142] Thus Nicholas Eftimiades's slim volume on Chinese intelligence operations usefully raises the issue of PRC espionage. But, in seeking to generate anxiety about Beijing, he neglects to put Chinese practice in context. Cases and methods he details parallel those David Kaplan attributes to Taiwan intelligence and practices revealed in the multinational analysis of Michael J. Glennon.[143] Levine and others such as Michel Oksenberg, David Lampton, and Barber Conable emphasize the continuing significance of U.S.-China relations. Fearing fundamental damage to the relationship, they argue for greater wisdom and patience alongside a broader appreciation of Chinese development and its importance in the future.[144]

At the same time, it also is apparent that diplomatic historians who do not specialize in Sino-American relations have found even less reason than heretofore to investigate the issues in the field. Michael Hogan, for instance, in his important collection of essays on the end of the Cold War neglected to look at the Chinese factor even though it can be said to have had a role in bringing about the collapse of the Soviet empire and even though the Cold War's end reshaped Sino-American relations.[145]

The direction that Sino-American relations will now take is a question both of policy relevance and of fundamental importance to development of the literature exploring U.S.-China interaction since 1945. The enormous progress of recent years clearly is in jeopardy. Whereas revelations may continue from Russian archives there seems less cause for optimism about Chinese materials as the PRC appears to be entering a prolonged era of political disarray and continuing frictions with the United States. Even in the U.S., where the principle of access to documents is institutionalized, the struggle over the parameters appears far from resolved. Regulations are not effectively enforced, government agencies continue to try to delay declassification mandates, and unreconstructed officials seem determined to protect secrecy without regard for the right of the public in a democracy to know what their national policies are or have been.

More optimism is warranted on the methodological front. The history of American-Chinese relations has changed and transformation will persist. There has been an abundance of innovative experimentation with approaches and concepts borrowed from political science, as in the work of Zhang Shu Guang, from political psychology, by Gordon Chang and He Di, from art and cultural history, by Warren I. Cohen, from the sociology of knowledge, by Qing Simei, from intellectual history, by Shaw Yu-ming and Paul Evans, and from cultural studies, as in my recent examination of Taiwan and Hong Kong.[146] Historians in the field have taken seriously the injunction to look beyond traditional policymakers and take seriously others who shape Sino-American interaction, as is apparent in the work of Leonard Kusnitz on public opinion, Robert Sutter on Congress, and my own writing on interest groups including businessmen, journalists, and missionaries.[147] They have analyzed how interaction in fields apart from political and security relations have impinged upon these concerns as in the writing of William Walker on opium or Denis Fred Simon on science and technology. Most have responded to the opportunities to make their studies truly bilateral, exploring Chinese interests, actions, motives, and perspectives alongside those of Americans, as in the analysis by Odd Arne Westad. They have also sought to place their studies in the context of world affairs, as becomes clear from a reading of the essays in *The Great Powers in East Asia*, making the examination of Sino-American relations truly a part of international history as well as an aspect of American history, American diplomatic history, and modern Chinese history.

There is, of course, room for new methodological approaches and a continuing need to fill in substantive gaps in our understanding of Sino-American relations. There clearly remains considerable distance between existing scholarship and the kind of syntheses that Robert McMahon searched for in 1988. Scholars have broadened the potential time frame for locating the arrival of the Cold War in China but have not come to fully satisfactory conclusions. Even on the much studied issue of lost opportunities for better Sino-American relations a final judgment has not been rendered. More work must be done to study officials who fashioned China policy in the U.S. and policy toward the U.S. in China. Covert activities, economic diplomacy, and the cultural aspects of Sino-American relations all needed further attention. The new frontier created by the entree to Soviet archives promises years of fruitful labor, answering a host of vital questions, which hopefully will also be addressed by access to Chinese materials.

Whatever the future impediments to development of the study of Sino-American relations since 1945, for many the most serious will be the necessity of moving forward without the guiding hand of Dorothy Borg. Her death in 1993 has removed the inspiration and energy that brought many scholars into the field and kept them there working late into the night, not daring to relax on weekends or take vacations that did not include a stop at some archive. Moreover the field has been doubly bereft, having also lost John K. Fairbank, whose extraordinary devotion to educating generations of specialists in Chinese history and Sino-American relations, not to mention his own scholarly contributions, fundamentally shaped the common enterprise.[148] Those of us who remain, however, have been given, through their lives and their insight, the clear mandate to persevere despite whatever barriers exist and foster both historical knowledge and contemporary understanding between China and the United States.

NOTES

1. Bruce Kuniholm, "Foreign Relations, Public Relations, Accountability, and Understanding," *Perspectives* 28 (May/June 1990): 1, 11–12; Warren I. Cohen, "Stop Falsifying U.S. History," *World Monitor* (October 1990): 14–17; Warren I. Cohen, "Omissions in the Historical Record," *Foreign Service Journal* (August 1990): 27–29. Correspondence and various articles on these issues were printed in the *Congressional Record*, 101st Congress, 2nd sess., October 19, 1990, pp. S16288-S16301.

2. The conference produced a volume: Warren I. Cohen ed., *New Frontiers in American-East Asian Relations* (New York: Columbia University Press, 1983).

3. Steven M. Goldstein and He Di, "New Chinese Sources on the History of the Cold War," *Cold War International History Project Bulletin* (Spring 1992): 4–6.

4. Robert J. McMahon, "The Cold War in Asia: Toward a New Synthesis?" *Diplomatic History* 12 (Summer 1988): 307–28.

5. Harry Harding and Yuan Ming ed., *Sino-American Relations 1945–1955: A Joint Reassessment of a Critical Decade* (Wilmington, DE: Scholarly Resources, 1989), xxi–xxii.

6. Akira Iriye, "Was There a Cold War in Asia?" in John Chay ed., *The Problems and Prospects of American-East Asian Relations* (Boulder, CO: Westview Press, 1977), 14.

7. Odd Arne Westad, *Cold War and Revolution: Soviet-American Rivalry and the Origins of the Chinese Civil War* (New York: Columbia University Press, 1993), 28, 32.

8. John W. Garver, *Chinese-Soviet Relations 1937–1945: The Diplomacy of Chinese Nationalism* (New York: Oxford University Press, 1988), 209.

9. Steven I. Levine, *Anvil of Victory: The Communist Revolution in Manchuria, 1945–1948* (New York: Columbia University Press, 1987), 238. Levine first set forth his views in "A New Look at American Mediation in the Chinese Civil War: The Marshall Mission and Manchuria," *Diplomatic History* 3 (1979).

10. Garver, *Chinese-Soviet Relations 1937–1945*, 210–30.

11. Westad, 165–78. Liu Xiaoyuan in his unpublished manuscript "A Partnership for Disorder: China, the United States, and Their Policies for Postwar Disposition of the Japanese Empire, 1941–1945," 300–301n2, pinpoints Garver's emphasis on nationalism in contrast to Westad's focus on partisan politics in their analyses of Chiang Kai-shek's activ-

ities. Liu maintains that his study demonstrates that Chiang was both a nationalist and a politician.

12. Arnold Xiangze Jiang, *The United States and China* (Chicago: University of Chicago Press, 1988).

13. Yang Kuisong, "The Soviet Factor and the CCP's Policy Toward the United States in the 1940s," *Chinese Historians* 5 (Spring 1992): 17–34.

14. Steven M. Goldstein, "Sino-American Relations, 1948–1950: Lost Chance or No Chance?" in Harding and Yuan, *Sino-American Relations*, 119–42. His earlier statement of the case appeared as "Chinese Communist Policy Toward the United States: Opportunities and Constraints, 1944–1950," in Dorothy Borg and Waldo Heinrichs eds., *Uncertain Years: Chinese-American Relations, 1947–1950* (New York: Columbia University Press, 1980), 235–78.

15. Shaw Yu-ming, "John Leighton Stuart and U.S.-Chinese Communist Rapprochement in 1949: Was There Another 'Lost Chance in China'?" *China Quarterly* (March 1982) and *An American Missionary in China: John Leighton Stuart and Chinese-American Relations* (Cambridge: Harvard University Press, 1992). See also John C. Brewer and Kenneth W. Rea, "Dr. John Leighton Stuart and U.S. Policy Toward China, 1946–1949," in Patricia Neils ed., *United States Attitudes and Policies toward China: The Impact of American Missionaries* (Armonk, NY: M. E. Sharpe, 1990), 230–44; Edmund S. Wehrle, "John Leighton Stuart's Role in the Marshall Mission Negotiations: The Kalgan Crisis," in ibid., 245–62.

16. Warren I. Cohen, "Conversations with Chinese Friends; Zhou Enlai's Associates Reflect on Chinese-American Relations in the 1940s and the Korean War," *Diplomatic History* 11 (Summer 1987): 287–88.

17. Ho Zhigong, " 'Lost Chance' or 'Inevitable Hostility?' Two Contending Interpretations of the Late 1940s Chinese-American Relations," *Society for Historians of American Foreign Relations Newsletter* 20 (September 1989): 76–77.

18. He Di, "Evolution," 31, 40, 43, 47. Nevertheless, he rejects the idea that openings for improvement had anything to do with factions in the CCP, which he claims ceased to exist after the 1945 Seventh Party Congress. Foreign policy lay firmly in the grasp of Mao Zedong.

19. Zhai Qiang, *The Dragon, the Lion, and the Eagle: Chinese-British-American Relations, 1949–1958* (Kent, OH: Kent State University Press, 1994), 26, and 15, 208.

20. Lowell Dittmer, *Sino-Soviet Normalization and Its International Implications, 1945–1990* (Seattle: University of Washington Press, 1992), 160–61, 164–65.

21. Qing Simei, "Chinese and American Conceptions Regarding Peace, Order and China's Modernization, 1945–1960," Ph.D. dissertation, Michigan State University, 1994.

22. Marc S. Gallicchio, *The Cold War Begins in Asia: American East Asian Policy and the Fall of the Japanese Empire* (New York: Columbia University Press, 1988), 37, 112, 133, 137–44.

23. For the history of the U.S. relationship with the Nationalist regime on the mainland and in Taiwan my own work is the only comprehensive source, see *Taiwan, Hong Kong and the United States, 1945–1992: Uncertain Friendships* (New York: Macmillan/Twayne, 1994).

24. McMahon, "The Cold War in Asia," 310.

25. Melvyn Leffler, *A Preponderance of Power: National Security, the Truman Administration, and the Cold War* (Stanford: Stanford University Press, 1992).

26. David McLean, "American Nationalism, the China Myth, and the Truman Doctrine: The Question of Accommodation with Peking, 1949–50," *Diplomatic History* 10 (Winter 1986): 25–42.

27. Robert Blum, *Drawing the Line: The Origin of the American Containment Policy in East Asia* (New York: Norton, 1982), 4–5.

28. Nancy Bernkopf Tucker, *Patterns in the Dust: Chinese-American Relations and the Recognition Controversy, 1949–1950* (New York: Columbia University Press, 1983) and "China's Place in the Cold War: The Acheson Plan," in Douglas Brinkley ed., *Dean Acheson and the Making of U.S. Foreign Policy* (New York: St. Martin's, 1993), 109–32.

29. Nancy Bernkopf Tucker, "American Policy Toward Sino-Japanese Trade in the Postwar Years: Politics and Prosperity," *Diplomatic History* 8 (Summer 1984): 183–208; Yasuhara Yoko, "Japan, Communist China, and Export Controls in Asia, 1948–1952," *Diplomatic History* 10 (Winter 1986): 75–90. Ronald McGlothlen has recently made the argument that concern about Japan's recovery dictated all Acheson's foreign policy decisions in Asia. *Controlling the Waves: Dean Acheson and U.S. Foreign Policy in Asia* (New York: Norton, 1993).

30. Bruce Cumings, *The Origins of the Korean War*, vol 2: *The Roaring of the Cataract, 1947–1950* (Princeton: Princeton University Press, 1990); June M. Grasso. *Truman's Two-China Policy, 1948–1950* (Armonk, NY: M. E. Sharpe, 1987).

31. Michael Schaller, "Consul General O. Edmund Clubb, John P. Davies, and the "Inevitability" of Conflict Between the United States and China, 1949–1950: A Comment and New Documentation," *Diplomatic History* 9 (Spring 1985): 149–60.

32. Cumings, *Roaring of the Cataract*, 417–23; John Lewis Gaddis. *The Long Peace: Inquiries into the History of the Cold War* (New York: Oxford University Press, 1987), 72–73.

33. He Di, " 'The Last Campaign to Unify China': The CCP's Unmaterialized Plan to Liberate Taiwan, 1949–1950," *Chinese Historians* 5 (Spring 1992): 12.

34. Re importance of Acheson speech to Chinese see He, "The Last Campaign," 7–8 which Chen also accepts, Chen, "The Sino-Soviet Alliance and China's Entry Into the Korean War," Working Paper #1, CWIHP, Woodrow Wilson Center, June 1992. On the Soviet side see Sergei N. Goncharov, John W. Lewis and Xue Litai. *Uncertain Partners: Stalin, Mao, and the Korean War* (Stanford: Stanford University Press, 1993) and Weathersby, "New Findings," 26. Cumings has rejected as "nonsense" the idea that Stalin would have approved Kim's plans because he believed the U.S. would not intervene. *The Roaring of the Cataract*, 448.

35. Goncharov, Lewis, and Xue, *Uncertain Partners*, 98–107 and passim; Tucker. *Patterns in the Dust*, 224n68.

36. Yang, "The Soviet Factor," 32; Chen "The Sino-Soviet Alliance," 19.

37. Hao Yufan and Zhai Zhihai, "China's Decision to Enter the Korean War: History Revisited," *China Quarterly* 121 (March 1990): 94–115; Zhang Shu Guang. *Deterrence and Strategic Culture: Chinese-American Confrontations, 1949–1958* (Ithaca: Cornell University Press, 1992), 15–16; Chen Xiaolu, "China's Policy Toward the United States, 1949–1955," in Harding and Yuan, *Sino-American Relations*, 189–91; Jonathan Pollack, "The Korean War and Sino-American Relations," ibid., 220.

38. Goncharov, Lewis and Xue, *Uncertain Partners*, 146–47.

39. Rosemary Foot, *The Wrong War: American Policy and the Dimensions of the Korean Conflict, 1950–1953* (Ithaca: Cornell University Press, 1985), 23–24; Foot, "Anglo-American Relations in the Korean Crisis: The British Effort to Avert an Expanded War, December 1950–January 1951," *Diplomatic History* 10 (Winter 1986): 43–57; William W. Stueck, "The Limits of Influence: British Policy and American Expansion of the War in Korea," *Pacific Historical Review* 55 (February 1986): 68–74.

40. Edward C. Keefer, "President Dwight D. Eisenhower and the End of the Korean War," *Diplomatic History* 10 (Summer 1986): 267–89.

41. Dean Rusk believed at the time and as late as 1991 when his memoirs were published that the Chinese were complicit. Dean Rusk (as told to Richard Rusk). *As I Saw It* (New York: Norton, 1990; paperback, New York: Penguin, 1991), 165.

42. Edward Crankshaw ed., *Khrushchev Remembers* (Boston: Little Brown, 1970), 368–70.

43. Goncharov, Lewis and Xue argue to the contrary that this was an important motive for Stalin. *Uncertain Partners*, 152.

44. Kathryn Weathersby, "New Findings on the Korean War," *Cold War International History Project Bulletin* (Fall 1993); Weathersby, "Soviet Aims in Korea and the Origins of the Korean War, 1945–1950," Working Paper #8, CWHIP, Woodrow Wilson Center.

45. Hao and Zhai, "China's Decision," 100.

46. Anthony Farrar-Hockley, "A Reminiscence of the Chinese People's Volunteers in the Korean War," *China Quarterly* 98 (June 1984): 287–304.

47. Chen Jian, "The Sino-Soviet Alliance," 21.

48. William W. Stueck, "The Korean War as International History," *Diplomatic History* 10 (Fall 1986): 291–309.

49. Zhang, *Strategic Deterrence*, 96.

50. Cohen, "Conversations," 288; Michael Hunt, "Beijing and the Korean Crisis, June 1950–June 1951," *Political Science Quarterly* 107 (Fall 1992): 464–65: Thomas J. Christensen, "Threats, Assurances, and the Last Chance for Peace: The Lessons of Mao's Korean War Telegrams," *International Security* 17 (Summer 1992): 122–54.

51. Russell Spurr, *Enter the Dragon: China's Undeclared War Against the U.S. in Korea, 1950–1951* (New York: Newmarket Press, 1988); Hao and Zhai, "China's Decision," 106–11. Michael Hunt, in his far more authoritative and useful account of the discussion among China's leaders, dismisses Spurr's version as "imaginative." Hunt, "Beijing and the Korean Crisis," 454n7. See also Zhang Xi, "Peng Dehuai and China's Entry Into the Korean War," *Chinese Historians* 6 (Spring 1993): 10–15.

52. Hunt, "Beijing and the Korean War," 476–78 and Zhang, 79–151.

53. Hunt, "Beijing and the Korean War," 466.

54. Burton I. Kaufman, *The Korean War: Challenges in Crisis, Credibility and Command* (New York: Knopf, 1986), 137–38.

55. Rosemary Foot, *A Substitute for Victory: The Politics of Peacemaking at the Korean Armistice Talks* (Ithaca: Cornell University Press, 1990).

56. Roger Dingman, "Atomic Diplomacy during the Korean War," *International Security* 13 (Winter 1988/89): 63–69, 76–77.

57. Daniel Calingaert, "Nuclear Weapons and the Korean War," *Journal of Strategic Studies* 11 (June 1988): 177–202; Rosemary Foot, "Nuclear Coercion and the Ending of the Korean War," *International Security* 13 (Winter 1988–89): 92–112; Mark A. Ryan. *Chinese Attitudes Toward Nuclear Weapons: China and the United States During the Korean War* (Armonk, NY: M. E. Sharpe, 1989), 152–77 and passim; John Wilson Lewis and Xue Litai. *China Builds the Bomb* (Stanford: Stanford University Press, 1988), 15.

58. Rosemary Foot, "Making Known the Unknown War: Policy Analysis of the Korean Conflict in the Last Decade," *Diplomatic History* 15 (Summer 1991): 411–31. Richard H. Immerman also appears to take seriously Ike's threats to use nuclear weapons in Korea because, he contends, Eisenhower presumed that they could be limited to tactical strikes, a view he would later abandon. Furthermore Immerman thinks Ike really believed that his nuclear threats had ended the war. "Confessions of an Eisenhower Revisionist: An Agonizing Reappraisal," *Diplomatic History* 14 (Summer 1990): 326n23 and 342n105.

59. Pollack, "The Korean War," 213–37; Pollack, "Into the Vortex: China, the Sino-Sovi-

et Alliance, and the Korean War," R-3910-RC, Rand Corporation, 1990; Hunt, "Beijing and the Korean War," 470–72; and see the older, but still useful study by Lawrence S. Weiss, "Storm Around the Cradle: The Korean War and the Early Years of the People's Republic of China," Ph.D. dissertation, Columbia University, 1981.

60. The most recent representation of this view was by Norman Graebner "Eisenhower and Communism: The Public Record of the 1950s," in Richard A. Melanson and David Mayers ed., *Reevaluating Eisenhower* (Chicago: University of Illinois Press, 1987), 67–87.

61. Robert P. Newman, *Owen Lattimore and the "Loss of China"* (Berkeley: University of California Press, 1992); Paul M. Evans. *John Fairbank and the American Understanding of Modern China* (New York: Basil Blackwell, 1988). See also Paul Gordon Lauren ed., *The China Hands' Legacy: Ethics and Diplomacy* (Boulder: Westview, 1986).

62. William O. Walker III, *Opium and Foreign Policy: The Anglo-American Search for Order in Asia, 1912–1954* (Chapel Hill: University of North Carolina Press, 1991), 216 and passim.

63. The standard works of Eisenhower revisionism include Robert A. Divine. *Eisenhower and the Cold War* (New York: Oxford University Press, 1981); Fred I. Greenstein. *The Hidden-Hand Presidency* (New York: Basic Books, 1982); Blanche Wiesen Cook. *The Declassified Eisenhower* (New York: Penguin, 1984); and Stephen E. Ambrose. *Eisenhower*, vol. 2: *The President* (New York: Simon and Schuster, 1984). Scholars have reacted positively and negatively to the new assessment of Ike, see Gary Reichard, "Eisenhower as President: The Changing View," *South Atlantic Quarterly* 77 (Summer 1979): 265–81; Mary McAuliffe, "Commentary: Eisenhower, the President," *Journal of American History* 68 (December 1981): 625–32; Robert Burk, "Eisenhower Revisionism Revisited: Reflections on Eisenhower Scholarship," *Historian* 50 (February 1988): 196–209; and especially Robert McMahon, "Eisenhower and Third World Nationalism: A Critique of the Revisionists," *Political Science Quarterly* 101 (1986): 453–73.

64. For the classic view of Dulles see Townsend Hoopes, *The Devil and John Foster Dulles* (Boston: Little Brown, 1973) and Foster Rhea Dulles. *American Policy Toward Communist China: The Historical Record, 1949–1969* (New York: Crowell, 1972) which is refuted by the essays in Richard H. Immerman ed., *John Foster Dulles and the Diplomacy of the Cold War* (Princeton: Princeton University Press, 1990). See also the thoughtful review of Immerman's volume by Robert Divine, "John Foster Dulles: What You See Is What You Get," *Diplomatic History* 15 (Spring 1991): 277–85.

65. David A. Mayers, "Eisenhower and Communism: Later Findings," in Melanson and Mayers, *Reevaluating Eisenhower*, 88–119 and Mayers. *Cracking the Monolith: U.S. Policy Against the Sino-Soviet Alliance, 1949–1955* (Baton Rouge: Louisiana State University Press, 1986). The earlier view was articulated forcefully by Foster Rhea Dulles. *American Policy Toward Communist China: The Historical Record, 1949–1969* (New York: Crowell, 1972), 133–34.

66. Nancy Bernkopf Tucker, "Cold War Contacts: America and China, 1952–1956," in Harry Harding and Yuan Ming ed., *Sino-American Relations, 1945–1955: A Joint Reassessment of a Critical Decade* (Wilmington, DE: Scholarly Resources, 1989), 238–66; Warren I. Cohen, "China in Japanese-American Relations," in Akira Iriye and Warren I. Cohen ed., *The United States and Japan in the Postwar World* (Lexington: University of Kentucky Press, 1989), 36–60; Qing Simei, "The Eisenhower Administration and Changes in Western Embargo Policy Against China, 1954–1958," in Cohen and Iriye eds., *Great Powers in East Asia, 1953–1960* (New York: Columbia University Press, 1990), 121–42.

67. Nancy Bernkopf Tucker, "John Foster Dulles and the Taiwan Roots of the 'Two Chinas' Policy," in Immerman, *Dulles*, 235–62; Wang Jisi makes the convincing argument that

the U.S. government sought to create two Chinas as early as the Korean War, "The Origins of America's 'Two Chinas' Policy," in Harding and Yuan, *Sino-American Relations*, 198–212.

68. John Lewis Gaddis, "The American 'Wedge' Strategy, 1949–1955," in Harding and Yuan, *Sino-American Relations*, 157–83, and in a longer version, "Dividing Adversaries: The United States and International Communism, 1945–1958," in Gaddis. *The Long Peace: Inquiries Into the History of the Cold War* (New York: Oxford University Press, 1987), 147–94.

69. Waldo Heinrichs, "Eisenhower and Sino-American Confrontation," in Warren I. Cohen and Akira Iriye eds., *The Great Powers*, 103.

70. James Shepley, "How Dulles Averted War," *Life* (January 16, 1956);

71. He Di and Gordon H. Chang, "The Absence of War in the U.S.-China Confrontation over Quemoy-Matsu in 1954–1955: Contingency, Luck, Deterrence?" *American Historical Review* 98 (December 1993): 1500–24.

72. He Di, "The Evolution of the People's Republic of China's Policy toward the Offshore Islands," in Cohen and Iriye, *Great Powers*, 222–45; Thomas E. Stolper. *China, Taiwan and the Offshore Islands* (Armonk, NY: M. E. Sharpe, 1985); Lewis and Xue. *China Builds the Bomb*, 22–34.

73. Gordon H. Chang, *Friends and Enemies: The United States, China, and the Soviet Union, 1948–1972* (Stanford: Stanford University Press, 1990), 116–42 and an earlier version of the essay "To the Nuclear Brink: Eisenhower, Dulles, and the Quemoy-Matsu Crisis," *International Security* (Spring 1988): 96–122; Leonard H. D. Gordon, "United States Opposition to Use of Force in the Taiwan Strait, 1954–1962," *Journal of American History* 72 (December 1985): 637–60; Ambrose, *Eisenhower*, 244–45.

74. Marc S. Gallicchio, "The Best Defense is a Good Offense: The Evolution of American Strategy in East Asia, 1953–1960," in Cohen and Iriye, *Great Powers*, 74–75.

75. Gallicchio, "The Best Defense," 78.

76. Zhai Qiang, "Britain, the United States, and the Jinmen-Mazu Crises 1954–55 and 1958," *Chinese Historians* 5 (Fall 1992).

77. Edwin W. Martin, *Divided Counsel: The Anglo-American Response to Communist Victory in China* (Lexington: University of Kentucky Press, 1986); Zhai, *The Dragon, the Lion, and the Eagle*; David C. Wolf, " 'To Secure a Convenience': Britain Recognizes China —1950," *Journal of Contemporary History* (April 1983): 299–326; Ritchie Ovendale, "Britain, the United States, and the Recognition of Communist China," *Historical Journal* 26 (March 1983): 139–58 and "Britain and the Cold War in Asia," in Ovendale ed., *The Foreign Policy of the British Labour Government, 1945–51* (Leicester, England: Leicester University Press, 1984).

78. Tracy Lee Steele, "Allied and Interdependent: British Policy During the Chinese Offshore Islands Crisis of 1958," in Anthony Gorst, Lewis Johnman, and W. Scott Lucas eds., *Contemporary British History, 1931–1961* (New York: Pinter, 1991), 232, 239; Zhai, "Britain," 40–41.

79. John Lewis and Xue Litai are wrong in portraying an American leadership anxious to sign a treaty but too busy to move ahead with it. *China Builds the Bomb*, 21; Tucker, "John Foster Dulles," 240–44; Chang Su-ya, "Reluctant Alliance: John Foster Dulles and the Making of the U.S.-R.O.C. Mutual Defense Treaty of 1954," in *Chinese Yearbook of International Law and Affairs* 12 (1992–1993): 501–46.

80. U. Alexis Johnson, *The Right Hand of Power* (Englewood Cliffs, N.J.: Prentice-Hall, 1984), 228–65.

81. Qing, "The Eisenhower Administration and Changes in Western Embargo Policy Against China," in Cohen and Iriye, *Great Powers*, 121–42; Burton I. Kaufman, "Eisenhow-

er's Foreign Economic Policy with Respect to East Asia," ibid., 104–12; Tucker, "A House Divided," ibid., 52–53. Qing sees the Eisenhower cabinet as uniformly opposed to relaxation of controls whereas Kaufman and I argue that Eisenhower had allies. See also Sayuri Shimizu, "Creating People of Plenty: The United States and Japan's Economic Alternatives, 1953–1958," Ph.D. dissertation, Cornell University, 1991.

82. Anna K. Nelson, "John Foster Dulles and the Bipartisan Congress," *Political Science Quarterly* 102 (Spring 1987): 50–55; John Rourke. *Congress and the Presidency in U.S. Foreign Policymaking, A Study of Interaction and Influence, 1945–1982* (Boulder: Westview, 1983), 86–87.

83. Robert Accinelli, "Eisenhower, Congress, and the 1954–55 Offshore Island Crisis," *Presidential Studies Quarterly* 20 (Spring 1990): 329–48.

84. Divine, "What You See," 284–85.

85. Arthur M. Schlesinger, Jr., *A Thousand Days: John F. Kennedy in the White House* (Boston: Houghton Mifflin, 1965). In his recently published essay Arthur Waldron accepts this view. He has not, however, consulted any of the new documentation on the question. "From Nonexistent to Almost Normal: U.S.-China Relations in the 1960s," in Diane B. Kunz ed., *The Diplomacy of the Crucial Decade: American Foreign Relations During the 1960s* (New York: Columbia University Press, 1994), 219.

86. Warren I. Cohen, *Dean Rusk* (Totowa, NJ: Cooper Square, 1980). Cohen argues that Rusk was more flexible than JFK on China in contrast to the views of most administration members who have written on the issue. Suggestive corroboration for Cohen came from the article by William P. Snyder, "Dean Rusk to John Foster Dulles, May–June 1953: The Office, the First 100 Days, and Red China," *Diplomatic History* 7 (Winter 1983): 84–86.

87. Thomas G. Paterson and many of the other contributors to the volume he edited: *Kennedy's Quest for Victory: American Foreign Policy, 1961–1963* (New York: Oxford University Press, 1989).

88. McGeorge Bundy. *Danger and Survival: Choices About the Bomb in the First Fifty Years* (New York: Vintage, 1988), 532.

89. Gordon H. Chang, "JFK, China and the Bomb," *Journal of American History* 75 (March 1988): 1287–1310 and *Friends and Enemies*, 228–52 and 292–93. Revelations about the extended espionage career of Larry Wu-tai Chin, a CIA analyst, suggest that the PRC could well have been informed about feasibility studies and top secret discussions. *New York Times*, January 6, 1986. Raymond Garthoff makes similar assertions about debates during the Johnson administration, claiming to have been personally involved in such discussions. Garthoff, *Detente and Confrontation*, 984n.

90. James Fetzer, "Clinging to Containment: China Policy," in Paterson, *Kennedy's Quest*, 181–84.

91. Leonard A. Kusnitz. *Public Opinion and Foreign Policy: America's China Policy, 1949–1979* (Westport, CT: Greenwood Press, 1984), 106.

92. Cohen, *Rusk*, 170; Robert J. MacMahon. *Cold War on the Periphery: The United States, India, and Pakistan* (New York: Columbia University Press, 1994).

93. Rusk, *As I Saw It*, 283, 428.

94. Kusnitz, *Public Opinion*, 106–7; Tucker, "Cold War Contacts," 256–57 (quote 257). Gordon Chang sees this less as a strategy than as evidence that "toward the end of the 1950's Washington began to consider Beijing America's most dangerous immediate enemy." Chang, *Friends and Enemies*, 292.

95. Nancy Bernkopf Tucker, "Threats, Opportunities and Frustrations in East Asia," in Warren I. Cohen and Nancy Bernkopf Tucker eds., *Lyndon Johnson Confronts the World* (New York: Cambridge University Press, 1994).

96. Chang, *Friends and Enemies*, 253–71.

97. George McT. Kahin. *Intervention: How America Became Involved in Vietnam* (Garden City, NY: Doubleday, 1987), 338–41.

98. Kusnitz, *Public Opinion*, 110–20.

99. Thomas Powers, *The Man Who Kept the Secrets: Richard Helms and the* CIA (New York: Pocket Books, 1979); Joseph Burkholder Smith, *Portrait of a Cold Warrior* (New York: Putnam, 1976); Victor Marchetti and John D. Marks, *The* CIA and the Cult of Intelligence (New York: Dell, 1980); Ray S. Cline, *Secrets, Spies and Scholars* (Washington, D.C.: Acropolis Books, 1976).

100. SC No. 10078/65, CIA, Office of Current Intelligence, "Probable Effects in China and Taiwan of a GRC Attack on the Mainland," August 18, 1965, National Security Files, Country File Vietnam, Bx 50–51, F: vol. 2: Special Intelligence Material 7/65–10/65, Lyndon Baines Johnson Library, Austin, TX.

101. William M. Leary and William Stueck, "The Chennault Plan to Save China: U.S. Containment in Asia and the Origins of the CIA's Aerial Empire, 1949–1950," *Diplomatic History* 8 (Fall 1984): 349–64; William M. Leary. *Perilous Missions* (University Station: University of Alabama, 1984). See also John Prados. *The Presidents' Secret Wars* (New York: Morrow, 1986).

102. John Ranelagh, *The Agency: The Rise and Decline of the* CIA (New York: Simon and Schuster, 1986); Tucker, "John Foster Dulles," 244–51; Alfred W. McCoy. *The Politics of Heroin in Southeast Asia* (New York: Harper, 1972); David Wise and Thomas B. Ross. *The Invisible Government* (New York: Random House, 1964).

103. Robert D. Schulzinger, "Complaints, Self-justifications, and Analysis: The Historiography of American Foreign Relations since 1969," *Diplomatic History* 15 (Spring 1991): 245–64.

104. Steven I. Levine, "China and America: The Resilient Relationship," *Current History* 91 (September 1992): 241–46.

105. Lowell Dittmer in his recent study *Sino-Soviet Normalization*, 147–255, uses the terms menage a trois and marriage to head four of his eight sections on the strategic triangle.

106. Allen S. Whiting noted war preparations in Beijing in "Sino-Soviet Relations in the 1980s," in Richard A. Melanson ed., *Neither Cold War Nor Detente?* (Charlottesville: University of Virginia Press, 1982), 92. Arkady Shevchenko describes the fear generated in Moscow by the thought of Chinese hordes pouring across the border and Defense Minister Andrei Grechko's view that nuclear weapons should be used so as "once and for all get rid of the Chinese threat." *Breaking with Moscow* (New York: Knopf, 1985), 164–65.

107. John W. Garver, *China's Decision for Rapprochement with the United States, 1968–1971* (Boulder: Westview, 1982), 149–58.

108. Banning N. Garrett and Bonnie S. Glaser, "From Nixon to Reagan: China's Changing Role in American Strategy," in Kenneth A. Oye, Robert J. Lieber, and Donald Rothchild eds., *Eagle Resurgent? The Reagan Era in American Foreign Policy* (Boston: Little Brown, 1987), 256–63.

109. Sadako Ogata, *Normalization with China: A Comparative Study of U.S. and Japanese Processes* (Berkeley: Institute of East Asian Studies, University of California, 1988). Differences between the United States and Japan regarding the issues of recognizing China dated back to the immediate postwar period, see Howard Schonberger, "Peacemaking in Asia: The United States, Great Britain, and the Japanese Decision to Recognize Nationalist China, 1951–52," *Diplomatic History* 10 (Winter 1986): 59–74.

110. Robert G. Sutter, *The China Quandary: Domestic Determinants of U.S. China Policy, 1972–1982* (Boulder: Westview, 1983).

111. Henry A. Kissinger, *The White House Years* (Boston: Little Brown, 1979) and *Years of Upheaval* (Boston: Little Brown, 1982). Kissinger makes yet another case for his crucial role in *Diplomacy* (New York: Simon and Schuster, 1994). See also H. R. Haldeman, *The Haldeman Diaries: Inside the Nixon White House* (New York: Putnam, 1994), 365, 367; Stephen E. Ambrose. *Nixon*, vol. 2: *The Triumph of a Politician, 1962–1972* (New York: Simon and Schuster, 1987), 454; John Prados, *Keepers of the Keys: A History of the National Security Council from Truman to Bush* (New York: Morrow, 1991), 321–22.

112. Tucker, *Uncertain Friendships*, 272n29.

113. Robert D. Schulzinger, *Henry Kissinger: Doctor of Diplomacy* (New York: Columbia University Press, 1989), 76–101.

114. Walter Isaacson, *Kissinger* (New York: Simon and Schuster, 1992), 334–36.

115. Marshall Green, Oral History Interview, Foreign Service Oral History Project, Georgetown University.

116. Haldeman, 271, 307, 319, 369, 414, 418, 420–22.

117. Richard Solomon, *Chinese Political Negotiating Behavior, 1967–1984: An Interpretive Assessment* (Santa Monica, CA: Rand Document #R-3299) and *U.S.-PRC Political Negotiations, 1967–1984: An Annotated Chronology* (Santa Monica, CA: Rand Document #R-3298); Jim Mann, "China's Invisible Weapon," *Los Angeles Times*, June 13, 1994, A1, A8.

118. Political scientists who have written on the complex process of decisionmaking in China during the 1970s include Jaw-ling Joanne Chang, *United States-China Normalization: An Evaluation of Foreign Policy Decision Making* (Baltimore: Maryland Studies in East Asian Law and Politics, 1986); Robert S. Ross, "From Lin Biao to Deng Xiaoping: Elite Instability and China's U.S. Policy," *China Quarterly* (June 1989): 265–99.

119. Zbigniew Brzezinski, *Power and Principle: Memoirs of the National Security Adviser, 1977–1981* (New York: Farrar, Straus, Giroux, 1983), 196–233. See also Jimmy Carter, *Keeping Faith* (New York: Bantam, 1982) and Gaddis Smith, *Morality, Reason and Power: American Diplomacy in the Carter Years* (New York: Hill and Wang, 1986).

120. Cyrus Vance, *Hard Choices: Critical Years in America's Foreign Policy* (New York: Simon and Schuster, 1983), 107–19. See also David S. McLellan, *Cyrus Vance* (Totowa, NJ: Roman and Allenheld, 1985).

121. James C. H. Shen, Taipei's last ambassador, produced the most impassioned indictment in *The U.S. and Free China: How the U.S. Sold Out Its Ally* (Washington, D.C.: Acropolis Books, 1983). Michel Oksenberg defended the administration's secrecy in "Congress, Executive-Legislative Relations, and American China Policy," in Edmund S. Muskie, Kenneth Rush, and Kenneth W. Thompson eds., *The President, the Congress, and Foreign Policy* (Lanham, MD: University Press of America, 1986) as does Jimmy Carter in his memoirs *Keeping Faith* (New York: Bantam, 1982).

122. Tucker, *Uncertain Friendships*, passim; David E. Kaplan, *Fires of the Dragon: Politics, Murder and the Kuomintang* (New York: Atheneum, 1992); Robert P. Newman, "Clandestine Chinese Nationalist Efforts to Punish Their American Detractors," *Diplomatic History* 7 (Summer 1983): 205–22.

123. Sutter, *China Quandary*; Lester Wolff and David L. Simon, *Legislative History of the Taiwan Relations Act* (Jamaica, NY: American Association for Chinese Studies, 1982); Louis W. Koenig, James C. Hsiung, and Chang King-yuh eds., *Congress, the Presidency, and the Taiwan Relations Act* (New York: Praeger, 1985); William B. Bader and Jeffrey T. Bergner ed., *The Taiwan Relations Act: A Decade of Implementation* (Indianapolis: Tango Press, 1989).

124. Edwin A. Winckler and Susan Greenhalgh eds., *Contemporary Approaches to the Political Economy of Taiwan* (Armonk, NY: M. E. Sharpe, 1988); K. T. Li, *The Evolution of Policy Behind Taiwan's Development Success* (New Haven: Yale University Press, 1988);

Shirley W. Y. Kuo, Gustav Ranis, and John C. H. Fei, *The Taiwan Success Story* (Boulder: Westview, 1981); Stephan Haggard, *Pathways from the Periphery* (Ithaca: Cornell University Press, 1990); Robert Wade, *Governing the Market* (Princeton: Princeton University Press, 1990); Tucker, *Uncertain Friendships*.

125. Martin L. Lasater, *The Taiwan Issue in Sino-American Relations* (Boulder: Westview, 1984) and *Policy in Evolution* (Boulder: Westview, 1989) and *U.S. Interests in the New Taiwan* (Boulder: Westview, 1993); A. James Gregor, *The China Connection* (Stanford: Stanford University Press, 1986); Robert L. Downen, *The Tattered China Card* (Washington, D.C.: Council for Social and Economic Studies, 1984).

126. Robert G. Sutter and William Johnson eds., *Taiwan in World Affairs* (Boulder: Westview, 1994); Robert G. Sutter. *Taiwan: Entering the 21st Century* (New York: University Press of America, 1988); Harvey Feldman, Michael Y. M. Kau, and Ilpyong J. Kim eds., *Taiwan in a Time of Transition* (New York: Paragon, 1988); Tien Hung-mao, *The Great Transition* (Stanford: Hoover Institution Press, 1989); Thomas B. Gold, *State and Society in the Taiwan Economic Miracle* (Armonk, NY: M.E. Sharpe, 1986); and Mark J. Cohen, *Taiwan at the Crossroads* (Washington, D.C.: Asia Resource Center, 1988) which focuses on human rights and independence issues.

127. A. Doak Barnett, *The FX Decision: "Another Crucial Moment" in U.S. China Taiwan Relations* (Washington, D.C.: Brookings, 1981). For a broader examination of Taiwan's defense posture written by a partisan of the Nationalists see Martin L. Lasater, *Taiwan: Facing Mounting Threats* (Washington, D.C.: Heritage Foundation, 1987).

128. Jonathan D. Pollack, *The Lessons of Coalition Politics: Sino-American Security Relations* (Santa Monica, CA: Rand Corporation, 1984).

129. Alexander M. Haig, Jr. *Caveat: Realism, Reagan, and Foreign Policy* (New York: Macmillan, 1984), 194–215. See also John W. Garver, "Arms Sales, the Taiwan Question, and Sino-U.S. Relations," *Orbis* 26 (Winter 1983): 999–1035.

130. George Shultz, *Turmoil and Triumph* (New York: Scribner, 1993), 381–99.

131. Garrett and Glaser, "From Nixon to Reagan," 290.

132. A. Doak Barnett, *The Making of Foreign Policy in China: Structure and Process* (Boulder, CO: Westview, 1985). See also Harry Harding ed., *China's Foreign Relations in the 1980s* (New Haven: Yale University Press, 1984); Thomas W. Robinson and David Shambaugh eds., *Chinese Foreign Policy: Theory and Practice* (New York: Oxford University Press, 1994); and the implications for foreign policy analysis of studies such as Frederick C. Teiwes, *Leadership, Legitimacy, and Conflict in China: From a Charismatic Mao to the Politics of Succession* (New York: M. E. Sharpe, 1984).

133. For a Chinese perspective that emphasizes the constructive nature of the relationship in the 1980s see Huan Guocang's "China's Policy Toward the United States," in Hao Yufan and Huan Guocang eds., *The Chinese View of the World* (New York: Pantheon, 1989), 141–73.

134. Joyce K. Kallgren and Denis Fred Simon eds., *Educational Exchanges: Essays on the Sino-American Experience* (Berkeley: Institute of East Asian Studies, University of California, 1987). See also David M. Lampton, *A Relationship Restored: Trends in U.S.-China Educational Exchanges, 1978–1984* (Washington, D.C.: National Academy Press, 1986).

135. R. David Arkush and Leo O. Lee eds., *Land Without Ghosts: Chinese Impressions of America from the Mid-Nineteenth Century to the Present* (Berkeley: University of California Press, 1989), 241–98 presents views of Chinese from the PRC and 203–39 include the reflections of Chinese from Taiwan.

136. David Shambaugh, *Beautiful Imperialist: China Perceives America, 1972–1990* (Princeton: Princeton University Press, 1991).

137. Nancy Bernkopf Tucker, "China and America: 1941–1991," *Foreign Affairs* 70 (Winter 1991/92): 75–92 explores the underlying problems in the relationship.

138. Robert S. Ross discusses the Bush administration's efforts to settle on a China policy in "National Security, Human Rights, and Domestic Politics: The Bush Administration and China," in Kenneth Oye, Robert Lieber and Donald Rothchild eds., *Eagle in a New World: American Grand Strategy in the Post-Cold War Era* (New York: HarperCollins, 1992), 281–313.

139. Roger W. Sullivan, "Discarding the China Card," *Foreign Policy* 86 (Spring 1992): 3–23.

140. Levine, "The Resilient Relationship," 242; Bruce Cumings, "The End of the 70-Years Crisis," *World Policy Journal* 8 (Spring 1991).

141. Levine, "The Resilient Relationship," 242; Tucker, "China and America," 92.

142. Steven W. Mosher has exploited the Tiananmen backlash but has also acted as a constant critical voice throughout the 1980s. See *China Misperceived: American Illusions and Chinese Reality* (New York: HarperCollins, 1990) which attacks virtually the entire American China watching community; *Journey to the Forbidden China* (1985) and *Broken Earth: The Rural Chinese* (1983) the original dissertation version of which threatened to disrupt U.S.-China academic exchange because of its alleged use of purloined source material.

143. Nicholas Eftimiades, *Chinese Intelligence Operations* (Annapolis, MD: Naval Institute Press, 1994); Kaplan, *Fires of the Dragon*, passim; Michael J. Glennon, "Liaison and the Law: Foreign Intelligence Agencies' Activities in the United States," *Harvard International Law Journal* 25 (Winter 1984): 1–42.

144. Michel Oksenberg, "The China Problem," *Foreign Affairs* 70 (Fall 1991): 1–16; Barber B. Conable, Jr. and David M. Lampton, "China: The Coming Power," *Foreign Affairs* 72 (Winter 1992/93): 133–49.

145. Michael J. Hogan ed., *The End of the Cold War: Its Meaning and Implications* (New York: Cambridge University Press, 1992).

146. Zhang, *Deterrence and Strategic Culture*; Chang and He, "The Absence of War"; Warren I. Cohen, *East Asian Art and American Culture* (New York: Columbia University Press, 1992); Qing Simei, "Chinese and American Conceptions"; Shaw, *An American Missionary*; Evans, *John Fairbank*; Tucker, *Uncertain Friendships*.

147. Kusnitz, *Public Opinion*; Sutter, *China Quandary*; Tucker, *Patterns*.

148. John King Fairbank, *Chinabound: A Fifty Year Memoir* (New York: Harper and Row, 1982); Paul A. Cohen and Merle Goldman, comp., *Fairbank Remembered* (Cambridge: Harvard University Press, 1992).

Chapter Ten

Recovery Through Dependency: American-Japanese Relations 1945–1970

MARC GALLICCHIO

One afternoon in the winter of 1985, a Japan specialist at the American embassy in Tokyo attempted to explain why his country's relationship with Japan was so unusual. He related that he had just spent the previous day drafting a cable to Washington in which he summarized Prime Minister Nakasone Yasuhiro's address to the Diet. Certain that his superiors would be interested in what, if anything, the prime minister had said about the troublesome issues of trade and burden sharing, the American foreign service officer ignored Nakasone's lengthy tribute to the generosity of the United States and went right to the meat of the message. A colleague who had just been posted to Tokyo looked over the draft and immediately complained that the summary made no mention of Nakasone's effusive praise of the United States. The veteran impatiently dismissed his greener colleague's complaint. "Oh, he always says that," he explained. His colleague, who had arrived in Japan after tours in several other countries, was not satisfied. "That's the point," he insisted "no one else does."

As the preceding anecdote suggests, the special relationship between the

United States and Japan has bred its own special frustrations. Japan, despite its great wealth, relies on the United States for its military security, making it both an economic rival of the United States and a dependent ally. Americans find this status dissonance all the more exasperating because it seems to have been the result of deliberate calculation on the part of Japanese officials. From the perspective of the 1990s it is all too easy to attribute extraordinary foresight to Japan's leaders. At a time when the temptation to read history backwards seems especially strong, we are fortunate to have scholars who are busy writing it forward.

When Carol Gluck published her essay on the historiography of the American Occupation of Japan a little more than ten years ago, she noted that few scholars had ventured beyond the period of the San Francisco conference to examine the dynamics of U.S.-Japan relations in the post-Occupation era. Several years later, Robert J. McMahon identified a similar void in the existing literature. As McMahon noted, this gap seemed all the more surprising given the deluge of scholarship on the 1950s produced by the Eisenhower revisionists.[1] In part, the frustratingly slow pace of the declassification of American archives helps to explain this oversight. But it also seems that other issues have held a stronger attraction for historians interested in American-East Asian relations. The Korean War, the near-catastrophic encounters in the Taiwan strait, and the deepening involvement in Vietnam all seemed more momentous. In contrast, U.S.-Japan relations after the Occupation seemed relatively free of the crises that convulsed much of Asia in the 1950s. For a time it seemed that the most important bilateral relationship in the world, to borrow from the rhetoric of American officials, would remain the least studied. That trend now seems to be ending. In recent years there has been an increase in the production of dissertations and scholarly articles on post-Occupation U.S.-Japan relations. Several surveys have also appeared, although like their sources, both archival and secondary, they tend to thin out as their narratives reach the mid-1960s.[2] The picture that emerges from these works is not simply a linear story of Japan's rise from the ashes of defeat. Although the recovery of Japan within the American alliance system is taken for granted today, it is becoming clear that officials in both countries never felt as complacent about the outcome of their policies.

For the most part, this essay will be concerned with the emerging body of post-Occupation scholarship. Carol Gluck's masterpiece conveniently included many works in progress that have since appeared in print. It would be redundant and a not a little foolhardy to attempt to go over that ground again. There are several recent works on the Occupation that seem especially deserving of attention, however, either because they attempt a comprehensive view of the Occupation or because their influence on subsequent scholarship has been noteworthy. One study that manages to do both is Howard Schonberger's *Aftermath of War*.[3] Although Schonberger did not address the social implications of the Occupation he nevertheless did provide what is to date the most thorough study of the economic and political dimensions of American policy. Using collective biography as an organizational device for managing the mountainous records of the Occupation, Schonberger personalized the efforts of the Occupationaires without downplaying the larger forces that shaped American policy. According to Schonberger, the limits of reform were self-imposed by the American decisions to maintain the imperial structure in modified form and work through the existing governmental apparatus. Nevertheless, liberal reform experienced a brief heyday before the Truman administration adopted the "reverse course" in 1947. Worsening relations with the Soviet Union, the impending collapse of Nationalist China, and growing fears that *zaibatsu* dissolution and other policies were creating an economically enfeebled Japan convinced American officials to abandon their experiment in reform. In the interest of stability, the Occupation moved to shore up the position of Japan's conservative elite and undermine that of the democratic Left. As Schonberger noted elsewhere, following this reverse in American policy "What reforms survived the Occupation period and remain a legacy today have done so largely in spite of, rather than because of, American policy after 1947."[4]

In all, Schonberger's accomplishment was substantial. He lucidly traced the development of American economic and political policies through the six years of the Occupation while showing how bureaucratic and international economic and political forces shaped those policies. In doing so he convincingly demonstrated that "American policymakers treated Japan not as an isolated experiment in social engineering but primarily within the framework of global economic concerns and Cold War fears of the Soviet Union and Communism."[5]

Several of the chapters in *Aftermath of War* appeared in early form in scholarly journals so that even before Schonberger's book appeared it seemed that a new consensus was forming on the main issues of the reverse course.[6] That apparent calm was quickly shattered, however, by Justin Williams, Sr.'s barbed rebuttal of the growing trend in Occupation scholarship. Williams, a former member of SCAP's government section, argued that there was no reverse course. Instead the American effort in Japan shifted emphasis from internal democratic reforms, which were nearly complete by 1947, to matters of broader foreign policy.[7] In short, Williams denied the connection between internal reforms and Cold War policy that Schonberger, John Dower, Michael Schaller,

William Borden, and others sought to make.[8] Moreover, Williams maintained that those who adhered to the idea of a reverse course were mistaken about the Occupation's main objectives. According to Williams, the Occupation sought to establish popular sovereignty in Japan and institute political and economic reforms similar to those that existed in the United States. When the Occupation failed to go farther, Williams claimed, Japanese communists, other radical leftists, and their sympathizers in SCAP felt betrayed.

In their rejoinders Dower and Schonberger pointed out that the reverse course was just that, a reversal of existing policies. The economic democratization of *zaibatsu* dissolution, about which Williams was somewhat blase, abruptly ended, union activists were purged from the work force and the right to organize curtailed, Japanese identified as militarists or ultra-nationalists were readmitted to public life, reparations to Japan's former enemies slowed, and American officials pressured Japan to rearm.

In an important first-person account, *Remaking Japan*, Theodore Cohen, a liberal member of the Economic and Scientific Section of SCAP, not only acknowledged the existence of a reverse course, but also found it starting a year earlier than most other scholars. According to Cohen the reverse course originated in the Republican congressional victory in 1946. From that point on, Cohen argues, congressional concern over the American taxpayer's burden in Japan rather than Cold War developments governed the course of the Occupation.[9] Nevertheless, Cohen regarded the Occupation as a success, although in some areas, such as civil service reform and the Public Service Law's restrictions on the right to strike, his own recommendations went unheeded.

Perhaps the most unusual and provocative perspective on the liberal phase of the Occupation and the subsequent reverse course has been offered by Tetsuya Kataoka.[10] Writing as a Japanese nationalist (he describes the postwar Japanese politicians he admires as *Gaullists*) Kataoka condemns the liberal enthusiasms of the Occupation and regards the reverse course as a necessary but incomplete redressing of earlier wrongs. In particular, Kataoka blames the Occupation for weakening the prewar politicians, such as Hatoyama Ichiro, whom he considers to have been democratic in inclination, in favor of what he terms a new class of bureaucratic politicians of whom Yoshida Shigeru was the leader.[11] Kataoka argues that the Occupation reformers were influenced by the Leftist Japan scholar E. H. Norman and the reform impulse of the New Deal. As a result, the liberals' desire to transform Japanese society grew out of their mistaken assumption that social structure determined a nation's foreign policy. Terming such thinking reductionist and the reforms it bred as "social engineering" Kataoka adopts the vocabulary of American neoconservatives to criticize the Occupation.[12] Although Kataoka's thesis positing an unarticulated compact between MacArthur and Yoshida and a subsequent struggle between the professional politicos and the new breed of bureaucratic politicians is intriguing, his critique of the liberal phase of the Occupation is less than compelling. After all, American conservatives also have held that social structure determines foreign policy and one could argue that the emergence of Japan as a modern state is best understood as one large exercise in "social engineering."

In his defense of the Occupation Justin Williams sought to draw the lines of the debate as starkly as possible, admitting no possibility for common ground. Nevertheless, the work of D. Clayton James would seem to suggest that some scholars could live with a combination of the two views. In the third volume of his biography *The Years of MacArthur*, James unhesitatingly employed the term "reverse course" to describe the changes in American policy.[13] Recognizing the importance of economic motives in the reverse course, James also suggested that some of SCAP's more controversial measures, such as revision of the National Public Service Law, were reactions to perceived threats to Japan's internal security. Ultimately, however, he concluded that "In the decades ahead, Japan would advance from apt student to master teacher on the subject of capitalism. Unhappily, though, many Japanese never did quite figure out what the 'occupationeers' meant by 'democracy' -especially after the reverse course."[14]

The historians of the reverse course share with Williams a sense of emotional commitment that informs their writing. As a result, there is in their work, Kataoka excepted, an implicit assumption, sometimes made explicit, that a truly democratic Japan could have emerged from the Occupation if American officials had not betrayed the forces of movement after 1947. This assumption deserves further examination for as Schonberger himself indicated, Japanese officials were often successful in thwarting American policies, even in the early phase of the Occupation. Greater attention to the reformers in Japan on the part of American scholars might move this debate in a new direction. In the meantime it seems likely that most students of American-East Asian relations will continue to agree that there was indeed a reverse course even if they disagree on the reasons for it.

One of the consequences of the recent work on the Occupation has been to reduce the role played by Douglas MacArthur to a more human scale. Scholars now recognize that much of the reform program carried out by MacArthur's headquarters originated in Washington, and historians of the reverse course have shown that after 1947 the Truman administration played an even greater role in developing and implementing policy. James's biography provided the fullest treatment of the general's role in the Occupation, but

Schonberger also devoted a chapter to MacArthur. Two other important works on the blue-eyed shogun appeared in the 1980s, Michael Schaller's *Douglas MacArthur: The Far Eastern General* and Richard Finn's *Winners in Peace: MacArthur, Yoshida, and Postwar Japan.*[15]

Schaller's provocative work vividly demonstrated how this most political of generals managed to politicize American policy toward East Asia in the Cold War. According to Schaller, despite his reputation as America's Far Eastern expert, MacArthur's views on the region remained remarkably unchanged from those held by his father at the turn of the century. Schaller's is essentially a political biography that effectively highlights the general's talent for shameless self-promotion. Insofar as the Occupation was concerned, Schaller argued that MacArthur's policies were best understood as an attempt to position himself as a presidential candidate in 1948, a view also supported by Schonberger.

D. Clayton James was more skeptical about the influence of MacArthur's political ambitions on his role as Supreme Commander. He argues that the general's call for an early end to the Occupation in 1947 came at a time when MacArthur had not yet committed himself to run for the Republican nomination. James also interprets the general's support for *zaibatsu* dissolution, despite strong criticism from Republicans, as the result of confusion over government policy and not, as Schaller and Schonberger argue, as an attempt to broaden his appeal to the electorate. All agree that MacArthur was naive about American politics, but it does seem doubtful that the general would have pressed for a policy, *zaibatsu* dissolution, that seemed likely to threaten the very nomination that he sought. On the other hand, it might be inappropriate to use conventional political wisdom to explain the motives of a man who detected a conspiracy behind nearly every order emanating from Washington and who thought Dwight Eisenhower could not be a "good Republican" because he had "Jewish blood in his veins."[16]

Although Schaller managed to shrink MacArthur to more human dimensions, one was left wondering how this seemingly hollow man managed to win the loyalty of those around him, and more important, the respect of the Japanese he ruled. While agreeing that MacArthur's legacy has been exaggerated, Richard Finn contends that the general's success owed much to the effective working relationship he developed with Yoshida Shigeru, the leading political figure during the Occupation. Initially critical of Yoshida's obstruction of Occupation policy, MacArthur welcomed the former diplomat's consolidation of his power in the January 1949 elections. As Finn and Kataoka show, the innate conservatism that bound the two men together also allowed Yoshida more freedom to maneuver.

Following the dismal results of MacArthur's candidacy and the implementation of the reverse course, the general's influence over the Occupation began to slip. By early 1950, as the Truman administration moved toward a peace treaty with Japan, John Foster Dulles assumed responsibility for concluding the Occupation on terms satisfactory to the United States. In the early 1960s, Frederick Dunn labeled the treaty an "American achievement." For good or ill, scholars continue to see it that way.

In contrast to Dunn, however, recent historians also see the peace treaty and the security treaty with the United States as Dulles's achievement. Before Dulles could begin his work, however, he needed to overcome the Pentagon's opposition to a peace treaty. In *The American Occupation of Japan: The Origins of the Cold War In Asia*, Michael Schaller places the peace treaty in the context of an expanding American military involvement in East Asia. In the process, he provides the most thorough analysis of the efforts of the Defense Department and its erratic secretary Louis Johnson to scuttle any treaty.[17] Indeed, as Schaller shows, it was not until the outbreak of the Korean War that the JCS relented with the understanding that the peace treaty would be followed by a separate security treaty providing the United States with base rights throughout Japan and a commitment by Japan to rearm. In *Aftermath of War*, Howard Schonberger took a similar approach to the peace and security treaties, concluding that together with the restrictions imposed on Japan's trade with the PRC they "severely compromised Japanese sovereignty and contributed to Cold War tensions."[18] John Dower further refined this line of interpretation by describing the security arrangements and the peace treaty as the culmination of a three stage transformation in American policy. In the initial phase, 1947–1949, American officials took steps, mainly economic, to deny Japan to the Soviet Union. During the next two years, their thinking turned to the problem of getting Japan to play a more positive role in Cold War strategy in the region. The final stage produced the peace and security treaties locking Tokyo into the American sponsored regional security system while simultaneously saddling Japan with a "subordinate independence."[19]

Yoshida would have preferred better terms, of course, but he was willing to pay a stiff price to end the occupation. Most scholars agree that Dulles held all the high cards in the negotiations except where the issue of military rearmament was concerned.[20] Seigen Miyasato, Richard Finn, and Roger Dingman all note that Yoshida was determined to postpone rearmament and rely on American forces, even as he pledged to rearm in his negotiations with Dulles.[21] In his important article on the impact of the Korean War on Japan, Dingman described how Dulles realized too late the "essential irrationality of the bargain that he had struck. . . . What reasonable Japanese politician would be willing to advocate spending billions of yen for rearmament to replace hard currency-producing protectors?"[22]

Although he had little choice but to hope for Yoshida's full cooperation in rearming Japan, Dulles left little to chance when it came to the question of restricting Japan's freedom to trade to with China. As Nancy Bernkopf Tucker has shown, Dean Acheson's State Department continued to weigh the merits of permitting Japanese trade with the PRC.[23] Both the Japanese and Americans saw China as an important source of raw materials and a natural outlet for Japanese manufactured goods. Acheson continued to consider allowing some form of commerce between Japan and China even after the outbreak of the Korean War. Dulles, however, sought to isolate the PRC as much as possible. As John Dower has shown in *Empire and Aftermath*, Dulles threatened to hold the peace treaty hostage in the U.S. Senate unless Yoshida pledged to recognize the Nationalists on Taiwan as the government of China. In addition, future American assistance was conditioned on Japanese participation in the economic blockade of China.[24] This agreement was sealed in the notorious "Yoshida letter" which was actually written by Dulles. Warren Cohen has added a new twist to this episode by arguing that the intended object of Dulles's blackmail was actually Acheson.[25] Dulles feared that Acheson would be swayed by British arguments in favor of leaving Japan free to trade with China in nonstrategic goods. In order to head off that possibility Dulles enlisted the support of his senatorial allies and went to work on Yoshida. Together with Tucker's article, Cohen's essay provided additional evidence supporting the argument advanced by both in their earlier work that Acheson intended to leave the door open to possible recognition of the PRC at some later date.

The negotiations for the peace and security treaties took place against a background of concern for Japan's economic recovery. As mentioned, the reverse course had been undertaken in large measure to revive Japan's moribund economy. Although the Korean War provided a much needed infusion of dollars for nonlethal war goods, the assistance provided by war-related purchases was expected to be temporary. The loss of the China market looked to be of more lasting consequence. According to William Borden, the Japanese dilemma was actually part of a larger structural problem in the American-dominated system of global capitalism that emerged after World War II. As early as 1947 it became obvious to American policymakers that their plans for a multilateral trading regime were foundering on the stagnant economies of their allies. Borden argued that the nagging dollar gap was eventually dealt with through a combination of military aid and purchases, opening of the American market and by linking the Japanese economy to the raw material producing areas of Southeast Asia. Borden introduced his thesis by noting that "Japanese colleagues have assured me that the basic themes of this work are old hat in Japan" but he added that "many cold-war-oriented and less economically astute American diplomatic historians would find unduly one-sided my insistence that economic policies loomed very large in American policy toward Europe and Japan, the core of American diplomacy, in the post-war period."[26]

Despite that immodest introduction, Borden failed to inoculate himself from criticism concerning his use of economic evidence. Roger Dingman welcomed Borden's effort to reconnect America's Japan policy to its broader global concerns, but he complained that among other failings, Borden never demonstrated how large Japan's dollar gap was relative to other countries. In "The Dagger and the Gift" Dingman also questioned Borden's assertion that the Korean War was "'the decisive event" in the revival and redirection of Japanese trade." Instead he argued that although the Korean War aided Japan's recovery, officials in Tokyo had already settled on the broad measures needed to produce recovery before the outbreak of the war. In the long run, Dingman suggests, it was these decisions that accounted for Japan's economic revival.[27]

Although Borden sought to place Japan policy into the broader context of an emerging world capitalist order dominated by the United States, it was his argument concerning Southeast Asia that gained the widest notice. Briefly put, Borden argued that the United States became involved in Vietnam in order to protect that area as a market and source of raw materials for a rein-dustrializing Japan. Andrew J. Rotter agreed. The *Path to Vietnam*, according to Rotter, led through Tokyo.[28] Howard Schonberger made a similar case in *Aftermath of War*. Michael Schaller also perceived a connection between American involvement in Southeast Asia and Japan's recovery. Although all of these authors recognized that security and economic concerns were inter-twined, Schaller tended to give more emphasis to military considerations than the others.

Historians have incorporated this "Great Crescent" thesis, to borrow a term used in State and Defense Department planning papers, into their secondary works with few changes. Variations can be found in Thomas McCormick's *America's Half Century*, Walter LaFeber's *The American Age*, Thomas Havens's *Fire Across the Sea*, and Marilyn B. Young's *The Vietnam Wars*.[29] The emergence of this thesis in the historiography of the Cold War marked an important moment for the scholars associated with the Wisconsin school, of which the late William Appleman Williams was the leading practitioner. Although the first generation of Williams's students had been inspired by the Vietnam War to find the roots of American imperialism, the connection between American intervention in Vietnam and the larger theme of Open Door imperialism remained elusive. The "Great Crescent" thesis not only made that connection explicit, but also placed it in the larger context of world systems theory then in vogue.[30]

Although the Great Crescent argument exhibited some of the same strengths of the Open Door thesis, particularly its presentation of a unifying theme in American foreign relations, it also shared some of the same weaknesses. Critics of the Open Door thesis have long noted that the abundance of rhetoric concerning American expansion in Asia was never matched by actual economic activity. Similarly, American policymakers said a great deal about forging the connection between the economies of Japan and Southeast Asia, but they did little to turn those visions into reality. As Dingman noted, Borden displayed a surprising tendency to take policy documents and congressional testimony on this subject at face value. Historians may wish to speak "truth to power," as Bruce Cumings has urged, but they should not assume that people in power speak the truth to each other.[31] According to Richard Finn, the idea of substituting Southeast Asia for China as Japan's main trading partner was a scheme cooked up in the Pentagon but left half-baked throughout the 1950s. Even Borden concedes that the Southeast Asian market never lived up to expectations during the period of American intervention and escalation.[32]

Although most historians agree that American officials worried about Japan's recovery during the 1940s and 1950s, they are less likely to concur on how the Truman and Eisenhower administrations sought to remedy that problem. In part, the disagreement among historians over the American role in resurrecting Japan's coprosperity sphere hinges on differing views of Dean Acheson's Asian policies. Warren Cohen and Nancy Bernkopf Tucker tend to see Acheson waging a losing battle to sever American ties to the Guomindang. For them Acheson's policy was one of delay and bureaucratic compromise while waiting for the dust to settle after the Chinese communist victory. Others see Acheson in command of the situation skillfully orchestrating a campaign to control the Asian rimlands. Ronald McGlothlen's *Controlling the Waves: Dean Acheson and U.S. Foreign Policy in Asia* is firmly in the latter camp. In this study of Acheson's tenure as Undersecretary of State, 1945–1947, and Secretary of State, 1949–1953, McGlothlen argues that although Acheson remained a Europeanist at heart, his Asian policy was shaped by an abiding concern for the economic reconstruction of Japan. Toward this end Acheson supported the reverse course and the lenient peace treaty and attempted to develop South Korea as an economic handmaiden to

Japan's reindustrialization. As Secretary of State he also fought attempts to block Japanese trade with the Chinese mainland while simultaneously plotting to depose Chiang on Taiwan, an island deemed important to Japan for its "strategic, economic, and psychological" significance.[33]

Although McGlothlen chose a narrative format for his study, his decision to treat American policy toward the PRC and Taiwan in separate chapters seems to have contributed to his overlooking important contradictions in his discussion of Acheson's grand design. It is not clear why Acheson would attach so much value to Taiwan while the possibility of a revived Japanese trade with the mainland existed. A more attractive Nationalist regime on Taiwan would strengthen the hand of those in the administration and congress who wanted to isolate the PRC. As long as a Nationalist regime survived on Taiwan the administration would find it difficult to cut its ties to the Guomindang. Why would Acheson pursue a policy that would complicate his efforts to open Japanese trade with the PRC? McGlothlen's apparent answer to this question is that the secretary recognized that one day Taiwan would become one of Japan's leading trading partners in Asia. Given Taiwan's weakened condition in 1950, however, this is tantamount to saying that Acheson was clairvoyant, which is a claim even the secretary never made for himself.[34]

McGlothlen also argued that Acheson's concern for Japan's recovery led him to support an American commitment to Vietnam, but here he added more nuance to the Great Crescent argument. At first, according to McGlothlen, Acheson offered assistance to the French in Vietnam in the hope of gaining French cooperation in Europe, but by late 1949 he "began to place new emphasis on Southeast Asia's potential role in Japanese trade, and on Vietnam's role in regional security."[35] Yet as McGlothlen shows elsewhere, by mid 1950 Japan had made significant progress toward recovery. The Japanese standard of living stood at 70 percent of its prewar level and industrial output reached 83 percent.[36] Japan was far from achieving prosperity, and its trade deficit ballooned to $640 million dollars in 1951, but were these conditions so troubling as to prompt an American commitment to Southeast Asia? It also remains unclear how Acheson came to believe that Indochina could serve Japan's recovery while it remained part of the French empire. For at the very moment that Americans were supposed to be hitching Japan's economy to the resources of the Southeast Asia, Acheson and others in the administration were also arguing that the defense of Southeast Asia was crucial for a European recovery.[37] Did American officials really expect the region to serve both ends? Did the supposedly masterful strategists of the Truman administration actually believe that the prosperity of most of the industrial world depended on the survival of a noncommunist Indochina? Acheson's policies and subsequent American efforts to revive Japan's economy suggest otherwise.

The system of economic and security arrangements that Truman bequeathed to his successor shaped the contours of American-Japanese relations over the next decade. The persistence of what Akira Iriye has dubbed the San Francisco system is somewhat remarkable given that the British, Japanese, Chinese Communists, and the Americans, or rather the American president, all sought to revise some part of it in the mid-1950s. Although we still await the release of further evidence from the PRC, Russia, and Japan, it seems plausible that historians will come to view this period in Asia as a missed opportunity to reduce Cold War tensions in Asia.

Although much scholarship has been devoted to the Sino-American conflict in the Taiwan Strait during this period, Japanese-American relations are also beginning to receive serious attention. In 1989 and 1990, Warren Cohen and Akira Iriye edited two important conference volumes, *The United States and Japan in the Postwar World* and *The Great Powers in East Asia*, both of which contained articles on the China question in American-Japanese relations. In "From the Yoshida Letter to the Nixon Shocks," Hosoya Chihiro identified the emergence of Hatoyama Ichiro as the head of the Japanese government in December 1954, as a turning point in Tokyo's diplomacy. Hatoyama hoped to establish better relations with the PRC and the Soviet Union while maintaining close ties to the United States. The prime minister encountered strong opposition, however, from within the newly merged Liberal Democratic Party (1955) and the foreign ministry. In part, the bureaucrats disapproved of any sharp departures from the policies established by Yoshida for fear of antagonizing the United States.[38]

Ironically, historians who have studied the Eisenhower administration's policy on the China question have found that the president also favored a lessening of restrictions on Sino-Japanese trade. Warren Cohen, Burton Kaufman, and Qing Simei agree that the president believed such restrictions were counterproductive and that they put more pressure on allied relations than on the PRC.[39] Sayuri Shimizu reached a similar conclusion in her dissertation "Creating a People of Plenty: The United States and Japan's Economic Alternatives, 1953–1958."[40] All identified the Joint Chiefs of Staff and Jiang Jieshi's (Chiang Kai-shek) congressional supporters as the major obstacles to such a plan. Eisenhower would have needed to work especially hard to win approval for the changes he desired in the trade regime. Instead, as Kaufman notes, Ike turned his attention to other matters that seemed more pressing after 1955. Allied pressure finally provided the impetus for ending the so-called China differential (the list of embargoed goods for China was larger than that for the Soviet Union) in 1957. Cohen agreed that Eisenhower was not willing to lead the fight for a new policy, but he credits the president for using allied pressure and the specter of Japanese textiles flooding American markets to outmaneuver Jiang's Washington allies. In contrast to Schonberger, who viewed the trade restrictions as a serious infringement on Japanese sovereignty, Cohen tended to view the matter as a more of a "nuisance" for Japan. In all, he concluded, the trade saga showed how weaker allies can achieve their goals through persistent and skillful diplomacy.

The China trade was an important and potentially explosive issue for Eisenhower, but it was only one element of the president's economic policy toward Japan. In her dissertation, Sayuri Shimizu shows how the United States explored various alternatives to help create a materially prosperous and politically stable Japan. Redirecting Japanese trade toward Southeast Asia was one possibility, but the Americans never committed the development aid necessary to make the project work, nor did the Japanese believe that regional integration alone would provide the key to Japan's recovery.[41] Removing restrictions on the China trade was another, somewhat more successful option. The ultimate course chosen by the administration, however, was the integration of Japan into the western economic system, a policy that was also welcomed by Japanese officials. To achieve this end Eisenhower championed Japanese membership in GATT and pushed for the opening of American markets to Japanese goods. The result was slow but steady progress. The Japanese confronted exclusionary measures even after joining GATT and the Eisenhower administration pressured Tokyo into "voluntary" quotas when complaints from American producers grew too loud to ignore. Nevertheless, Shimizu concludes that "the Eisenhower administration used its power quite well in helping to rebuild the Japanese economy. It generally succeeded in meeting Japan's economic needs and demands, and attained the mutual goal of creating a self-supporting Japanese economy."[42]

We are now beginning to construct a clearer picture of how the Eisenhower administration dealt with the problem of Japan's recovery, although, we need more discussion of the Japanese side along the lines of Hosoya's essay. For example, we have no English language study of the Foreign Ministry comparable to Chalmers Johnson's MITI and The Japanese Miracle.[43] Moreover, those that exist tend to be based on memoir and journalistic accounts. The opening of Japanese archives for this period would be welcomed; unfortunately it is not to be expected anytime soon.

Although American officials initially were happy to see Hatoyama replace Yoshida, they soon regarded the new prime minister as unreliable. It seems particularly revealing that given Eisenhower's own views on trade with China, the United States and Japan were not able to cooperate more closely. In part, it would seem that the inability of both leaders to quell the dissent within their own governments helps to explain their failure to build a mutually acceptable policy. Owing to domestic opposition, the president was unwilling to go beyond eliminating the China differential. More significant changes would have to wait. It also seems clear, however, that Hatoyama's pursuit of a rapprochement with the PRC *and* the Soviet Union raised fears in Washington that substantial modifications in one element of the San Francisco system might lead to an unraveling of the whole web of American-made security arrangements in the Western Pacific. As the current writer has suggested, Hatoyama's desire to reach an accord with the Soviet Union over the Northern Territories dispute compounded Dulles's worries over Tokyo's errant attitudes on Chinese trade. A compromise on the territorial dispute, Dulles feared, would remove a major irritant in Japan-Soviet relations and focus Japanese attention on the return of Okinawa.[44] This was too much too soon. Dulles responded by threatening to make permanent American control over Okinawa. If, as scholars have recently suggested, the Eisenhower administration pursued a policy of detente with the Soviet Union in the mid-1950s, it nevertheless seems certain that the Americans believed that the stakes were too high to allow the Japanese to play their own hand.

In the decade after the Occupation, American officials continued to doubt Japan's commitment to the alliance. Thus even though Hatoyama did not wish to sever the American connection, the smallest signs of independence in Tokyo rang alarm bells in Washington. For American officials, the lagging pace of Japanese rearmament provided the most persistent evidence of Japan's lukewarm support. Japanese officials made occasional concessions, but for the most part they kept to their goal concentrating on economic recovery, leaving defense to the United States. As H. W. Brands has pointed out, Eisenhower was particularly sensitive to arguments that emphasized the delicate balance between military spending and economic growth.[45]

In the final analysis, the president favored a healthy Japanese economy over a strong military. The JCS were less easily reconciled to this arrangement. Martin Weinstein's *Japan's Postwar Defense Policy, 1947–1968* continues to be the point of departure for historians interested in Japan's military policy.[46] Weinstein argued that Japanese officials took advantage of the bipolar nature of Cold War tensions to develop a coherent and nonprovocative strategy that protected their country at minimum cost. According to Weinstein, references to public opinion and the "Peace Constitution" are not sufficient to explain why Japan stalled on rearmament. In order to understand Japan's military policy one needs to look to the conscious choices made by LDP leaders. Where

Weinstein sees a policy shaped by consensus, James Auer and Aaron Patrick Forsberg see a policy achieved by default.[47] Forsberg argues that LDP members never reached an agreement on defense policy to match the general understanding on economic goals. No institutions in defense or political affairs emerged to match the Ministry of International Trade and Industry. Nevertheless, Forsberg's treatment of the "revisionist" ministries of Hatoyama and Kishi seems to reinforce Weinstein's conclusion that the failures of both governments revealed the underlying support for Yoshida's approach to defense issues. Tetsuya Kataoka ruefully agrees. According to Forsberg, opposition from Japan's regional neighbors further limited Japan's ability to rearm or assume a more active role in foreign affairs. It seems doubtful, however, that regional opposition could have prevented a more rapid remilitarization if Japanese leaders had desired it. As the current writer has suggested, given the importance that the New Look strategy placed on cooperative action, the Americans almost certainly would have found a way to overcome allied fears of Japan if Tokyo had been willing to increase the pace of rearmament.[48]

Although the Americans remained disappointed in Japanese military spending during the 1950s, U.S. and Self-Defense Forces began to cooperate more closely in defense planning. Thus, as Weinstein indicates, by the end of the decade Japanese leaders could reasonably expect that their hopes for revision of the security treaty would be met when the pact came up for renewal in 1960. In particular, Japanese officials wanted the new treaty to contain a U.S. pledge to defend Japan and a provision for prior consultation on the use of American forces stationed in Japan in operations outside the home islands. Japanese leaders also wanted to remove from the existing agreement the humiliating clause that allowed the U.S. to use its forces to maintain internal security in Japan. The ensuing public turmoil in Tokyo shocked American officials especially since the new treaty seemed to contain the provisions Japanese officials wanted most. The political upheaval produced by the debate over treaty revision received its fullest treatment in George Packard's *Protest in Tokyo* (1966).

Recent studies by Tadashi Aruga and John Welfield support Packard's earlier conclusion that the opponents of the treaty were more anti-Kishi than anti-American.[49] Aruga also concluded that Japan's political dependence transformed the protests into an act of immature national self-assertion. According to Aruga, opponents of the treaty knew they could take to the streets without permanently alienating their American protectors. American indulgence, he concludes, essentially kept the crisis from seriously affecting the alliance. Welfield suggests that the furor over the treaty showed that political leaders, the foreign policy elite, and the foreign policy public continued to favor the Yoshida policy of passive defense and alignment with the U.S. In contrast, Kishi seemed to represent a more activist policy that carried disturbing reminders of Japan's militaristic past. Welfield also suggested that there was less to the agreement than met the eye. The provision on mutual security only made explicit what the commingling of forces had already made a reality. As for agreements on prior consultation and internal security, both gave the U.S. sufficient latitude to act as they would have under the old treaty.

It is hard to quarrel with the conclusions of Weinstein and Welfield that Yoshida's defense policy served Japan well during the 1950s. Yet in attempting to assess the role of military policy in American-Japanese relations during this period, it might also be helpful if historians consider what was missing from the relationship. In the decade after the Occupation Japanese officers began attending American military schools and representatives of both forces in Japan cooperated more closely on strategic planning. Nevertheless, it does not appear that these lower-level contacts favorably influenced American policy at higher levels. Unlike Nationalist China, no one spoke for Japan in the JCS, Defense Department or National Security Council. The pervasive belief that Japan was not doing enough for its own defense meant that Tokyo could not count on supporters to make its views known in the executive branch.

The extent to which the presence of friendly voices in the higher counsels of government might have deflected policies inimical to Japan cannot be known. It is clear, however, that American military authorities could obstruct policies beneficial to Japan when they so desired. The issue of Okinawa reversion is a case in point. Okinawa's unique legal status after the Pacific War and its impact on U.S.-Japan relations led to several studies by political scientists in the 1970s.[50] The role of the island's military bases in the Vietnam war also called attention to the paradoxical situation of American forces claiming to wage a war for democracy from a semicolonial possession.[51] More recently, L. Eve Armentrout Ma has described how American land practices became the catalyst for Japanese nationalism on Okinawa.[52] According to Armentrout Ma, in the absence of the bases issue, ties of language and culture would not have been enough to inspire the reversion movement. Indeed, as Timothy Maga shows, the Kennedy administration explored other alternatives to reversion even as it decided to gradually relinquish administrative control to the islanders in the aftermath of the 1960 treaty crisis.[53]

Much to the consternation of the ambassador in Tokyo and other American diplomats, the High Commissioner, General Paul Caraway, blocked these efforts until his retirement in 1964. Caraway receives special mention in the memoirs of John K. Emmerson, U. Alexis Johnson, and Edwin O. Reischauer.[54] According to the usually reserved Ambassador Reischauer, the general was "rigid" "bull-headed" and "autocratic." Caraway's obstructionism highlights the special position of the High Commissioner, which in itself explains why the JCS were so reluctant to surrender control over the island.

In *Empire in Eclipse*, a study of Japan's foreign policy since 1945, John Welfield uses the Okinawa controversy to illuminate the connection between factional politics in the LDP and the debate over an "Asianist" or "pro-American" foreign policy. Making extensive use of newspapers in Japan and the United States, Welfield explains that by the mid-1960s the Secretary of Defense was finally able to convince the Joint Chiefs that administrative control over the Ryukyus (of which Okinawa was a part) was no longer needed for strategic purposes. State Department officials hoped to reward the pro-American Sato Eisaku by reaching an agreement on reversion. Despite the long-awaited approval of the Joint Chiefs and Defense Department, congressional opposition delayed the agreement until after Richard Nixon became president. The Nixon-Sato communique, like the 1960 security treaty, seemed to contain important loopholes on the question of introducing nuclear weapons onto the island. Fortunately, neither side ever found it necessary to test their interpretation of the agreement. Welfield's conclusion on the Okinawa controversy is similar in tone to Warren Cohen's assessment of the China trade question. In securing reversion, Japan had "reasserted its sovereignty over a strategically important piece of real estate inhabited by nearly a million former Japanese subjects . . ." while managing to "stand exactly where it stood in 1951—allied to the United States, but with no military commitments beyond its shores."[55]

This situation seemed less satisfactory to American officials than Japanese. The return of Okinawa came at the end of a decade of disillusionment and frustration in Washington over Japan's role in the Vietnam War. Roger Buckley suggests that the Americans were partly to blame for their own disappointment. He notes that in the immediate aftermath of the security treaty crisis the Kennedy administration asked so little of Japan that it could not be turned down.[56] Similarly, Prime Minister Ikeda pledged his support to anticommunism but committed his government to doubling Japanese income in five years. Neither side was prepared for the demands on the alliance that escalation in Vietnam would create.

Walter LaFeber highlights the economic issues underlying the political tensions in this period.[57] In the United States, it was frustrating enough to watch Japan's economy thrive as America's stagnated. But for the Nixon administration, Japan's unwillingness to help pay for the war seemed especially threatening because it weakened America's ability to fulfill what the president saw as its necessary geopolitical role. LaFeber concludes that normalization of relations with the PRC, and the threat to block the import of Japanese textiles, the so-called "Nixon-shocks," signaled an end to an era in American-Japanese relations. The relationship had become more "natural" suggests LaFeber, with "competition" replacing "harmony" and "partnership." With the emergence of detente, Japan began to pursue a more independent foreign policy.

Roger Buckley is more skeptical concerning Japan's assertion of an independent course. "The familiar twin Japanese objectives of economic security and military links to Washington were still firmly in place once the excitement and noise had subsided."[58] The rapid development of Japan as a foreign aid donor seems to underscore this point. Robert M. Orr, Jr. skillfully employs bureaucratic analysis in *The Emergence of Japan's Foreign Aid Power* to show how Japanese administrators frequently used American pressure to prod their colleagues in other agencies to shape aid programs in such a way as to serve Japan's interests *and* satisfy American requests.[59]

Nevertheless, the Vietnam era can be seen as a watershed of some kind in American-Japanese relations. Thomas Havens suggests that American conduct in the war forced Japanese citizens to develop a more practical view of their ally. The Japanese antiwar movement was not vehemently anti-American, but it was harshly critical of American policy.[60] Before the war, the Japanese ranked the United States as their most admired country. By the end of the war the U.S. placed third behind France and Switzerland. The Nixon shocks added to the feeling of disillusionment, but perhaps more significant were the changing fortunes of both countries' economies. Rising Japanese self-confidence and increasing American self-criticism, suggests Akira Iriye, "may have served to equalize the two peoples' self-perception."[61]

In the last decade historians have begun to ask how the United States might have aided Japan's economic resurgence and thus contributed to this equalization of perception. At present, scholars concur on several basic points. Most agree that the U.S.-Japan security arrangement benefitted Japan by transferring Tokyo's defense burden onto the shoulders of American taxpayers. They also recognize the importance of the military purchases and technology transfers that accompanied the Korean and Vietnam wars. The gradual opening of American markets to Japanese goods in the 1950s and 1960s, while the U.S. acquiesced in restrictive practices by Japan, is credited with furthering this economic expansion.[62] Theodore Cohen went a step further and in somewhat self-congratulatory fashion identified the economic democratization measures of the early Occupation (particularly land and labor reform) with creating a new domestic market in which Japanese firms could test and improve their products.[63]

Although they agree upon the relative importance of the developments just mentioned, various scholars have been quick to remind students of the internal decisions and structural changes that shaped Japan's own brand of capitalism. As mentioned, Roger Dingman argues that before the Korean War, Japan's governing elite established the policies that would produce Japan's recovery. Similarly, John Dower points out how the demands of the Pacific War led to the emergence of a bureaucratic elite that grew in power during the Occupation and came to exercise unprecedented influence over Japan's economic development.[64] In this way, Dower sees the emergence of Japan's "guided capitalism" rooted in the past as opposed to the many current commentators who treat the emergence of "Japan Inc." as strictly a postwar phenomenon. Mark Mason's study of ten American companies that tried to enter the Japanese market through direct investment in the years 1899–1990 underscores the need to take the long view. Mason found that by 1930, after an initial period of encouragement, business elites and the Japanese government moved to impose restrictions on foreign direct investment. These practices continued after the war, abetted this time by American Occupation authorities who shielded the Japanese economy from outside competition.[65]

Bruce Cumings and James Fallows have also developed this theme. Both argue that Japan's postwar growth should be seen as part of the nation's late and thus historically different approach to industrialization.[66] Instead of following the Anglo-American or "cosmopolitan" model of capitalism posed by Adam Smith, Japan followed the "nationalist" path to development marked out by others, particularly the German economist Friedrich List. In recent decades, as a result of this difference in economic philosophies, American free traders have found themselves operating under one set of rules while Japan plays by another. This situation is bitterly ironic, Fallows suggests, because American development in the nineteenth century also depended heavily on the visible hand of the state.[67]

Although we are beginning to see more scholarship devoted to placing Japan's economic expansion into a historical perspective, much of the work on this subject is still prescriptive or admonitory in nature. Much as Enlightenment philosophers used the perceived wisdom of other societies to recommend improvements in their own, American commentators have employed the image of a disciplined Japan to urge reforms at home. David Halberstam's richly detailed saga of the Ford and Nissan automobile companies chronicles the creeping complacency that many, including many Japanese, see as the root cause of America's relative decline.[68] While such case studies are needed, Halberstam's allegory should be balanced against works such as Mark Mason's study of American multinationals. Mason debunks many of the myths about American indifference or inattentiveness to the demands of the Japanese market and shows how even those firms that outperform Japanese companies in the international marketplace cannot overcome the numerous restrictions placed on their activities within Japan. The realization that the United States and its one-time junior partner operate on fundamentally different economic principles poses a challenge to future relations, argues John Dower, especially since capitalism in the late twentieth century seems to be transforming the structures of both societies at an accelerating rate.[69]

During this century periods of competition and conflict in U.S.-Japan relations have usually revived traditional images of the other on both sides of the Pacific. The postwar era is different, however, in that citizens of both countries have been in much closer contact than in any previous period. Historians are now beginning to ask if that unprecedented level of contact has improved mutual perceptions and understanding. Akira Iriye has sketched the broad outlines of the social and cultural interaction of the two peoples, but more fine-grained studies are needed. In his biography of MacArthur, D. Clayton James conveniently summarized the findings of many of the studies discussed by Carol Gluck, although the conclusions are his own.[70] In examining public health policy, educational and local government reform, women's rights, press censorship, and MacArthur's missionary activities, James notes that in many instances there existed a considerable gulf between the letter of SCAP directives and their implementation, but he nevertheless concludes with a favorable overall evaluation of the Occupation. To support his assessment, James cites opinion polls showing that in May 1952, 47 percent of respondents answered yes to the question "Do you think the UN Occupation has had good effects on the people?" Another 39 percent said they "did not know" and 14 percent replied with a definite "no." James sees in this and other polls evidence of a willingness on the part of Japanese to think that the Americans meant well even when they resorted to autocratic means to democratize Japan. "If contemporary Japanese forgive SCAP's blunders and admire its idealistic goals," he writes "maybe historians and biographers henceforth will grant MacArthur's wish, after all, and record that his career reached its zenith in Japan."[71]

The relative harmony that was established during the Occupation seems all the more remarkable in light of the war's brutality and the racism exhibited by both sides in the conflict. In "Trans-Pacific Racism: The U.S. Occupation of Japan" Yukiko Koshiro carries forward the themes presented in John Dower's *War Without Mercy*.[72] Dower had suggested that once the war ended American images of the Japanese as subhuman beasts underwent a

transformation. The American conquerors still viewed the Japanese as infe-
riors, but now their new wards were seen as children in need of training.
Koshiro expands upon this theme and finds that Americans and Japanese
eventually dealt with racial matters by reverting to long-established mutual
images. According to Koshiro, Japan had developed a dual identity to coin-
cide with its emergence as a great power in the early twentieth century. As the
West's best pupils, the Japanese were both "honorary whites" and members
of the undesirable non-white races. During the Occupation and the Cold
War American policies encouraged this dual self-image in order to alienate
Japan from the revolutionary nations of Asia and ensure Japan's alignment
with the west. According to Koshiro, the Occupation avoided any discussion
of racial equality, thereby missing a chance to place American-Japanese relations on a new footing. The reversion to hierarchy, she suggests, served both
nations' interests, but left the invidious race question lurking just beneath
the surface of Japanese-American relations.[73] Koshiro has demonstrated the
symmetry between prewar and postwar images, but it seems that where the
Japanese are concerned she underestimates the legacy of the Pacific War. In
explaining Japan's "psychological detachment" from Asia some acknowl-
edgement has to be made of the ill feeling that other Asians held toward their
former invaders.

Following the Korean War, Japanese may have wished to preserve their
sense of racial purity, but as Roger Dingman shows, that conflict guaranteed
that the Japanese would have to live with a substantial American presence in
their midst.[74] Just when it seemed that Japan might be rid of the most visible
signs of foreign interference the war intervened. American officials were suddenly forced to reverse their previous plans for the reduction of armed forces
on the home islands. The continued and enlarged American presence,
according to Dingman, redirected the pattern of cross-cultural contact from
elite exchanges to the more widely diffused realm of popular culture. This was
a true exchange, he suggests, providing Japanese with exposure to American
popular culture and also a test market for consumer goods later produced for
export. Of course familiarity does not necessarily breed understanding, as
Dingman shows elsewhere. In recounting the tragic story of the *Lucky Dragon*, a Japanese tuna boat doused by radioactive fallout in 1954, Dingman
shows how latent racism surfaced in the Japanese-American quarrel over
medical treatment for the exposed crew members.[75]

The *Lucky Dragon* episode also fueled the ban-the-bomb movement in
Japan and highlighted the tension between Japan's dependence on the American nuclear deterrent and the strong public desire to control or eliminate the
fearsome weapons that had become the "cardinal instrument of American

national security policy."[76] The Japanese government's squeamishness over rearmament and the public's abhorrence of nuclear weapons probably did more to shape the attitudes of American policymakers than the numerous private contacts between Japanese and Americans. Speaking of Yoshida's resistance to military spending, Dulles complained that in Japan, "There has not been any rebirth of moral strength as in the case of Germany."[77]

Of course the Japanese saw things differently. Akira Iriye argues that Japan did undergo a rebirth, from predatory imperialist to peaceful international-ist.[78] Unfortunately, Japan adopted the vocabulary and principles of interna-tionalism at the moment when American internationalists, most notably Dulles, were adopting the language and logic of geopolitics. Predictably, what the Japanese termed a conversion, Americans called opportunism. Whatever one may conclude about the purity of Japanese motives, it seems clear that there were obvious limits to their commitment to progressive international-ism. In describing the overwhelming desire on the part of Japanese to be rid of the mixed-race children in their midst, Yukiko Koshiro concludes that "The ideals of a new Japan—a democratic and cosmopolitan nation as a creator of a new civilization for the sake of the world—did not include racial tolerance for these children."[79] Moreover, even Japanese peace activists exhibited a nationalist strain by emphasizing what the Pacific War had done to them and not what Japan had done to its neighbors. As John Dower notes, "From the perspective of Japan's Asian victims, such an appeal would seem shockingly parochial rather than internationalist."[80]

In general, the existing scholarship indicates that in the 1950s and 1960s most Japanese maintained a positive image toward the United States. Although they were fearful of being dragged into one of the Cold War's con-flicts, they nevertheless retained a tolerant, even admiring attitude toward the United States.

Americans perceived the Japanese in similarly benign terms, when they thought of them at all. In the aftermath of the Vietnam War, these images began to change. The creation of the Japan Foundation indicated the signifi-cance Tokyo attached to improving cultural relations. By targeting the Unit-ed States as the major recipient of foundation money and programs the Japanese government also signaled its belief that American efforts to under-stand Japan had been insufficient. Such measures certainly seemed warrant-ed. By the mid-1970s it was clear to observers that many American officials had never developed the same degree of comfort with Japanese leaders as they had with Europeans.[81] The flow of popular books on the Japanese economic miracle, many of which are of more value to historians as cultural artifacts than as guides to Japan's development, did little to stop the periodic eruptions

of anti-Japanese prejudice. As Iriye has observed, American and Japanese officials now realized that the traditional subjects of diplomacy, security, and
trade, clearly had a cultural dimension. Or as James Fallows wrote in *More
Like Us*, "culture matters."[82]

As historians begin to approach the subject of cultural interaction after the
Vietnam War, their studies will of necessity become more fragmented and
particular. Although it might have been possible at one time to broadly divide
public opinion into elite and mass perceptions, such categories no longer
seem safe even for the purpose of generalization. Regional differences are just
one of the other considerations that will have to be taken into account. Citizens in places that identify with the Pacific basin, such as Seattle, and the
inhabitants of towns in the Midwest that depend on Japanese direct investment, are likely to hold attitudes far different from those of auto workers in
Detroit or steel workers in Western Pennsylvania.[83] It is, of course, too early
to tell what these developments might mean for the future of the Pacific
alliance.

As far as historians of American-Japanese relations are concerned, the lagging pace of declassification will mean that the more accessible field of cultural relations will hold more opportunity for research in the immediate
future. For those historians of American foreign relations who are more concerned with the ways in which governments interact, the American response
to the revisionist cabinets of Hatoyama and Kishi still seem promising areas
of study.

At this writing, the other side of the great divide, the post-Vietnam era in
American-Japanese relations, largely remains uncharted territory. Narratives
covering the period tend to dissolve into general discussions of Japan's rise
and America's relative decline. Chronologies collapse in on themselves, leaving an impression that history has ended with the arrival of Japan as an economic superpower.[84] The lack of distance from the events of the past two
decades helps to explain the lumping of the events of this period into an
undifferentiated mass but it also seems that the recent scholarship on the
years before Vietnam reinforces this tendency. One comes away from reading
this body of impressive scholarship with the sense that by the early 1950s
American and Japanese officials had created the grooves in which policy
would run for the next twenty years. But one also learns from the best of these
works the degree to which officials in both countries debated the wisdom of
these policies, tested other options, and frustrated each others' plans. In
adding dimension and definition to post-Occupation history, this last decade
of scholarship has left us better able to understand the role of American-
Japanese relations in Japan's recovery.

Acknowledgment

I wish to thank John Dower, Miles Fletcher, and Michael Schaller for their helpful comments and criticisms of an earlier draft of this paper. I am also grateful to Augie Nigro and Christopher Ryan for their valuable research assistance.

NOTES

1. Carol Gluck, "Entangling Illusions—Japanese and American Views of the Occupation" in Warren I. Cohen, ed., *New Frontiers in American-East Asian Relations: Essays Presented to Dorothy Borg* (New York: Columbia University Press, 1983), 170–236; Robert J, McMahon, "The Cold War in Asia: Toward A New Synthesis?" *Diplomatic History* 12:3 (Summer 1988): 307–327.

2. See John Hunter Boyle, *Modern Japan: The American Nexus* (Orlando: Harcourt Brace Jovanovich, 1993) for a an excellent introduction to the political, economic, and cultural sides to the relationship. Roger Buckley, *US-Japan Diplomacy: 1945–1990* (Cambridge: Cambridge University Press, 1992) is a critical essay on the political and economic relations between the two countries that is probably of more value to readers already familiar with the main scholarly debates on the subject.

3. Howard Schonberger, *Aftermath of War: Americans and the Remaking of Japan, 1945–1952* (Kent, OH: Kent State University Press, 1989).

4. See Justin Williams, Sr. "American Democratization Policy for Occupied Japan: Correcting the Revisionist Version," and rejoinders by John Dower and Howard Schonberger, *Pacific Historical Review* 57 (May 1988): 179–201, 202–208, 209–218.

5. Schonberger also hoped to prove that American policy "rested primarily on enlightened self-interest more than generosity or goodwill." But it is doubtful that many historians needed convincing on this point. Schonberger, *Aftermath of War*, 10.

6. See McMahon, "The Cold War In Asia," 321–323.

7. Justin Williams Sr. "American Democratization Policy," 185–186. Another study that treats the post-1947 policies as a "shift in emphasis" or "reorientation" is Robert A. Pollard, *Economic Security and the Origins of the Cold War, 1945–1950* (New York: Columbia University Press, 1985), 186–187.

8. John Dower, "Occupied Japan as History and Occupation History as Politics," *Journal of Asian Studies* 34, no. 2 (February, 1975): idem, *Empire and Aftermath: Yoshida Shigeru and the Japanese Experience, 1878–1954* (Cambridge: Harvard University Press, 1979) Michael Schaller, *The American Occupation of Japan: The Origins of the Cold War in Asia* (New York: Oxford University Press, 1985); William Borden, *The Pacific Alliance: United States Foreign Economic Policy and Japanese Trade Recovery, 1947–1955* (Madison: University of Wisconsin Press, 1984).

9. Theodore Cohen, *Remaking Japan: The American Occupation As New Deal* (New York: The Free Press, 1987), 309–311.

10. Tetsuya Kataoka, *The Price of A Constitution: The Origin of Japan's Postwar Politics* (New York: Crane Russak, 1991).

11. On the emergence of a new class of bureaucratic politician see also Gary D. Allinson, "The Structure and Transformation of Conservative Rule," in Andrew Gordon, ed., *Postwar Japan as History* (Berkeley: University of California Press, 1993), 123–144.

12. As John Dower has noted, one's assessment of the Occupation depends on how one interprets the prewar period in Japanese politics. Those scholars and officials who defended American Occupation policies and who opposed more far-reaching economic and political reform tended to characterize the 1920s as an era of democratic growth led by moderate politicians. The main task of the Occupation, they argued, was to remove the militarists from power so these Japanese "moderates" could return Japan to the course it had been on before the military seized power in the 1930s. Although Kataoka's criticism of the Occupation as "social engineering" echoes American neoconservatives of the 1980s, his description of Japanese politics in the 1920s and of the democratic advances in that period is similar to the views expressed by more traditional American conservatives, such as Joseph Grew and John McCloy, immediately after the war. Compare Kataoka's description of Hatoyama as "thoroughly wedded to parliamentary democracy and constitutional government," with Dower's sketch of the same man as "a former purgee with a record of support not only for Japanese aggression in the recent war but also for the suppression of dissent in the 1920s and 1930s. Kataoka, ibid., 134; Dower, "Peace and Democracy in Two Systems: External Policy and Internal Conflict," in Gordon, ed., *Postwar Japan as History* 15.

13. D. Clayton James, *The Years of MacArthur*, III, *Triumph and Disaster, 1945–1964* (Boston: Houghton Mifflin, 1985), 247.

14. Ibid., 247.

15. Michael Schaller, *Douglas MacArthur: The Far Eastern General* (New York: Oxford University Press, 1989); Richard B. Finn, *Winners in Peace: MacArthur, Yoshida, and Postwar Japan* (Berkeley: University of California Press, 1992).

16. Schaller, *MacArthur*, 149.

17. Schaller, *The Occupation of Japan*.

18. This actually represents a moderating of Schonberger's earlier conclusion that the treaties created a "fraudulent independence under U.S. hegemony." McMahon, "Cold War In Asia," 323; Schonberger, *Aftermath of War*, 278.

19. "Occupied Japan and the Cold War in Asia," in John W. Dower, *Japan in War and Peace: Selected Essays* (New York: New Press, 1993), 155–207. Dower's stages describe the general outline of policy, but they do not exclude the existence of some overlap from one to the other. For example, MacArthur's decision to grant immunity from war crimes prosecution to the Japanese officials involved in the notorious biological warfare experiments on American, Australian, British, Chinese, and Russian prisoners was made in 1947. According to a recent study, American officials traded the grant of immunity for the unit's data which the Americans thought important to national security. The revelation of this secret arrangement adds a new dimension to the term "victor's justice" when applied to the Tokyo War Crimes trials. See Peter Williams and David Wallace *Unit 731 Japan's Secret Biological Warfare in World War II* (New York, The Free Press, 1989).

20. Michael M. Yoshitsu, *Japan and the San Francisco Peace Settlement* (New York: Columbia University Press, 1983), 99–100.

21. Seigen Miyasato, "John Foster Dulles and the Peace Settlement with Japan," in Richard Immerman, ed., *John Foster Dulles and the Diplomacy of the Cold War* (Princeton: Princeton University Press, 1990), 189–212; Roger Dingman, "The Dagger and the Gift: The Impact of the Korean War on Japan," *The Journal of American East Asian Relations* 2 (Spring 1993): 29–55.

22. Dingman, "Dagger and the Gift," 40.

23. Nancy Bernkopf Tucker, "American Policy Toward Sino-Japanese Trade in the Postwar Years: Politics and Prosperity" *Diplomatic History* 8, no. 3 (Summer 1984): 183–208. On the system of restrictions eventually imposed see Yoko Yasuhara, "Japan, Communist

China, and Export Controls in Asia, 1951–1952" *Diplomatic History* 10, no. 1 (Winter 1986): 75–90.

24. John Dower, *Empire and Aftermath*, 400–414.

25. Warren I. Cohen, "China in Japanese-American Relations," in Akira Iriye and Warren I. Cohen eds., *The United States and Japan in the Postwar World* (Lexington: University of Kentucky Press, 1989), 36–60.

26. Borden, *Pacific Alliance*, x–xi.

27. Dingman, "The Dagger and the Gift," 41–46, and idem, review of Borden, *The Pacific Alliance* in *The Journal of American History* (March 1985): 908–909.

28. Andrew J. Rotter, *The Path to Vietnam: Origins of the American Commitment to Southeast Asia* (Ithaca: Cornell University Press, 1987).

29. Thomas McCormick, *America's Half-Century: United States Foreign Policy in the Cold War* (Baltimore: Johns Hopkins University Press, 1989), 114–118; Walter LaFeber, *The American Age: U.S. Foreign Policy at Home and Abroad Since 1896* 2nd. ed. (New York: Norton, 1989), 518–521; Thomas R. H. Havens, *Fire Across the Sea: The Vietnam War and Japan, 1965–1975* (Princeton: Princeton University Press, 1987), vii; Marilyn B. Young, *The Vietnam Wars: 1945–1990* (New York: HarperCollins, 1991), 25.

30. The development and dissemination of the Great Crescent thesis owed much to the sharing of ideas by Thomas McCormick, Walter LaFeber, and Howard Schonberger, all of whom were students of Williams. William Borden wrote his thesis while working at Wisconsin with McCormick and John Dower. Andrew Rotter took his PhD at Stanford but he started work on the project that eventually became his dissertation while he was a student of Walter LaFeber's. Thomas McCormick acknowledged his debt to Borden and Rotter in his own contribution to William Appleman Williams, Thomas McCormick, Lloyd Gardner, and Walter LaFeber, editors, *America in Vietnam: A Documentary History* (Garden City, NY: Anchor Press, 1985).

31. This expression is used by Bruce Cumings in a recent essay that, among other things, refers to Borden's work as a model for other historians. Cumings, " 'Revising Postrevisionism,' or, The Poverty of Theory in Diplomatic History," *Diplomatic History* 17, no. 4 (Fall 1993): 539–570.

32. Borden and other proponents of the Great Crescent argument maintain that despite the initial weak growth in the region, American officials remained attracted by the economic potential of Southeast Asia. This emphasis on American policymakers' concern with the economic potential of an area, despite disappointing initial returns, is similar to the argument Open Door scholars use to counter critics who point to the lack of American investment in Asia at the turn of the century. U.S. investment in northeast Asia may have been slight, they argue, but American officials remained intent on positioning the nation to control the future development of the region.

33. Ronald L. McGlothlen, *Controlling the Waves: Dean Acheson and U.S. Foreign Policy in Asia* (New York: Norton, 1993), 134.

34. Ibid, 134.

35. Ibid, 201.

36. Ibid, 39.

37. Melvyn Leffler, "The United States and the Strategic Dimensions of the Marshall Plan," *Diplomatic History* (Summer 1988): 304.

38. Chihiro Hosoya, "From the Yoshida Letter to the Nixon Shock," in Cohen and Iriye, eds., *The United States and Japan*, 21–35.

39. Cohen, "China in Japanese-American Relations," in Cohen and Iriye eds., *The United States and Japan*, 36–60; Burton Kaufman, "Eisenhower's Foreign Economic Policy With

Respect to Asia," and Qing Simei "The Eisenhower Administration and Changes in Western Embargo Policy Against China," in Warren I. Cohen and Akira Iriye, eds., *The Great Powers in East Asia, 1953–1960*, 104–120, 121–142.

40. Sayuri Shimizu, "Creating People of Plenty: The United States and Japan's Economic Alternatives, 1953–1958" (Ph.D. diss., Cornell University, 1991).

41. Akio Watanabe, "Southeast Asia in U.S.-Japanese Relations," in Cohen and Iriye, eds. *The United States and Japan*, 80–95.

42. Ibid., 376.

43. Of course research along these lines may prove disappointing. John Dower concludes that after the Yoshida letter and the security treaty tied Japan to the U.S., the Foreign Ministry became little more than an office for translating American policy. Dower, *Yoshida*, 414.

44. Marc Gallicchio, "The Kuriles Controversy: U.S. Diplomacy in the Soviet-Japan Border Dispute, 1941–1956" *Pacific Historical Review* 50, no. 1 (February 1991): 69–101; and Fuji Kamiya, "The Northern Territories: 130 Years of Japanese Talks with Czarist Russia and the Soviet Union," in Donald S. Zagoria ed., *Soviet Policy in East Asia* (New Haven: Yale University Press, 1982), 121–152.

45. H. W. Brands, Jr., "The United States and the Reemergence of Independent Japan," *Pacific Affairs* 59, no. 3 (Fall 1986): 387–401.

46. Martin Weinstein, *Japan's Postwar Defense Policy, 1947–1968* (New York: Columbia University Press, 1971).

47. James E. Auer, *The Postwar Rearmament of Japanese Maritime Forces, 1945–1971* (New York: Praeger, 1972); Aaron Patrick Forsberg, "America and the Resurgence of Postwar Japan: After the Occupation" (Ph.D. diss., University of Texas, 1992).

48. John Welfield observes that the Eisenhower administration's shift in emphasis from increasing the size of the Japanese Self-Defense forces to improving their firepower through high-technology weaponry helped to reduce the friction between the two governments. The greater reliance on jet aircraft and missile systems created a new source of tension, however, by placing new demands on Japanese farm land through runway extensions and site developments. See John Welfield, *Empire in Eclipse: Japan in the Postwar American Alliance System* (London: Athlone Press, 1988), 109–113; and Marc Gallicchio, "The Best Defense is a Good Offense," in Cohen and Iriye, *Great Powers in East Asia*, 63–85. For the JCS's frustrations with Japanese military spending see Robert J. Watson, *History of the Joint Chiefs of Staff* 5 *The Joint Chiefs of Staff and National Policy, 1953–1954* (Washington: GPO, 1986), 267–279.

49. George R. Packard III, *Protest in Tokyo* (Princeton: Princeton University Press, 1966); Tadashi Aruga, "The Security Treaty Revision of 1960," in Cohen and Iriye eds. *The United States and Japan*, 61–79; Welfield, *Empire in Eclipse*.

50. See for example Akio Watanabe, *The Okinawa Problem* (Carlton, Australia: Melbourne University Press, 1970).

51. Mark Selden, "Okinawa and American Security Imperialism," in Mark Selden ed., *Remaking Asia* (New York: Pantheon, 1974), 279–302.

52. L. Eve Armentrout Ma, "The Explosive Nature of Okinawa's 'Land Issue' or 'Base Issue,' 1945–1947: A Dilemma of United States Military Policy," *The Journal of American East Asian Relations* 1, no. 4 (Winter 1992): 435–464.

53. Timothy P. Maga, *John F. Kennedy and the New Pacific Community, 1961–1963* (New York: St. Martin's Press, 1990), 99–110.

54. Edwin O. Reischauer, *My Life Between Japan and America* (New York, Harper & Row, 1986), 204–206; John K. Emmerson, *The Japanese Thread: A Life in the U.S. Foreign Service*

(New York: Holt, 1978), 377; U. Alexis Johnson, *The Right Hand of Power* (Englewood Cliffs, NJ: Prentice-Hall, ., 1984), 456.

55. Welfield, *Empire in Eclipse*, 251.

56. Buckley, *US-Japan Alliance Diplomacy*, 104–110.

57. Walter LaFeber, "Decline of Relations During the Vietnam War," in Cohen and Iriye eds., *The United States and Japan*, 96–117.

58. Buckley, *US-Japan Alliance*, 133. See also Bruce Cumings, "Japan's Position in the World System," in Gordon, ed., *Postwar Japan as History*, 34–63.

59. Robert M. Orr, Jr., *The Emergence of Japan's Foreign Aid Power* (New York: Columbia University Press, 1990).

60. Havens, *Fire Across the Sea*.

61. Akira Iriye, *Across the Pacific: An Inner History of American-East Asian Relations* revised edition (Chicago: Imprint Publications, 1992), 348.

62. John Dower refers to an American "economic umbrella." Dower, "Peace and Democracy in Two Systems," p. 13.

63. Cohen, *Remaking Japan*, 457–459.

64. "The Useful War," in Dower, *Japan in War and Peace*, 9–32.

65. Mark Mason, *American Multinationals and Japan: The Political Economy of Japanese Capital Controls, 1899–1980* (Cambridge: Harvard Council on East Asian Studies, 1992). See also Dennis J. Encarnation, *Rivals Beyond Trade: America Versus Japan in Global Competition* (Ithaca: Cornell University Press, 1992).

66. Bruce Cumings, "Archaeology, Descent, Emergence: Japan in British/American Hegemony, 1900–1950" in Masao Miyoshi and H. D. Harootunian, eds. *Japan in the World* (Durham: Duke University Press, 1993), 70–114; James Fallows, *Looking at the Sun: The Rise of the New East Asian Economic and Political System* (New York: Pantheon, 1994).

67. Interestingly it seems neither Fallows nor Cumings are aware that List's theories owed much to the American economist Mathew Carey. Cumings, "Japan in British\American Hegemony," 86, n. 12. On Carey and List see Kenneth Wyer Rowe, *Mathew Carey: A Study in American Economic Development* (Baltimore: Johns Hopkins University Press, 1933), 117–118 ; A. D. H. Kaplan, *Henry Charles Carey: A Study in Economic Thought* (Baltimore: The Johns Hopkins University Press, 1931), 28–30, 46–47, 46 n.61; and Tetsuo Najita, "Japan's Industrial Revolution in Historical Perspective," in Miyoshi and Harootunian, eds., *Japan in the World*, 24. I am grateful to Sally Griffith for the references to the works by Rowe and Kaplan.

68. David Halberstam, *The Reckoning* (New York: Morrow, 1986).

69. "Fear and Prejudice in U.S.—Japan Relations," in Dower, *Japan in War and Peace*, 305–314.

70. James, *MacArthur*, 273–308.

71. James, *MacArthur*, 307–308. Toshio Nishi presents a favorable assessment of the Occupation's education reforms in *Unconditional Democracy: Education and Politics in Occupied Japan, 1945–1952* (Stanford: Hoover Institution Press, 1982). Kyoko Hirano offers a mixed review of Occupation censorship and oversight of Japan's film industry in *Mr. Smith Goes to Tokyo: Japanese Cinema under the American Occupation, 1945–1952* (Washington: Smithsonian Institution Press, 1992). Hirano contends that the reverse course was evident in American film policy as early as 1946, particularly where representations of the emperor were concerned, but she also argues that Japanese producers and directors found American oversight less onerous than their own government's censorship had been before and during the Pacific War.

72. Yukiko Koshiro, "Trans-Pacific Racism: The U.S. Occupation of Japan" (Ph.D. diss,

Columbia University, 1992); John W. Dower, *War Without Mercy: Race and Power in the Pacific War* (New York: Pantheon, 1986).

73. On the postwar persistence of traditional racial stereotypes on both sides of the Pacific see "Fear and Prejudice in U.S.-Japan Relations" Dower, *Japan in War and Peace*, 301–335.

74. Dingman, "The Dagger and the Gift."

75. Roger Dingman, "Alliance in Crisis: The Lucky Dragon Incident and Japanese-American Relations," in Cohen and Iriye eds., *The Great Powers in East Asia*, 187–214.

76. Ibid., 206.

77. Quoted in Gallicchio, "Kuriles Controversy," 94.

78. Akira Iriye, "War, Peace and U.S.-Japanese Relations," in Cohen and Iriye eds., *The United States and Japan*, 191–208.

79. Koshiro, "Trans-Pacific Racism," 9:29.

80. Dower, "Peace and Democracy in Two Systems," in Gordon, ed., *Postwar Japan as History*, 10.

81. See Richard J. Barnet, *The Alliance: America, Europe, Japan, Makers of the Postwar World* (New York: Simon and Schuster, 1983), 389.

82. James Fallows *More Like Us: Putting America's Native Strengths and Traditional Values to Work to Overcome the Asian Challenge* (Boston: Houghton Mifflin, 1989).

83. Bruce Cumings notes a similar dichotomy in American business elites. Representatives of competitive high-technology industries favor free trade, those in older low-technology industries support some form of protection. Cumings, "Japan's Place in the Postwar System," in Gordon, ed., *Postwar Japan as History*, 54.

84. John Dower makes the important point that although Americans came to see Japan as an economic superpower in the 1970s, the term Japan as Number One was first used in 1979, the Nixon shocks and oil embargoes of that decade left many Japanese conscious of the tenuousness of their prosperity. Dower, "Peace and Democracy in Two Systems," in Gordon, ed., *Postwar Japan as History*, 29.

Part Three

Chapter Eleven

The Unfathomable Other: Historical Studies of U.S.-Philippine Relations

GLENN ANTHONY MAY

Let me begin by making three possibly self-evident observations about the history of U.S.-Philippine relations. First of all, its parameters are distressingly broad—considerably broader, I would argue, than those of any other field under consideration in this volume. That is so because the Philippines, unlike China, Japan, Vietnam, and Korea, was, for almost fifty years, a formal colony of the United States. Hence, under the rubric of U.S.-Philippine relations, one typically considers not only such activities as diplomacy, missionary endeavors, trade, military involvements, cultural contacts, and the like—the sort of things that other historians of U.S.-Asian relations are wont to discuss in their writings—but also the formulation, execution, and impact of U.S. colonial policies as well as Filipino reactions to those policies and Filipino interactions with the many agents of U.S. colonialism.[1]

To put the point another way, the history of U.S.-Philippine relations is not really one field, but at least two, one of which bears some resemblance to the histories of America's relations with most other nation-states, and the second of which does not. What that second field *does* resemble is British (or

French or German or Spanish) imperial history, a highly developed academic specialty outside the United States which has generated a massive corpus of scholarship.[2]

A second observation follows from the first. Because the U.S.-Philippine colonial relationship has been seen as a component of U.S.-Philippine or U.S.Asian relations, it has often been conceptualized in peculiar—and, in my view, inappropriate—ways. Many of the American scholars who have undertaken studies of that relationship have received their academic training in U.S. diplomatic history, exposed throughout their careers to a scholarly literature that pays particular attention to policy formation in metropolitan capitals and to interactions and diplomatic exchanges between U.S. officials and their opposite numbers in other independent nation-states. When such interactions are discussed by diplomatic historians, they are depicted, much of the time, as a series of dyadic relationships—confrontations between John Quincy Adams, on the one hand, and Castlereagh or Canning, on the other; or between Charles Francis Adams and Lord John Russell; or Truman and Molotov; or Kissinger and Le Duc Tho; collaborative initiatives by Theodore Roosevelt and Sir Cecil Spring Rice; or by House and Grey; or Franklin Roosevelt and Churchill. To be sure, there are good reasons why diplomatic historians have adopted this literary convention, since dyadic relationships of that kind actually exist in the world of diplomacy. But the reasons are less compelling when the subject under examination is not diplomacy, but rather colonial rule. The administration of a colony is, after all, a very different thing from the negotiation of a treaty: colonial officials have far more power than diplomats; they also deal with different issues; they also interact with a greater range of people. In fact, in the Philippines under U.S. rule, there were no opposite numbers comparable to a Canning, Molotov, or Grey.[3]

In light of all that, then, it is at once striking and unsettling that so much of the literature about the U.S.-Philippine colonial relationship attempts to tell the story in terms of dyads. It tells us about the alliances between Taft and Pardo de Tavera; Forbes and Osmeña; Harrison and Quezon; and MacArthur and Quezon. It also tells us about confrontations between Wright and Pardo de Tavera; Wood and Quezon; and MacArthur and Osmeña. The episodes discussed are often memorable and dramatic; the plot lines are clearly drawn, easy to follow. But the entire construction is, at bottom, artificial—the product of a misguided effort to create the illusion that the colonial encounter was something akin to a diplomatic one. Beyond that, the actual stuff of colonial rule—the formation of policies, their execution, the day-to-day activities of thousands of American colonial officials, the reaction of Filipinos to all that—is, more often than not, largely ignored. In effect, then, a good deal of what has been written about the U.S.-Philippine colonial relationship is both misleading and conceptually flawed.

My third point relates to the entire body of scholarship on the history of U.S.-Philippine relations. While it cannot be denied that first-rate books and articles have been written, the sad truth is that a large number of them—in particular, many of the ones written on this side of the Pacific—are strikingly asymmetrical, far more valuable for their findings about the American side of the encounter than the Filipino. In part, that asymmetry can be explained by the fact that many American scholars simply lack the linguistic competence to do justice to the Filipino actors; in part, by their limited knowledge of Philippine society and culture; in part, by the relative paucity of insightful scholarly literature about things Filipino upon which they can rely. Indeed, a case can be made that, despite the merits of much of the scholarship, we have not yet made substantial progress in understanding the dynamics of the Philippine-American historical relationship.

I

The principal purpose of this essay is to assess the scholarship produced about U.S.-Philippine relations since Peter Stanley published his excellent overview of the field, "The Forgotten Philippines," in 1972.[4] Because of space limitations, I will restrict myself to evaluating four different categories of scholarship: studies of U.S.-Philippine relations before the establishment of formal colonial rule; those on the colonial period; those on the years since independence; and surveys of the entire history of U.S.-Philippine relations.[5]

Although most of the literature on the history of U.S.-Philippine relations deals with the period following America's acquisition of the Philippines at the turn of this century, a few studies of earlier interactions are worth noting. Commercial contacts between the United States and the Philippines actually began in the late eighteenth century, as U.S. merchant ships engaged in trade with the Spanish colony. Then, in the nineteenth century, various foreign nationals, including some Americans, opened commercial houses in Manila, and over the course of several decades those businesses played a prominent role in transforming the archipelago's economy, fueling and financing the expansion of cash-cropping and, along the way, helping to incorporate the colony into the world market economy. The classic account of the role of American entrepreneurs in this process of transformation was written by Benito Legarda in the 1950s.[6] More recently, however, Norman Owen, whose research has focused on the Bikol region of the Philippines, has modified some of Legarda's conclusions. While acknowledging that American merchant houses in Bikol and other parts of the archipelago played a catalytic role in Philippine economic development, Owen demonstrates that they were, on balance, grossly mismanaged enterprises. He also points out that Spanish merchants in the provinces contributed far more to the nineteenth-century economic transformation of the archipelago than has heretofore been acknowledged.[7]

The subject of U.S. acquisition of the Philippines has long been the subject of debate among historians. At bottom, they have differed on two interrelated questions. First, was the U.S. acquisition of the Philippines an economically motivated act? According to John Grenville and George Young, writing in the 1960s, Commodore George Dewey's descent on Manila at the outset of the Spanish-American War was primarily a strategic decision, intended to neutralize the Spanish fleet, not to acquire an Asian empire.[8] But other scholars writing in the same decade—most notably, Thomas McCormick—depicted it as an economic act, a logical step in an emerging, self-conscious policy of gaining bases that would permit the United States to exploit the China market.[9] More recently, Luzviminda Francisco and Jonathan Fast have written a book in which they argue that U.S. interest in the Philippines actually issued from a conspiracy between corporate interests and the McKinley administration to gain access to the archipelago's sugar lands. While they have done a considerable amount of research and uncovered valuable data on the connections between the sugar trust and U.S. policymakers, their book ultimately fails to convince, however, because their argument rests too much on circumstantial evidence.[10]

The second key question relates specifically to U.S. president William McKinley: how can his actions in the months preceding the decision to acquire the Philippines be understood? There are two schools of thought on McKinley's behavior. In the eyes of some—McCormick, H. Wayne Morgan, and, most recently, Lewis Gould—the president took a very early fancy to the idea of taking the Philippines and, once he did, pursued a consistent policy of promoting that objective. But other historians—Ernest May in the 1960s and David Trask in the 1980s—portray the president as indecisive, a waffler who had no clear idea about what to do with (or about) the Philippines for several months after Dewey's victory and who made up his mind only after the American public clearly signaled to him that they favored acquisition. The studies of all the aforementioned scholars are valuable, and the ones by Gould and Trask are especially well-researched on the Philippine decision. Still, in this reader's eyes, none of them is wholly convincing, for the simple reason that the surviving documentation about McKinley himself is scant and contradictory. Unless new sources surface, the debate about McKinley is certain to continue.[11]

One episode in the history of U.S.-Philippine relations that has attracted much attention over the past two decades is the Philippine-American War, the turn-of-the-century struggle between U.S. military units and the forces of Emilio Aguinaldo, the president of the first Philippine Republic. On this side of the Pacific, much of the literature about the war has been, to a certain extent, polemical in tone. John Morgan Gates's *Schoolbooks and Krags*, published in 1973, is essentially an apologia for the U.S. military effort in the Philippines.[12] Gates's principal argument is that, from the outset, the U.S. Army placed as much emphasis on "benevolent" policies—among them, the creation of Filipino-run local governments in occupied areas and the opening of public schools—as on the application of force. Gates also downplays the much-criticized destructiveness of U.S. military operations in the final stages of the war. While conceding that General Jacob Smith's campaign on the island of Samar in 1901 did "irreparable damage," he defends the equally controversial policies of General J. Franklin Bell in southwestern Luzon, characterizing them as "a credit to the American Army in the Philippines and a masterpiece of counter-guerrilla warfare."

A better-researched and somewhat muted defense of the U.S. military can be found in Brian Linn's *The U.S. Army and Counterinsurgency in the Philippines, 1899–1902*.[13] A study of U.S. military operations in four different regions of the island of Luzon, Linn's monograph makes the important point that U.S. success in the conflict was due in no small measure to the decentralization of the U.S. command system. Facing different challenges from their Filipino enemy in different areas, U.S. commanders had the flexibility to tailor their policies to local conditions. Rather than seeing the war as a single struggle between Americans and Filipinos, then, Linn depicts it as a collection of independent local ones.

Much more critical of the U.S. Army's activities in the Philippine-American War is Stuart Creighton Miller. Claiming (and demonstrating) that American commanders deceived the Filipino leaders about U.S. intentions in the months preceding the outbreak of the conflict, that U.S. soldiers held racist attitudes toward Filipinos, and that they were guilty of many atrocities, and also charging that the campaigns of Smith and Bell were inhumane and appallingly destructive, Miller concludes that the Philippine conflict was a "sordid episode" in U.S. history.[14]

All three of those books have considerable merits, but all can also be faulted in various ways. Of the three authors, only Linn has used extensively the two largest collections of archival records relating to the war—the "Philippine

Insurgent Records" (PIR), a mammoth collection of documents captured by the U.S. Army from the Filipino forces, and the records of U.S. military units that served in the Philippine conflict, housed in the U.S. National Archives.[15] Gates may be right that the U.S. command introduced policies intended to win hearts and minds, but an examination of the complete historical record reveals that at the local level they were often not carried out. Miller may be right that the Americans did atrocious things in the Philippines, but he pays little attention to atrocities committed by the Filipinos and overstates the destructiveness of U.S. policies. Furthermore, all three are much weaker on the Filipino side of the conflict than on the American. Only Linn has used sources generated by Filipinos to any extent, and even he relies primarily on translated documents in the "Selected Documents" series of the PIR, which amount to about 15 percent of the entire collection.

What we find in all three books, I would argue, is essentially monofocal history—useful, often insightful, and provocative contributions to an ongoing dialogue in the scholarly community about the ways in which the United States has conducted warfare in the so-called Third World. The protagonists are Americans. Filipinos appear as, at best, supporting actors. The historical context in which these Filipinos operated is either ignored or sketchily described.

One book about the conflict that aims to be bifocal is David Haward Bain's *Sitting in Darkness: Americans in the Philippines*.[16] Published by a major commercial press and apparently intended for the mass market, Bain's book attempts to tell the story of two leading figures in the Philippine-American War—Emilio Aguinaldo, the Filipino commander (and president of the Philippine Republic), and Frederick Funston, the self-promoting U.S. brigadier who captured him. Unfortunately, the book is highly problematic. Bain's discussion of Aguinaldo, for example, is based in large part on two published "memoirs," both of which are, unknown to Bain, highly unreliable sources. One of them was entirely ghostwritten and, toward the end of his life, Aguinaldo disowned it, claiming it was untrustworthy. The other, which Bain describes as a translation of a memoir written in Tagalog, is not a translation at all, but rather a brief, incompetent, English-language summary of the original, filled with misinterpretations and mistakes and missing much important material from the Tagalog original.[17] Bain is also unaware of recent scholarship on Aguinaldo, most of it published in the Philippines. In light of all the above, it is perhaps predictable that Bain gets so much wrong. He presents Aguinaldo as a heroic figure who had widespread popular support during his struggle against the Americans. (Aguinaldo, he tells us, was "emblematic of [Filipino] aspirations.") But, in fact, as my discussion of the literature about the Filipino side of the war should make clear, Aguinaldo was nothing of the sort.

Over the past twenty years or so, our knowledge of that other side of the conflict has increased enormously. In 1972, when Peter Stanley published his state-of-the-field survey, the most influential book on the subject was Teodoro Agoncillo's *Malolos: The Crisis of the Republic*, which had appeared twelve years earlier.[18] The thesis of Agoncillo's lengthy monograph is that the Filipino resistance to the Americans was fueled by the Filipino lower classes and that the indigenous upper classes—including Trinidad H. Pardo de Tavera, Benito Legarda, and other wealthy, educated, influential men— betrayed the incipient Philippine nation by collaborating with the enemy. Agoncillo's analysis still finds its way into textbooks used in Philippine universities; indeed, a slightly modified version of it can be found in a very popular one written by Renato Constantino.[19] But recent scholarship has shown that it is incorrect.

In fact, one important reason for the failure of the Filipino war effort is that popular support for it was seriously undermined by Aguinaldo's own policies. In a daring, insightful book about Philippine popular uprisings, Reynaldo Ileto has argued that, in the revolution against Spain that immediately preceded the Philippine-American War, the Filipino leader Andres Bonifacio was able to mobilize mass support by appealing to the millenarian aspirations of the lower classes. According to Ileto, Bonifacio's goal in the revolution was "*kalayaan*"—a Tagalog word that, in our own day, is translated as independence, but at the time connoted, in addition to political autonomy, a condition of bliss, brotherhood, abundance, and equality. Put another way, Bonifacio did not aim simply to make the Philippines independent; he was also calling on the lower classes to take part in a social revolution—a fact that might help to explain why they rallied to his side. Ileto sees Aguinaldo, Bonifacio's chief rival in that earlier revolutionary movement and the man who eventually ordered his execution, in a very different light. In his view, Aguinaldo's goal was to achieve political autonomy alone; his war effort did not hold out the hope of radical social change and it consequently had limited popular appeal.[20] A doctoral dissertation by Milagros Guerrero complements Ileto's study. Guerrero has demonstrated that Filipino peasants were dissatisfied with Aguinaldo because his decrees ignored their interests and reinforced the power of local elites. Himself a member of the provincial socioeconomic elite, Aguinaldo was interested only in pursuing policies palatable to, and winning the adherence of, members of his own social class. During the Philippine-American war, peasants manifested their discontent by seizing property of the wealthy and refusing to obey Aguinaldo's officials.[21]

If Agoncillo's account can be faulted for exaggerating the extent of lower-class support for the war effort, it also severely underestimates the contributions of upper-class Filipinos. My own book, *Battle for Batangas: A Philippine Province at War*, and studies by Norman Owen, William Henry Scott, and other scholars tell us that, for much of the war, the key players in the indigenous resistance were well-off, politically influential, educated Filipinos in the provinces. Such people led the military units that fought against the Americans. They also organized and coordinated local efforts to aid the Filipino soldiers in the field. Rather than being a popular struggle undermined by the elites, the Filipino resistance was, in reality, elite-generated, elite-directed, and elite-sustained.[22]

One additional war-related issue that has received attention of late has been the demographic/epidemiological consequences of the conflict. Over the years, wild assertions have been made about the level of mortality during the war, with some writers claiming that Filipino deaths numbered in the millions and that U.S. military policies were largely responsible for most of them. My own research on the province of Batangas—a place where, it has often been claimed, mortality levels were extraordinarily high—demonstrates that such assertions are far from the mark. Examination of parish records reveals that death rates in Batangas actually began to soar in 1897, two years before the outbreak of the Philippine-American War, primarily as a consequence of the combined effects of malnutrition and a malaria epidemic that were byproducts of the earlier revolution against Spain. To a certain extent, then, the high level of mortality during the Philippine-American War was due to preexisting epidemiological and ecological conditions.

Of considerably greater significance is a brilliant book by Ken De Bevoise, which places the morbidity and mortality crises that occurred at the time of the Philippine-American War in the context of nineteenth-century epidemiological developments. Based on thorough research in Philippine and U.S. archives, De Bevoise's study shows that the epidemics that plagued the Philippines in the wartime period—malaria, smallpox, cholera, etc.—all had their origins in complex longterm ecological/biological dynamics, and that while the war doubtless made some things worse it alone cannot explain the heavy loss of life that took place.[23]

II

Let me turn now from the Philippine-American War to the era of U.S. colonial rule. Many of the early studies of U.S. colonial policy in the Philippines were written by the policymakers themselves—among them, Dean C. Worcester and W. Cameron Forbes—and the authors tended, not surprisingly, to see the Americans in a consistently favorable light and to overstate their accomplishments.[24] Such blatant apologias for U.S. colonialism went out of fashion some time ago, but that is not to say that the U.S. colonial record is without current-day defenders. The most noteworthy of these, and also the most prolific, is Lewis E. Gleeck, Jr., a retired U.S. foreign service officer, who since 1974 has written more than a dozen books about the American experience in the Philippines.

Gleeck's work varies considerably in quality. At his best—for example, in his book about American governors general and high commissioners in the Philippines—he sheds much light on the personalities and objectives of U.S. policymakers and the development of U.S. policies.[25] But, at other times, he appears to be a cheerleader. The principal theme of most of Gleeck's books is that the United States was, on balance, a uniquely benevolent and effective colonial power, that it both meant well and did much good. Like Worcester and Forbes before him, Gleeck often appears to overemphasize the continuities and achievements of U.S. policymaking, to ignore or discount the internal inconsistencies as well as the blatant racism and ethnocentrism of the policymakers, and to be somewhat dismissive of leading Filipino actors.[26]

A very different view of U.S. colonial rule can be found in the books of Renato Constantino, a leading figure in the "nationalist" school of Philippine historiography.[27] Relentlessly critical of U.S. policies toward the Philippines, Constantino depicts the mother country as devious, oppressive, and completely self-interested. A recurrent refrain in his books is that the United States was, from the outset, intent on exploiting the Philippines, principally by promoting American economic interests at the expense of the Filipino people. He also faults American educational efforts in the Philippines, an area of U.S. colonial policy that defenders like Gleeck have extolled; in his view, the school system introduced in the archipelago by the United States aimed to "miseducate" the Filipinos by transplanting American values and fostering an adulation of false heroes. Some of the criticisms found in these books echo ones made earlier by the well-known Marxist writer and former revolutionary William J. Pomeroy.[28]

One observation worth making about both the apologists of U.S. empire and the critics is that, while they disagree fundamentally about the objectives of U.S. policy, they actually agree on one key point—to wit, that in its almost half-century of colonial rule, the United States had a substantial impact on the Philippines. Apologists see the impact as beneficial, critics see it as detrimental, but both are absolutely certain that the Americans introduced significant economic, political, social, and cultural changes.

Not all the literature on the U.S. colonial period is so polemical in tone. Perhaps the most influential and certainly the most elegantly written study of the subject is Peter Stanley's *A Nation in the Making: The Philippines and the United States, 1899–1921*.[29] In that book, Stanley describes the evolution during the "Taft era" (1900–1913) of a paternalistic U.S. policy toward the Philippines, envisaging "indefinite retention" of the archipelago, and the subsequent shift after 1913 to one attempting in the long run to prepare the Filipinos for independence and in the short run to concede them greater control over the insular government. Stanley also tells us an enormous amount about the thoughts and actions of the Filipino political leaders with whom U.S. policymakers regularly interacted—among them Trinidad H. Pardo de Tavera, a key player in the period 1900–1907, and Manuel Quezon and Sergio Osmeña, two prominent members of the Philippine Assembly, the national legislative body established by the Americans in 1907. The enduring virtue of Stanley's book is the author's demonstration that all of those Philippine leaders had well-developed, nuanced agendas of their own, and that Quezon and Osmeña, in particular, played a clever double game, adopting a public posture of dogged commitment to the goal of immediate self-rule while privately harboring doubts about the readiness of the Philippines for independence and sometimes even cooperating with U.S. colonial officials to halt movement in that direction.

Stanley's book is a marvelous achievement. In conception as well as in execution, it is comparable to another classic study of U.S.-Asian relations, Michael Hunt's *Frontier Defense and the Open Door: Manchuria in Chinese-American Relations, 1895–1911*.[30] But that last statement should not necessarily be interpreted as unqualified praise, for, as I have suggested earlier, there is a world of difference between the sort of diplomatic exchanges Hunt is writing about and the interactions between rulers and ruled described by Stanley. While it is true that Filipino politicos like Quezon and Osmeña were not merely passive onlookers, the amount of power they (or any other Filipino) wielded in the colonial scheme of things was, at least up to 1935, fairly limited—far more limited than that of Chinese policymakers in their dealings with the United States. Furthermore, while Stanley provides us with an understanding of a few important Filipino leaders, we learn very little about the millions of Filipinos who lived outside the metropolitan capital.

The early years of U.S. colonial rule are also examined in my own book, *Social Engineering in the Philippines*.[31] Modeled somewhat more on studies of European colonialism than on studies of U.S. diplomacy, it focuses on three areas of U.S. colonial rule in the Philippines: political education (preparation of Filipinos for self-government), primary schooling, and measures undertaken to change the Philippine economy. The book can best be understood in the context of the aforementioned debate about the impact of U.S. colonialism on the archipelago. Its principal argument is that, while Americans often stated that they wanted to change the Philippines in fundamental ways and made earnest efforts to achieve their objectives, their actual record of accomplishment was disappointing. In the field of education, for example, partly because of disagreements among the successive directors of the educational system about the type of schooling that was most suitable for Filipinos, partly because of a lack of funding, and partly because of the enormity of the task confronting them, the Americans did not make a great deal of headway. Economic development was frustrated by a different problem—a division of opinion between the U.S. Philippine Commission, the principal policymaking body in the archipelago, which favored the growth of cash-cropping and wanted to provide attractive incentives to American investors, and the U.S. Congress, which opposed that approach, reflecting the sentiments of constituents from sugar- and tobacco-producing states who feared Filipino competition in those crops. Hence, in my view, both the defenders of U.S. colonialism like Gleeck and the critics like Constantino have erred by exaggerating the impact of U.S. policies on the Philippines; whether one views U.S. policies as benevolent or malevolent, it seems clear that they changed relatively little.

Useful insights into U.S. colonialism can also be found in several essays in *Compadre Colonialism: Studies on the Philippines Under American Rule*, edited by Norman G. Owen.[32] In one of them, Michael Cullinane shows that Filipino elites from the Spanish period continued to dominate Philippine local governments during the Taft era and that U.S. colonial officials constantly fretted about the "corruption" of those governments. In another, Owen argues convincingly that, in the economic sphere, U.S. colonial policy did not transform the archipelago. Both contributions lend credence to the notion that the U.S. colonial period in the Philippines featured far more continuity than change. Frank Golay provides further confirmation of that point in a piece that appears in *Reappraising an Empire*, a volume of essays edited by Stanley; he argues that U.S. efforts to modernize and democratize the Philippines were undercut by revenue shortages, due to resistance by Philippine elites to taxation.[33]

Several scholarly studies have dealt with the institutional structure of the U.S. colonial empire. Romeo Cruz, relying largely on material gathered in U.S. archives, has produced a detailed account of the organization, functions, and personnel of the Bureau of Insular Affairs (BIA), the branch of the War Department in Washington charged with overseeing U.S. administration of the Philippines. As institutional history and as a description of the BIA's day-to-day operations, Cruz's book has value, but, as Cruz himself points out, the BIA generally concerned itself with routine administration and its influence on "basic American colonial policy" was minimal.[34]

Some historians have dealt in depth with U.S. policymakers. Oscar Alfonso's study of Theodore Roosevelt's role in Philippine policymaking has both the strengths and weaknesses of Cruz's book. While it tells us much about the U.S. president's thinking about the islands, it also proves fairly conclusively that Roosevelt had little impact on major policy decisions.[35] Much more significant is Rodney Sullivan's study of Dean C. Worcester, who served from 1900 to 1913 as a member of the Philippine Commission. Extremely well-researched, the book tells us about Worcester's career as an academic botanist and zoologist at the University of Michigan, his lengthy scientific field trips to the Philippines in the 1880s and early 1890s, and his subsequent emergence as an authority on the Philippines. Sullivan also tells us about Worcester's career as a colonial administrator. As secretary of the interior in the Philippines, Worcester was responsible for the administration of the territories inhabited by "non-Christian" peoples, agriculture, public health, and various other things. By and large, he views Worcester as a failure: his agricultural and public health policies were poorly conceived; his public land policies were severely criticized by Filipino politicians.[36] Worcester is also the subject of a brief, clever, soft-core psychological sketch by Peter Stanley, which appears in *Reappraising an Empire*.[37] Very useful synopses of the Philippine careers of the twelve men who occupied the top position in the U.S. colonial bureaucracy in the archipelago can be found in Gleeck's aforementioned book on the governors general and high commissioners.[38]

The American whose name is most often associated with the Philippines is, of course, Douglas MacArthur, and his Philippine experiences are the subject of a monograph by Carol Petillo. First stationed in the Philippines in 1903 as a young U.S. Army officer, MacArthur returned to the colony for two assignments in the 1920s, and served as military adviser to the Philippine Commonwealth Government between 1935 and 1941. Thereafter, as USAFFE commander, he was first badly beaten in the Philippines by the Japanese in 1941–42 and returned in triumph to the archipelago in 1944. Adopting an Eriksonian approach to her subject, Petillo makes a case that the Philippines became for MacArthur "a place where he could test himself with less threat than he perceived in the rest of the world." Petillo has also made important factual findings, the most noteworthy of which is that MacArthur received a payment of $500,000 from Commonwealth president Manuel Quezon just before his departure from the Philippines in 1942. But, unfortunately, the book deals superficially with the Filipinos MacArthur interacted with and the author's comments about MacArthur's celebrated liaison with the Filipina Isabel Rosario Cooper—e.g., "Isabel, small, soft-spoken and of another race, offered no threat to his masculinity"—may be more revealing about Petillo's own attitudes about race and gender than MacArthur's.[39]

Lower-ranking U.S. colonial officials have also been studied by historians. James Halsema, a retired foreign service officer, has written a biography of his father, E. J. Halsema, who served as an engineer in the Bureau of Public Works and later as the appointed mayor of the city of Baguio. Although Halsema did a fair amount of research in American archives, his book suffers from a certain shallowness because only a handful of his father's papers have survived.[40] Peter Gowing, who spent much of life as a missionary educator, has written several books on Muslim Filipinos, one of which, *Mandate in Moroland: The American Government of Muslim Filipinos, 1899–1920*, is an examination of the four U.S. officials charged with developing policy toward the Muslims during the early colonial period: Leonard Wood, Tasker Bliss, John J. Pershing, and Frank Carpenter. Gowing provides a wealth of data about specific policies—public health, education, taxation, and so on—but, because his focus is entirely on the American policymakers, we learn next to nothing about Muslim perspectives.[41] Much more enlightening is Frank Jenista's monograph, *The White Apos: American Governors on the Cordillera Central*, which probes both the policies of U.S. colonial officials who served in the upland region of northern Luzon and the interactions between those Americans and the upland peoples. Jenista's most intriguing findings relate to the longterm sexual liaisons established between the Americans and the local women. The sexual dimension of the U.S. colonial relationship is important, but up to now few scholars have looked into it.[42]

Colonial officials were not the only Americans who resided in the Philippines during the U.S. colonial period. The activities of those other Americans—a very mixed bag of entrepreneurs, shopkeepers, adventurers, and romantics—have been explored most seriously by Lewis Gleeck. His book *The Manila Americans (1901–1964)* is full of information, rather chaotically assembled, about the expatriate community—its leaders, clubs, and other organizations; the hotels and bars its members frequented; the businesses they ran; the newspapers they read.[43] The best book on Protestant missionaries in the Philippines has been written by Kenton Clymer. Superbly researched, Clymer's study shows that, while the Protestant denominations that attempted to proselytize in the Philippines adopted a public stance of cooperating with each other, their relations were, in reality, often conflictual and filled with mistrust. Clymer also provides insights into the missionary mentality, revealing to us the ethnocentrism, rabid anti-Catholicism, and cultural insensitivity of those men and women who served in the Philippines. Despite the book's many merits, though, it hardly touches on indigenous reactions to the missionaries and exaggerates the impact of missionary activities.[44] Narrower in scope is Anne Kwantes's monograph on Presbyterian missionaries. Although Kwantes asserts repeatedly that the missionaries were agents of important social change, her assertions remain unproven, since she limits herself to missionary sources and hence sees their activities entirely through their eyes.[45]

On the Filipino side of the Philippine-American encounter, the scholarship of the past two decades has been decidedly mixed. Vicente Albano Pacis has written a competent biography of the Philippine political leader Sergio Osmeña, and a book by Aruna Gopinath is informative about the political maneuvers of Commonwealth president Manuel Quezon, Osmeña's sometime ally and sometime rival. Bernadita Reyes Churchill has produced an exhaustive examination of the efforts, sometimes half-hearted, of Philippine political leaders to prod the U.S. Congress to pass independence legislation.[46] Yet all three of these books are lacking in two important respects: they fail to explain the cultural and political contexts in which those Filipino political influentials operated, and, partly as a consequence of that, they never provide us with a satisfactory explanation of why those men acted as they did. For insight into such things, a reader would be better advised to turn to Stanley's *A Nation in the Making* or to the books of Theodore Friend and Bonifacio Salamanca, published in the 1960s.[47]

In fact, over the decades, one of the major problems in the field of Philippine-American studies has been the failure of Filipino scholars and non-Filipino specialists on Philippine history to produce a substantial body of culturally informed literature about Filipino actors—a literature that might provide the Americanists who venture into the field some guidance in understanding Filipino realities. But, in recent years, there are hints that the situation may be changing. The important work by Ileto and Guerrero on the Philippine-American War, discussed above, are signs of the change. So too are five superb essays about Philippine politics during the colonial period that have appeared in two separate edited volumes—Stanley's *Reappraising an Empire* and Ruby Paredes's *Philippine Colonial Democracy*.[48]

The principal point of four of those studies—one essay by Paredes on the Federal Party, the political organization that cooperated with the U.S. Philippine Commission at the beginning of the American colonial era; two by

Michael Cullinane, the first on the early political career of Manuel Quezon and the other on Sergio Osmeña's rise to power; and one by Alfred McCoy on Quezon's authoritarian tendencies during the Commonwealth period (1935–41)—is that Philippine colonial politics was, at its core, clientelist politics. Philippine politicians rose to prominence in the American era as a result of patronage they received from U.S. officials. The Federalistas, for example, were essentially clients of Taft; Quezon owed his early success to a Constabulary officer named Harry Bandholtz; and Osmeña relied to a certain extent on W. Cameron Forbes, a member of the Philippine Commission. Even in the Commonwealth period, when the Philippines was quasi-independent and Quezon was busy consolidating his control over the political system, the Commonwealth president continued to seek assistance from American patrons like High Commissioner Frank Murphy in order to promote his objectives. Here then was a fundamental truth about Philippine political life: however skillful Filipino politicians may have been in mobilizing followers, they always knew that power ultimately resided in the mother country.

A fifth essay by Reynaldo Ileto provides further insight into the dynamics of colonial politics. Intended as a corrective to traditional accounts that focus narrowly on the activities of visible metropolitan influentials, Ileto's piece examines the phenomenon of popular radicalism in central Luzon in the first decade and a half of U.S. rule. Ileto's argument is that millenarian notions similar to those earlier articulated by the revolutionary leader Andres Bonifacio were widely held by common men and women in the provinces, that such people fully believed that a new era of *kalayaan* was at hand, and that both American officials and Filipino politicians were forever alert to the danger of popular uprisings. In Ileto's view, given the strength of such popular attitudes, politicians like Quezon had no choice but to demand immediate independence, even though they personally may have been inclined to favor a continuation of U.S. rule. One thing that seems clear from these five essays is that during the U.S. colonial period Filipino politicians were, in a sense, trapped between two antipodal constituencies—foreign patrons who expected them to cooperate in carrying out the policy goals of the mother country and the lower classes who had their own more radical agenda. Under the circumstances, is it any wonder that men like Quezon and Osmeña often appeared to be inconsistent or two-faced?

As Ileto's essay suggests, the era of U.S. colonial rule was by no means uniformly tranquil, and on a number of occasions popular uprisings and other disturbances took place. Valuable discussions of those uprisings appear in books written by David J. Sturtevant and, again, Ileto.[49] Sturtevant's study, a survey of popular discontent between 1840 and 1940, is heavily influenced by the ideas of the brilliant Indonesianist Harry Benda. Sturtevant, like Benda before him, attempts to understand popular uprisings by situating them on a developmental continuum: some he views as traditional (or mystical, or religious) in nature; others strike him as more modern (or secular, or sophisticated).[50] In his book, he traces "the transition from mysticism to relative sophistication" in Philippine popular uprisings—which is to say, from nativist/millenarian movements of the mid-nineteenth century to patriotic secret societies in the 1920s to the "modern" Sakdal movement of the 1930s, with its more conventional (i.e., more "western") political agenda. Quite different in approach is Ileto's book, covering the period 1840 to 1910. Whereas Sturtevant attempts to document change, Ileto is struck by the continuities between those movements, and whereas Sturtevant tends to see mystical/millenarian movements as quaint and irrational, Ileto argues persuasively that they issued from a coherent, rational world view shared by the lower-class participants.

Finally, there is a mountain of data about the Philippine-American colonial encounter in the many books and articles that have been written over the past twenty-plus years on Philippine local history. Since the appearance of John Larkin's pioneering local history *The Pampangans* in 1972, more than two dozen regional, provincial, and municipal histories have been published, most of which deal to some extent with the American colonial period. The scholarship varies greatly in quality, ranging from unreconstructed antiquarianism to first-rate social history. Furthermore, there is so much of it that one wonders whether any useful generalizations can be made about the lot. Still, those caveats notwithstanding, I will make three simple points about what those local histories tell us about developments in the Philippines during the U.S. colonial period.

First, it seems clear that, for at least several decades, the introduction of American political institutions did not appreciably alter political life at the local level: landed families that had dominated local politics in the Spanish era continued to hold power. Second, in many parts of the Philippines, the coming of U.S. rule resulted in a steady accumulation of wealth by landed elites and a concomitant decline in the living conditions of holders of small plots, tenants, and wage laborers. To some extent, these developments can be understood as a continuation of ones begun in the last century and a half of Spanish rule, as cash-cropping replaced subsistence agriculture and landowners with means were inclined to increase the size of their estates at the expense of smallholders. But the situation was exacerbated by the U.S. connection, particularly by the establishment of virtual free trade between the United States and the Philippines, which increasingly tied the archipelago to the U.S.

economy, guaranteed landowners a favorable market for their cash crops, and gave them an added incentive to expand their holdings. Third, in those areas where disparities between rich and poor were growing, rural disturbances became more prevalent and labor organizations began to emerge. Although a few of these local histories claim that the U.S. colonial period brought progress, an even larger number suggest that, on balance, the average Filipino may have been better off before the coming of the Americans than after.[51]

III

In 1946, the colonial relationship came to an end and the Philippines at last achieved independence. But exactly how independent was the new nation-state? That straightforward question has been addressed time and again by writers, and the answer that many of them have reached is that the change in flag and status did not appear to be so consequential. The case has been stated most baldly by five authors who occupy positions on the left of the political spectrum: Jose Maria Sison (the Philippine communist leader who has used the pen name Amado Guerrero), the Philippine nationalists Renato and Letizia Constantino, the American Marxist William Pomeroy, and Stephen Shalom.[52] All of them maintain that, in the aftermath of World War II, the United States and a succession of Philippine presidents established a mutually beneficial, cooperative, neocolonial relationship, one in which the United States exercised inordinate influence over its former colony. In exchange for U.S. support and financial assistance, Philippine leaders conceded the United States important military bases (Subic Bay Naval Base, Clark Air Base, etc.) and valuable trade and investment advantages in the Philippines. Furthermore, throughout the post-independence era, the U.S. Central Intelligence Agency, the U.S. Embassy, U.S. aid agencies, and, more recently, U.S.-dominated multilateral lending agencies (the World Bank, the IMF) essentially dictated Philippine government policies. Within the Philippines itself, this relationship proved beneficial to established elites, who were able to maintain their dominant position in society, but disastrous to common men and women, who became progressively impoverished.

Others who have written about specific aspects of postwar U.S.-Philippine relations have reached somewhat similar conclusions. In a well-researched article, Bonifacio Salamanca has shown that even *before* the Philippines received independence, three successive Philippine presidents (Quezon, Osmeña, and Manuel Roxas) had indicated their willingness to grant military bases to the United States.[53] An excellent unpublished doctoral dissertation by Ronald Edgerton explains how the first president of the independent Philippines, Roxas, believing that his country's future depended on continued cooperation with the former colonial power, made other major concessions to the Americans.[54] Three different books denounce the policies of the multilateral lending agencies, asserting that they have forced the Philippines to adopt development strategies that have wrecked the economy and especially hurt the country's poor.[55] James Putzel, in a book documenting the failure of agrarian reform in the postwar Philippines, has shown that the U.S. government has consistently blocked truly redistributive agrarian reform programs.[56] Support for the notion that the United States has exercised undue influence in the Philippines has come as well from books written by two former CIA operatives. In a self-adulatory memoir, Edward G. Lansdale, the famed psywar and counterinsurgency specialist, explains how he contributed to the defeat of the HMB (Huks), the peasant-based guerrilla organization that rebelled against the Philippine government shortly after independence, and subsequently orchestrated the successful presidential campaign of Ramón Magsaysay in 1953. (In a biography of Lansdale, Cecil Currey essentially accepts Lansdale's analysis, but he provides a wealth of additional data.)[57] Joseph B. Smith, who was assigned to the Philippines after Magsaysay's death in 1957, discusses in his own revealing book the agency's efforts to influence Philippine elections over the next few years.[58]

There can, of course, be little doubt that officials of the U.S. government and organizations like the IMF and World Bank have exercised influence in the Philippines. But a number of scholars have raised questions about the extent and pervasiveness of that influence. In a recent article, Dennis Merrill shows that American efforts to reform the administration of President Elpidio Quirino were largely unsuccessful, because Quirino either resisted or circumvented American supervision.[59]

Lewis Gleeck, in *The Third Philippine Republic* indicates that most presidents in the Philippines between 1946 and 1972 were far more independent actors than they have generally been credited with being and also that the U.S. role in determining the outcome of Philippine elections has been grossly exaggerated.[60] Furthermore, Nick Cullather, in several outstanding articles and an edited collection of sources, has documented the ways in which the Magsaysay and Garcia administrations regularly pursued their own agendas and/or promoted the agendas of their domestic allies, often at the expense of U.S. interests. Cullather's discussion of Magsaysay is especially astute. Typically depicted as a crude, uneducated, easily manipulated tool of the CIA and the U.S. mission, Magsaysay was, instead, a clever manipulator, who used the American connection for his own purposes and whose poor record on reform can be explained by his intimate ties to landholding elites and old-guard politicians.[61] Magsaysay's defenders, including Lansdale, often contrasted him favorably to the Vietnamese leader Ngo Dinh Diem, claiming that Magsaysay, unlike Diem, was willing to do the things that would rally popular support; the curious truth of the matter is that Magsaysay differed from Diem more in style than in substance.

It also seems clear that, despite assertions to the contrary by both defenders and critics of post-independence U.S. policy toward the Philippines, the defeat of the HMB guerrillas was not due primarily, or even substantially, to the assistance provided the Philippine government by the United States. As Benedict Kerkvliet has shown in a fascinating study of the Huk uprising, the Huks failed because they self-destructed. For one, they made serious tactical mis takes, choosing to engage the government in conventional battles at a time when they simply lacked the manpower and firepower to succeed. Second, and more important, there was a yawning gulf between the objectives of the poor peasants who joined the movement and those of the Philippine Communist Party (PKP) leaders who tried to direct it. The former had relatively modest, conservative goals—to get a larger share of the harvest from landlords, to end the government's discriminatory and repressive practices, to gain access to credit—whereas the latter aimed to confiscate estates and nationalize the economy. In the end, the Philippine government was able to exploit those differences and detach the peasant rank and file from the movement by making token concessions.[62]

Raymond Bonner's book *Waltzing with a Dictator: the Marcoses and the Making of American Policy* furnishes additional evidence that there were definite limits to America's ability to control Philippine leaders.[63] An account of U.S relations with Marcos from the Johnson administration to Marcos's fall from power, it reveals that, while different U.S. presidents apparently had different objectives in the Philippines, all of them essentially pursued the same policy—that of supporting Marcos. Even President Carter's administration, ostensibly committed to human rights, winked at obvious abuses by Marcos's government and decided to maintain Marcos's friendship. In fact, rather than being strongarmed by the United States, Marcos managed, most of the time, to outwit the Americans. By cleverly playing the cards at his disposal—that is, by emphasizing his opposition to communism and engaging in tough negotiations on the renewal of the military bases agreement—he got what he wanted: military and economic aid, IMF and World Bank loans, and external validation.

A few other studies that deal with post-independence U.S.-Philippine relations are worth noting. Lewis Gleeck's *Dissolving the Colonial Bond: American*

Ambassadors to the Philippines, 1946–1984 contains useful biographical sketches and his short book on the American entrepreneur and political meddler Harry Stonehill affords intriguing insights into U.S. business practices in the Philippines and the workings of Philippine politics.[64] Several books deal with the now-dead military bases issue, but since most of the key documents relating to recent negotiations are not available, those studies can hardly be considered definitive.[65] Much the same can also be said about the extensive literature on U.S. involvement in the fall of Marcos, the coming to power of Cory Aquino, and the ongoing revolution of the New People's Army. Although some of those books—ones by Lewis Simons, Sandra Burton, and Richard Kessler, for example—are extremely informative, it seems unlikely that they will ultimately pass the test of time.[66]

The literature discussed thus far tends to focus narrowly on U.S.-Philippine bilateral relations, but, as we all know, both nation-states operated in a larger world and their relations with each other were often affected by external developments. A number of studies shed light on the international context in which U.S. and Filipino policymakers operated. Douglas Macdonald, Andrew Rotter, Robert Blum, and others have examined in depth the changes in U.S. policy toward Southeast Asia that issued directly from the fall of China and the onset of the Korean War—changes that included a growing concern for the perceived failings of the Quirino administration in the Philippines and the decision by policymakers in Washington to intervene more actively in Philippine affairs. In a comprehensive survey of U.S.-Southeast Asian relations in the period 1940–1950, Gary Hess had shown that the longstanding U.S. policy of supporting elite interests in the Philippines actually mirrored a region-wide policy of promoting political stability through the cultivation of pro-Western elites.[67] Such studies serve as valuable correctives to the tendency of specialists on U.S.-Philippine relations to picture those interactions as "special" and unique, and one can only hope that, as more archival records become available, more scholarship of this kind will be produced.

IV

The last category of scholarship I want to examine—surveys of the U.S.-Philippine historical relationship—includes only two books, both published within the past few years: Stanley Karnow's *In Our Image* and H. W. Brands's *Bound to Empire*.[68] Karnow's book, for which he received a Pulitzer Prize, is a first-rate work of synthesis. Although he has dipped a bit into manuscript collections and conducted many interviews, the book's arguments and conclusions rest squarely on the secondary literature, which Karnow has read and digested. His focus is primarily on the Americans, whom he portrays as sometimes well-intentioned, sometimes not, but almost always ineffective. His major argument is that, while American policymakers in the colonial period aimed to create a nation in their own image, they essentially failed, partly because they underestimated the task confronting them and partly because they made serious mistakes. In the post–World War II era, U.S. policymakers did no better. MacArthur restored to power old elites, who promptly attacked and suppressed lower-class guerrilla units that had fought against the Japanese. CIA operatives intervened, not always cunningly, in Philippine politics; various U.S. administrations supported the dictator Ferdinand Marcos, and Ronald Reagan continued to stand by him virtually to the day he fled from Malacanāng Palace.

Engagingly written, filled with marvelous anecdotes and apt turns of phrase, Karnow's book, like most works of historical synthesis, does not necessarily tell us much that scholars don't already know. Like most syntheses, moreover, its strongest chapters are those about which historians have done the most research (the colonial period, World War II, the years immediately following independence) and its weakest are those which have not been well-served by scholars (in particular, the years 1954–1972, treated in a single chapter). Karnow makes an effort to tell us about Filipino leaders from time to time—for instance, Quezon and Marcos, who have been much-discussed in the literature—but, over all, *In Our Image* is a book about the U.S. side of the Philippine-American encounter. Its protagonists are McKinley, Taft, Forbes, Harrison, Wood, MacArthur, Lansdale, and Reagan.

Brands's *Bound to Empire* is a very different kind of book. Whereas Karnow has exhausted the secondary literature, Brands has plunged into the archives: his footnotes indicate that he has looked at seventy-seven manuscript collections in the United States and the Philippines, including the papers of key U.S. policymakers (Taft, Forbes, Harrison, Wood, FDR, Sayre, MacArthur, Dulles, Johnson) and important Filipino politicians (Quezon, Laurel, Roxas, Quirino, Garcia, Romulo). While his book builds to a certain extent on the findings of other scholars, it sometimes goes well beyond them—as, for instance, in his four chapters covering the period 1944–1964, which are filled with valuable new information derived from his digging in the archives. *Bound to Empire* is, therefore, a combination of research monograph and historical synthesis. What is more, Brands makes a determined effort—far more than Karnow, I would argue—to tell the Filipino side of things. There is much more in his book about Filipino actors, a lot of it derived from the material he has uncovered in the archives.

But, as it happens, Brands's detailed examination of the Filipino "other," something that could have been the book's chief virtue, turns out to be its chief deficiency. As a description of Filipino realities, *Bound to Empire* is problematic. Part of the problem is Brands's conceptualization of the Philippine-American historical experience as a series of dyadic personal relationships between U.S. policymakers and Filipino politicos—a conceptualization that, as I have already indicated, can be found in books that preceded his, likewise written by historians with a background in the history of U.S. foreign relations (Stanley, Theodore Friend, Michael Onorato, and others). In Brands's book, the diplomatic dyad is elevated to paradigmatic status, even when the author is discussing the grossly asymmetrical relationships of the colonial era. My point here is not that relationships did not exist between Pardo de Tavera and Taft or Osmeña and Forbes or Quezon and MacArthur; of course they did and, as the work of Paredes, Cullinane, and McCoy make clear, they are eminently worthy of exploration. But there was a difference between the dyads of the colonial period and those of the post-independence era; more important, there was a lot more to the U.S.-Philippine encounter than dyads, *especially* in the colonial period. If, as Brands claims in his introduction, his primary interest is in examining the Americans and Filipinos who wielded power, he might best be advised, for the colonial period at least, not to focus solely on the Filipino holders of national office, whose range of authority was delimited, but rather on provincial political influentials, economic elites, leaders of labor unions, and millenarian movements.

But even as an examination of national political figures, Brands's book has problems. While he has immersed himself in thousands of documents written by Filipinos, Brands does not have enough understanding of Philippine society, culture, and history to make maximal use of them. On occasion, it is true, he provides important insights—as in his observation that Filipino elites "spoke the language of Filipino nationalism while relying on the United States." But, too much of the time, his interpretive strategy is to compare Filipino politicians and politics, either implicitly or explicitly, to the only yardstick he feels comfortable with, American politicians and politics. And when he does that, he invariably finds them wanting—self-serving, devious, or simply corrupt. In Brands's version of the Philippine-American past, American officials attempt to carry out programs or policies, but Filipinos—with the exception of Magsaysay, perhaps—only aspire to get elected or to fill their pockets.

It would be wrong to think that Brands is the only American to present such a view of Filipino political behavior. One can point to many whose approach has been similar, including not a few makers of U.S. policy from

Taft down to the present. But, whether he has company or not, it appears to me that such a view of Filipino political leaders is, at bottom, an ethnocentric one; Filipinos are being expected to measure up to American notions of appropriate conduct—notions that, by the way, as Brands himself recognizes, Americans often don't measure up to either.

How then can we explain this Filipino other? The first step, I would argue, is to abandon the idea that Filipino politics is in any sense deficient (i.e., corrupt) if it deviates from our own. The second is to try to explain why, in addition to the reasons that have already been discussed, Filipino politicians have operated as they have.

One possible key to understanding Philippine political behavior is to recognize that, dating from the Spanish period, politics has been understood by Filipinos as primarily a struggle over economic resources. Under the Spanish colonial system, the Spaniards placed political power over Philippine municipalities in the hands of local officials chosen by a limited electorate. Electoral contests were extremely vicious, largely because the stakes—control over licenses, monopolies, road-building, and the like—were perceived to be so high. If, then, Philippine governments in the years after the U.S. takeover failed to approximate American models, that may have been because indigenous understandings of the function of politics were so different.[69]

Furthermore, there is evidence in the anthropological literature that cultural values as well as historical experience may help to explain the nature of Philippine politics. In an intriguing study of Manileño's conceptions of the difference between public and private property, Richard Stone has found that, by and large, no such distinctions are recognized by most people. Cab drivers, for example, do not consider that the roads they operate their vehicles on are public property; rather, they feel that any space their vehicles occupy or any unoccupied space they claim by means of a hand signal belongs to them. Squatters have much the same attitude about public land they reside on. What an outsider might consider illegal behavior (the violation of posted traffic rules, in the case of driving; squatting; or even, in the case of government officials, dipping into the public treasury), many Filipinos might very well see as acceptable conduct. In the Philippines, the clear lines that westerners tend to draw between public and private simply do not exist.[70]

A third point to be made concerns the nature of the Philippine state. One unfortunate consequence of the colonial experience has been that many of the new states that emerged from it were fundamentally weak, decentralized, often artificial creations, with boundaries that did not necessarily correspond to ethnolinguistic or cultural realities. The Philippines was one of these, a col-

302 Glenn Anthony May

lection of islands and ethnolinguistic groups that may have shared certain cultural characteristics and colonial experiences but not necessarily any deep sense of loyalty to a unitary nation-state. Like many of those new states, moreover, the Philippines was poor, a fact that limited the ability of the government to integrate the population effectively and to exercise control over it.[71]

That third point is directed related to the fourth. The Philippines, like China, is a place where family ties are incredibly strong and where families—including political families—typically operate as a unit to maximize collective resources and to promote collective ends. Free to operate in the regional context with limited intervention from the weak state, Philippine families have used a Philippine equivalent of *guan xi* to gain, exercise, and maintain political power; once in control of political power, they have used it to enrich themselves. For much of the twentieth century, therefore, the weak Philippine state has been obliged to contend with powerful families which have controlled towns, provinces, even entire regions, and the ability of metropolitan politicians to get elected and to rule has been dependent on their success in forging alliances with such families. And, not surprisingly perhaps, in this nation-state where politics has long been conceived as a means of accumulating resources, the forging of those alliances has involved the granting to allies of considerable favors.

In light of all the above, it seems strange, and downright silly, to attempt to portray Filipino political leaders in the way that Brands and other scholars have tried to portray them. Clearly, they do not measure up to American yardsticks; just as clearly, given the nature of their society, we have no right to expect them to. If our objective as historians of U.S.-Asian relations is to understand both the American and Asian actors, we must avoid the temptation to see those actors through a single set of lenses. To understand the "other," one must appreciate the culture of the "other." If we do otherwise, we run the risk of replicating in our books the same cultural biases that we find in the correspondence of the long-dead American policymakers we study.

V

Having examined the literature of the recent past, I now turn, in conclusion, to the future. Clearly, as I have hinted all too often in the preceding pages, much of the history of U.S.-Philippine relations remains to be written. For the colonial period, partly because of the tendency of U.S.-based historians to focus on high policy, many important topics have thus far been largely ignored: U.S. health and agricultural programs, ecological and environmental questions, secondary and university education, imperial architecture, the impact of U.S. colonialism on gender issues, and the like. For the post-independence era, the literature is skimpy on everything except formal government-to-government (and agency-to-government) contacts, and very little of it, including the examinations of formal interactions, has been based on archival sources.

But, in a sense, the real challenge confronting the field is not that of exploring topics heretofore neglected, but rather that of approaching the subject matter in very different ways. It would be useful, for example, if more scholars of the colonial period attempted to see U.S. colonialism in a comparative context. Theodore Friend has written a suggestive study contrasting Filipino and Javanese responses to the Japanese occupation in World War II, and it is easy to imagine that other studies of this genre—e.g., ones comparing U.S. educational policies in the Philippines to those in French Indochina or British Malaya—might be equally informative.[72] The field would richer too if more scholars of the post-independence era made an effort to place U.S.-Philippine relations in the context of historical developments in the entire Asia-Pacific region.

What is needed, above all, is more research and much more culturally sensitive writing about the Filipino side of the U.S.-Philippine relationship. Part of the responsibility for doing that will obviously fall to bona fide specialists on Philippine history—whether Philippine nationals or area specialists from other countries—who can build on the pathbreaking, recent work of Ileto, Guerrero, Paredes, Cullinane, and McCoy. But part of it will also fall to historians of U.S. foreign relations and other Americanists, two groups of scholars whose record of accomplishments to date, while not without its triumphs, has been, on balance, something less than stellar. A necessary first step in changing that state of affairs will be to train a cadre of young historians with the linguistic competence to read the available sources. By my estimate, Philippine archives contain hundreds of thousands of Philippine-language documents with information bearing on the U.S.-Philippine relationship, and, up to now, very few of them have been examined by any scholar, Filipino or non-Filipino. To tell the story of the Filipino side of those interactions—to demystify the Filipino "other"—historians of U.S.-Philippine relations must begin at long last to take those sources into account.

NOTES

1. I realize, of course, that for considerably shorter periods, U.S. relations with both Japan (after World War II) and South Vietnam (especially between 1965 and 1973) bore a certain resemblance to those with the Philippines during the era of U.S. colonial rule;

among other things, in both cases, important decisions were made by the United States about matters that, had Japan or South Vietnam been truly independent nation-states at the time, it would not have been permitted to make. I will not presume to determine whether it ultimately makes sense for historians of U.S.-Japanese relations or U.S.-Vietnamese relations to consider those shorter periods of U.S. suzerainty as conceptually separate categories of analysis.

One other qualification should be stated. I do not mean to suggest that *all* types of interactions between Americans and Filipinos in the colonial period were necessarily different from those in the post-independence era. Indeed, if one is studying nongovernmental actors, it is hard to see much difference between what occurred before 1946 and what occurred afterward (except, perhaps, that in the earlier period such actors—for example, missionaries, people engaged in business—could get considerably more assistance from the U.S. government). I am grateful to Roger Dingman for drawing my attention to this issue and to Bill Brands for commenting thoughtfully on it.

2. Why do we lump two such different fields under the heading of U.S.-Philippine relations? Most probably because we have no other choice. While it might make more sense to place the topic under the heading of U.S. imperial history, the simple truth of the matter is that the American academy recognizes no such separate field. There are perhaps understandable reasons for that state of affairs, not the least of which is that the formal U.S. empire was, compared to the British, small, short-lived, seemingly inconsequential. Yet, whatever the reasons, the result is that, if we are to consider the U.S.-Philippine colonial relationship at all in an American academic context, it must be done, *faute de mieux*, under the heading of U.S.-Philippine or U.S.-Asian relations.

3. I am indebted to Alfred W. McCoy, a leading historian of the Philippines, for this point about dyads. McCoy first made it in a penetrating review of H. W. Brands's book, *Bound to Empire: The United States and the Philippines*, which appeared in the *Journal of Asian Studies* 52 (Aug. 1993): 772–73.

4. Peter W. Stanley, "The Forgotten Philippines," in *American-East Asian Relations: A Survey*, ed. Ernest R. May and James C. Thomson, Jr. (Cambridge: Harvard University Press, 1972), 291–316. Also see Glenn Anthony May, "The State of Philippine-American Studies," in May, *A Past Recovered: Essays in Philippine History and Historiography* (Quezon City: New Day Publishers, 1987), 174–89.

5. Among the many important subjects I am unable to discuss are U.S.-Philippine cultural relations (including popular culture), immigration, and interactions during World War II. In the case of World War II, there is a voluminous literature dealing with combined military actions at the time of the Japanese invasion, guerrilla activities during the war, interned Americans, MacArthur's return and its aftermath, and so forth.

6. Benito F. Legarda, Jr., "Foreign Trade, Economic Change and Entrepreneurship in the Nineteenth Century Philippines" (Ph.D. diss., Harvard University, 1955).

7. Norman G. Owen, "Americans in the Abaca Trade: Peele, Hubbell & Co., 1856–1875," in *Reappraising an Empire: New Perspectives on Philippine-American History*, ed. Peter W. Stanley (Cambridge: Harvard University Press, 1984), 201–30; Owen, *Prosperity Without Progress: Manila Hemp and Material Life in the Colonial Philippines* (Berkeley: University of California Press, 1984); Owen, "Abaca in Kabikolan: Prosperity Without Progress," in *Philippine Social History: Global Trade and Local Transformations*, ed. Alfred W. McCoy and Ed. C de Jesus (Quezon City: Ateneo de Manila University Press, 1982): 191–216.

8. John A. S. Grenville and George B. Young, *Politics, Strategy, and American Diplomacy: Studies in Foreign Policy, 1873–1917* (New Haven: Yale University Press, 1966), 267–96.

9. Thomas McCormick, "Insular Imperialism and the Open Door: The China Market

and the Spanish-American War," *Pacific Historical Review* 32 (May 1963): 155–69; McCormick, *China Market: America's Quest for Informal Empire, 1893–1901* (Chicago: Quadrangle Books, 1967), 107–25; Walter LaFeber, *The New Empire: An Interpretation of American Expansion, 1860–1898* (Ithaca: Cornell University Press, 1963), 361–62, 408–17.

10. Luzviminda Bartolome Francisco and Jonathan Shepard Fast, *Conspiracy for Empire: Big Business, Corruption and the Politics of Imperialism in America, 1876–1907* (Quezon City: Foundation for Nationalist Studies, 1985).

11. McCormick, *China Market*, 107–25; H. Wayne Morgan, *William McKinley and His America* (Syracuse: Syracuse University Press, 1963), 388–413; Morgan, *America's Road to Empire: The War with Spain and Overseas Expansion* (New York: Wiley, 1965); Lewis L Gould, *The Spanish-American War and President McKinley* (Lawrence: University Press of Kansas, 1982); Ernest R. May, *Imperial Democracy: The Emergence of America as a Great Power* (New York: Harcourt, 1961); David Trask, *The War with Spain in 1898* (New York: Macmillan, 1981); Also consult Ephraim K. Smith, "A Question from Which We Could Not Escape: William McKinley and the Decision to Acquire the Philippine Islands," *Diplomatic History* 9 (Fall 1985): 363–75, and Louis Halle, *The United States Acquires the Philippines* (Lanham, MD: University Press of America, 1985); John L. Offner, *An Unwanted War: The Diplomacy of the United States and Spain Over Cuba, 1895–1898* (Chapel Hill: University of North Carolina Press, 1992.).

12. John Morgan Gates, *Schoolbooks and Krags: The United States Army in the Philippines, 1898–1902* (Westport: Greenwood Press, 1973).

13. Brian Linn's *The U.S. Army and Counterinsurgency in the Philippines, 1899–1902* (Chapel Hill: University of North Carolina Press, 1989).

14. Stuart Creighton Miller, *"Benevolent Assimilation": The American Conquest of the Philippines, 1899–1903* (New Haven: Yale University Press, 1982).

15. The original PIR documents were returned to the Philippines in the 1950s and are now held in the Philippine National Library, where they have been renamed the "Philippine Revolutionary Papers." A microfilmed copy of the originals was retained by the U.S. National Archives. Most of the records of U.S. military units that served in the Philippines can be found in Record Group 395 of the U.S. National Archives. To use that collection, one should first consult a valuable unpublished finding aid, available at the Archives: U.S. National Archives and Records Service, "A Preliminary Inventory of U.S. Army Overseas Operations and Commands, 1898–1942," 2 vols., 1971.

16. David Haward Bain's *Sitting in Darkness: Americans in the Philippines* (Boston: Houghton Mifflin, 1984). For other views of the U.S. military effort, see Richard E. Welch, Jr., *Response to Imperialism: the United States and the Philippine-American War, 1899–1902* (Chapel Hill: University of North Carolina Press, 1979); Welch, "American Atrocities in the Philippines: The Indictment and the Response," *Pacific Historical Review* 43 (May 1974): 233–53; Russell Roth, *Muddy Glory: America's "Indian Wars" in the Philippines, 1899–1935* (W. Hanover, Mass.: Christopher Publishing House, 1981); Brian McAllister Linn, "Intelligence and Low-Intensity Conflict in the Philippine War," *Intelligence and National Security* 6 (1991): 90–114; Sara Bunnett, ed., *Manila Envelopes: Oregon Volunteer Lt. George F. Telfer's Spanish-American War Letters* (Portland: Oregon Historical Society Press, 1987); Allan R. Millett, *The General: Robert L. Bullard and Officership in the United States Army* (Westport: Greenwood Press, 1975): Kenneth Ray Young, *The General's General: The Life and Times of Arthur MacArthur* (Boulder: Westview Press, 1994); Willard B. Gatewood, Jr., *Black Americans and the White Man's Burden, 1898–1903* (Urbana: University of Illinois Press, 1975); Lewis E. Gleeck, Jr., "The California Volunteers of 1898," *Bulletin of the American Historical Collection* 14 (Oct.–Dec. 1986): 7–38; Gleeck, "Lucban Besieged by Filipino

Guerillas (1899–1901)," *Bulletin of the American Historical Collection* 17 (July-Sept. 1989): 77–85.

17. The Tagalog original is Emilio Aguinaldo, *Mga Gunita ng Himagsikan* (Manila: n.p., 1964). I have compared the original to the translation used by Bain.

18. Teodoro Agoncillo's *Malolos: The Crisis of the Republic* (Quezon City: University of the Philippines, 1960).

19. Renato Constantino, with the collaboration of Letizia R. Constantino, *The Philippines: A Past Revisited* (Manila: By the author, 1975). One finds a similar argument in O. D. Corpuz, *The Roots of the Philippine Nation*, 2 vols. (Quezon City: Aklahi Foundation, 1989), 2:403–82.

20. Reynaldo C. Ileto, *Pasyon and Revolution: Popular Movements in the Philippines, 1840–1910* (Quezon City: Ateneo de Manila University Press, 1979).

21. Milagros C. Guerrero, "Luzon at War: Contradictions in Philippine Society, 1898–1902" (Ph.D. diss., University of Michigan, 1977), 48–70, 133, 140–49. For a defense of Aguinaldo, see Alfredo B. Saulo, *Emilio Aguinaldo: Generalissimo and President of the First Philippine Republic—First Republic in Asia* (Quezon City: Phoenix Publishing House, 1983); and Saulo, *The Truth about Aguinaldo and Other Heroes* (Quezon City: Phoenix Publishing House, 1987).

22. Glenn Anthony May, *Battle for Batangas: A Philippine Province at War* (New Haven: Yale University Press, 1991). See also chs. 5–7 in May, *A Past Recovered: Essays on Philippine History and Historiography* (Quezon City: New Day Publishers, 1987); Norman G. Owen, "Winding Down the War in Albay, 1900–1903," *Pacific Historical Review* 48 (Nov. 1979): 557–89; Stephen Henry Totanes, "Sorsogon's Principalia and the Policy of Pacification, 1900–1903," *Philippine Studies* 38 (Fourth Quarter 1990): 477–99; William Henry Scott, *Ilocano Responses to American Aggression, 1900–1901* (Quezon City: New Day Publishers, 1986); Orlino Ochosa, *The Tinio Brigade: Anti-American Resistance in the Ilocos Provinces, 1899–1901* (Quezon City: New Day Publishers, 1991); Ma. Fe Hernaez Romero, *Negros Occidental Between Two Foreign Powers, 1888–1909* (Bacolod City: Negros Occidental Historical Commission, 1974), 124–214; Luis Camara Dery, *From Ibalon to Sorsogon: A Historical Survey of Sorsogon Province to 1905* (Quezon City: New Day Publishers, 1991), 146–202; John A. Larkin, *The Pampangans: Colonial Society in a Philippine Province* (Berkeley: University of California Press, 1972), 117–28; Alfred W. McCoy, " 'Muy Noble y Muy Leal': Revolution and Counterrevolution in the Western Visayas, Philippines, 1896–1907," unpublished research paper, Research School of Pacific Studies, Australian National University, 1978; Peter Schreurs, *Angry Days in Mindanao* (Cebu City: San Carlos Publications, 1987); John N. Schumacher, S.J., *Revolutionary Clergy: The Filipino Clergy and the Nationalist Movement, 1850–1903* (Quezon City: Ateneo de Manila University Press, 1981); Schumacher, "Recent Perspectives on the Revolution," *Philippine Studies* 30 (Fourth Quarter 1982): 445–92; Rosario Mendoza Cortes, *Pangasinan, 1801–1900: The Beginnings of Modernization* (Quezon City: New Day Publishers, 1990); Caridad Aldecoa-Rodriguez, *Negros Oriental and the Philippine Revolution* (Dumaguete City: Provincial Government of Negros Oriental, 1983); Elsie Ramos, "Tayabas, 1571–1907" (M.A. thesis, University of the Philippines, 1992), 119–88; Evelyn Tan Cullamar, *Babaylanism in Negros, 1896–1907* (Quezon City: New Day Publishers, 1986).

23. Glenn Anthony May, "150,000 Missing Filipinos: A Demographic Crisis in Batangas, 1887–1903," in May, *Past Recovered*, 66–97; May, *Battle*, 25–27, 60–61, 205–07, 262–67, 271–75; Ken De Bevoise, *The Philippine Disease Regime: Epidemics in the Nineteenth-Century Total Environment* (Princeton: Princeton University Press, forthcoming); De Bevoise, "Until God Knows When: Smallpox in the Late-Colonial Philippines," *Pacific Historical*

Review 59 (May 1990): 149–85. See also Reynaldo C. Ileto, "Cholera and the Origins of the American Sanitary Regime in the Philippines," in *Imperial Medicine and Indigenous Societies*, ed. David Arnold (Manchester: Manchester University Press, 1988), 125–48; John Morgan Gates, "War-Related Deaths in the Philippines," *Pacific Historical Review* 53 (Nov. 1983): 367–78.

24. See, for example, Dean C. Worcester, *The Philippines Past and Present*, 2 vols. (New York: Macmillan, 1914); W. Cameron Forbes, *The Philippine Islands* (Boston: Houghton Mifflin, 1928); Joseph Ralston Hayden, *The Philippines: A Study in National Development* (New York: Macmillan, 1942).

25. Lewis E. Gleeck, Jr., *The American Governors General and High Commissioners in the Philippines* (Quezon City: New Day Publishers, 1986).

26. See, for example, Lewis E. Gleeck, Jr., *American Institutions in the Philippines (1898–1941)* (Manila: Historical Conservation Society, 1976); Gleeck, *The American Half-Century (1898–1946)* (Manila: Historical Conservation Society, 1984).

27. Renato Constantino, *Past Revisited*; Renato Constantino and Letizia R. Constantino, *The Philippines: The Continuing Past* (Quezon City: Foundation for Nationalist Studies, 1978).

28. William J. Pomeroy, *American Neo-Colonialism: Its Emergence in the Philippines and Asia* (New York: International Publishers Co., 1970).

29. Peter Stanley, *A Nation in the Making: The Philippines and the United States, 1899–1921* (Cambridge: Harvard University Press, 1974).

30. Michael Hunt, *Frontier Defense and the Open Door: Manchuria in Chinese-American Relations, 1895–1911* (New Haven: Yale University Press, 1973).

31. Glenn Anthony May, *Social Engineering in the Philippines: The Aims, Execution, and Impact of American Colonial Policy, 1900–1913* (Westport: Greenwood Press, 1980).

32. Norman G. Owen, ed., *Compadre Colonialism: Studies on the Philippines Under American Rule* (Ann Arbor: Center for South and Southeast Asian Studies, University of Michigan, 1971).

33. Frank H. Golay, "The Search for Revenues," in *Reappraising an Empire*, ed. Stanley, 231–60. For other insights into U.S. economic policies, see Norman G. Owen, ed., *The Philippine Economy and the United States: Studies in Past and Future Interactions* (Ann Arbor: Center for South and Southeast Asian Studies, University of Michigan, 1983).

34. Romeo V. Cruz, *America's Colonial Desk and the Philippines, 1898–1934* (Quezon City: University of the Philippines Press, 1974). Also see Visitacion R. De la Torre, *History of the Philippine Civil Service* (Quezon City: New Day Publishers, 1986), and, on the legal system, Winfred L. Thompson, "Law and Legitimacy: The Taft Commission and the Establishment of a Government of Law in the Philippines, 1900–1901," *Pilipinas* 8 (Spring 1987): 11–28.

35. Oscar Alfonso, *Theodore Roosevelt and the Philippines, 1897–1909* (Quezon City: University of the Philippines Press, 1970).

36. Rodney J. Sullivan, *Exemplar of Americanism: The Philippine Career of Dean C. Worcester* (Ann Arbor: Center for South and Southeast Asian Studies, University of Michigan, 1991).

37. Peter W. Stanley, " 'The Voice of Worcester Is the Voice of God': How One American Found Fulfillment in the Philippines," in *Reappraising an Empire*, ed. Stanley, 117–41.

38. Gleeck, *Governors General.* For other studies of important U.S. officials see Sidney Fine, *Frank Murphy: The New Deal Years* (Chicago: University of Chicago Press, 1979); David Vawter DuFault, "Francis B. Sayre and the Commonwealth of the Philippines, 1936–1942" (Ph.D. diss., University of Oregon, 1972); Kenton J. Clymer, "Humanitarian

Imperialism: David Prescott Barrows and the White Man's Burden in the Philippines,"
Pacific Historical Review 44 (Nov. 1976): 495–517; Victor J. Sevilla, *Justices of the Supreme
Court of the Philippines: Their Lives and Outstanding Decisions*, 3 vols. (Quezon City: New
Day Publishers, 1984–85). For information on the president of an investigatory commis-
sion that came to the Philippines before the Taft Commission, see Maynard Moser, *Jacob
Gould Schurman: Scholar, Political Activist, and Ambassador of Good Will* (New York: Arno
Press, 1982).

39. Carol Petillo, *Douglas MacArthur: The Philippine Years* (Bloomington: Indiana Uni-
versity Press, 1981). For Petillo's comments about Cooper, see pages 150–54, 164–66. On
MacArthur, also consult D. Clayton James, *The Years of MacArthur*, 3 vols. (Boston:
Houghton Mifflin, 1970–85), and Ricardo Trota Jose, *The Philippine Army, 1935–1942*
(Quezon City: Ateneo de Manila University Press, 1992).

40. James J. Halsema, *E.J. Halsema, Colonial Engineer: A Biography* (Quezon City: New
Day Publishers, 1991).

41. Peter Gowing, *Mandate in Moroland: The American Government of Muslim Filipinos,
1899–1920* (Quezon City: New Day Publishers, 1977). On U.S. policies toward the Muslims,
consult as well Henry F. Funtecha, *American Military Occupation of the Lake Lanao Region,
1901–1913* (Marawi City: University Research Center, Mindanao State University, 1979);
and Lewis E. Gleeck, Jr., "The American Encounter with the Moros and Wild Tribesmen,"
Bulletin of the American Historical Collection 19 (April–June 1991): 33–52.

42. Frank Jenista, *The White Apos: American Governors on the Cordillera Central* (Quezon City: New Day Publishers, 1987).

43. Lewis Gleeck, *The Manila Americans (1901–1964)* (Manila: Carmelo & Bauermann,
1977). Also consult Gleeck, *Americans on the Philippine Frontiers* (Manila: Carmelo &
Bauermann, 1974); Gleeck, *American Business and Philippine Economic Development*
(Manila: Carmelo & Bauermann, 1975); Gleeck, *The History of the Jewish Community of
Manila* (Manila: By the author, n.d.); Ronald J. Edgerton, "Americans, Cowboys, and Cat-
tlemen on the Mindanao Frontier," in *Reappraising an Empire*, ed. Stanley, 171–97.

44. Kenton J. Clymer, *Protestant Missionaries in the Philippines, 1898–1916: An Inquiry
into the American Colonial Mentality* (Urbana: University of Illinois Press, 1986). Also consult Clymer "The Methodist Response to Philippine Nationalism, 1899–1916," *Church History* 47 (Dec. 1978): 421–33; Clymer, "The Episcopal Missionary Encounters with Roman
Catholicism in the Philippines, 1901–1916," *Philippine Studies* 28 (First Quarter 1980):
86–97; "Methodist Missionaries and Roman Catholicism in the Philippines, 1899–1916"
Methodist History 18 (April 1980): 171–78; "Religion and American Imperialism:
Methodist Missionaries in the Philippine Islands, 1899–1914," *Pacific Historical Review* 49
(Feb. 1980): 29–50.

45. Anne C. Kwantes, *Presbyterian Missionaries in the Philippines: Conduits of Social
Change (1899–1910)* (Quezon City: New Day Publishers, 1989). On missionaries, also con-
sult Clifford E. Barry Nobes, *Apo Padi (An Autobiography)* (Quezon City: New Day Pub-
lishers, 1988); Michael C. Reilly, "Charles Henry Brent: Philippine Missionary and Ecu-
menicist," *Philippine Studies* 24 (Third Quarter 1976): 303–25; Milton Walter Meyer, "The
Course of Early Baptist Missions in the Philippines (I)," *Bulletin of the American Historical
Collection* 15 (April–June 1987): 7–23; Meyer, "The Course of Early Baptist Missions in the
Philippines (II)," *Bulletin of the American Historical Collection* 15 (July–Sept. 1987): 38–57.

46. Vicente Albano Pacis, *President Sergio Osmeña*, 2 vols. (Quezon City: Phoenix Press,
1971); Aruna Gopinath, *Manuel L. Quezon: The Tutelary Democrat* (Quezon City: New Day
Publishers, 1987); Bernadita Reyes Churchill, *The Philippine Independence Missions to the
United States, 1919–1934* (Manila: National Historical Institute, 1983). Also consult Rolan-

do M. Gripaldo, "The Quezon-Winslow Correspondence: A Friendship Turned Sour," *Philippine Studies* 32 (Second Quarter 1984): 129–62; Gerald E. Wheeler, "Quezon and the High Commissioners," *Bulletin of the American Historical Collection* 9 (April–June 1981): 26–45; and Esteban A. De Ocampo, with the collaboration of Alfredo Saulo, *First Filipino Diplomat: Felipe Agoncillo (1859–1941)* (Manila: National Historical Institute, 1977).

47. Theodore Friend, *Between Two Empires: The Ordeal of the Philippines, 1929–1946* (New Haven: Yale University Press, 1965); Bonifacio Salamanca, *The Filipino Reaction to American Rule, 1901–1913* (Hamden, CT: Shoe String Press, 1968).

48. See the essays by Michael Cullinane and Reynaldo Ileto in *Reappraising an Empire*, ed. Stanley, 59–113; and the introduction by Paredes and the essays by Paredes, Cullinane, and Alfred McCoy in *Philippine Colonial Democracy*, ed. Ruby R. Paredes (New Haven: Yale University Southeast Asia Studies, 1988), 1–12, 41–160.

49. David J. Sturtevant, *Popular Uprisings in the Philippines, 1840–1940* (Ithaca: Cornell University Press, 1976); Ileto, *Pasyon*. Also consult Alfred McCoy, "*Baylan*: Animist Religion and Philippine Peasant Ideology," *Philippine Quarterly of Society and Culture* 10 (1982): 141–94; McCoy, "Culture and Consciousness in a Philippine City," *Philippine Studies* 30 (Second Quarter 1982);157–203; McCoy, "The Iloilo General Strike: Defeat of a Proletariat in a Philippine Colonial City," *Journal of Southeast Asian Studies* 15 (Sept. 1984): 330–64; Melinda Tria Kerkvliet, *Manila Workers' Unions, 1900–1950* (Quezon City: New Day Publishers, 1992); Benedict J. Kerkvliet, *The Huk Rebellion: A Study of Peasant Revolt in the Philippines* (Berkeley: University of California Press, 1977); Michael J. Connolly, S.J., *Church Lands and Peasant Unrest in the Philippines: Agrarian Conflict in 20th-Century Luzon* (Quezon City: Ateneo de Manila University Press, 1992); Samuel K. Tan, *The Filipino Muslim Armed Struggle, 1900–1972* (Manila: Filipinas Foundation, 1977); Motoe Terami-Wada, "The Sakdal Movement, 1930–34," *Philippine Studies* 36 (Second Quarter 1988): 131–50; Terami-Wada, "Benigno Ramos and the Sakdal Movement," *Philippine Studies* (Fourth Quarter 1988): 427–42; James C. Biedzynski, "American Perceptions of the Sakdals," *Bulletin of the American Historical Collection* 18 (July–Sept. 1990): 85–94.

50. Benda briefly sketched his ideas in "Peasant Movements in Colonial Southeast Asia," in Harry J. Benda, *Continuity and Change in Southeast Asia: Collected Journal Articles of Harry J. Benda* (New Haven: Yale University Southeast Asia Studies, 1972), 221–35. Another book that uses Benda's approach is Sartono Kartodirdjo, *Protest Movements in Rural Java: A Study of Agrarian Unrest in the Nineteenth and Early Twentieth Centuries* (Singapore: Oxford University Press, 1973) .

51. John A. Larkin, *The Pampangans: Colonial Society in a Philippine Province* (Berkeley: University of California Press, 1972); Larkin, *Sugar and the Origins of Modern Philippine Society* (Berkeley: University of California Press, 1993); Volker Schult, *Mindoro: A Social History of a Philippine Island in the 20th Century; A Case Study of a Delayed Developmental Process* (Manila: Divine Word, 1991); McCoy and de Jesus, eds., *Philippine Social History*; Kerkvliet, *Huk Rebellion*; Lewis E. Gleeck, Jr., *Laguna in American Times: Coconuts and Revolucionarios* (Manila: Historical Conservation Society, 1981); Gleeck, *Nueva Ecija in American Times: Homesteaders, Hacenderos, and Politicos* (Manila: Historical Conservation Society, 1981); Gleeck, "Pangasinan in American Times (1899–1946)," serialized in *Bulletin of the American Historical Collection* 11 (Jan.–March 1983): 7–45; 11 (April–June 1983): 40–84; 11 (July–Sept. 1983): 41–74; 11 (Oct.–Dec. 1983): 61–94; Alfred W. McCoy, "Ylo-ilo: Factional Conflict in a Colonial Economy, Iloilo Province, Philippines, 1937–1955" (Ph.D. diss., Yale University, 1977); Rosario Mendoza Cortes, *Pangasinan, 1901–1986: A Political, Socioeconomic and Cultural History* (Quezon City: New Day Publishers, 1990); Resil B. Mojares, *Theater in Society, Society in Theater: Social History of a Cebuano Village,*

1840–1940 (Quezon City: Ateneo de Manila University Press, 1985); Ma Fe Hernaez Romero, *Negros Occidental*; Jaime B. Veneracion, *Kasaysayan ng Bulakan* (Cologne, Germany: BAKAS, 1986); Violeta B. Lopez-Gonzaga, *The Socio-Politics of Sugar: Wealth, Power Formation and Change in Negros, 1899–1985* (Bacolod City: Social Research Center, University of St. La Salle, 1989); Lopez-Gonzaga, *The Negrense: A Social History of an Elite Class* (Bacolod City: Institute for Social Research and Development, University of St. La Salle, 1991); Howard T. Fry, *A History of the Mountain Province* (Quezon City: New Day Publishers, 1983); Daniel F. Doeppers, *Manila, 1900–1941: Social Change in a Late Colonial Metropolis* (New Haven: Yale University Southeast Asia Studies, 1984); Doeppers, "Mortgage Loans and Lending Institutions in Pre-War Manila," *Philippine Studies* 31 (Second Quarter 1983): 189–215; Doeppers, "Metropolitan Manila in the Great Depression: Crisis for Whom?" *Journal of Asian Studies* 50 (Aug. 1991): 511–35; Caridad Aldecoa-Rodriguez, *Negros Oriental from American Rule to the Present* (Dumaguete City: Provincial Government of Negros Oriental, 1989); Mardonio M. Lao, "The Economy of the Bukidnon Plateau During the American Period," *Philippine Studies* 35 (Third Quarter 1987): 316–31; Shinzo Hayase, "American Colonial Policy and the Japanese Abaca Industry in Davao, 1898–1941," *Philippine Studies* 33 (Fourth Quarter 1985): 505–17.

52. Amado Guerrero, *Philippine Society and Revolution* (Manila: Pulang Tala Publications, 1971); Constantino and Constantino, *Continuing Past*; William J. Pomeroy, *An American Made Tragedy: Neocolonialism and Dictatorship in the Philippines* (New York: International Publishers, 1974); Stephen Rosskamm Shalom, *The United States and the Philippines: A Study of Neocolonialism* (Philadelphia: Institute for the Study of Human Issues, 1981). Also see Gabriel Kolko, *Confronting the Third World: United States Foreign Policy, 1945–1980* (New York: Pantheon Books, 1988).

53. Bonifacio Salamanca, "Quezon, Osmeña and Roxas and the American Military Presence in the Philippines," *Philippine Studies* 37 (Third Quarter 1989): 301–16.

54. Ronald K. Edgerton, "The Politics of Reconstruction in the Philippines, 1945–1948" (Ph.D. diss., University of Michigan, 1975). Also see Vivian Tan, "Unequal Partners: United States Policy Toward the Philippines and the Philippine Trade Act of 1946," *Pilipinas* 8 (Spring 1987): 1–10.

55. Robin Broad, *Unequal Alliance: the World Bank, the International Monetary Fund, and the Philippines* (Berkeley: University of California Press, 1988); Walden Bello, David Kinley, and Elaine Elinson, *Development Debacle: the World Bank in the Philippines* (San Francisco: Institute for Food and Development Policy, 1982); Vivencio R. Jose, ed., *Mortgaging the Future: the World Bank and IMF in the Philippines* (Quezon City: Foundation for Nationalist Studies, 1982).

56. James Putzel, *A Captive Land: the Politics of Agrarian Reform in the Philippines* (London: Catholic Institute for International Relations, 1992). Also see Paul M. Monk, *Truth and Power: Robert M. Hardie and Land Reform Debates in the Philippines, 1950–1987* (Clayton, Vic.: Centre of Southeast Asian Studies, Monash University, 1990).

57. Edward Geary Lansdale, *In the Midst of Wars: an American's Mission to Southeast Asia* (New York: Harper & Row, 1972); Cecil B. Currey, *Edward Lansdale: the Unquiet American* (Boston: Houghton Mifflin, 1988).

58. Joseph Burkholder Smith, *Portrait of a Cold Warrior* (New York: Putnam, 1976).

59. Dennis Merrill, "Shaping Third World Development: U.S. Foreign Aid and Supervision in the Philippines, 1948–1953," *Journal of American-East Asian Relations* 2 (Summer 1993): 137–59. Another important article that makes the case that Quirino attempted to pursue an independent course, albeit not always successfully, is Roger Dingman, "The Diplomacy of Dependency: The Philippines and Peacemaking with Japan, 1945–52," *Jour-*

nal of Southeast Asian Studies 17 (Sept. 1986): 307–21. For an earlier view of the Quirino period see Richard E. Welch, Jr., "America's Philippine Policy in the Quirino Years (1948–1953): A Study in Patron-Client Diplomacy," in *Reappraising an Empire*, ed. Stanley, 285–306; and, for recent defenses of Quirino, see Salvador P. Lopez, *Elpidio Quirino—The Judgment of History* (Manila: Elpidio Quirino Foundation, 1990), and Raissa Espinosa-Robles, *To Fight Without End: The Story of a Misunderstood President* (Makati: Ayala Foundation, 1990).

60. Lewis E. Gleeck, Jr., *The Third Philippine Republic, 1946–1972* (Quezon City: New Day Publishers, 1993).

61. Nick Cullather, "America's Boy? Ramon Magsaysay and the Illusion of Influence," *Pacific Historical Review* 62 (Aug. 1993): 305–38; Cullather, "The United States, American Business, and the Origins of the Philippine Central Bank," *Bulletin of the American Historical Collection* 20 (Oct.–Dec. 1992): 80–99; Cullather, ed., *Managing Nationalism: United States National Security Documents on the Philippines* (Quezon City: New Day Publishers, 1992). Also see Cullather, "The Limits of Multilateralism: Making Policy for the Philippines, 1945–1950," *International History Review* 13 (Feb. 1991): 70–95. Unfortunately, Cullather's book *Illusions of Influence: The Political Economy of United States-Philippines Relations, 1942–1960* (Stanford: Stanford University Press, 1994) appeared too late for me to consider it in this essay.

Doubts have been raised, as well, about the extent of U.S. economic influence in the Philippines and the role of the World Bank and the IMF in the Philippine economy. See several articles in Norman G. Owen, ed., *Philippine Economy*, and Glenn Anthony May, "The Special Relationship on Trial," in May, *Past Recovered*, 190–205.

62. Kerkvliet, *Huk Rebellion*; D. Michael Shafer, *Deadly Paradigms: The Failure of U.S. Counterinsurgency Policy* (Princeton: Princeton University Press, 1988). Also see Eduardo Lachica, *Huk: Philippine Agrarian Society in Revolt* (Manila: Solidaridad Publishing House, 1971). A very useful, well-researched account of U.S. efforts to deal with the Huk rebellion can be found in Douglas J. Macdonald, *Adventures in Chaos: American Intervention for Reform in the Third World* (Cambridge: Harvard University Press, 1992), but Macdonald grossly exaggerates the importance of U.S. policies in bringing about the Huks' defeat.

63. Raymond Bonner, *Waltzing with a Dictator: the Marcoses and the Making of American Policy* (New York: Random House, 1987).

64. Lewis E. Gleeck, Jr., *Dissolving the Colonial Bond: American Ambassadors to the Philippines, 1946–1984* (Quezon City: New Day Publishers, 1988); Gleeck, *The Rise and Fall of Harry Stonehill in the Philippines: An American Tragedy* (Manila: By the author, 1989). Also consult Thomas B. Buell, *The Quiet Warrior: A Biography of Admiral Raymond A. Spruance* (Boston: Little Brown, 1974).

65. Patricia Ann Paez, *The Bases Factor: Realpolitik of RP-US Relations* (Manila: CSIS, 1985); Roland G. Simbulan, *The Bases of Our Insecurity: A Study of the U.S. Military Bases in the Philippines* (Quezon City: Balai Fellowship, Inc., 1985); Eduardo Z. Romualdez, *A Question of Sovereignty: The Military Bases in the Philippines, 1944–1979* (Manila: By the author, 1980); William E. Berry, *U.S. Bases in the Philippines: The Evolution of the Special Relationship* (Boulder: Westview Press, 1989).

66. See, for example, Lewis Simons, *Worth Dying For* (New York: Morrow, 1987); Sandra Burton, *Impossible Dream: the Marcoses, the Aquinos, and the Unfinished Revolution* (New York: Warner Books, 1989); Richard J. Kessler, *Rebellion and Repression in the Philippines* (New Haven: Yale University Press, 1989); Aurora Javate-De Dios, Petronilo Bn. Daroy, and Lorna Kalaw-Tirol, eds., *Dictatorship and Revolution: Roots of People's Power* (Metro-Manila: Conspectus, 1988); Lewis E. Gleeck, Jr., *President Marcos and the Philippine*

Political Culture (Manila: By the author, 1987); Walden Bello, *U.S. Sponsored Low-Intensity Conflict in the Philippines* (San Francisco: Institute for Food and Development Policy, 1987); Gareth Porter, *The Politics of Counterinsurgency in the Philippines: Military and Political Options* ((Honolulu: Center for Philippine Studies, University of Hawaii, 1987); Lucy Komisar, *Cory Aquino: The Story of a Revolution* (New York: George Braziller, 1987); Miguela G. Yap, *The Making of Cory* (Quezon City: New Day Publishers, 1987).

67. Macdonald, *Adventures*; Andrew J. Rotter, *The Path to Vietnam: Origins of American Commitment to Southeast Asia* (Ithaca: Cornell University Press, 1987); Robert M. Blum, *Drawing the Line: The Origins of American Containment Policy in East Asia* (New York: Norton, 1982); Gary Hess, *The United States' Emergence as a Southeast Asian Power, 1940–1950* (New York: Columbia University Press, 1987). On the international context, also consult Michael Schaller, *The American Occupation of Japan: The Origins of the Cold War in Asia* (New York: Oxford University Press, 1985).

68. Stanley Karnow, *In Our Image: America's Empire in the Philippines* (New York: Random House, 1989); H. W. Brands, *Bound to Empire: The United States and the Philippines* (New York: Oxford University Press, 1992).

69. See Glenn Anthony May, "Civic Ritual and Political Reality: Municipal Elections in the Late-19th-Century Philippines," in *Philippine Colonial Democracy*, ed. Paredes, 13–40.

70. Richard L. Stone, *Philippine Urbanization: The Politics of Public and Private Property in Greater Manila* (DeKalb, Ill.: Northern Illinois University, Center for Southeast Asia Studies, 1973). This is not to say that Filipinos themselves do not complain about governmental corruption. Some of them have, of course, adopted certain "western" values. In addition, out-of-office politicians often complain about the corruption of those in office; that is to say, they appeal to a western standard when the politicians being held to it are their opponents.

71. This point and the next are discussed at considerable length in an enormously important collection of essays: Alfred W. McCoy, ed. *An Anarchy of Families: State and Family in the Philippines* (Madison: University of Wisconsin Center for Southeast Asian Studies, 1993). See, in particular, McCoy's introduction to the volume.

72. Theodore Friend, *The Blue-Eyed Enemy: Japan Against the West in Java and Luzon, 1942–1945* (Princeton: Princeton University Press, 1988).

Chapter Twelve

U.S.-Vietnamese Relations:
A Historiographical Survey

ROBERT J. McMAHON

In striking contrast to each of the other topics under consideration at this conference, the burgeoning scholarly literature on the United States and Vietnam revolves almost exclusively around an *event* rather than a *relationship*. The Vietnam war, that wrenching conflict that so divided and still divides Americans, stands as the singular reason for almost all of the books and articles on the Vietnamese-American encounter that continue to pour forth with such astonishing regularity. The conflict that ultimately claimed more than two million Asian and almost 60,000 American lives provides the indispensable *raison d'être* for the vast bulk of that now extensive literature. Not surprisingly, most scholars have concentrated on the period of most active U.S. involvement during the 1960s and early 1970s. Even those authors examining earlier and later periods of U.S.-Vietnamese relations, however, have proven unable to escape the long shadow cast by the war. Thus specialists investigating the early development of ties between the United States and Vietnam invariably search for a proper prelude to that bloody and protracted conflict while those investigating events since 1975 typically seek an appropriate epilogue.

To an even greater extent than studies of U.S. relations with China, Japan, Korea, and the Philippines, scholarship on the United States and Vietnam is slanted heavily toward American sources and perspectives. As with nearly all of the countless memoirs, novels, songs, films, and television programs inspired by the war, the historical literature focuses on the *American* experience in Vietnam. In most of the books and articles produced by academic and nonacademic experts alike the Vietnamese remain in the shadows, much as they do in the diverse offerings of American popular culture. Although a small group of Asian specialists has provided a useful counterpoint to this dominant trend, the literature on the United States and Vietnam remains overwhelmed by American scholars asking American-oriented questions and seeking answers in documents produced by Americans. This is a matter of considerable irony since few would dispute the fact that both the origins and the denouement of the war have roots that lie deep in Vietnamese soil. Indeed, the ultimate failure of the United States to achieve its objectives in that embattled land simply cannot be understood without an appreciation of the dynamics of modern Vietnamese history. But the Vietnam war, alas, has failed as of yet to produce its Bruce Cumings.

For all its American-centeredness, the extensive corpus of scholarship on the United States and Vietnam defies easy categorization. It ranges widely to embrace not only traditional studies in diplomatic, military, and political history, but also such disparate fields as economics, sociology, social psychology, cultural studies, gender studies, intellectual and social history, literature, journalism, and ethics. Most books and articles focus especially, however, on one or more of several core issues. A first set of issues concerns American motivations. Why did the United States intervene militarily in Vietnam? Why did policymakers in Washington come to view Vietnam as so important to U.S. national security that they committed more than half a million U.S. troops there? What mix of strategic, economic, political, ideological, or psychological forces influenced American thinking? A second set concerns U.S. strategy. Why did the United States choose to fight the war in the way that it did? Why, in the end, did it lose? Might a more positive outcome have been possible had different tactics and a different strategy been followed? A final set interrogates the results and meaning of the war. What have been the consequences of the long struggle over Indochina? For the United States? For Vietnam? For the world? What lessons does that struggle hold for the future?

I will try to summarize briefly the major lines of debate that have developed around those first two sets of questions, emphasizing principal areas of agreement as well as continuing points of controversy. I will also discuss a few of the more notable works that push the boundaries of the current debate in exciting new directions. Finally, I will conclude with some general thoughts about potentially fruitful avenues for future research.

It must be stated from the outset that no consensus has yet emerged among scholars with regard to the core questions noted above; nor is it likely that one ever will. Although a surprising degree of convergence has occurred on a number of discrete issues, the root debates about the origins, course, and meaning of the Vietnam war divide scholars today almost as deeply as they did while the war was still being fought. Because those questions in their essence cut right to the heart of such fundamental issues as the purpose of U.S. foreign relations, the nature of American society, and the meaning of the American historical experience, it would take a confident positivist or a hopeless naif to expect their resolution. Historians of the Vietnam war can no more expect agreement about such inherently unresolvable issues than historians of the American revolution, the Civil War, or the New Deal can expect scholarly consensus about debates that have raged far longer and just as intensely.

The literature on the Vietnam war has in some respects followed a curiously distinctive pattern. As Robert A. Divine noted in a perceptive review essay that appeared in 1988, scholarly appraisals of the American record in Vietnam reversed the pattern that had obtained following previous American conflicts. During and immediately after both World Wars nearly all historical accounts reflected and bolstered official policy. The Cold War initially met with similar treatment from the first wave of historians. In the case of Vietnam, however, scholars adopted from the outset a highly critical stance toward governmental policy, a stance both fueled and reinforced by the war's unpopularity at home. Only in the wake of North Vietnam's successful reunification of the country in 1975 did a revisionist school of thought emerge; and then it "came in the form of a belated justification of U.S. policy, rather than the usual critique."[1]

The fact that most early analysts of the war in Vietnam found fault with U.S. policy should not, though, be allowed to obscure the profound differences that separated their various interpretive approaches. Writing in 1979, Leslie H. Gelb and Richard K. Betts identified no less than nine distinct explanations advanced by experts during the 1960s and 1970s for America's failed intervention in Vietnam. They ranged from economic imperialism to idealistic imperialism, from bureaucratic politics to domestic politics, and from misperceptions and ethnocentrism to ideological blinders and the imperatives of international power politics.[2] Put another way, early writers agreed that the United States failed to achieve its objectives in Vietnam and tended to concur in the judgment that intervention amounted to a policy blunder of colossal proportions. They differed over *why* the United States failed, however, and they bickered about the relative importance of the different factors that prompted and sustained U.S. intervention.

Two diametrically opposed positions can be discerned within this early babble of competing explanations, positions which continue to be reflected in the more recent scholarship. One, which might be termed the liberal realist critique, characterizes the Vietnam war as an avoidable tragedy. If only American policymakers had reached a more measured and realistic assessment of the limited interests at stake for the United States in Southeast Asia, this view holds, the tragedy could have been averted. If only they had recognized the limitations of American power, another variant of this argument goes, or if only they had appreciated the irresistible appeal of revolutionary nationalism within Vietnam, then the United States could have been spared the unnecessary agony of the war.[3] The other position, which is sometimes termed the radical revisionist stance, takes a dramatically different tack, characterizing the Vietnam war as a necessary and logical consequence of America's position as global hegemon. Given the economic and strategic needs of the American political economy, this view posits, communist expansion and indigenous revolutions had to be resisted in Vietnam and elsewhere. The Vietnam war, then, was not a preventable accident attributable to policy mistakes and misperceptions, according to the radical critique, but the inevitable outcome of a rapacious superpower's need to establish its global supremacy, ensure widespread compliance with its dictates, and crush all challenges to its dominance.[4]

At the close of the 1970s, only a few years after communist forces marched triumphantly into Saigon, George C. Herring published a masterful synthesis of the former perspective. Within the confines of a remarkably compact, lively, and fast-paced narrative, Herring drew from a variety of primary and secondary sources to produce the most compelling overall interpretation of the Vietnam war to date. *America's Longest War* dwells at length on the mistakes, blunders, and misperceptions that plagued the U.S. effort in Vietnam from its very inception. "By wrongly attributing the Vietnamese conflict to external sources," Herring argues, American leaders "drastically misjudged its internal dynamics" and "elevated into a major international conflict what might have remained a localized struggle."[5] Distancing his own views from some of the more unsophisticated and apologetic of those within the liberal realist camp, Herring insists that the "disastrous" policy pursued by the United States in Vietnam "was not primarily a result of errors of judgment or of the personality quirks of the policymakers." On the contrary, he sees U.S. intervention as

"a logical, if not inevitable, outgrowth of a world view and a policy, the policy of containment, which Americans in and out of government accepted
without serious question for more than two decades."[6] In other words, the
Vietnam war cannot be dismissed simply as an accident, but neither can it be
construed as inevitable. It was, rather, the logical result of an illogical global
strategy since containment, at least insofar as U.S. officials applied it to Southeast Asia, suffered from fatally flawed premises.

Herring's skillful overview, revised and updated in 1986, continues to exert
a powerful impact on the Vietnam war literature. The book succeeded in part
because it both reflected and reformulated a perspective already subscribed to
by the majority of academic and nonacademic specialists on the war; it did so,
moreover, within the contours of a highly engaging and effective narrative
structure. Although Herring's liberal realist perspective continues to be challenged from the left (and, since the early 1980s, the right as well) it remains
the dominant paradigm. A measure of the success of *America's Longest War*
can be glimpsed from a brief survey of the other major overviews that have
followed in its wake.

Journalist Stanley Karnow, in a 1983 book that served as a companion
piece to the acclaimed PBS documentary series, "Vietnam: A Television History," echoed many of Herring's conclusions. Although the colorful personality sketches, ample anecdotal material, and rich descriptive passages so prized
by journalists come at the expense of analytical rigor, *Vietnam: A History*, like
America's Longest War, essentially ascribes American failure to the misappro-
priation to Southeast Asia of a foreign-policy strategy designed for Europe.
Karnow's interpretive judgments all fall comfortably within the boundaries of
the liberal realist school of thought. In his rendering, America's Vietnam policy abounds in arrogance, errors of judgment, and cultural misperceptions—
but there is nothing *inevitable* about any of this.[7]

In one of the more recent—and more effective—surveys of the American-
Vietnamese relationship, Gary R. Hess builds on the liberal realist position. In
a brief but admirably balanced and insightful book, he contradicts none of
Herring's major arguments. Hess does, to be sure, pay a bit more attention to
the Vietnamese side of the conflict. "It is essential to understand Vietnamese
history and culture," he states categorically, "in order to appreciate the American role in that country"—a contention that few could dispute. As a specialist primarily in American diplomatic history, however, his guiding questions
remain American-centered ones. Addressing directly one of the most vexing
of those questions, Hess posits that the intermixture of several factors best
explains why "such a relatively small and obscure country" became "of overriding importance to the United States." He lists them as follows:

"A global strategy that looked upon the confrontation with the Communist powers as a 'zero-sum game' and cast Southeast Asian nations into potential 'dominoes'; the 'lessons of the past' that taught the importance of halting aggression and thus perceived Vietnam as another place where the Communist powers were 'testing' Western resolve; the parallel growth of U.S. commitment and 'credibility' that made disengagement tantamount to surrendering America's position of world leadership; and the historic conviction of American mission that encouraged leaders, as well as civilian and military personnel in the field, to see in Vietnam an opportunity to realize Western ideals."[8]

Hess's liberal use of quotation marks in that summary passage suggests that, like Herring, Karnow, and the other liberal realists, he sees American policy as rooted essentially in a series of illusions. The clear implication of his analysis is that there were no falling dominoes; that U.S. decisionmakers misread the lessons of history; that they exaggerated both the communist threat to Southeast Asia and the extent to which America's credibility as a global power was being tested there; and that Vietnam, in actuality, held negligible material, strategic, or geopolitical value to the United States.

American intervention in what amounted to a civil struggle among Vietnamese, then, could—nay, *should*—have been avoided. No appreciable damage to American security or prestige would have resulted from a policy of strict nonintervention, according to the liberal realist view, since few tangible interests—or nontangible ones for that matter—were at stake. However purposeful and deliberate the decisions of the Truman, Eisenhower, Kennedy, Johnson, and Nixon administrations were at the time, wiser and more prudent leaders would presumably have weighed the likely risks and benefits with greater care—and decided against military involvement.

That basic view, for all the variations in emphasis, approach, and tone that naturally distinguish the work of individual authors, provides the overarching interpretive scaffolding for the vast bulk of the books and articles written about the Vietnamese-American relationship in general and the Vietnam war in particular. In addition to the books by Herring, Karnow, and Hess, popular interpretive overviews by such diverse authors as George McT. Kahin, William S. Turley, Marilyn Blatt Young, Anthony Short, James S. Olson and Randy Roberts, Paul Kattenberg, James Pinckney Harrison, Michael Maclear, James William Gibson, George Donnelson Moss, Hugh Higgins, and William C. Duiker all adhere to the basic tenets of the liberal realist position.[9] Significant differences abound, of course. Turley, a specialist in Southeast Asian history, devotes much more sustained attention to the Vietnamese side of the equation, arguing that U.S. intervention was a doomed attempt "to reverse historical trends that were firmly established long before U.S. troops arrived."[10] Young, who takes the story of Vietnamese-American relations up to 1990, offers a more biting indictment of the U.S. civilian and military officers who, in her judgment, callously savaged a land and a people. In their broader interpretive assessments, though, both Turley and Young echo and support the principal arguments of the avoidable tragedy school of thought. Thus Turley in the end faults the United States first and foremost for making "commitments out of proportion to its interests."[11]

The emergence in the early 1980s of a full-blown conservative assault on some of the core assumptions of the liberal realist school actually did little to undermine its widespread acceptance within the scholarly mainstream. The politically driven and frequently intemperate arguments of those who advanced the thesis that the war really could have been won may ironically have strengthened the appeal of authors whose criticisms and caveats seemed so moderate and reasonable by comparison. In the 1980 presidential campaign, candidate Ronald Reagan, in a celebrated remark, proudly referred to the Vietnam conflict as "a noble war." Journalist Norman Podhoretz picked up that theme two years later with a book-length brief for the defense. He apologetically justified American intervention as "an act of prudent idealism whose moral soundness has been so overwhelmingly vindicated by the hideous consequences of our defeat."[12] With the addition of several thoughtful analyses of the military dimensions of the war by such former U.S. Army officers as Harry G. Summers, Jr., Bruce Palmer, Jr., and Philip B. Davidson, a new conservative position on the war appeared for a time to be in the ascendancy.[13] Certainly conservatives outside and inside academe were laboring mightily to cobble together a new consensus—one that presumably could explain and rationalize the American defeat without in the process hamstringing the future use of U.S. military power.

From the vantage point of the mid-1990s, however, those efforts appear clearly to have fallen well short of the mark. The work of Summers, Palmer, Davidson, and their followers must, of course, be distinguished from the work of Podhoretz and other polemicists who were always more concerned with shattering the anti-interventionist ethos spawned by the Vietnam war than with making a serious contribution to the understanding of a complex conflict. The military writers, Vietnam veterans all, have made valuable contributions to the scholarship on the war. Their studies have, for example, called needed attention to the grievous shortcomings of both American tactics and American strategy in Vietnam. Summers, Palmer, and Davidson argue persuasively that both U.S. civilian leaders and their military advisers violated the most basic rules of strategy since they never developed realistic plans for achieving U.S. politico-military goals in Vietnam. Nor did either group manage to reconcile tactics with strategy—a cardinal sin to all serious students of military history.

The deficiencies that inhere in each of the alternative courses of military action that these writers propose severely weaken their overall analysis of the war, however, as several excellent critiques have so convincingly pointed out.[14] Certainly increasing American troop strength dramatically, as Summers's prescriptions for sealing infiltration routes into South Vietnam would have required, could never have gained popular acceptance in the United States. Nor would it have resolved the underlying issues that caused the guerrilla insurgency in the first place.

The conservative critique of the liberal realist position at best nibbles around the edges of that perspective; it fails to directly confront—no less contradict—its central premises. As they did back in the 1960s and 1970s, the radical revisionists still offer the most serious, most thoughtful, and most challenging alternative perspective on the Vietnam war.

Gabriel Kolko's seminal book, *Anatomy of a War: Vietnam, the United States, and the Modern Historical Experience*, published in 1985, offers the most sophisticated and comprehensive formulation of that perspective. Summarized most baldly, Kolko sees U.S. intervention as the inevitable consequence of a set of structural imperatives flowing from America's position as the dominant power within the world capitalist system. The needs of the American political economy for increased trade and investment outlets, for greater access to external sources of important raw materials, and for closer integration between capitalist core nations and the developing countries of the Third World periphery set it on a collision course with revolutionary nationalist movements. "Washington's ambition to guide and integrate the world's political and economic system," Kolko asserts, stands as the "goal which was surely the most important cause of its intervention in the Vietnam conflict after 1950."[15] A conflict such as that which occurred in Vietnam, in his view, quite simply had to take place *somewhere* during the post World War II era. "It was scarcely accidental," Kolko insists, "but rather the logical outcome of contemporary U.S. ambition, strength, and weakness."[16]

Although careful readers can certainly discern much common ground between a Kolko and a Herring on certain discrete points of analysis and interpretation, their overarching explanations for U.S. intervention in Vietnam—and for U.S. withdrawal and defeat—stand fundamentally in conflict. The liberal realist conception of the Vietnam war as an accidental tragedy caused by misplaced fears and perceptual blunders simply cannot be reconciled with the radical revisionist conception of the conflict as the inevitable consequence of America's drive for global hegemony. Those conflicting perspectives create a basic fault line within the scholarly literature. That fault line can be detected not just in the broad overviews of the U.S.-Vietnamese relationship that I have been discussing up to now. It is evident also in the extensive monographic and article literature to which I now turn, a vast and rapidly growing body of work which can best be grouped around different chronological periods and particular topical areas.

Scholars have offered a wide variety of explanations for the deepening U.S. involvement in Southeast Asia in the aftermath of World War II. On one basic point, however, there has been virtual unanimity: nearly all specialists now agree that the American commitment to the French at the end of the 1940s stemmed from deliberate and purposeful calculations about broader U.S. Cold War objectives. Whether those objectives were primarily economic in character, as Kolko and the radical revisionists posit, or the product instead of strategic, ideological, political, or psychological forces, remains, however, a major point of contention.

In one of the most carefully researched investigations of this early period, Andrew J. Rotter makes a strong case for the centrality of economic considerations. Following the classic revisionist framework set forth by William Appleman Williams, he postulates that the American search for an open world dictated that Southeast Asia, with its important economic ties to such core areas as Western Europe and Japan, be stabilized and reconstructed— and, in the process, inoculated against the dangerous virus of communism. Rotter's important book, *The Path to Vietnam*, details, in his words, "U.S. postwar efforts to reconstruct the global political economy, in which effort Southeast Asia, and especially Vietnam, would play a critical role."[17] Writing in a similar vein, William Borden, Thomas McCormick, and Patrick J. Hearden, among others, argue that American calculations about the needs of the capitalist world economy as a whole shaped the U.S. decision to help France suppress the Vietminh insurgency. They contend that the American commitment to the French was influenced most directly by the perceived need to reinvigorate sputtering economic recoveries in Western Europe and Japan by ensuring the availability of Southeast Asian resources and markets.[18]

Those authors, especially Rotter and Borden, construct their propositions about American behavior upon such an impressive empirical foundation that nearly all serious students of the Vietnamese-American encounter have been influenced by their work. Specialists in the early Cold War period now concede that a crucial relationship obtained between U.S. support for the French and the U.S. effort to stimulate the recovery and reintegration of Japan and

Western Europe. But can U.S. motivations best be understood as exclusively, or even primarily, *economic* ones? Or might other considerations of equal or greater weight have also conditioned U.S. actions?

Those crucial issues have generated a plethora of different approaches and emphases. Robert M. Blum, for example, stresses the political context of U.S. commitments in Southeast Asia, arguing that the wrenching domestic debate over who "lost" China reinforced the Truman administration's inclination to pursue a more activist policy in Vietnam. In large part, he suggests, the administration sought to steal the political thunder from its increasingly virulent Republican critics.[19] Michael Schaller, in an excellent study of the U.S. occupation of Japan, agrees that America's intervention in Vietnam was prompted by its overriding commitment to Japanese economic recovery. But, unlike Borden, he sees the strategic strands of that policy as tightly interwoven with its economic strands; the geopolitical priority of containing the Soviet Union and, after 1949, China matched or exceeded the economic priorities that also shaped U.S. policy.[20] The work of Gary R. Hess, George C. Herring, Ronald H. Spector, Lloyd C. Gardner, Richard H. Immerman, and other specialists also point more toward a multicausal explanation of the initial U.S. commitment to the French.[21]

Those authors generally acknowledge the validity of the revisionist contention that America's intervention in Vietnam grew in large measure from its effort to link the economies of Southeast Asia's emerging nations more closely to the core areas of Western Europe and Japan. They do not necessarily interpret that policy, however, as one *determined* by material needs. In his masterful study of the overall national security policy of the Truman administration, Melvyn P. Leffler argues that the material underpinnings of American policy toward Southeast Asia were, in fact, less significant than the strategic underpinnings. Above all else, he avers, the United States sought to create for itself favorable correlations of economic-military power in core and peripheral areas. Such favorable correlations of power—which meant, in effect, a preponderance of power for the United States—were needed to ensure not only America's physical security but the survival of its political values, institutional arrangements, and ideological predilections. U.S. officials looked at the shattered, wartorn world of the late 1940s as an unusually dangerous one that afforded countless opportunities for Soviet expansion and subversion. In Leffler's framework, geopolitical fears prompted U.S. efforts to integrate periphery with core in Southeast Asia, and elsewhere, far more than the economic ambitions that served to reinforce those efforts.[22]

This debate about the initial U.S. commitment in Vietnam, for all its nuance and sophistication, and for all the wealth of documentary evidence that has nourished it, defies simple resolution. Indeed, it exposes in micro-cosm the essential fault line that still divides—and still defines—the field of American diplomatic history. Do the economic expansionist designs of the modern American state determine U.S. foreign policy? Or do other factors, such as fears about potential external threats, whether genuine or imagined, or some other combination of political, ideological, bureaucratic, and psychological variables drive that policy? Did American officials ever truly worry about external threats? Or did they simply manipulate a malleable public to back an expansionist policy by cynically manufacturing fears about illusory foreign perils? The weight of the empirical evidence offered by Leffler for the national security thesis he advances is nothing short of staggering. Yet it has thus far won few converts among those already committed to the view that the American empire, like all empires, grew out of the material imperatives embedded in the very nature of the world capitalist system. Bruce Cumings, one of the most perceptive and imaginative of those who subscribe to the latter perspective, recently chided Leffler for what he considers a false reification of the national security concept. Cumings insists that geopolitical imperatives often reinforced, but always remained subordinate to, economic impera-tives.[23] That perspective represents more than just a reversal of Leffler's order. It serves, instead, as a powerful and necessary reminder that, in the broadest sense, historical debates about American intervention in Vietnam remain inseparable from those concerning the origins of the Cold War and, even more basically, those surrounding the core purpose and meaning of U.S. for-eign policy.

The steady escalation of the American political, economic, and military commitment in Indochina during the 1950s and 1960s has generated an enormous literature—and, not surprisingly, equal controversy. For all the breadth, diversity, and complexity of the scholarly work subsumed under this general topic, though, most books and articles have aggregated around just a handful of perceived turning points in U.S. policy: the Eisenhower adminis-tration's response to the crushing French defeat at Dienbienphu in 1954 and its role at the Geneva Conference of that same year; the Kennedy administra-tion's gravitation toward the option of incremental escalation; and the John-son administration's reluctant embrace of full-scale war in the spring of 1965.

A few deceptively simple questions have shaped the essential contours of the resulting historical literature treating these years. What perceived stakes, scholars ask, could possibly have justified the expenditure of billions of U.S. dollars and the deployment of millions of U.S. troops? And precisely how, they ask, did the Eisenhower, Kennedy, and Johnson administrations reach the decisions that led to ever-greater U.S. commitments in Indochina? At the risk once again of oversimplification, the most basic split among scholars concerns not the relative wisdom of U.S. decisions; those decisions have drawn remarkably few defenders over the years. Rather, it pits those authors who believe that America's spiraling commitments resulted from a series of misplaced fears, misperceptions, or miscalculations—the accidental tragedy perspective—against those who are convinced that those commitments resulted from the cold logic of empire—those convinced, in Bruce Cuming's apt summation, that "the Vietnam war was important to shore up the periphery around the world."[24]

A vigorous scholarly debate has emerged in recent years about Eisenhower's foreign policy, a debate which has, in turn, exerted a powerful impact on studies of U.S.-Vietnamese relations during the 1950s. Convinced that Eisenhower had been judged too harshly by earlier critics, the first wave of Eisenhower revisionists cited Ike's shrewd avoidance of overseas interventions as one of the hallmarks of his diplomacy. His firm decision against intervention at Dienbienphu serves for these authors as a prime case in point. Eisenhower resisted withering pressures, both from French leaders and from officials within his own administration, to mount a last-ditch effort to save the French garrison at that besieged fortress. Scholars differ about the relative strength of those pressures, just as they disagree about the circumstances under which Eisenhower might have opted for intervention.[25] In the end, however, they invariably applaud his prudence. George C. Herring and Richard H. Immerman probably best captured the scholarly consensus that still prevails in an incisive 1984 article. "There seems little reason to quarrel with the view that the administration acted wisely in staying out of war in 1954," they concluded.[26]

A few recent studies have opened up the interpretive lens to include the entirety of the Eisenhower record in Vietnam, including the crucial post-1954 period. That wider focus has raised profound doubts about Eisenhower's alleged prudence and wisdom. Two books have proved especially valuable in this regard. George McT. Kahin's *Intervention* blasts the Eisenhower administration for its role in giving birth to the South Vietnamese government of Ngo Dinh Diem. Kahin calls the decision to back Diem one of the most fateful—and most foolish—of America's entire thirty-year adventure in Vietnam. Gambling that the aloof Catholic patrician could establish a secure and prosperous anti-communist regime in the south, the Eisenhower administration instead wound up tying itself to a woefully unrepresentative and undemocratic elite. That decision just sowed the seeds for future political, economic, and security problems.[27] David Anderson's *Trapped By Success*, the most comprehensive account to date of the Vietnam policy of the Eisenhower administration, offers a similarly harsh indictment. Anderson demonstrates persuasively that only a massive infusion of U.S. economic and military aid managed to keep the Diem regime afloat between 1954 and 1961; yet that aid never proved sufficient to transform South Vietnam into a viable nation. Instead, he argues that the Eisenhower administration became intoxicated by its illusory achievement in South Vietnam, foolishly touting the Saigon regime as the "miracle" of Southeast Asia and trapping "itself and its successors into a commitment to the survival of its own counterfeit creation."[28]

The role played by the John F. Kennedy administration in the deepening American involvement in Vietnam has sparked even greater scholarly scrutiny. Most historians agree that Kennedy's decisions brought incremental, but not dramatic, escalation and that he left his successors with stronger, but still limited, U.S. ties to South Vietnam. They differ on almost all other critical questions, including the underlying rationale for Kennedy's decisions, the significance of Vietnam to overall American foreign policy objectives, the nature and strength of both Diem's regime and the Vietcong insurgency, the precise role of the United States in the coup against Diem, and the broader impact of Diem's ouster on both the stability of the Saigon regime and the U.S.-Vietnamese relationship.

Most scholars concur that broader global interests and fears conditioned Kennedy's response to the spreading insurgency within South Vietnam. But what, precisely, were those interests and fears? On that basic point, historians have diverged rather sharply. R. B. Smith, in a challenging multivolume work he has entitled *An International History of the Vietnam War*, argues that Kennedy (and Johnson after him) had little choice but to respond to an aggressive Sino-Soviet challenge in Vietnam; to do otherwise, he contends, would have risked a serious blow to American power and prestige.[29] Ironically, scholars on the left, although far more critical of U.S. intervention than Smith, accept some of his premises—albeit with a very different twist.

The radical revisionists, too, see real interests and real fears driving Kennedy's commitments. U.S. interests in Vietnam during the Kennedy and Johnson presidencies, according to Thomas J. McCormick, stemmed from the longstanding U.S. "commitment to economic integration within Asia and the important role of Southeast Asian raw materials, food, markets, and investment opportunities for sustaining Japanese economic growth."[30] U.S. fears derived especially from the dangerous precedents that might be established by a communist victory in Vietnam, precedents that might encourage revolutionaries elsewhere while dealing a severe blow to U.S. credibility. American officialdom recognized, in McCormick's words, that "empires were of a piece, and the loss of one member affected the organic health of the whole."[31] Patrick Hearden strikes a similar interpretive chord. Kennedy and his advisers recognized that a communist insurgency in Vietnam could severely harm American global interests. "American leaders feared," Hearden says, "that rebel groups throughout the Third World would be emboldened if the United States appeared weak and hesitant in the face of the communist challenge in South Vietnam. Thus they felt compelled to maintain the prestige and credibility of the United States as a vital part of their commitment to perpetuate the Pax Americana."[32]

Before turning to the liberal realist perspective, an issue that has garnered considerable attention of late requires at least a mention. Some of his former associates and supporters (joined by a noted filmmaker) now argue that Kennedy would have avoided committing U.S. combat troops to Vietnam. They cite as evidence a handful of statements that JFK made late in 1963 which expressed a growing skepticism about U.S. involvement in Vietnam and the fact that he had actually ordered at that time a modest reduction in the number of U.S. advisers stationed there. In a balanced and well researched recent study, John M. Newman develops this case at great length.[33] Yet neither Newman nor any of the other proponents of this view have produced any evidence that Kennedy had reexamined the core assumption upon which U.S. involvement had been based: namely, that the preservation of a noncommunist South Vietnam was vital to American global interests. The fact that Kennedy's closest national security advisers were the very men whose advice Lyndon Johnson followed when he decided to commit U.S. combat forces in the spring of 1965 suggests the strong likelihood that Kennedy would have followed a similar course.

The more vital debate among scholars of the Kennedy and Johnson period concerns the forces that most influenced U.S. escalation in Vietnam. As noted earlier, the liberal realists tend to view American escalation as stemming from a global containment strategy that led U.S. leaders to oppose reflexively communist advances anywhere on the global chessboard. Like McCormick, Hearden, and Kolko, they stress the U.S. fixation with the credibility of its power as well as the persistent U.S. fear about falling dominoes. Unlike those historians, however, the liberal realists tend to emphasize the illusory nature of U.S. fears, suggesting that America's preoccupation with prestige and reputation was as foolish as was its obsession with falling dominoes. The liberal realists also attach much greater weight to other causal factors. Stephen Pelz and Larry Bassett and Larry Berman, for example, contend that Kennedy and Johnson were influenced strongly by political factors. Both presidents sought to avoid a debilitating debate over "who lost Vietnam" and both sought to hold intact a shaky Democratic coalition; each of those goals seemed to require a firm demonstration of their anticommunist credentials.

In LBJ's case, Berman claims that the overriding goal of buying time for an ambitious domestic reform agenda proved to be the single most powerful influence on the pace and extent of troop deployments in Vietnam.[34] Other writers stress the personal dynamic, or the role of the advisory system, or the peculiarities of bureaucratic politics as factors that helped shape U.S. decisionmaking.[35]

These basic interpretive differences regarding the *why* of U.S. intervention derive in considerable measure from contrasting approaches to historical evidence. The liberal realists concentrate especially on the decisionmaking process within the U.S. Government. Their conclusions about the factors that most influenced U.S. behavior derive from a close reading of the numerous memoranda, cables, policy papers, and records of meetings that have been declassified and made available to scholars. That traditional method of diplomatic history rests on the eminently logical proposition that what is most important is what officials say is most important at the time, especially that which is expressed during closed meetings and in private statements and remarks. During their frequent deliberations about Vietnam policy, decisionmakers in the Kennedy and Johnson administrations rarely talked about the need to integrate Southeast Asia or the importance of Japanese economic revitalization; according to this method for measuring evidence, then, those factors could not have been of decisive importance.

But, the radical revisionists would counter, unquestioned assumptions also invariably shape policy decisions. Assumptions about the overall goals and needs of the United States and the larger world system are so universally embraced by elites within the public and private sectors that they need not be articulated. The relative significance of those core ideas cannot, consequently, be deduced from a simple accounting of the frequency with which they are mentioned during policy debates. If that claim contains merit, and it certainly seems to, then how, exactly, do historians identify these assumptions? And how, precisely, do they evaluate their influence on policy? What method of scholarly investigation can historians employ, in other words, if they are inclined to believe that what is not said may be as salient to policy decisions as what is said?

Bruce Cumings argues that theory—world-systems theory in particular— offers a reliable guide. He makes that case quite explicitly in his critique, alluded to earlier, of Melvyn Leffler's *A Preponderance of Power*. Contrasting that book with Thomas McCormick's interpretive overview of U.S. foreign policy since World War II, *America's Half-Century*, Cumings says that the latter study offers superior analytical insights. Why? Because, Cumings suggests, of the richness of the world-systems perspective that guided McCormick and the contrasting paucity of theory undergirding Leffler's work. It matters little to Cumings that McCormick cited not a single source in his book whereas Leffler drew from thousands of primary documents. Quite to the contrary, he says that the analytical superiority of *America's Half-Century* "interrogates the idea that evidence is only found in the archives."[36]

Those contrasting approaches to theory and to evidence certainly help explain why a sizable fault line still runs through the literature on American foreign policy—and, inevitably, through the literature on Vietnamese-American relations. Even if that fissure can never fully be closed, future scholars of the U.S.-Vietnamese encounter can certainly seek to narrow it. They should, for example, investigate particular issues and topics that lend themselves to a more direct engagement between the arguments of the liberal realists and those of the radical revisionists. By advancing and testing hypotheses situated at the nexus between the theoretical and the empirical, they can help bridge some of the gap between theory-driven and document-driven approaches. Theories about state behavior, after all, can only be validated by focusing on specific cases and drawing, in the process, on all historical evidence relevant to those cases. Invariably, some hypotheses—and some larger theoretical frameworks—will be strengthened by such a method of scholarly exploration; others will be weakened; still others will need to be rejected entirely.

The literature on American deescalation in Vietnam, and more particularly that work dealing with the domestic and systemic crises precipitated by the Tet offensive of 1968, serves as an excellent case in point. In *Anatomy of a War*, Gabriel Kolko demonstrated conclusively that a symbiotic relationship obtained between the dollar/gold crisis of that year and the Johnson administration's subsequent decision to set a ceiling on American troop levels and to open negotiations with North Vietnam. Previous authors, liberal and radical alike, had almost completely ignored that relationship. Now, they generally acknowledge it, paying a least a nod to Kolko's pioneering study. Is that because they have been persuaded by the theoretical assumptions about the behavior of global hegemons that informed Kolko's analysis? More likely, they have been impressed by the documentary evidence Kolko has marshalled to demonstrate the point. Policymakers did discuss at great length the ramifications of the Vietnam stalemate on the health of the American economy and on Washington's relationship with its most important allies. The weight of documentary evidence is so great that it simply can no longer be ignored.

Larger issues relating to U.S. deescalation, not surprisingly, remain matters of sharp dispute among specialists. Did the United States begin the painful process of extrication from Vietnam, first under Johnson and then under Nixon and Ford, as a result primarily of pragmatic calculations about the crippling costs of empire? Did Tet, then, represent the high water mark of the American empire? In short, is the theory correct? Kolko states the case for those propositions with uncharacteristic clarity. "Tet revealed that it was time to focus on the limits of the system," he writes. "To have pursued the scale of escalation to an even higher level would have wreaked an untold amount of damage on America's economic position at home and abroad, on its military power elsewhere, and on its political life—a price scarcely any serious person proposed to pay."[37] Tet, in his view thus forced "a long-postponed confrontation with reality."[38]

All hegemons must at some point face inevitable limitations on their power, world-systems theorists tell us. The Tet offensive of 1968, according to Kolko, became that point for the United States. Is that theoretical framework adequate for understanding America's post-Tet behavior? This complex issue demands much closer historical scrutiny than it has thus far received. How, for example, did private elites respond to the Vietnam war in the wake of the Tet offensive? And how and why had their views changed over time? Or had they? Remarkably, in view of the countless studies produced about the United States in Vietnam, not a single monograph has investigated the evolving attitudes and interests of American businessmen, industrialists, and bankers toward the Vietnam war. Nor has anyone yet investigated the attitudes and interests of American labor or other key interest groups. Even Congressional and public opinion toward the war have received far less systematic attention than each deserves; and despite the attention lavished on the media for its role during the Vietnam war, fundamental questions about the media's role within American society and the complex relationship between the media and the state during the Vietnam era have yet to be addressed adequately.

With the exception of Kolko and a mere handful of other scholars, most specialists have analyzed the origins, course, and denouement of American intervention in Vietnam as if policy elites operated in some kind of curious isolation from the rest of American society. We need to know much more about the conjunction between state and society—one of the crucial insights of the corporatists—if we are to fully comprehend the meaning of the Vietnam war in its widest context. If theory helps point us to the obvious conclusion that there *must* be some connection between state and society in the development of any nation's foreign policy, it is evidence—plied from archives, to be sure, but not *just* from archives—that will fill in the blanks. Otherwise, the conjunction will remain fuzzy and unspecific. Kolko's insights about the Tet offensive hardly offer the last word. Rather, they should open up an important new avenue for scholarly research about the Vietnam war, one that seeks to connect that war to the larger society that supported, sustained, and ultimately turned against that effort. We need to interrogate much more fully and imaginatively than we have the relationship between state and society that made possible a war such as Vietnam.[39]

Some of the recent work on the war has begun such an effort by focusing on the counterproductive methods employed by the United States in combatting the North Vietnamese and their Vietcong allies. Loren Baritz and James William Gibson have, for example, suggested that a blind faith in technological superiority and managerial sophistication spawned a self-defeating U.S. military strategy.[40] To pose the question at the heart of their books even more broadly, however, one might ask: how did the cultural values of American society condition American behavior in Vietnam? This question has multiple dimensions. To address them adequately the historian of the Vietnam war must be willing to borrow approaches and insights from other scholarly disciplines.

To the extent, for example, that preconceptions about race and gender form an integral part of the American cultural system, how might those factors have influenced American attitudes and actions? Although George Herring, Sandra Taylor, and others have offered richly suggestive comments about the influence of racial stereotypes on U.S. policy in Vietnam, much more work clearly needs to be done with regard to the intersection between race, culture, and power.[41] How could the United States denigrate one group of Vietnamese with demeaning racial pejoratives while trying at the very same time to work with another group of Vietnamese? John Dower's incisive study of the Pacific War might serve as an instructive model for historians interested in exploring such complex issues.[42] Susan Jeffords's application of the insights of feminist scholarship to American behavior in Vietnam advances another intriguing set of questions for scholars intent on exploring the cultural dimensions of the war.[43] "Vietnam was the funeral of the myth of legitimate male power," *Time* magazine essayist Lance Morrow recently suggested, picking up on one of her themes.[44] Does such a notion make sense? Can it offer any important insights to scholars of the Vietnam war? Down what routes will this cultural approach take scholars? And how might those routes complement—or contradict—those that privilege political economy, strategy, or other noncultural variables? Clearly the traditional methods and theories of the diplomatic historian will need to be broadened before such provocative questions can be fruitfully pursued.

The Vietnamese dimension of the conflict, despite its obvious importance, still ranks among the most amazingly neglected aspects of the entire war. We need to know much more about the nature of the *interaction* between the United States and Vietnam, both North and South. We also need to explore more fully the conjunction between Vietnamese realities and American goals and actions. To what extent did the history, culture, economics, and politics of Vietnam influence American behavior? In view of those factors, to what extent were American goals achievable in any meaningful sense? Needless to say, those are extraordinarily complex questions. To explore them fully one needs a degree of expertise on both the Vietnamese and American sides of the story that few scholars currently possess.[45] In his fine, American-centered study of U.S. policy during the 1950s, David Anderson pointedly emphasizes the limitations imposed on American ambitions by the realities of Vietnamese society. "The historical, social and economic mosaic of Vietnam's village-based culture," he suggests, "was resistant to American outside manipulation and much too complex and embedded to be changed quickly by American wealth and good intentions."[46] Yet Anderson's training and expertise do not allow him to probe that suggestive theme very deeply. Microstudies at the village or provincial level can prove enormously enlightening in that regard, as the older works by Jeffrey Race and Joseph Trullinger attest, and the fine recent study by Eric Bergerud has powerfully reconfirmed.[47] Additional work in that vein will likely reveal more about the Vietnam war and those who fought it and lived it than can any further additions to the already voluminous literature on decisionmaking in Washington.

Finally, continued exploration of the war's international dimensions, including the role of such other actors in the drama as the Soviet Union, China, Japan, Korea, Thailand, the Philippines, Indonesia, and Australia, can also contribute to a deeper understanding of the Vietnam conflict. The interests, fears, and ambitions of other nations inevitably affected both the course of the war and the ability of the main contestants to achieve their goals; so, too, did the fluctuating set of opportunities and constraints offered by the larger international system. The slow trickle of documentary evidence emerging from long-closed archives in China and the former Soviet Union raises the possibility that the Vietnamese policy of America's principal adversaries—and Hanoi's principal allies—may soon be much more fully understood. The few groundbreaking studies that have already appeared offer grounds for cautious optimism on that score.[48] A truly international history of the Vietnam war, however, remains a distant and elusive goal. Such an account would have to examine the origins, course, and impact of the conflict not only in its American and Vietnamese dimensions but in regional and global systemic terms as well. One can only hope that an event which must surely rank among this century's most seminal will someday find a historian with the necessary breadth, wisdom, and perspective to write such a study.

In conclusion, the literature on the Vietnamese-American encounter, for all its vastness and for all its diversity (and this paper has just touched the surface), has tended to focus on an event rather than a relationship. The voluminous corpus of scholarship generated by that event has provoked, informed, and challenged. It has not, however, produced a consensus with regard to the most basic questions and issues. Nor is it likely to any time soon. The basic fault line that still divides scholars can, nonetheless, be narrowed, especially if scholars prove willing to engage each other more directly and if they prove willing to advance hypotheses that are susceptible to empirical verification. One of the most promising areas for such work lies within identifiable points of conjunction between the perceived needs of the American state and the society from which those needs ultimately derive—and from which support must ultimately be gained and sustained. Another concerns the Vietnamese side of a relationship that up to now has been represented in an appallingly one-sided fashion in the literature. Until scholars with the necessary training, skills, and commitment to explore both sides of the Vietnamese-American encounter add their voices to the old and new debates, this subfield will remain woefully unbalanced. The Vietnamese-American relationship must ultimately be examined and understood in terms of *both* American history *and* Vietnamese history, in the way that such scholars as Michael Hunt, Akira Iriye, Bruce Cumings, and others have done for the U.S. encounter with China, Japan, and Korea. Otherwise our vision of the Vietnam war will remain far too exclusively the product of American sources and American perspectives.

NOTES

1. Robert A. Divine, "Vietnam Reconsidered," *Diplomatic History*, 12 (Winter 1988): 79–93. The quote is from p. 80.

2. Leslie H. Gelb and Richard K. Betts, *The Irony of Vietnam: The System Worked* (Washington, D.C.: Brookings Institution, 1979).

3. This viewpoint characterized such notable early studies as Robert Shaplen, *The Lost Revolution* (New York: Harper & Row, 1965); Arthur M. Schlesinger, Jr., *The Bitter Heritage: Vietnam and American Democracy* (Boston: Houghton Mifflin, 1967); George McT. Kahin and John W. Lewis, *The United States in Vietnam* (New York, 1969); and David Halberstam, *The Best and the Brightest* (New York: Random House, 1972).

4. See, for example, Gabriel Kolko, *The Roots of American Foreign Policy: An Analysis of Power and Purpose* (Boston: Beacon, 1969).

5. George C. Herring, *America's Longest War: The United States and Vietnam, 1950–1975* (2nd rev. ed., New York: Knopf, 1986), 279.

6. *Ibid.*, xii.

7. Stanley Karnow, *Vietnam: A History* (New York: Viking Press, 1983).

8. Gary R. Hess, *Vietnam and the United States: Origins and Legacy of War* (Boston: Twayne, 1990), 172–73.

9. George McT. Kahin, *Intervention: How America Became Involved in Vietnam* (New York: Knopf, 1986); William S. Turley, *The Second Indochina War: A Short Political and Military History, 1954–1975* (Boulder, CO: Westview Press, 1986); Marilyn Blatt Young, *The Vietnam Wars, 1945–1990* (New York: HarperCollins, 1991); Anthony Short, *The Origins of the Vietnam War* (London: Longman, 1989); James S. Olson and Randy Roberts, *Where the Domino Fell: America and Vietnam, 1945–1990* (New York: St. Martin's, 1991); Paul Kattenburg, *The Vietnam Trauma in American Foreign Policy* (New Brunswick, N.J.: Transaction, 1980); James Pinckney Harrison, *The Endless War: Fifty Years of Struggle in Vietnam* (New York: Free Press, 1982); Michael Maclear, *The Ten Thousand Day War: Vietnam, 1945–1975* (New York: Avon, 1981); James William Gibson, *The Perfect War: The War We Couldn't Lose and How We Did* (New York: Random House, 1986); George Donelson Moss, *Vietnam: An American Ordeal* (Englewood Cliffs, N.J.: Prentice-Hall 1990; 2nd rev. ed., 1994); Hugh Higgins, *Vietnam* (London: Heineman, 1975; 2nd rev. ed., 1982); and William J. Duiker, *U.S. Containment Policy and the Conflict in Indochina* (Stanford: Stanford University Press, 1994).

10. Turley, *The Second Indochina War*, 1.

11. Young, *The Vietnam Wars*, 200.

12. Norman Podhoretz, *Why We Were in Vietnam* (New York: Simon and Schuster, 1982), 210. For a similar view, see Richard M. Nixon, *No More Vietnams* (New York: Avon, 1985).

13. Harry G. Summers, Jr., *On Strategy: A Critical Analysis of the Vietnam War* (New York: Dell, 1984; first published in 1982 by Presidio Press); Bruce Palmer, Jr., *The Twenty-five Year War: America's Military Role in Vietnam* (Lexington: University of Kentucky Press, 1984); Phillip B. Davidson, *Vietnam at War: The History, 1946–1975* (New York: Oxford University Press, 1988). Two books by academic specialists bear many resemblances to these works. See Guenther Lewy, *America in Vietnam* (New York: Oxford University Press, 1978); Timothy J. Lomperis, *The War Everyone Lost—and Won: America's Intervention in Viet Nam's Twin Struggles* (Baton Rouge: Louisiana University Press, 1984; 2nd rev. ed., 1993, published by Congressional Quarterly Press).

14. See especially George C. Herring, "American Strategy in Vietnam: The Postwar Debate," *Military Affairs*, 46 (1982): 57–63; Gary R. Hess, "The Military Perspective on Strategy in Vietnam: Harry G. Summers's, *On Strategy* and Bruce Palmer's, *The 25-Year War*," *Diplomatic History*, 10 (Winter 1986): 91–106; Jeffrey P. Kimball, "The Stab-in-the-Back Legend and the Vietnam War," *Armed Forces and Society*, 14 (Spring 1988): 433–458.

Gary R. Hess has identified another strain in the revisionist historiography. A few authors, whom he terms "hearts-and-minds revisionists," argue that the war might have been won if civilian pacification efforts had only been pursued more effectively and less emphasis had been devoted to conventional military actions. See, for example, Andrew F. Krepinevich, *The Army and Vietnam* (Baltimore: Johns Hopkins University Press, 1986); Larry E. Cable, *Conflict of Myths: The Development of Counterinsurgency Doctrine and the Vietnam War* (New York: New York University Press, 1988); and Larry E. Cable, *Unholy Grail: The US and the Wars in Vietnam, 1965–1968* (London: Routledge, 1991). The views of John Paul Vann, a leading proponent of the pacification program, are expertly set forth in Neil Sheehan, *A Bright Shining Lie: John Paul Vann and America in Vietnam* (New York: Random House, 1988). For Hess's critique of the "hearts-and-mind" approach, see Gary R. Hess, "The Unending Debate: Historians and the Vietnam War," *Diplomatic History*, 18 (Spring 1994): 242–243.

15. Gabriel Kolko, *Anatomy of a War: Vietnam, the United States, and the Modern Historical Experience* (New York: Pantheon, 1985), 548.

16. *Ibid.*, 557.

17. Andrew J. Rotter, *The Path to Vietnam: Origins of the American Commitment to Southeast Asia* (Ithaca: Cornell University Press, 1987), x. See also Rotter's important article, "The Triangular Route to Vietnam: The United States, Great Britain, and Southeast Asia, 1945–1950," *International History Review*, 6 (August 1984): 404–23.

18. William S. Borden, *The Pacific Alliance: United States Foreign Economic Policy and Japanese Trade Recovery, 1947–1955* (Madison: University of Wisconsin Press, 1984); Thomas McCormick, "Introduction: Crisis, Commitment, and Counterrevolution, 1945–1952," in *America in Vietnam: A Documentary History*, William Appleman Williams, Thomas McCormick, Lloyd Gardner, and Walter LaFeber, eds. (New York: Norton, 1985), 45–60; Thomas J. McCormick, *America's Half-Century: United States Foreign Policy in the Cold War* (Baltimore: Johns Hopkins University Press, 1989); Thomas J. McCormick, "American Hegemony and the Roots of the Vietnam War," in *Vietnam: Four American Perspectives*, Patrick J. Hearden, ed. (West Lafayette, IN: Purdue University Press, 1990), 83–107; and Patrick J. Hearden, *The Tragedy of Vietnam* (New York: HarperCollins, 1991). See also Howard B. Schonberger, "The Cold War and the American Empire in Asia," *Radical History Review*, no 33 (1985): 140–48.

19. Robert M. Blum, *Drawing the Line: The Origin of the American Containment Poicy in East Asia* (New York: Norton, 1982).

20. Michael Schaller, *The American Occupation of Japan: the Origins of the Cold War in Asia* (New York: Oxford University Press, 1985). See also Schaller's important article, "Securing the Great Crescent: Occupied Japan and the Origins of Containment in Southeast Asia," *Journal of American History*, 69 (September 1982): 392–414.

21. Gary R. Hess, *The United States' Emergence as a Southeast Asian Power, 1940–1950* (New York: Columbia University Press, 1987); Gary R. Hess, "The First American Commitment in Indochina: The Acceptance of the 'Bao Dai' Solution, 1950," *Diplomatic History*, 2 (Fall 1978): 331–50; George C. Herring, "The Truman Administration and the Restoration of French Sovereignty in Indochina," *Diplomatic History*, 1 (Spring 1977): 97–117; Ronald H. Spector, *Advice and Support: The Early Years of the U.S. Army in Vietnam, 1941–1960* (New York: Free Press, 1985); Lloyd C. Gardner, *Approaching Vietnam: From World War II through Dienbienphu, 1941–1954* (New York: Norton, 1988); Richard H. Immerman, "Prologue: Perceptions by the United States of Its Interests in Indochina," in *Dien Bien Phu and the Crisis of Franco-American Relations, 1945–1955*, Lawrence S. Kaplan, Denise Artaud, and Mark R. Rubin, eds. (Wilmington, Del.: Scholarly Resources, 1990), 1–26; and Robert J. McMahon, "Harry S. Truman and the Roots of U.S. Involvement in Indochina, 1945–1953," in *Shadow on the White House: Presidents and the Vietnam War, 1945–1975*, David L. Anderson, ed. (Lawrence: University Press of Kansas, 1993), 19–42; and Duiker, *U.S. Containment Policy and the Conflict in Indonesia*.

22. Melvyn P. Leffler, *A Preponderance of Power: National Security, the Truman Administration, and the Cold War* (Stanford: Stanford University Press, 1992).

23. " 'Revising Postrevisionism,' or, The Poverty of Theory in Diplomatic History," *Diplomatic History*, 17 (Fall 1993): 539–569. See especially 561–566.

24. *Ibid.*, 565. McCormick presents this case more fully, arguing the Korean and Viet-

nam conflicts together constituted a "Rimlands War" that "was fought as part of a general strategy to integrate the periphery more effectively into core economies and part of a specific strategy to sustain Japanese economic recovery, ensure its participation in the world-sytem and keep open the option that China itself might someday be restored to that system and led down a capitalist road." See McCormick, *America's Half-Century*, 111.

25. For the Eisenhower revisionist perspective, see especially Herbert Parmet, *Eisenhower and the American Crusades* (New York: Macmillan, 1972); Robert A. Divine, *Eisenhower and the Cold War* (New York: Oxford University Press, 1981); Stephen E. Ambrose, *Eisenhower*, vol. II, *The President* (New York: Simon and Schuster, 1984). For works dealing more specifically with Dienbienphu, see John Prados, *"The Sky Would Fall": Operation Vulture, the U.S. Bombing Mission, Indochina, 1954* (New York: Doubleday, 1983); Melanie Billings-Yun, *Decision Against War: Eisenhower and Dien Bien Phu, 1954* (New York: Columbia University Press, 1988); George C. Herring and Richard H. Immerman, "Eisenhower, Dulles, and Dienbienphu: 'The Day We Didn't Go to War' Revisited," *Journal of American History*, 71 (September 1984): 343–363; Richard H. Immerman, "Between the Unattainable and the Unacceptable: Eisenhower and Dienbienphu," in *Reevaluating Eisenhower: American Foreign Policy in the Fifties*, Richard A. Melanson and David Mayers, eds. (Urbana: University of Illinois Press, 1987), 120–154; and the essays in Kaplan, Artaud, and Rubin, eds., *Dien Bien Phu*.

26. Herring and Immerman, "Eisenhower, Dulles, and Dienbienphu," 363.

27. Kahin, *Intervention*.

28. David L. Anderson, *Trapped By Success: The Eisenhower Administration and Vietnam, 1953–61* (New York: Columbia University Press, 1991). The quote is from 197.

29. R. B. Smith, *An International History of the Vietnam War*, vol. I, *Revolution Versus Containment, 1955–61* (New York: St. Martin's 1983); and vol. II, *The Stuggle for Southeast Asia, 1961–65* (New York: St. Martin's, 1985).

30. McCormick, *America's Half-Century*, 147.

31. *Ibid.*, 148.

32. Hearden, *Tragedy of Vietnam*, 76. For a similar perspective, see Noam Chomsky, *Rethinking Camelot: JFK, the Vietnam War, and U.S. Political Culture* (Boston: South End Press, 1993).

33. John M. Newman, *JFK and Vietnam: Deception, Intrigue, and the Struggle for Power* (New York: Warner Books, 1992).

34. Lawrence J. Bassett and Stephen E. Pelz, "The Failed Search for Victory: Vietnam and the Politics of War," in *Kennedy's Quest for Victory: American Foreign Policy, 1961–1963*, Thomas G. Paterson, ed. (New York: Oxford Univesity Press, 1989), 223–52; Larry Berman, *Planning a Tragedy: The Americanization of the War in Vietnam* (New York: Norton, 1982).

35. In addition to the broad overviews discussed above (and cited in notes 5–9), the following recent studies also fall within the eclectic boundaries of the liberal realist school: Brian VanDeMark, *Into the Quagmire: Lyndon Johnson and the Escalation of the Vietnam War* (New York: Oxford University Press, 1991); David L. DiLeo, *George Ball, Vietnam, and the Rethinking of Containment* (Chapel Hill: University of North Carolina Press, 1991); John P. Burke and Fred I. Greenstein, *How Presidents Test Reality: Decisions on Vietnam, 1954 and 1965* (New York, 1991); David M. Barrett, *Uncertain Warriors: Lyndon B. Johnson and His Vietnam Advisers* (Lawrence: University Press of Kansas, 1993); Gary R. Hess, "Commitment in the Age of Counter-insurgency: Kennedy's Vietnam Options and Decisions, 1961–1963," in *Shadow on the White House*, 63–86; George C. Herring, *LBJ and Vietnam: A Different Kind of War* (Austin: University of Texas Press, 1994); Robert D. Schulzinger, " 'It's Easy to Win a War on Paper': The United States and Vietnam,

1961–1968," in *The Diplomacy of the Crucial Decade: American Foreign Relations During the 1960s*, Diane B. Kunz, ed. (New York: Columbia University Press, 1994), pp. 183–218; Walter LaFeber, "Johnson, Vietnam, and Tocqueville," in *Lyndon Johnson Confronts the World: American Foreign Policy, 1963–1968*, Warren I. Cohen and Nancy Bernkopf Tucker, eds. (New York: Cambridge University Press, 1994), pp. 31–55; Richard H. Immerman, " 'A Time in the Tide of Men's Affairs': Lyndon Johnson and Vietnam," in *Lyndon Johnson Confronts the World*, pp. 57–97; and H. W. Brands, *The Wages of Globalism: Lyndon Johnson and the Limits of American Power* (New York: Oxford University Press, 1995), pp. 219–253. The imaginative study by Yuen Foong Khong, *Analogies at War: Korea, Munich, Dien Bien Phu, and the Vietnam Decisions of 1965* (Princeton: Princeton University Press, 1992), which utilizes cognitive psychology to probe the worldviews of Johnson administration officials, might also be grouped within the liberal realist tradition.

36. Cumings, " 'Revising Postrevisionism'," 566.

37. Kolko, *Anatomy of a War*, 335

38. *Ibid.*, 334.

39. For further discussion of these points, see Robert J. McMahon, "Nixon, Kissinger, and the Costs of Empire," *Peace and Change* 20 (April 1995), 215–23.

40. Loren Baritz, *Backfire: A History of How American Culture Led Us into Vietnam* (New York: Morrow, 1985); Gibson, *Perfect War*.

41. George C. Herring, " 'Peoples Quite Apart': Americans, South Vietnamese, and the War in Vietnam," *Diplomatic History*, 14 (Winter 1990), 1–23; Sandra C. Taylor, "Lyndon Johnson and the Vietnamese," in *Shadow on the White House*, 113–29.

42. John W. Dower, *War Without Mercy: Race and Power in the Pacific War* (New York: Pantheon, 1985).

43. Susan Jeffords, *The Remasculinization of America: Gender and the Vietnam War* (Bloomington: Indiana University Press, 1989).

44. Lance Morrow, "Men: Are They Really That Bad?" *Time*, 143 (February 14, 1994), 58.

45. Two younger scholars whose work may meet those exacting standards are Mark Bradley and Robert Brigham. For their preliminary assessment of available Vietnamese sources on the war, see Mark Bradley and Robert Brigham, "Vietnamese Archives and Scholarship on the Cold War Period: Two Reports," Working Paper No. 7, Cold War International History Project, Woodrow Wilson International Center for Scholars, September 1993.

46. Anderson, *Trapped by Success*, 90.

47. Jeffrey Race, *War Comes to Long An: Revolutionary Conflict in a Vietnamese Province* (Berkeley: University of California Press, 1972); James Walker Trullinger, Jr., *Village At War* (New York: Longman, 1980); Eric M. Bergerud, *The Dynamics of Defeat: The Vietnam War in Hau Nghia Province* (Boulder, CO: Westview, 1991).

48. See, for example, John W. Garver, "The Chinese Threat in the Vietnam War," *Parameters*, 22 (Spring 1992): 73–85; Qiang Zhai, "Transplanting the Chinese Model: Chinese Military Advisers and the First Vietnam War, 1950–1954," *Journal of Military History*, 57 (October 1993): 689–715; Chen Jian, "China and the First Indo-China War, 1950–1954," *China Quarterly*, 133 (March 1993): 85–110; and Chen Jian, "China's Involvement with the Vietnam War, 1964–1969," *China Quarterly*, forthcoming.

Chapter Thirteen

Bringing Korea Back In:
Structured Absence, Glaring Presence, and Invisibility

BRUCE CUMINGS

Consider this statement on Korean history around the time of Christ:

> The significance of sinicised Choson, and later settlements in Korea spon-
> sored by the Han emperors, lay in their long-term cultural influence on
> Japan. In time the Korean peninsula became the main conduit through
> which Chinese culture flowed to the Japanese islands.

This was written in 1993.[1] It could have been written at any time since Japan
rose up more quickly in the Western imagination than did Korea, namely,
after 1868; but not before. What's wrong with the quotation? First, Korea was
never "Sinicized," although it came close in the period 1392–1910 (that is,
outside the time nearly two millennia ago to which this author refers). Certainly it was not Sinicized when walled mini-states contested for power on the
peninsula, in the centuries just after Christ. Second: Is there no other significance to Korea than its "long-term" effects in conducting Chinese influence
by remote control to Japan? Was that influence unchanged by its passage

through Korean hands? Did China exercise no "cultural influence" on Korea, but only on Japan? If not, why not? If so, why emphasize and dwell upon Japan, and not Korea?

From the inroads of the Western imperial powers in East Asia right down to the moment at which I am writing, non-Koreans have had trouble taking Koreans seriously, in understanding Koreans as actors in history. The history of the past century, in which Korea fell victim to imperialism and could not establish its own constructions of the past, makes us think that if Koreans are Confucians, or Buddhists, or establish a civil service exam system, they must therefore have become "Sinicized." The world is more complex than that, and Korean history is stronger than that.

Now consider this statement:

> Korean Americans know themselves to be individuals with roots and con-
> text, people with rich and complex histories, thoughts, feelings, and flam-
> boyant dreams. But most Americans see us primarily through the lens of
> race; they see us as all alike and caring only about ourselves.[2]

Today there are more than a million Korean-Americans, living all over the country but with big clusters in Los Angeles and New York. They are mostly invisible to the dominant white majority, until they start showing up in big numbers at elite universities (in which case they become a "model minority") or in big numbers after the 1992 Los Angeles disorders—in which case they become an aggrieved minority put upon by Afro-Americans, just like the aggrieved white majority: "victims" of black violence. In the aftermath Elaine Kim wrote that the worst thing was the lack of *voice* for the Korean who experienced the riots. Korean-Americans could not "speak" in any relevant way, in this very recent American experience.[3]

It is one thing for Ted Koppel and *ABC Nightline*[4] to forget that Koreans can speak for themselves. It is quite another for some of the most recent scholarly literature to continue whiting out Koreans as actors in history, or to shine a brilliant light upon South Korea as a "miracle" economy, with the same blinding effect. Ralph Ellison's *Invisible Man* should have taught us that you are stereotyped when people cannot see you and look right through you, or when they spotlight you for attributes they never thought you had: "a cred-it to your race."

In this essay I would like to examine some new literature on Korean-American relations (conceived broadly), in the light, the shadows, and the darkness of this theme.

New Light on Korean-American First Encounters

There is a further curiosity, an intensifying subtlety in human stereotyping, which is to credit you with things you did not do, or claim a presence when there was an absence, so that you will feel good about yourself. 1982 was the centennial of the U.S.-Korean Treaty of Amity and Commerce, occasioning an outpouring of commemorative volumes which, predictably, did not move the scholarly literature forward one iota. Over and over the assembled scholars announced the importance of this, Korea's first "modern" treaty, convened and duly signed by two sovereign, independent, and equal nations.[5] One volume acknowledged a bit of strain between the two countries, owing to unrequited passion: the Korean people "have kept a sort of one-sided 'love affair' with the United States for a very long time," but the American people have still not responded sufficiently to their assiduous courting."[6]

It was of course the second such treaty, but the first was with Japan (in 1876) and Koreans perceive that to be mere prelude to Japan swallowing their country, so prefer to ignore that one. It was a classic unequal treaty of the imperial era. Not-very-sovereign Korea's politically dictated absence in 1882 turns into its fictive presence in 1982, all in the waving of a celebratory wand. As we will see, this wand also let the current Korean regime under Chun Doo Hwan—the most unpopular in South Korean history, which also detonated the worst anti-Americanism in history—off without criticism or remotely objective analysis—hardly a surprise considering that funding sources in Seoul paid for most of the 1982 conferences and volumes.

Fortunately we now have a good biography of the American who negotiated the 1882 treaty, Commodore Robert W. Shufeldt. Li Hung-chang, great "self-strengthener" of late-nineteenth-century China, secretly negotiated the Korean deal with Shufeldt in Tientsin, even to the point of selecting Korea's new national flag (and still the flag of South Korea). They then presented the finished document to the Koreans. As Frederick Drake aptly put it, Shufeldt "was discussing the treaty with the viceroy of Chihli ... writing it in Tientsin in the Chinese language, and arranging it through the agency of China's diplomats for a Korean official he had never formally met and had seldom seen!"[7]

A Chinese official took Shufeldt to Inchon to sign the treaty, weighing anchor in heavy fog on the ship *Swatara* on May 8, 1882 and arriving off Korea the next day. On May 20 Shufeldt presented his credentials to Korean officials, with this prefatory flourish: "Great America. Imperial Decree of Commodore Shufeldt U.S.N. Special Envoy with full power." He came ashore two days later to sign the treaty. Little noticed back home, the achievement nonetheless duly impressed the commodore: he had accomplished, he later wrote, "the feat of bringing the last of the exclusive countries within the pale of Western Civilization."[8]

Li Hung-chang made sure that another naval officer arrived to sign the British treaty five days later, and a German envoy arrived by June. All three treaties were identical in substance, and they signaled Li's success at taking over Korea's foreign policy; all he had really wanted to do was find a way to protect China's eastern flank.[9] As for Shufeldt, he was proud to the point of prurience with his climactic feat: he now hoped that Korea and China would come to look beyond Japan for the source of the rising sun, and then (mixing metaphors), come together on the bridal couch with a new American empire of the Pacific:

> as everything that is bright comes from the East—even as the sun rises in the East & as still the Star of Empire westward takes its way—so China must look to the shores of America for a new Civilization & a more vigorous regeneration. This is the natural course of events, the true march of human progress, the irresistible flow of the human tide. . . . The pacific [sic] is the ocean bride of America—China & Japan & Corea—with their innumerable islands, hanging like necklaces about them, are the bridesmaids, California is the nuptial couch, the bridal chamber, where all the wealth of the Orient will be brought to celebrate the wedding. Let us as Americans—see to it that the 'bridegroom cometh' . . . let us determine while yet in our power, that no commercial rival or hostile flag can float with impunity over the long swell of the Pacific [sic] sea. . . . It is on this ocean that the East & the West have thus come together, reaching the point where search for Empire ceases & human power attains its climax.[10]

The three Western nations got extraterritorial rights in Korea for their citizens, consular representation, fixed tariffs, port concessions, and other benefits; Korea got a routinely commonplace "use of good offices" clause that, ever since, has been misinterpreted by Koreans who think it meant the U.S. would or should protect them from Japan. The main point is made by a fine historian: the treaties "violated Korean sovereignty,"[11] whether under the old rules or the new. With the 1882 agreements Korea was fully hooked into the system of unequal treaties, a process begun by Japan and finished by China—both of which were then subject to the same system.

If, for the centennial cheerleaders, the United States was the white-gloved benefactor of Korea in the early period, Japan and Russia were the blackguards. We now have a new study of Japan's encroachment on Korea by Peter Duus. Although it breaks much new ground in examining the economic activities of Japanese merchants and textile industrialists in Korea, it merely repeats the common scholarly view that an enlightened and terribly modern Meiji leadership had to drag recalcitrant old Korea kicking and screaming into the late-nineteenth century international system.[12] As for Russia, the late and indefatigable George Lensen plowed up entirely new territory in his two-volume study of Russian diplomacy in Korea, based on deep archival research and published exactly in the same centennial year of 1982. Out of it comes a Russian diplomacy more benign than either England's or Japan's, and certainly no more self-interested than America's. Lensen has a sober analysis of Russian aims in Korea, arguing that the Tsars never were willing to do much to get from Korea the infamous "warm water port" that subsequent generations assumed to have been the daily goal of Moscow's diplomacy, and no longer desired it at all after leasing Port Arthur on the China mainland.[13]

Lensen was even able to deconstruct the hoary myths surrounding King Kojong's sojourn in the Russian legation in 1896–97: it turns out to have been Kojong who hastened to the Russian embrace, not vice-versa. On the morning of February 11, 1896, in order to escape Japanese ministrations, the king and his crown prince disguised themselves as court ladies and fled to the Russian legation. There they remained for almost exactly one year.[14] Kojong quickly fired his pro-Japanese cabinet, but he did not really become a creature of the Russians. He continued to work with another indefatigable man, the American Horace Allen, and was "more Japanophobe than Russophile," in Lensen's words. Although the Russians were like every other foreign mission in believing the Koreans hapless and unable to govern themselves without a strong foreign hand behind the king, they interfered little in the internal affairs of Korea during the period that Kojong was in the legation, and it was Kojong who feared returning to his own palace. Thus he was no Tsarist prisoner.[15] (Arguments to the contrary are many, and Lensen discusses them, but they are usually shaped not by the facts but either by the interests of British and Japanese diplomacy at the time, or the posthaste hindsight that came with the arrival of Soviet troops in Korea after World War II.)

During Kojong's sojourn with the Russians, however, Tokyo and Moscow began conjuring with the idea of dividing Korea into spheres of influence. Negotiations in May 1896 in Moscow nearly yielded a partition of Korea along a mid-peninsula boundary line, although apparently not at the 38th or 39th parallel as many historians have claimed. Their agreement did result, however, in the creation of a demilitarized zone between their respective forces.[16]

Other recent archivally based work on the late nineteenth century would also include Jongsuk Chay's *Diplomacy of Asymmetry*,[17] which seeks to fill the gap in studies of late-nineteenth century Korean-American relations that, he says, opened up between *God, Mammon and the Japanese* in 1944 and everything since: that is, Chay thinks there is no work that surpasses Fred Harvey Harrington's. Neither do I, and that is still true in 1995. Chay's book is a serious work of history, drawing upon primary sources in English, Korean, and Japanese (although mostly American-based English sources), and it will reward particularly people looking for an overview of the period 1866–1910. Robert Swartout's study of Owen Denney[18] is nicely done and will hold the interest of specialists; like the Chay volume it makes no new departures either in interpretation or historical method. Yur-bok Lee took as his subject the German adviser to Korea, Paul Georg von Möllendorff, an eccentric and colorful figure who "went Korean," learning the language, dressing in the garb of a Korean official, and introducing any number of progressive ideas to his Korean counterparts.[19] If this study does not bear directly on Korean-American relations, it is well-done (if traditional) diplomatic history and provides insight into the German models of development that Japan and Korea have often favored over comparable American models.

Korean Eclipse

Much of the existing writing on Japan's seizure and colonization of Korea virtually whites out any Korean role in a crucial period of modern history that lasted forty years, from 1905 to 1945. For one thing Koreans don't write much twentieth-century history based in primary materials, and neither do the Japanese. The colonial period was a virtual "black box" for decades in the literature. For another, historians in both Koreas indulge in myths that no one collaborated except a handful of "national traitors" (the South) or that everyone resisted except for classes of sordid compradors and pusillanimous aristocrats (the North). It cannot have been that way, and of course it wasn't. Several recent archivally based studies have unflinchingly illuminated the real history of the colonial period, locating the starting point of a particular model of Korean industrialization, documenting the resistance of Kim Il Sung and his allies for the first time, and examining some of the most appalling experiences Koreans suffered under Japanese rule.

Carter Eckert has identified the kernel of Japan's colonial "administrative guidance" in the Government-General's Industrial Commission of 1921, which for the first time called for supports to Korea's fledgling textile industry and for it to produce not just for the domestic market, but especially for exports to the Asian continent, where Korean goods would have a price advantage. This was by no means a purely "top-down" exercise, either, for

Koreans were part of the Commission and quickly called for state subsidies and hothouse "protection" for Korean companies.[20] That Japan had much larger ideas in mind, however, is obvious in the proposal for "General Industrial Policy" put before the 1921 conference:

> Since Korea is a part of the imperial domain, industrial plans for Korea should be in conformity with imperial industrial policy. Such a policy must provide for economic conditions in adjacent areas, based on [Korea's] geographical position amid Japan, China, and the Russian Far East.

One of the Japanese delegates explained that Korean industry would be integral to the empire-wide planning going on in Tokyo, and would require some protection if it were to accept its proper place in "a single, coexistent, coprosperous Japanese-Korean unit."[21]

As the 1920s drew to a close and the depression dawned, Japan girded its loins at home for trade competition, inaugurating tendencies in its political economy that remain prominent today; here was an early version of what is now termed "export-led development." Both Chalmers Johnson and Miles Fletcher date the origins of Japan's national industrial strategy and "administrative guidance" from the mid- to late 1920s. The Export Association Law of 1925 was an important turning point, stimulating industrial reorganization, cartels, and various state subsidies to exporters.[22] Also visible at this early point was the developmental model of state-sponsored loans at preferential interests rates as a means to shape industrial development and take advantage of "product cycle" advantages that Jung-en Woo has explored, yielding firms whose paid-in capital was often much less than their outstanding debt. Businessmen did not offer shares on a stock market, but went to state banks for their capital. Strategic investment decisions were in the hands of state bureaucrats, state banks, and state corporations (like the Oriental Development Company), meaning that policy could move "swiftly and *sequentially*," in Woo's words, and in ways that influenced South Korea in the 1960s and 1970s.

By the mid-1930s this sort of financing had became a standard practice: the key institution at the nexus of this model was the Korean Industrial Bank (*Chōsen Shokusan Ginkō*), the main source of capital for big Korean firms. Koreans were gaining experience in this bank; about half of its employees were Korean by the end of the colonial period. Meanwhile the Bank of Chōsen played the role of central bank and provisioned capital throughout the imperial realm in Northeast China. It had twenty branches in Manchukuo, served as fiscal agent for Japan's Kwantung Army, and also had an office in New York to vacuum up American loans for colonial expansion. On the side it "trafficked in opium, silver and textile smuggling," and participated in the ill-famed Nishihara Loan, designed to buy off Chinese opposition to Japan's "twenty-one demands," about nineteen of which bit off pieces of Chinese sovereignty. Most important for Korea, however, was the Industrial Bank's role under Ariga Mitsutoyo (1919–1937) in "jump-starting Korea's first industrial and commercial entrepreneurs, men such as Min T'ae-shik, Min Kyu-sik, Pak Hông-sik, and Kim Yôn-su."[23]

Government-General subsidies to Korea's first "chaebôl" or conglomerate began in 1924 with Kim Sông-su's Kyôngbang Textile Company, amounting to 4 percent of its capital, and continued every year thereafter until 1935 (except for the depression year of 1932–33), by which time they accounted for one-quarter of the firm's capital. Kim Sông-su got loans from the Industrial Bank of ¥80,000 in 1920 and one triple that size in 1929, allowing a major expansion of his textile business. For the next decade Kyôngbang got several million yen worth of loans from this bank, so that by 1945 its ¥22 million outstanding debt was more than twice the company's worth.[24]

The modal *zaibatsu* organization was not Kim's, however, but Noguchi Jun's "new" one, a very close model for postwar South Korea's *chaebôl* (the characters are the same as for *zaibatsu*). Noguchi, who was known as the "king" of Korean industry, had his own little empire in the colony that accounted for more than one-third of Japan's total direct investment in Korea and included firms dealing in magnesium, coal, oil, explosives, aluminum, and zinc, in addition to his major firms in chemicals. He also built 90 percent of Korea's electric resources, including the great Suiho Dam on the Yalu, second in the world only to Boulder Dam. In Barbara Molony's recent study, we find located in northern Korea the second-largest chemical complex in the world, one which provided the starting point for North Korea's postwar chemicals industry, something integral to its self-reliant industrial policy— just as it was to Japan's.[25] Noguchi's main plant, the Chösen Nitrogenous Fertilizer Company, was at Hûngnam. It made ammonium sulfates and phosphates, most of which went to Japan. As Hermann Lautensach shows in the best study of Korean geography and resources in the colonial period, long unavailable in English, in 1936 its production was one-eighth of that in the whole German empire—and Germany was the largest producer of chemicals in the world. Noguchi was able to build this huge complex because of nearby hydroelectric facilities which provided cheap energy, especially the Chosin (Changjin) Reservoir.[26]

Noguchi explained at another industrial commission in 1936 how he integrated Korean workers into his industrial combine, a policy that Chun Doo Hwan returned to in the 1980s to keep out "disguised workers," that is, students who tried to organize labor in the factories:

the Koreans I employed as workers [at first] were generally graduates of higher common school. But Russian communism was rampant in North and South Hamgyông Provinces, and scores of arrests were carried out around this time. On each such occasion many of the criminals came from my factory. . . . I decided from that time on never to employ any higher common school graduates in my factories . . . the higher common schools are spending a good sum of money on producing people not very useful to business.[27]

Hermann Lautensach was no apologist for colonialism, but he was much impressed by the rapid development of Korea in the late 1930s. Here was an "obvious, indeed astonishing success," even if the development was "oriented toward the needs of the empire." This, combined with a succession of excellent harvests in 1936–38, yielded the idea of a "Korean boom:" with "the rapid development of all of Korea's economic capacity . . . a certain amount of prosperity is beginning to enter even the farmer's huts."[28] The northeast corner of Korea, long backward, was "experiencing an upswing unlike any other part of Korea," mainly because of its incorporation into Manchukuo trading networks.[29]

Also in this region existed the only serious resistance to Japanese rule in or near Korea by the 1930s, namely, the guerrilla resistance led by Kim Il Sung, Kim Ch'aek, Ch'oe Yong-gôn, Ch'oe Hyôn, and several other people who would structure the high leadership of postwar North Korea for many decades. Wada Haruki, a superb historian at Tokyo University, is using Russian, Chinese, American, Japanese, and North Korean archival materials to assess the rise to power of Kim Il Sung, the nature of the North Korean regime, its relations with the USSR and China, and its responsibility for the outbreak of the Korean War. Thus far he has published one book in Japanese,[30] which is now the definitive text on the Korean anti-Japanese movement in 1930s Manchuria and one with the original argument that the postwar Democratic People's Republic of Korea is a singular "guerrilla state," founded on the political, military, and social experience of the Manchurian guerrillas. After decades of hagiography by North Koreans and the diametric opposite by South Koreans (seeking to deny that Kim Il Sung was anything but an imposter), we can now locate and understand the colonial background of one of the Kims who would influence postwar history.

Another such Kim was Kim Sông-su, the core figure in a group of landlords and industrialists from southwestern Korea, who got very rich in the colonial period and later played major roles in postwar South Korea. Kim was born into a wealthy, aristocratic family that possessed something more like a plantation of rice paddies rather than the typically small farms that dotted

Korea. The ancestral spread was near the coast in Koch'ang where North and South Chôlla Provinces come together, and where the family's influence is still strongly felt. Kim founded the *Tonga ilbo* (*East Asia Daily*), the leading Korean newspaper after 1920, and the Kobu School in Chôlla and Posông College, later Korea University, in Seoul—where his statue stood until the 1980s, when radical students demanded that it be removed. Besides land-holdings, the core of this fortune was the aforementioned Kyôngsông Textile Company. Sông-su's brother Kim Yôn-su ran this enterprise, which by the 1940s had become Korea's first multinational firm, with a new factory in Manchuria. Its interests included three ginning factories, a huge factory for spinning and weaving in Seoul's Yôngdûngp'o industrial district, a bleaching and dyeing factory, silk thread and cloth factories; also industries such as ball bearings, brewing, gold mining, real estate, metal, oil refining, and even air-craft. In his study of this important family, Carter Eckert does not flinch from documenting its collaboration with Japanese militarism in the 1940s.[31]

If there was growth enough in the colony for some Koreans to do well, there was uprooting and dislocation enough for a huge number of Koreans to do badly. I have documented in my earlier work this vast population move-ment in the last decade of colonial rule,[32] but we have a new book by George Hicks on the mobilization of enormous numbers of Korean women for sex-ual slavery. These "comfort women" became a major issue in recent years between Japan and Korea. The issue was "settled" superficially in 1994 when the Japanese offered $20,000 in compensation to the survivors. One reason why the Japanese were able to keep the lid on this story for so long was that the South Korean government was not interested in opening it up, as many of the women had been mobilized not only by Japanese officials, but also by Koreans. Japanese colonialism fractured the Korean national psyche, pitting Korean against Korean with consequences that continue down to our time.

Somewhere between 100,000 and 200,000 Korean women were mobilized into this slavery, along with smaller numbers of Filipinos, Chinese, and a handful of Westerners. Pae Pong Gi was the first Korean woman to come for-ward and tell her story with her identity unprotected, in Yamatani Tetsuo's 1979 film, *An Old Lady In Okinawa*. "Like so many other comfort women," Hicks writes, she "remained in the same role with the American Occupation Forces on Okinawa." Yun Chong Mo's novel, *My Mother was a Military Com-fort Woman*," was inspired by "the sight of a drunken American soldier drag-ging a girl by the hair in a Seoul street."[33] There is a direct step from this recent literature to a new study by Saundra Sturdevant and Brenda Stoltzsfus, crank-ing open the lid on the multitudes of Korean women who have serviced the American military presence in Korea over the past fifty years.[34]

Hicks also has a fascinating account of another colonial "mobilization detail." In late 1944 Japanese authorities dragooned some 7,000 Koreans to build a huge, labyrinthine underground bunker near Mount Fuji for the Imperial household and other high officials of government; it was preparatory to the "decisive battle for the Homeland" that never came, and was completed just before Japan surrendered. An untold number of Koreans died during the hasty, pell-mell blasting out tunnels and caves, with little or no precaution for their safety (at least 1000 perished), and persistent rumors claim that those laborers who constructed the Emperor's inner sanctum were later killed because of the secrets they knew. Here too, women were thrown into a "comfort" station for the construction workers, "housed in a refitted silkworm workshop" which the police rented from its owner.[35]

World War II ended with tens of thousands of Koreans annihilated in Hiroshima and Nagasaki—most of them conscripted laborers in war industries. This awful insult to the human fodder that Japanese leaders moved hither and thither in their empire was not the final one, however; after the war the last irradiated survivors anyone cared about were the Koreans, written off on racial grounds by Tokyo and given no help from a Seoul government ashamed of their existence.

It Wasn't a Korean War?

The collapse of the Soviet Union and the partial opening of some of its archives has occasioned a new literature on the Korean War. By and large this literature reflects the continuing influence of the Korean national division and the continuing cold war on the peninsula, neither of them ended yet in spite of proclamations about "the end of history" on a world scale since 1989. Some of this work is archivally based, and some of it is war-fixated. By war-fixated I mean the ideological construction of the Korean War as a war which was not about Korea, but a conflict limited to the time period 1950–53, detonated by Soviet-American rivalry, maybe with the Chinese revolution thrown in; the most important question to be asked is who can be blamed for starting it; the second-ranking question is why did the Chinese join the war? To answer these questions you need to read the archives in Washington, Moscow and Beijing. The war-fixated literature has its own way of whiting out Koreans and their history, with the way inaugurated and lit by the man who directed the American intervention in Korea, Secretary of State Dean Acheson.

In one of Acheson's first attempts to construct the history of the Korean War, something he later did with such polished ventriloquy that most of his core judgments have entered the American literature as considered conclusions,[36] he remarked that it "isn't a Korean War." He started this way:

> Korea is not a local situation. It is not the great value of Korea itself which led to the attack. It isn't that *they* [sic] wanted square miles in Korea. But it was the spearpoint of a drive made by the whole Communist control group on the entire power position of the West—primarily in the East, but also affecting the whole world. Surely their purpose was to solidify Korea—but it was also to unsettle Japan, South East Asia, Philippines, and to gain all of South East Asia, and to effect situation also in Europe. That is what the war in Korea is being fought about.

And he went on, "instead of doing what the enemy set out to do, the enemy has done the exact opposite. Nothing they could have done would be more calculated to defeat their own purpose. It is all their own stupidity." Korea was a "testing ground" for both sides, "that is the global strategy of the global purpose of both sides. It isn't a Korean war on either side."[37]

Such thinking extruded most of what I discussed in my study of the Korean War, that is, it extruded Koreans and their history, deemed irrelevant to the real issues.[38] The current rewriting of Korean War history is based on scattered and often privileged access to Soviet and Chinese documents, with no scholar given full access. This literature is one-sided and premature. It is one-sided in that it purports to write the history of the Korean War without using Korean sources. It is premature in that no serious historian ought to make judgments about specific documents without access to the full run of similar documents, since it is not the "smoking gun" document but the weight of the evidence that makes it possible to render mature historical judgment. Moreover, the emphasis on Moscow's documents has directed attention away from Washington's documents—both those that have appeared and those that have not. We need balanced attention to what we already know from Washington's side, rather than yet another attempt to refight the Cold War by citing Moscow's documents in isolation.

Based on the documentation from the early American occupation of South Korea, there is no longer the slightest question that the U.S. moved as quickly as one could imagine to set up a government with separate executive, police, and military arms in September–November 1945. It matters little what the Soviets may or may not have been doing in Pyongyang, because the American authors of these decisions instantly assumed the worst about Moscow's intentions, but more important, they could not govern their zone without suppressing the many leftwing organizations that sprouted in southern Korea. When central figures (like Acheson) got hold of Korea policy circa

1947, they could only imagine that this separated government could sustain itself by restitching its economic ties with a reindustrialized Japan, and that became the policy that governed the American intervention in Korea in 1950—quite irrespective of what the Soviets, the Chinese, or the North Koreans might have been doing. This we know because of the archival work done by William Borden and Michael Schaller, tied to a theory of political economy *without which* this episode would have remained unexplained, no matter how good the documents.[39]

In 1977 U.S. declassification authorities released several thousand archival boxes of North Korean materials seized during MacArthur's march to the Yalu. Several scholars—including Haruki Wada, Dae-Sook Suh, Charles Armstrong, and myself—have used these materials. They document many things, but the main point is this: why privilege a document from Washington, Moscow, or Beijing over Korean *captured* documents, which cannot have been combed by declassification censors (at least not those in Pyongyang)? I am unaware of any citation of these materials in the post-Cold War literature, including the best of it.[40]

Scholars focusing on Soviet and Chinese documents show no interest in the coup d'etat Dean Rusk and others were running against Chiang Kai-shek on the last weekend in June 1950. No interest in the secret testimony of the American commander in Korea in the summer of 1949 that South Koreans were lunging across the parallel and starting most of the fighting, much of it substantial and involving hundreds of troops, in the period May–December 1949. No interest in Dean Acheson's knowledge of this, which prompted him to get the United Nations to send military observers to Korea to watch the North *and leash the South*. No interest in John Foster Dulles's many retrospective statements during Eisenhower-era national security council meetings, that if a new Korean War starts, we won't know how it started.

From the new Soviet and Chinese documents we have learned that Kim Il Sung secretly visited both Moscow and Beijing in the spring of 1950, had discussions with both Stalin and Mao about his plans to vanquish the South (both of them appearing wary and reluctant, but ultimately supportive), and that the Russians later shipped military materiel as additions to what they had left in or sold to North Korea earlier, while the Chinese facilitated the flow back to Korea of thousands of Korean soldiers who fought in the Chinese civil war.

Mostly missing is the context of these visits, a war situation that had been bubbling since the spring of 1949, one in which Syngman Rhee was at least as assiduous (if not as successful) in seeking great-power backing from MacArthur in Tokyo and whoever would listen in Washington, either for an attack on the North (his maximum goal) or an American defense if the North attacked (his minimum goal, which I argued he had achieved in late 1949 through the good offices of intelligence operator M. Preston Goodfellow). Still misunderstood is the simple fact that Washington always assumed that Stalin and Mao backed Kim, regardless of the evidence; still unapprehended is Kim and his regime (now that of his son), which showed remarkable staying power since the "revolutions of 1989," and which can hardly be accounted for by support from Moscow and Beijing, or old stories about Kim licking Stalin's boots to get what he wanted.

The continuing immaturity of studies of this war can be seen in the blithe and often unconscious assumption that one can write the Korean War without Koreans (even to write a definitive "dictionary" of the war without them[41]), or that Koreans are not capable of striking a blow in history when stacked up against the great centers of world politics like Washington, Moscow, and Beijing, or that when they do (even if on behalf of Moscow), their actions become "reckless war-making of the worst kind."[42] A person who had immersed himself in the Korean materials before and during the war could never say such a thing, because the overwhelming testimony of the Korean evidence is that this war had long indigenous beginnings before the end of the Pacific War, let alone the Cold War, and that not one Korean of significance (save a handful of mendicants who spent most of their time massaging the American ego), took the 38th parallel as a line dividing anything but one people with a national integrity going back a millennium. So: reckless war-making, or Koreans invading Korea?

The North Koreans crossed a line that the U.S. thoughtlessly and single-handedly dictated in 1945. The American Occupation proceeded to set up a quasi-colonial government of Koreans staffed from the hirelings of Japanese imperialism, and to place at the forefront of the South Korean army and police people who had fought against the Allies in the Pacific War. Even the very Korean quislings who had tracked Kim and his guerrilla allies in the Manchurian fastness on behalf of Japanese militarism were posted at the most sensitive spots along the 38th parallel in the summer of 1949. That Kim Il Sung's June 1950 act can still be seen as reckless war-making is merely to inscribe on the scholar a kind of auto-induced injury saying, "I cannot think beyond the ideological boundaries established by my country—even after the conflict which established those boundaries has disappeared." It is this nystagmus-like attention span[43] that is the tell-tale sign that the quasi-archivists are still fighting the Cold War.

Americans are by no means alone in whiting out Korean history. If you have any doubt that the Chinese can be just as cavalier and arrogant as anyone else in dismissing Koreans, read Russell Spurr's book on China's entry into the war. Basing his research almost entirely on Chinese informants, Spurr can barely find a single Korean who made a difference in the Korean War, but he does repeat any number of stereotypes of Koreans as hot-blooded, garlic-eating swine who rarely if ever make a difference in battle and are utterly indifferent to the carnage around them.[44]

There is a last genre of work on the Korean War by scholars who use archives, read voraciously in any archive they can get their hands on, and have found a way to step outside state-constructed discourses on Korea. Not so curiously, several of them are British diplomatic historians: Rosemary Foot, Peter Lowe, Callum MacDonald.[45] They are limited to English-language archives, but they have used them (mainly here and in England) to rewrite the history of the Korean War and to establish a high standard for scholarship on the subject. With their work and that of some American scholars, a new threshold has been reached where one can actually debate the events of the Korean War and their significance with people who know what they are talking about.

Not a Korean War? Until a truly multi-archival *consciousness* develops among American diplomatic historians, people will continue to grind axes as if the mute objects of their attentions did not or do not or will not count, a long tradition in the literature going back to Tyler Dennett, but a tradition that now needs a polite burial.

Korean Miracle?

There is now a large literature on Korean development, almost always meaning *South* Korean development (North Korea's stunning absence in much of the literature is another kind of whiting-out or structured absence[46]). Books by Jung-en Woo, Alice Amsden, and Stephan Haggard have done much to remedy the inability of many experts—especially economists—to explain Korea's rapid industrialization.[47]

For Alice Amsden, South Korea succeeded where others failed precisely by "getting prices wrong," in her wonderful phrase. Using theories of "late development" she argues that Korea progressed by intensive technological learning and adaptation. The essence of Woo's argument is this:[48] "The Korean state has moved from a dependent, penetrated status to one of relative autonomy by positioning itself astride the flow of foreign capital, refracting capital in a prismatic fashion to fund rising industries, create mammoth firms, buttress its social support, and in dialectical fashion wrest national autonomy from the external system."

This Korea was dependent: almost completely so. First it was a colony, then it was occupied by a foreign army, then the U.S. retrieved it from oblivion in the summer of 1950. It was penetrated, not least by an American general commanding its army and full divisions of foreign troops. Lacking much domestic capital, the state found a way to use foreign capital and earnings both to reward its friends and promote efficient production. It fostered one rising industry after another, starting with simple assembly operations and ending with microprocessors. It created from scratch octopus-like firms now known to the world as *chaebŏl*. In conditions of often stunning political and social dislocation, it worked effectively to build support and slowly to legitimate its hell-bent-for-leather development program. Ultimately it will wrest from the great powers who divided it a unified Korea which will be among the advanced industrial nations of the next century.

South Korea, truncated into half a country, with almost no natural resources, a thoroughly uprooted and aggrieved population, no domestic capital to speak of, a minuscule domestic market and a workforce long claimed to be lazy louts (a common Japanese refrain): and still here is this industrial country, this "Miracle on the Han." There you have it: no capitalists, no Protestant ethic, no merchants, no money, no market, no resources, no get-up-and-go, not to mention no discernible history of commerce, foreign trade, or industrial development, so on and so forth: And yet there it is. By no means did Koreans "do it" alone, however.

W. W. Rostow had stimulated an enormous debate with his 1960 book, *The Stages of Economic Growth* (subtitled *A Non-Communist Manifesto*), which inaugurated the new, Kennedy-style concern with "nation-building" and economic development. Rostow had been teaching at the Center for International Affairs at Massachusetts Institute of Technology, which had prepared policy papers for the incoming administration that quickly began to influence policy.[49] Rostow was then named a national security adviser to President Kennedy, and he hit the ground running. Within weeks of the inauguration he and his close associate, Robert Komer, had taken a close look at South Korea and argued that in spite of its truncated and isolated condition, it had strong human resources and was an ideal place to develop light industries for export. In a March 15, 1961 memo called "Action in Korea," Komer outlined "the major thrust of U.S. effort[s] over the next decade:" (1) "crash economic development," (2) "creation of light labor-intensive industry," and vigorous U.S. action "in directing and supervising ROK [Republic of Korea] economic development." Komer and Rostow thought Korea had one major, underutilized resource: its people.[50] A major revision of U.S. Korea policy in 1965 embodied the new American judgments. Although it restated Korea's use as a strategic backstop for Japan, it now also touted the ROK as an example, like Taiwan, that "the non-Communist approach to nation-building pays off," and among eight policy goals, number two was "economic growth averaging at least six percent per year" over the five years from 1966–71. Nor was the U.S. unhappy with the strong role of the state in the Korean market: it wished to promote "whatever appears to be the most effective division between the public and private sectors."[51]

Rostow, as Woo points out, was a Schumpeterian: he believed in big leaps forward, not incremental change. When Joel Bernstein, director of the AID mission in Korea, complained that Korean future projections were much too optimistic, the Koreans quoted Rostow back to him. As Bernstein wrote to Rostow,

> You are being quoted as saying that conventional economists always underestimate demand for the products needed in a growing economy, that Korea should not worry about overcapacity because demand is always underestimated, that estimates of requirements should be made in the ordinary way and then everything should be doubled, and that economic development is too serious a matter to leave to economists who do not understand it adequately.

The Koreans, Bernstein thought, had a "damn the torpedoes" attitude, and still did not understand "the principle of marginal utility."[52] Rarely have we had a better example of conventional American economics confronting neo-mercantilism; Bernstein did not win, of course, because the Koreans were right: Rostow was just as Schumpeterian as they were.

The highly conscious agents of the miracle on the Han were state bureaucrats willing to hand out something for something: no-cost money if you put it to good use, building up another industrial prodigy. "Policy loans" for export performance. Then there was so-called "negative interest." That was the rate Park Chung Hee would give you on a few million dollars, if you would throw it into electronics or steel. In Korea the state deployed money in the magical way that Joseph Schumpeter imagined,[53] as a mysterious poof of energy for the incessant innovation that he saw as the motive force of growth. A man goes to a bank with an idea for a better mousetrap, the banker signs a piece of paper, greenbacks pour out like Christmas cookies and all the mice run for cover. If in the American system it is typically the private bank and the entrepreneur whose symbiosis creates this energy, Schumpeter also said that institutions could perform this function—which they did in Korea, even if *chaebôl* coupling with finance ministry isn't quite as romantic. It isn't too hard to imagine the incentive, however, if the bank rate is 20 percent per annum on loans, and the state gives you one for 10 percent, or even 5. People come running for money like that, but they had to perform to keep it coming.

If this system worked intermittently in the 1960s, it worked like clockwork in the 1970s and became the essence of the "Korean model." With huge amounts of petrodollars sloshing through world markets after the OPEC quadrupling of oil prices, with bankers begging people to take loans, the Korean state mediated that flood of money, pointing it toward the immensely expensive "Six Industries" of Park's "big push." For the next fifteen years, Korea borrowed abroad at Latin American rates: foreign debt rose 42 percent shortly after the oil shock, but investment also shot up, to a historic high of 32 percent of GNP in 1974. By the end of the decade Korea was among the big four debtors in the world, led by Brazil; its foreign borrowing from 1976–1979 placed it third, behind Mexico and Brazil, but in the decade 1967–78, Korean debt grew 15-fold, twice the rate of all less-developed countries and well ahead of Mexican and Brazilian borrowing. Korea also, however, grew by an average of 11 percent from 1973 to 1978, with heavy industry accounting for 70 percent of total manufacturing investment. To get the big loans of that period, however, you had to be big already: a *chaebôl*. To keep getting them, you "had to be gigantic."[54]

The central element in the Korean model, then, is finance: and "the main goal of Korea's finance was to hemorrhage as much capital as possible into the heavy industrialization program." According to Jung-en Woo:

> The financial policy . . . was this: the government set financial prices at an artificial low to subsidize import-substituting, heavy, chemical, and export industries. . . . The political economy of this bifurcated financial system was illiberal, undemocratic, and statist. . . . Every bank in the nation was owned and controlled by the state; bankers were bureaucrats and not entrepreneurs, they thought in terms of GNP and not profit, and they loaned to those favored by the state.[55]

The average cost of such loans through much of the 1970s was minus 6.7 percent, whereas the curb rate was also positive, well above the inflation rate. The result was that each favored *chaebôl* "for all practical purposes, was a private agency of public purpose."[56] The public purpose, of course, was to herd them into specific, selected industries that would build the "rich country, strong army" of Park's dreams.

The question for Korea is how a state bureaucracy could allocate credit resources efficiently, that is, rationally; and how could they be wizards of finance, gnomes of Seoul, when every political calculation would push in the

direction of rewarding friends and benefactors at the expense of the com-
monweal? The answer to this question comes in several Korean parts.

First, political leaders do not pay attention to efficiency and rationality, but
to political and, in this case, national efficacy.[57] All kinds of risks disappear
when a company knows that a long-term investment has the backing and the
resources of a highly nationalistic political leadership behind it (like the
American aerospace industry in the 1960s). Second, the Korean ideal of the
civil servant does produce many well-educated people devoted to what is best
for their country and government, and by the 1960s there were many foreign-
trained technocrats who knew how to plan and allocate resources. Third,
there *were* many rewards for friends.

When we compare the work by Amsden and Woo to a much more conventional literature on Korea's "modernization," we return ourselves to the
huzzahs for our good Korean friends found in the 1982 centennial literature,
or the one-eye-to-the-Cold-War biases of so much Korean War literature.
The best example is the Harvard project on the modernization of the Republic of Korea (1945–1975), which occupies a space between the laudatory and
the scholarly genres; its six volumes are useful and represented a milestone in
the serious study of the South Korean economy.[58] But the intellectual basis of
the entire enterprise is an uncritical set of assumptions that South Korean
development not only conforms to the European model of Enlightenment
progress and continuous development toward liberal democracy (or soon
will if it hasn't yet), but also that it can be a model for other developing countries. This project, undertaken jointly by the Harvard Institute for International Development and the Korea Development Institute, presented its "twin
objectives" as follows: "to examine the elements underlying the remarkable
growth of the Korean economy and the distribution of the fruits of that
growth, together with the associated changes in society and government; and
to evaluate the importance of foreign economic assistance, particularly
American assistance, in promoting these changes."[59]

Left out was all that Amsden and Woo speak of, not to mention the
extreme labor agitation and extraordinary political upheaval that accompanied the "Miracle on the Han."

In spite of Korea's continuing growth, all was not rosy in Korean-American relations during the 1970s, even by official accounts. There arose something called "Koreagate," which added a new stereotype to the Korean image
in the U.S.: bribery and corruption. The late Robert Boettcher left an excellent account of this episode, a book that never got the attention it deserved.
This was a thoroughly investigated scandal, at least by the U.S. House International Affairs Committee team under Congressman Donald Fraser, a

Democrat from Minnesota (the Justice Department was much less enthusiastic in getting to the bottom of it).

The scandal had its origins in President Nixon's determination to withdraw part of the American troop contingent from Korea, as part of his "doctrine" of getting Asians to fight Asian wars, especially the Vietnam War which he was systematically escalating with an eye toward eventually winding it down. Park Chung Hee and his allies were absolutely appalled by Nixon's plans, and desperately sought to counter them. In early 1970, for example, Prime Minister Chông Il-gwôn told the American Ambassador, William Porter, that if Nixon tried to take U.S. troops out, he would lie down on the runway so the planes couldn't take off. "Do that, my good friend," Porter replied, "but let me take a picture before the planes begin to roll."[60]

It was actually Vice-President Spiro Agnew who lowered the boom, however, in a bizarre six-hour meeting in August 1970 with Park Chung Hee in which Agnew was denied lunch, coffee, or even a trip to the rest room. One of Agnew's aides remarked that this grueling session was "brutal and absolutely offensive," a performance by a head of state "unlike any I had ever seen." It was all to no avail, however; three days later about 10,000 American troops—rolled out of Korea. Shortly thereafter, in a meeting on August 26, 1970, Park started the influence-peddling ball rolling, hoping to make up in a Democratic-controlled Congress what he had lost in the Nixon White House.[61]

Soon a retinue of Korean Central Intelligence Agency (KCIA) operatives working out of the Korean Embassy in Washington, the Unification Church, and other front organizations, began bribing influential Americans to build up Seoul's influence in the U.S. The prime targets were sitting Congressmen. Even the Ambassador, Kim Dong Jo, got into the act, stuffing envelopes with $100 bills and distributing them on Capitol Hill. The immediate goal was to reverse Nixon's troop withdrawal policy, or assure that no more American troops would leave Korea. But there were many other targets, including several universities that housed critics of the human rights violations of the Park regime.[62] The key—and colorful—figure in this scandal was Tongsun Park, a rice merchant, lobbyist, and *bon vivant* who was under KCIA direction by 1971 if not earlier; Bo Hi Pak, a KCIA officer and later Reverend Mun Sun Myung's righthand man and translator, was another key Koreagate operator.[63]

During the Carter administration the investigation fizzled, and some observers wondered if that might be because so many Democrats were targets of the influence-peddling effort. The Fraser investigation left scholars with a fine study of Korean-American relations in the 1960s and 1970s, however.

The late Donald S. MacDonald also produced a useful survey of U.S.-Korean relations, based on access to much documentation that still remains classified.[64] We are now getting some historical distance on the 1960s, which is reflected in the new information in this study. MacDonald, long a Foreign Service officer and later a scholar of Korea, based his book almost entirely on internal State Department records; it was written for State Department use when he was head of the Korea desk and much later was declassified. MacDonald added a new introduction but otherwise left his study alone.

This book illustrates both the strengths and weaknesses of a diplomatic history based in sources that diplomats write and think to be important: it is full of interesting information and documentation (although several scholars have used the same files for the period 1945–53), and it misses a lot—especially the military side, which has been so important in the U.S. relationship with Korea. MacDonald's sources are very good on the Eisenhower administration, and there are several revelations about the reasons why John Foster Dulles wanted to install nuclear weapons in Korea in 1957–58 (in part to stabilize and forestall an attack by Rhee on the North). Anyone who wants a handy interpretive summary of two decades of diplomacy could hardly do better than to start here. MacDonald's rather bland study becomes more interesting when placed alongside the views of Koreans critical of the American role in Korea in the same period; such views can be sampled in mild form in the compendium, *Alliance Under Tension*.[65]

Not So Miraculous

The Park regime ended in 1979, and out of the resulting turmoil came the Kwangju Rebellion, now a touchstone of Korean-American relations. These disorders had their origin in a declining Korean economy and resulting mass protests in August 1979 that soon led to the assassination of Park by the head of the KCIA, Kim Chae-gyu, on October 29, 1979. Gen. Chun Doo Hwan seized power within the forces of order in a shootout on December 12, 1979, but had not yet made himself President. In late April 1980, however, miners took over a small town near the East coast and Chun named himself head of the KCIA, while keeping his post as head of the Army Security Command. A few weeks earlier the American commander, Gen. John Wickham, had given his blessing to the Korean military's role in politics, which included "being watchdogs on political activity that could be de-stabilizing, and in a way making judgments about the eligibility and reliability of political candidates."[66]

After Chun's actions, demonstrators took to the streets all over the country. By mid-May tens of thousands of students and common people flooded Korea's cities, with demonstrations of at least 50,000 in Seoul. On May 17,

General Chun tried to complete his coup: he declared martial law, closed the universities, dissolved the legislature and banned all political activity, and arrested thousands of political leaders and dissidents in the midnight hours of May 17–18. He also set up a special committee for national security measures, making himself head of the standing committee of the same group. With this action, Chun detonated the Kwangju Rebellion. On May 18 about 500 people took to Kwangju's streets, demanding repeal of martial law. Elite paratroopers landed in the city and began the indiscriminate murder of students, women, children. By May 21 hundreds of thousands of local people had driven the soldiers from the city, which citizen's councils controlled for the next five days. These councils determined that 500 people had already died, with some 960 missing.[67] The citizen's councils appealed to the U.S. Embassy for intervention, but it was left to Gen. Wickham to release the Twentieth Division of the ROK Army from its duties along the demilitarized zone.

Loudspeakers from helicopters warned Kwangju's citizens that the Twentieth Division would enter the city at dawn on May 27; all were to disarm and return to their homes. At 3 A.M. the soldiers came in shooting, killing scores more people who had refused to put down weapons that they had seized from local armories. These units were disciplined, however, and quickly secured the city. Now Chun moved to complete the coup d'etat he had begun on December 12, arresting Kim Dae Jung and blaming the rebellion on him, knocking together an "electoral college" under the barely disguised Yushin system and making himself President of the Fifth Republic. Gen. Roh Tae Woo was one of his closest associates in the suppression of Kwangju and the seizure of power. It will probably never be known how many people died in the Kwangju Rebellion, but Kwangju's death statistics, which had had a monthly average of 2,300, soared to 4,900 deaths in May 1980.[68]

After a show trial that found Kim guilty, his execution was pending when tremendous American pressure was brought to bear to keep him alive. He was given life in prison, and then two years later allowed to go into exile in the U.S. President Ronald Reagan then hurried to invite Chun to Washington as the President's first visiting head of state after his inauguration. His aides told reporters that the U.S. was anxious to shore up relations with Seoul lest North Korea try to fish in troubled waters. Thereafter the Reagan administration sold Chun 36 F-16 jetfighters, added about 4,000 Americans to the existing troop commitment, and established new intelligence facilities.

There may not have been an American alternative to turning a cold shoulder to the citizens of Kwangju, since to deny Chun troops or take the side of Kwangju would have been an intervention with no precedent since the 1940s. But it made hash of Jimmy Carter's human rights policies,[69] and the United

States paid dearly for that inaction in Korean attitudes toward the U.S. Kwangju was Korea's *Tiananmen* nightmare, in which students and young people were slaughtered on the same or greater scale as in "People's" China in June 1989.

Chun had himself inaugurated President in February 1981. In the same year he purged or proscribed the political activities of 800 politicians, 8,000 officials in government and business, and threw some 37,000 journalists, students, teachers, labor organizers, and civil servants into "Purification Camps" in remote mountain areas; some 200 labor leaders were among them. They were said to be boot camps for political miscreants, who would see the error of their ways after lots of pushups, marathon running, small-group criticism and self-criticism, and ideological exhortation.

In one of the 1982 centennial celebrations, Youngnok Koo concluded the volume with this observation:

> The United States, once dimly perceived as no more than a huge, obscure, strange, distant nation, has come to be seen as a familiar and important ally by the Korean people over the past hundred years. According to a recent Dong-A Ilbo and Korea University joint survey, the U.S. was ranked first among the best-liked nations. . . . Yet Korea's high regard for America is not reciprocated; Korea ranked only twelfth, along with Thailand, in a similar survey conducted in the U.S.[70]

This is right about what Americans think of Korea and Koreans, but dead wrong about what Koreans think of Americans. All these celebrations occurred in what was probably the worst period in Korean-American relations in history, namely, the early 1980s aftermath of Kwangju and Chun Doo Hwan's draconian dictatorship that followed it, both of which touched off such violent anti-Americanism that the American Embassy in Seoul came to be surrounded with impervious walls, gates, and granite barriers such as you might find in Beirut. Somehow the celebratory scholars were able to ignore all this, too: the Koo-Suh volume has no index entry for Kwangju.[71]

For several years thereafter it seemed that the Chun regime was stable. All the pundits said it was stable,[72] and American policy determined to keep it so by unprecedented postings of two career CIA employees successively as ambassadors (James Lilley and Donald Gregg). And yet in 1987 it came apart at the seams in a popular mobilization very reminiscent of the ones that would topple East European communist regimes two years later. In spite of the nationwide distaste for Chun's Fifth Republic, obvious to anyone willing to listen to Koreans in the 1980s, in 1987 Chun determined to hand pick his successor and continue to hold power behind the scenes; he had hit one big firm after another for contributions to set up a so-called Ilhae Foundation ("Ilhae" was Chun's penname) from which to continue to rule the roost. In the spring of that year another student had been tortured to death by the police; they claimed it was an accident, but the cover-up of the case unraveled and touched off nationwide demonstrations on June 10. Catholic fathers at the Myôngdong Cathedral harbored students wanted by the authorities, and those still protesting were subjected to merciless repression by riot police. In this atmosphere the ruling party nominated Roh Tae Woo to succeed Chun under the existing anti-democratic system, without any real presidential election. Massive protests ensued, with middle class people now cheering and often joining protesters. From June 10 through 20, all streets in urban areas were virtual battlefields. A mass movement for democracy, embracing students, workers, and many in the middle class, finally brought a democratic breakthrough in Korea—just as similar movements had in the Philippines a year earlier, and as they would in Eastern Europe two years later.[73]

The Reagan Administration was now concerned that a full-fledged revolution might topple the regime. In late June various Americans sought to convince Chun and Roh to change their policies. On June 29, 1987 General Roh Tae Woo announced direct presidential elections for December 1987, an open campaign without threats of repression, amnesties for political prisoners including Kim Dae Jung, guarantees of basic rights, and revision or abolishment of the current Press Law.[74] This was a watershed event, and showed Roh to be a far shrewder politician than Chun; by this simple stroke Roh made himself a plausible candidate in the next election. When the opposition split he proceeded to win it, and ruled until the next election (in 1992) finally got the military out of Korean politics.

Following on the June 1987 breakthrough Korean labor suddenly became extremely active, belying much punditry about its "weakness." In September 1977 *Fortune* magazine had this to say about business in Korea: "What positively delights American business men in Korea is the Confucian work ethic.... Work, as Koreans see it, is not a hardship. It is a heaven-sent opportunity to help family and nation. The fact that filial piety extends to the boss-worker relationship comes as a further surprise to Americans accustomed to labor wrangling at home."[75]

Korean labor was also said to be "weak,"[76] presumably another good thing (even if American business quickly found out that it wasn't so). It is one thing for *Fortune* to say such things; that is the job of its writers. I still do not understand why the immense sacrifice that the Korean people made to drag their country into the late twentieth century should merit such uncritical enthusiasm from academics who presumably are not paid for their views.

For many years the Urban Industrial Mission (UIM), an organization run by Christians, sought to make Korean workers aware of their rights. George Ogle, a Methodist missionary who first arrived in Korea in 1954, worked with the UIM for twelve years until the Park regime deported him in 1974. (Ogle had defended eight men who had been tortured into confessing that they were part of a communist conspiracy.) He later wrote an excellent study of Korean labor, which, along with Jang Jip Choi's superb study,[77] has added much depth to our understanding. Ogle thought the Korean labor movement of the 1970s and 1980s played a major role in transforming the Korean system away from harsh authoritarianism, much like the Solidarity movement in Poland. Unlike Solidarity, however, the sacrifices of Korean workers have been met in the West with a "stony silence."[78]

It would be difficult to overestimate the importance of the 1988 Summer Olympics to the Chun and Roh governments of the 1980s, since this was to be the coming-out party for the Miracle on the Han, just as the 1964 Olympics had brought Japan's economic prowess to the world's attentions. It is also doubtful that Roh Tae Woo would have made the dramatic announcement about direct elections on June 29, 1987 had the Olympics not been pending.

The games went off with only the North Koreans and Cubans boycotting, and for the first time since 1976 the Americans and the Russians were both there, and the competition was splendid. The opening ceremony was a magnificent homage to Korean culture, both the high if constricted one of the Confucians and the low but diverse and vital one of the masses. The organic choreography of masses of people was worthy of a Kim Il Sung extravaganza (and often like it). Predictably the herd of foreign journalists who descended for a look at Korea did not like what they saw: too noisy, too spicy, too proud, too nationalistic, these people. Thus the commentary ranged from the blatant racism of P. J. O'Rourke in *Rolling Stone* to the more subtle aversions and aspersions of Ian Buruma in *The New York Review of Books*.[79]

Michael Shapiro also went to Korea in the Olympic year, and wrote a fine book about it. If you stand on a street corner in Seoul, you are not likely to see Chông Chu-yong or Kim Woo Chung. You will see cab drivers honking in the gridlocked traffic, shoeshine boys, tea-room waitresses hustling by with a takeout order, old ladies selling apples, young officeworkers in black pants and white shirt, bus girls in blue uniforms leaning out of the back door of a bus to announce the destination, old men heaving along under A-frames or pulling two-wheeled carts, women with sleeping babies strapped to their backs trying to maneuver enormous sidewalk vending wagons festooned with hats and wigs, delivery boys balancing ten auto tires behind the seat of their motorbikes, scooting in and out of traffic. Mr. Shapiro wrote about these people.[80]

South Korea under the Kim Young Sam government inaugurated in 1993 has made much progress toward a truly democratic system, but it is not there yet. In the summer of 1994 the regime carried out large numbers of arrests in the aftermath of Kim Il Sung's death, under the draconian National Security Law (NSL) that has been in force since 1948, albeit with many revisions. Fortunately we now have an English excerpt of Park Won Soon's three-volume study of this law. Park, a well-known lawyer who has defended many human rights victims in Korea, wrote that the NSL embraces every aspect of political, social, and artistic life, not excluding even professor's lecture notes (under the NSL two professors were arrested in the summer of 1994 for not being sufficiently critical of the South Korean left). The current NSL states that "any person who praises or encourages" anti-State activities can be prosecuted; since North Korea is an "anti-State entity" according to legal interpretations of this law, you could go to jail for offering condolences on Kim Il Sung's death—which hundreds of people did. But you might also simply drink a bit too much and say the wrong thing; in one case a person was prosecuted for "a statement benefitting the enemy while drunk." People spirited away under the NSL "have no idea where they were taken to and their families have no recourse to find out their whereabouts." Under this law Seoul keeps politically "unconverted" leftists in jail from as far back as the Korean War: as of 1992 two had been incarcerated more than forty years, with Kim Sôn-myông having served forty-three years for being a guerrilla in the South during the war.[81] In August 1994 the U.S. State Department took the unusual step of publicly condemning the NSL; as long as it is on the books, there will be no possibility of reconciliation with North Korea.

South Korea in the 1980s changed markedly in its historiography, with lots of good work appearing by courageous historians. It was a different kind of quasi-archival work, a deeply revisionist look at the origins of the Republic of Korea and the Korean War. This work is extensive and need not be enumerated, but it has the following characteristics: first, a concern for the mass of the Korean population, after generations of scholarship only about the elite; second, a harsh look at the role of the United States in the 1940s transition from Japanese to South Korean rule; third, a radical and didactic concern for using the past to criticize the present and shape the future; and finally, not much—or not enough—concern with primary research (although many new sources on the late 1940s have been uncovered by some practitioners of "the new history").

Historian Shim Chi-yôn has produced a number of books on the late

1940s, focusing on the major political parties of the period and greatly increasing our knowledge; he also produced an interesting study on the U.S.-Soviet Joint Commissions in 1946 and 1947.[82] Ch'oe Sang-yong's critical study of the U.S. Occupation first emerged as a dissertation at Tokyo University under the guidance of Prof. Sakamoto Yoshikazu; when he returned to Seoul after completing it in the early 1970s, the KCIA read passages out loud from it while torturing him, with the phone off the hook so his wife could hear his screaming. Now his study is published,[83] and he teaches at Korea University. Yi U-jae has done excellent work on peasants' and workers' movements in the early postwar period, both on his own and in collaboration with others.[84]

The previously forbidden subject of South Korea's leftwing people's committees, which emerged in the wake of Japan's defeat and which governed affairs in many counties for months and even years thereafter, has also gotten attention since the mid 1980s with much new information coming available. Historians from the southwestern Chôlla provinces, in which the Left was strongest and which suffered the severest repression in the postwar period, have been particularly active. This work comes from historians like An Chong-ch'ôl, and novelistic chroniclers of postwar history like Ch'oe Myông-hui. (Ms. Ch'oe comes from Namwôn, a hotbed of rebellion in 1945–50, and the headquarters of the US-ROK guerrilla suppression command in 1949–50.) People in Namwôn not only had strong people's committees but often supported the North Koreans when they occupied the area in the summer of 1950. When Republic of Korea forces retook the area, they massacred so many people that the living honor the dead in mass ancestor worship, on the anniversary day of specific massacres.[85]

The Kwangju Rebellion provoked more anti-American criticism than any event since the period before the Korean War, and an immense outpouring of writing once Chun Doo Hwan was overthrown. The brutal suppression of this rebellion, with American acquiescence if not outright support, was the subject of several National Assembly inquiries in the early 1990s and still gnaws at the heart of the relationship.

The emergence of a directly elected President and National Assembly in early 1993, getting the military out of power for the first time since 1961, combined with the end of the Cold War and the collapse of European communism, has somewhat attenuated the radical thrust behind the new history. But its influence is sufficient to lead to continuing demands for the rewriting of centrally vetted school textbooks (for example, the reconstitution of the October 1946 uprisings as a patriotic people's struggle, rather than a treacherous riot[86]).

Visible Koreans?

Koreans are now in the American midst, as we saw at the beginning of this essay, with large numbers of Korean-American students now attending the best colleges in the country. The Korean presence in America is not recent, however, but goes back to the turn of the century when some 7,000 immigrants were brought into Hawaii to cut sugar cane. It was never very large until changes in the immigration laws in 1965, but then immigration to the U.S. accelerated rapidly. According to U.S. Naturalization and Immigration figures (which probably understate the numbers quite a bit), there were but ten Korean immigrants to the U.S. in the year 1950, 1,507 a decade later, nearly 10,000 in 1970, and 32,158 in 1975. The 1970 census reported 8,881 Koreans in Los Angeles County, which other sources thought was less than 50 percent of the real total. There were also about 13,000 Koreans born in the U.S. by 1975, perhaps 10,000 of whom antedated the 1965 changes. Today there are more than a million Korean-Americans, living all over the country but with big clusters in Los Angeles and New York.

If Koreans in America were dutiful, hardworking laborers useful for sugar cane cutting at the beginning of this century,[87] by its end they have become a "model minority," held up to others as an example of bootstrapping your way to Horatio Alger success without help from the federal government or the welfare state.[88] None of these stereotypes have made Korean-Americans happy because they lump a diverse population under a catch-all rubric, but this one is decidedly preferable to the previous ones. The latest version, unfortunately, has put Korean-Americans at loggerheads not with whites, but with African Americans. Racial disputes have broken out between Koreans and blacks in New York, Chicago, Philadelphia and many other places, but nothing was more disheartening then the example of poor Koreans arming themselves against poor blacks, Hispanics, and whites in the 1992 Los Angeles riots.

Those Koreans who run liquor stores or "swapmeets" in the Los Angeles ghetto are just a step above poverty themselves, but (like Jews in the past) they became a target of wrath just because they are there and not in a pleasant suburb. Many Afro-Americans complain that Korean businesspeople are racists and do not treat them with dignity, which may well be true in many cases— but that makes Koreans no different than white Americans. Furthermore many Korean-Americans have shared the poverty and racial degradation of American society, and often have a much more sympathetic understanding of African American problems than do whites.

The case of Soon Ja Du was an important prelude to the 1992 Los Angeles riots. An immigrant shopkeeper with rudimentary English, in March 1991 she shot and killed Latasha Harlins in a dispute over a $1.79 bottle of orange juice, as the security cameras whirred. Over and over the television media played this videotape, inflaming black passions and shaming Koreans, while whites stood by watching as if uninvolved: "every time it played it made black people hate Koreans."[89] Soon a court acquitted Ms. Du of any wrongdoing. LA's "black-Korean conflict" was tailor-made for the towering cynicism of Hollywood writers, who in a film called *Falling Down* presented your stereotypical rude and crude Korean shopkeeper, who gets what he deserves from an enraged white man—a guy who's "not gonna take it anymore"—played by Michael Douglas. It seems a perfect example of the divide-and-rule tactics that whites have long used, whether consciously or unconsciously, to assure that they do not face a unified multiracial opposition from below.[90]

The subsequent riots in April 1992 were the worst experience imaginable for the growing numbers of Korean-Americans in the U.S. Day after day the TV networks showed ruined Korean shops, young Koreans arming themselves against young rioters, enormously unproportional property losses (Korean businesses lost at least $400 million, far higher than any other group), and endless harping on the theme of black vs. Korean, despised minority vs. model minority. As Elaine Kim wrote,

> It is difficult to describe how disempowered and frustrated many Korean Americans felt.... [They] shared the anguish and despair of the Los Angeles *tongp'o* [community] which everyone seemed to have abandoned—the police and fire departments, black and white political leaders, the Asian and Pacific American advocates who tried to dissociate themselves from us because our tragedy disrupted their narrow and risk-free focus on white violence against Asians. At the same time, while the Korean Americans at the center of the storm were mostly voiceless and all but invisible (except when stereotyped as hysterically inarticulate, and mostly female, ruined shopkeepers or gun-wielding male merchants on rooftops concerned only about their property), we repeatedly witnessed Americans of African, European and, to a slightly lesser extent, Chinese and Japanese descent discussing publicly the significance of what was happening.[91]

Rarely if ever did any media analyst point out that the Koreans had bought their stores from African-Americans, who had bought them from Jews after the Watts riots a generation earlier; or that the Korean merchants were often the poorest segment of Korean businesspeople in the U.S., doing a job and providing a service that most others would reject.

In the mid-1970s about 85 percent of Korean-Americans were in the working class, and only 5 percent were professionals; yet upwards of 70 percent of Korean immigrants had been professionals back home. In Southern California in the 1970s there were about 600 immigrant physicians with no license to practice medicine, who found jobs as health care workers or hospital clerks.[92] Many more are professionals by now, living in the suburbs, but the majority of professionals who emigrated still do not work in positions commensurate with their skills and backgrounds, and the majority of the community is still working class.

This is important evidence, large grains of salt, to take while you read about Koreans as a "model minority." A person with a college degree from Korea who brings his family to New York and runs a vegetable store for ten years—a very common phenomenon—is not going to be happy with his status; probably there won't be much he can do about his own, but he and his wife will work their fingers to the bone to assure that their offspring will regain the status that the father had in Korea, namely, a college degree and a professional career. Maybe the family will be lucky and get a child into a top university; then they will encourage that child to specialize in the sciences, since in so many other fields there are "glass ceilings" that prevent Korean-Americans from getting top jobs—especially in American corporations, which at the top levels remain overwhelmingly a segregated minority of white males.

Visible Koreans: The U.S.-North Korean Nuclear Crisis

If Koreans in the American midst are less than visible, a North Korea potentially armed with nuclear weapons was a highly visible presence in the early 1990s, represented almost always as a Saddam Hussein-substitute trope: "renegade state led by crazed dictator seeking weapons of mass destruction."

Since I read the daily North Korean press and the country has been familiar to me for almost three decades, I cannot put myself into the shoes of Americans who see such things, especially since the majority were born after the Korean War. What must they think? Didn't we beat a country by that name at some distant point in the past? Does this have something to do with that "forgotten war" in the 1950s? Why is North Korea, long-term Soviet puppet and communist hellhole, not down the post-Cold War drain yet? Who was Kim Il Sung, father to psychotic son Kim Jong Il—can he be the same Kim Il Sung whom my Dad told me General MacArthur fought against?

Print and television reporters mindlessly repeated Pentagon and White House caricatures of North Korea and its "nuclear bomb," in spite of their (regrettably *post-facto*) protests about how the Pentagon herded the media like cattle during the Persian Gulf War of 1990–91, and in spite of some excellent recent work on U.S. nuclear policies in Korea.[93] For anyone who tried to read the many stories, there was a disturbingly mimetic quality to print and television stories on North Korean nukes. Over and over again the same unexamined facts and assumptions intruded every article.

David Sanger, a reporter for the *New York Times* asserts that North Korea is a menace, about to collapse, unyielding to international inspections, and probably capable of building a bomb from 50 tons of uranium or small amounts of extracted plutonium, it is not clear which. That North Korea is a menace has been a standard since 1946, when Kim Il Sung came to power and when the first alarms began about an attack on the South. That it will collapse any day now has been a stock line since the Berlin Wall fell.[94] Reporters routinely say that North Korea has refused inspections: yet by November 1993 North Korea had allowed six formal inspections of its Yongbyon site by the International Atomic Energy Agency (IAEA), in the period May 1992–February 1993. Indeed, Sanger had reported one of Les Aspin's aides as saying, "we have no evidence that they are extracting or reprocessing plutonium." Sanger then adds that in the past the CIA has said "it suspects North Korea already has enough plutonium to make at least one crude weapon."[95] That is, a CIA estimate one day is turned into Mr. Sanger's statement the next that "there is evidence" of this.

On the weekend of November 5–7, 1993, coinciding with Defense Secretary Les Aspin's visit to Seoul, from *CBS Evening News* to the Fox Network, even to National Public Radio, wild charges circulated about crazed North Koreans readying an atomic bomb, forbidding access to international inspectors, and concentrating 70 percent of their army on the border with South Korea—the implication being that they might attack at any minute. On Sunday, November 7, President Clinton told *Meet the Press* that "any attack on South Korea is an attack on the U.S.,"[96] and on November 18 *CBS Evening News* again ran a scare story saying North Korean nukes are the single greatest threat to world peace today. Within a few days, it turned out that this hysteric press hoopla had been generated out of a couple of comments by an official traveling with Aspin.

In June 1994 the widely ridiculed Jimmy Carter stepped in and solved the Korean crisis, but doing what no American leader had ever imagined doing before: he went to Pyongyang and talked directly with Kim Il Sung. It may be forgotten now, but the main press reaction to his diplomacy was an endless series of articles, cartoons, depicting the "Carterization" of President Bill Clinton. Soon after Kim Il Sung passed on, and the American media outdid its earlier racist imagery by depicting North Korea as a "headless beast"

(*Newsweek*'s post-mortem on Kim's death)[97] armed with nuclear weapons and sure to be an even worse "loose cannon" under heir-apparent Kim Jong Il, widely assumed to be a dissolute, drunken, dangerous if not insane, replica of his father. *Plus ça change.* . . .

Conclusion

What can be said in the way of work that ought to be done, work that needs doing, in the field of Korean-American relations? The early history of the relationship is still in dire need of people who will examine the record without trying to predict the past by reference to present needs, especially the perceived need to sustain friendly relations between the two countries. Although no one has yet matched Harrington's masterful 1944 account of the American triptych in East Asia, the missionary/businessman/diplomat (that is, God, mammon, and the combination of all three in Horace Allen), it would be good to get beyond that triptych and think more systematically about the U.S.-Korean interaction (as Japanese scholars are now doing in regard to U.S.-Japan relations, using world-systems theory). My own sense is that a kind of trilateral relationship between British/American hegemony and the relevant countries in East Asia goes a long way toward explaining the diplomacy of the region from the turn of the century into the 1930s.[98] We still need to penetrate more deeply into the black hole of Korea and Manchuria in the 1930s, particularly the informal role many Americans played in Japanese development plans for the region in spite of the rumored "closing" of the Open Door.[99]

In the postwar period, we know almost nothing about the most important and sustained official (and unofficial) relationship between Americans and Koreans, namely the connection between the two sets of military and intelligence organizations. Interviews with people who served for decades at the nexus of the two armies, like James Hausman, have provided much tantalizing information.[100] But no one, to my knowledge, is doing serious archival work on this subject even though American-side military archives are now mostly open into the late 1960s. As for the intelligence archives, our glorious "post-Cold War world" has not yet produced an American CIA willing to open its own archives; by contrast, KGB history looks positively transparent in 1995.

I would like to close on a different note, however, by saying that my conclusion to the earlier volume in this series of books dedicated to Dorothy Borg (Dorothy's memory deserves many more such dedications), argued that soon Korea would again begin to move in the orbit of East Asia, and its close, at times intense, relations with the United States would eventually come to be seen as anomalous in its long history. I was premature by a decade, but not about the cause: the end of the Cold War has spawned a revival of relations among Japan, China, South Korea and Russia, and for the first time South Korean diplomacy is asserting independence of Washington and negotiating horizontally (Tokyo, Beijing, and Moscow) as well as vertically (i.e., with Washington, which more or less controlled South Korean diplomacy from 1945 to 1989). It's just that the Cold War could have and should have ended ten years before it did;[101] if it had, I could claim to have been right.

Notes

1. Arthur Cotterell *East Asia: From Chinese Predominance to the Rise of the Pacific Rim* (New York: Oxford University Pres, 1993), 46–47.

2. Elaine H. Kim in Karin Aguilar-San Juan, ed. *The State of Asian America* (Boston: South End Press, 1994), 73.

3. Ibid., 71–72. See also Kim, "Home is Where the Han Is: A Korean American Perspective on the Los Angeles Upheavals," *Social Justice* 20, nos. 1, 2 (Spring–Summer 1993).

4. Kim argued that Koppel had no articulate Korean voices in the several shows ABC did on the 1992 events, until he finally found Korean-Americans who were articulate speakers of English (like herself) to showcase briefly. Kim in Aguilar-San Juan, *State of Asian America*, 73.

5. See for example Youngnok Koo and Dae-sook Suh, *Korea and the United States: A Century of Cooperation* (Honolulu: University of Hawaii Press, 1984). I presented a paper to the conference at the University of Hawaii that preceded this volume, but the editors excluded it from the conference volume, presumably on political grounds.

6. See Tae-Hwan Kwak, ed., *U.S.-Korean Relations, 1882–1982* (Seoul: Kyungnam University Press, 1983), x. In spite of its celebratory theme, there are still several good articles in the Kwak volume. For example Gerard H. Clarfield accurately says that the U.S. intervened in Korea, Taiwan, and Indochina in 1950 primarily to bolster a reviving Japanese economy; he is just off by three years in saying the decisions were all taken in 1950. See "The Last Domino: American, Japan, and the Blair House Decisions," 54–64.

7. Frederick C. Drake, *The Empire of the Seas: A Biography of Rear Admiral Robert Wilson Shufeldt, USN* (Honolulu: University of Hawaii Press, 1984), 292.

8. Ibid., 296–98.

9. Kwang-Ching Liu, foreword to Key-Hiuk Kim, *The Last Phase of the East Asian World Order* (Berkeley: University of California Press, 1980), xvi-xvii.

10. Quoted in Drake *The Empire of the Seas*, 115–16.

11. Woo-keun Han, *The History of Korea* (Honolulu: University of Hawaii Press, 1974), 387.

12. Peter Duus, *The Abacus and the Sword* (Berkeley: University of California Press, 1995).

13. George Alexander Lensen, *Balance of Intrigue: International Rivalry in Korea and Manchuria, 1884–1899*, 2 vols (Tallahassee: Florida State University Press, 1982), 850–54.

14. Ibid., 583–84.

15. Ibid., 591.

16. Ibid., 630–34.

17. Jongsuk Chay, *Diplomacy of Asymmetry: Korean-American Relations to 1910* (Honolulu, University of Hawaii Press, 1990).

18. Robert R. Swartout, Jr., *Mandarins, Gunboats, and Power Poitics: Owen Nickerson Denny and the International Rivalries in Korea* (Honolulu, University of Hawaii Press, 1980).

19. Yur-Bok Lee, *West Goes East: Paul Georg von Möllendorff and Great Power Imperialism in Late Yi Korea* (Honolulu, University of Hawaii Press, 1988).

20. Carter J. Eckert, et al., *Korea Old and New* (Cambridge: Korea Institute, Harvard University, 1990), 44, 82–84.

21. Quoted in Ibid., 115, 128.

22. Chalmers Johnson, *MITI and the Japanese Miracle* (Berkeley, University of California Press, 1982); William Miles Fletcher III, *The Japanese Business Community and National Trade Policy, 1920–1942* (Chapel Hill, University of North Carolina Press, 1989).

23. Jung-en Woo, *Race to the Swift: State and Finance in Korean Industrialization* (New York: Columbia University Press, 1991), 23–30. See also Dennis McNamara, *The Colonial Origins of Korean Enterprise* (New York: Cambridge University Press, 1990).

24. Eckert *Korea Old and New*, 85–86.

25. Barbara Molony, *Technology and Investment: the Prewar Japanese Chemical Industry* (Cambridge: Harvard University Press, 1990).

26. Hermann Lautensach, *Korea: A Geography Based on the Author's Travels and Literature* (Berlin: Springer-Verlag, 1945), 400.

27. Eckert, *Korea Old and New*, 119, 149.

28. Lautensach, *Korea: A Geography*, 383, 386–87.

29. Ibid., 204–207.

30. Wada Haruki, *Kin Nichi-sei to Manshu konichi senso* [Kim Il Sung and the Anti-Japanese War in Manchuria] (Tokyo: Heibon-sha, 1992).

31. Eckert, *Korea Old and New*, 58.

32. Bruce Cumings, *The Origins of the Korean War: Liberation and the Emergence of Separate Regimes, 1945–47* (Princeton: Princeton University Press, 1981).

33. George Hicks, *The Comfort Women: Sex Slaves of the Japanese Forces* (New York: Norton, 1995), 136, 140, 206–207. As Hicks acknowledges, the seminal study on this subject was Kim Il-myôn's *The Emperor's Forces and Korean Comfort Women*. Yun Chong Mo's book, mentioned in the text, was also a milestone, as was Yoshida Seiji's revelations in *My War Crimes: The Forced Draft of Koreans*. (Tokyo, 1983).

34. Sandra Sturdevant and Brenda Stoltzsfus, *Let the Good Times Roll: Prostitution and the U.S. Military in Asia* (New York: The New Press, 1992).

35. Hicks *Comfort Women*, 70–71.

36. Perhaps the best example is Michael Walzer's defense of the first Korean War (for containment) and his criticism of the second Korean War (for rollback) in Just and Unjust Wars: A Moral Argument with Historical Illustrations (New York: Basic Books, 1977), 117–123.

37. Truman Library, Papers of Dean Acheson, "Notes on Meetings," May 16, 1951.

38. Cumings, *Origins of the Korean War*.

39. William S. Borden, *The Pacific Alliance: United States Foreign Economic Policy and Japanese Trade Recovery, 1947–1955* (Madison: University of Wisconsin Press, 1984), and Michael Schaller, *The American Occupation of Japan: The Origins of the Cold War in Asia* (New York: Oxford University Press, 1985).

40. The best includes Sergei N. Goncharov, John W. Lewis, and Xue Litai, *Uncertain Part-*

ners: Stalin, Mao and the Korean War (Stanford, Stanford University Press, 1993); Michael H. Hunt, "Beijing and the Korean Crisis," *Political Science Quarterly* (fall 1992), 453–478; and Kathryn Weathersby's articles in the Wilson Center Cold War History project.

41. James Matray and his collaborators demonstrate that even something so august as an historical dictionary is a shaped and constructed text; this one dates the war from 1950, thus betraying its American blinders, and includes lots of weightless Westerners while excluding many weighty Koreans. See James I. Matray, ed., *Historical Dictionary of the Korean War* (New York, Greenwood Press, 1991).

42. Goncharov et al., *Uncertain Partners*, 214.

43. Nystagmus is the term for the odd behavior of pigeons when confronted with a top spinning in one direction in front of them. Stop the spinning, and the pigeon's head keeps flipping in the same direction.

44. Russell Spurr, *Enter the Dragon: China's Undeclared War Against the U.S. in Korea, 1950–51* (New York: Newmarket Press, 1988), 4–5. 12, 246, for example. I was a reader of this manuscript and recommended that it not be published, because of what I considered to be factual errors and racism.

45. Rosemary Foot, *The Wrong War: American Policy and the Dimensions of the Korean Conflict, 1950–1953* (Ithaca, Cornell University Press, 1985); also Foot, *A Substitute for Victory: The Politics of Peacemaking at the Korean Armistice Talks* (Cornell University Press, 1990); Peter Lowe, *The Origins of the Korean War* (New York, Longman, 1986); Callum MacDonald, *Korea: The War Before Vietnam* (Ames, University of Iowa Press, 1986); also MacDonald, *Britain and the Korean War* (New York, Oxford University Press, 1990).

46. In a recent modern history of Korea designed to redress the absence of twentieth-century coverage in the extant general histories, there is no chapter on North Korea. See Eckert et.al., *Korea Old and New*.

47. Alice Amsden, *Asia's Next Giant* (New York: Cambridge University Press, 1989). See also Stephan Haggard, *Pathways From the Periphery: The Politics of Growth in the Newly Industrializing Countries* (Ithaca: Cornell University Press, 1990), which treats South Korea as one of four case studies of policy choice in industrialization.

48. Woo, *Race to the Swift*, 6–7.

49. Woo, *Race to the Swift*, 70; Donald MacDonald, *U.S.-Korean Relations from Liberation to Self-Reliance* (Boulder, Colorado: Westview Press, 1992), 26–27.

50. Woo, *Race to the Swift*, 76–77. Komer was with the CIA Office of National Estimates in the 1950s, but moved to the NSC in 1960.

51. MacDonald, *U.S.-Korean Relations from Liberation to Self-Reliance*, 31–32.

52. Quoted in Woo, *Race to the Swift*, 99.

53. This is derived from many conversations with Meredith Woo-Cumings, a rock-ribbed Schumpeterian.

54. Woo, *Race to the Swift*, 149–53.

55. Ibid., 159.

56. Ibid., 169.

57. Ibid., 11.

58. The primary volume is Edward S. Mason, Mahn Je Kim, Dwight H. Perkins, Kwang Suk Kim and David C. Cole, *The Economic and Social Modernization of the Republic of Korea* (Cambridge: Harvard East Asian monographs, 1980).

59. Ibid., v. On the next page the authors laud "the development of Korean entrepreneurship," refer to "an industrious and disciplined labor force," and say that the interconnection of government and private initiative in Korea has been "remarkably productive." The only references to the Korean Central Intelligence Agency (KCIA), the most extensive,

repressive and anti-democratic institution in South Korean life, say that this organization played a good role in keeping President Park well informed (260, 488).

60. Robert Boettcher with Gordon L. Freedman. *Gifts of Deceit: Sun Myung Moon, Tongsun Park, and the Korean Scandal* (New York: Holt, 1980), 91.

61. Ibid., 96. Years later newspapers revealed that American intelligence had monitored the August 26 Blue House meeting, sending Park into another fit of rage.

62. All the information in my discussion of "Koreagate" comes from Boettcher (1980) and the investigation that Boettcher ran under Donald Fraser's direction, with which I consulted at the time and which ultimately produced many published volumes of evidence and testimony (see the list in Boettcher's book, 351–52). This information came under oath and under threat of perjury, and is therefore much better than most other sources on Korean-American relations and on the Park regime and how it operated.

63. Boettcher *Gifts of Deceit*, 214–15.

64. MacDonald, *U.S.-Korean Relations from Liberation to Self-Reliance.*

65. Manwoo Lee, Ronald D. MacLaurin, and Chung-in Moon, *Alliance Under Tension: The Evolution of South Korean-U.S. Relations* (Seoul: Kyungnam University Press, 1988).

66. Asian *Wall Street Journal*, March 11, 1980, quoted in George Ogle, *South Korea: Dissent Within the Economic Miracle* (Atlantic Highlands, N.J.: Zed Books, 1990), 95–96.

67. These figures were compiled in September 1980 by the most important watchdog group in the U.S., the North American Coalition on Human Rights in Korea, led by Rev. Pharis Harvey. Japanese network television covered the entire rebellion closely, filming many of the worst atrocities.

68. *Lost Victory: An Overview of the Korean People's Struggle for Democracy in 1987.* ed. Christian Institute for the Study of Justice and Development (Seoul: Minjungsa, 1988), 30–32.

69. Like everything else in the Carter administration, Kwangju also fell between the stools of incessant NSC-State Department feuds between cold warriors and moderates, except that in this case Richard Holbrooke of the State Department also counseled a prudent silence; there was, he thought, far too much "attention to Kwangjoo [sic]" without consideration of the "broader questions" of Korean security and the like, which had not been properly addressed. (*New York Times*, May 29, 1980.) Holbrooke had also helped to reverse Carter's policy of withdrawing troops from Korea; after Reagan defeated Carter in the 1980 elections, Holbrooke became a well-paid consultant to the Hyundai Corporation.

70. Koo and Suh, *Korea and the United States*, 353.

71. Instead Koo wrote that "warm feelings on both sides have been generated by Chun Doo Hwan's preelection [sic] visit to President Reagan and by the renewed United States resolve to defend Korea." Ibid., 364. Kwak, *U.S.-Korean Relations*, cited above, note 6, likewise has no index entry for Kwangju.

72. See for example Harold Hinton, *Korea Under New Leadership* (New York: Praeger, 1983).

73. We now have an excellent study of the events in 1987, *Lost Victory* (1988). See also the good study by Kie-duck Park, "Fading Reformism in New Democracies: A Comparative Study of Regime Consolidation in Korea and the Philippines," (Ph.D. dissertation, University of Chicago, 1993).

74. Roh's declaration is in *Lost Victory* (1988), 308–13.

75. Quoted in *South Korea: Dissent Within the Economic Miracle*, 76.

76. Haggard, *Pathways from the Periphery.*

77. Jang Jip Choi, *Labor and Authoritarianism in Korea* (Seoul: Korean University Press, 1989).

78. Ogle, *South Korea*, xiii–xiv.

79. O'Rourke did a sort of racist potpourri/travelogue in *Rolling Stone* (October 1988), dwelling on Korean facial features that he found outlandish. Buruma compared the 1988 games to those Hitler sponsored in 1936; after visiting Korea's Independence Hall he asked if his "revulsion" against Korean nationalism was "a sign of decadence," or is there something "to the idea of the rise and fall of national, even racial vigor?" See Ian Buruma. "Jingo Olympics," *New York Review of Books* (November 10, 1988).

80. Shapiro, *The Shadow in the Sun: A Korean Year of Love and Sorrow* (New York: Atlantic Monthly Press, 1990), 40, 61–67, 91–94.

81. Won Soon Park. *The National Security Law* (Los Angeles: Korea Network for the UN World Conference on Human Rights, 1993), 26, 37–38, 57, 62, 122–23.

82. Shim Chi-yôn, *Inmin-dang Yôn'gu* [On the People's Party] (Seoul: Kyungnam University Press, 1991); Shim, *Han'guk Minju-dang Yôn'gu* [On the Korean Democratic Party], 2 vols. (Seoul: Ch'angjak kwa pip'yông-sa, 1982, 1984); Mi-So Kongdong Wiwônhoe [The U.S.-Soviet Joint Commission] (Seoul, Ch'onggye yôn'guso, 1989).

83. Ch'oe Sang-yong, *Migunjông kwa Hanguk minjokjuûi* [The American military government and Korean nationalism] (Seoul: Nanam sinsô, 1988).

84. A useful collection of his and others' work is *Yôksa wa kidokkyo*, no. 9, *Nongch'ôn hyônsil kwa nongmin undong* [History and Christianity, no. 9, Realities of the villages and peasant movements] (Seoul: Minjung-sa, 1984).

85. See for example An Chong-ch'ôl, *Kwangju-Chônnam Chibang Hyôndaesa Yôn'gu* [The modern regional history of Kwangju and South Cholla Province] (Seoul: Hanol Academy, 1991); Ch'oe Myông-hûi, *Honbul* [Fire spirit], 3 vols (Seoul: 1985–92). In the past few years the magazine *Mal* and the newspaper *Han'gyore sinmun* have documented several massacres in which hundreds died after the Rhee regime reoccupied South Korea; this is only the tip of a rather appalling iceberg, and the record of South Korean political repression in occupied North Korea remains to be fully unearthed. All this is not to say that the North did not also commit atrocities; but to say so does not surprise anyone. My own work (in *Origins*, vol. 2) and that of Callum MacDonald suggests that the record will eventually show that the Rhee regime was the more atrocious during the Korean War, and that Americans who accompanied South Korean army and police units knew well what was going on.

86. *Han'guk ilbo*, March 15, 1994.

87. Horace Allen told Sanford E. Dole, Governor of Hawaii, that Koreans were superior to Chinese—"a patient, hard-working, docile race, easy to control from their long habit of obedience." Quoted in Bong-youn Choy, *Koreans in America* (Chicago: Nelson-Hall, 1979), 74.

88. See many examples of the latter stereotype in Won Yong-Jin, " 'Model-Minority' Strategy and Asian-Americans' Tactics," *Korea Journal* 34, no. 2 (Summer 1994): 57–66.

89. Warren Lee, *A Dream for South Central: The Autobiographic of an Afro-Americanized Korean Christian Minister* (San Francisco: Warren Lee, 1993), 74.

90. Ibid., 76–77.

91. Elaine H. Kim in Aguilar-San Juan, ed., *The State of Asian America*, 71–72. See also Elaine Kim, "Home is Where the Han Is: A Korean American Perspective on the Los Angeles Upheavals," *Social Justice*, 20, nos. 1, 2 (Spring–Summer 1993).

92. Choy *Koreans in America*, 218–19, 226, 249–50.

93. The best book-length study of nuclear issues in Korea is Peter Hayes, *Pacific Powderkeg: American Nuclear Dilemmas in Korea* (Lexington, MA: Lexington Books, 1991).

94. See for example Nick Eberstadt, "The Coming Collapse of North Korea," *Wall Street Journal*, June 26, 1990.

95. David E. Sanger, *The New York Times*, November 4, 1993.

96. *New York Times*, Nov. 8, 1993

97. Another example would be "The threat From North Korea," *Time* (June 13, 1994).

98. Cumings, "Archaeology, Descent, Emergence," in H.D. Harootunian and Masao Miyoshi, eds., *Japan in the World* (Durham, Duke University Press, 1993), 79–111.

99. A graduate student at the University of Chicago, Haruo Iguchi, is doing ground-breaking archival work on this subject, with special attention to the Ayukawa "new zaibatsu" group.

100. Thames Television (London), interview taken in 1988.

101. As I argued in "The Seventy Years' Crisis," *World Policy Journal* (Spring 1991).

Epilogue

American-East Asian Relations in the 21st Century

ERNEST R. MAY

In the early 1970s, a group of historians gathered at Cuernavaca, Mexico, to discuss the state of knowledge about American-East Asian relations. The two people who had pressed hardest for this inventory-taking were John King Fairbank, the great Sinologist, and Dr. Dorothy Borg, an independent scholar whose works included the prize-winning volume, *The United States and the Far Eastern Crisis of 1933–1938*. The reports at Cuernavaca were subsequently printed as *American-East Asian Relations, A Survey*.

Partly to keep the account current and partly to remind the world how much remained unknown, Dorothy Borg prodded Warren Cohen into organizing a follow-on meeting approximately a decade later. From it came a volume, edited by him, entitled *New Frontiers in American-East Asian Relations: Essays presented to Dorothy Borg*.

John Fairbank and Dorothy Borg have both died since then. Their spirits, however, have hovered over Warren Cohen, inspiring him to organize this conference at the Wilson Center to assay work of the last decade and to review the agenda still open. My assignment is to speculate about trends that may be evident when Warren—or whoever else the ghosts of John and Dorothy possess—reviews this field the next time around.

Historians, being wise and cautious folk, usually refrain from speaking about the future. We plead that it is our business to look in the opposite direction. While economists and political scientists do deal with the future, they have artful ways of not committing themselves to predictions for which they can be held accountable. If events don't match their models, they explain that models capture only aspects of reality. "Externalities" are to blame for events going awry. On this logic, some economists and social scientists have built great reputations without ever getting anything quite right. Even intelligence analysts, who are paid to make predictions, do so often in language so delphic that they can claim later to have been right, no matter what. Stepping where not only social scientists and intelligence analysts but even my valiant fellow historian, Paul Kennedy, might hesitate to tread, I will venture a few guesses about trends likely over the next decade or two.

First, however, I will ply my trade and speak of the past. Damon Runyon once said, "The race may not be to the swift nor the battle to the strong, but that's the way to bet." In forecasting, the preferred bet is nearly always on continuity. This is even true for weather. If you say that the weather tomorrow will be like the weather today, you may frequently be wrong, but you are apt to be right more often than wrong. In some years, you could even win money off Willard Scott. A look ahead should therefore start with a long look backward in order to describe trends of the past that could stretch into the future.

Over the more than two centuries since the first formal contacts, American-East Asia relationships have varied from exploitation (often mutual exploitation) to conflict to cooperation. The general trend has been toward a lessening in exploitation and conflict and an increase in cooperation.

In the nineteenth century and well into the twentieth century, the American approach to most of the Chinese culture area in East Asia was exploitative. Americans went there to make money off people whom they thought backward and ignorant, at least in the sense of not knowing as much as they about how to make things, to sell them, and to profit from them. Other Americans went to Asia for missionary purposes—in President William McKinley's famous words about the Filipinos, "to uplift and Christianize them."

At the turn of the century, when members of the Boxer Society in China were in arms against foreigners, Finley Peter Dunne described how Americans and other Westerners approached China. His fictional Chicago barkeeper, "Mr. Dooley," said to his friend, Hennessy:

" 'Th'Lord f'rgive f'r sayin'it, Hinnissy, but if I was a Chinyman, which I will
fight anny man for sayin', an'was livin' at home, I'd tuck me shirt into me
pants . . . an'take a fall out iv the in-vader if it cost me me life. Here am I,
Hop Lung Dooley, r-runnin'me little liquor store an' p'rhaps raisin' a family in th' town iv Koochoo. I don't like foreigners there anny more thin I do
here. Along comes a bald-headed man with chin whiskers from Baraboo,
Wisconsin, an'says he: 'Benightened an' haythen Dooley, 'says he, 'ye have
no God,' he says. 'I have,' says I. 'I have a lot iv them,' says I. 'Ye ar-re an
oncultivated an'foul crather,' he says. 'I have come six thousan' miles f'r to
hist ye fr'm the mire iv ignorance an' irreligion in which ye live to th' lofty
plane iv Baraboo,' he says . . .

"Th' nex' day in comes a man with a suit iv clothes that looks a tablecloth in a section house, an' says he:. . . . 'I riprisint Armour an' Company, an' I'm here to make ye
change ye'er dite,' he says. 'Hinceforth ye'll ate th' canned roast beef iv the merry ol'
stock yards or I'll have a file iv sojers in to fill ye full iv ondygestible lead,' he says. An'
afther him comes th' man with Aunt Miranda's Pan Cakes an' Flaked Bran an' . . .
othr ririsintatives iv Western Civilization."

Though Dunne obviously sided with the Chinese, he was equally obviously
hopeful that they would surge into the Western twentieth century. Mr. Dooley finished by saying to his friend,

"it looks to me as though Westhern Civilization was in f'r a bump . . . .
[T]wuddn't surprise me if whin theygot through batin' us at home, they
might say to thimselves: 'Well, here goes f'r a jaunt ar-roun' the wurruld.'
Th' time may come, Hinnissy, whin ye'll be squirtin' wather over Hop Lee's
shirt while a man named Chow Fung kicks down ye'er sign an' heaves rocks
through ye'er windy."

In fact, as we now know well, exploitation ran both ways. John Fairbank
exposed in several works the extent to which, in the nineteenth century, Chinese officials manipulated the greed, illusions, and ignorance of Americans in
order to pit them against other barbarians. Michael Hunt has detailed how
this manipulation continued through the Boxer period and the decade or so
thereafter. The Open Door policy and "dollar diplomacy," so often ascribed to
machinations by American imperialists or their English friends, were at least
as much the handiwork of Zhang Zhidong (Chang Chih-tung), Wu Tingfang,
and others in or around the Chinese imperial court.

Unquestionably, the relationship was unequal. Americans had little success
in exploiting China. As often noted by critics of America's pre-1949 commitment to China, actual trade and investment remained minimal. Missionaries
sent from the United States to China probably had more influence on Ameri-

cans than on Chinese. The Chinese were relatively more successful in exploiting the Americans, in the sense of being able to use them in balance of power diplomacy. But Americans suffered little from failing to find their fabled "four hundred million customers." Chinese, on the other hand, suffered a great deal for not having enough unity, economic and administrative wherewithal, and European-style coercive power to make their diplomatic jiujitsu effective.

After 1949, the American relationship with the rump Republic of China worked more equally for both parties. The United States successfully exploited Taiwan both economically and militarily. As of 1970, when the American-PRC relationship began to change, Taiwan was an important U.S. trading partner and the locale for about 3 percent of U.S. foreign direct investment in Asia. It was also a key location for U.S. intelligence-gathering. The Republic of China, however, enjoyed at least equal success in exploiting the United States. Its military alliance with the United States was the key, probably, to its survival as a nation. It owed to the United States its status as a permanent member of the UN Security Council, and it was consistently one of the largest recipients of American aid, both economic and military. In total grants and credits, between 1945 and 1970, it ranked behind Japan but ahead of Israel.

Elsewhere in the Chinese culture area and in regions to the south and west, pre-World War II relationships were minimal. The Philippines were, of course, an exception. There, Americans were successful exploiters, enjoying privileged access to resources and possessing both military and naval bases. The reverse exploitation was largely that of a small class among the Philippine elite, who secured political and economic dominance by influencing Americans in the Philippines and pulling strings in Washington.

After World War II, mutual exploitation became more the rule not only in the Philippines but elsewhere as well. Americans expanded trade and investment throughout Southeast Asia. Also, the United States established a string of bases—Tan Son Nhut, Camranh Bay, Luang Prabang, Udorn, Utapao, and Sattahip, among others. But the American commitment to containing the People's Republic of China gave Southeast Asian elites enormous leverage. This translated into political, economic, and military support being provided even when American decisionmakers had strong misgivings about how such support was to be used and by whom.

South Vietnam is the signal example. During World War II, non-Communist Vietnamese nationalists gained American sympathy. In the first postwar decade, this gave them some leverage against their French masters. When the Geneva accords of 1954 allowed South Vietnam to function independently, non-Communist nationalists, particularly a Roman Catholic minority led by Ngo Dinh Diem, used every device to secure continued U.S. backing. The more their regime was threatened by communist guerrillas, the more money and other support Washington supplied.

Americans, of course, expected to benefit. The Cold War had come to be seen as a delicately balanced global contest where any gain by the supposed Sino-Soviet bloc could have a cascading "domino effect," jeopardizing the entire Western position. Though Vietnam itself was not important to Americans either economically or strategically, American officials hoped that their clients in South Vietnam would, by remaining in place, provide defense in depth for Thailand, Malaysia, and lands beyond.

When Washington finally became nervous and pressed the South Vietnamese to do more for themselves, American officials obtained a result that horrified most of them. South Vietnam's generals responded to the American urging, like English courtiers to Henry II's exclamation about the "turbulent priest," by assassinating Diem and his relatives. The resultant sense of complicity and guilt locked Americans into alliance with the South Vietnamese even after Washington concluded that the generals in charge came from "the bottom of the barrel." It took years of grueling warfare and a near revolt among Americans of draft age before the United States could detach itself.

In the end, this particular case of mutual exploitation was terribly costly for all parties. Long before the final victory of the North Vietnamese, the war had destroyed much of the natural wealth of South Vietnam and taken from its villagers and townspeople the comparative independence and prosperity that had differentiated them from people in the north. North Vietnam itself was ravaged by American bombing. According to the best available estimates, North Vietnamese deaths, military and civilian, military and civilian, totalled around three million. Though individuals such as Singapore strong man Lee Kwan Yew contend that "dominoes" would have fallen had the United States not fought the war in Vietnam, most retrospective analysis questions whether Americans gained anything from their involvement in Vietnam other than long suppurating wounds within.

With lower stakes, this pattern repeated itself elsewhere. Thailand, for example, received economic and military aid on a huge scale, and Washington found itself making promises to Thailand that it had never made to allies in Europe. Where the North Atlantic Treaty pledged the United States to "the preservation of peace and security" and to act only according to "constitutional processes," statements by Secretary of State Dean Rusk and President Lyndon Johnson defined the security of Thailand as a "vital interest" of the United States. In secret, the Johnson Administration agreed to contingency plans that meant automatic war if Thailand were invaded. Farther away from the theater of the Vietnam War, in Pakistan, as Robert McMahon has recently shown, the United States was pulled similarly into extensive economic and military commitments.

When the verb "to exploit" is used, one tends to visualize the strong taking advantage of the weak. Historically, the pattern in American-East Asian relations was more often one of mutual exploitation, with the United States, the stronger power, not necessarily getting more than it gave. This is a not uncommon pattern. Scholarly work on Africa initiated by Ronald Robinson and John Gallagher has turned up abundant evidence of European governments being used by their colonies or dependencies. Some of the most interesting new documents opened as a result of the collapse of the Soviet Union and of China's version of *glas'nost* suggest something similar for the socialist world. Mao appears to have had considerable influence over Stalin's policies in Asia and, in the crises preceding the erection of the Berlin Wall, Khrushchev seems to have acted almost as a puppet of East German leader Walter Ulbricht. In any case, exploitation, often mutual, has been one pattern in past American-East Asian relations. Conflict has, of course, been a second pattern. In the nineteenth and early twentieth centuries, the relationship between the United States and Japan never became exploitative on either side. Like the Americans in their relations with Europeans, the Japanese guarded their independence until their country was too well consolidated to seem an inviting area for informal colonization. Japan stepped forth in the 1890s first as a rival of Western powers in China and elsewhere in the Pacific, then increasingly as a claimant for hegemony.

The resultant clash of interests was intensified by a concomitant clash of prejudices. Both Japanese and Americans tended to think of themselves as chosen people. American racial discrimination infuriated Japanese. Failure of the Japanese to acknowledge and accept inferiority infuriated Americans. The American diplomat-banker Willard Straight wrote to a friend early in the twentieth century, " I now find myself hating the Japanese more than anything else in the world. It is due I presume to the constant strain of having to be polite and to seek favors from a yellow people." On the eve of Pearl Harbor, American military analysts discounted Japan's air forces on the ground that Japanese were not physically up to flying high-speed missions. "[T]he Japanese as a race have defects of the tubes of the inner ear ... [and] are generally myopic. ... ," wrote one, noting also "Japanese children receive fewer mechanical toys and less mechanical training than those of any other race."

Whether conflict of interest between Americans and Japanese would have led to the Pacific War, absent arrogant racism on both sides, is obviously a moot question. What is important is the fact that one cannot explain the intensity of American-Japanese differences or the rapid progress toward hostility solely in terms of competition for national advantage or power or both. To some extent, American-Japanese antagonism in the early twentieth century and again in the 1930s has to be understood, as Akira Iriye has often argued, in terms of unreconciled self-images. The gap was simply too wide between the views Japanese had of themselves and the views of them obviously held by Americans and vice versa.

The other, more recent example of conflict is the American relationship with mainland China. The two nations fought a war in Korea. Each maintained—and still maintains—powerful military forces targeted against the other's. Here, clashes of interest seem more nearly sufficient for explanation. On the other hand, the two nations would probably not have menaced one another so openly or so ferociously had it not been for their deep religious differences—Confucius and Marx on one side, St. Paul and Alfred Marshall on the other. Thus, alongside a historic pattern of mutual exploitation stands a historic pattern of conflict, augmented in the one instance by unreasoned, in the other by reasoned, prejudice.

The third pattern to be found in the past is one of cooperation, even collaboration. In the 1920s, Americans and Japanese worked together despite disdain for and misunderstanding of one another. The same has been true more or less continuously since World War II. After the early 1970s, the relationship between Americans and Chinese turned in the same direction. While the level of U.S.-PRC cooperation has never approached that between the United States and Japan, the trend has nevertheless run more or less steadily away from the intense hostility of earlier years. And the American relationship with the Republic of China has also, as mentioned earlier, moved from one of mutual exploitation to one of cooperation.

The preconditions for these cooperative relationships seem to have been three. First, there developed a sense of shared interest. In the mutually exploitative relationship, each party pursued its own interests. While Zhang Zhidong allowed Americans to acquire concessions and mission stations in China, it was not because he thought them useful to Chinese as well as to Americans; it was solely because he wanted to buy opportunity to use Americans against other barbarians. By contrast, Zhou Enlai and Richard Nixon both wanted a rapprochement because both believed that China and the United States had a common interest in containing the Soviet Union. Diem wanted Americans in Vietnam in order to bolster his regime both against North Vietnam and against its competitors in the south. The current government of Vietnam seeks normalization of relations with the United States on a premise that Vietnamese and Americans will both benefit from increases in trade and investment.

Second, both parties in a cooperative relationship need to be confident of their own national independence and identity. This was lacking in China before the Communist revolution and in most of Southeast Asia before the 1980s. It was lacking even in Thailand despite that nation's having enjoyed formal independence since 1350—four centuries longer than the United States. For practical purposes, the Thai government, into the 1970s, was playing the same game as Zhang Zhidong. Only with the ebbing of the great power conflict in Asia and the extraordinary political and economic development of the region in the last decade or so have Thailand and other Southeast Asian lands acquired the footing necessary for the transition to a cooperative relationship with the United States.

Third, the parties in a cooperative relationship need some degree of mutual understanding. Earlier, this was absent in American relations with all peoples of Asia, not just the Japanese. On the American side, the operative image of Chinese tended to be either Charlie Chan or Fu Manchu. On the side of Chinese or Vietnamese or others, images of the United States were equally crude. In *The Making of a Special Relationship*, Michael Hunt cites as a particularly sophisticated Chinese reference work Wei Yüan's treatise of the 1840s, characterizing Americans as "docile, good-natured, mild, and honest." Asian images of Americans tended to vacillate between this, the noble savage, and the bloodthirsty aggressor of Maoist posters. The transition to cooperation required some refining of stereotypes.

Turning now from past to future, the question is whether cooperation will continue or whether one of the other past tendencies will reassert itself or whether chances favor some line of development foreshadowed perhaps in past American-European or U.S.-Latin American relationships but not in past American relationships with Asia.

It probably has to be assumed that conditions shaping future American-East Asian relations will be radically different from those of all but the very recent past. For one thing, affairs in the world seem likely to be less often comprehensible as *international* relations. Though the dominant unit in most of modern political history has been the sovereign nation state, this has become progressively less true. The sovereign nation state has been losing both coherence and competence, and there is no evident reason for the trend to run otherwise, for the nation state has been increasingly constrained from within and challenged from without.

The United States makes a good test case for this proportion. Though early in becoming a nation, the United States was late in becoming a nation state. Most of the founders of the American republic wanted something more like the Dutch or Swiss confederacies than like a European dynastic state, and they got their wish. Not until after the Civil War did "United States" become in common use a singular noun. Previously, Americans said "the United States are . . ." Not until the Great Depression did the national government have more than a symbolic role in the lives of most citizens. With World War II and the Cold War, however, the United States became a nation state with a vengeance. Even with an executive and a Congress in constant tension, the United States stretched its domain to an extent and in ways that would have been the envy of Philip II or Louis XIV. Also, it built a military establishment of Napoleonic dimensions.

But the United States became a nation state just as the nation state was approaching sunset. In America as in other parts of the world, nonsovereign political, economic, and social groups were already becoming forces able to frustrate the state and its organs, if not to compete with them. Brian Balogh's recent book, *Chain Reaction*, provides an example. It shows how worried private citizens developed sufficient expertise and political influence to challenge government agencies that had previously monopolized both knowledge about and responsibility for nuclear energy. Multinational business and financial institutions have defied control from any national capitals, and religious and ethnic groups, with links across borders, have shaped state action in ways uncommon earlier. American policies toward Israel and Cuba offer illustrations.

The core capacity of the nation state—its ability to make war—has grown enormously and yet paradoxically become increasingly nonfunctional. Nuclear weapons are in part accountable. Awareness of their potential destructiveness forced all parties to the Cold War strategic arms competition to recognize that the costs of war could easily exceed any imaginable national gain. The North Koreans or someone else may demonstrate soon that nuclear weapons *can* be used, but President Clinton stated an almost certain truth when he said that the nation which first broke the nuclear taboo would suffer such destruction as to become unrecognizable. It is not only nuclear forces, however that have become nonfunctional. Despite the dazzling performance of the U.S.-led coalition in the Gulf War of 1991, Saddam Hussein still rules in Baghdad. (And George Bush is in retirement in Houston.) Russian military forces have found it extremely difficult to control events in Russia's "near abroad," as prolonged fighting in Chechnya bore witness. Over the imaginable future, military force seems likely to be a much smaller factor in world affairs than in most of the remembered past.

Another new condition that will environ future American-East Asian relations is the continuing revolution in telecommunications. Marshall McLuhan was not wrong in writing in 1964 in *Understanding Media* of the world's becoming a "global village." He was just premature. Coupled with the near universality of access to television sets, geostationary satellites and the technologies loosely known as "cable" have made it possible for almost any event anywhere to be observed by audiences everywhere. The whole world watched and participated vicariously in the revolutions in Eastern Europe and the former Soviet Union. The demonstration in Tiananmen Square in June 1989 occurred in part because the two and half million television receivers in China had carried pictures of demonstrations in Leipzig, Dresden, Berlin, Prague, Budapest, and Moscow.

In parallel, the development of the telefax machine, the personal computer, the modem, and the computer network, have created large transnational societies linked electronically rather than geographically. The Middle East peace process exemplifies the effects. When the process first gained momentum through President Carter's Camp David initiative, the principal parties made artful use of then existing communications technology. The Israelis and the Egyptians both hired American public relations firms. They did their utmost to shape newspaper and magazine stories. They paid particular attention to getting favorable coverage on major television networks both in the United States and in Europe.

In the 1990s, the pace of the peace process was dictated in part by relentless coverage from Ted Turner's Cable News Network (CNN), which had only come into being the year after Carter's Camp David talks. Debates among Israelis and among Jews worldwide and debates among Palestinians and other Arabs took place not only in personal meetings, over the telephone, and via cable among elites; they took place equally crucially in thousand of fax and computer network exchanges going household to household. At this moment, we have no idea just how this transformation in global communications will affect relations among peoples of the world, but it is hard not to assume that—like the transformation in the functionality of military force—it will make the future different from any known past.

A third new condition particularly affecting American-East Asian relations is the apparent shift in the world's center of gravity. Those of us traditionally educated find it hard not to think of history as marching straight from ancient Athens to present-day Georgetown, interrupted only by the long "dark ages," but in fact Europe was usually only a secondary center of civilization. Only gradually after the fifteenth century and particularly after the beginning of industrialization did Europe become effectively the hub of world affairs. Then, in the course of the nineteenth and early twentieth centuries, that hub shifted visibly in the direction of North America.

In the past few decades but especially in the last decade and a half, that shift seems to have resumed. Despite the formation of the European Union and the prospect that it will eventually extend from the Atlantic to the Urals, Europe is increasingly an enclave. It does not have even the centrality that it possessed during the Cold War, when the contest over Germany was pivotal. Like Marshall McLuhan, the great British historian, A.J.P. Taylor, sometimes penned premature truths. One was his observation about the effect of American intervention in World War I—false as to 1917 but perhaps true by now: "Henceforward," wrote Taylor, "what had been the center of the world became merely 'the European question.' "[4]

If interstate transactions are less important in world affairs but economic transactions are more important, it is easy to make a case that the world's center of gravity is rapidly moving toward Asia. According to World Bank estimates, aggregate gross domestic product in East Asia equalled only one-third that of the United States and Canada in 1970; by 1991 it equalled more than seventy-five per cent. By U.S. Commerce Department calculations, gross product in East Asia in 1980 was less than half that of OECD Europe. By 1990 it was more than two-thirds. One of the World Bank's most recent publications is *The East Asian Miracle*, analyzing the post-1970 experience of Japan, Hong Kong, South Korea, Singapore, Taiwan, Indonesia, Malaysia, and Thailand. If trends of the past two decades continue even sluggishly during the decades ahead, East Asia will before long outproduce both North America and Europe.

Samuel Huntington has argued that, as international struggle becomes less feasible and less common, the world is likely to see intercivilizational struggles. This has been disputed, both on the ground that his Hobbesian premises are questionable and on the ground that "civilization" is too loose an aggregate term. Now turning his *Foreign Affairs* article into a book, Huntington may demolish both objections. In any case, it seems hard not to assume that relationships among groups defined less by nationality than by ethnicity or religion or culture will become increasingly important. Given the multiplicity of ethnic and religious groups in Asia and the varieties among Asian cultures, this argues that relations between the West and Asia will be prominent features in whatever world systems develop in decades to come. Note, for example, that the largest and most populous Muslim country is not in the Middle East. It is Indonesia.

With the nation state in retreat, the "global village" becoming reality, and the world's center of gravity shifting toward Asia, the possible paths for future American-East Asian relations seem to be three: toward separation, toward renewed antagonism, or toward some form of integration.

None of these three lines of development is unimaginable. A good deal of anxious writing has already gone to the possibility that the world will divide into protectionist trading blocs, one based on the Deutschmark, one on the dollar, and one on the yen. If economic linkages were in fact to be artificially interrupted, cultural linkages could also be interrupted. Reduced travel and scholarly exchange would affect the degree of interest in Asia among Americans and in America among Asians. We would stop watching each other and stop trying to network our PCs.

Alternatively, competition of one kind or another could make Americans and Asians antagonists. Current scare writings, exemplified by George Freedman's *The Coming War with Japan* and Michael Crichton's novel, *Red Sun Rising*, suppose antagonism arising out of economic competition. Paul Kennedy's discussion in *Preparing for the Twenty-first Century* of the possible consequences of a Chinese breakup supposes that geopolitical competition could come to center in Asia as it once centered in Europe. Still another possibility would turn on revival of ideological antagonism like that of the early Cold War. After all, talk of the demise of communism seems premature, to say the least, given that a quarter of the earth's population still pays nominal homage to Marx and Lenin. If antagonism of any sort developed, it would hardly be between the United States on one side and a united Japan, China, and Southeast Asia on the other. On the contrary, it would surely involve cross-cultural alliances of some kind, if only between certain American firms and certain Asian firms or certain religious groups on both sides of the Pacific.

The third imaginable path could involve some separation, even into mark, dollar, and yen blocs, and continued competition, but with separation not spelling mutual isolation and competition not turning into hostility. The economies would continue to grow into one another. Chryslers could perhaps come to be produced as yen-earners as Hondas are now produced as dollar-earners. Travel and scholarly exchange, abetted by television, telefax, and computer networks, possibly even by usable translation software, could increase levels of mutual interest and understanding. The societies and cultures would obviously remain different. They might, indeed, become increasingly distinctive. But the general condition would be that evoked by the title of a recent Council on Foreign Relations book by Alan D. Romberg and Tadashi Yamamoto comparing American and Japanese societies—*Same Bed, Different Dreams*.

Partly remembering Damon Runyon and weather prophecy, I come out expecting American–East Asian relations to follow the third of these paths rather than the first or second. Effective separation seems to me too hard to achieve, given not only current levels of economic integration but also current levels of cultural interpenetration. In 1941 not many Americans could mount a protest against the military analysts who talked about the Japanese being myopic and not having mechanical toys. In Japan, only a small minority knew enough about the United States to see how reckless and dangerous were the policies of General Tojo's cabinet. Now, there are legions on both sides of the Pacific able expertly to pooh-pooh writings about coming economic wars and, moreover, to lobby effectively against policies that might produce such wars.

Economic, social and cultural interpenetration—some of it evident to me on any day when I cross Harvard Yard and see a student population heavily Asian or Asian-American—works against antagonism. We have large numbers of hostages on one another's territories. It will be very easy for their numbers to increase, very hard for them to go down.

So, to connect these musings about the future with the essays presented here: What do these surmises bode for historical writing about American-East Asian relations? Here, my best guess is that, if American-East Asian relations continue to evolve as in the current decade, writings about their history a decade or two decades hence will look much like writings now.

The Ph.D. dissertations of recent years surely provide an index to scholarly books of the near future, at least in the United States and the U.K. A number of these dissertations deal with old topics and themes, deepening our knowledge of exploitation or conflict prior to the 1970s. Many make use of Asian sources, particularly newly available Chinese sources, highlighting the Asian side of American-East Asian relations and, in the process, adding significantly to earlier evidence on the extent to which those relations were mutually exploitative.

The majority of recent dissertations, however, deal with comparatively new topics or themes. A few, for example, treat American-East Asian economic relations, but not in the vein of "open door imperialism" writing which, whatever its force as political analysis, revealed little about actual exchanges of goods and services. They have more affinity with business history studies such as those of Mira Wilkins on the automobile trade, and of Irvine Anderson on Standard Vacuum oil in China, and of Miles Fletcher on business firms and Japanese trade policy. Two deal, for example, with the effects of post-World War II occupation on the economies of Japan and Korea. One gives historical dimension to economists' debates about why the Korean economy grew more rapidly and robustly than that of Brazil. Another looks at the question of how much growth in East Asian economies was due to government roles. One other explores the important but highly technical question of how exchange rate mechanisms evolved.

A larger number of dissertations on newer topics and themes have some type of cultural focus. One popular subject is the press, but not with the old-fashioned concentration on editorials that were probably widely ignored. Many of these recent dissertations try to explain news reportage or to winkle out of news stories underlying cultural images. A 1991 Temple University dissertation, for example, compared coverage of the Korean War in the *New York Times* with that in the *Asahi Shimbun*. One completed at Rutgers University in the same year sought to establish the role of Henry Luce in shaping American images of China in the 1930s.

The chances are that the dissertations of the next decade—hence the books of the decade after that—will deepen these lines of inquiry. We will continue to learn about past exploitation and conflict, especially as illuminated by Asian sources or newly opened U.S. sources, such as those of CIA and other intelligence agencies. But we will learn even more about the evolution of cooperation, and we will gain enhanced knowledge about the mechanisms that, in the past, have either promoted or inhibited American comprehension of East Asian cultures or East Asian comprehension of American cultures.

I hope that this forecast is not too rosy. It troubles me to think that deepened and prolonged cooperation would probably have seemed much the best bet on the future had a conference on American-East Asian relations been held on these premises in 1929 or, indeed, as late as the summer of 1931, five months before the Manchurian crisis. But my odds board today would carry cooperation as the favorite—not more than two-to-one against. (Remember that, after the Bay of Pigs debâcle, when President Kennedy's aides asked the Joint Chiefs of Staff why they had given the operation a "fair chance of success," they explained that, to them, "fair chance of success" meant three-to-one against.) Antagonism seems to me to have less than a fair chance—around five-to-one. Separation, meaning effective mutual isolation, comes in a loser at eight-to-one or worse.

And I hope that these bets turn out right for scholarly as well as personal reasons. We already know a great deal about exploitation and conflict. We know very little about how cooperation comes about and is sustained or not sustained. As Thomas Hardy comments in *The Dynasts*, "war makes rattling good history, but peace is poor reading." It will do us good if we can learn more about the processes of peace—perhaps even how to make them "rattling good history."

Index